MICHAEL FOLEY AND JOHN E. OWENS

Congress and the presidency

Institutional politics in a separated system

MANCHESTER UNIVERSITY PRESS

MANCHESTER AND NEW YORK

distributed exclusively in the USA and Canada by St Martin's Press

Copyright © Michael Foley and John E. Owens 1996

Published by Manchester University Press
Oxford Road, Manchester M13 9NR, UK
and Room 400, 175 Fifth Avenue, New York, NY 10010, USA

Distributed exclusively in the USA and Canada
by St Martin's Press, Inc., 175 Fifth Avenue, New York,
NY 10010, USA

British Library Cataloguing-in-Publication Data
A catalogue record for this book is available from the British Library

Library of Congress Cataloging-in-Publication Data
Foley, Michael, 1948–
    Congress and the presidency: institutional politics in a
separated system / Michael Foley and John E. Owens.
        p. cm.
    Includes index.
    ISBN 1-7190-3883-9. — ISBN 7190-3884-7 (alk. paper)
        1. Separation of powers—United States. 2. United States
Congress. 3. Presidents—United States. 4. United States—
Foreign relations. I. Owens, John E. II. Title.
JK305.F64 1996
320.473—dc20   95–21418
                                                                  CIP

ISBN 0 7190 3883 9   *hardback*
ISBN 0 7190 3884 7   *paperback*

First published 1996

00 99 98 97 96   10 9 8 7 6 5 4 3 2 1

Typeset by Carnegie Publishing, 18 Maynard Street, Preston, England
Printed in Great Britain by Redwood Books, Trowbridge

Contents

Contents

List of figures and tables

Figures

Tables

List of figures and tables

Series editor's foreword

The Politics Today series has been running successfully since the late 1970s, aimed mainly at an undergraduate audience. After over a decade in which a dozen or more titles have been produced, some of which have run to multiple editions, Manchester University Press thought it time to launch a new politics series, aimed at a different audience and a different need.

The Political Analyses series is prompted by the relative dearth of research-based political science series, which persists despite the fecund source of publication ideas provided by current political developments.

In the United Kingdom we observe, for example: the rapid evolution of Labour politics as the party seeks to find a reliable electoral base; the continuing development of the post-Thatcher Conservative Party; the growth of pressure group activity and lobbying in modern British politics; and the irresistible moves towards constitutional reform of an arguably outdated state.

Elsewhere, there are even more themes upon which to draw: for example, the ending of the Thatcher–Reagan axis; the parallel collapse of communism in Europe and Russia; and the gradual retreat of socialism from the former heartlands in Western Europe.

This series will seek to explore some of these new ideas to a depth beyond the scope of the Politics Today series – whilst maintaining a similar direct and accessible style – and to serve the audience of academics, practitioners and the well-informed reader, as well as undergraduates. The series has three editors, Bill Jones and Michael Moran, who will concentrate on domestic UK topics, and Michael Clarke, who will attend to international issues.

Bill Jones

Preface and acknowledgements

This study arose from a view shared by the authors that a new combined study of the Congress and the presidency was now long overdue. Even before the important changes which occurred after the Republicans won control of both houses of Congress in the 1994 mid-term elections, Congress' institutional structure in the late 1980s and early 1990s was very different from that which had existed in the 1970s. It seemed to us that these changes as well as Congress' increasingly bureaucratic character and the many important theoretical developments associated with Congress – notably purposive explanations of legislative behaviour – were insufficiently recognised and examined in existing book-length studies. While scholarly and popular interest in the presidency has always been greater than that given to Congress, it appeared that existing studies of the presidency neither took account of the level of popular disenchantment with the cult of the strong presidency, nor recognised the extent to which presidents had used their high profile positions to distance themselves from the federal bureaucracy as a way of advancing their own political status. But even more important than these specific concerns about the state of congressional and presidential analysis was the strong sense that most books on these central institutions were either 'Congress-centred' or 'presidency-centred'. As a consequence, there is no up-do-date study which adequately considers the Congress and the presidency both as single and co-equal institutions within America's separated system. This book is intended to correct that deficiency.

Every work of scholarly endeavour builds on the work of previous and contemporary generations. This is no less true of this work. Readers will readily identify our substantial debts to other scholars. Less visible are the debts we have incurred to colleagues in the United States and Britain and to our respective graduate students and research assistants. Eric Uslaner read and made comments on a number of chapters in the book. We thank him for helping us avoid a number of mistakes and pitfalls. Glenn Parker provided us with codings from his own work that enabled us to analyse up-to-date survey data on voters' likes and dislikes of congressional candidates. Tom Mann, Charles O. Jones, and Bert Rockman helped provide a congenial and rewarding scholarly environment during Owens' stays at the Brookings Institution in Washington; Tom Mann, director of the

Preface and acknowledgements

Governmental Studies Program at Brookings also kindly provided office facilities which made the tasks of researching and seeking out information much easier than would otherwise have been the case. We would also like to thank the numerous members of Congress, White House and congressional staff assistants, Congressional Research Service officials, and journalists who provided vital detailed information for the study. Owens would also like to thank Denise Lievesley, Eric Tanenbaum, Simon Musgrave and other staff at the ESRC Data Archive at the University of Essex for satisfying seemingly endless requests for machine-readable data from the ICPSR at Michigan and for providing research facilities. On many occasions, the impressive staff at the Reference Center at the American Embassy in London responded in a timely manner to a number of urgent requests for information. For this, we wish to thank them. The book would not have been completed without the assistance of our graduate students and research assistants who performed essential research and preparatory tasks well and with good humour. These include most notably Josephine Bowen, Kirstie Godwin of the US Election Project at the University of Westminster, Julian Kirby, and Ali Tajvidi. Others who assisted at various stages were Giles Alston, Mary King, Jeff Sachs and Dana Lansky. We would also like to thank our respective institutions – the Department of International Politics at the University of Wales and the School of Social and Policy Sciences at the University of Westminster – and the Nuffield Foundation for invaluable financial support; also Richard Purslow and his staff at Manchester University Press for their support, encouragement and professionalism in helping produce the book in final form. Finally, we both owe a huge debt to our families without whose love and support this project would not have been possible. As a token of our deep appreciation, we dedicate the book to them.

Michael Foley
John E. Owens
Aberystwyth and Colchester
May 1995

CHAPTER I

Introduction

Over the last three decades, the power, roles, and internal organisation of America's foremost political institutions have changed in important ways. Although no major amendments to the United States Constitution have been approved during this period, the ways the Congress and the presidency operate – both as separate and coordinate institutions in competition (and sometimes in cooperation) with one another – have rendered the practice and substance of American politics and policy-making almost unrecognisable.

Thirty years ago, the United States was approaching the culmination of what James Sundquist has called 'the cult of the strong presidency'.[1] Twenty years after the death of Franklin Roosevelt, the power-maximising presidency which he epitomised remained firmly in place – buoyed by intense and widespread demands for internal social and political reform, and the martial tones of American foreign policy objectives – that, in President Kennedy's words, the United States would 'pay any price, bear any burden, meet any hardship, support any friend, oppose any foe, in order to assure the survival and success of liberty'.[2] If the American people were going to be led, if the fragmented system created by the Constitution's framers was going to work, what James MacGregor Burns calls 'the crucible of leadership' had to be the presidency.[3] 'What is good for the country', argued Richard Neustadt, an adviser to Kennedy, 'is good for the president, and *vice versa*.'[4] With rare exceptions, political commentators celebrated an extremely expansive concept of presidential power.

In contrast with the exalted role accorded the presidency, Congress was a constant target of derision – stale, moribund, ineffective, unrepresentative, poorly designed and ill equipped to exercise leadership on the major national issues of the time, and insufficiently expert to compete effectively with the expert specialists housed in the executive. 'Old ideas, old values, old beliefs die hard in Congress,' observed Samuel Huntington. 'The structure of Congress encourages their perpetuation. The newcomer to Congress is repeatedly warned that "to get along he (sic) must go along". To go along means to adjust to the prevailing mores and attitudes of the Inner Club. The more the young congressman desires a career in the House or the Senate, the more readily he makes the necessary adjustments.'[5] Parochialism, structural fragmentations, and the committee and seniority systems – which gave power to those from one-party states who did not represent the mainstream of American politics – made congressional claims to national policy leadership transparently vacuous. Congress' willingness even to make such claims was in doubt. For more than three decades, Congress had permitted – even encouraged – the president and the rest of the executive to take more power and responsibility. In times of crisis – manufactured or real – Congress deliberated but ultimately looked to the other end of Pennsylvania Avenue to the White House for policy proposals, draft legislation, and leadership. Epitomising congressional compliance, in 1965 both the House and the Senate consented almost unanimously to President Johnson's Gulf of Tonkin Resolution for unlimited military intervention in southeast Asia. In consequence, Congress in the 1960s was at the margins of policy leadership and relegated to being 'the spokesman for the interests of unorganised individuals'.[6]

Without accepting some of the more grandiose claims made for political institutions – for example, that they are equipped with larger and more profound ideas than individuals who comprise them[7] – how they relate to one another and how they are organised internally influences the capacity of a political system to be democratic, and the quality of its democracy. In profound ways, the choices made by the framers of the American Constitution in 1787 affected and continue to affect the conduct of American politics and government. Those same choices have also stimulated lively debates among critics who in recent years have variously bemoaned the incapacity of Congress, the abuses of presidential power, and the prevalence of division and 'gridlock'. The United States has a separated system, not a presidential or a parliamentary system.[8] It is not a system of separated powers but a 'government of separated institutions sharing powers'.[9] The system's institutional structure is about the most complex in any liberal democratic system. While the system in Britain leans towards strong executive-dominated party government, and those in Germany and Italy have executives which are constantly at the mercy of shifting parliamentary coalitions, the American system is unique in the degree to which power is shared not only between the Congress and the president, but also between the House of Representatives and the Senate, between the national government and the fifty states, between various other institutions not mentioned in the Constitution – all checked by an independent Supreme Court charged with interpreting the original document.

The institutional structure bestowed by the Constitution's framers was not designed to produce effective or powerful government. Dissatisfied with the undemocratic, executive-dominated British system, they were most concerned with devising a balanced system which would embody the principle of limited government, which would not threaten the liberties of individual citizens, which would be based on the consent of those who participated in it, and which would insulate government from the plebiscitary effects of direct majority rule. According to James Madison's dictum: 'Ambition must be made to counteract ambition . . .

to control the abuses of government'.[10] Thus, the Constitution did not give the Congress complete legislative power but insisted that for a bill to become law it must be signed by the president who would have the power to veto. If, however, two-thirds majorities in both houses could be mustered, the president's veto could be overridden. Nor was the president given a completely free hand in appointments to the executive; the advice and consent of the Senate were required. Other constitutional provisions built in similar mechanisms – some quite ingenious – requiring the participation of one branch of government in the affairs of others. The anticipated effects of making governing institutions both independent of and dependent on one another were that any attempt by one branch to act forcefully or to change the balance among institutions would provoke – as in Newtonian physics – an equal and opposite reaction from the other. Thus, Sundquist has observed: 'The Constitution, in effect, put two combatants into the ring and sounded the bell that sent them into endless battle.'[11]

Institutional competition – rooted in the Constitution's insistence on separate powers, different electoral bases and periods of office, staggered elections, and its multiple ambiguities – has been the hallmark of the American system. Institutional competition and power-sharing have also provided fertile ground for continuing political and academic discourse about which institutions are predominant and/or powerful in a particular period of history, and about the degree to which Congress and the president compete and cooperate in creating national policy.

The expectation of the framers was that Congress would be the dominant institution of the national government. Any visitor to Washington, D.C. today will notice that it is the buildings of the Congress on Capitol Hill which occupy the highest terrain – deliberately so – not the White House. Congress remained the dominant institution, particularly in domestic affairs, until an abrupt change caused by the inauguration of 'King' Andrew Jackson.[12] Jackson's successors, however, had neither the inclination nor the capacity to emulate his pre-eminence until Abraham Lincoln entered office in 1861. Lincoln dominated Congress for most of the Civil War. Following his death, the post-bellum reconstruction period was dominated by the radical Republicans who ruled the government almost like a British cabinet from Capitol Hill. From the 1870s onwards, a number of presidents attempted to battle with Congress on patronage issues but left legislative leadership to Congress. Although the power of the presidency was augmented exponentially in the twentieth century – notably during and after Franklin Roosevelt's presidency (1933–45) – the period has witnessed a similar see-sawing in the pre-eminence and power of the two branches. Apart from Franklin Roosevelt's presidency, and to a lesser extent those of Theodore Roosevelt (1901–9), Woodrow Wilson (1913–21), Lyndon Johnson (1963–9), and Ronald Reagan's in his first year, the remaining periods are characterised to a greater or lesser extent as periods of congressional dominance. Implicit in identifying periods of congressional and presidential predominance – as well as those frequently forgotten periods when power relations between the two institutions were balanced or stalemated[13] – is the idea that the Constitution does not tell us everything about congressional–presidential relations. This is because the framers of the Constitution did not anticipate – and would not have welcomed – either the democratisation of the United States or efforts made through successive party systems and the enhancement of the president's legislative, public communications, and administrative capacities. These important developments – largely ratified by the Supreme Court – permitted presidents at times to circumvent the system's strong bias to inaction and to pursue pro-active public policies, particularly in moments of crisis. In consequence, congressional–presidential relations have differed in many important respects from how they were envisaged by the framers, particularly over the last sixty years.

The same forces which have altered congressional–presidential relations have also ushered in equally important changes in the internal organisation of Congress and the presidency. In the period immediately after the founding of the American Republic, the legislative and executive branches were substantially inchoate institutions. As the primary location of the federal government, Congress soon developed fairly elaborate internal structures but for the first seventy-five years of its existence it was comprised of transient, amateur politicians who were often poorly educated and received little assistance from professionals. Presidents, in contrast, usually had extensive political experience but little administrative capacity directly under their control. As Americans approach the end of the twentieth century, their primary national governing institutions are very different. Both the Congress and the presidency are massive, sprawling bureaucracies, each organised internally with labyrinthine complexity, and each containing multiple divisions and specialisations of labour.

Thus, just as scholars have identified changes over time in the balance of power between the Congress and the president, so they have identified different periods in the organisational developments of both these institutions. Over time, the balance of power between central party leaders and committees has alternated. One hundred years ago, Congress remained in the grip of central party leaders who dominated the committee systems. By the middle decades of the twentieth century, strong central party leadership had given way to committee government and strong committee chairs. After the early 1970s, committee government gave way to subcommittee power. Throughout most of America's political history the presidency was in its traditional form – with a small staff, little funding independent from the executive departments, highly dependent on Congress for cabinet appointments, and typically unable to exercise legislative leadership. Today, largely as a result of changes consolidated by Franklin Roosevelt, the modern presidency is an enormous bureaucracy with huge responsibilities for legislative leadership, foreign policy-making, and symbolic leadership of the country. The presidency as a institution is multi-layered and frequently characterised by rivalries between suborganisations, so that any contemporary president faces a problem familiar in Congress: how to get all the different parts of the institution – let alone all the different parts of the executive branch – working together with the president. Institutionalised pluralism is then an important feature of the internal organisational developments of both these institutions as well as a major dynamic of the separated system as a whole.

The approach adopted in this book is unashamedly institutionalist. We seek to understand the contemporary conditions of the Congress and the presidency as America's foremost governing institutions. We adopt an institutional approach partly for the reason, discussed earlier, that America's political system has a pronounced, self-consciously institutional character; and partly because of a belief in the importance of political institutions as important variables affecting political outcomes.

Understanding the collective performance of political institutions and processes – as distinct from the behaviour of individual politicians and officials – is rightly a major concern of political science. The study of American political institutions has a long and impressive history which dates back to the work of Alexander Hamilton, John Jay, and James Madison in the Federalist Papers. Over recent decades, it has embraced the important theoretical work of the 'new institutionalists' who, borrowing from the economic sphere, have explored why institutions exist and what impact they have on collective actions.[14]

As a result of new institutionalist thinking, it is now commonly accepted that political institutions like the American Congress and the presidency, and the political processes they encompass, play a decisive role in determining collective political, social, and economic outcomes in the United States. Politicians and other political actors do not operate in a vacuum but are located in institutional environments. The collective actions of political actors are not simply the sum of their individual actions. Individuals behave and interact within political and social structures – comprising rules, patterns of behaviour, and organisations – which aggregate their individual activities and influence collective results. In this sense, political institutions provide added value, including identity and direction, to the activities of individual actors. Their rules, norms of behaviour, and organisational structures influence individual members' values, beliefs, and behaviour.[15] Collective political outcomes depend, therefore, not only on the characteristics, predicaments, and motives of individuals but also on institutional rules, norms, and organisational frameworks which structure individual actors' behaviour and condition individual roles, norms, and values. Recognising these interactions and focusing particularly on developments since 1960, this study examines both the historical development of the Congress and the presidency as separate institutions of American national government, as well as the changing dynamic relations between them. It pays considerable attention to the institutional designs of Congress and the presidency and how they have changed over time in response to internal pressures (such as changing memberships) and external factors (such as electoral change and new interactions with other institutions). We seek to explain how organisational structures, along with formal and informal decision rules, influence the politics and behaviour of the Congress and the presidency.

In contrast with other studies of the Congress and the presidency, which tend to emphasise one institution to near the exclusion of the other, our focus is directed to both bodies, as co-equal institutions in a separated system. The study is divided into three separate sections – the Congress is deliberately chosen as the focus of the first section, the second then considers the presidency, and the final section examines changing congressional–presidential relations over the last thirty years. Each of the first two sections considers in separate chapters how each institution has developed historically; how each interacts with the American electorate; how each is currently organised formally and informally; and how and why each makes the decisions that it does.

The first section considers first Congress' steady institutionalisation over more than two centuries. Chapter 2 shows how over this period Congress was transformed from an unstructured representative and legislative body in the eighteenth and early nineteenth centuries into a highly institutionalised legislative organisation in the late twentieth century with complex structures, procedures, norms, and traditions. Institutional change is considered within four eras encompassing the institution's history and explained as democratic responses to shifts in American politics and society over time. Chapter 3 focuses on the changing relationship between members of Congress and their constituents. It demonstrates the importance of the electoral connection in contemporary congressional politics – how pervasive is candidate-centred politics, how contemporary members of Congress must be attentive to their voters, recognise changing conditions in their districts and states, develop their own unique home styles, muster their own resources to win re-election, and constantly court their re-election constituencies. Chapters 4 and 5 focus on Congress in Washington. Beginning with a description of a busy congressional week, the first of these two chapters emphasises Congress' multi-dimensional and fragmented character and its related need for complex, flexible, and elaborate organisational structures. Unusually for examinations of congressional organisation, the chapter explores how individual members of Congress are able to use the substantial resources available in their personal offices to pursue policy entrepreneurship. It then examines in depth the continuing importance of Congress' work horses – the committees systems. In Chapter 5, we consider the changing roles of central party leaders and party organisations as they seek to counteract the endemic institutional fragmentation associated with individual and committee activity, and attempt to organise, inform, broker, and even manage and lead, their party colleagues. The second part of the chapter explores the effect of party, constituency, ideology, and interest groups on individual legislators' decision-making behaviour.

The second section of the study begins in Chapter 6 by reviewing the institutionalisation of the presidency and the growth of the 'modern' presidency in the twentieth century. It explains how the presidency has become institutionalised in response to the expanding need to supervise the burgeoning executive establishment. Chapter 7 explores the growing importance of the public presidency: how presidents are commonly seen as party leaders without parties to lead; how in the absence of a supportive party they seek to generate a personal following and maintain their popularity by 'going public'; how much of the energy expended in the White House is today geared to attending to the mass media; and how their other responsibilities restrict their ability to engage in the sort of permanent electoral campaign necessary for maintaining popular support. Chapter 8 considers the nature of presidential decision-making. It surveys the political and structural constraints which condition the president's position inside the executive branch and examines presidential efforts to capture the initiative in decision-making. Following a review of the president's decisional resources, ranging from the cabinet and sub-cabinet groupings to the White House staff and the president's own personality and experience, the chapter considers competing explanations of presidential behaviour which link together inputs, processes, and outputs.

In the third and final section, we consider the changing relationships between the Congress and the president. The framers of the American Constitution invited a contest between these two institutions. Chapter 9 examines how contemporary Congresses and presidents have responded to this invitation in the legislative arena. The chapter traces how beginning with Franklin Roosevelt modern presidents assumed the role of legislative leader of Congress; and how, as a result, presidency-centred interpretations consumed the literature on legislative relations. Borrowing from a different literature tradition, the chapter emphasises how the business of legislating in America's separated system is really a shared process. Having explained how the separated system introduced great fluidity and imprecision into congressional–presidential legislative relations, Chapter 10 explores the different elements of the separation of powers principle and the ways in which the Supreme Court has sought to resolve the jurisdictional disputes that have inevitably arisen between the Congress and the presidency. The main debates and key cases are discussed and analysed. The chapter illustrates the different ways in which the separation of powers, as the central organising principle of the national government, continues to structure the calculations, tactics, and vocabulary of Washington politics. In addition to acknowledging the role of the judiciary in managing inter-branch disputes, the chapter goes on to examine both the limits of reciprocal control and the conventions that foster day-to-day cooperation within a separated system. Chapter 11 shifts the focus of the study to policy-making. Here, we explore the profound influence that congressional–presidential relations have on the policy-making capacity of American national government. For this purpose, the chapter examines the character and implications of two controversies which are arguably the most significant and very often the least well understood points of friction within the separated system.

The final chapter focuses on the Congress and the presidency within the broader contexts of the political system and American society. We show how the idea of institutional duality has remained central to the operation and understanding of government within Washington. We explain how institutional differences between the Congress and the presidency are closely correlated to the expression of political differences even to the extent of defining the nature of issues and structuring the organisation of political disputes. Despite the popular emphasis given to the presidency-centred perspective, it is the institutional duality of the presidency and Congress which characterises national policy-making and generates a persistent dispute over the functional costs of such a disjunction in government. In the 1990s, this duality has prompted renewed debate about the relative advantages and disadvantages of single-party and split-party control of government. Our view of the separated system is more sanguine. When there is sufficient political will, support, and negotiating skill available, Congress and the presidency can and do move in concert as representative governing institutions thereby bridging the distance between the institutions.

The main purpose of the book is to provide a vehicle for understanding how the Congress and the presidency have changed over recent decades, to explain the changes in terms of wider developments in American politics, to demonstrate how these changes are accommodated within America's separated system, and to reassert the importance of institutions in this unique political system.

Notes

1 James L. Sundquist, 'Congress and the President: Enemies Or Partners?' in Lawrence C. Dodd and Bruce I. Oppenheimer (eds), *Congress Reconsidered* (New York: Praeger, 1977), p. 223. See also Thomas E. Cronin, *The State of the Presidency* (Boston: Little Brown, 1975), chapter 2.

2 John F. Kennedy, Inaugural Address, January 21, 1961.

3 James MacGregor Burns, *Presidential Government. The Crucible of Leadership* (Boston: Houghton Mifflin, 1965).

4 Richard E. Neustadt, *Presidential Power* (New York: John Wiley, 1960), p. 185.

5 Samuel P. Huntongton, 'Congressional Responses to the Twentieth Century', in David B. Truman (ed.), *The Congress and America's Future* (Eaglewood Cliffs, NJ: Prentice-Hall, 1965), p. 16.

6 Huntington, 'Congressional Responses to the Twentieth Century', p. 23.

7 See, for example, Samuel P. Huntington, *Political Order in Changing Societies* (New Haven, CT: Yale University Press, 1968), p. 10.

8 Charles O. Jones, *The Presidency in a Separated System* (Washington, D.C.: The Brookings Institution, 1994).

9 Neustadt, *Presidential Power*, p. 42.

10 James Madison, Alexander Hamilton, and John Jay, *The Federalist Papers* (New York and Toronto: New American Library, 1961), no. 51, p. 322.

11 James L. Sundquist, *The Decline and Resurgence of Congress* (Washington, D.C.: The Brookings Institution, 1981), p. 16.

12 *Ibid.*, pp. 23–9.

13 Jones, *The Presidency in a Separated System*, p. 291.

14 The 'new instituionalist' approach has its origins in Ronald H. Coarse, 'The Nature of the Firm', *Economica*, 4 (1937).

15 James G. Marsh and Johan P. Olsen, 'The New Institutionalism: Organisational Factors in Political Life', *American Political Science Review*, 78 (1984), pp. 734–49; and Matthew D. McCubbins and Terry Sullivan (eds), *Congress: Structure and Policy* (Cambridge and New York: Cambridge University Press, 1987).

PART I

Congress

CHAPTER 2

The dynamics of institutional change in Congress

Just over a hundred years ago today, Woodrow Wilson praised the brevity of the United States Constitution. 'The fact that it attempts nothing more is its great strength', argued the future president, 'because if the Framers had gone beyond more than elementary provisions, the document's elasticity and adaptability would have been lost; and thus its ability to endure and survive.'[1] Article 1 of the Constitution granted Congress specifically enumerated powers and provided rules for electing its members and how often it should meet, but no mention was made of how the national legislature would organise itself – except that the presiding officer of the House of Representatives (the Speaker) should be elected and that the vice president (and in his absence, the president *pro tempore*) should preside over the Senate – and no mention was made of political parties or congressional committees. The Constitution's brevity allowed the Congress almost complete freedom to evolve its own organisational framework, internal rules, and behavioural norms. Brevity and silence also allowed the institution to change over time.

How and why Congress' internal organisation and status have changed over more than 200 years provides the focus for this chapter. For the Congress of the mid-1990s is very different from that envisaged in 1787; and very different from the institution which developed in the nineteenth century. Even the Congress of the 1940s or the 1970s is very different from the contemporary institution. Over more than two centuries, Congress has been transformed from an informal, non-specialised representative and legislative assembly, attempting to fulfil the republican aspirations of post-revolutionary Americans, into a complex, highly specialised, rather bureaucratic institution which acts in the late twentieth century like a complete government intervening in all policy areas and at every stage of the policy-making process. These changes were responses not only to internal congressional politics, but also to what Woodrow Wilson called 'the voices in the air which cannot be misunderstood'[2] – political, economic, and social changes which transformed the nature of problems facing constituents, and thus the public policies they were willing to support, and compelled changes in Congress' internal structure and behaviour to enable it to respond.

Before the constitution

Those who thought about republican government in the America of the 1770s and 1780s insisted on its representativeness, particularly that it should represent local people. When the American colonists declared independence from Britain in 1776, their major complaint was that George III's Parliament had violated a basic axiom of the 1689 Bill of Rights: that there should be no taxation without representation. As Thomas Jefferson, James Madison, and other revolutionary leaders understood it, the British system of parliamentary government established by the so-called Glorious Revolution allowed only those authorised by the people – elected representatives – to consent to taxation. Since the colonists were not permitted to elect any members of the British House of Commons three thousand miles away in Westminster, and had not authorised any to consent to taxation on their behalf, the actions of Parliament were illegitimate.

The representational imperative

When they set about creating America's first system of government under the Articles of Confederation of 1777, the leaders of the newly created United States not surprisingly drew some obvious lessons from their struggles with the un-democratic British Parliament. In the new Continental Congress, a political representative would not only be chosen by his constituents; he would also be one of them, would live among them, and in the words of John Adams 'think, feel, reason, and act like them.'[3]

Yet, it was not long before this insistence upon a locally oriented concept of representation became a major problem. Those elected as members of the Continental Congress were manifestly representatives of particular communities and states, but they were not necessarily well qualified to make laws and public policy for the new nation. Even if it was supposed that they were well qualified, would they act always in the best interests of the collectivity of American people and the new American state without losing or setting aside their local identities and their constituents' particular interests? The experiences of the Continental Congress and, even more so, the state legislatures were not comforting. If anything, these representative bodies were 'too democratic'. Their members tended to hold very parochial outlooks or were beholden to local interests which were at best partisan and at worst corrupt. By the mid-1780s, a major change in prevailing opinion had occurred. Many American leaders now saw the popular sovereignty of legislative government as the greatest threat to America's fragile democracy; as the Continental Congress acted as little more than an assembly of ambassadors of the individual states, and as representatives and the majority factions in state legislatures abused and misused powers granted them in the name of the people. Although the Articles of Confederation granted the Continental Congress important powers (but not the power to tax or legislate), almost the only way the national government could act was through the states: congressional resolutions were regarded by the individual states merely as recommendations which may or may not be enforced; ratification and subsequent amendment of the Articles required the consent of all thirteen states; and members of Congress were delegates of the states paid from state funds and prohibited from serving more than three years in any six-year period. Leadership of the Continental Congress was also unstable, confused, and weak.[4] By the time the war with Britain ended in October 1781, the states had lost interest in America's now forgotten first system of government, and the Continental Congress was homeless and inert.

Congress in the new Constitution

The delegates of the individual states who met in Philadelphia in the summer of 1787 to write a new national Constitution faced the classic dilemma of democratic government: how to provide for representative government which would be responsive to the needs and demands of constituents, and yet provide government strong enough to take decisive action in promoting 'the aggregate interests of the community' while avoiding the worst excesses of 'the spirit of locality' (Madison) and 'elective despotism' (Jefferson) which had characterised representative government in the individual states.

Congress, rather than the executive, was given the primary task of resolving this dilemma. Consistent with the Whig view – that the right to govern was contingent on the people retaining the right to choose a body of people to represent them and through such a body to have a voice in the making of all laws – Madison insisted that '[i]n republican government, the legislative authority necessarily predominates'.[5] The very first sentence of the new Constitution specifically granted all legislative power to the Congress. Section 8 of Article 1 then provided Congress with formidable powers to tax, spend, and 'provide for the common defense and general welfare of the United States' – powers which affected virtually all areas of civil society. The same section also gave the national legislature substantial powers in the areas of foreign policy (to declare war, and make treaties with other countries), appointments to other branches of government (to advise and consent to presidents' nominations, and to impeach), foreign and inter-state commerce, national security (to raise and maintain armed forces), selecting the president (in case of stalemate in the electoral college, presidential disability or resignation), and proposing constitutional amendments. Members of Congress then would have a dual role in which they would be required to make laws for the collectivity of American people and the new American state, *and* represent the parochial interests of the people.

Congress' dual role was reinforced by the invention of a new national vision of popular representation which, according to Madison, should rest alongside, even above, locally oriented representation. The authority of national

15

governmental institutions would rest on a new concept of 'the American people' constituted as a separate and superior entity over and above governments and peoples of the individual states. Thus, the Constitution begins with an overtly nationalist preamble: 'We the people of the United States . . .', although 'the people' did not include most women, any native Americans, or most southern blacks. The national vision of popular sovereignty would be achieved and the excesses of locally oriented representation would be reduced through direct popular elections of the national government. All sixty-five members of the new House of Representatives would be directly elected in national elections every two years, and each legislator would represent an enormous district of about 30,000 electors apportioned to the states on the basis of their populations. It is a mute point whether such a small legislature with such large districts charged by the Constitution to originate money bills mollified the fears of ordinary electors who a few years earlier had marched under the banner 'no taxation without representation'. Following the practice of the states, the one-chamber Continental Congress was replaced by a new bicameral legislature the second chamber of which – a small Senate chosen by the state legislatures and (hopefully) composed of men with broader visions and more stable temperaments – would check the likely 'fickleness and passion' (Madison) of the directly elected House. Regardless of population size, each state would elect two senators for six-year terms, with one third of the chamber retiring every two years, thereby ensuring that the smaller states would not be constantly outvoted by their larger neighbours.

The institutional development of Congress

For any governmental organisation in a large society to be viable, for it to be able to perform the tasks it has been given – to allocate values authoritatively, make laws, resolve societal problems, settle conflicts, represent the people, and so forth – it must be institutionalised. It must develop and sustain regular and stable rules, generate normative patterns of behaviour, and establish internal structures which help the institution serve its purposes. In the case of collective institutions such as legislatures, they must develop organisational mechanisms (e.g. leadership structures, party organisations, and divisions of labour) that aggregate the actions of individual members and socialise them into the institution's internal processes, norms, and values. Applied to the United States Congress, we can say that the institution's organisational structures, rules, and norms interact with and are influenced over time by the changing needs of members and the numerous political, economic, and social forces existing within the wider society.[6] In turn, these internal arrangements and structures also influence the attitudes, expectations, and behaviour of the members, as well as the institution's collective outcomes such as legislative decisions (see Figure 2.1).

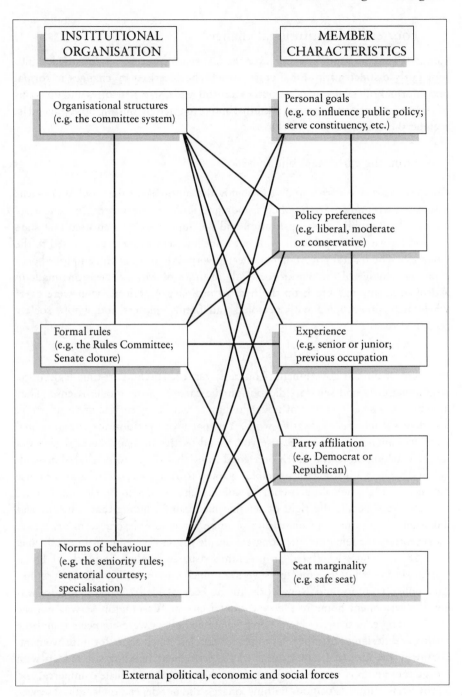

Figure 2.1 Explaining the dynamics of congressional change. *Source*: see text.

Four eras of institutional change

Congress' organisational history over the last two centuries may be divided into four fairly distinct institutional eras[7] – each characterised by changes in formal and informal rules, members' resources, central leadership structures and divisions of labour, and decision-making patterns; and prompted by shifting policy agendas, memberships, and varying workloads.

From the early Republic to 1860

Congress' first era – from 1787 to roughly the outbreak of the Civil War – was associated with an agrarian policy agenda and limited government. In these early days of the Republic, the Constitution and the Supreme Court ensured that state and local government performed all but a specific set of functions granted to the Congress. The federal government collected very little income and employed only a tiny percentage of the workforce. Only in times of war did decisions made in Washington impinge much on the lives of ordinary Americans who were over-whelmingly preoccupied with personal and family matters and whose society remained rural.

A Congress of amateur legislators

In an era of limited government, Congress was a leisurely, part-time legislature. House members and senators did not pursue careers in the modern sense. They attended to a small amount of undemanding constituency service and undertook less than six months' legislative work. Yet, party competition for congressional seats was intense – if only because voters and parties in many states regarded a job in Washington as too much of a good thing that ought to be shared around. When Abraham Lincoln, for example, wanted to run for re-election as a House member in 1848, he told a friend: 'If nobody else wishes to be elected, I could not refuse the people the right of sending me again.' Finding that someone else did want his job, he kept his earlier promise to serve only one term.[8] Even so, the incentives for remaining in Congress during this era were far from irresistible. Until 1800, Congress suffered an itinerant existence resident variously at Phila-delphia, Princeton (where members were crammed into the college teaching room), Annapolis, Trenton, and New York (in the Federal Hall). When Congress was given a permanent home in the new capital city at Washington, it was not for another ten years that the House and Senate chambers were connected, and the quality and design of members' accommodation left much room for improvement. For many decades, the new capital was a permanent building site ridden with mosquitoes and boasting few 'respectable' white people, very little commerce, and a provincial culture.[9] Positions within Congress did not depend on length of service (seniority), so major political figures like Henry Clay and Daniel Webster drifted in and out of the Congress as convenience dictated, with the result that membership of Congress was extremely unstable. The mean age of House members hovered around 43, usually more than half the membership was newly elected, and the mean term of service was just two terms (four years). In the Senate, service was more a hobby than a profession. In the space of twelve years between 1789 and 1801, as many as 94 individuals became senators, representing 32 states, and of these 33 resigned before completing their terms. Even up to the Civil War, most senators served only three to four years of their six-year terms.[10]

Either because of or in spite of the high turnover in membership, Congress did not enjoy a favourable reputation. After the entry of many western states in the early nineteenth century, the legislature developed a reputation as a vulgar, unruly, even chaotic and violent, body as James Sterling Young's splendid description shows:

> Congress at work was Hyde Park set down in the lobby of a busy hotel – hortatory outcry in milling throngs, all wearing hats as if just arrived or on the verge of departure, variously attired in the fashions of faraway places. Comings and goings were continual – to the rostrum to see the clerk, to the anterooms to meet friends, to the Speaker's chair in a sudden surge to hear the results of a vote, to the firesides for hasty caucuses and strategy-planning sessions. Some gave audiences to the speaker of the moment; some sat at their desks reading or catching up on correspondence; some stood chatting with lady friends invited on the floor; others dozed, feet propped high. Page boys weaved through the crown, 'little Mercuries' bearing messages, pitchers of water for parched throats, bundles of documents, calling out members' names, distributing mail just arrived on the stagecoach. Quills scratched, bond crackled as knuckles rapped the sand off wet ink, countless newspapers rustled. Desk drawers banged, feet shuffled in a sea of documents strewn on the floor. Bird dogs fresh from the hunt bounded in with their masters, yapping accompaniment to contenders for attention, contenders for power. Some government! 'Babeltown,' a legislator called it.[11]

The situation in the Senate was no better. During the debate on the 1850 Compromise, Senator Harry S. 'Hangman' Foote (D.MS) wielded a pistol at Missouri's Thomas Hart Benton. Only the intervention of other senators prevented bloodshed. Six years later, during the debate on the Kansas statehood bill, two South Carolina representatives entered the Senate chamber and bludgeoned Senator Charles Sumner (R.MA) as he sat at his desk.

During this first institutional era, there was really no established hierarchy among national governmental institutions. The balance of power shifted between the House and the Senate, and less often from Congress to the president (during the presidencies of Jefferson and Jackson). Within this highly fluid institutional environment, members of Congress did not develop deep loyalties to one particular branch of government. Henry Clay of Kentucky, for example, entered the House at the age of 34 after having served two terms in the Senate, was elected Speaker eight months later, resigned after three years to negotiate the Treaty of Ghent on behalf of President Madison, was re-elected to the House where he was again promptly elected Speaker in 1815. He resigned in 1820, returned three years later, was again elected Speaker for another two years, and then became a senator. Even the Senate, which included the leading statesmen of the day and was the primary forum for the great anti-slavery debates before the Civil War, was 'an honorific nothing' during this era.[12]

Early institutionalisation

Spurred on by a desire to establish congressional pre-eminence in national policy-making and to affirm the new government's success,[13] Congress assumed some of the characteristics of a modern legislature right from the outset. Helped by the election of a majority of 'legislatively socialised' members like Madison who had been members of the Constitutional Convention, state legislatures, state constitutional conventions or the Continental Congress, Congress soon established a framework of formal rules and structures. The First Congress which convened in New York in 1789 successfully established procedures for developing specific policies; created a division of labour; devised mechanisms for receiving demands and producing decisions; and approved rules which guaranteed the expression of minority views and the assertion of majority rule. Thereafter, the small number of elite careerists – like Madison, Jefferson (who as vice president wrote the *Manual of Parliamentary Procedures* for the Senate), Clay, and John C. Calhoun – who wished to develop personal power bases and bolster congressional resistance to executive encroachment retained a close interest in procedural matters. Facing relatively few constituency demands, needing to spend little time in Washington, and able to participate in a genuinely deliberative body, most of the amateur politicians of the early Congresses saw little need for elaborate internal organisations and structures.

The development of standing committee systems

In the early Congresses, members were unwilling to entrust important legislative responsibilities to small subgroups of members for any significant length of time. Most House business was conducted in the Committee of the Whole, following the precedents established by the British House of Commons, colonial assemblies, and state legislatures in which many members had served. Once members agreed on general principles, a bill was then sent to a special select committee composed of specialist members who drafted legislative language. Within a few decades, however, these arrangements became unworkable. The new country's expansion westwards, the War of 1812, a larger membership (182 after 1813, 234 after 1853), and greater congressional determination to resist executive influence (especially during the Washington, Jefferson, and Jackson presidencies), encouraged the House's workload to grow enormously. A more differentiated standing committee system was required which would allow legislators to focus in greater detail and on a continuing basis on such important subjects as taxation, appropriations, and inter-state commerce; and allow Congress as a governing institution to accumulate experience and expertise independent from the executive. Prompted by these pressures, the House was transformed during Clay's speakership (1811–14, 1815–21, 1823–5) from an institution which principally did its business on the floor and in select committees to one in which legislating by specialised standing committees became the norm. Between 1809 and 1825, the number of House standing committees grew from 10 to 28, and the percentage of House bills referred to standing committees grew from 47 to 93 per cent. A system of 12 standing committees was established by the Senate in 1816 with similar effects.[14]

In the ensuing decades leading up to the outbreak of the Civil War, committees were transformed from loose aggregations of *ad hoc* units appointed for specific legislative purposes into formalised systems whose members owed their appointment and advancement increasingly to party leaders and a 'sort of conditional seniority'.[15] The broader significance of this change was that independently from the president Congress embedded within its rules new divisions and specialisations of labour which significantly decentralised internal operations and gave subgroups of legislators increasingly important personal stakes in policy-making within discrete subject jurisdictions.

Weak central leadership

Having opted for internal divisions and specialisations of labour, deciding which members would be assigned to which committees became a highly charged business. In the House, the assignment of members to committees was linked inevitably with electing the Speaker whose supporters expected to receive plum committee assignments and chairs. Not surprisingly, speakership elections were often fierce and tenure of the office short (usually about three years). Although few Speakers achieved Henry Clay's stature and influence, the office was an immensely important source of power not only in the appointment of committee members and chairs but also in facilitating and guiding the development of (party) legislation, mediating parliamentary disputes, and scheduling legislation. At this time, however, the Speaker was not the majority party's floor leader in the House. This role was usually left to the chair of the Ways and Means Committee, or to assertive presidents.[16]

In the smaller more intimate Senate, centralised leadership was resisted much more strongly. The common view was expressed by Senator Daniel Webster when he declared in 1830 that the chamber was a 'Senate of equals, of men and individual honor and personal character, and of absolute independence' who knew no master and acknowledged no dictator.[17] The chair of the majority caucus performed official duties at the beginning of each Congress. To the extent that effective leadership was exercised – to make committee assignments, schedule and manage important legislation on the floor, and apply party discipline – it was exercised by the chamber's intellectual leaders and leading debaters.[18]

From the Civil War to the 1910s

Congress' second institutional era – from the Civil War until the 1910s – was a period of dramatic change. As politicians opted to pursue congressional careers with much greater enthusiasm and purpose, the national legislature became fully institutionalised. Although throughout this period Congress remained a part-time legislature, meeting usually for only six months a year, its membership became professionalised, more party-dominated, and more centrally directed and its internal structure assumed more complex organisation, and new formal rules and behavioural norms.

From about 1860 until after the first decade of the new century, the United States experienced a period of remarkable economic, social, and political change. Industrialisation accelerated, inter-state commerce flourished, and the size of the country grew as more new states were admitted. The Civil War initiated the process of clarifying the Constitution's ambiguities and establishing the supremacy of the federal government. After the Civil War, the national government's economic power grew phenomenally generating in its wake powerful new democratic pressures which propelled previously unknown problems on to the national policy agenda. And, it was Congress rather than the president which responded to these new pressures and greatly enhanced its power. By the 1880s the legislature – generally under the control of the Republican Party – had become in Wilson's famous words 'the predominant and controlling force, the centre and source of all motive and of all regulative power'.[19]

The beginning of Congressional careerism

With Congress ascendant, the presidency in eclipse, federal spending more than quadrupling,[20] and the post-war reconstruction policy agenda a burgeoning responsibility, patterns of congressional recruitment changed significantly. Party leaders and citizens back home began to appreciate better the advantages of sending the same representative or senator to Washington election after election: members of Congress could perform better their representative and legislative responsibilities the longer they served, or so it was thought. Nowhere was this reasoning better appreciated than in the south after 1877 when leaders and voters saw that by returning the same (Democratic) members their states could accrue seniority more quickly and thereby greater power and influence; but other parties in regions and states dominated by one party – Republicans in the midwest and rural north-east and Democrats in urban working-class areas – also recognised

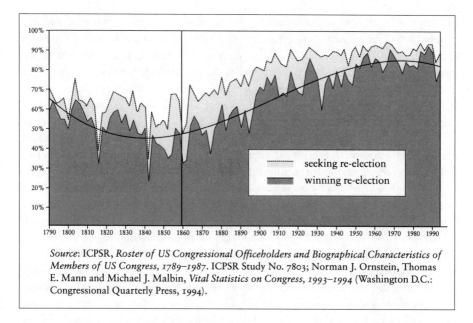

Source: ICPSR, *Roster of US Congressional Officeholders and Biographical Characteristics of Members of US Congress, 1789–1987*. ICPSR Study No. 7803; Norman J. Ornstein, Thomas E. Mann and Michael J. Malbin, *Vital Statistics on Congress, 1993–1994* (Washington D.C.: Congressional Quarterly Press, 1994).

Figure 2.2 Percentages of members of the US House of Representatives seeking and winning re-election.

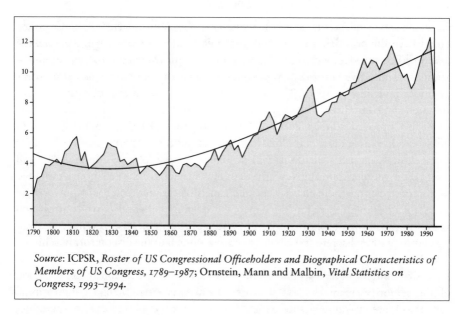

Source: ICPSR, *Roster of US Congressional Officeholders and Biographical Characteristics of Members of US Congress, 1789–1987*; Ornstein, Mann and Malbin, *Vital Statistics on Congress, 1993–1994*.

Figure 2.3 Mean years served by Members of the US House of Representatives, 1790–1994.

the same advantages. In consequence, the value of a congressional seat and the probability of re-election rose sharply (see Figure 2.2) and the mean length of House service increased (see Figure 2.3). So, although they still needed to be nominated by their state and district parties during this era, members increasingly opted to remain longer in Congress as life in the now magnificent capital city was much more to their liking; as the rapid expansion of Congress' workload into important areas such as the tariff, monetary policy, race, and federal patronage offered them more exciting and rewarding opportunities for power and influence; and as they came increasingly to regard their jobs in Washington as attractive full-time careers suitable for ambitious, college-educated, professionals.[21]

Nelson Polsby has observed that '[u]ntil a deliberative body has some minimum amount of work to do, the necessity for interaction among its members remains slight, and, having no purpose, coordination by means of a division of labor, rules and regulations, precedents and so on, seem unlikely to develop.'[22] The growth of congressional careerism after the Civil War stimulated legislative institutionalisation and professionalism. As career expectations soared and as a greater sense of institutional identity and loyalty developed, representatives and senators moved to adopt more complex, regular, and explicit forms of legislative organisation with clear divisions and specialisations of labour to handle better their increased numbers and workloads.

The institutionalisation of standing committees

Faced by new and complex areas of public policy and insistent that Congress rather than the president initiate policy, the new career-oriented members moved to strengthen the standing committee systems to facilitate greater subject specialisation and legislative activism. By 1913, the number of committees had risen to 61 in the House and 74 in the Senate.[23] Over this period, many committees also acquired subcommittees, were assigned more or less permanent rooms in the Capitol, employed staff (a total of 100 by 1890), and began routinely to hire full-time clerks. Greater complexity in the committees systems produced major changes in Congress' organisational structure, modes of decision-making, and internal power distribution. New divisions and specialisations of labour developed as committees and their chairs acquired much of the authority and power they enjoy today – able to act fairly independent of chambers and party control, and possessing exclusive authority to authorise, appropriate, raise revenue, and kill legislation within discrete subject jurisdictions – much to the discomfort of scholars like Wilson.[24]

Committee power was underpinned by careerism and incipient solidification of the seniority norm. As the seniority norm was strengthened congressional careerists were guaranteed automatic advancement on committees and, therefore, greater predictability in pursuing their congressional careers. Seniority became a more or less inviolable 'rule' in the Senate after 1877. In the House, it became institutionalised much more gradually as formal assignment power was retained by the Speaker. By 1885, seniority was undoubtedly an important criterion for appointing the major committee chairs but there was no assumption or expectation that the chair of a committee would be reappointed to the same committee in a subsequent Congress or that members could retain their committee assignments (committee property rights) in successive Congresses.[25] Indeed, it was more likely that a member who chaired a minor committee successfully would be promoted by the Speaker to the chair of a more important one. Powerful Speakers also tended to violate seniority by naming minority as well as majority members to committees.[26]

Besides strengthening the standing committees, Congress' more career-oriented legislators also voted themselves new personal staff assistance and other resources. Individual senators were authorised to employ a single staffer (at $6 a day) in 1885; representatives were allowed to do the same in 1893 (at $100 a month). Between 1880 and 1910, House administrative spending more than doubled to $5 million, new office buildings were completed for members and their staff (in 1908 and 1909), the research facilities of the Library of Congress were expanded (1899) and augmented by a specialist Legislative Reference Service (1914), and a new Office of Legislative Counsel was created (1918) to help members draft legislation.

By the 1910s then Congress had truly discarded the part-time amateur aura of the early nineteenth century when the average member's office was under his hat and most of his time was spent on or around the House or Senate floor. Instead, the House and the Senate had adopted the trappings of a modern professional legislature which was increasingly bureaucratic with relatively small numbers of members conducting most of the floor business and the rest summoned to the floor from offices and committee rooms by electric signals.[27]

The strengthening of party leadership

Congress' second institutional era coincided with a period of party government. As the party system stabilised in the late nineteenth century around clearly defined constituency bases, producing large numbers of safe seats for each, central party leaders in the House were able to command cohesive majorities.[28] So, when legislation was especially important to the majority party House Speakers like James G. Blaine (R.ME, 1869–74), John G. Carlisle (D.KY, 1883–8), Thomas B. Reed (R.ME, 1889–90, 1895–8), and Joseph G. Cannon (D.IL, 1903–10) ignored seniority and committee property rights in their assignments and appointed favoured allies in order to assure majority party control, encourage greater policy coherence, and reduce legislative unpredictability.[29] With the House's adoption of the Reed Rules in 1890, the majority party through the Speaker (who usually chaired the Rules Committee) took a much firmer grip of the floor agenda regardless of its plurality. As a result, it was able to control the timing and content of floor bills, to prevent the minority from obstructing the majority by reducing the number for a quorum and limiting dilatory motions; and by referring all public bills to standing committees who then reported to the floor thereby allowing only nominal floor debate on amendments approved by the Rules Committee. In 1899, a separately designated position of majority floor leader was created thereby reinforcing the institutionalisation of central party leadership.

Leadership of the Senate remained as sporadic and *ad hoc* after the Civil War as before. The chair of the majority caucus remained the official leader but the position was a weak one because party unity was usually elusive. Powerful senators, who were also state party bosses – like Roscoe Conkling (R.NY), William Allison (R.IO), and Nelson Aldrich (R.RI) – exercised a sort of factionalised unofficial leadership but this was principally for organisational purposes, notably controlling committee assignments. After the mid-1880s the position of majority floor leader – the nearest equivalent to the House Speaker – became associated with the chair of the majority caucus or conference but the holder of the position was not expected to supervise and direct the majority party and often held the position only for a year. This situation changed between 1911 and 1915 as a result of Progressive insurgency when Senate Democrats merged the posts of floor leader and caucus chair to create the single office of majority leader. When Democrats won control of the presidency in 1912, they elected an ally of President Wilson, John W. Kern (D.IN), as majority leader. Kern assumed primary responsibility for directing the president's legislative programme through the Senate and assigning sympathetic committee members and chairs.[30] The introduction of new rules to expedite Senate business – such as the Anthony Rule of 1870 for speeding action on non-controversial business and the cloture rule of 1917 by which filibusters could be terminated on the vote of two-thirds of the members present – also strengthened the hand of party managers.

Emerging House–Senate differences

Notwithstanding this strengthening of party authority in both houses, organisational divergence between the House and Senate grew significantly during this era. Differences arose largely from the increasing disparity in the sizes of the two chambers and execution of their separate constitutional responsibilities. The political conflict over slavery before the Civil War had constrained the expansion of the frontier westwards. With slavery abolished, the construction of transcontinental railroads, and opening up of new markets and resources, twelve new states were admitted to the union between 1863 and 1912. As a result, the Senate grew from 72 to 96 members, while membership in the House increased from 241 to its present size of 435, reflecting a quadrupling of population. Of course, the House had always been larger than the Senate, but now the combined effects of its larger size and the requirements of party government made it imperative that the popular chamber acquire even more complex organisation, new formal rules, more rigid procedures, a more elaborate committee system, and a more bureaucratic aura. The Senate meanwhile was better able retain its individualistic stately tradition with a minimum of formal rules (just 40 in 1884).

As the size and functions of the federal government grew and its proclivity for military and political intervention overseas increased, the roles of the House and the Senate in relation to one another underwent significant change. The House continued to initiate all spending and tax legislation, as the Constitution required, and became increasingly involved in tariff, monetary, and regulatory policy, but the political power and status of the Senate soared as its special constitutional responsibilities for overseeing the appointment of executive officials and for ratifying treaties became much more significant, and as the emerging mass media paid senators greater attention. By the end of the century, the Senate was successfully challenging the pre-eminence of the House; the distinctive roles of each chamber had become more clearly delineated; and bicameral policy-making had become decidedly more problematic.

From the 1910s to the early 1970s

In the wake of Progressive insurgency, the appeal of party rule as a principle of government declined after 1910. Power within Congress shifted to the decentralised and increasingly autonomous committee systems. Committee jurisdictions were formalised in House and Senate rules; seniority and committee property rights norms became entrenched (notably in the appointment of committee chairs); the number of standing committees was reduced; committee memberships became increasingly stable, expert, and distinctive; committees' legislative resources improved; and their recommendations came to be more readily accepted by colleagues on the House and Senate floors.

The revolt against central control

As membership of the House and Senate stabilised – in response to rising careerism and the fall in turnover (see Figures 2.2 and 2.3) and the probability that no new states would be admitted to the union[31] – congressional Progressives became increasingly frustrated by their respective party leaders' inability to respond to the newly emerging industrial and urban political agenda, and to accommodate their individual career ambitions.

In a dramatic series of events in the 1910s the nagging conflict between insurgent Progressives and Republican leaders of the House came to a head. The immediate cause of what became a revolt was the action taken by the autocratic Speaker 'Uncle Joe' Joseph G. Cannon (R.IL, 1903–11) to reduce the Progressives' influence. Violating fairly well established seniority and committee property rights norms, by which the chair of a committee was assigned to the majority member with the longest continuous service and which permitted members to remain on committees as long as they wished, Cannon moved to punish dissident members of his party who would not submit to party discipline. Between 1907 and 1910, he removed seven incumbent committee chairs (four without giving them new committee assignments), skipped over the most senior ranking majority members to appoint favoured allies to the chairs of ten other committees, and transferred a ranking Republican member of one committee to a lowly position on another. Led by George W. Norris (R.NB) and John M. Nelson (R.WI), Republican Progressives combined with the minority Democrats in 1910 to strip Cannon of his power to appoint committee members and chairs, removed him as chair of the Rules Committee, and tripled the size of the committee by adding ten new members. When Democrats organised the House in 1911, power to assign members to committees was assumed by the party caucuses and their respective committees on committees, which in the case of House Democrats comprised Democratic members of the Ways and Means Committee.

In the Senate, a Progressive-inspired thrust also resulted in more decentralised decision-making. At the same time that Senate Democrats elected Kern as majority leader in 1913, they also gave committees greater autonomy and allowed a majority of committee members to call meetings, elect subcommittees, and appoint conferees with the House. Reinforced subsequently by the ratification of the 17th amendment to the Constitution in 1913, the effect on party government was almost immediate. President Wilson's heavy legislative programme became stalled. Over a period of a few years, the party system which had formerly linked senators downwards to a state party organisation and state legislature (which had formerly appointed them) and upwards to the party caucuses in the Senate (which ordered Senate business and dispensed jobs in the federal bureaucracy through the corrupt spoils system and senatorial courtesy) had been destroyed. Senators would henceforth build personal organisations independent of state party organisations and develop their own political records based on their own policy preferences and re-election needs. In this process, Senate party leaders lost what control they had and well disciplined party caucuses became a phenomenon of the past.[32]

The consolidation of committee government and baronial power

After the 1910s, congressional politics was transformed into committee government as power within the House and the Senate was transferred to autonomous committees which were given jurisdictions over fairly tightly defined parcels of subjects, which developed their own norms and orientations, and with which legislators' personal careers became increasingly identified and evaluated. In the previous eras, committees had conducted hearings and drafted legislation, but their activities had been controlled largely by central leaders. Now that the power of central leaders and party caucuses was curtailed, committee members – and especially chairs – moved quickly to bolster their institutional positions, establish their autonomy from central leaders (and relatively inactive party caucuses), and protect themselves from the public gaze. In one of the first moves to consolidate committee power (and in anticipation of the new Budget and Accounting Act of 1921), the House moved in 1920 to reconcentrate its appropriations authority in a reconstituted Appropriations Committee with separate subcommittees exercising jurisdiction over single appropriations bills. The Senate followed in 1922. It was, however, changes in the House Rules Committee which symbolised most forcefully the new power of committees, and the problems it posed for majority rule. Under the previous conditions of centralised party government in the House established by the Reed Rules, the Speaker controlled the Rules Committee and was in a position to prevent the committee from blocking the majority party's programme. Still in full possession of its 1890 powers, the Rules Committee now enjoyed considerable autonomy under conditions of committee government, and could, if it so wished, dictate what legislation the House could approve regardless of the wishes of the majority or public opinion. In the late 1930s, majority Democrats were made painfully aware of the committee's autonomous power as conservative opposition to the New Deal grew. Conservative Democrats opposed to many New Deal programmes and the massive increase in federal and presidential power it entailed dominated this important 'gatekeeping' committee and were able to prevent a Democratic president and Democratic majorities in Congress from enacting New Deal legislation.

Committee government and chair power during this third institutional era were to a great extent founded on the seniority and committee property rights norms. In the House, these norms became almost inviolable for committee as-signments in 1919;[33] much earlier, as we have explained, in the Senate. The chief beneficiaries of these norms and committee autonomy after the 1930s were con-servative southern Democrats who comprised a large proportion of the party following Democratic losses in non-southern seats in the 1920s. When the Demo-crats took control of the House and Senate with huge majorities in 1933, it was these southerners who chaired almost all the important House committees and more than half those in the Senate – in far greater proportions than their numeric representation justified. After the 1936 elections, they used the vantage points of their committee bastions to frustrate the legislative efforts of the Roosevelt Administration and their congressional party's leaders. These confrontations signalled the emergence of an era of committee government.

In the immediate post-war period, Congress moved to consolidate committee government and reinforce the power of committee chairs or 'barons'. The Legis-lative Reorganisation Act of 1946 reduced the number of House standing com-mittees from 33 to 15 and the Senate's from 48 to 19. Before 1946, major committees like the Banking and Currency Committee usually had only a clerk and a couple of stenographers even though members were expected to process legislation of huge national and international importance. Under the provisions of the 1946 Act, committees were authorised to hire up to four professional and six clerical staff (except the Appropriations Committees which could appoint as many as they wished). So began a trend which by 1973 had led to House committee staff increasing more than 1,000 per cent and Senate committee staff by almost 400 per cent. With the passage of the 1946 Act and the reappearance of split-party control of Congress and the presidency in 1947 and 1953 committees entered a golden age which lasted well into the 1960s in which central party leaders were consigned to the margins directing most of their energies to brokering deals among mostly conservative committee chairs. Congressional power did not rest with Congress as a whole or in central leaders but with full standing committees and their chairs who had the power to shape legislation and deny the wishes of party majorities.

Under conditions of committee government, each committee was assigned a specific policy jurisdiction; each had the authority and the capacity to develop policy expertise independently of the executive; each had a budget to hire staff, write legislation, and conduct investigations; and each had a chair whose formal position owed nothing to his popularity, representativeness, or support from central leaders and everything to having accumulated the longest continuous period on the committee. It is no wonder, so the story goes, that when President Truman created the new Department of Defense, it was suggested that Carl Vinson (D.GA), chair of the House Armed Services Committee, would make a good Secretary of Defense. According to the story, Vinson replied: 'Shucks, I'd rather run the Pentagon from up here!'[34] In the Senate, the power of committee chairs was further enhanced by their ability to control committee assignments through the Democratic Steering Committee and by their membership of other major committees they did not chair.

Emerging problems of committee government

While committee government provided Congress as an institution with a much-needed system of specialised advice outside the tight strictures of party government, and individual members with opportunities to pursue their personal career aspirations, it posed fundamental problems for a legislature which was supposed to operate by majority rule and exercise important representative and law-making functions. First was the problem of leadership.[35] Although the Speaker in the House and the majority leader in the Senate were not exactly powerless, often they were unable to speak persuasively for their chamber and command party majorities because unlike their predecessors Reed and Cannon their party's constituency bases were divided. Even such able and prestigious leaders as Speaker Sam Rayburn (D.TX, 1940–6, 1949–52, 1955–61) and Senate majority leader Lyndon Johnson (D.TX, 1953–61) were obliged by the constraints of a divided majority party and of committee government to adopt highly personalised accommodative, brokerage leadership styles which consisted primarily of mediating conflicts between autonomous committee leaders and party factions.[36]

Second, there was the related problem of democratic accountability and responsibility. This was particularly acute when the Democrats were the majority. As a result of many senior non-southern Democrats losing their seats in the 1946 mid-term elections, when the Democrats regained control of Congress in 1948 it was typically southern conservatives re-elected from the one-party south who claimed committee chairs and negotiated with Democratic and Republican administrations. Because central party leaders did not have the power to discipline committee members and chairs like 'Judge' Howard Smith (D.VA), chair of the Rules Committee (1955–66) or James O. Eastland (D.MS), chair of the Senate Judiciary Committee (1956–78) – who obstructed party legislation – majority Democrats could not give those who had voted for them any reasonable assurance that campaign promises would be legislated; nor could the party be held democratically responsible for its successes and failures. Congress' democratic accountability was further weakened by the invisibility of committee activities to the American public: committee business was often conducted in secret; committees and subcommittees were numerous; and jurisdictions confusing and overlapping. By fragmenting power within Congress, committee government also made the coordination of legislative business difficult. Nowhere was this problem more apparent than in budgetary policy where three different sets of committees were involved – the relevant authorisation committees, Appropriations Committees, and the Ways and Means and Finance Committees. One consequence of the fragmented committee system was that Congress surrendered substantial responsibility for coordinating budgetary decisions to the Bureau of the Budget within the executive.[37]

What held together the fragmented committee system and perpetuated conservative power was a set of overarching norms (in the House) and folkways (in the Senate) into which new congressional recruits were socialised. New members were expected to serve a long apprenticeship; pursue their legislative responsibilities diligently; work hard on committee legislation; develop a policy specialism (especially in the House); avoid debating the broad direction of policy; maintain the prestige of their chamber; avoid self-serving acts of publicity; be courteous to seniors; and exchange favours with other members (reciprocity).[38]

From the 1970s to the present

Even as the golden age of committee government reached its apotheosis in the 1940s and 1950s, the seeds of revolt had already been sown. Congress is a representative institution as well as a law-making body. As the Progressive revolt demonstrated at the beginning of the century, representational pressures cannot long be suppressed. When Congress moved in the 1940s to streamline and modernise its committee system, it made the institution's internal structure very hierarchical. The number of members benefiting directly from committee government was small, while the amount of power forfeited to committees and their chairs by rank and file members was large.

From the late 1950s on, new representational forces gained momentum, resulting in the 1970s in the most comprehensive reform of Congress' internal distribution of power since the 1910s and a much more assertive legislature. Out of this reform process emerged a new institutional era in which Congress took steps to becoming a complete government, intervening in all areas of policy (domestic and foreign), often in opposition to the president. Within Congress, power was further decentralised from full committees and their chairs to subcommittees and to individual members as the House and the Senate became much less hierarchical and more democratic, and as members came to act more for themselves rather than for their party or the president. Organisational, behavioural, and stylistic differences between the House and the Senate also narrowed as senators began increasingly to compete with their House colleagues to deliver efficient service to their increasingly attentive constituents, and the House became a fully-fledged overseer of foreign and military policy.

Membership change

The origins of the new institutional era lay in the elections of 1958 when a new generation of activist liberal northern Democrats – less willing to uphold the traditional norms of apprenticeship, restricted activism, and deference, and more determined to challenge conservative power – were elected to the 86th Congress (1959–60).[39] Immediately, they organised into the Democratic Study Group in the House, and in 1961, with a new activist Democratic administration persuaded Speaker Rayburn to reform the conservative-dominated Rules Committee. The committee was enlarged from twelve to fifteen members, allowing Rayburn to appoint two new Democrats loyal to the party's national programme. Four years later, the '21 day rule' was reintroduced to foreclose delays by the Rules Committee. The increase in liberal representation was soon reflected in the 1960s in assignments to important committees like Appropriations and even more so on authorising committees where they proceeded to initiate a basket of entitlement programmes (such as Medicare and Medicaid, and income maintenance programmes) outside the discretion of the Appropriations Committees. As congressional workloads increased (see Figure 2.4) and became more complex, and as members demanded more opportunities to demonstrate their leadership in specific policy specialisms, the number of subcommittees grew phenomenally – reaching 133 in the House and 99 in the Senate by 1967.

In the early 1970s the pace of internal congressional reform quickened. With economic stagnation deepening, a new emphasis on popular participation and environmental degradation, growing disenchantment with government and leaders (fuelled by the failures of President Johnson's Great Society, Vietnam and Watergate, and the growth of the 'imperial presidency'),[40] and the emergence of

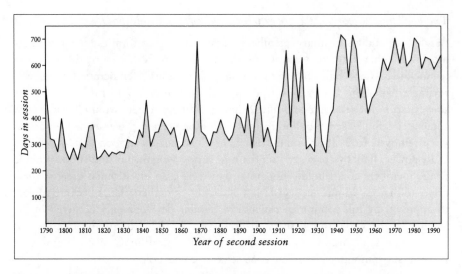

Figure 2.4 Number of days House of Representatives in session, 1789–1994.

new, more heterogeneous constituency groups, the number of members retiring voluntarily rose sharply (see the top line of Figure 2.2). In their places were elected a wave of new, younger, skilled, more ambitious and more enterprising activists schooled in the civil rights and consumer movements of the 1960s who insisted that Congress better accommodate constituents' needs, and assert its autonomy from the executive. As a result, rights and opportunities of individual committee members were enhanced, Congress' budgetary procedures were reformed, individual members' resources were further improved, the public's access to congressional deliberations was increased through electronic voting in the House and an end to secret voting in committees. Committee staffs and member resources were also expanded in the 1970s to allow members to travel more to their districts. New resource agencies such as the Congressional Budget Office and the Office of Technology Assessment were established to conduct independent policy analysis; and the budgets of the General Accounting Office and the Congressional Research Service were increased. Most significantly, as Congress' institutional capacity was expanded, Congress became more assertive in its relations with the executive – even when the president was of the same party as the majority in Congress. Symptomatic of Congress' increased assertiveness was the passage of the War Powers Resolution in 1973, restricting the president's capacity to commit American troops abroad. In the following year, the Budget and Impoundment Control Act introduced new congressional controls over presidential budgetary decisions; and throughout the 1970s and 1980s, Congress made increasing use of the legislative veto and oversight to bring the executive to heel.

The challenge to committee government and chairmanship power

Besides expanding ordinary members' rights and opportunities, the reformers moved in other ways to make Congress less hierarchical, less rigid, and more democratic. After a half century of dormancy, the House Democratic Caucus was revitalised in 1969. Under new Caucus rules, seniority would no longer be the sole criterion for selecting committee chairs; in future, chairs would be subject to Caucus election by secret ballot. In 1975, as a direct result, three senior Democrats were removed from their committee chairs. In other attacks on committee and chair power, limits were placed on the number of assignments and subcommittee chairs members could hold. Subcommittees were also given much greater autonomy to process committee legislation and after 1977 their chairs became subject to approval by full committee caucuses.[41] Similar developments occurred in the Senate. In the early 1970s, secret ballots were introduced for the elections of committee chairs and in the late 1970s senators placed limits on the number of full and subcommittee chairs any one senator could hold.

Greater internal democracy/flatter authority structure

The overall effect of these changes was to flatten Congress' hierarchical power structure and limit the ability of a small number of senior members to dictate policy. Once the bastions of congressional power in the golden age, standing committees and their chairs found after the mid-1970s that their wings had been severely clipped and the seniority norm sharply devalued as they were forced to become much more beholden to their party's caucus.

In other reforms introduced in the 1970s, rank and file members demanded and received a stronger voice in the conduct of business in their chambers. House Democratic Caucus rules were revised to ensure that the preferences of party majorities prevailed. Fairly small numbers of members were permitted to call Caucus meetings. Caucus majorities were permitted to instruct majority members of the Rules Committee to grant rules allowing floor consideration of named bills; and the Speaker was authorised to ensure that Caucus opinions on particular bills were adequately represented on conference committees with the Senate. Traditional norms and folkways – apprenticeship, specialisation, reciprocity, and legislative work – which reinforced the committee and seniority systems in the previous era were undermined as much greater emphasis was placed on individualism and a new type of collegialism.

Under these new conditions, House members and senators were encouraged to participate in a much wider range of policy areas than their predecessors, to broaden their interests outside their committee assignments, to collaborate with a much wider range of colleagues, and to challenge bills reported to the floor, even by the most prestigious committees.[42] In consequence, a wider range of members in both houses were able to make their reputations and meet the demands of their constituents in a larger number of policy-making arenas – on the floor of their chamber, in party committees and caucuses, in *ad hoc* groups and coalitions, in the mass media, as well as in the committee and subcommittees of which they are members. As a consequence of their increased staff and other resources, relatively junior members with good staff could acquire influence by providing their colleagues with expertise in policy areas like the budget, environment, military procurement, agriculture, and banking which became increasingly technical and even more specialised.[43] Finally, the enhancement of their official resources enabled members to adopt positions on a far wider range of issues than did their predecessors and to counter the efforts of opponents who made use of their public voting records.[44]

Strengthening central leadership structures

The curtailing of committee and chair power and the movement towards greater internal democracy served to generate important questions which had been raised at the very foundation of the Republic about Congress' capacity to represent and make laws. Fearing a legislative free-for-all, House Democrats sought to counterbalance their decentralising reforms by strengthening the powers of the Speaker and by making the holder of the office more accountable to the Democratic Caucus. In 1973, the Caucus moved to appoint the Speaker, the Majority Leader, and the Majority Whip to the Democratic Committee on Committees, thereby strengthening the party leadership's influence over committee assignments. In 1974, House Democrats created a new Democratic Steering and Policy Committee with responsibility for policy development, establishing legislative priorities, and assigning House Democrats to committees. The Speaker chaired the committee and appointed a quarter of its members. Subsequently, the Speaker was given the power to refer bills simultaneously and sequentially to several committees (multiple referral), to create *ad hoc* committees, to set time limits for committee deliberations, and to appoint and remove members of the Rules Committee. Besides increasing party control, these reforms also undercut further the power of full committees and their chairs.

As the congressional policy agenda of the 1980s and 1990s became fixated with the budget deficit, constricting opportunities for legislative individualism and policy activism, and as majority Democrats became more united ideologically, the power of central party leaders was further strengthened. In the House, Democratic Speakers 'Tip' O'Neill (D.MA, 1977–86), Jim Wright (D.TX, 1987–9), and Tom Foley (D.WA, 1989–94) exploited opportunities provided by the new congressional budget process created by the 1974, 1985, and 1990 Budget Acts to centralise budget decision-making and enhance their influence. Other unrelated legislative issues were bundled together into huge omnibus bills all or parts of which were then referred by central party leaders sequentially to one or more committees. Extensive procedural devices, such as special rules, were also used to structure members' voting choices and enhance the prospects of passage of majority legislation on the floor. With Republican presidents in the White House and Democrats retaining control of Congress, O'Neill, Wright, and Foley assumed the mantle of leader of the opposition frequently appearing on television to reply to presidential messages and publicising alternative Democratic policy proposals. In 1992, Speaker Foley orchestrated removal of the chair of a House select committee. Over the same period, Senate majority leaders also increased their control of the floor timetable by restricting senators' individual privileges and by introducing weekly scheduling of business, as part of broader efforts to enhance coordination and predictability.

By 1994, then, a new consolidation and centralisation of power had occurred in the House, to a much lesser extent in the Senate. In both houses, however, congressional decision-making was much more democratic, more individualistic, and more collegial than in earlier eras. Following their resounding victories in the 1994 mid-term elections, the new House Republican majority further strengthened the power of central party leaders, albeit subject to rank and file controls and term limits.

The Republican takeover of 1994

In a bold move unprecedented since the days of Speaker Cannon, at the beginning of the 104th Congress (1995–6) the House Republican Conference – swollen by a large influx of freshmen – allowed Newt Gingrich (R.GA), the first Republican Speaker in forty years, to dictate the choice of committee chairs, in three cases passing over more senior members. House Republicans also gave Gingrich additional influence over Republican committee assignments, over the referral of bills to committees, and the administration of the House. In the style of a prime minister, Gingrich also assumed even greater responsibility than his Democratic predecessors for this party's public and media relations demanding, for example, a half-hour slot on prime-time television to address the American people. While the powers of the Speaker were further increased, the position of committees was weakened as the new Republican majority severely cut committee budgets, implemented six-year term limits for committee and subcommittee chairs, reduced committee memberships, and proposed to remove rules restrictions on floor amendments to committee bills. Three full committees and thirty-one House subcommittees were also abolished. However, even as the power of the Speaker was increased and that of committees made much more dependent on central leaders, the more open, participatory, and collegial congressional culture created in the 1970s and 1980s continues. With Gingrich's support, as many as twenty freshmen and sophomores (members with one term of service) were appointed to subcommittee chairs, and many others to prestigious committees and leadership positions. In one important area, a sharp reversal of the Democratic trend toward a more decentralised House has occurred. A number of important powers formerly held by the committee 'barons' have been reinstated. Chairs now have complete control over committee budgets and subcommittee staffs, are permitted to appoint subcommittee chairs (if necessary, violating seniority), and may convene committee hearings at short notice. This will mean that at least in the short term Republican subcommittee chairs will find it much more difficult to develop autonomous fiefdoms as Democratic chairs did from the 1970s onwards. Perhaps indicative of the future should the Democrats regain control of the House was the rejection by the House Democratic Caucus in December 1994 of a move to give their leader power to select committee ranking members. While internal change in the House has been fairly dramatic, that in the more individualistic Senate has been minimal, except for substantial cuts in committee budgets.

These important changes introduced in 1994 and 1995 neatly underline a point which has always been true of Congress over the long term: that it is a

Table 2.1. Four eras of institutional change in Congress

	External Influences	Membership Characteristics	Central Leadership Organs	Divisions of Labour
ERA I – 1789–1860	Agrarian society; limited government; sectionalism; emerging party system	Amateur legislators; transient House and Senate membership; minimum resources; undemanding constituency responsibilities	Generally weak; chambers dominanted by a few elite careerists and leading debaters or occasionally by a strong president	Shift from Committee of the Whole House to standing committee systems; informal divisions and specialisations of labour
ERA II – 1860–1910s	Rapid industrialisation; pressures for increased government; sectionalism; strengthened party system; Republican domination; Progressivism	Growth of careerism; more stable membership; expanding member resources; legislative professionalisation; growing House–Senate divergences	Strong central party leadership in the House; factionalised leadership in Senate; enforcement of majority rule through formal rules	Committee systems institutionalised; growing divisions and specialisations of labour; strengthening of seniority and committee property rights
ERA III – 1910s–1970s	Advanced industrial society; mass politics; increased federal government intervention; Democratic domination after 1932	Professional career legislators; stable membership; conservative coalition; strong norms and folkways	Weak, personalised broker-style central leadership dependent on committees and presidential leadership	Institutionalisation of seniority, committee property rights and committee government; strong chairs; conservative domination
ERA IV – 1970s–now	Expansion of big government; participatory democracy; more demanding constituents; growing disenchantment with government and politicians; technocracy; mass media politics; declining party system; split-party government; deficit politics	Reform activists; individualism and collegialism; decline of traditional norms and folkways; incumbency embedded; more extensive constituency service; growing importance of expertise; increases in members' official resources	Stronger centralised leadership controls over floor and committees; greater party unity; influential party caucuses; enhanced media and party roles; centralised budgeting	Committees and chairs weakened and subjected to stronger party and floor controls; subcommittee and individual member power increased; expansion of committee resources; greater differentiation between committees

Source: see text.

quintessentially dynamic legislature, not only in the sense that it makes national policy, but also in the ways it responds organisationally and procedurally to the changing currents of American politics. It is not a plebiscitary conveyor of popular and transient sentiments but a deliberative body designed to filter public opinion through its internal procedures and deliver considered policy outcomes. Over this period, Congress was transformed from an unstructured representative and legislative body in the eighteenth and early nineteenth century into a highly institutionalised legislative organisation in the late twentieth century with complex structures, procedures, norms and traditions. Without ignoring crucial organisational and behavioural differences between the House and the Senate, we have placed institutional change within four eras, the chief characteristics of which are summarised in Table 2.1. The changes associated with each era have been explained as democratic responses to shifts in American politics and society over time. As the problems confronting constituents change – and therefore the policy positions and agendas that they will support – existing political alignments shift and Congress' membership changes. Over time, new members sharing common perceptions of the dominant issues of the time come to dominate the legislature. In order to promote the newly emerging policy agenda, and regardless of their partisan, ideological, and constituency differences, they find that they need to change Congress' structure and processes to make the institution respond better to their needs and the needs of those who elect them. If they succeed, a new institutional era is inaugurated.

In the next three chapters, we focus specifically on the contemporary era, to examine how Congress – America's most democratic institution – operates today. We begin by exploring the electoral connection between present-day members and their constituencies.

Notes

1   Woodrow Wilson, *Congressional Government. A Study in American Politics* (Baltimore and London: Johns Hopkins Press, 1981. Originally published 1885), p. 29.

2   *Ibid.*, p. 54.

3   Quoted in Edmund S. Morgan, *Inventing the People. The Rise of Popular Sovereignty in England and America* (New York and London: W. W. Norton, 1988), p. 241.

4   Calvin Jillson and Rick K. Wilson, *Congressional Dynamics. Structure, Coordination, and Choice in the First American Congress, 1774–1789* (Stanford, CA: Stanford University Press, 1994), esp. chapters 3–5.

5   James Madison, Alexander Hamilton, and John Jay, *The Federalist Papers* (New York and Toronto: New American Library, 1961), no. 51, p. 322.

6   James G. Marsh and Johan P. Olsen, 'The New Institutionalism: Organisational Factors in Political Life', *American Political Science Review*, 78 (1984), pp. 734–49; Nelson W. Polsby, 'The Institutionalization of the US House of Representatives', *American Political Science Review*, 62 (1968), pp. 144–68.

7   On congressional change, see Lawrence C. Dodd, 'The Cycles of Legislative Change',

in Herbert F. Weisberg (ed.), *Political Science: The Science of Politics* (New York: Agathon, 1986), pp. 82–104; Lawrence C. Dodd, 'A Theory of Congressional Cycles: Solving the Puzzle of Change' in Gerald C. Wright, Leroy N. Rieselbach, and Lawrence C. Dodd (eds), *Congress and Policy Change* (New York: Agathon Press, 1986), pp. 3–44.

8   Quoted in Neil MacNeil, *Forge of Democracy. The House of Representatives* (New York: David McKay, 1963), p. 124.

9   James Sterling Young, *The Washington Community, 1800–1828* (New York and London: Harcourt, Brace Jovanovich, 1966), pp. 44–5, 22–8.

10 H. Douglas Price, 'Congress and the Evolution of Legislative "Professionalism"', in Norman J. Ornstein, (ed.), *Congress in Change* (New York: Praeger, 1975), pp. 5 and 7; Nelson C. Dometrius and Lee Sigelman, 'Costs, Benefits and Careers in the US House of Representatives: A Developmental Approach', *Congress and the Presidency*, 18 (1991), pp. 55–75, 66–7; Randall B. Ripley, *Power in the Senate* (New York: St. Martin's Press, 1969), p. 43.

11 Young, *The Washington Community*, pp. 96–7. See also Alexis de Tocqueville, *Democracy in America*, vol. i (New York: Harper Collins, 1969), p. 200.

12 Price, 'Congress and the Evolution of Legislative "Professionalism"', p. 6.

13 Jack Van Der Silk, 'The Early Institutionalisation of Congress', *Congress and the Presidency*, 16 (1989), p. 2; Joel H. Silbey, '"Our Successors Will Have an Easier Task": The First Congress under the Constitution, 1789–1791', *This Constitution*, 17 (1987), p. 4; and Jillson and Wilson, *Congressional Dynamics*.

14 Gerald Gamm and Kenneth A. Shepsle, 'Emergence of Legislative Institutions: Standing Committees in the House and Senate, 1810–1825', *Legislative Studies Quarterly*, 14 (1989), p. 47; Elaine K. Swift, 'Reconstitutive Change in the US Congress: The Early Senate, 1789–1841', *Legislative Studies Quarterly*, 14 (1989), pp. 175–203; Thomas W. Skladony, 'The House Goes To Work: Select and Standing Committees in the US House of Representatives, 1789–1828', *Congress and the Presidency*, 12 (1985), pp. 165–87; Joseph Cooper, *The Origins of the Standing Committees and the Development of the Modern House* (Houston, TX: Rice University Press, 1970); and MacNeil, *Forge of Democracy*, pp. 149–50.

15 H. Douglas Price, 'Careers and Committees in the American Congress: The Problem of Structural Change', in William O. Aydelotte (ed.), *The History of Parliamentary Behavior* (Princeton, NJ: Princeton University Press, 1977), pp. 42–3.

16 Garrison Nelson, 'Leadership Position-Holding in the United States House of Representatives', *Capitol Studies*, 4 (1976), pp. 11–36; John F. Hoadley, *Origins of American Political Parties, 1789–1803*, (Lexington, KY: University Press of Kentucky, 1986), pp. 47–53; Young, *The Washington Community*, ch. 6.

17 Congressional Quarterly, *Guide to the Congress of the United States: Origins, History and Procedure* (Washington, D.C.: Congressional Quarterly, 1971), p. 83.

18 Margaret Munk, 'Origin and Development of the Party Floor Leadership in the United States Senate', *Capitol Studies*, 2 (1974), pp. 23–4; Young, *The Washington Community*, pp. 157–63.

19 Wilson, *Congressional Government*, p. 31.

20 Morris P. Fiorina, David W. Rohde, and Peter Wissel, 'Historical Change in House Turnover' in Ornstein, *Congress in Change*, p. 37.

21 Allan G. Bogue, Jerome M. Clubb, Carroll R. McKibbin, and Santa A. Traugott,

'Members of the House of Representatives and the Process of Modernisation, 1789–1960', *Journal of American History*, 63 (1976), pp. 275–302, p. 283.

22   Polsby, 'The Institutionalization of the US House of Representatives', p. 165.

23   George B. Galloway, *History of the House of Representatives* (New York: Thomas Crowell, 1969), p. 65.

24   Wilson, *Congressional Government*, p. 69.

25   Ripley, *Power in the Senate*, pp. 42–4; Robert W. Packwood, 'The Senate Seniority System' in Ornstein, *Congress in Change*, pp. 60–71; Nelson W. Polsby, Miriam Gallagher, and Barry R. Rundquist, 'The Growth of the Seniority System in the US House of Representatives', *American Political Science Review*, 63 (1969), table 1.

26   Lauros G. McConachie, *Congressional Committees* (New York: Thomas Crowell, 1898), pp. 159–60, 165.

27   George Rothwell Brown, *The Leadership of Congress* (Indianapolis: Bobbs-Merrill, 1922), pp. 250–1.

28   Joseph Cooper and David W. Brady, 'Institutional Context and Leadership Style: The House From Cannon to Rayburn', *American Political Science Review*, 75 (1981), p. 415.

29   James Bryce, *The American Commonwealth* (London and New York: Macmillan and Co, 1888), pp. 185–7.

30   David J. Rothman, *Politics and Power: The United States Senate 1869–1901* (Cambridge, MA: Harvard University Press, 1966), pp. 29 and 34; Munk, 'Origin and Development of the Party Floor Leadership', pp. 27–8; Joseph S. Clark, *The Senate Establishment* (New York: Hill and Wang, 1963), pp. 24–8; Ripley, *Power in the Senate*, p. 26; Congressional Quarterly, *Guide to Congress* (Washington, D.C.: Congressional Quarterly, 1982), 3rd edn, pp. 98–9.

31   In 1915, the membership of the House was frozen at 435 to avoid overcrowding.

32   Brown, *The Leadership of Congress*, pp. 195–7, 257–8, 275; Rothman, *Politics and Power*, p. 90.

33   Michael Abram and Joseph Cooper, 'The Rise of Seniority in the House of Representatives', *Polity*, 1 (1968), p. 70.

34   See Richard Bolling, *House Out Of Order* (New York: Dutton, 1965), p. 65.

35   Lawrence C. Dodd and Richard L. Schott, *Congress and the Administrative State* (New York and Chichester: Wiley, 1979), pp. 74–8.

36   Cooper and Brady, 'Institutional Context and Leadership Style', pp. 422–4; Randall B. Ripley, *Party Leaders in the House of Representatives* (Washington, D.C.: The Brookings Institution, 1967), p. 92; Rowland Evans and Robert Novak, *Lyndon B. Johnson: The Exercise of Power* (New York: New American Library, 1966); and Ralph K. Huitt, 'Democratic Party Leadership in the Senate', *American Political Science Review*, 55 (1961), pp. 333–44.

37   Allen Schick, 'The Three-Ring Budget Process: The Appropriations, Tax, and Budget Committees in Congress', in Thomas E. Mann and Norman J. Ornstein (eds), *The New Congress* (Washington, D.C.: American Enterprise Institute, 1981).

38   Donald R. Matthews, *US Senators and Their Worlds* (New York: Vintage Books, 1960); Herbert B. Asher, 'The Learning of Legislative Norms', *American Political Science Review*, 67 (1973), pp. 499–513; David W. Rohde, Norman J. Ornstein, and Robert l. Peabody, 'Political Change and Legislative Norms in the US Senate, 1957–74', in Glenn R. Parker (ed.), *Studies of Congress* (Washington, D.C.: Congressional Quarterly Press, 1985).

39   Michael Foley, *The New Senate. Liberal Influence on a Conservative Institution, 1959–1972* (New Haven and London: Yale University Press, 1980); Clark, *The Senate Establishment*; Lawrence C. Dodd and Bruce I. Oppenheimer, 'The House in Transition: Change and Consolidation' and Norman J. Ornstein, Robert L. Peabody, and David W. Rohde, 'The Changing Senate: From the 1950s to the 1970s', both in Lawrence C. Dodd and Bruce I. Oppenheimer (eds), *Congress Reconsidered*, 2nd edn (Washington, D.C.: Congressional Quarterly Press, 1981).

40   Arthur S. Schlesinger, *The Imperial Presidency* (Boston: Houghton Mifflin, 1973).

41   See Roger H. Davidson and Walter J. Oleszek, *Congress Against Itself* (Bloomington, IN: Indiana University Press, 1977); Leroy N. Rieselbach, *Congressional Reform . The Changing Modern Congress* (Washington, D.C.: Congressional Quarterly Press, 1994); Dodd and Oppenheimer, 'The House in Transition'; Ornstein, Peabody, and Rohde, 'The Changing Senate'; James L. Sundquist, *The Decline and Resurgence of Congress* (Washington, D.C.: The Brookings Institution, 1981).

42   Steven S. Smith, *Call To Order. Floor Politics in the House and Senate* (Washington, D.C.: The Brookings Institution, 1989); Steven S. Smith, 'New Patterns of Decision-making in Congress' in John E. Chubb and Paul E. Peterson (eds), *The New Direction in American Politics* (Washington, D.C.: The Brookings Institution, 1989); Burdett A. Loomis, 'The "Me Decade" and the Changing Context of House Leadership" in Frank H. Mackaman (ed.), *Understanding Congressional Leadership* (Washington, D.C.: Congressional Quarterly Press, 1981), pp. 157–79; cf. Edward V. Schneier, 'Norms and Folkways in Congress: How Much Has Actually Changed?' *Congress and the Presidency*, 15 (1988): 117–38

43   Lawrence C. Dodd, 'The Rise of the Technocratic Congress: Congressional Reform in the 1970s' in Richard A. Harris and Sidney M. Milkis (eds), *Remaking American Politics* (Boulder and London: Westview, 1989).

44   Burdett A. Loomis, *The New American Politician: Ambition, Entrepreneurship, and the Changing Face of Political Life* (New York: Basic Books, 1988); Charles S. Bullock and Burdett A. Loomis, 'The Changing Congressional Career', in Lawrence C. Dodd and Bruce I. Oppenheimer (eds), *Congress Reconsidered*, 3rd edn (Washington, D.C.: Congressional Quarterly Press, 1985); and Herbert A. Asher, 'The Changing Status of the Freshman Congressman', in Ornstein, *Congress in Change*.

CHAPTER 3

Congress' electoral connection

The framers of the Constitution prescribed that Congress would write and approve laws but first and foremost the national legislature would be a representative assembly. In Federalist Paper number 52 James Madison insisted:

> As it is essential to liberty that the government in general should have a common interest with the people, so it is particularly essential that the branch of it under consideration should have an immediate dependence on, and an intimate sympathy with, the people.

Over 200 years later, the most important task for prospective members of Congress is not to persuade local voters that the president or their party's presidential candidate is popular and responsive to their needs and demands. It is that they – and only they – will truly represent the local community and will remain close to the people back home once elected. 'If you elect me to Congress,' declared Arkansas Democrat Bill McCuen in his bid to win a House seat in 1992, 'you're not sending me away forever. I'm taking you with me.'[1] This representative imperative is so strong that even incumbent House members and senators who can usually depend on being re-elected go to extraordinary lengths to avoid charges that they have 'gone native' in Washington, become beholden to the 'special interests', or lost touch with their constituents. So, a television advertisement for House Agriculture Committee chairman Kika de la Garza told voters in 1994: 'Most politicians go to Washington and you never see them again. Not Kika de la Garza . . . [He returns to the district] almost every weekend . . . Today in Washington they call him Mr. Chairman. But in South Texas, we still call him "Kika".'[2] As public trust and confidence in the federal government has deteriorated (falling from 74 per cent public confidence in 1972 to just 42 per cent in 1992),[3] the incentives for members of Congress to project themselves as local politicians unconnected with Congress in Washington has increased dramatically.

Once elected, local voters *expect* their member of Congress to provide high quality service to the state or district, to be accessible, to communicate with them frequently, and to promote their causes and interests, even at the expense of broader general interests. Even a powerful chairman must find time and resources to accommodate mundane, even trivial, requests from his/her constituents. When House members and senators decide how they will spend their time, when they decide whether or not to take an interest in a particular bill or subject, when they choose a committee or subcommittee to join, and when they decide how to vote on the budget, health care, crime or any other issue, they will first consider their constituencies. What David Mayhew calls the 'electoral connection'[4] is hugely important – in many situations, paramount.

The nature of congressional elections

In the United States, elections are seen as the primary (to some, the only) mechanisms by which citizens influence the composition of government and the making of public policy, and the only opportunities to exercise their political rights and responsibilities and hold politicians publicly accountable. Something like 521,000 political offices are filled by election – many more than in any other country. Despite the frequency of elections and the common usage of such phrases as 'American democracy', elections for the Congress do not encourage broadly based participation. Nor do they provide American citizens with a more or less equal ability to influence government decisions, or ensure public competition among candidates. Figure 3.1 shows that only about half the voting age population participate in congressional elections during presidential election years and barely a third in mid-term elections. In contrast with other liberal democratic societies, American voters' propensity to vote is strongly correlated with the amount of formal education they have received, and to a lesser extent with age and living outside the south.[5] Most congressional elections – particularly for the House of

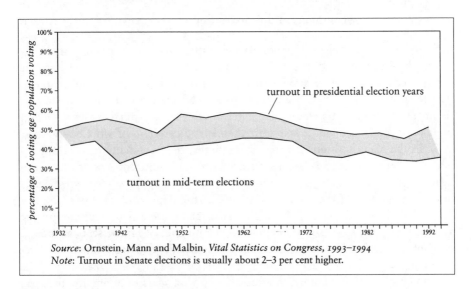

Source: Ornstein, Mann and Malbin, *Vital Statistics on Congress, 1993–1994*
Note: Turnout in Senate elections is usually about 2–3 per cent higher.

Figure 3.1 Voter turnout in House elections, 1932–1994.

Representatives – attract very little media attention and most campaigns are sporadic and amateurish. It is not surprisingly then that levels of voter interest are low. Survey evidence from the American National Election Study (ANES) shows that significant numbers of citizens are not interested in congressional campaigns or who wins them. In the 1992 elections, for example, 35 per cent of voters said they cared little about the outcome, but voted nonetheless; 29 per cent did not even know which party controlled Congress at the time. As we will see from the subsequent discussion, other features of congressional elections suggest a limited democratic basis.

The formal context of congressional representation

In common with other liberal democratic systems of Anglo-Saxon origin, members of Congress are elected by simple majority voting. Originally, the Constitution provided only for the House to be popularly elected for two-year terms; senators would be elected indirectly by state legislatures for six-year terms. Only since the middle of the nineteenth century has the House been elected from single-member constituencies, and only since 1913 have senators been elected directly. Candidates for congressional office must meet few formal constitutional requirements: House members must be at least 25 years old and have held US citizenship for at least 7 years; senators must be at least 30 and have held citizenship for 9 years. Both House members and senators must be residents of the state which elects them. Within certain constitutional limits, individual states decide who can vote.

House apportionment and redistricting

Because the House is elected by populations rather than by geographic areas, the geographic distribution of the voting age population and where district lines are drawn (redistricting) have crucial effects upon the composition of the chamber. Article 1, Section 2 of the Constitution provides for the redistribution or reapportionment of House seats among the states after every decennial census to reflect population shifts. Individual states are then left to determine district boundaries.

In the eighteenth and nineteenth centuries, the potentially painful process whereby states lost seats as a consequence of reapportionment – or as a result of new states being admitted to the union – was avoided by the simple expedient of increasing the size of the House. However, as the population expanded rapidly in the late nineteenth century, fears grew that the House was becoming too large and cumbersome, so in 1915 Congress set the number of House seats at today's total of 435. After House membership was capped,[6] reapportionment and redistricting became much more controversial processes, especially when large shifts in population occurred among the states. Following years of acrimony, the 1929 Reapportionment Act effectively delegated the task of reapportioning seats to the

Bureau of the Census, and after 1941, a complex mathematical formula known as the Hill method of equal proportions was used to minimise the proportional difference between the average district size in any two states. In the reapportionment which followed the 1990 census, 19 seats, mainly in the north east and midwest, were redistributed to southern and western states giving representatives from these states a House majority for the first time ever. In common with previous reappointments a number of incumbents were forced into contesting districts which were drastically redrawn or where other incumbents were also running.

Once seats are reapportioned, state governors are required to agree new congressional district lines with their state legislatures. Until very recently, redistricting was a somewhat haphazard, often non-existent, process. For example, before the mid-1960s, Louisiana had not redrawn its congressional districts since 1912. Georgia, Wisconsin, Colorado, and South Carolina had not done so since the early 1930s. Various attempts were made in the early twentieth century – notably in the 1901 Reapportionment Act – to require that districts be composed of 'contiguous and compact territory . . . containing nearly as practicable an equal number of inhabitants', but these requirements were widely ignored. By the early 1960s, the huge disparities in district populations had become a national scandal. Particularly egregious were the disparities between densely populated urban districts and sparsely populated rural seats. Twenty mainly urban districts contained over 600,000 people in 1960, while eighteen mainly rural districts contained less than 250,000. The difference between the largest district (Texas 5th) and the smallest (Oklahoma 4th) was almost three quarters of a million people.[7] Following a long campaign, the United States Supreme Court moved to rectify these imbalances and institutionalise the principle of one vote one value. In *Wesberry* v. *Sanders* (1964), the Court ruled that Article 1, Section 2 of the Constitution meant that 'as nearly as practicable one man's vote in a congressional election is to be worth as much as another's.' Three years later, Congress prohibited at-large elections in states which elected more than one member, and the Court insisted that states draw congressional districts as equally as possible and to take account of population shifts within states' boundaries.

Despite these and subsequent actions, even now all congressional districts do not have equal populations – for the obvious reasons that state populations vary and the Constitution requires every state to have at least one representative regardless of population. In the 1990 census, for example, Alaska, Vermont, and Wyoming all had populations below the 572,466 equal proportions quota but nevertheless each was given its constitutional minimum. In contrast, the most populous district – Montana's at-large district – is the largest in American history with a population of 803,655, 76 per cent larger than the smallest – Wyoming's at-large district – with just 455,975 people. Even in multi-member states, discrepancies in populations persist: each of Kansas' districts have populations of 621,400 whereas Rhode Island's have 503,000.

One important consequence of the Court's requirement for population equality is that many House districts are not meaningful political communities because they do not coincide with local city, county, or state legislative district boundaries which typically form the bases of local party activities. As a result, it is argued, electoral connections between national and local political representatives are weakened. This complaint was given added weight after the 1990 reapportionment because 19 specific majority–minority districts were created. Following Court decisions in *Thornburg v. Gingles* (1986), *Garza v. County of Los Angeles* (1990), and *Grove v. Emison* (1993), states were authorised to ignore county and other local political boundaries in order to create majority–minority districts and increase the number of black and Hispanic House members. North Carolina's majority–minority 12th district looks like an inverted dinosaur as it straggles along 160 miles of Inter-state Highway–85 between Durham and Charlotte, is barely contiguous, and is certainly not compact; while the state's 6th district is divided into three non-contiguous parts. These and minority–majority districts in Florida, Georgia, Louisiana, New York, and Texas have become the subject of intense litigation.[8]

While this sort of racial gerrymandering is relatively recent, partisan gerrymandering has a much longer history. Court requirements that districts be of equal size have done little to discourage the practice; and now that detailed census data and sophisticated computer software are available state governors and legislatures have been able to effect gerrymanders far more ingenious than Elbridge Gerry's original (failed) efforts in Massachusetts in 1812. In one of the best recent examples, Texas Democrats approved a redistricting plan, following the 1990 reapportionment, which drew congressional boundaries along extremely convoluted routes through Dallas, Houston, and San Antonio. Their purpose was to protect all 19 House Democratic incumbents, concentrate as many Republican voters as possible into just eight districts, and secure control of the state's three new districts. Judging by the 1992 and 1994 election results, the Texan gerrymander was extremely successful: Democrats won 22 of the state's 30 seats on the basis of just 50 per cent of the popular vote. Partisan gerrymanders are not always effective. Either a ruling party attempts to maximise its seats and risks creating marginal districts which are difficult to win or hold; or it adopts a minimal strategy, ensuring larger majorities in a smaller number or seats which waste votes and reduce its chances of capturing other more marginal seats. Georgia's ruling Democrats pursued the former strategy following the 1990 reapportionment and came badly unstuck. In attempting to unseat the state's only Republican – the House minority's whip, Newt Gingrich – in the state's 6th district, the ruling Democrats made two other seats highly marginal; in the 1992 elections, Republicans won both marginal seats, including one held by a Democratic incumbent, and defeated another two Democratic incumbents in 1994 thereby increasing their state delegation from one to five. Attempts to persuade the Supreme Court to rule partisan gerrymandering unconstitutional were rejected in *Davis* v. *Bandemer* (1986) and *Badham* v. *Eu* (1989).

Senate apportionment

Representation in the Senate is, of course, based on fixed geographical areas. Regardless of population size, every state is guaranteed two seats which cannot be denied without its consent. Until the 17th amendment was ratified in 1913, senators were indirectly elected by state legislatures – in keeping with the framers' desires for the second chamber to provide stability and continuity as a counter-balance to the more volatile, popularly elected House. For the same reasons senators serve staggered six-year terms with a third of seats up for re-election every two years. Table 3.1 shows those seats up for re-election in 1996 and 1998.

Table 3.1 Classes of Senate seats, 1996–1998

State	Current Senator	Party	First Elected	State	Current Senator	Party	First Elected
Class 2 – Up for Election in 1996 (33)							
Alabama	Howell Heflin*	Dem	1978	Montana	Max Baucus	Dem	1978
Alaska	Ted Stevens	Rep	1970	Nebraska	James Exon*	Dem	1978
Arkansas	David Pryor*	Dem	1978	New Hampshire	Robert Smith	Rep	1990
Colorado	Hank Brown*	Rep	1990	New Jersey	Bill Bradley*	Dem	1978
Delaware	Joseph Biden	Dem	1972	New Mexico	Pete Domenici	Rep	1972
Georgia	Sam Nunn*	Dem	1972	North Carolina	Jesse Helms	Rep	1972
Idaho	Larry Craig	Rep	1990	Oklahoma	James Inhofe	Rep	1994
Illinois	Paul Simon*	Dem	1984	Oregon	Mark Hatfield	Rep	1966
Iowa	Tom Harkin	Dem	1984	Rhode Island	Claiborne Pell*	Dem	1960
Kansas	Nancy Kassebaum*	Rep	1978	South Carolina	Stron Thurmond	Rep	1954
Kentucky	Mitch McConnell	Rep	1984	South Dakota	Larry Pressler	Rep	1978
Louisiana	Bennett Johnston*	Dem	1972	Tennessee	Fred Thompson	Rep	1994
Maine	William Cohen	Rep	1978	Texas	Phil Gramm	Rep	1984
Massachusetts	John Kerry	Dem	1984	Virginia	John Warner	Rep	1978
Michigan	Carl Levin	Dem	1978	West Virginia	Jay Rockefeller	Dem	1984
Minnesota	Paul Wellstone	Dem	1990	Wyoming	Alan Simpson	Rep	1978
Mississippi	Thad Cochran	Rep	1978				
Class 3 – Up for Election in 1998 (34)							
Alabama	Richard Shelby	Rep	1986	Maryland	Barbara Mikulski	Dem	1986
Alaska	Frank Murkowski	Rep	1980	Missouri	Kit Bond	Rep	1986
Arizona	John McCain	Rep	1986	Nevada	Harry Reid	Dem	1986
Arkansas	Dale Bumpers	Dem	1974	New Hampshire	Judd Gregg	Rep	1992

State	Current Senator	Party	First Elected	State	Current Senator	Party	First Elected
California	Barbara Boxer	Dem	1992	New York	Alfonse D'Amato	Rep	1980
Colorado	Ben Nighthorse Campbell	Rep	1992	North Carolina	Lauch Faircloth	Rep	1992
Connecticut	Christopher Dodd	Dem	1980	North Dakota	Byron Dorgan	Dem	1992
Florida	Bob Graham	Dem	1986	Ohio	John Glenn	Dem	1974
Georgia	Paul Coverdell	Rep	1992	Oklahoma	Don Nickles	Rep	1980
Hawaii	Daniel Inouye	Dem	1962	Oregon	Bob Packwood	Rep	1968
Idaho	Kirk Kempthorne	Rep	1992	Pennsylvania	Arlen Specter	Rep	1980
Illinois	Carol Moseley-Braun	Dem	1992	South Carolina	Ernest Hollings	Dem	1966
Indiana	Daniel Coats	Rep	1990	South Dakota	Tom Daschle	Dem	1986
Iowa	Charles Grassley	Rep	1980	Utah	Robert Bennett	Rep	1992
Kansas	Bob Dole	Rep	1968	Vermont	Patrick Leahy	Dem	1974
Kentucky	Wendell Ford	Dem	1974	Washington	Patty Murray	Dem	1992
Louisiana	John Breaux	Dem	1986	Wisconsin	Russell Feingold	Dem	1992

* senator has announced his/her retirement

Equal state representation in the Senate means that senators' constituencies vary considerably in size and composition. In today's Senate – to use the most extreme example – Senators Barbara Boxer and Diane Feinstein of California represent almost 30 million people – 66 times as many people as do Senators Alan Simpson and Craig Thomas of Wyoming who represent just over 450,000. In aggregate, the combination of equal representation and unequal populations means that, as intended by the Constitution, small states have a significant representational advantage. Currently, 74 out of 100 senators represent just one-third of the country's population, while 16 senators represent just over half. This bias towards rural and small state representation also has important partisan and ideological implications which have benefited Republicans in recent years. Republican strength in the eight smallest (and more conservative) states won the party a Senate majority between 1981 and 1986, on the basis of a nationwide minority of popular votes.[9]

State election laws

Although Congress sets the date for general elections – on the Tuesday after the first Monday in November in every even year – there is no national congressional election process. Instead, each state decides the date by which candidates must put their names forward (or 'file for the ballot'), the precise processes by which the parties choose their nominees, and various electoral registration requirements. (Most states require advance personal registration but some, like Minnesota and Maine also permit voters to register on election day.) In consequence, an intricate patchwork quilt of state laws and regulations governs congressional election processes necessitating a formal election timetable which includes many different events occurring on different days in different states over about eight months. Table 3.2 show the 29 dates of events in the 1993–4 electoral cycle.

Table 3.2. The 1994 congressional election calendar

Date	Event	Date	Event	Date	Event
March 8	Texas primary	June 21	South Dakota runoff	Sept. 13	Arizona primary
March 15	Illinois primary	June 28	Utah primary		Connecticut primary
April 12	Texas runoff		Alabama runoff		District of Columbia primary
May 3	Indiana primary		Mississippi runoff		Maryland primary
	North Carolina primary	July 19	Georgia primary		Minnesota primary
May 10	Nebraska primary	Aug. 2	Kansas primary		New Hampshire primary
	Pennsylvania primary		Michigan primary		New York primary
	West Virginia primary		Missouri primary		Rhode Island primary
May 17	Oregon primary	Aug.4	Tennessee primary		Vermont primary
May 24	Arkansas primary	Aug. 9	Colorado primary		Virgin Islands primary
	Idaho primary		South Carolina primary		Wisconsin primary
	Kentucky primary		Georgia runoff	Sept. 17	Hawaii primary
May 31	North Carolina runoff	Aug. 16	Wyoming primary	Sept. 20	Massachusetts primary
June 7	Alabama primary	Aug. 23	Alaska primary		Washington primary
	California primary		Oklahoma primary		Oklahoma runoff
	Iowa primary		South Carolina runoff	Oct. 1	Louisiana primary
	Mississippi primary	Sept. 3	Guam primary	Oct. 4	Florida runoff
	Montana primary	Sept. 6	Nevada primary	Nov. 8	American Samoa primary
	New Mexico	Sept. 8	Florida primary		Louisiana runoff
	South Dakota primary	Sept. 10	Delaware primary	Nov. 22	American Samoa runoff
June 14	Maine primary				
	North Dakota primary				
	Virginia primary*				
	Arkansas runoff				

Source: Federal Election Commission.
Note: * Parties in Virginia may choose to nominate candidates by convention rather than by primary.

Most states require direct primary elections in which voters rather than party activists decide who will be a party's nominee and 13 states allow or require party conventions to choose nominees. Eight states require state party conventions to endorse specific candidates before the primary (pre-primary endorsements) in order to help voters choose; another 18 states allow parties to endorse candidates. State laws also regulate who can participate in primaries: 26 states have closed primaries, which require voters to register with a party first in order to qualify to vote; another 10 states allow voters to decide on election day in which primary they will vote. Currently, Louisiana holds open primaries in which all candidates – Democrats, Republicans, independents and others – contest the same primary. A candidate winning 50 per cent of the primary vote is automatically elected without the need for a further ballot in November. Where no candidate wins a majority, the two leading candidates contest the general election. In yet another variant, Alaska and Washington hold 'blanket' or 'jungle' primaries in which all candidates appear on the same primary ballot, with the candidate winning the largest number of votes for each party progressing to the general election. Ten southern states, South Dakota, American Samoa, and Guam require second runoff primaries if no candidate receives a required percentage of votes cast . In Alabama, Arkansas, Florida, Georgia, Louisiana, Mississippi, Oklahoma, South Carolina, and Texas, the winning candidate is required to gain 50 per cent of the primary vote; in North Carolina, 40 per cent; and in South Dakota, 35 per cent. The effects of this floor can be decisive. In the 1992 Georgia Senate race, incumbent Democratic Senator Wyche Fowler won only 49.2 per cent of the vote in a three-cornered race; and went on to lose his seat in the runoff to Republican Paul Coverdell who won 50.6 per cent.

The imposition over recent years of term limits for members of Congress by 22 states may further complicate the congressional election process. However, at the time of writing, federal courts have judged state term limit laws un-constitutional – because they add a further qualification for membership of Congress besides age, residency, and citizenship – and congressional Republicans' proposals for a constitutional amendment foundered in the House in early 1995, even though opinion polls report support for the proposals running at 70 per cent in favour.

Congressional recruitment

State electoral laws represent one important set of contextual factors with which candidates must contend in their efforts to reach Capitol Hill. A second set are social, economic, political, demographic, and geographic.

Constituency diversity

No House district or state is identical and none is socially or culturally monolithic. Even though House districts contain roughly the same number of constituents, they vary widely according to geography, demography, economy, politics, and the way the mass media are organised. Seeking nomination or election from a seat in a huge rural district like at-large Alaska (586,000 square miles) or Montana (147,046 square miles) – the geographic equivalent of the distance from Chicago to Washington and thousands of miles from the capital – is bound to be different from seeking a seat covering 10 or 11 square miles in downtown Brooklyn or Manhattan. Other differences are significant:

- Some districts and states are wealthier than others. Median family income (1990) in Connecticut is twice that in Mississippi. Variations across House districts are even wider: families in Maryland's 8th district (Washington suburbs) had a median income of $64,199 while those in New York's 16th district (South Bronx) had a median income of $16,683 and almost 40 per cent of families living in poverty.

- The economic bases of constituencies vary: Michigan's 9th and 16th districts (Flint, Pontiac, and Dearborn) are dominated by the motor industry; Washington's 2nd and 7th districts (Puget Sound and Seattle) by the giant Boeing Aircraft Corporation; Iowa's 5th (northwest) and Kansas' 1st district (rural west) by agricultural production; Virginia's 8th and Maryland's 4th, 5th, and 8th districts by federal government employment; Virginia's 2nd and 8th districts (Norfolk and Washington suburbs) and South Carolina's 1st district (Charleston) by the military or military contractors; and so on.

- Ethnic contexts vary: 74 per cent of the residents of New York's 11th district (central Brooklyn) are black; 84 per cent of the population of California's 33rd district (east central Los Angeles) are Hispanic; 22 per cent of Arizona's 6th district (which includes the Navajo Reservation) and 20 per cent of New Mexico's 3rd district (north and east central) are Native Americans. Jews are prominent in New York's 8th and 9th districts (parts of Manhattan and Brooklyn), Italian-Americans in New York's 13th district (Staten Island and south-west Brooklyn), Asian-Americans in California's 8th district (San Francisco), and Irish-Americans in Massachusetts' 9th district (Boston). Other districts and states have virtually no ethnic minorities – Vermont's at-large district is almost exclusively white, as are many of Minnesota's districts. Other districts and many states are thoroughly cosmopolitan: California's 9th district is 32 per cent black, 12 per cent Hispanic, 16 per cent Asian, and 28 per cent of English, German, and Irish ancestry; New Mexico's 3rd district is 35 per cent Hispanic, 21 per cent Native American, 32 per cent English, German, and Irish.

- Certain districts have atypical age distributions: over one-third of the voting age population in Florida's 13th and 22nd districts are over 65, whereas almost a quarter of California's 33rd district (east central Los Angeles) are under 24.[10]

- Political traditions are ideological diverse – ranging from Utah, probably the most conservative state, to Massachusetts, the most liberal.[11]

- Many House districts are safe for one party. New York's 11th district (central Brooklyn) is solidly Democratic, giving Bill Clinton 57 per cent in 1992, whereas districts like Indiana's 6th district are solidly Republican.

51

Other districts (like California's 1st district), and almost all states, are thoroughly competitive.

- Largely as a function of state registration laws, turnout varies across districts and states. In 1994, 57 per cent of the voting age population turned out in Wyoming's at-large House district but only 10 per cent in California's 33rd district; and 63 per cent in the Senate election in Wyoming compared with 31 per cent in West Virginia.

- Finally, how communications media are organised varies. Some districts – like Connecticut's 1st (Hartford), Indiana's 10th (Indianapolis), or Tennessee's 5th (Nashville) – and most states (but especially Rhode Island and Utah) – coincide almost exactly with specific newspaper, television, and radio markets. Others do not. Senators from Florida and Mississippi,[12] for example, must cope with several markets, as must most House candidates and particularly those contesting seats in densely populated conurbations in New York City or Los Angeles or sparsely populated rural areas like Iowa's 3rd district (which includes six media markets). Candidates in states like New Jersey and Connecticut must also contend with out-of-state media.

Party organisations

Unlike Britain, where strong party organisations recruit candidates for office and structure politicians' careers, America's days when party leaders controlled nominations have long passed. Although the two major parties still dominate House and Senate elections,[13] the effect of the direct primary system is to undermine the influence of party organisations. Some House districts boast strong party organisations which can guarantee the nomination of faithful lieutenants – as, for example, in Cook County (Chicago) and Nassau County (New York)[14] – but these are exceptions. Even in those House districts where party organisations are strong, insurgents are frequently successful in challenging organisation candidates; as, for example, Floyd Flake in 1986 when he defeated an incumbent supported by the Queens Borough Democratic organisation in New York City's 6th congressional district. There remain no examples of party organisations successfully controlling nominations for the Senate. While party organisations no longer control congressional nominations, national, state, and local party leaders are often active recruiting candidates, many of whom already have a history of considerable party involvement.[15] In 1994, for example, local Republican officials successfully coaxed Mark Neumann (R.WI) into mounting a second challenge to the newly elected Democratic incumbent in Wisconsin's 1st district; and Senate minority leader Robert Dole and National Republican Senatorial Committee chair Phil Gramm were involved in recruiting a Republican candidate for the Senate race in New Jersey against incumbent Senator Frank Lautenberg. Similarly, in

1992, both parties' congressional campaign committees made special efforts to recruit women candidates.[16]

Political ambition

Contemporary congressional recruitment depends most importantly on the personal initiative of individual candidates. 'People nominate themselves', Alan Ehrenhart has observed. 'That is, they offer themselves as candidates, raise money, organise campaigns, create their own publicity, and make decisions themselves . . . Candidates do not win because they have party support. They do not win because they have business or labor support. They win because they are motivated to set out on their own and find votes.'[17] Indeed, the decision to run for Congress is usually a very personal one made by people who are self-starters – highly motivated, politically ambitious men and women – who enter the political arena on their own initiative to pursue their own and their supporters' agendas, and who are willing to put themselves (and their families) through a very arduous experience which may not achieve the desired objective. In the words of former US Senator Thomas Eagleton: 'Today, you are either a self-starter or a no-starter.'[18]

If politically ambitious self-starters are successful in recruiting state and local party committees to help mobilise voters and recruit volunteer workers, all well and good. If they can obtain useful electoral services from the national party organisations – money, professional campaign advice, state-of-the-art television and radio production facilities, help with direct mail shots to contributors and voters, public opinion surveys, phone banks, and up-to-date information on unfolding issues – even better. Since the 1970s the national and congressional campaign committees of the parties have come to play major roles in fund raising, media consultancy, issue research, and opinion polling in congressional cam-paigns; and, on a nationwide basis, in coordinating and monitoring daily develop-ments in the most competitive districts and states.[19] But, a much more important influence on congressional recruitment than these party efforts are the individual candidate's liking for politics and their personal political ambition.

The most effective congressional candidates are the so-called quality candi-dates. Most of these will be men and women who have already invested heavily in political careers and who are now seeking to move up the promotion ladder. If they are candidates for the House, the quality candidates will probably be state legislators or local government officials. If they are candidates for the Senate, they will most likely be House members. Being a senator, with its smaller member-ship, longer terms, and more democratic internal structure, is regarded as being at the top or near the top of the political career ladder. Only one former senator has subsequently run for the House in the post-war period whereas numerous House members have run for the Senate. Senators are also regarded as being a step away from the presidency. In the 104th Congress (1995–6), no fewer than

13 senators (Biden, Dole, Glenn, Gramm, Harkin, Hollings, Kennedy, Kerrey, Lugar, Pressler, Simon, Specter, and Thurmond) were or had been presidential or vice presidential candidates. Not all quality candidates, however, are politically experienced. Some are political amateurs who might be just as well known and appealing to voters as experienced politicians: an athlete (like former New York Knicks basketball star, Senator Bill Bradley or Congressman Steve Largent, the former receiver for the Seattle Seahawks), an astronaut (like Senators John Glenn or Harrison Schmidt), an entertainer (like Senator Fred Thompson or Congressmen Ben Jones or Sonny Bono), a television journalist (like Congresswoman Marjorie Margolies-Mezvinsky or 1992 California Senate candidate Bruce Herschensohn), a former Vietnam POW (like Senator John McCain or 1994 Virginia senatorial candidate Oliver North), a multimillionaire (like Senator Herb Kohl or Congressman Michael Huffington), or even a transplant surgeon (like Senator Bill Frist).[20]

Political ambition is not everything, of course. Quality candidates and their potential financial supporters need to make some important strategic calculations. They need to evaluate their chances of winning before deciding whether or not to enter a race – and thereby risk losing their current office, if they hold one – and they need to assess the quality of the opportunities available to them, partly on the basis of whether national economic and political conditions favour their party in a particular year, the quality of their opponents, and their likely success in mustering sufficient resources.[21]

Opportunity and incumbency

In most congressional elections there are no real prospects of beginning a congressional career – simply because most seats are already held by somebody else. Indeed, the most outstanding feature of recent congressional elections is the power of incumbency. Once elected, members of Congress – especially House members – usually stay in office for as long as they want. Since 1960, 91 per cent of House incumbents and 84 per cent of incumbent senators have sought re-election, and of those, respectively, 93 per cent and 70 per cent have been re-elected (see Table 3.3). A significant minority of House incumbents do not even face major party opposition – about 16 per cent in the 1980s down to 7 per cent in 1994. Because incumbency is so strong an influence, voluntary retirement is the main cause of House turnover, not electoral defeat. This was true even in 1992 and 1994 when historically high numbers of incumbents lost. Somewhat ironically given the framers' expectations that the Senate's membership would be more stable, a higher proportion of senators lose their re-election bids.[22]

Table 3.3. House and senate incumbents
seeking and winning re-election, 1960–1994

Year	Retiring	Total	Defeated in primary	Defeated in general election	Re-elected	Re-elected members as percentage of all seats up for re-election
		Seeking Re-election				
HOUSE						
1980	34	398 (91.5%)	6 (1.5%)	31 (7.8%)	361 (90.7%)	83.0%
1982	40	393 (90.3%)	10 (2.5%)	29 (7.4%)	354 (90.1%)	81.4%
1984	22	411 (94.0%)	3 (0.7%)	16 (3.9%)	392 (95.4%)	90.1%
1986	40	394 (90.3%)	3 (0.5%)	6 (1.5%)	385 (97.7%)	88.5%
1988	23	409 (93.8%)	1 (0.2%)	6 (1.5%)	402 (98.3%)	92.4%
1990	27	406 (93.3%)	1 (0.2%)	15 (3.7%)	390 (96.0%)	89.7%
1992	65	368 (84.6%)	19 (5.2%)	24 (6.5%)	325 (88.3%)	74.7%
1994	48	387 (89.0%)	4 (1.0%)	34 (8.8%)	349 (90.2%)	80.0%
Means	37 (8.5%)	395 (90.1%)	6 (1.3%)	20 (4.6%)	369 (93.4%)	85.0%
SENATE						
1980	5	29 (85.3%)	4 (11.8%)	9 (26.5%)	16 (55.2%)	47.1%
1982	3	30 (90.9%)	0 (0%)	2 (6.1%)	28 (93.3%)	84.8%
1984	4	29 (87.9%)	0 (0%)	3 (9.1%)	26 (89.6%)	78.8%
1986	6	28 (82.4%)	0 (0%)	7 (20.6%)	21 (75.0%)	61.8%
1988	6	27 (81.8%)	0 (0%)	4 (12.1%)	23 (85.2%)	69.7%
1990	3	32 (91.4%)	0 (0%)	1 (2.9%)	31 (96.9%)	88.6%
1992	7	28 (80.0%)	1 (2.9%)	4 (11.4%)	23 (82.1%)	65.7%
1994	9	26 (74.3%)	0 (0%)	2 (7.7%)	24 (92.3%)	68.6%
Means	5 (15.9%)	28 (84.3%)	1 (1.8%)	4 (12.4%)	24 (83.7%)	73.6%

Source: Ornstein, Mann, and Malbin, *Vital Statistics On Congress, 1993–1994* Tables 2.7 and 2.8
Note: Retirees include those running for other offices but exclude those who died or resigned before the election.

Types of opportunity seats

Because incumbents usually win re-election, just three types of seats offer good opportunities for new recruits. One type is *open* seats, where there is no incumbent running. Between 1982 and 1994, a mean 11 per cent of House seats (47 districts) were open; about one in seven contests in Senate elections. All House open seats do not offer good prospects for newcomers because even though the incumbent party's new candidate usually receives a lower percentage of the vote than his/her predecessor – the so-called retirement slump – many open seats are safe for one party. Between 1968 and 1990, Democrats won just over three-quarters of their House open seats and Republicans about two-thirds of theirs.[23] Even in the electoral upheavals of 1994, over half the House open seats were won by the party which held them previously. The same is not true of Senate open seats which are almost universally competitive. Since reconstruction, only Arkansas and Louisiana have so far not elected a Republican senator; West Virginia not since the 1930s. Since 1939, only Kansas has not elected a Democratic senator. Whereas in 1959, 14 states split their representation between the parties, in 1993 the number had reached 20.

The second type of opportunity seats are the *marginals*, where the incumbent won narrowly last time or is perceived as vulnerable. Marginal seats are much more difficult to define than open seats because some incumbents regularly achieve less than 60 per cent (the conventional lower bound for marginality), or even less than 55 per cent, of the vote but are not regarded as vulnerable, while others receive up to 65 per cent and lose. In 1994, 6 of the 34 House incumbents who lost had received over 60 per cent of the popular vote in 1992. On these figures, House incumbents are 'unsafe at any margin'.[24]

The third type of opportunity occurs in House seats which have been *redistricted*. Particularly in states which lose seats, sometimes previously secure incumbents are forced into seeking re-election in new less sympathetic districts, occasionally against another incumbent. In the 1992 House elections, for example, Congressman Stephen Solarz (D.NY), a nine-term incumbent and one of the House's most able leaders on foreign affairs elected from a strong Jewish constituency, was forced by his state's redistricting plan to seek re-election in a newly drawn predominantly Hispanic district. Predictably, Solarz lost to a Hispanic candidate, Nydia Velázquez, the first Puerto Rican woman in Congress. In this example, the seat in question remained firmly in Democratic hands. Not so Georgia 3rd district where redistricting robbed five-term Democrat Richard Ray of his traditional political base and provided an excellent opportunity for Mac Collins who took the seat for the Republicans. Not surprisingly, incumbent House members devote considerable efforts, not always successful, to persuading their state legislatures to create favourable district lines.[25]

The third type of opportunity seat in Senate elections are those of *appointed senators*. Being appointed as an interim senator by a state governor does not lead automatically to success in the subsequent special or general election. Of the ten interim appointments made between 1980 and 1995, two did not run in the subsequent general election, three lost, and five were elected.

National conditions

National conditions, personalities, and issues also condition the calculus of congressional recruitment. If the economy is doing well and the president is popular, prospective candidates for the opposing party – particularly the experienced quality candidates – will rationalise that their chances of defeating an incumbent of the president's party are slim, and most likely will delay a challenge until next time. Potential financial contributors and national party strategists will probably reach the same conclusion and decide to channel their resources into shoring up support for favoured incumbents. Should the economy not be growing and the president's popularity vulnerable, experienced quality candidates of the opposing party (and their supporters) will likely view the prospects of winning as high; so nominations to challenge incumbents will become more competitive and their ability to raise campaign money will improve. Generally, therefore, when national conditions favour a party, large numbers of quality candidates with well-financed campaigns will run for that party; when a party is not favoured, it will concentrate on supporting its incumbents, and challengers and candidates in open seats will be of a low quality and receive weak support.[26] Even so, in some election years, political neophytes apparently defy this strategic rationale, run primarily in re-sponse to local circumstances, and win. In the 1994 elections, two-thirds of the Republican challengers who defeated House Democrats and over half of the Republican winners in House open seats had no previous elective experience. In the Senate race in Tennessee, Democratic incumbent Jim Sasser was beaten in his re-election bid by a Republican with no previous elective experience.[27]

Whether or not there is a presidential contest is also important. In every mid-term election since 1934 the president's party has lost seats in the House and on all but three occasions in the Senate. In the 1994 mid-term elections, President Clinton's Democratic Party lost 53 House seats and following the defection of Democrat Senator Richard Shelby to the Republicans, 8 seats in the Senate. One explanation for mid-term losses is that without the added attraction of a presi-dential contest, voter support for the president's party falls, as does voter turnout – usually by about 13 per cent in mid-term elections – a loss of 23 million voters or 54,000 in each congressional district.[28] A more conventional alternative explan-ation is that mid-term elections are referendums on the performance of the president midway through his/her term. Voters' evaluations of the president are effectively transferred to the party's congressional candidates.[29]

National conditions also affect the number of retirements which, as we have explained, have a crucial effect upon aggregate results. Incumbents of the un-favoured party are likely to reason that they may lose, or that it just not worth the effort seeking re-election for yet another term, and so retire. Undoubtedly, it was the likely prospects of losing which explains the historically high numbers of retirements in 1992 and 1994.

Recruitment and money

Campaigning for Congress is not only about winning votes. It is also about acquiring resources – particularly money – and the strategic decisions made by potential financial contributors.[30]

Congressional elections are hugely expensive – certainly more expensive than in Britain, but probably not as expensive as elections to the Japanese Diet. In 1994, the mean cost of a Senate contest was $9 million, and that of a House race just under $950,000. Total congressional spending for the 1993–4 electoral

Table 3.4. House and Senate campaign spending 1986–1994, by type of seat

| Election Year | Total Expenditure by All Candidates | | All Candidates | | General Election Expenditures | | | | | | | |
| | | | | | Incumbents | | Challengers | | Open Seats | | All Seats | |
	Total	Mean per contest	Total	Mean per contest	Total	Mean	Total	Mean	Total	Mean	Democrats	Republicans
HOUSE												
1986	$238.9m.	$548,080	$210.3m.	$483,540	$132.1m.	$334,380	$41.1m.	$124,833	$37.1m.	$431,279	$113.0m.	$97.3m.
1988	$256.0m.	$588,552	$223.1m.	$512,782	$156.0m.	£378,544	$41.6m.	$119,598	$24.7m.	$465,472	$123.0m.	$99.2m.
1990	$265.8m.	$611,080	$231.3m.	$531,724	$163.4m.	$400,441	$37.2m.	$110,655	$29.8m.	$495,833	$131.2m.	$99.2m.
1992	$407.6m.	$937,011	$332.7m.	$764,805	$204.6m.	$582,906	$63.3m.	$177,781	$61.2m.	$424,931	$187.0m.	$142.1m.
1994	$405.7m.	$932,529	$343.3m.	$789,103	$209.3m.	$546,475	$73.8m.	$212,709	$57.5m.	$611,489	$185.4m.	$155.2m.
SENATE												
1986	$211.6m.	$6,413,333	$189.7m.	$5,747,575	$89.3m.	$3.3m.	$53.4m.	$1.9m.	$47.0m.	$3.4m.	$80.8m.	$108.8m.
1988	$200.8m.	$6,095,454	$185.0m.	$5,605,151	$101.2m.	$3.7m.	$49.1m.	$1.8m.	$34.6m.	$2.9m.	$97.0m.	$88.0m.
1990	$180.4m.	$5,155,143	$172.4m.	$4,925,714	$113.4m.	$3.5m.	$49.4m.	$1.7m.	$9.6m.	$1.6m.	$83.7m.	$88.7m.
1992	$272.1m.	$7,772,857	$195.3m.	$5,597,143	$100.3m.	$3.7m.	$56.3m.	$1.9m.	$38.2m.	$2.7m.	$98.5m.	$96.7m.
1994	$318.4m.	$9,096,857	$272.1m.	$7,775,143	$115.1m.	$4.4m.	$101.6m.	$3.9m.	$54.0m.	$3.0m.	$116.3m.	$154.3m.

Source: Federal Election Commission.

cycle was $724 million, more than double the total for 1981–2. In 1994, a new record was set for a single race when Senator Diane Feinstein and Congressman Michael Huffington spent a total of $44.5 million in the California Senate race; the most expensive House race also involved Huffington in the contest for California's 22nd district in 1992 when the candidates spent $6.1 million. The ability of candidates, especially challengers and those contesting open seats, to run viable campaigns depends greatly on the availability of sufficient money; which, in turn, depends greatly on strategic calculations made by financial contributors of the likelihood that their favoured candidates will win.

Most financial contributors play safe and give most of their money to incumbents. In the last five elections, contributions to incumbents accounted for over half total spending in Senate elections and almost two-thirds of House expenditures (see Table 3.4). In individual races, House incumbents now spend between three or four times as much as challengers, while incumbent senators spend more than twice as much as their challengers (although this was not the case in 1994). As Figure 3.2 shows, the gap between incumbents' and challengers' spending over recent years has widened sharply. Even when they lose their seats, House incumbents typically spend significantly more than their winning challengers – on average 54 per cent more in 1994 (see Figure 3.3). Incumbent Dan Rostenkowski (D.IL) lost his seat in 1994 even though he spent over $2.5 million; his winning opponent spent only $116,000. Incumbents generally find raising money easier than do challengers because they have access to contributions from wealthy political action committees (PACs) and their parties. PACs contribute about half House incumbents' receipts and about 40 per cent of incumbent senators'. About 40 percent of PAC contributions to incumbents are made by business, 30 per cent by non-connected groups (including ideological and single-issue groups like Emily's List), 20 per cent by labour unions, and the rest by trade, membership, and health groups, and others. In 1992, the Federal Election Commission (FEC) allowed national party committees to give up to $95,240 in direct and coordinated spending to each House candidate, and as much as $2,492,145 to Senate candidates. However, parties also distribute substantial sums of unregulated 'soft money' usually provided by businesses for use in state and local elections, and given directly to state and local party organisations.[31]

While incumbents usually have little trouble acquiring funds, challengers and many candidates in open seats find fund raising a truly daunting task requiring considerable time, effort, and money. Many prospective candidates are deterred from running. In 1993, for example, Republican Congressman Dick Zimmer had to abandon a bid for the Republican nomination in the New Jersey Senate race against multimillionaire incumbent Senator Frank Lautenberg, after calculating he would need to raise $8 million – $22,000 a day – to fund a competitive challenge. Although the minimum is lower for House races, non-incumbents need to raise at least $200,000 just to run a viable campaign.[32] Particularly at the nomination/primary stage, the task of raising early 'seed' money – so important to organising and planning a worthwhile campaign and going on to raise even more money – is difficult and time-consuming. When he ran in a Democratic primary in 1986, Congressman David Price (D.NC) had to take out a second

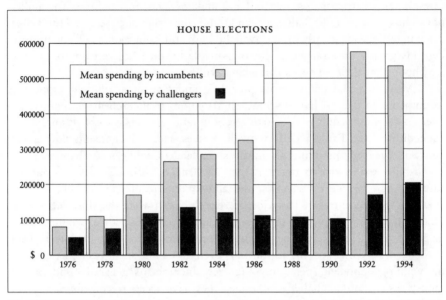

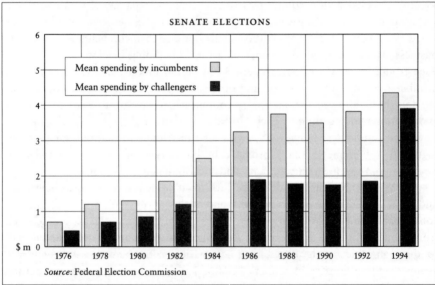

Figure 3.2. The gap between general elections campaign spending by incumbents and their challengers, 1976–1994.

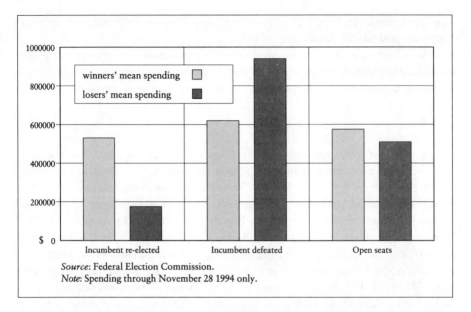

Source: Federal Election Commission.
Note: Spending through November 28 1994 only.

Figure 3.3. General election campaign spending by winners and losers by type of contest, 1994 House elections.

mortgage on the family home, knowing that success in both the primary and general election was directly related to how much money he could raise and spend.[33]

The more money challengers and candidates in open seats raise, the better their chances of winning. Figure 3.3 shows that the 34 winning House challengers in 1994 spent an average $612,611 compared with a mean $161,575 spent by the losing challengers. In Senate races, the two winning challengers spent an average $6.6 million compared with a mean $3.5 million spent by the losing challengers.[34] Money is an even stronger determinant of electoral success in open seats. Not surprisingly, open seat elections are often the most expensive – because they tend to be the most competitive, attract the strongest candidates, and are the targets of considerable spending by national party committees.[35] Winning candidates in House and Senate open seats typically spend almost twice as much as losers, although not in 1994 (see Figure 3.3). Again, however, it must be stressed that spending more than one's opponent in an open seat is no guarantee of victory. In the 1994 House elections, for example, 16 losers in the 52 open seats spent more than the winners – in one case (Wyoming's at-large district) by a margin of almost five to one.

Faced with financial demands of this order, candidates with large personal fortunes – like Michael Huffington who spent $27.8 million of his own money to finance his losing campaign for the Senate in California or Herb Kohl (D.WI) who spent almost $6.8 million of his own money to retain his Senate seat in 1994 – have a considerable advantage.

Candidate quality, opportunity, national conditions, and resources are the keys to congressional elections. Let us now consider how these factors interacted to influence congressional recruitment for the 104th Congress (1995–6).

Recruiting the 104th Congress

To say the least, the 1994 mid-term elections were highly unusual. For the first time in forty years, the Republicans won majorities in both houses. Last time mid-term elections were held with a Democrat in the White House (in 1978), Republicans picked up only 15 House seats. This time they won 54. Various factors have been cited to explain the Republican victory – the unpopularity of Democratic president Bill Clinton, the Republicans' much trumpeted but not well known 'Contract With America', the lingering effects of redistricting, issues such as taxation, the budget deficit, crime, economic insecurity, health care proposals, and widespread disgust with Congress (just 16 per cent approval ratings). Notwithstanding the undoubted importance of these factors, it is also clear from the high number of opportunity seats that a dramatic change in political direction was possible, even likely. In the House, the second largest number of voluntary retirements in the twentieth century meant that 52 seats (12 per cent) were open. Nine seats were open in the Senate – a quarter of all contests, and the highest number since 1980. Given that the Democratic majority in the House was just 78, and 10 in the Senate, having lost 10 House seats and gained none in the Senate in 1992 when Clinton won the presidency, Democrats were vulnerable. Many other House and Senate seats were marginal the last time they were contested: 160 House seats (37 per cent) were won by less than 60 per cent in 1992, 88 by Democrats; 13 Senate seats were marginal, 8 held by Democrats (see Table 3.5).

Table 3.5. What happened in the 'opportunity seats' in 1994?

	HOUSE			SENATE		
	Number of seats	Won by Democrats	Won by Republicans	Number of seats	Won by Democrats	Won by Republicans
Where Democratic incumbent retiring or seeking other office	28	8 (28.6%)	20 (71.4%)	6	0	6 (100%)
Where Democratic incumbent vulnerable to primary defeat	3	2 (66.7%)	1 (33.3%)	0	0	0
Where Republican incumbent retiring or seeking other office	20	4 (25%)	16 (75%)	3	0	3 (100%)
Where Republican incumbent vulnerable to primary defeat	1	0	1 (100%)	0	0	0

	HOUSE			SENATE		
	Number of seats	Won by Democrats	Won by Republicans	Number of seats	Won by Democrats	Won by Republicans
Where Democratic incumbent won by 50.0–54.9% in last election	48	27 (56.3%)	21 (43.8%)	6	6 (100%)	0
Where Democratic incumbent won by 55.0–59.9% in last election	40	33 (82.5%)	7 (17.5%)	2	1 (50%)	1 (50%)
Where Republican incumbent won by 50.0–54.9% in last election	44	0	44 (100%)	5	0	5 (100%)
Where Republican incumbent won by 55.0–59.9% in last election	28	0	28 (100%)	1	0	1 (100%)

Source: US Election Project

How political ambition and electoral opportunity interacted in recruiting candidates can be seen from Table 3.6. The table shows that 52 per cent of candidates (54) running in House open seats had previously been elected to public office, including a state Supreme Court justice, and 32 state legislators. Among Senate candidates, political experience was even more prevalent: 83 per cent of those running in open seats but only 42 per cent of challengers running against incumbents had previous elective experience. Continuing an established trend, the

Table 3.6. The value of political experience
in House and Senate elections, 1994

	HOUSE			SENATE		
	Number of districts	Politically Experienced Candidates		Number of states	Politically Experienced Candidates	
Type of Seat		N	%		N	%
OPEN SEATS						
Democratic candidate contested seat	52	32	61.5%	9	8	88.8%
Democratic candidate won seat	14	13	92.9%	0	0	0
Republican candidate contested seat	52	22	42.3%	9	7	77.7%
Republican candidate won seat	38	18	47.4%	9	7	77.7%
INCUMBENTS' SEATS						
Democratic challenger defeated incumbent in primary election	2	2	100.0%	0	0	0
Democratic challenger defeated Republican incumbent in general election	0	0	0	0	0	0
Republican challenger defeated incumbent in primary election	1	0	0	0	0	0
Republican challenger defeated Democratic incumbent in general election	34	15	44.1%	2	1	50%

Source: Congressional Quarterly.

bias towards the politically experienced was stronger among Democrats, especially among winners. Perhaps surprisingly, more than half the Republican winners in both open and incumbent-held seats had no previous political experience. As we showed earlier, however, despite their inexperience, these candidates were well-financed and able to take advantage of favourable national conditions. Most importantly, they capitalised effectively on the concerns of key blocs of voters (particularly white men in the south) over specific salient issues – particularly taxation, the budget deficit, gun control, abortion, and gay rights – as well as general disenchantment with Congress. For the first time in decades, voters were able to assign blame unequivocally to single-party Democratic government. As a result, Republicans retained the support of their party identifiers in a mid-term election for the first time since 1980; and won the support of a majority of independents, who now account for about a third of voters, and significant support from those who had voted for Ross Perot in 1992. While Republicans mobilised their voters, Democrats were much less successful, in part because the Clinton Administration had alienated many of their party's core constituencies who on election day did not turn out to vote.

The 1994 election outcome turned on the results in the opportunity seats. Republicans did best in the open seats (lines 1 to 4, Table 3.5) winning almost three out of four, including 21 formerly held by Democrats (lines 1 and 2); Democrats won only four districts previously held by Republicans (lines 3 and 4). Republicans also did well in marginal districts (lines 5 to 8) although not as well as in Democratic open seats, and many of these results were extremely close. Indeed, had just 19,500 voters in 13 races voted Democratic, Democrats would have retained control of the House. Democrats won none of the Republicans' marginal seats. The Senate results followed a similar pattern. Republicans regained control for the first time since 1986 primarily by winning all nine open seats, including six previously held by Democrats. However, they succeeded in defeating only one of eight incumbent Democratic senators who were marginal last time; and one who was considered safe.

Inevitably, there were some surprise results not accounted for in the list of opportunity seats. Six House Democratic incumbents who lost were favoured by Congressional Quarterly just two weeks before the election. Two – Dan Rostenkowski (D.IL) and David Price (D.NC) – were regarded as safe. Seeking his nineteenth term in a solid Democratic district, Rostenkowski was under federal indictment for fraud and lost to an unknown political novice. Price, a four-term incumbent representing the most progressive district in North Carolina, lost to a local policy chief who had no previous political experience by 1,200 votes. Given some surprise results should be expected, and that 155 House winners (84 Democrats, 71 Republicans) received less than 60 per cent of the vote, there is considerable scope for membership change in 1996 – at least in the House.

The new Congress

The election of Republican majorities in both houses for the first time since 1952, and the defeat of 34 House Democratic incumbents made significant differences to Congress' ideological and demographic composition, as well as to the institution's policy agenda and internal operations. Not surprisingly, the members of the 1994 House class were younger than the 87 departing members – lowering the mean age from 53.7 to 52.2 years.[36] Well over half the new members were under 45 (compared with just 21 per cent of incumbents); the youngest member was only 27 when elected. For the second Congress in succession, the length of service of House members fell – from four to three terms; and from 10. 6 to under 10 years. This means that over half the members of the 104th Congress have been elected since 1990 – with obvious consequences for Congress' institutional stability. Apart from their youth, the most remarkable features of the 1994 class were their relative lack of political experience, lower levels of education, and self-conscious 'outsider' image. Just over half of the newcomers had held previous elective offices, compared with 72 per cent of the 1992 intake. Given that 61 out of the class of 72 were Republicans, it was not surprising that representation by business people and bankers increased while those with careers formerly in education declined. In common with a long established trend, no blue collar/working-class members were elected. Eight of the House freshmen were millionaires. Unlike the 1992 intake, which included a record number of women, blacks, and Hispanic members, the new class of 1994 was much less demographically diverse. The number of women increased by one to 49 – just 11 per cent of the House. Only three more black members were elected (including a second Republican) bringing the total in the House to 39 (9 per cent, compared with 12 per cent of the US population), and the number of Hispanics (18) and Asian and Pacific Islanders (6) remained the same.

Like their colleagues in the House, the eleven new senators in 1994 were younger than those they replaced, although the mean age of all senators continued to rise to more than 58 – the highest since the 1960s. In contrast with the House, all but two of the new senators (82 per cent) had previous elective experience, usually as House members. Senator Carol Moseley-Braun (D.IL) remained the only black member although one more woman (Republican Senator Olympia Snowe of Maine) was elected bringing the total to eight. Changes in senators' occupational and educational backgrounds were minimal. Two of the new senators were millionaires.

Importantly for President Clinton, not only were most new members Republicans, they were much more conservative than those they replaced. On the basis of Congressional Quarterly's conservative coalition and presidential support scores, retiring and defeated House members and senators were more liberal or moderate and far more supportive of President Clinton than their colleagues. Given the inclusion of so many conservative Republicans in the 1994 intakes, it was likely that the 104th Congress would be much more polarised between liberals and conservatives than its predecessors, and much less supportive of President Clinton. Less predictable was the change in the political influence of various states. On the basis of 'clout ratings' devised by *Roll Call*, which ranks states according to the size of their delegations, number of committee chairmanships and ranking memberships, number of members on the important committees, leadership posts, the amount each state receives in federal funds on a per capita basis, proportion of majority members in House and Senate delegations, and seniority, some states increased their influence in Congress and some lost influence. California, the largest state, retained its premier position as the state with the most clout, but New York was replaced by Texas in 2nd position. Florida moved up from 12th to 6th, Kansas from 23rd to 14th, and Georgia from 37th to 16th. In contrast, the positions of Kentucky, Maryland, and West Virginia fell substantially.[37]

While the 1994 elections brought considerable change to Congress' membership, it is important to stress that most incumbents were returned to Washington: 90 per cent of House members and 92 per cent of senators seeking re-election were re-elected

Incumbents and their constituents

Why incumbents seek and win re-election on a regular basis has been a subject of considerable academic interest over the last twenty years. In a pathbreaking study, David Mayhew explained the decline in House turnover as a function of the falling number of marginal seats: in 1948, Democratic candidates won between 45 and 55 per cent of the vote in 27 per cent of House districts but by the 1970s only a handful of House members won by these tight margins and over 75 per cent of incumbents seeking re-election won by more than 60 per cent.[38] Mayhew ascribed the declining competitiveness of House elections to incumbents' ability to insulate themselves from adverse partisan swings in popular opinion, although Fiorina has shown that the vanishing marginals did not deny Republicans control of the House when they won a majority of the national vote.[39]

Electoral diversity and the growth of candidate-centred politics

Whether the decline in marginals is as significant as Mayhew claims has been questioned. Gary Jacobson has suggested that the declining marginals are essentially a symptom of a more dissaggregated, disjointed electoral process in which contemporary House elections are shaped more by the interactions of local *and* national factors rather than by national tides alone. The causes of this greater diversity are the declining importance of partisanship in the entire electoral system – in elections for president as well as for Congress[40] – and the growth of a more candidate-centred and candidate-influenced electoral politics. The consequences are that far more House seats are now winnable by both parties. Until the mid-1960s, competition between the two parties was confined to a particular subset of House seats which frequently changed hands election after election. Since the mid-1960s, party competition has been more dispersed across a larger number of districts.[41] So, when an incumbent retires, both parties have an opportunity to exploit: although the likelihood of any particular seat switching parties in two successive elections has also been reduced. Between 1946 and 1966, over one-third of those members who entered the House by winning a seat from the other party were defeated in their first attempt to win re-election. After 1966, 11 out of 12 freshmen were re-elected after one term. The recent electoral history of Rhode Island's 1st district shows this phenomenon in classic form. Between 1960 and 1988, the district was represented by a Democrat, Fernand St Germain who lost his re-election bid as a result of scandal. The previously safe Democratic seat elected a Republican who then went on to win between 55 and 70 per cent of the vote in subsequent elections until he ran for the Senate in 1994. Against the national tide, the seat provided Democrats with one of only four victories in open seats and will likely remain in the party's hands for some time. Just as freshmen have been able to win election, so a much larger number of senior House incumbents have been able to hold on to seats which previously they would have lost in countervailing partisan tides. One recent study has shown that between 1950 and 1988 incumbency increased the vote for each party in Senate elections by a mean 6.5 per cent; and in House elections in the 1980s, incumbency was worth an additional 10 per cent of the vote.[42] According to Jacobson, the vanishing marginals deprived Republicans of House majorities in 1966, 1968, 1972, 1980, and 1984.[43]

Reaching out to constituents

Once they are elected, incumbents are able to insulate themselves from adverse partisan swings by exploiting the considerable latitude which Congress' institutional organisation allows to develop highly individualistic Washington careers and to expend considerable time and energy cultivating their constituents' support. One of the most important decisions a representative or senator makes when he/she arrives in Washington is how much time he/she will devote to legislating and other Washington-based activities, and how much time and energy will be spent on cultivating constituency support. Table 3.7 shows how one member – Senator Carl Levin (D.MI) – divided his time over one week in 1993. Apart from spending the weekend in his district, something like a third of appointments within the senator's packed schedule involved direct personal meetings with constituents. Many others undoubtedly had a direct bearing on them as well. The time spent by contemporary legislators on constituency-related activities is considerable.

Most House members wage a continuous re-election campaign. Almost as soon as one election has ended, the next one begins.[44] Senators' longer terms allow them to concentrate their first three to four years attending to matters of state in Washington leaving the final two or three years for re-election activities. Patterns of fund raising by senators, visits to their states, and voting behaviour tend to be governed by these different phases of activity.[45]

Table 3.7. Senator Carl Levin's schedule, May 24–29 1993

Monday 24 May	1.35 pm	Flight from Detroit to Washington
	3.00	Meeting with constituent and staff on labour legislation
	3.30	Meeting with staff on appointment of official to a Michigan state park
	4.00	Meeting with AFL-CIO and other senator on FDR Commission
	5.00	Reception with other senators sponsored by Senator Dodd
	5.00	Meeting with Clinton Administration nominee to Defense Department
	5.30	Meeting with Senate Armed Services Committee staff on foreign trip
Tuesday 25 May	8.15 am	Meeting with Senate Governmental Affairs Committee staff
	8.30	Meeting of Senators' Urban Issues Group
	9.30	Hearing of Nuclear Deterrence Subcommittee of Senate Armed Services Committee
	9.30	Nomination hearing of Senate Governmental Affairs Committee
	12.00	Photo session with Michigan school children on Senate steps
	12.15	Senator Dodd's Forum for Clinton ambassador Strobe Talbott
	12.30	Democratic Conference on campaign finance bill
	1.15 pm	Celebration for car manufacturers and unions with President Clinton
	2.30	Meeting with staff and lobbyist on health care legislation
	2.30	Nomination hearings Senate Armed Services Committee
	4.00	Meeting with Michigan labor union members on health care legislation
	4.45	Meeting with other senator on campaign finance legislation
	4.45	Record tape on NAFTA
	6.00	Buffet Dinner hosted by car manufacturers and unions
Wednesday 26 May	9.30 am	Hearing of Nuclear Deterrence Subcommittee of Senate Armed Services Committee
	12.00	Meeting with staff on gift legislation
	1.30 pm	Meeting with representative of National Cancer Society
	4.00	Meeting with staff and Michigan small business people on NAFTA
	4.30	Meeting with Michigan electricity company on legislation
	5.00	Meeting with foreign government official on foreign trip
	5.30	Meeting with another senator on legislation
Thursday 27 May	8.35 am	Telephone call to Michigan TV station on auto industry celebration and NAFTA
	8.45	Meeting with Government Operations staff on Great Lakes
	9.30	Telephone call to Treasury Under Secretary on legislation
	10.45	Meeting with Interior Secretary and congressman on legislation

	12.00	Photo session with Michigan school children on Senate steps
	12.30	Lunch with Democratic Policy Committee and Clinton administration officials
	2.30 pm	Meeting with executive from major company in Michigan
	2.30	Hearing of Defense Technology Subcommittee of Senate Armed Services Committee
	4.30	Meeting with Senator Riegle (MI) on federal appointments
	6.55	Television appearance
Friday 28 May	9.00 am	Meeting with law students in Court programme
	9.30	Meeting with staff on bonus legislation
	9.30	Briefing from CIA
	10.00	Meeting with Detroit city councilman
	11.00	Radio Phone Press Conference
	12.30 pm	Meeting with staff on National Security Council
	1.30	Record video tape on NAFTA
	2.00	Meeting of Friday Group
	4.25	Flight from Washington to Detroit

Source: Senator Levin's Office.

Home styles

For a member of the House and Senate to enjoy a long congressional career, he/she must cultivate an effective 'home style' among those groups of voters he/she expects to rely on for re-election.[46] Incumbents tend not to perceive or relate to all members of their geographical constituency in the same way and to the same extent. They differentiate among three or four nested constituencies. Closest to them is their personal constituency comprising a small number of the incumbent's most trusted friends and acquaintances. This is part of a wider circle – their primary constituency (not to be confused with those who vote for him/her in a primary election) – comprising those active supporters who recruited the member as a candidate initially and now make tangible and positive contributions (finance, voluntary help, etc.) to re-elect him/her. However, it is primarily towards their re-election constituency that members direct their home style – to those voters whom the House member or senator thinks will vote for him/her (middle-class voters, conservatives, liberals, pro-choicers, 'yuppies', 'traditional Democratic voters', and so forth) – and, in the cases of senators and a few House members, towards a national constituency.[47]

Incumbents' home styles are reflected in how much and what kinds of attention they pay to their re-election constituencies; how they present themselves to those constituents and others; and how they explain their behaviour in Washington. Styles vary considerably according to incumbents' personalities, the character of their constituencies, and the strategies they pursue towards particular constituencies. The home styles of some members – like Senator Robert Byrd (D.WV) or Congressman Henry Gonzalez (D.TX) – emphasise close personal contact.

Others, like those of Senators Jesse Helms (R.NC) or Daniel Patrick Moynihan (D.NY), emphasise particular policy positions; others still stress their local political leadership or emphasise constituency service. Congressman John Murtha (D.PA), for example, stresses his ability to channel federal dollars into his south-west Pennsylvania district; in 1990, he campaigned for re-election on the slogan 'Experience . . . Makes it Happen'.[48] Regardless of specific content, what most home styles have in common is an emphasis on the member's fit with his/her re-election constituency and a set of strategic perceptions about particular sets of voters who need to be accommodated.

Strategic politicians (again)

Incumbents spend so much time developing their home styles as part of a strategy to make themselves look unbeatable, thereby discouraging opposition and encouraging their own supporters.[49] Their evident success in deterring formidable opponents explains why most face weak, inexperienced, and reluctant challengers who typically lack the money and organisation to launch a serious challenge. Probably the best example in recent years was twenty-term Congressman William Natcher (D.KY) who spent only $6,623 in 1992 to win re-election with 61 per cent of the vote. His opponent – a 25-year-old student with no previous electoral experience – spent just $1,125. Not all incumbents can realistically expect to spend as little as Natcher. So, well before the next election, they accumulate millions of dollars in the bank as a deterrent against potential quality opponents and to persuade potential financial supporters that they are unlikely to be defeated. One year before the 1994 elections, for example, Congressman Chuck Schumer, a Democrat representing a safe Democratic seat in New York City, had over $2.1 million in the bank while Senator Edward Kennedy (D.MA) had over $2.5 million. In the event, Schumer spent just under $160,000 to defeat a weak opponent who spent a mere $14,000; Kennedy found himself in a tighter than usual race in which his opponent spent $8 million to his $11 million. But, to reiterate, the optimal strategy is to deter opposition. Schumer's was successful; Kennedy's was not, even though he won. Seeking to beat an opponent by outspending him/her is a poor second best alternative which is likely to be perceived as a sign of electoral vulnerability and help a challenger raise money.[50] Because almost all Senate seats are competitive, the ability of incumbent senators to pursue deterrent strategies is much more limited. Few do not face quality opponents.

Cultivating constituency trust

Regardless of presentational differences, the essence of an effective home style is to promote an aura of trust among prospective supporters back home. That is, the individual member of Congress wishes to demonstrate that he/she is qualified to hold the office (including whether he/she is honest), that he/she can identify with the attitudes, beliefs, and perceptions of his/her constituents, that he/she can empathise with the problems and perceptions of constituents whose support they seek, and that he/she is accessible to voters.[51] In an era when Congress' reputation is low, it is also helpful if members are able to convey a sense that they are different from, and better than, most of their colleagues.

House members and senators employ a variety of strategies to cultivate an aura of trust. They allocate their time and energy, their staff and other resources to reflect their re-election constituencies' interest and concerns. They advertise themselves and their activities to the folks back home in ways which will engender positive images; they take positions favoured by their re-election constituencies; they express support for popular local causes; when asked, they explain in intelligible language how and why they supported and protected re-election constituencies when they voted on legislation in Washington; and they claim personal responsibility for 'bringing home the bacon' – research grants, housing and urban aid, military contracts and so forth – to their states and districts.

They demonstrate their accessibility by frequent contact with their constituents – in person, by mail, or through the mass media. Helped by generous travel allowances and the scheduling of 'non-legislative' work periods during congressional sessions, incumbents make frequent visits to their constituencies.[52] Thanks to the congressional frank (worth about $163,000 per member in 1994 now cut by the Republican Congress to $108,000), members make extensive use of the mail to maintain contact with their constituents especially in election year. The visitor to members' Capitol Hill or constituency offices frequently encounters numerous bundles of letters, newsletters, press releases, video and audio cassettes for radio and television (prepared free in Congress' excellent television and radio broadcasting facilities) strewn across floors and desks ready for distribution free.[53] Typically, mail is devoid of partisan, ideological, and policy content; and is often frivolous – congratulations letters to high school students, competition winners, scholarship; cards for bereavements, anniversaries, birthday cards, and so on. Most House members and senators also employ press secretaries and other staff to publicise their activities through the public media. All circulate newsletters which convey typically bland messages, avoid controversial items, express positions supported by most constituents, claim credit for non-controversial local benefits, and announce visits to the district or state.

Mainly because they have smaller constituencies, House members' contact with constituents is typically direct, through personal visits, letters, and telephone calls. As a result, House members tend to know their constituencies more intimately than their Senate colleagues. They are also better able to control their press, by maintaining close contacts with local journalists, and by providing them with ready-packaged news on slack days. In the event that incumbents face strong opposition at the next election, they can expect extensive and favourable publicity for initiatives they have taken. It is rare for House races to be covered by television, even rarer for members' voting records to be closely scrutinised in the media at election time.[54] In contrast, senators find it far more difficult to promote home styles based on personal accessibility and constituents' trust. Their longer terms and larger, more heterogeneous, and diffuse re-election constituencies make them more remote from their supporters, steer them into more controversies, and compel them to be more dependent on the vagaries of the mass media for contacts with constituents. Because the Senate occupies a more exalted and more exclusive position in the hierarchy of governmental institutions, and because senators exercise exclusive powers over the ratification of treaties (like the INF Treaty in 1988 and the new Strategic Arms Reduction Treaty of 1991), have special responsibilities in foreign policy-making, and advise and consent to executive and judicial appointments, senators are compelled more than their House colleagues to articulate policy preferences and, as a result, cannot so easily avoid discussion of salient and controversial national issues. Witness the furore in many states during the 1992 elections which followed the harsh questioning of Anita Hill during the Senate hearings on the nomination of Clarence Thomas to the Supreme Court in 1991. Senators also find themselves more often in the crossfire of divergent local opinion stimulated by interest groups and attentive voters through the media.[55]

Servicing constituencies

Although good constituency service has long been regarded as an important part of the job of being a member of Congress,[56] the need to cultivate trust has led incumbents to devote much greater attention to and allocate more resources to servicing their constituents over the last thirty or so years. Answering enquiries from and undertaking casework on behalf of the folks back home has effectively transformed incumbents into legislative ombudsmen and women.[57] Some members go to quite extraordinary lengths to demonstrate their attentiveness to constituents' demands. A few years ago, for example, San Antonio Congressman Albert Bustamente (D.TX) tried to persuade the US Naval Academy to release an exceptionally gifted basketball player from military duty so that he could play for his district's local NBA team, the San Antonio Spurs.[58] The causes of greater constituency attentiveness are readily identifiable: the growth of the federal administrative state in such areas as education, health care, housing and urban development, poverty, science and space, business regulation, environmental and consumer protection after the 1960s; the resulting rise in constituents' enquiries; the increasing numbers of newly elected members eager to extend their re-election constituencies in districts and states not particularly sympathetic to their political outlooks; and the greater proclivity of members to vote themselves more resources to undertake these activities. Surveys conducted by the American National Election Study between 1978 and 1992 show that between 10 and 15 per cent of American adults contacted their member of Congress or senator (equivalent to between 55,000 and 85,000 constituents in the average congressional district) at some time, including 6 per cent who wanted to give their opinion on a particular issue. House members surveyed in 1986 reported 1,153 contacts per week per member and just over 200 pieces of casework.[59] Senators receive even more, especially those representing the largest states. Incoming mail to House members and senators is currently running at about 70 million pieces for the House and 40 million for the Senate. In order to cope with these volumes of enquiries, members receive – in addition to their salaries of $133,644 (1995) – generous travel, office, personal staff and communications allowances which over a two-year House term are worth about $1.8 million per member and over a six-year Senate term between $12 and $15 million per senator; even more for committee chairs and party leaders. With these allowances, House members can employ up to eighteen personal staff full-time, and up to four other positions filled by part-timers, interns, shared employees, or temporary staffers; and senators an average of forty personal staffers with senators from the largest states employing over seventy. Not surprisingly, in view of the attention and energy they devote to constituency communications, members now assign twice as many staff to offices in their districts and states than they did in 1972. In 1993, over 60 per cent of House members operated at least two district offices and 54 per cent of senators had at least four offices in their states; 72 per cent of House members deployed at least 40 per cent of their staff in their districts, while 70 per cent of senators employed at least 30 per cent in their states. Sometimes over half a senator's state-based staff are employed exclusively on casework.

The strategic rationales for such concentrations of resources are obvious: constituency service is a relatively cost-free, non-controversial way for incumbents to bolster their credentials for re-election.[60] Incumbents undertake these tasks not only because it is their job but because they wish to inspire trust among constituents who will hopefully reward them with support at the next election. Acquiring constituents' trust gives incumbents licence to do and say what they want on matters of public policy when they are in Washington, and scope to adjust their issue positions as the next election approaches. Constant attention to constituents can even compensate incumbents whose policy views are out of tune with their districts or states.[61] Congress' most respected party leaders and policy experts are able to pursue energetic Washington careers on the basis of unassailable electoral support back home.

Satisfying voters

The efficacy of cultivating trust and providing good constituency service is vindicated by ANES surveys which demonstrate repeatedly that voters evaluate incumbents primarily according to their constituency attentiveness, personal qualities, and experience – rather than by their party connections, ideology, or positions on domestic of foreign policy issues (see Table 3.8). At election time, almost all voters recognise the names of incumbent House members but only about half recognise the names of their challengers. Incumbent senators' names are recognised by even higher percentages but, again reinforcing differences between House and

Senate elections, so are challengers' (see Table 3.9). One of the advantages which Senate candidate Bill Frist had in challenging incumbent Senator Jim Sasser (D.TN) in the 1994 race was that he was well known and (as a transplant surgeon) trusted by voters. Generally, however, voters are much more likely to rate incumbents more positively than challengers. The difference between ratings of House incumbents and challengers is particularly striking; and is twice that for Senate incumbents and their challengers (which helps explain why incumbent senators have lower re-election rates than their House colleagues).

Table 3.8. Voters' likes and dislikes of their House member, 1984–1992

	DEMOCRATIC INCUMBENTS					REPUBLICAN INCUMBENTS					BOTH PARTIES
	1984	1986	1988	1990	1992	1984	1986	1988	1990	1992	Mean
Experience	18.8%	18.8%	9.9%	19.0%	14.7%	22.2%	22.3%	12.5%	15.8%	13.1%	16.7%
Trust	13.3%	17.5%	11.4%	17.1%	16.9%	15.3%	16.8%	9.4%	15.4%	13.3%	14.6%
Leadership Qualities	4.3%	2.3%	4.0%	4.6%	2.5%	4.9%	2.8%	2.6%	1.3%	2.5%	3.1%
Constituency Attention	24.4%	33.8%	32.4%	31.5%	24.4%	25.6%	29.8%	32.4%	28.3%	25.3%	28.7%
Personal Qualities	28.2%	24.2%	19.7%	27.1%	21.2%	21.0%	27.5%	15.1%	22.9%	18.3%	22.5%
Party Connections	4.3%	6.9%	4.8%	5.7%	8.7%	9.2%	11.3%	6.5%	3.3%	6.3%	6.2%
Ideology	5.8%	11.2%	12.3%	10.3%	9.4%	7.5%	8.0%	12.8%	8.8%	11.4%	9.8%
Domestic Policy	8.4%	19.3%	13.3%	23.8%	17.3%	6.6%	9.9%	9.4%	12.9%	9.5%	13.0%
Foreign Policy	1.6%	4.8%	2.5%	2.4%	1.1%	2.3%	2.8%	2.3%	0.4%	0.3%	2.1%
Group Connections	10.7%	19.1%	16.2%	11.0%	8.9%	6.1%	6.3%	6.5%	7.9%	6.8%	10.0%
Miscellaneous	1.8%	3.4%	4.0%	4.1%	4.6%	3.2%	4.7%	3.1%	5.0%	6.5%	4.0%

Source: Warren E. Miller *et al.* and the National Election Studies, *American National Election Studies, 1984–1992*. *ICPSR Study Numbers 8475 and 3172* (Ann Arbor, MI: ICPSR, 1984–1993).
Notes: Data based on responses of those who voted for House candidates in districts contested by an incumbent. The definition of trust is taken from Glenn R. Parker, 'The Role of Constituent Trust in Congressional Elections', *Public Opinion Quarterly*, 53 (1989), pp. 182–3.

Table 3.9. Percentages of voters who recognised House and Senate candidates' names, 1980–1992

Year	Incumbents (%)	Challengers (%)	Incumbent-Challenger Difference (%)	Candidates in Open Seats (%)
		HOUSE		
1980	92	54	−38	82
1982	94	62	−32	77
1984	91	54	−37	80
1986	91	46	−45	84
1988	95	58	−37	72
1990	93	39	−54	80
1992	94	63	−31	80
Mean	93	54	−39	79

	SENATE			
1980	99	81	−18	89
1982	97	78	−19	95
1986*	97	77	−20	94
1988	98	80	−18	97
1990	96	70	−26	89
1992	97	87	−10	96
Mean	97	79	−18	93

Source: American National Election Studies, 1980–1992. Cumulative Data File. ICPSR No. 8475 and ICPSR No. 6067.
* Note: No data were available for Senate candidates in 1984

Not surprisingly, House incumbents have more contact with voters than their challengers (although not in 1992); while voters' contacts with incumbent senators and their challengers is generally much higher (Table 3.10). The differences between House and Senate challengers is most noticeable in contacts through the mass media, especially television and newspapers. Being better known to voters matters, of course, because the more familiar voters are with a candidate (usually the incumbent) the more likely they are to vote for him/her. Only about 2 per cent of voters in House elections and 3 per cent of voters in Senate elections vote for candidates who are less familiar than their own; more than half House voters and less than half of Senate voters defect to candidates with whom they are more familiar. Independent voters (who claim no identification with either the Democratic or Republican parties) tend to vote for the better-known House candidate more than 80 per cent of the time, and the better known Senate candidate 95 per cent of the time.[62]

Table 3.10. Voters' contact with House and Senate incumbents and challengers, 1990 and 1992

		HOUSE			SENATE		
Percentage of voters who:	Election Year	Incumbents	Challengers	Difference	Incumbents	Challengers	Difference
Had some contact	1990	78	23	−55	na	na	na
	1992	67	67	0	na	na	na
Had personal contact	1990	12	1	−11	23	10	−13
	1992	10	9	−1	15	4	−11
Attended meeting	1990	12	2	−10	24	9	−15
	1992	7	7	0	18	6	−12
Met with staff	1990	8	1	−7	17	9	−8
	1992	6	5	−1	14	5	−9
Received mail	1990	51	7	−44	83	55	−23
	1992	37	36	−1	69	41	−27

		HOUSE			SENATE		
Percentage of voters who:	Election Year	Incumbents	Challengers	Difference	Incumbents	Challengers	Difference
Read in newspaper	1990	48	13	−35	89	76	−13
	1992	39	39	0	82	65	−17
Heard on radio	1990	26	6	−20	59	49	−10
	1992	19	19	0	52	42	−10
Saw on television	1990	48	13	−35	95	78	−17
	1992	43	42	−1	90	75	−15
Had contact through friends	1990	23	4	−19	32	18	−14
	1992	17	17	0	25	11	−14

Source: American National Election Studies, Cumulative Data File, 1952–1990. ICPSR 8475, 6067 and 9580.

Presentation or representation?

Notwithstanding the substantial number of retirements and electoral defeats of incumbents in 1992 and 1994, incumbents appear to be doing the right things to win re-election, as far as the voters are concerned. Although they are highly critical of Congress as a collective policy-making institution, Americans love *their* member of Congress whom they evaluate on the basis of constituency attentiveness and personal style. Thus, a *Times Mirror* survey conducted a few days before the 1994 mid-term elections showed that 58 per cent of respondents 'would like to see their representative in Congress re-elected', but only 31 per cent said that they would like to 'see most members of Congress re-elected'.[63] Most incumbents are re-elected and popular with their constituents because they behave strategically as rational and self-interested politicians. Preferring little or no electoral competition, they project home styles which foster voters' trust, develop unique and individualistic relationships with constituents, and portray themselves as electorally invincible so as to discourage opposition. To state this, however, is not to ignore the frequent criticism of members of Congress, that they emphasise presentation at the expense of substance. Yet, home styles are not entirely self-serving. Although congressional elections do not meet fully the requirements of full participatory democracy, it is clear nevertheless that members need to find effective ways of keeping voters and the media informed about public issues, in part to relegitimise their election. As they pursue their Washington careers and become increasingly involved in the details of public policy-making, the greatest risk incumbents take is neglecting their re-election constituencies. Most of the time, most House incumbents probably do find it relatively easy to emphasise non-controversial constituency service and escape penetrating questions on policy issues in their interactions with constituents; but more informed citizens, opposition candidates, interest groups, and the media can and do call them to account, and as the ANES results in Table 3.8 show increasingly congressional voters are evaluating incumbents according to their ideological and policy preferences. Moreover, as the results of the 1992 and 1994 elections demonstrate, voters do take their revenge if they suspect a breach of trust albeit more frequently in Senate than House elections.

What is most clear from this chapter is that a considerable amount of members' activity during and between elections is devoted to serving constituents and winning re-election. Contemporary electoral circumstances require incumbent House members and senators to be attentive to their voters, to recognise shifting conditions in their districts and states, to muster their own resources to win re-election, and to construct and maintain their own re-election constituencies. Individual members of the House and Senate develop unique and individualistic home styles which they project to their re-election constituencies. When they arrive in Washington to represent their constituencies and formulate public policy, we should also expect them to behave in unique and individualistic ways. With this in mind, we explain in the next chapter how the organisation of both houses of Congress reflects the differentiations among members' electoral connections.

Notes

1   Quoted in Jeffrey L. Katz, 'Candidates Move to Outside as Tactic To Win Races', *Congressional Quarterly Weekly Report*, May 2 1993, p. 1176.
2   Quoted in Stuart Rothenberg, 'Campaigning', *Roll Call*, March 7 1994, p. 32.
3   Timothy J. Conlan, 'Federal, State, Or Local? Trends in the Public's Judgement', *Public Perspective*, 7 (1993), pp. 3–5.
4   The phrase is Mayhew's. David R. Mayhew, *Congress: The Electoral Connection* (New Haven, CT and London: Yale University Press, 1974).
5   Raymond E. Wolfinger and Steven J. Rosenstone, *Who Votes?* (New Haven, CT and London: Yale University Press, 1980); Raymond E. Wolfinger, Steven J. Rosenstone, and Richard A. McIntosh, 'Presidential and Congressional Voters Compared', *American Politics Quarterly*, 9 (1981), p. 255.
6   Currently, the House also has four non-voting delegates – from American Samoa (1981), District of Columbia (1971), Guam (1972), and Virgin Islands (1976) and one resident commissioner for Puerto Rico (1976) – bringing the total to 440. Proposals were made in 1994 to grant delegate status also to the resident representative of the Northern Marianas Islands. Puerto Rico's delegate or Resident Commissioner is elected for four years; the others for two years. Although not technically members of the House, in the 103rd Congress (1993–4) majority Democrats allowed delegates to vote in certain circumstances. Delegates may also speak on the floor, serve and vote on committees, and even hold committee chairmanships. Republicans ended delegate voting in 1995.
7   See Gordon E. Baker, *The Reapportionment Revolution. Representation, Political Power and the Supreme Court* (New York: Random House, 1966.), pp. 78–9.
8   In *Shaw* v. *Reno* (1993), the Supreme Court rejected the constitutionality of North Carolina's 12th district, ruling that states had not been given a '*carte blanche* to engage in racial gerrymandering' and requiring them to demonstrate a 'compelling

state interest' other than race before allowing such districts. By March 1995, federal judges had also ruled minority–majority districts in Georgia, Louisiana, and Texas as the products of racial gerrymandering.

9   John T. Pothier, 'The Partisan Bias in Senate Elections', *American Politics Quarterly*, 12 (1984), pp. 88–100.

10 Congressional Quarterly, *Congressional Districts in the 1990s. A Portrait of America* (Washington, D.C.: Congressional Quarterly, 1993).

11 Gerald C. Wright, Robert S. Erikson, and John P. McIver, 'Measuring State Partisanship and Ideology with Survey Data', *Journal of Politics*, 47 (1985), pp. 478–9.

12 Charles Stewart and Mark Reynolds, 'Television Markets and US Senate Elections', *Legislative Studies Quarterly*, 15 (1990), pp. 495–523.

13 Currently, the House includes only one independent – Congressman Bernie Sanders (Vermont) – a self-described socialist elected in 1990, who is associated with the House Democratic Caucus. In recent decades, two independents have sat in the Senate but both caucused with one of of the parties: James Buckley (NY, 1970–6), a conservative who caucused with Republicans, and Senator Harry Flood Byrd of Virginia who was appointed as a Democrat in 1965, elected as a Democrat in 1966, re-elected as an independent in 1970 and 1976, and caucused with the Democrats.

14 William O. Lipinski (D.IL), for example, is a product of the Cook County Democratic machine. After serving a lengthy apprenticeship in other offices, Lipinski was nominated in 1982 by the Democratic organisation to challenge the incumbent Democrat (previously favoured by the organisation) who refused to retire. As the organisation's committeeman for Chicago's 23rd Ward, Lipinski won the Democratic primary handsomely, and subsequently the general election. When Chicago lost a congressional district, as a result of reapportionment in 1990, Lipinski again beat a fellow Democratic incumbent in the primary with the solid support of the intact Democratic machine. Political machines are, of course, not confined to the Democratic Party. Nassau County (New York) is the home of a powerful Republican Party machine which for many decades controlled nominations in New York's 4th (formerly 5th) congressional district.

15 Paul S. Herrnson, *Party Campaigning in the 1980s* (Cambridge and London: Harvard University Press, 1988); Thomas A. Kazee and Mary C. Thornberry, 'Where's the Party? Congressional Candidate Recruitment and American Party Organisations', *Western Political Quarterly*, 43 (1990), p. 76.

16 Robert Biersack and Paul S. Herrnson, 'Political Parties and the Year of the Woman' in Elizabeth Adell Cook, Sue Thomas, and Clyde Wilcox (eds), *The Year of the Woman. Myths and Realities* (Boulder, CO and Oxford: Westview Press, 1994), p. 166.

17 Alan Ehrenhart, *The United States of Ambition: Politicians, Power, and the Pursuit of Office* (New York: Times Books/Random House, 1991), p. 17. See also Joseph A. Schlesinger, *Ambition and Politics* (Chicago: Rand McNally, 1966); Linda L. Fowler and Robert D. McClure, *Political Ambition. Who Decides to Run for Congress* (New Haven and London: Yale University Press, 1989).

18 Lawrence N. Hansen, 'The Vanishing American Candidate', unpublished manuscript (The Joyce Foundation, 1991) quoted in Thomas A. Kazee (ed.), *Who Runs For Congress. Ambition, Context and Candidate Emergence* (Washington, D.C.: Congress Quarterly Press, 1994), p. 167. See also David E. Price, *The Congressional Experience. A View From the Hill* (Boulder and Oxford: Westview Press, 1992),

p. 10; Herrnson, *Party Campaigning in the 1980s*, p. 86; and Allen D. Hertzke, 'Vanishing Candidates in the 2nd District of Colorado', in Kazee, *Who Runs For Congress*, pp. 82–100.

19   Herrnson, *Party Campaigning in the 1980s*.

20   The amateur candidate typology is Canon's. See David T. Canon, *Actors, Athletes and Astronauts. Political Amateurs in the United States Congress* (Chicago and London: University of Chicago Press, 1990).

21   Gary C. Jacobson and Samuel Kernell, *Strategy and Choice in Congressional Elections*, 2nd edn (New Haven: Yale University Press, 1983), esp. chapter 3; David W. Rohde, 'Risk-Bearing and Progressive Ambition: The Case of the United States House of Representatives', *American Journal of Political Science*, 23 (1979), pp. 1–26.

22   But see Amihai Glazer and Bernard Grofman, 'Two Plus Two Plus Two Equals Six: Tenure of Office of Senators and Representatives, 1953–1983', *Legislative Studies Quarterly*, 12 (1987), pp. 555–63.

23   Gary C. Jacobson, 'The Persistence of Democratic House Majorities' in Gary W. Cox and Samuel Kernell, *The Politics of Divided Government* (Boulder and Oxford: Westview Press, 1991), p. 62.

24   Thomas E. Mann, *Unsafe at Any Margin. Interpreting Congressional Elections* (Washington, D.C. and London: American Enterprise Institute, 1978); Gary C. Jacobson, *The Politics of Congressional Elections*, 3rd edn (New York: Harper Collins, 1992), p. 34.

25   See, for example, Chuck Alston, 'Incumbents Share the Wealth, With Redistricting in Mind', *Congressional Quarterly Weekly Report*, May 25 1991, pp. 1343–50.

26   Jacobson, *The Politics of Congressional Elections*, p. 171; Jacobson and Kernell, *Strategy and Choice*, pp. 23, 33, 49–59; Gary Jacobson, 'Strategic Politicians and the Dynamics of US House Elections, 1946–1986', *American Political Science Review*, 83 (1989), pp. 775–93; and Linda L. Fowler, *Candidates, Congress, and the American Democracy* (Ann Arbor, MI: University of Michigan Press, 1993).

27   John E. Owens, 'The 1994 US Mid-Term Elections', *Politics Review*, 4 (1995), p. 5.

28   Angus Campbell, 'Surge and Decline: A Study of Electoral Change', *Public Opinion Quarterly*, 24 (1960), pp. 397–418; and James E. Campbell, *The Presidential Pulse of Congressional Elections* (Lexington, KY: University of Kentucky Press, 1993).

29   Edward R. Tufte, Political Control of the Economy (Princeton, NJ: Princeton University Press, 1978), and Campbell, *The Presidential Pulse of Congressional Elections*; cf. Kazee, *Who Runs For Congress*, p. 179.

30   Paul S. Herrnson, *Congressional Elections. Campaigning at Home and in Washington* (Washington, D.C.: Congressional Quarterly Press, 1995).

31   Joshua Goldstein, *The $43 Million Loophole. Soft Money in the 1990 Congressional Elections* (Washington, D.C.: Center for Responsive Politics, 1991).

32   Quoted in Sara Fritz and Dwight Morris, *Gold-Plated Politics. Running For Congress in the 1990s* (Washington, D.C.: Congressional Quarterly Press, 1992), p. 89.

33   Price, *The Congressional Experience*, pp. 13–14.

34   Excluding the huge expenditures by losing challengers Michael Huffington and Oliver North in California and Virginia decreases the mean to just $1.5 million.

35   Gary C. Jacobson, *Money in Congressional Elections* (New Haven: Yale University Press, 1980); Gary C. Jacobson, 'The Effect of Campaign Spending in House Elections: New Evidence for Old Arguments', *American Journal of Political Science*, 34 (1990), pp. 334–62.

36 Donna Cassata, 'Freshman Class Boasts Resumés To Back Up "Outsider" Image', *Congressional Quarterly Weekly Report*, November 12 1994, p. 12.

37 Benjamin Sheffner, 'After Revolution, Who Has Clout?', *Roll Call*, January 23 1995, pp. B8–B9.

38 David R. Mayhew, 'Congressional Elections: The Case of the Vanishing Marginals', *Polity*, 6 (1974), pp. 295–317.

39 Morris P. Fiorina, *Congress. Keystone of the Washington Establishment*, 2nd edn (New Haven and London: Yale University Press, 1989), pp. 136–7.

40 Walter Dean Burnham, 'The Changing Shape of the American Political Universe', *American Political Science Review*, 59 (1965), pp. 27–8; Martin P. Wattenberg, *The Decline of American Political Parties 1952–1988* (Cambridge, MA: Harvard University Press, 1986).

41 Mann, *Unsafe At Any Margin*, p. 90.

42 Michael Krashinsky and William J. Milne, 'The Effects of Incumbency in US Congressional Elections, 1950–1988', *Legislative Studies Quarterly*, 18 (1993), pp. 321–44.

43 Gary C. Jacobson, *The Electoral Origins of Divided Government. Competition in US House Elections, 1946–1986* (Boulder, CO and Oxford: Westview Press, 1990), pp. 58–9; Jacobson, 'The Persistence of Democratic House Majorities', pp. 19–20.

44 Richard F. Fenno, *Home Style: House Members in Their Districts* (Boston and Toronto: Little Brown, 1978), p. 15.

45 Richard F. Fenno, *The United States Senate. A Bicameral Perspective* (Washington, D.C. and London: American Enterprise Institute, 1982), p. 29; Martin Thomas, 'Electoral Proximity and Senatorial Roll Call Voting', *American Political Science Review*, 80 (1986); 253–83.

46 The following discussion relies heavily on Richard F. Fenno, *Home Style*, ch. 1, and Fenno, *The United States Senate*.

47 Fenno, *The United States Senate*, p. 16.

48 Mary Jacoby, 'Murtha Brings Home Bacon to Pennsylvania,' *Roll Call*, February 24 1994, p. 12, but see Robert M. Stein and Kenneth N. Bickers, 'Congressional Elections and the Pork Barrel', *Journal of Politics*, 56 (1994), pp. 377–99.

49 Fenno, *The United States Senate*, p. 26.

50 See Jacobson, 'The Effect of Campaign Spending in House Elections', pp. 335–62; cf. Donald P. Green and Jonathan S. Krasno, 'Salvation for the Spendthrift Incumbents: Reestimating the Effects of Campaign Spending in House Elections', *American Journal of Political Science*, 32 (1988), pp. 884–907; Lyn Ragsdale and Timothy E. Cook, 'Representatives; Actions and Challengers' Reactions: Limits to Candidate Connections in the House', *American Journal of Political Science*, 31 (1987), pp. 45–81.

51 Fenno, *Home Style*, pp. 57–61 and William T. Bianco, *Trust. Representatives and Constituents* (Ann Arbor, MI: University of Michigan Press,1994).

52 Glenn R. Parker, *Homeward Bound. Explaining Changes in Congressional Behaviour* (Pittsburgh: University of Pittsburgh Press, 1986), pp. 74–5, 78–9.

53 In 1992, House members sent out over 563 million pieces of mail – almost two pieces per man, woman, and child; senators almost 93 million pieces. John Pontius, *US Congress Official Mail Costs: FY 1972 to FY 1993* (est.) (Washington, D.C.: Congressional Research Service, January 12 1993), p. 3.

54 Fenno, *Home Style*, pp. 110–13, 138–9, 205–6; Timothy E. Cook, *Making Laws and Making News. Media Strategies in the US House of Representatives* (Washington,

D.C.: The Brookings Institution, 1989, ch. 5; Stephanie Greco Larson, *Creating Consent of the Governed. A Member of Congress and the Local Media* (Carbondale, IL: Southern Illinois University, 1992); Stephen Hess, *Live From Capitol Hill. Studies of Congress and the Media* (Washington, D.C.: The Brookings Institution, 1991); Peter Clarke and Susan H. Evans, *Covering Campaigns. Journalism in Congressional Elections* (Stanford, CA: Stanford University Press, 1983); Edie N. Goldenberg and Michael W. Traugott, *Campaigning for Congress* (Washington, D.C.: Congressional Quarterly Press, 1984), pp. 128–30.

55 Fenno, *The United States Senate*, pp. 13, 18–19; Jonathan S. Krasno, *Challengers, Competition and Re-election. Comparing Senate and House Elections* (New Haven, CT and London: Yale University Press, 1994) and Alan I. Abramowitz and Jeffrey A. Segal, *Senate Elections* (Ann Arbor, MI: University of Michigan Press, 1992); John R. Hibbing and John R. Alford, 'Constituency Population and Representation in the US Senate', *Legislative Studies Quarterly*, 15 (1990), pp. 581–99.

56 See, for example, Noble Cunningham, *Circular Letters of Congressman, 1789–1839* (Chapel Hill, NC: University of North Carolina Press, 1978).

57 Fiorina, *Congress*.

58 Quoted in Glenn R. Parker, 'Home Styles – Then and Now' in Christopher J. Deering (ed.), *Congressional Politics* (Chicago, IL: Dorsey Press, 1989), p. 40.

59 Cited in John R. Johannes, 'Individual Outputs: Legislators and Constituency Service', in Deering, *Congressional Politics*, p. 92.

60 See Douglas Rivers and Morris P. Fiorina, 'Constituency Service, Reputation, and the Incumbency Advantage' in Morris P. Fiorina and David W. Rohde, *Home Style and Washington Work. Studies in Congressional Politics* (Ann Arbor, MI: University of Michigan press, 1989), pp. 17–45; Price, *The Congressional Experience*, pp. 118–19; and Stephen E. Frantzich, *Write Your Congressman. Constituent Communications and Representation* (New York: Praeger, 1986).

61 Robert P. Weber, 'Home Style and Committee Behavior: The Case of Richard Nolan', in Fiorina and Rohde, *Home Style and Washington Work*, pp. 73–4.

62 Jacobson, *The Politics of Congressional Elections*, pp. 118–19.

63 Richard F. Fenno, 'If, As Ralph Nader Says, Congress Is "The Broken Branch", How Come We Love Our Congressmen So Much?' in Norman J. Ornstein (ed.), *Congress in Change* (New York: Praeger, 1975), pp. 277–87; Glenn R. Parker and Roger H. Davidson, 'Why Do Americans Love Their Congressmen So Much More Than Their Congress?' *Legislative Studies Quarterly*, 4 (1979), pp. 53–61; Kelly D. Patterson and David B. Magleby, 'Public Support for Congress', *Public Opinion Quarterly*, 56 (1992), pp. 539–51; Karlyn Bowman and Everett Carll Ladd, 'Public Opinion Toward Congress: A Historical Overview', in Thomas E. Mann and Norman J. Ornstein (eds), *Congress, the Press, and the Public* (Washington, D.C.: The Brookings Institution, pp. 45–58; and Nelson W. Polsby, 'Congress-Bashing for Beginners', *The Public Interest*, 100 (1990), pp. 15–23.

Congress as an organisation: member enterprises and committees

Congress was intended by the Constitution's framers to be both a law-making institution and a representative assembly. Those elected to the national legislature – from diverse constituencies and with various backgrounds, experiences, opinions, and preferences – were expected to represent the people in the making of national policy. In the next two chapters, we explore how in the 1990s members of the House and the Senate organise Congress to fulfil its representative and law-making responsibilities. The general theme running through both chapters is that Congress continues to function as a significant and autonomous representative and governing institution within the American national political system because both houses recruit ambitious entrepreneurial politicians who are overwhelmingly sympathetic to the principles of 'separated institutions sharing power','diffused responsibility, mixed representation, and institutional competition';[1] and because Congress' internal organisational structures are well suited to defending the institution's autonomy and scope of action against swelling presidentialism, executive expertise and coordinated power, and the ever-growing complexity of public problems at home and abroad.

The determination of contemporary members of Congress to resist devoting their Washington careers exclusively or primarily to promoting their own re-election prospects and to insist that the national legislature actively and genuinely shares in national policy-making is readily apparent. The immediate impression of the visitor to Capitol Hill is of an extremely active, lively, if bureaucratic and expensive organisation. Americans spend more than $2.4 billion a year (1995) on today's Congress – about $4.5 million a year for every member, and more than double the money appropriated for 1977. In the 1990s, the House of Representatives remains in session for 280 to 290 days a year, six to seven hours a day; the Senate, between 280 and 300 days, eight to nine hours a day. In any one Congress, between 6,000 and 8,000 bills are introduced into the House (14 to 19 bills per member); between 3,000 and 4,500 bills (30 to 45 each) in the Senate. Out of these totals, only about 1,000 bills pass into law. Over the same period, House members record between 700 and 1,000 votes (two to four a day) and attend over 5,000 committee meetings; senators record between 450 and 800 votes (one to three a day) and attend over 2,000 meetings. The toll this work load has on the quality of life of members and their families is well recognised.

Congress is not only a veritable hotbed of activity. It is also a sprawling, rather bureaucratic, institution which operates in many different arenas. Compared with the more intimate and cramped conditions of British MPs in the Palace of Westminster, members of Congress are housed in eight large office buildings located around Capitol Hill – five for senators and eight for House members – spread over an area of approximately 1.8 square miles. Besides the 540 members of Congress (100 senators, 435 representatives, 4 delegates, and 1 resident commissioner), these buildings accommodate over 27,000 members of staff – more than in each of the departments of Education, Energy, Housing and Urban Development, Labor, and State; and more than in any other legislature in the world.

To appreciate the range, variety and intensity of congressional activities, it is useful to examine what happens in Congress during one particular week. We have chosen the week of May 24–28 1993. We will then explain in the remainder of the chapter how the House and Senate organise to do their work, focusing in particular on members' personal offices and the highly important committee systems. The role of party organisations and leaders will be considered in the next chapter.

A week in Congress

A presidential week

The first important point to note about our chosen week is that ostensibly it was a 'presidential' week dominated by President Clinton's attempts to gain congressional approval for his first budget. Following what the *Washington Post* called 'a disastrous week' for the president – an expensive haircut on the tarmac at Los Angeles airport, a charge of nepotism over plans to reorganise the White House travel office, continuing controversy over the president's proposal to end the ban on gays in the military, apparent prevarication over Bosnia, and widespread accusations that his presidency lacked overall direction in domestic and foreign policy – Congress would decide in this week whether or not Clinton's presidency and the Democratic Party would pass its first important legislative test. As in preceding weeks, the week's television and print news was dominated by pleas from the president and executive officials for congressional support, and criticisms of his proposals from conservative Democratic and Republican opponents in both houses. On Monday, May 24, Congressman Charles Stenholm (D.TX), the leading conservative Democratic critic in the House, announced that the reconciliation bill (to be debated on Thursday) lacked the required 218 votes for passage; further cuts in entitlement spending were demanded, a less onerous energy tax, or both. On Tuesday and Wednesday, White House officials held a number of lengthy, well-publicised meetings with congressional critics while the president sought to shore up support among liberal supporters. Early on Wednesday morning, Clinton answered voters' questions at a 'town meeting' in the Rose Garden of the White House, which was broadcast to a nationwide audience on CBS Morning News. On the same day, former presidential candidate Ross Perot made a personal attack on Clinton on television, questioning whether the president had the ability to hold a middle management position in private industry. The week's high point arrived late on Thursday evening when to the obvious relief of the president and the House leadership, the House finally approved the reconciliation bill but only by six votes. The closeness of the president's victory served to intensify speculation about the bill's likely fate in the Senate where a number of conservative Democrats had already voiced opposition.

Table 4.1. Variety and complexity in congressional committee activity, May 24–29 1993

Monday	The House Appropriations Committee made its 602(b) allocations dividing up over $500 billion in discretionary federal spending for the 1994 fiscal year among its 13 subcommittees. The committee also marked up and reported out a trimmed-down version of the president's economic stimulus bill appropriating $931.5 million in spending for summer jobs, construction work, additional community police. On the Senate side, two different Appropriations subcommittees held hearings on the public health service and on marketing and inspection services operated by the US Department of Agriculture; and the Senate Banking, Housing and Urban Affairs Committee and the Commerce, Science, and Transportation Committee heard testimony on the president's nominations to various posts in executive departments.
Tuesday	The House Energy and Commerce Committee approved part of a bill preventing employers from hiring permanent replacement workers when full-time employees go on strike. The Senate Commerce, Science, and Transportation Committee approved a Clinton Administration proposal to sell off radio spectrum licences to stimulate the cellular telephone industry; and reported out bills to encourage high technology research by American industry, to promote the wearing of safety helmets by child cyclists, and to eliminate fraud and harassment by telephone. Other committees heard testimony on Indian food and nutrition programmes, federal aid for education, money laundering, environmental quality, and international economic and exchange rate policies.
Wednesday	The Senate Labor and Human Resources Committee approved legislation to create a National Skills Standards Board. The House Merchant Marine and Fisheries Committee reported a bill continuing shipping subsidies; and three Appropriations subcommittees reported out bills appropriating $25 billion in spending, including aid to Russia and the former Soviet Republics. The East Asian and Pacific Affairs Subcommittee of the Senate Foreign Relations Committee also heard evidence on the likely implications of North Korea's withdrawal from the Nuclear Non-Proliferation Treaty. Other committees and subcommittees held hearings on drug abuse, chemical defence programmes, equal employment practices, student loans, intelligence programmes, and coal mine safety.
Thursday	The Senate Judiciary Committee reported out legislation to prevent and punish offenders who violently assaulted women. A House Appropriations subcommittee approved over $68 billion in spending for veterans, housing and environment and space programmes. The Senate Banking Committee reported legislation tightening federal regulation of government securities markets, and the House Public Works and Transportation Committee approved another part of the striker replacement bill. Hearings were held on drink driving, environmental issues associated with military base closures, foreign and Native American graves, military tactics, and natural disasters.
Friday	A subcommittee of the Senate Judiciary Committee heard testimony on terrorism, asylum issues, and immigration policy.

Source: Congressional Record.

The committees' week

While the media was speculating over the beleaguered president's ability to win congressional support for his economic programme, there was much else going on in Congress during this week which attracted much less media attention. Both the House and the Senate had their own very busy schedules. Numerous committees were busy working on subjects ranging from $1.5 trillion in federal spending to safety helmets for child cyclists (see Table 4.1).

Table 4.2. House and Senate committee and subcommittee meetings, May 24–28 1993

Committee	Number of meetings on each day					Totals	Number of Markups	Number of Closed Meetings
	24	25	26	27	28			
HOUSE								
Agriculture	0	0	0	0	0	0	0	0
Appropriations	1	0	4	2	0	7	5	0
Armed Services	0	2	1	1	0	4	0	1
Banking, Finance and Urban Affairs	0	1	1	2	0	4	0	0
Budget	0	0	0	0	0	0	0	0
District of Columbia	0	0	0	0	0	0	0	0
Education and Labor	0	2	1	2	0	5	0	0
Energy and Commerce	0	2	3	3	0	8	3	0
Foreign Affairs	0	2	2	0	0	4	4	0
Government Operations	0	1	1	2	0	4	0	0
House Administration	0	0	1	0	0	1	0	0
Judiciary	0	0	0	2	0	2	0	0
Merchant Marine and Fisheries	0	2	1	1	0	4	1	0
Natural Resources	0	2	0	2	0	4	1	0
Post Office and Civil Service	0	0	0	1	0	1	0	0
Public Works and Transportation	0	0	2	1	0	3	1	0
Rules	0	1	1	0	0	2	0	0
Science, Space and Technology	0	1	1	1	0	3	0	0
Small Business	0	1	1	1	0	3	0	0
Standards of Official Conduct	0	0	0	0	0	0	0	0
Veterans' Affairs	0	0	0	0	0	0	0	0
Ways and Means	0	1	0	3	0	4	0	0
Permanent Select Intelligence	0	0	1	0	0	1	0	0
Joint Organisation of Congress	0	1	0	0	0	1	0	0
Totals	1	19	22	24	0	65	15	1

	SENATE							
Agriculture, Nutrition and Forestry	0	1	0	0	0	1	0	0
Appropriations	2	1	5	3	0	11	0	1
Armed Services	1	3	1	1	0	7	0	0
Banking, Housing and Urban Affairs	1	1	0	1	0	3	1	0
Budget	0	0	0	0	0	0	0	0
Commerce, Science and Transportation	1	1	2	2	0	6	0	0
Energy and Natural Resources	0	1	1	1	0	3	1	0
Environment and Public Works	0	2	0	1	0	3	0	0
Finance	0	0	0	0	0	0	0	0
Foreign Relations	0	0	1	3	0	4	0	0
Governmental Affairs	0	1	1	0	0	2	0	0
Indian Affairs	0	1	0	2	0	3	0	0
Judiciary	0	2	0	1	1	4	1	0
Labor and Human Resources	0	0	2	0	0	2	1	0
Rules and Administration	0	0	0	0	0	0	0	0
Select Ethics	0	0	0	0	0	0	0	0
Select Intelligence	0	0	1	1	0	2	0	2
Small Business	0	0	0	0	0	0	0	0
Special Aging	0	1	0	0	0	1	0	0
Veterans' Affairs	0	0	0	0	0	0	0	0
Joint Organisation of Congress	0	0	0	0	0	0	0	0
Totals	5	15	14	16	1	51	4	3

Source: 'Today in Congress', *Washington Post*, May 24–29 1993.

During this week, the House held 65 full committee and subcommittee meetings (about 20 a day) and the Senate 52 (about 17 a day) – making a total of 117 meetings, only three of which related to the budget reconciliation bill (Table 4.2). Many of these meetings were scheduled simultaneously, requiring many legislators to be in several places at the same time. Managing to attend so many committee (and other) meetings is a major problem for members of Congress. A second interesting point about Table 4.2 is that very few of these meetings were held to 'mark up' bills i.e. to amend their language, usually with the help of staff, before reporting them to the House or Senate floor. Not surprisingly for a week in May during the first session of a Congress, most committee meetings were hearings at which lobby groups, experts, executive officials, and occasionally private citizens provide testimony on proposed legislation or specific topics of concern; meetings to mark up bills tend to be later in the session, or in the second session simply because few bills are ready. A third point is that during this week most committee meetings were open to the public (and sometimes to television cameras); only four meetings were closed – all concerned with intelligence and military policy. Before Congress adopted so-called 'sunshine laws' in 1973, between 30 and 40 per cent of meetings were closed. Now, less than 10 per cent are closed. Fourth, although the House held more committee meetings, senators had more meetings in relation to their numbers. Fifth, the table shows that most committee meetings were held on Tuesday, Wednesday, and Thursday. While no longer the part-time body of earlier eras, today's Congress is essentially a three-day, Tuesday to Thursday, operation.[2] Sixth, almost all committee meetings were held in the morning, leaving time for floor and other activities in the afternoon and evening. Finally, although not shown in the table, most committee meetings were actually meetings of subcommittees (76 per cent in the House, 46 per cent in the Senate) – again because insufficient time had passed in the first session for legislation to be considered by full committees. Subcommittee activity is greater in the House because of the chamber's larger size and the unwieldy size of many full committees.

The week on the floors

Besides a full timetable of committee meetings, members had heavy schedules on the House and Senate floors. Apart from the president's budget bill, which was debated for five hours, the House debated 16 other bills (nine of which were passed) for almost 44 hours, recorded 23 roll call votes, and received four presidential messages. The Senate debated 26 bills for 43 hours (21 of which were approved), recorded 12 roll call votes, consented to 61 presidential nominations (including Roberta Achtenberg as assistant secretary for Fair Housing and Equal Opportunity, the first avowed lesbian appointed to high federal office), and received three presidential messages. Apart from the budget, the House debated and passed a resolution under the War Powers Resolution authorising the deployment of American troops in Somalia; approved supplemental appropriations and a much-reduced version of the president's economic stimulus package; authorised the Department of Veteran Affairs to provide further financial assistance to colleges and universities; and passed legislation requiring federal agencies to adopt measurable performance goals (part of the president's 'reinvent government' plan). The Senate reauthorised the Office of Refugees Resettlement; approved a major overhaul of the 1872 Mining Act; passed legislation for redundant CIA employees; and spent almost one-third of its week (188 pages of the *Congressional Record*, 11 recorded votes over five days) locked in a lengthy debate on controversial new campaign finance legislation. After years of controversy, the House and the Senate also agreed a conference bill reauthorising the National Institutes of Health, codifying President Clinton's decisions to allow foetal tissue research, and prohibiting the permanent admission into the United States of people with HIV (the AIDS virus).

Apart from their complexity and controversiality, it is important to note

87

that during this week, many if not most of the issues considered by Congress on the floors and in committee were *not* recommended or actively promoted by the president. In order for Congress to consider issues of such variety and complexity, enormous demands must be placed on members and their staffs – in terms of expertise, time, energy, coordination of activities in multiple arenas, publicising of issues, and representation of diverse interests. We will explain later how Congress' institutional structures are geared to helping members meet these demands. Before leaving this week, let us turn briefly to how House and Senate central party leaders spent their time.

The week for the party leaders

A glance at the schedule of House Speaker Tom Foley (D.WA) (Table 4.3) – who was subsequently defeated for re-election in 1994 – shows that he spent his week engrossed in building a coalition to win passage of the president's budget reconciliation bill – consulting with the president, the Director of the Office of Management and Budget, other Democratic leaders in the House and Senate (including the Democratic Whip Task Force), key groups of House Democrats (including the Congressional Black Caucus, House Democratic freshmen, the Hispanic Caucus, and the Conservative Democratic Forum), the Democratic Caucus (of all House Democrats), and individual House members. If we were to examine the schedule of the House Minority Leader Bob Michel (R.IL), we would find it rather less hectic and less concerned with legislative management. Michel attended a number of party meetings – including the House Republican Conference (of all House Republicans), the influential SOS and Chowder and Marching Society, a meeting of Republican whips – to discuss party tactics on the budget reconciliation package, but he also found time to attend to more routine party/electoral matters including a meeting of the Committee on Committees to assign new members to committees, a discussion forum on health care, as well as various fund-raising events and a regular meeting with lobbyists. The schedule for Senator Dole (R.KS), the Senate Minority Leader – who became the Majority Leader after January 1995 – also differed but in other ways. Reflecting his status as a sort of leader of the opposition (and then a likely Republican contender for the presidency in 1996), the senator spent a considerable part of his week meeting other Republican leaders, conferring with lobbyists, and attending a number of fund-raising events (including some on a whistle-stop trip to Texas to support the Republican candidate in a special election for a Senate seat). As we noted in the previous chapter, senators – and particularly party leaders – perceive themselves and are perceived to have national constituencies much more than House members and leaders.

If we were to examine how other members spent this week, most likely we would find other important differences. We should, however, also expect strong

Table 4.3. House Speaker Tom Foley's schedule, May 24–27 1993

Date	Time	Meeting
Monday May 24	2.00 pm	Meeting with Congressional Black Caucus
	3.00	House of Representatives Convenes
	3.15	Daily Leadership Press Conference
	5.00	Meeting with Senator Majority Leader Mitchell and House Majority Leader Gephardt
Tuesday May 25	8.30 am	Meeting with President Clinton and House Whip Task Force on budget reconciliation
	10.00	Meeting with President Clinton, House Majority Leader Gephardt, and House Democratic Freshmen on budget reconciliation
	11.45	Daily Leadership Press Conference
	12.00	House of Representatives Convenes
	2.00 pm	Meeting with Hispanic Caucus
	4.30	Television interview with Bernie Shaw on CNN
	5.00	Meeting with Congressman Charles Stenholm (D.TX), leader of the Conservative Democratic Forum, and House Majority Leader Gephardt on budget reconciliation
	6.30	Meeting with House Democratic Freshmen on budget reconciliation
Wednesday May 26	8.30 am	Meeting of House Democratic Caucus
	9.45	Daily Leadership Press Conference
	10.00	House of Representative Convenes
	11.30 am – midnight	For the rest of the day until about midnight, the Speaker telephoned and received individual House members in his office. He also met Leon Panetta, Director of the Office of Management and Budget; and talked with President Clinton at least three times keeping him apprised of member support
Thursday May 27	9.00 am	Meeting with House Democratic Whips
	10.45	Daily leadership press conference
	11.00	House of Representatives Convenes
		The rest of the day was spent contacting individual members and meeting with House Democratic Whip Bonior
	9.15 pm – 11.30 pm	Following the final passage of the Reconciliation bill, contacted the press in his home district in Washington state, and held a press conference with the Democratic leadership

Source: Jeff Biggs, press secretary to the Speaker.

similarities. All three leaders found time at various points in the week to make contact with constituents back home. Speaker Foley telephoned the press in Spokane; Senator Dole made time to be photographed with a dentist and his family from Kansas, and Congressman Michel spent his weekend in his district. A second similarity is the busy and hurried nature of these leaders' working weeks. We could not obtain the Senate Majority Leader's schedule but it is worth mentioning that two weeks later as one of the authors was ambling down the steep stairs of the Capitol Building on the Senate side, the 60-year-old Senator George Mitchell

(D.ME) was vaulting up the stairs two at a time on his way to the Senate chamber. Like the schedules of the other leaders, his was probably long, crowded, and touched on many different aspects of congressional life.

This brief review of this week in Congress tells us much about the work of Congress, its size, and organisation. First, we have seen that members of the House and Senate work within a variety of different arenas, venues, and contexts which compete for their attention, time, and energy. We have discussed only committee, floor and party leaders' activities. Space precludes discussion of activities in the numerous informal caucuses (21 in the Senate in 1993, ranging from the Caucus on Deficit Reduction and Economic Growth to the Western States Senate Coalition, 84 in the House) and other arenas in Washington and the rest of the country, where members and their staffs talk to interest group representatives, administration officials, civil servants, state and local officials, the press, attentive constituents, academics, and others who wish to be represented.

A second important finding is that once ambitious entrepreneurial politicians get to Washington as members of Congress they are not totally absorbed by re-election concerns. They involve themselves heavily in a wide variety of important policy matters – ranging from the budget, through crimes against women, striker replacement, the treatment of immigrants infected with AIDS, and industrial subsidies, to Somalia, North Korea, Cuba, and aid to Russia. And their involvement in policy matters in committees, on the floor, and elsewhere is informed by the knowledge that what Congress does and says matters.

A third point brings us to the focus of the rest of this chapter. In order for Congress to cope with the vast amounts of political and policy traffic it encounters from day to day and hour to hour, to represent and make laws, the institution requires complex organisational structures.

Congress and the problem of representation

Unlike the British House of Commons, representation in the United States Congress is not funnelled (more or less) tidily through parties – particularly the majority party, which controls the executive. Rather the issue is fudged. Simultaneously, Congress is supposed to represent particularistic or local constituencies as well as national and general ones – individuals or groups of citizens who have similar interests or opinions (blacks, the elderly, farmers, and so on), who may or may not reside within specific geographic boundaries; the entire populations of districts and states who are held to share certain interests and opinions; and the entire country or 'the public interest', most obviously in matters of economic, foreign, and national security policy. When they decide how to spend their time and energy in Washington and elsewhere, and when they make decisions on matters of public policy, House members and senators are supposed somehow to resolve the confusions and dilemmas arising from these different, and often competing, representations. They are supposed to satisfy both the particularistic and collective demands and needs of citizens.[3] In Edmund Burke's words, a distinction should be made between 'a congress of ambassadors from different and hostile interests, which interests each must maintain, as an agent and an advocate, against other agents and advocates' *and* 'a deliberative assembly of one nation, with one interest, that of the whole – where not local prejudices ought to guide, but the general good, resulting from the general reason of the whole'.[4]

In practice, the confusions and dilemmas of representation are not resolvable. Thus, Roger Davidson has argued:

> There is not one single Congress, but two. Though inextricably bound together, they are analytically and even physically distinct. One of these two bodies is Congress as an institution. It acts as a collegial body, performing its institutional duties and deliberating on legislative issues. The second Congress is the 540 individual lawmakers . . . acting on their own. They come from diverse backgrounds and follow various paths to win office. Their electoral fortunes depend not so much on what Congress does as an institution, but on how they cultivate support and good will of voters hundreds or thousands of miles away – voters shared by hardly any of their colleagues on Capitol Hill.[5]

To some extent, all legislative bodies combine collective and individualistic components. All are collectivities of individual representatives who reflect the wishes of particular electoral coalitions. In the British House of Commons, representation emphasises the collective: most MPs win election because they bear a particular party label, not because of their individual qualities; and so, once elected, they are expected to toe the party line in the belief that their loyalty to the party will benefit all party MPs and in many cases lead to promotion to the party hierarchy. In the Congress, the problem of competing representations is left unresolved or fudged. With far less guidance from party incentives, individual members must decide their own representational calculus and they must decide for themselves what sort of organisational structure best serves their representational aspirations. An important consequence of this fudging of the representation problem is that the contemporary Congress has multiple institutional structures. In early 1995, the House and Senate boasted over 1,000 organisations with their own staffs – even after the new House Republican majority cut three House committees, 31 subcommittees, and curtailed sharply the activities of informal caucuses. This total includes 640 members' offices, 36 standing committees, 4 select and special committees, 3 joint committees, 154 subcommittees, 17 party committees, 22 party leadership offices, 10 task forces, and 120 informal caucuses. Before examining in detail three sets of organisations – members' individual offices and standing committees and subcommittees in this chapter, and party leaderships in the next chapter – it is important to recognise some important organisational differences between the House and the Senate.

House–Senate differences

Ross Baker has argued that the characteristics of Edmund Burke's 'Congress of ambassadors' are more commonly found in the House; whereas those of his 'deliberative assembly of one nation' are more likely to be found in the Senate.[6] While this contrast is surely too stark and gives too little attention to similarities between the chambers, it points nevertheless to important organisational differences between the House and Senate. These differences arise largely from different membership sizes, lengths of terms served, constituency sizes and nature, and in their constitutional powers.

Differences in membership sizes produce significant differences between House and Senate rules. Being larger, procedural rules in the House are much more formalised, less flexible, more comprehensive (650 pages in the 103rd Congress), and impose more severe restraints on members than is the case in the Senate. The primary purpose of House rules is to ensure that a voting majority – specifically, a party majority acting through the Speaker and other majority leaders – can control the policy agenda, schedule, and floor proceedings effectively. Whereas the House is a majoritarian, more bureaucratic, and hierarchical institution, the Senate is more personal and individualistic and upholds minority power. It has fewer rules (just 90 pages), which are deliberately flexible and designed to promote and preserve the legislative prerogatives of individual senators, and uphold the chamber's tradition of mutual accommodation.

The degree to which subject specialisation and levels of expertise are encouraged in the respective chambers also varies. With a membership less than a quarter the size of the House, and the need for senators to cover the same policy ground, House members are seen as 'the reluctant specialists' compared with 'the glittering generalists' in the Senate.[7] With few exceptions (notably the budget and foreign policy), it is to House members and House committees and subcommittees that Congress looks to provide the detailed expertise necessary to develop the nitty gritty details essential for sound legislation. House members devote far more attention and energy to their committee work than do most senators. Indeed, the House's work is dominated by committees and subcommittees to an extent which would be alien to the Senate. Without prior use of House committees and subcommittees, Congress could not even function as an autonomous law-making body. Senators tend to be more concerned with the general direction of national policy – 'the articulation of interests, agenda-setting, and the promotion of policy' – and are sometimes disparaged by House colleagues for their low levels of policy expertise.[8]

We should keep these important differences in mind as we examine the three structures of congressional organisation.

In the last chapter, we made the point that contemporary House members and senators are elected and re-elected because of their own individual efforts, rather than as a result of the support of the president or other party leaders, party organisations, or interest groups. Once elected, it is logical that these ambitious entrepreneurial politicians should want to represent their constituents vigorously and play a meaningful role in the making of national policy. In a pathbreaking study, Richard Fenno showed that all members of Congress hold three basic personal political goals: re-election or serving their constituents, exercising influence in the chamber, and making good public policy. All members probably hold all three of these goals but each member has his/her own individual combination of priorities and intensities.[9] How members employ their time and energy once they arrive in Washington, how they behave, and what positions they take on public issues reflect the priorities and intensities they give to different goals. In short, the behaviour of members of Congress is purposive and discretion-maximising.[10] In Chapter 2, we showed how since the eighteenth century Congress has organised itself to reflect the internal demands of its members and the external demands of the electorate. In the contemporary era of 'individualised pluralism'[11] – where representatives and senators are in business for themselves – the same imperatives determine legislative organisation.

Members' personal enterprises

Just as these freewheeling entrepreneurs create personal organisations to win election, once they are in Congress, they build up their own personal enterprises to pursue their personal legislative and policy interests. Varying in complexity, structure, and function, these enterprises shape and constrain the behaviour of individual members in the House and the Senate.[12]

Much to the astonishment of foreign legislators visiting Capitol Hill, members of Congress occupy large suites of offices. House members have two to three office suites in one of the three House office buildings on the south side of the Capitol, while senators occupy more luxurious suites of five to eight rooms in one of three Senate office buildings on the north side. Apart from this spacious accommodation, members also have substantial institutional resources to run their personal offices – currently, about $750,000 per annum for each House member for travel, office, staff, and communications; and between $2 million and $2.5 million each for senators. Although sizeable proportions of these resources are used to provide constituent services from offices in their districts and states, substantial resources are used to hire staff to help them with their legislative and other work in Washington. During the 103rd Congress (1993–4), for example, House members employed on average seven staff and senators about 21 each in their personal offices in Washington. During the summer months, these totals are usually inflated by a small army of student interns.

Table 4.4 shows just how elaborate, even bureaucratic, members' personal offices have become. Organisation within them is often hierarchical; and functional divisions typically specialised. Although job titles vary, most members' personal offices are directed by an administrative assistant (AA) or staff director who is closest to the House member or senator. Most offices also include a legislative director who is responsible for researching and drafting legislation in committee and on the floor, and for liaising with interest groups; an office manager, who supervises the administration of the office and controls the member's diary or schedule; at least one press secretary; a number of legislative assistants (LAs); a systems manager or computer operator; and various clerical assistants and/or secretaries. As the table shows, legislative assistants are typically assigned to specific policy areas. Congressman Obey (D.WI) has four specialists each with responsibilities for at least four policy specialisms whereas in the much larger staff of Senator Levin (D.MI) seven specialists concentrate on a narrower range of subjects. Positions in House offices tend to be more differentiated, and more hierarchically organised whereas a more free-ranging style tends to prevail in senators' offices.

Table 4.4. Positions in members' personal offices in Washington, 1993

Position	Legislative Responsibilites	Name
CONGRESSMAN DAVID OBEY (D.WI)		
Staff Director	appropriations; budget	Joe Crapa
Personal Secretary/executive assistant		Carly Burns
Legislative Director	agriculture; budget/taxes; transportation	Paul Carver
Press secretary/senior writer		Jack Kole
Legislative assistant	Appropriations Committee; education, energy/environment, communications; immigration	Annes Georges
Legislative assistant	foreign affairs; defense; veterans, trade	Michael Marek
Legislative assistant	Appropriations Committee; health/human services; aging; banking consumers; housing; judiciary	Kathy Sykes
Computer manager		Michelle Montgomery
2 Staff assistants		
1 Legislative correspondent		
SENATOR CARL LEVIN (D.MI)		
Administrative assistant		Gordon Kerr
Personal Secretary		Willie Blacklow
Deputy press secretary/ Michigan liaison		Armetta Parker
Office manager		Barbara Cantrall
Legislative Director	taxation; budget; economy; housing	Chuck Cutolo
Legislative assistant	judiciary; transportation	Alison Pascale

Legislative assistant	defense	Richard Fieldhouse
Legislative assistant	defense	David Lewis
Legislative assistant	energy; environment; agriculture	Chris Miller
Legislative assistant	health; education; social services	Jackie Parker
Legislative assistant	banking; foreign affairs	John Sheridan
Policy Adviser		Steve Snider
3 legislative correspondents		
Executive secretary		Helen Galen
Legislative secretary		Dwanda Glenn
3 Staff assistants		
Secretary to Administrative Assistant		Devera Levin
Systems manatger/mailroom supervisor		David Bolyard
3 CMS specialists		

Source: Ann L. Brownson ed., *1993 Congressional Staff Directory 1* (Mount Vernon, VA: Staff Directories, Ltd., 1993).

Note: CMS specialists operate the Congressional Management (Computing) System to reply to constituents' mail.

With unlimited access to these resources, as well as to the Congressional Research Service (CRS), the Congressional Budget Office (CBO), and the Office of Technology Assessment (OTA) – all separate from any resources available to committees and party organisations of which they are members – individual House members and senators can become 'policy entrepreneurs'[13] in whichever subject areas they choose, independent from the executive, central party leaders and committee chairs, and they can serve their constituents at the same time. Typically, they assign staff in their personal offices to monitoring the progress of bills and amendments, keeping them informed on arcane subjects, liaise with political allies within Washington's issue networks, publicise their own policy proposals, and generally try to influence Congress' agenda. Unlike resources available through committees and parties which are shared with and controlled by others, these official resources are exclusively for the members' own use. Moreover,

> the member is working with and through associated staff personnel who share an identity and a set of goals not because of the payroll they are on, the office they work in, or the tasks they perform, but because of their loyalty and commitment to that particular member.[14]

Particularly for junior members, the potential benefits of these personal resources are enormous. Unlike their seniors, they do not enjoy privileged access to committee and party resources and so can use these resources to influence the policy agenda inside and outside Congress. Even the most junior members after a few months in Congress can make an impression, as can their personal staff.[15] The potential consequences for Congress' internal distribution of power and the institution's ability to retain its scope and autonomy in national government and policy-making are obvious.

Legislation and law-making

The job of members of Congress is to make public policy as well as represent their constituents. Notwithstanding their preoccupation with servicing their constituents, House members and senators devote considerable time and energy to legislating (Table 4.5). Inevitably, the processes of writing legislation – especially for such a large and varied country as the United States – are rather more complex than servicing the needs and demands of constituents. It is not surprising, therefore, that Congress is subject to continual public and media criticism for the ways it writes legislation, in almost all areas of public policy. Among congressional and academic critics, it is argued, Congress performs better as a representative institution than as a law-making body. Thus, Morris Fiorina observes: 'Through a complex mixture of accident and intention, we have constructed for ourselves a system that articulates interests superbly but aggregates them poorly.'[16] Whether Fiorina's dichotomy between representation and policy-making is a real one is questionable – voters and interests also influence how Congress organises itself

Table 4.5. Percentage of time spent by members of Congress
on various representational activities, 1993

Activity	HOUSE MEMBERS				SENATORS			
	Great Deal	Moderate Amount	Only a Little	Almost None	Great Deal	Moderate Amount	Only a Little	Almost None
Meeting with citizens in district	73.6	24.8	1.5	0	39.1	60.9	0	0
Attending committee hearings	48.1	45.0	7.0	0	50.0	50.0	0	0
Meeting with constituents in Washington	43.4	51.2	5.4	0	54.2	45.8	0	0
Meeting in Washington on legislative issues	42.6	50.4	7.0	0	16.7	83.3	0	0
Studying about legislation	23.7	57.3	16.8	2.3	33.3	50.0	16.7	0
Working with LSOs and informal groups	8.4	44.3	33.6	13.7	4.2	37.5	50.0	8.3
Attending floor debate	6.2	38.0	41.9	13.9	12.5	33.3	54.2	0
Managing the office	7.6	46.6	36.6	9.2	0	33.3	50.0	16.7
Fundraising	5.4	31.0	45.7	17.8	8.7	43.5	39.1	8.7
Working on coalition-building	6.1	31.3	43.5	19.1	4.2	41.7	41.7	12.5
Oversight of administrative agencies	6.2	21.7	41.9	30.2	0	26.1	52.2	21.7
Giving speeches outside district	5.4	23.1	47.7	23.9	0	25.0	58.3	16.7

Members were asked: 'How much time do you spend on the various activities listed below? Would you say you spend a great deal of time, a moderate amount of time, only a little time, or almost no time on . . . ?' The table shows percentages of respondents who indicated different times spent.

Source: US. Congress. Joint Committee on the Organisation of Congress, *Organisation of the Congress, Final Report*, Vol. II, 103rd Congress, First Session, Appendix B, pp. 275–80.

Note: LSO is a legislative service organisation, such as the Congressional Black Caucus.

thereby ensuring that the tasks of representation *and* public policy-making are complementary and interdependent – he and others rightly point to Congress' difficulty in reaching policy decisions.

Characteristics of the legislative process in Congress

A number of enduring characteristics of the congressional process explain why Congress often finds it difficult to make policy. Each is consistent with the themes of diffused responsibility, mixed representation, and institutional competition embedded in the Constitution.

First, the responsibilities for collecting policy-related information and processing legislation is dispersed among multifarious units within fairly discrete jurisdictions, with the inevitable consequence that the legislative process is highly fragmented. Broad policy areas such as the budget, environmental policy, health care, and trade are subdivided and parcelled out to various standing committees and their subcommittees. Hearings conducted by the Joint Committee on the Organisation of Congress in 1993 revealed, for example, that as many as 52 different House and Senate committees and subcommittees had jurisdiction over programmes for children and families; that the Environmental Protection Agency answered to 90 committees and subcommittees; and that 107 committees and subcommittees claimed some oversight role over the Pentagon.[17] If any spending is involved, the process is even more complex: programmes must be authorised (by House and Senate authorising committees), appropriations made (by the appropriations committees), revenues or borrowing raised (by the revenues committees), and revenue and spending reconciled in a complete budget (by the budget committees) (Table 4.6). Overlapping and dispersed committee responsibilities, often encouraged and reinforced by interest group activities, frequently cause inter-committee jurisdictional disputes and vitiate the formulation of coherent and/or comprehensive legislation.

Second, as the Constitution's framers intended, the legislative process in Congress is deliberately cumbersome. Once a bill or resolution is introduced into the House or Senate (see Table 4.7), it is referred to one or more committees and then usually to one or more subcommittees. The views of executive departments and agencies are requested; hearings are held before the committee(s) or subcommittee(s), or both, to receive testimony from various lobby groups, executive agencies, members of Congress, local and state government officials, outside experts, and private citizens interested in the measure. Sometimes investigations are conducted by committee or subcommittee staff, and their conclusions and recommendations considered by committee and/or subcommittee members. If subcommittee or committee members wish, the measure is then taken up, scheduled for 'mark-up' (the meetings at which members decide the content of bills and vote on amendments), and reported out to the House or Senate floor. If the

Table 4.6. Types of House and Senate committees
according to budget functions

	Authorising Committees	Appropriations Committees	Revenue Committees	Budget Committees
Number	14 in House; 15 in Senate e.g. House Agriculture	House and Senate Appropriations Committees	House Ways and Means and Senate Finance Committees	House and Senate Budget Committees
Functions	Report authorising and entitlement legislation; oversee executive agencies; submit views and estimates to Budget Committee on matters in their jurisdiction; recommend changes to law pursuant to reconciliation instructions; submit CBO cost estimates in reports on their legislation	Report regular and supplemental appropriations bills; review proposed budgetary rescissions (cancellations of budget authority) and deferrals (of budget authority); submit views and estimates to Budget Committees on federal spending; include limits on credit programmes in appropriations bills; establish rules for renewing programmes; establish account structure for federal agencies	Report revenue legislation; report legislation on public debt, social security, and certain other entitlements; submit views and estimates to Budget Committee on matters in their jurisdiction; recommend changes in laws pursuant to reconciliation instructions	Report budget resolution; draft reconciliation instructions and compile reconciliation bill; allocate new budget authority, outlays, and new entitlement and credit authority to committees; monitor budget and advise Congress on its status; (Senate) reports resolutions waiving certain budget procedures.

Source: Allen Schick with Robert Keith and Edward Davis, *Manual on the Federal Budget Process* (Washington, D.C.: CRS Report 91–902 GOV, December 24 1991).

measure is reported out in the House, the committee chair is then instructed to seek a rule from the Rules Committee which, if granted, determines for how long the bill will be debated on the floor, whether or not and to what extent it will be open to floor amendments, and in which order amendments will be considered. If the measure passes the House floor, it then goes to the Senate where it is subject to a similar series of legislative stages, except that the Senate has no Rules Committee; instead, the Senate Majority Leader plays the equivalent role of 'traffic cop' following consultations with interested senators. In practice, as in the case of President Clinton's health bill in 1994, both houses may consider important legislation simultaneously; or one may consider legislation first. (Largely for symbolic reasons now, revenue raising measures and appropriations bills originate in the House; treaties are considered first by the Senate.) The Senate has sole jurisdiction over the approval of important executive nominations. If a measure is to proceed for the president's signature, any substantive differences (which are often significant) in the bills passed by the respective houses must be reconciled in a House–Senate conference committee.

Third, besides being lengthy and cumbersome, the legislative process is cumulative and sequential. In no other legislature in the world is there a more

Table 4.7. How a bill becomes a law: decision points in the congressional process

HOUSE		SENATE
Introduced by a member; receives an HR number		Introduced by a member; received an S number
Referred to one or more of 19 committees by the Speaker (in practice, by the parliamentarian)		Referred to one or more of 17 committees by the Senate president
May be referred to a subcommittee by committee majority		May be referred to a subcommittee by committee chair
Comments solicited from appropriate executive agency		Comments solicited from appropriate executive agency
May be hearings convened by committee and/or subcommittee		May be hearings convened by committee or subcommittee
Reported to floor or killed		Reported to floor or killed
Placed on one of 5 calendars		Placed on one of 2 calendars
Granted rule (or not) by the Rules Committee, specifying the length and conditions of debate e.g. which amendments will be voted on		Granted by unanimous consent or majority vote (or not at all), specifying the length and conditions of debate e.g. which amendments will be voted on
Debated, amendments considered, and voted on floor (voice, standing, electronically recorded yeas and nays); motion to recommit offered (usually tabled)		Debated for an unlimited time, unless established by unanimous agreement, amendments considered, and voted on floor (voice, standing, or recorded yeas and nays); motion to reconsider offered (usually tabled)
Sent to the Senate; House acts first on revenue and appropriations bills		Sent to the House; House acts first on revenue and appropriations bills
	If bills are different either one house accepts the other's version or a conference is requested	
Conference reported voted on, subject to no amendments		Conference reported on, subject to no amendments
	Sent to the president who either (a) signs it (and it becomes law), (b) vetoes it (and it returns to both houses which each need to muster a two-thirds vote to override the veto), (c) does not sign the bill while Congress is in session (and bill becomes law after 10 days), or (d) does not sign the bill and Congress adjourns before the 10-day period (and the bill is killed by a pocket veto)	
	Enumerated and assigned either a public or private law number (e.g. PL 1, 104th Congress)	

Source: Congressional Quarterly, *Congress and the Nation VIII, 1989–92* (Washington, D.C.: Congressional Quarterly, 1993); and Walter J. Oleszek, *Congressional Procedures and the Policy Process* (Washington, D.C.: Congressional Quarterly, 1989).

complex pattern of serial decision-making; in no other legislature in the world is the veto emphasised more.[18] At any point along the way, a measure may not be considered, delayed, amended (sometimes beyond recognition), or defeated. Strategically placed committees, interest groups, or individual members of Congress can obstruct the process at something like fifty veto points along the way – double this number, if expenditure is involved. For a measure to proceed, its supporters must assemble a succession of majorities at each step or veto point. The process has been likened by one observer to 'those beloved but nerve-wracking board games of childhood in which a series of perils had to be survived before one's counter could be brought home safely'.[19] Small wonder is it that only a small proportion of measures introduced actually pass into law – in the 103rd Congress (1993–4), just 473 (4.8 per cent) out of a total of 9,824 bills and joint resolutions. Budget legislation must also meet a sequence of deadlines (see Figure 4.1).

Fourth, Congress' decentralised character and weak party organisation (to be discussed in Chapter 5) combine to ensure that bargaining and compromise are important features of the legislative process. Votes and favours must be traded ('logrolling'), arms must be twisted, and compromises reached in order to construct winning coalitions at each decision point.

Fifth, the legislative process works in a two-year cycle which effectively places a limit on the time available. For any measure to reach the statute book, the House and Senate and the president must all give their approval to it by the end of the Congress in which it was introduced. Failure to complete action on any measure before Congress adjourns *sine die* means that it dies automatically. For the measure to be enacted in a future Congress, it must be reintroduced and legislated through the same cumbersome, veto-ridden, time-limited process. In these circumstances, delay and expedition become major allies for the measure's supporters and opponents.

Sixth, the processes by which Congress sets its agenda, considers policy options and makes decisions is influenced greatly by a mass of complex written rules and procedures. As a result, policy decisions are often expressed in procedural actions. Party leaders, for example, have a variety of procedural devices at their disposal to protect their party's interests. Sometimes, they package a number of bills into one larger omnibus bill, so as to spare party colleagues the costs of casting difficult votes which will upset their constituents; or, they employ so-called 'fast track' procedures, such as suspending the rules, to win approval of legislation which is electorally important for the party. The complexity of congressional rules and procedures often means that skilled parliamentarians with detailed knowledge of the rules are able to use their expertise to further particular policy objectives. 'If you let me write the procedure,' Congressman John Dingell (D.MI) once told members of the Rules Committee, 'and I let you write the substance, I'll screw you every time.' As the powerful chair of the House Energy and

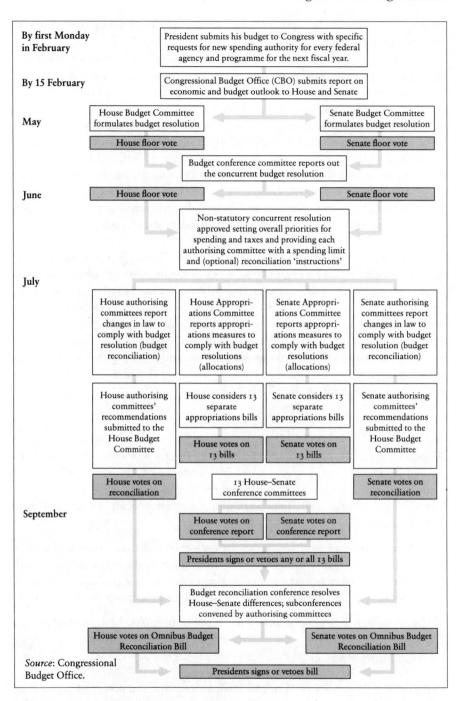

Figure 4.1. The congressional budget process.

Commerce Committee between 1981 and 1994, Dingell utilised his parliamentary skills to great effect on many occasions.

Seventh, congressional proceedings are governed by informal written precedents and prescriptive norms as well as formal written rules. Previous rulings or precedents by the House Speaker and the presiding officer of the Senate constitute a sort of unwritten law of Congress which allows variations in the applications of rules.[20] Much of the authority of the House Rules Committee, for example, is based solely on precedent. Despite a significant deterioration or, in certain cases, complete disappearance of some norms and folkways since the 1950s, active participation, collegiality, 'doing your homework', seniority and committee property rights are still very powerful norms in the 1990s. And, despite the contemporary emphasis on individualism and personal entrepreneurship, there remains a sizeable residue of older institutional loyalty and 'communitarian sentiment'.[21]

Finally, in a system of separated institutions sharing power, other parts of the government, including executive agencies (sometimes the president), state and local government officials, and sometimes the courts are heavily involved in the legislative process. Different parts of Congress – members, members' personal staff, committee staff, party leaders and their staffs, support agencies' staffs – interact with executive agency personnel, interest group representatives, 'policy wonks' in the various think tanks in Washington, and other highly knowledgeable 'policy watchers' within issue and policy networks.[22] These interactions both inform and complicate the legislative process.

The committee system

Woodrow Wilson's declaration more than 100 years ago that 'Congress in its committee rooms is Congress at work'[23] undoubtedly remains valid today. Testifying before the Joint Committee on the Organisation of Congress in 1993, House Public Works and Transportation Committee chair Norman Mineta (D.CA) observed:

> A great deal has been said about the importance of committees to the work of Congress, and that is absolutely true. Much of the real legislative work that is done day in and day out is done in the committees, and if that were not so, Congress simply would not be able to function.[24]

Why are committees so important? What is the institutional basis of their power?

Committee power

Kenneth Shepsle and Barry Weingast have argued that the power of committees is based on three crucial functions: gatekeeping – the ability to determine which legislative measures will proceed to the floor; information advantage – the capacity to apply their cumulative policy expertise to legislation; and proposal power – the power to develop and shape congressional policy. Underpinning these foundations are powerful norms – of deference and reciprocity – which determine that those who are not members of the reporting committee respect committee decisions, and those who are members of the reporting committee will reciprocate by respecting the decisions of other committees when they report legislation. And cementing committee power is the *ex post veto* which gives the members of a reporting committee a second chance at the penultimate stage of the legislative process – as members of a House–Senate conference committee – to use their power to negotiate adjustments to the bill or to insist unilaterally on the provisions in their original bill. In either case, the conference committee in effect presents both chambers with a *fait accompli* which both are reluctant to reject.[25]

Committee power then has a negative and a positive component.[26] The *negative* or gatekeeping power comprises their ability to restrict the choices available to colleagues in the parent chamber: to kill legislation, if necessary, by refusing to report it to the floor; to use the *ex post veto*; and to obtain the protection of restrictive rules. Negative power is bound up with the legislative process' sequential and iterative character, and with its procedural formality. For a measure to win House and Senate approval, it needs to be recommended by at least one committee. *Positive* or proposal power is less directly related to Congress' procedures. It is the power to propose policy prescriptions, to circumvent the floor, and to persuade a majority of committee non-members, with the help of party leaders, to vote against their own policy preferences in favour of a committee's recommendations.

Negative committee power is particularly important in the House because of the stringency of the chamber's germaneness rule which makes it difficult for committee non-members to circumvent a committee by offering floor amendments. It remains formidable today. Before he was defeated in 1994, Congressman Dan Glickman (D.KS), for example, spent eight years trying to extract liability reform legislation for small aircraft manufacturers out of the House Judiciary Committee over the opposition of its chair Jack Brooks (D.TX) and various clientele groups. Ultimately, Glickman – himself a committee chair – had to file a discharge petition to move his bill to the floor. Negative committee power is often reinforced by other floor procedures, such as so-called 'amendment trees' which limit the number and type of amendments that may be pending at any one time (if there is not a special rule or unanimous consent agreement that provides otherwise). Floor managers of committee bills – usually the full committee or subcommittee chair – are recognised to speak and offer defensive amendments on behalf of the committee before any other members are recognised or their amendments considered; and bill managers are recognised before other members to offer second degree amendments designed to counter or dilute hostile amendments and/or consolidate support for a bill.[27] Floor consideration of bills title by title and section by section, House special rules, and Senate unanimous consent requests also effectively preclude certain types of hostile amendments. Even if bill managers do not actually use negative committee power to the full, the threat of its use often gives committees additional leverage with which to bargain for support for a measure.

Positive committee power is weaker, but far from insignificant. Committees are expected to propose and report legislative measures to the floors. They have wide discretion to write the contents of bills as they wish; and on the floor they can exploit their recognition privileges to change proposals (by accepting amendments, for example) which take account of changing legislative circumstances. Of course, positive committee power does not mean that all proposals are accepted on the floor. Majority party leaders may refuse to schedule a measure; floor majorities may refuse to consider a measure; and committee recommendations may be overturned in the other chamber or in a conference committee. Even so, it is the committees more than any other set of legislative organisations in Congress who set the parameters of legislation within their chambers and if a bill goes to a conference committee. As Congress' gatekeepers, committees are also able to filter political and policy information before it reaches the floor; and when a bill reported by a committee is considered on the floor, committee specialists are likely to be more persuasive than committee non-members because they know the bill's content and politics better than their colleagues. Having substantial informational and staff resources, committee leaders also know which interests are for and against the measure, so they can better anticipate what pre-emptive action must be taken to avoid defeat or a floor challenge. Well before a bill reaches the floor, they will have had opportunities to devise a legislative stratagem, draft protective amendments, and monitor developments in the other chamber with a view to anticipating conference negotiations. Committee leaders will also have taken advantage of their long-standing personal relationships to generate floor support among those who are less concerned – even indifferent – to their committee's proposals, and request smooth and timely floor consideration of bills from well-placed allies.

For all these reasons – gatekeeping, expertise and informational advantage, proposal power, norms, procedural advantages, and leaders' personal relations – and because the majority party controls the floor as well as the committees and subcommittees – committees are immensely powerful. Even though individual members of Congress now have greater capacities to challenge committee recommendations if they wish, and committees have lost autonomy and power – particularly those responsible for authorising programmes and influencing foreign policy[28] – it is still extremely rare for a committee's policy recommendations not to be supported by a majority on the floor; and inconceivable that the vast majority of proposals enacted into law in any Congress will not bear the unmistakable fingerprints of the relevant House and Senate committees.

The committee system serves both the institutional needs of Congress as a collective body, and the personal political interests and needs of individual members. For the collective institution, committees provide for divisions and specialisations of labour which enable both chambers to process large volumes and wide varieties of legislative proposals simultaneously; they facilitate the acquisition and utilisation of valuable political and policy information and expertise about how programmes and agencies are performing and how they affect the daily lives of citizens and private organisations; and, in an institution replete with veto points, they provide arenas in which relatively small numbers of members are able to effect the compromises and bargains necessary to carry proposals into legislation. For individual members, committees provide opportunities to serve their constituencies, exercise influence in Washington, and make good public policy, specialising and developing policy skills, expertise and congressional influence in the specific policy areas which most interest them or are important to their constituents. When individual members of Congress think about the committees they would like to join, and when they become members of particular committees, '[e]ach member . . . wants his committee service to bring him some benefit in terms of goals he holds as an individual congressman.'[29] If committees did not perform these functions for individual members, they would not exist.

Of course, whether committees and their members always play positive roles in the legislative process is questionable. Congress has a long record of obstructing or emasculating important legislation. We need not revisit the heyday of Senator Joe McCarthy (R.WI) to view some of the shortcomings of committees' investigative roles. The Senate Judiciary Committee's questioning of Anita Hill during their 1991 hearings on the nomination of Clarence Thomas to the Supreme Court and the House Banking Committee's less than penetrating hearings on the Whitewater affair in 1994 offer more recent proof. We should also question whether the much vaunted subject specialisation, expertise, and experience, which committees are said to foster, lead automatically to the development of good public policy or to committee members who are expert, effective, or innovative. Committee hearings are often sparsely attended by members. Between 20 and 30 per cent of committee members do not even attend committee and subcommittee mark-ups and barely one-third (often less) actively participate in writing up a bill.[30] Contemporary pressures on members to spend more time and energy on providing constituency services and generating campaign funds for re-election purposes mean that they must spend less time and energy on committees developing legislative specialisms (see Table 4.5). The larger number of committee assignments which House members and senators now hold compared with the 1950s and 1960s – 4.7 for House members, 10.2 for senators – means that the attention they can give to the subject matter of any one committee is necessarily diluted. It is hardly surprising that members complain that they cannot devote sufficient time to legislative activities.[31]

Committee types and numbers

We may speak of Congress having a committee system; but congressional committees differ widely in the tasks they perform, in their jurisdictions, degrees of influence, status and autonomy, expertise, domination by their chairs, subcommittee structures and orientation, and in the extent to which they are constrained by external agencies – such as the parent chamber, the executive, members of clientele groups, and members of the two main political parties.

All congressional committees are empowered to study and report findings but not all receive, write, or report legislation. Those that are empowered to receive, write, and report legislation and conduct investigations – the House and Senate standing committees – are the most important. Other types of committees – *ad hoc*, select, special, joint committees – do not have legislative powers and are, therefore, rarely influential. Standing committees are permanently established in every Congress by the rules of each house which also name them, set out their specific jurisdictions and responsibilities, and establish most of their procedures. In the Democratic 103rd Congress (1993–4), there were 22 standing committees in the House and 17 in the Senate. When House Republicans organised the 104th Congress (1995–6), they eliminated three standing committees (District of Columbia; Merchant, Marine and Fisheries; and Post Office and Civil Service); renamed ten others to reflect better their conservative policy agenda (Table 4.8); reduced committee budgets; cut the memberships of most committees thereby reducing the pool of committee assignments by about 13 per cent; and altered many committee jurisdictions, most notably those of Commerce (contracted) and Transportation and Infrastructure (expanded).

Table 4.8. House and Senate committees and subcommittees in the 104th Congress, with former names and party ratios

HOUSE		
	104th Congress	103rd Congress
Name and Party Ratio	Subcommittees and Party Ratios	Name and Party Ratio
Agriculture (27R–22D)	Department Operations, Nutrition, and Foreign Agriculture (12–10); General Farm Commodities (10–8); Livestock, Dairy, and Poultry (7–5); Resource Conservation, Research, and Forestry (12–10); Risk Management and Speciality Crops (8–7)	Agriculture (27D–19R)
Appropriations (32R–24D)	Agriculture (7–4); Commerce, Justice, State, and Judiciary (5–3); District of Columbia (5–3); Energy and Water Development (6–3); Foreign Operations, Export Financing, and Related Programs (9–4); Interior (8–4); Labor, Health and Human Services, and Education (8–5); Legislative (5–3); Military Construction (7–4); National Security (9–5); Transportation (8–4); Treasury, Postal Service, and General Government (5–3); and Veterans Affairs, HUD, and Independent Agencies (8–4)	Appropriations (37D–23R)

Banking and Financial Services (27R–22D–1I)	Capital Markets, Securities and Government-Sponsored Enterprises (11–9); Domestic and International Monetary Policy (11–9); Financial Institutions and Consumer Credit (12–10); General Oversight and Investigations (6–4); Housing and Community Opportunity (12–10)	Banking, Finance, and Urban Affairs (30D–20R–1I)
Budget (24R–18D)	none	Budget (26D–17R)
Commerce (25R–21D)	Commerce, Trade, and Hazardous Materials (11–9); Energy and Power (11–9); Health and Environment (14–11); Oversight and Investigations (7–6); Telecommunications and Finance (14–11)	Energy and Commerce (27D–17R)
Economic and Educational Opportunities (24R–19D)	Early Childhood, Youth, and Families (10–8); Employer-Employee Relations (8–6); Oversight and Investigations (8–6); Postsecondary Education, Training, and Lifelong Learning (9–7); Worker Protections (9–7)	Education and Labor (24D–15R)
Government Reform and Oversight (22R–11D)	Civil Service (5–3); District of Columbia (5–3); Government Management, Information, and Technology (8–6); Human Resources and Intergovernmental Affairs (9–7); National Economic Growth, Natural Resources, and Regulatory Affairs (8–6); National Security, International Affairs, and Criminal Justice (8–7); Postal Service (6–4)	Government Operations (25D–16R–1I)
House Oversight (7R–5D)	none	House Administration (12D–7R)
International Relations (22R–19D)	Africa (7–5); Asia and the Pacific (8–6); International Economic Policy and Trade (8–6); International Operations and Human Rights (8–6); Western Hemisphere (7–5)	Foreign Affairs (26D–18R)
Judiciary (20R–15D)	Commercial and Administrative Law (6–4); Constitution (8–5); Courts and Intellectual Property (9–6); Crime (8–5); Immigration and Claims (7–5)	Judiciary (21D–14R)
National Security (30R–25D)	Military Installations and Facilities (10–8); Military Personnel (9–7); Military Procurement (15–12); Military Readiness (11–9); Military Research and Development (14–11)	Armed Services (33D–22R)
Resources (25R–20D)	Energy and Mineral Resources (8–6); Fisheries, Wildlife, and Oceans (8–6); National Parks, Forests, and Lans (14–11); Native American and Insular Affairs (6–5); Water and Power Resources (11–9)	Natural Resources (24D–15R)
Rules (9R–4D)	Legislative Process (5–2); Rules of the House (5–2)	Rules (9D–4D)
Science (27R–23D)	Basic Research (14–11); Energy and Environment (15–12); Space and Aeronautics (12–10); Technology (7–5)	Science, Space, & Technology (33D–22R)
Small Business (22R–19D)	Government Programs (7–5); Procurement, Exports, and Business Opportunities (8–6); Regulation and Paperwork (8–6); Tax and Finance (8–6)	Small Business (27D–18R)
Standards of Official Conduct (5R–5D)	none	Standards of Official Conduct (7D–7R)
Transportation and Infrastructure (33R–28D)	Aviation (15–12); Coast Guard and Marine Transportation (6–4); Public Buildings and Economic Development (5–4); Railroads (8–6); Surface Transportation (20–16)	Public Works and Transportation (38D–25R)
Veterans Affairs (19R–15D)	Compensation, Pension, Insurance, and Memorial Affairs (6–4); Education, Training, Employment, and Housing (6–4); Hospitals and Health Care (11–9)	Veterans Affairs (21D–14R)

Ways and Means (21R–15D)	Health (8–5); Oversight (7–4); Social Security (7–4); Trade (9–6)	Ways and Means (24D–14R)

SENATE

	104th Congress	103rd Congress
Name and Party Ratios		**Name and Party Ratio**
Agriculture, Nutrition, and Forestry (9R–8D)	Production and Price Competitiveness (5–4); Marketing, Inspection, and Product Promotion (5–4); Forestry, Conservations, and Rural Revitalisation (4–3); Research, Nutrition, and General Legislation (4–3)	Agriculture, Nutrition, and Forestry (10D–8R)
Appropriations (15R–13D)	Agriculture, Rural Development, and Related Agencies (6–5); Commerce, Justice, State, and Judiciary (6–5); Defense (9–8); District of Columbia (2–1); Energy and Water Development (7–6); Foreign Operations (7–6); Interior and Related Agencies (8–7); Labor, Health and Human Services, and Education (8–7); Legislative Branch (3–2); Military Construction (4–3); Transportation and Related Agencies (6–5); Treasury, Postal Service, and General Government (3–2); and Veterans Affairs, HUD, and Independent Agencies (6–5)	Appropriations (16D–13R)
Armed Services (11R–10D)	Air/Land Forces (7–6); Acquisition and Technology (4–3); Personnel (4–3); Readiness (5–4); Seapower (5–4); Strategic Forces (6–5)	Armed Services (11D–10R)
Banking, Housing, and Urban Affairs (11R–10D)	Financial Institutions and Regulatory Relief (7–5); Housing Opportunities and Community Development (4–3); HUD Oversight and Structure (3–2); International Finance and Monetary Policy (5–4); Securities (5–4)	Banking, Housing, and Urban Affairs (11R–10D)
Budget (12R–10D)	none	Budget (12D–9R)
Commerce, Science, and Transportation (10R–9D)	Aviation (8–7); Communications (8–7); Consumer Affairs, Foreign Commerce, and Tourism (5–4); Oceans and Fisheries (4–3); Science, Technology, and Space (5–4); Surface Transportation and Merchant Marine (6–5)	Commerce, Science, and Transportation (11D–9R)
Energy and Natural Resources (12R–10D)	Energy Production and Regulation (5–4); Energy Research and Development (5–3); Forests and Public Land Management (6–4); Parks, Historical Preservation, and Recreation (4–3)	Energy and Natural Resources (11D–9R)
Environment and Public Works (9R–7D)	Clean Air, Wetlands, Private Property, and Nuclear Safety (4–3); Drinking Water, Fisheries, and Wildlife (5–4); Tranportation and Infrastructure (5–4); Superfund, Waste Control, and Risk Assessment (4–3)	Environment and Public Works (9R–7DR)
Finance (11R–9D)	International Trade (7–7); Medicaid and Health Care for Low-Income Families (3–3); Social Security and Family Policy (4–4); Taxation and IRS Oversight (9–5)	Finance (10D–7R)
Foreign Relations	African Affairs (3–2); East Asian and Pacific Affairs (5–4); European Affairs (5–4); International Economic Policy, Export, and Trade Promotion (4–3); International Operations (5–4); Near Eastern and South Asian Affairs (5–4); Western Hemisphere and Peace Corps Affairs (4–3)	Foreign Relations (11D–8R)
Governmental Affairs (8R–7D)	Oversight of Government Management (4–4); Permanent Investigations (7–7); Post Office and Civil Service (3–3)	Governmental Affairs (8D–5R)
Indian Affairs (9R–8D)	none	Indian Affairs (10D–8R)

Judiciary (10R–8D)	Antritrust, Business Rights and Competition (4–3); Immigration (4–3); Administrative Oversight and the Courts (4–3); Terrorism, Technology, and Government Information (4–3); Constitution, Federalism, and Property Rights (5–3); Youth Violence (3–2)	Judiciary (10D–8R)
Labor and Human Resources (9R–7D)	Aging (4–3); Children and Families (5–4); Disability Policy (4–3); Education, Arts, and Humanities (9–7)	Labor and Human Resources (10D–7R)
Rules and Administration (9R–7D)	none	Rules and Administration (9D–7R)
Small Business (10R–9D)	none	Small Business (12D–9R)
Veterans Affairs (7R–5D)	none	Veterans Affairs (7D–5R)

Unlike the temporary, government-dominated standing committees in the British House of Commons, whose role is limited to legislative functions, congressional standing committees perform both legislative and investigative roles. Independent of party leaders and the executive, they (i) identify, investigate and study public problems; (ii) consider proposals sent them by individual members, the party leadership and the president; (iii) they convene hearings at which interested parties testify; (iv) sift through testimony; iv) publish reports of their findings; (v) decide what needs to be done; (vi) draft legislative language; (vii) and report out legislation. Most standing committees have more or less permanent subcommittees. Following the implementation of the so-called 'Subcommittee Bill of Rights' in 1973, which curtailed the discretional power of House full committee chairs over their creation, memberships, jurisdictions, agendas, budgets, and staff, subcommittees have proliferated. In the 103rd Congress, (1993–4), there were 204 subcommittees – reduced by Republicans in the 104th Congress to 154. Most legislation in the House (but not the Senate) is now considered first by subcommittees. In the 100th Congress (1987–8), 80 per cent of legislative measures in the House were reported out by subcommittees, double the percentage in the 91st Congress. In the Senate, only 46 per cent were reported by subcommittees.[32]

The House subcommittee system is highly structured. Between 1975 and 1994, House rules approved by Democratic majorities, required each standing committee (except Budget, which has only non-legislative task forces) with more than twenty members to establish at least four subcommittees. Subsequently, under a 1993 rule of the House Democratic Caucus, the number of subcommittees on each committee was limited to six for 'major' committees and five for 'non-major' committees (except Government Operations and House Administration which were limited to six). No limits were placed on 'exclusive' committees.[33] Membership of any one subcommittee was restricted to no more than 60 per cent of full committee members. Under rules adopted by the Republican-controlled

House in January 1995, no committee was allowed more than five subcommittees – except Appropriations which was limited to thirteen; Government Reform and Oversight to seven; and Transportation and Infrastructure to six.

In contrast, subcommittees in the Senate are highly unstructured. Although the total number of subcommittees is effectively limited by restrictions on the number of subcommittee assignments any senator may have, full committee chairs continue to exercise wide discretion and usually create subcommittees for as many majority party senators who wish to chair them. Thus, during the 103rd Congress (1993–4), two committees (Commerce, Science and Transportation and Finance) had eight subcommittees while four (Budget, Indian Affairs, and two select committees) had none; the mean was about five subcommittees per committee. The new Republican majority in the Senate moved in January 1995 to reduce the number of subcommittees to a mean of four per committee. Committee chairs determine the size of Senate subcommittees.

In order to appreciate fully the extent and range of committee activities, we should pause to note not only the sheer number of committees but also the astonishing range of subject jurisdictions (see Table 4.8). Table 4.9 extends this image by showing the extent and intensity of committee activities in the 102nd Congress (1991–2). During this two-year period no less than 8,051 committee meetings were scheduled (5,479 in the House, 2,572 in the Senate) and 1,682 measures were reported by committees.

Table 4.9. House and Senate committee activities
and workloads, 102nd Congress

Standing Committee	Membership	Staff	Measures Referred	Measures Reported	Measures Referred and Passed House	Measures Referred and Became Law	Hearings and Meetings Scheduled
HOUSE							
Agriculture	47	68	290	42	47	27	211
Appropriations	60	214	168	34	38	33	968
Armed Services	56	82	388	21	29	10	324
Banking, Finance, and Urban Affairs	51	102	456	19	33	14	297
Budget	43	104	1	1	1	0	94
District of Columbia	12	38	45	14	12	6	44
Education and Labor	43	115	647	36	56	28	290
Energy and Commerce	44	144	1102	69	69	32	397
Foreign Affairs	45	102	639	13	95	23	406
Government Operations	42	88	248	8	12	5	260
House Administration	19	68	326	15	41	12	78
Judiciary	35	73	1003	126	87	40	274

Merchant Marine and Fisheries	48	78	345	79	58	22	178
Natural Resources	443	82	568	131	144	80	345
Post Office and Civil Service	24	80	721	13	192	165	172
Public Works and Transportation	63	88	434	42	58	24	204
Rules	13	45	398	203	193	0	111
Science, Space, & Technology	55	91	177	26	26	11	297
Small Business	45	51	61	5	5	2	114
Standards of Official Conduct	14	12	3	1	1	0	27
Veterans Affairs	35	46	221	21	33	19	93
Ways and Means	38	138	1994	86	72	23	295
Select Aging	68	36	0	0	0	0	103
Select Children, Youth, and Families	36	19	0	0	0	0	24
Select Hunger	32	15	0	0	0	0	41
Select Intelligence	19	27	20	3	4	3	73
Select Narcotics, Abuse and Control	36	15	0	0	0	0	27
SENATE							
Agriculture, Nutrition and Forestry	18	37	128	8	19	11	62
Appropriations	29	78	152	35	34	31	399
Armed Services	20	51	151	40	31	5	195
Banking, Housing, and Urban Affairs	19	54	189	12	18	10	172
Budget	21	57	141	6	1	0	45
Commerce, Science, and Transportation	20	75	256	61	43	20	172
Energy and Natural Resources	20	49	373	120	104	56	180
Environment and Public Works	17	41	248	20	35	20	145
Finance	20	61	990	28	13	6	146
Foreign Relations	19	65	327	62	59	7	309
Government Affairs	13	112	231	36	33	23	209
Judiciary	18	122	732	150	191	123	206
Labor and Human Resources	17	126	359	45	35	23	190
Rules and Administration	16	25	123	31	37	4	38
Small Business	21	25	23	3	4	3	50

Veterans' Affairs	12	22	130	20	21	13	54
Select Aging	21	30	1	1	0	0	19
Select Ethics	6	11	0	0	0	0	13
Select Indian Affairs	18	25	71	41	30	10	105
Select Intelligence	17	37	12	4	2	2	66

Source: US Congress. Joint Committee on the Organisation of Congress, *Committee System Background Materials* (1993).

It will be apparent from Tables 4.8 and 4.9 that the sizes of committee memberships and party ratios (majority to minority) vary considerably. Both are negotiated by majority and minority party leaders in each chamber at the beginning of each Congress. In the House, committee sizes ranged from 61 (Transportation and Infrastructure) to 10 (Standards of Official Conduct); and in the Senate, from 28 (Appropriations) to 6 (Select Ethics). Committee sizes usually reflect relative workloads and attractiveness to members, although in the Senate, committee sizes are also constrained by a 1977 rule (unless an exemption is granted to an individual senator) which limits the number of assignments senators may hold on different types of committees. Party ratios reflect those of the parent chamber, but with some important qualifications. Until 1994, Democratic Caucus rules assured effective control of the House by insisting that all standing committees (with the exception of Standards of Official Conduct) had three Democrats for every two Republicans. Thus, during the 103rd Congress (1993–4), Democratic majorities on the important Appropriations, Budget, Energy and Commerce, Rules, and Ways and Means committees were disproportionately greater than the House majority; and on subcommittees still greater. On eleven of the thirteen Appropriations subcommittees, and to lesser degrees on other subcommittees, Republicans were outnumbered 2:1 even though they constituted about 40 per cent of the full House. In the 104th Congress (1995–6), committee ratios were aligned much more closely with the 53:47 ratio in the full House. However, the majority Republicans followed the Democrats' practice by ensuring that ratios on Appropriations, Budget, House Oversight, and Ways and Means were disproportionately higher. Majority parties in the Senate tend not to inflate committee ratios for fear that a disgruntled minority might obstruct business. On some subcommittees (e.g. on the Finance Committee), the number of minority members equals that of majority members. These lower disparities sometimes deprive the majority party of effective control. Democrats' slim two-vote margin on the Senate Finance Committee in 1993, for example, enabled conservative Democratic Senator David Boren (D.OK) to kill President Clinton's proposed Btu energy tax in June 1993 by threatening to vote with committee Republicans against the president's entire budget.

As we have suggested already, House committees tend to be more important than Senate committees. Senate committees do not define or channel senators' Washington activities or augment their influence in the chamber to the same extent that House committees do for House members. Senate floor action is at least as important as action taken by Senate committees, partly because germaneness rules are much more lax. Senators also serve on many more committees than do their House colleagues, and typically develop interests beyond their committee assignments. Essentially, Senate committees are arenas for senators' individual activities rather than communal workplaces.[34] They can be bypassed more easily than can House committees; their recommendations to the floor are far less influential on the chamber floor; their members are less concerned about their committees' collective reputations; they are less autonomous within the chamber; their memberships are less expert; and they are less strongly led.[35]

Variations in committee prestige and attractiveness

Within both houses some committees are more prestigious and more attractive than others. As the national agenda became engrossed by deficit politics and fiscal restraint in the 1980s and 1990s, and as the preferences of individual House members and senators came to reflect this agenda, power shifted within the House (much less so in the Senate) to those committees dealing primarily with money: in particular to Appropriations, Budget, and Ways and Means. By the early 1990s, these three committees together with Rules and Energy and Commerce, the one authorising committee which continued to play an active role in the contemporary agenda, came to form a new committee oligarchy.[36] Not to be confused with an older committee oligarchy, discussed in Chapter 2, based on seniority and underpinning committee government in the 1940s and 1950s, the emergence of this new oligarchy was influenced primarily by the changing policy agenda. Its development has caused other authorisation committees – concerned with substantive policy areas such as agriculture, banking and housing, education and labour, foreign affairs, and so forth – to be relegated *de facto* to more peripheral roles. If anything, the Clinton Administration's focus on budgetary and health care issues in 1993 and 1994 reinforced this oligarchy because the same committees considered this legislation. Given the policy agenda contained in the new Republican majority's Contract With America, the committee oligarchy after 1994 is slightly different. The Appropriations, Budget, and Ways and Means Committees have undoubtedly retained their central places, but this group has been joined by the previously dormant House Oversight (formerly House Administration) and Judiciary Committees which have been given central roles in enacting the Republican Contract With America. House Oversight has been assigned the task of reducing the costs of running the House while Judiciary was given responsibility for about half the legislation promised in the Contract With America, including the balanced budget amendment, a new crime bill, term-limits, and prison reform.[37]

The upshot of greater differentiation in the contemporary House is that committees such as Agriculture, Banking, Education and Labor (now Economic and Educational Opportunities), Resources, Science, and Veterans Affairs are much less attractive. Typically, they recruit large numbers of new members who have failed to win other preferred assignments.[38] At the beginning of the 104th Congress, for example, 49 per cent of the Small Business Committee, 44 per cent of the Science Committee, and over a quarter of the Banking, Economic and Educational Opportunities, Government Reform and Oversight, Resources, and Veterans committees were new members of the House. In sharp contrast, only 13 per cent of Appropriations, 8 per cent of House Oversight, Rules, and Ways and Means were freshmen. The silver lining for members who join less attractive committees is that promotion up the committee seniority ladder often is rapid. A member might reasonably expect to be chair of a subcommittee on committees such as Agriculture, Banking, Economic and Educational Opportunities, Government Reform and Oversight, Small Business, and Veterans – with the resources and influence such a position brings – after just two or three terms, even less. In January 1995, in an extraordinary development three Republican freshmen were appointed (under House Republican rules) to subcommittee chairs by their full committee chair. Once members of these less attractive committees rise to middle-ranking positions, the prospect of further promotion to a chair within a few years often deters them from seeking transfers to more prestigious committees. In contrast, gaining a subcommittee chair on the Appropriations, Ways and Means, or National Security requires between eleven and fifteen years' service.[39]

Even so, notwithstanding these differences among committees in prestige and attractiveness, we should note that not all members of Congress want to join the same 'elite' committees – because all do not share the same goals. As Fenno has shown, not all members want to exercise influence within their chamber by becoming a member of a prestigious committee. Many members prefer to join committees which allow them to pursue what they regard as good public policy, or concentrate on serving their constituents. Thus, at the beginning of the 103rd Congress, newly-elected Democrat Paul McHale (D.PA) wanted to use his twenty years' experience in the Marine Corps to shape US military policies: he sought and won a seat on the House Armed Services Committee. Chicago Democrat Bobby Rush sought and won a seat on the House Banking, Finance and Urban Affairs Committee because he wanted to have 'a direct impact on economic revitalisation of cities and close-in suburbs'.[40] Congresswoman Maria Cantwell (D.WA) opted for Public Works and Transportation because she had promised during her campaign to do something to improve mass transit for her district's long-distance commuters. Freshman Senator Ben Nighthorse Campbell (D.CO) wanted his assignments to the Energy and Natural Resources and Indian Affairs committees because they reflected his state's mining interests and his ethnicity.

The relationship between specific committee assignments and the personal goals and interests of members has enabled scholars to develop a useful typology of committees shown in Table 4.10 which distinguishes among prestige, policy, and constituency committees on the basis of members' motivations:[41] prestige committees are those which attract members most interested in exercising influence in their chamber; policy committees comprise members who are driven primarily by their pursuit of 'good public policy'; and constituency committees consist of members motivated primarily by serving their constituencies. We will refer to these different types of committees in later discussions.

Table 4.10. House and Senate committees types by preference motivations of new House members and senators

HOUSE	SENATE
Prestige Committees	**Policy Committees**
Appropriations	Budget
Budget	Foreign Relations
Rules	Governmental Affairs
Ways and Means	Judiciary
	Labor and Human Resources
Policy Committees	
Banking, Finance, and Urban Affairs (now Banking and Financial Services)	**Mixed Policy/Constituency Committees**
Education and Labor (now Economic and Educational Opportunities	Armed Services
Energy and Commerce (now Commerce)	Banking, Housing, and Urban Affairs
Foreign Affairs (now International Relations)	Finance
Government Operations (now Government Reform and Oversight)	Small Business
Judiciary	
	Constituency Committees
Constituency Committees	Agriculture, Nutrition and Forestry
Agriculture	Appropriations
Armed Services (now National Security)	Commence, Science, and Transportation
Merchant Marine and Fisheries (now abolished)	Energy and Natural Resources
Natural Resources (now Resources)	Environment and Public Works
Public Works and Transportation (now Transportation and Infrastructure)	
Science, Space, & Technology (now Science)	**Unrequested Committees**
Small Business	Rules and Administration
Veterans' Affairs	Veterans' Affairs
Unrequested Committees	
District of Columbia (now abolished)	
House Administration (now House Oversight)*	
Post Office and Civil Service (now abolished)	
Standards of Official Conduct	

Source: Steven S. Smith and Christopher J. Deering, *Committees in Congress* 2nd edn (Washington, D.C.: Congressional Quarterly Press, 1990), pp. 87 and 101.

* *Note:* It is unlikely that after 1994 the House Oversight remained in this category. See text.

Having suggested now that the processes by which members seek and are assigned to committees are important, let us explain how they work.

Committee assignment processes

First, it is important to note that there is nothing in the rules of either the House or Senate which entitles any member to join any committee. Assignment of members to the more than 2,000 committee seats in the House and over 1,000 in the Senate is entirely a party matter. Members in both houses and in both parties serve at the discretion of their party colleagues and, if they so wish, may remove them from a committee entirely or strip them of their seniority.[42]

Each party in each house has a different committee assignment system.

House systems

The rules limit all members to two standing committees and four subcommittees. Republican Conference and Democratic Caucus rules impose further limitations as follows:

1. *Republicans*

Assignments are made by a 27-member Steering Committee of the Republican Conference chaired by the House Speaker, and comprising the Majority Leader, the Majority Whip, the chairs of the House Republican Conference and the National Republican Congressional Committee, four committee chairs (Appropriations, Budget, Ways and Means, and Rules), a representative of the sophomore class (those in their second term), three representatives of the freshman class, and nine regional representatives. Effectively, the Republican Leader controls about a quarter of the votes on the committee. He/she also appoints Republicans to the Oversight Committee. Assignments are ratified by the Republican Conference.

Republicans are limited to one 'red' committee (Appropriations, Commerce, Rules, and Ways and Means) or two 'white' committees (Agriculture, Banking, International Relations, Judiciary, National Security, Resources, Science, and Transportation and Infrastructure). 'Blue' committees (Budget, Economic and Educational Opportunities, Government Reform and Oversight, House Oversight, Small Business and Veterans' Affairs) are unrestricted.

2. *Democrats*

Assignments are made by the 34-member Democratic Steering and Policy Committee chaired by the Democratic Leader and comprising 12 regional representatives, 11 party leaders and 10 other appointees (which include the chairs/ranking members of the Appropriations, Commerce, Rules, and Ways and Means committees). Decisions on assignments are subject to confirmation by the House Democratic Caucus. The Democratic Leader alone makes appointments to the Oversight Committee.

Democrats may sit either on one exclusive committee (Appropriations, Rules, and Ways and Means); or one major committee (Agriculture, Banking, Economic and Educational Opportunities, Commerce, International Relations, Judiciary, National Security, and Transportation and Infrastructure) and one non-major committee (Budget, Government Reform and Oversight, House Oversight, Resources, Science, Small Business, and Veterans' Affairs) or two non major committees. The Standards of Official Conduct Committee is exempt.

Senate systems

In the Senate, Rule V categorises all committees, including joint committees, into major or 'A' committees (Agriculture, Nutrition and Forestry; Appropriations; Armed Services; Banking, Housing and Urban Affairs; Budget; Commerce, Science and Transportation; Energy and Natural Resources; Environment and Public Works; Finance; Foreign Relations; Governmental Affairs; Judiciary; and Labor and Human Resources); minor or 'B' committees (Rules and Administration, Small Business; Veterans' Affairs; Select Aging; Select Intelligence; and Joint Economic); and exempt or 'C' committees (Ethics; Indian Affairs; and Joint Taxation). Senators are limited to no more than two 'A' and one 'B' committees, with unrestricted service on 'C' committees. However, over 20 senators usually obtain waivers of the rule to allow them to sit on three committees. Vacancies are filled strictly by seniority.

Informal restrictions usually prevent senators from the same state having the same assignment, although in the 103rd Congress, Senators Murray and Gorton of Washington were both members of the Appropriations Committee.

1. *Republicans*

Republican senators are assigned by a Committee on Committees which is appointed by the chair of the Republican Conference, subject to ratification by the full Conference. The committee comprises eight members including the Republican Leader who serves as an ex-officio member. Members are prohibited from holding seats on more than one major 'A' committee before all Republicans are assigned at least one. The Republican Conference does not vote on the committee's decisions but, instead, assignments strictly follow seniority with new members being assigned to committees last. Like the Democrats, Republican senators are usually prohibited from sitting on more than one of the four or five (including Budget) most important committees.

2. *Democrats*

Senators are assigned by a Steering Committee whose size is set by the Democratic Conference (19 members in the 104th Congress). The Steering Committee, including its chair, is appointed by the Democratic Leader who usually appoints himself. Steering Committee decisions are subject to approval by the full Democratic Conference. Since the introduction of the

'Johnson rule' in the 1950s, each Democrat has been guaranteed a seat on one of the four most important committees (usually Appropriations, Armed Services, Finance, and Foreign Relations or Commerce, Science, and Technology).

In all four systems, party leaders play influential roles and, particularly in the House, are usually in strong positions to insist on an assignment being given to a particular member. In 1993, for example, the House leadership and Dan Rostenkowski (D.IL), Ways and Means chair and DSPC member, insisted that Mel Reynolds (D.IL) receive the only Democratic vacancy on the Ways and Means Committee. Robert Menendez (D.NJ), who was from the same state as the retiring member of the committee, was denied the seat evidently because he represented an anti-tax state. When he was Speaker, 'Tip' O'Neill often provided the Democratic Steering and Policy Committee (DSPC) with leadership support scores when they considered members' requests to transfer committees.[43] At the beginning of the 104th Congress (1995–6), Speaker Newt Gingrich (R.GA) played a decisive role in the assignment of House Republicans, ensuring that new members were appointed to positions on the most prestigious committees, including seven on Appropriations, six on Budget, one on Rules, and three on Ways and Means. More unusually, in 1993 President Clinton lobbied personally for a Ways and Means seat for Congressman William Jefferson (D.LA) who had helped run his presidential campaign in Louisiana.[44] In the Senate, the views of committee chairs are very important. For example, in 1993, Appropriations Committee chair Robert Byrd (D.WV) requested and received seniority for freshman Senator Patty Murray (D.WA) whom he wished to be assigned to his committee instead of the slightly more senior Senator Diane Feinstein (D.CA) who supported a line-item veto of budget items which Byrd vehemently opposed.

When they decide the suitability of members for particular committees, assignment committees and party leaders take into consideration a number of factors: the member's/party's electoral needs, party harmony, whether the seat was previously occupied by a member from the same state or same region, the member's party loyalty and policy views, the applicant's seniority, whether a member has failed to win another assignment, whether he/she is a 'responsible' legislator, what expertise, ability, and experience the member can offer, ideology (liberal, moderate, or conservative), which groups or colleagues have endorsed the application, the candidate's acceptability to the committee chair, and whether or not the member has already been assigned temporarily to the same committee.[45]

Whether an individual member receives his/her desired assignment depends on whether there are vacancies on the particular committee, the level of competition for the vacancies, and the efforts of the assignee.[46] Inevitably, the process is convoluted and often unsystematic, involving complex and difficult calculations for many members. Because existing committee members have the right to remain on their committees as long as they wish – the committee property rights norm

– the number of vacancies is usually limited. Competition for positions on the most desirable committees is always intense and the potential for party disharmony considerable.[47] In order to minimise party disharmony and help members win the assignments which will help their careers, the parties have introduced the formal and informal mechanisms described above which restrict the members of certain types of committees to one assignment.[48] However, waivers to the rules limiting assignments are frequently granted by the Democratic Caucus and Republican Conference in order to accommodate the requests of individual members, to ensure a party balance on certain committees, and to fill vacancies on unpopular panels. In the 103rd Congress, as many as one in five House members received a waiver.

House subcommittee assignments are made by the full committee chair in the case of Republicans, but he/she will not assign members to a second sub-committee until all members have received one assignment. Democrats are assigned by the party caucus of Democrats on each committee: members bid for assignments on the basis of full committee seniority; no member may receive a second subcom-mittee assignment until all Democrats have one assignment they want.

One important consequence of the largely self-selective nature of the assign-ment process is that many committees are unrepresentative of their parent cham-bers; with obvious implications for the internal distribution of House and Senate power and the nature of public policy decisions. Members from urban and finan-cial centres tend to be attracted to the banking committees (in the 103rd Congress, 42 per cent of the House committee and 19 per cent of the Senate committee represented eastern constituencies), westerners to the House Resources and Senate Energy and Natural Resources Committee (respectively, 56 per cent and 50 per

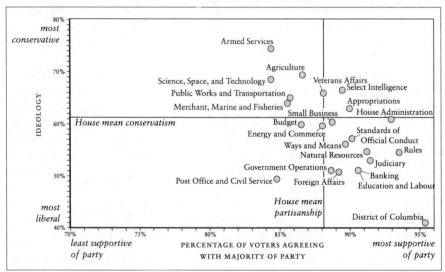

Figure 4.2. House committee conservatism and partisanship, 103rd Congress.

cent in the 104th Congress), those from farming areas to the agriculture commit-tees, those from constituencies with substantial military interests to the National Security and Armed Services committees, those representing ports to the Trans-portation and Infrastructure Committee, and so on. Typically, these geographical and interest biases translate into ideological biases. Figure 4.2 shows that more than half the House committees in the 103rd Congress were overrepresented by liberals (notably District of Columbia, Post Office, Foreign Affairs, Education and Labor, Banking, and Government Operations); and the rest by conservatives (notably Armed Services, Agriculture, and Space). The same was also true of Senate committees. Biases are often stronger in subcommittee memberships.

One effect of overrepresentation is that interest groups concentrate their lobbying efforts and campaign contributions on the members of full committees and subcommittees which handle the legislation and issues which most interest them. A study of the behaviour of PACs in the 1992 elections, for example, showed that nine of the top ten House recipients and five of the top Senate recipients of campaign contributions from agribusiness PACs were members of the House and Senate Agriculture committees. House Agriculture chair, 'Kika' de la Garza (D.TX) received over 50 per cent of his campaign funds from these sources. In the same elections, six of the top ten House recipients of money from communications and electronic industry PACs served on the House Energy and Commerce, and and six of the top ten Senate recipients were members of the Senate Commerce, Science and Transportation Committee. House Energy and Commerce chair John Dingell received as much as 10 per cent of his funds from these sources and another 8 per cent from the energy and natural resources industries.[49] As three House and two Senate committees began to consider health care legislation in the 103rd Congress, another study showed that members of these five committees received over $8 million from health care-related PACs between January 1993 and March 1994.[50] Some writers have used data such as these to argue that geographic and ideological overrepresentation of certain constituencies on committees and subcommittees results in decisions heavily favourable towards interests under their purview.[51] However, while various stud-ies have hinted at or identified general effects, none provides systematic support for the view that overrepresentation significantly affects policy outcomes when other factors are controlled. There is evidence, however, to suggest that PAC money does mobilise already sympathetic members to more active support for PACs' interests in committee.[52]

Variations in committee behaviour and organisation

We have noted already that committees differ according to their powers, prestige and attractiveness, and their representativeness. They are also organised differ-ently. Because their members tend to share similar goals and because they have distinctive subject jurisdictions, each committee operates within a distinctive political environment comprising the parent chamber, and the expectations of influential external actors such as executive officials, client interest groups, and the parties (particularly, their congressional leaders) which together constitute the committee's policy coalitions. This political environment effectively sets the parameters within which the committee operates. Thus, Richard Fenno's study of various committees in the 1950s and 1960s found that Foreign Affairs was constrained primarily by the executive's demands and expectations, Ways and Means by those of the parent House, and Post Office and Interior by clientele groups. The strategies committee members adopted to accommodate their individual goals to the committee's political environment and to make decisions also varied from committee to committee. Appropriations and Ways and Means members wanted to demonstrate their influence and responsiveness to the parent chamber, while Education and Labor Committee members wished to pursue policy partisanship and Interior Committee members were guided by a desire to process and win passage of all constituency-supported bills requested by members.[53]

Within the constraints imposed by parent chambers, the degree to which committees work through their subcommittees also varies. Steven Smith and Christopher Deering have shown that besides the thirteen subcommittees of the Appropriations committees – which effectively write the annual and supplemental appropriations bills – the most active House subcommittees were those of policy committees (see Table 4.11). On these committees, policy-oriented activists found more autonomous subcommittees best suited to serving their personal goals, sometimes at some cost to committee harmony; subcommittees tended to be less active on constituency committees. In the early and mid-1990s, subcommittees of the Energy and Commerce Committee – notably those on Health and Environment chaired by Henry Waxman (D.CA), Oversight and Investigations chaired by full committee chair John Dingell, and Telecommunications and Finance chaired by Edward Markey (D.MA) – were among the most active in the House. On some House committees, however – particularly prestige committees – subcommittee activity is more limited. The Rules Committee, for example, rarely refers legislation to its subcommittees; while the Ways and Means Committee under Rostenkowski's chair restricted subcommittee autonomy.[54] Committee rules sometimes restrict subcommittee activity: the rules of the Ways and Means Committee, for example, require that all amendments to the income tax sections of the Internal Revenue Code be considered in the full committee; while those of the Natural Resources Committee stipulate full committee consideration of legislation relating to Native Americans. Following the Republicans taking control of the House in 1995, it was unclear how much autonomy subcommittees would be allowed. Full committee chairs (and the Speaker) regained control over the appointment of subcommittee chairs and members and over subcommittee budgets, but they lost the right also to chair a subcommittee on the same committee and the power to appoint their own staff to subcommittees in addition to those appointed by subcommittee chairs.

In Senate committees, of course, the question of subcommittee influence – as distinct from the influence of individual senators – is much less relevant because committees are less important. What happens on the Senate floor is as important as committee action. Not surprisingly, there is greater variation in the internal structure of committees than in the House. With certain exceptions (for example, Appropriations and Judiciary), subcommittees do not mark up or report legislation; their principal purpose being to hold hearings on behalf of the full committee. Some barely function at all: in the 103rd Congress (1993–4), for example, subcommittees of the Senate Agriculture and Finance committees did not even have separate office space (nor separate staff in the latter case); and only one subcommittee was consistently active on the Banking Committee – two held no meetings at all in 1993. As part of their efforts to meet party requirements that committee budgets should be cut by 25 per cent, many Republican chairs reduced the number of subcommittees on their committees in early 1995.

Committee leadership

The primary role of committees in the legislative process means that committee leadership is very important to Congress' ultimate decisions. Usually, the most important member of a full committee or subcommittee is the chair. House and Senate committee chairs continue to exercise enormous power on behalf of their committee. This is despite the reforms of the 1970s which devalued their powers and status by proliferating subcommittee leadership positions (113 in the 103rd House or 44 per cent of all majority Democrats), and despite the greater accountability of Republican chairs to the Speaker after 1994. It was no wonder that President Clinton went to Chicago in 1994 to campaign in the Democratic primary for Dan Rostenkowski, the Ways and Means chair, whose political skills and strong support for health care legislation were seen as crucial to the success of the president's proposals.

With only two exceptions in the fifty years before 1970, House committee chairs and ranking minority members were selected exclusively by seniority: the longest serving member of each party became chair and ranking minority member, respectively. Under Democratic majorities, Democratic Caucus rules required House committee chairs (except the chair of the Rules Committee who was nominated by the Speaker) and the chairs of the thirteen subcommittees of the Appropriations and Ways and Means committees to be nominated at the beginning of each Congress by the Democratic Steering and Policy Committee (DSPC); and approved by the full Caucus. In the event that the Caucus rejected a nomination and the DSPC did not nominate the next most senior majority member of the committee, the full Caucus could nominate any other majority committee member.

Subcommittee chairs were elected by a secret ballot of all committee Democrats from among the most senior Democratic members of full committees.

Major changes to the positions of House committee chairs were implemented at the beginning of the 104th Congress (1995–6) following the election of a Republican majority. In a sharp reversal of Democratic practice, full committee chairs were chosen effectively by the new Speaker Gingrich; although nominally by the Republican Steering Committee dominated by Gingrich and subject to confirmation by secret ballot in the Republican Conference. More dramatically, House rules were changed to implement a House Republican Conference rule adopted in December 1992 which prohibited all full and subcommittee chairs from holding their offices for more than six consecutive years, excluding prior service. As a result of these new term limits, all 20 full and 86 subcommittee chairs apparently will be required to resign their posts in 2001. In further moves, both parties changed their rules to prohibit members holding more than one chair or ranking member position on either a full or subcommittee. In consequence, more than thirty Republicans were required to give up their additional posts in January 1995.

The cumulative effect of rules introduced by the parties since the 1970s has been to devalue the seniority norm in the selection of committee and subcommittee leaders. Although the Democratic procedures continued to favour the reappointment of incumbent chairs, between 1975 and 1994 five full committee chairs were deposed and replaced by less senior – in some cases, substantially less senior – colleagues. F. Edward Hebert (D.LA) of Armed Services, Wright Patman (D.TX) of Banking, and W. R. Poage (D.TX) of Agriculture were deposed in 1975; Melvin Price (D.IL) of Armed Services was deposed in 1985; and Glenn Anderson (D.CA) and Frank Annunzio (D.IL) in 1990. Hebert, Poage, and Anderson were replaced by the second ranking committee Democrat but Annunzio was replaced by the third ranking, Patman by the fourth, and Price by the seventh. Other chairs were also challenged – notably Henry Gonzalez (D.TX) of Banking in 1990 and G. V. 'Sonny' Montgomery (D.MS) of Veterans Affairs in 1992, both of whom received substantial negative votes against them in the Caucus. (Montgomery won by only eight votes against the committee's fourth ranking Democrat.) Most recently, in 1994, the House Democratic Caucus violated the seniority norm to elect David Obey (D.WI) as chair of the prestigious Appropriations Committee instead of the second ranking member. Obey not only became the youngest chair of the committee since 1919 but was only the fifth ranking Democrat on the committee. In January 1995, the devaluation process was taken even further in a move which echoed the days of Speaker Joe Cannon at the beginning of the century. The new House Speaker Newt Gingrich passed over the most senior Republicans on three committees to nominate more assertive conservatives to the chairs of Appropriations, Commerce, and Judiciary – Robert Livingston (R.LA), Thomas Bliley (R.VA), and Henry Hyde (R.IL). Nominating Livingston to the Appropriations chair, Gingrich and the Steering Committee passed over four more senior Republicans. At the same time, Democrats also deposed Charlie Rose (D.NC) as the ranking minority member on the House Oversight Committee after he challenged Richard Gephardt for Democratic leadership.

Seniority has also been violated increasingly in elections of subcommittee chairs. In the mid-1970s and 1980s, the bids of a number of senior Democrats for subcommittee chairs were rejected by committee colleagues. In 1989, for example, Romano Mazzoli (D.TN) was voted out of his chair of the House Judiciary Subcommittee on Immigration, Refugees and International Law and replaced by the thirteenth ranking member Bruce Morrison (D.CT). Three years later, Democrats changed their rules to allow the DSPC to recommend for whatever reason the removal of subcommittee chairs. Following a close House vote on President Clinton's budget reconciliation package in May 1993, 81 House Democrats called a full meeting of the Democratic Caucus to invoke this rule against 11 subcommittee chairs who voted against the president's package. The Caucus decided to take no action. When the Republicans took control of the House in 1995, they appointed three freshmen members – Linda Smith (R.WA), David McIntosh (R.IN), and Tom Davis (R.VA) – who were immediately appointed to chairs of subcommittees on the Small Business and Government Reform and Oversight committees, passing over two more senior members in the last two cases. Even so, despite the increasing number of violations and challenges, seniority remains the norm in the selection of House committee chairs. In 1995, only seven full committee House chairs were not the most senior members of their committee – in one case because the most senior member was already chair of another committee. However, as these incidents demonstrate, seniority is no longer the only criterion for selecting chairs.

Seniority is an even stronger norm in the selection of Senate chairs and ranking members. Both parties follow chamber rather than committee seniority, subject to ratification by their conferences and a secret ballot on any nominee if one-fifth of senators so request (Rule IV). Thus, when Republican senators on the Foreign Relations Committee supported the second ranking senator Richard Lugar (R.IN) for the committee chair in 1984, the most senior Republican Jesse Helms (R.NC) invoked the ratification rule and was subsequently elected chair. In December 1994, the Republican Conference also refused the claim of Senator John Warner (R.VA) for the chair of the Rules and Administration in favour of the existing ranking member, Senator Ted Stevens (R.AK), who had greater chamber seniority. In March 1995, the Republican Conference also rejected a request from conservative senators that Senator Mark Hatfield (R.OR) should be removed from the chair of the Appropriations Committee following his vote against the party's balanced budget amendment.

As in the House, Senate rules prohibit members from chairing more than one full committee, and limit full committee chairs to one subcommittee on 'A' committees and one on 'B' and 'C' committees (see above, p. 117). Majority senators who do not hold full committee chairs are limited to chairing three subcommittees. In the 104th Congress, only eleven Republican senators (mostly freshmen) did not chair any subcommittee (21 per cent); whereas almost half chaired at least two subcommittees and almost all full committee chairs also chaired a subcommittee. By tradition, the minority party limits any senator to one full committee ranking position. Subcommittee chairs are chosen by full committee chairs, usually in collaboration with and agreement by majority members of the full committee.

Rightly, several arguments are made against the seniority norm: (1) that it is incompatible with majority party rule and, therefore, undemocratic; (2) that it does not ensure the selection of able and competent leaders, and may actually thwart the promotion of talented juniors; (3) that it favours those geographic areas dominated by a single party and not representative of the mainstream of the majority party; and (4) that it favours the retention of committee chairs who may no longer function adequately. Both parties uphold seniority in both houses, however, because it is a simple and predictable mechanism for choosing committee leaders which limits internal party divisions and removes the need for members to choose between competing candidates. Individual members support seniority because it rewards experience and provides Congress with institutional memory. Most of those who hold chairs are a committee's most experienced members; and even if they are not, they have normally sat on the committee for at least 15 years. (In 1995, the mean length of committee service of House chairs was 18 years, with five members having served over 20 years; the mean length of service for Senate chairs was 22 years.) Typically, they are among the most expert members of their committee, who have dealt with the same or similar policy problems and political constituencies, heard the same arguments, and interrogated the same witnesses over many years.[55] All these factors tend to strengthen Congress' capacity to represent and make public policy.

Moreover, increased party control over leadership selection has addressed some of the criticisms of seniority – at least, to some extent. The increased willingness of the Democratic Caucus and the Republican Conference to violate seniority in the choice of House committee chairs – seen graphically in the election of Obey in 1994 and in the appointment of Bliley, Hyde, and Livingston in 1995 – undoubtedly serves to remind contemporary committee chairs in the most forceful manner that they are responsible to committee and party members. Indeed, it was Obey himself who insisted in a letter to committee Democrats bidding for the chair of the Appropriations Committee that: 'Holding a chair entails the responsibility of pursuing the collective agenda of the party and the House . . . not the individual agenda of a particular member who happened to be fortunate to be granted the authority.'[56] Even the most powerful committee chairs must cooperate with and be responsive to their party colleagues. In the 104th Congress (1995–6), party control over committee chairs was particularly transparent as chairs strove to implement the party's Contract With America expeditiously, sometimes against their own inclinations to defend their committee's resources. Observing that he had no control over legislative scheduling in his committee, House Judiciary chair Henry Hyde (R.IL) conceded in 1995, 'I am really a sub-chair' to the party leadership.[57]

Chair power

Although it is less apparent when a party gains control of Congress after years as a seemingly permanent minority, winning the support and harnessing the positive power of a committee chair is usually critical to sponsors (and opponents) of legislation. Even more important is the negative power of chairs to delay its consideration – even when favoured by a committee majority or approved by a subcommittee. Rules and procedures designed to allow committee members to circumvent their chair are cumbersome and rarely used. A committee's capacity to exert its positive and negative power rests to a large extent on the chair's formal powers: (i) to decide which bills will be considered; (ii) to influence the content of legislation falling within its jurisdiction; (iii) to initiate investigations and reports, and manage information; (iv) to convene meetings; (v) to assign members to conference committees (subject to limitations); and (vi) to manage the committee's public relations. These powers are further enhanced by the positive power which accrues to chairs through control of a substantial budget, and the appointment, dismissal, supervision, and direction of a large committee staff (subject to provision for subcommittees and minority members). In 1994, House committee budgets ranged from almost $20 million a year and more than 200 staff for the Appropriations Committee to less than $1 million for the Standards of Official Conduct Committee. In the Senate, where full committee chairs exercise even greater control over the appointment, dismissal, and allocation of committee staff, annual budgets vary from over $5 million for Appropriations, Governmental Affairs, Judiciary, and Labor and Human Resources to just over $1 million for Small Business. Like many personal staff, a large number of committee staffers are renowned for their policy entrepreneurial activities, expertise, and influence. They are typically well-educated and well-connected into Washington's issue networks[58] and, like members' personal staffs, their numbers have increased rapidly over recent decades.

Effective committee leadership does not depend only on formal powers and control over vast resources. Not every committee chair is powerful; and few are powerful on all issues at all times. The personality and skill of individual leaders are important factors. Contemporary congressional commentators often recall stories about committee chairs such as Robert Byrd of Senate Appropriations, Dan Rostenkowski of Ways and Means, John Dingell of Energy and Commerce, and Jack Brooks (D.TX), chair of the House Judiciary Committee, who employed sanctions and coercion to reach their objectives. Byrd, for example, as chair of the Senate Appropriations Committee between 1986 and 1994, was likened to a benevolent dictator reminiscent of the pre-reform Congress. When Senator Don Nickles (R.OK) proposed that federal spending be capped in 1990, Byrd retaliated by deleting appropriations to help start an Amtrak railway service in Oklahoma. In a second incident, in February 1994, Byrd agreed to hold hearings in the Appropriations Committee on balanced budget legislation proposed by fellow Democrat Paul Simon of Illinois but opposed by Byrd. Byrd then proceeded to stack the witness list with administration officials, academics and professional economists who opposed the measure; and scheduled Simon's appearance in support on the very last day.[59] In the House, powerful chairmanship is often associated with John Dingell of the Energy and Commerce Committee. During the 98th Congress (1983–4), Dingell delayed marking up the Natural Gas Policy Act because he feared that pro-regulation committee members had the votes to win amendments which would adversely affect high energy consuming states, such as Michigan, his home state. When Dingell finally scheduled a mark-up, a committee member boasted to Dingell: 'John, we've got the votes.' Dingell replied, 'Yeah, but I've got the gavel.' After losing two test votes, Dingell adjourned the committee delaying consideration of the bill indefinitely.[60]

While Byrd, Dingell, and others were domineering, other chairs – like Claiborne Pell (D.RI) of Senate Foreign Relations (1987–94) and Henry Gonzalez (D.TX) of House Banking, Finance and Urban Affairs Committee (1989–94) –

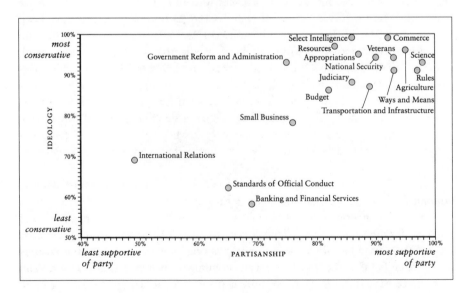

Figure 4.3. House chairs' conservatism and partisanship, 104th Congress (based on voting in 103rd Congress).

often were portrayed as weak and ineffective. Committee leadership styles vary widely as do chairs' ideologies and partisanship (Figure 4.3). Even so, it would be a mistake to assume that committee leadership rests solely on the personal characteristics of leaders. Leadership also depends on the context in which leadership is attempted and the nature of the issues being considered.[61]

In the previous discussion, we noted how committees differed according to the personal goals of their members, their political environments, and strategic premises or decision rules. Figure 4.1 showed how some committees are more conservative and more partisan than others. Committees such as House Education and Labor, Rules, and Ways and Means and Senate Finance are highly partisan; whereas House Appropriations, Foreign Affairs, Public Works and Transportation, Veterans' Affairs, and the Senate Commerce, Science and Transportation were highly bipartisan. House Banking, and Senate Energy and Natural Resources and Judiciary tend to be riven by ideological divisions; whereas House Merchant Marine and Fisheries and House and Senate Agriculture tend to divide along regional lines. These contextual factors affect not only how committees make decisions and what decisions they make, but also the effectiveness of chairs' leadership styles. Prestige and policy committees like Energy and Commerce, Ways and Means, Senate Appropriations, and Senate Labor and Human Resources lack consensus on many major issues within their jurisdictions.[62] In consequence, their chairs – Dingell, Rostenkowski, Byrd, and Edward Kennedy (D.MA) – tend to be 'policy combatants who draw upon their formal and personal resources to further a cause'. In contrast, chairs of constituency committees – 'Kika' de la Garza (D.TX) of House Agriculture, Bill Clay (D.MO) Post Office and Civil Service, and Senator J. Bennett Johnston (D.LA) of Senate Energy and Natural Resources – were expected to pursue more predictable, consensual styles which helped maintain the flow of federal largess to their constituencies. It is this marriage of style and context which goes far in explaining effective committee leadership. Even the most 'powerful' committee chairs do not get their way always. Energy and Commerce chair John Dingell – an ardent supporter of health care reform – suffered an embarrassing defeat in 1994 when he failed to move a health reform bill through his committee. No committee chair wins on every issue, even on important ones.

In the contemporary party-oriented context of the contemporary House, committee chairs' scope of action is constrained much more than their predecessors by the need to demonstrate a willingness to cooperate with and be responsive to party colleagues and leaders. Thus, even the forceful former Ways and Means chair, Dan Rostenkowski was 'constantly calling caucuses . . . meeting with us all the time [so that] he knows what his committee members want'. Energy and Commerce chair John Dingell carefully cultivated loyal lieutenants among more junior committee members.[63] Wary of their colleagues in the Democratic Caucus, sitting and prospective Democratic House chairs – including southern Democratic chairs (usually more conservative than their northern colleagues) – voted much more frequently with their party's majority than in the days of committee government.[64] Figure 4.2 suggests that even before the decisive intervention of Speaker Gingrich in the appointment of Republican chairs at the beginning of the 104th Congress (1995–6), most would be loyal to their party. Only 5 out of 20 chairs had party unity scores below 80 per cent in the previous Congress. Thus, Judiciary chair Henry Hyde (R.IL) felt compelled in early 1995 to push a proposal included in the Republican Contract With America for a constitutional amendment to impose term limits on members of Congress even though personally he opposed the measure.

Having stressed the increasing importance of party, we turn in the next chapter to examine the congressional party systems and the extent to which they are able to counter the fragmentation generated by individualism, policy entrepreneurship, and the committee systems, when legislation reaches the floor.

Notes

1   Richard Neustadt, *Presidential Power* (New York: John Wiley, 1960), p. 28; Charles O. Jones, *The Presidency in a Separated System* (Washington, D.C.: The Brookings Institution, 1994).

2   The Senate is supposed to have a formalised system whereby senators spend three full five-day weeks 'on' (in Washington working on legislative business) and one week 'off' (dealing with constituency demands in the state and elsewhere).

3   Robert Weissberg, 'Collective vs. Dyadic Representation in Congress', *American Political Science Review*, 72 (1978), pp. 535–7; Thomas E. Cavanagh, 'The Calculus of Representation: A Congressional Perspective', *Western Political Quarterly*, 35 (1982), pp. 120–9.

4   Edmund Burke, 'Speech to the Electors of Bristol' (1774). Quoted in Hanna Fenichel Pitkin, *The Concept of Representation* (Berkeley, CA: University of California Press, 1967), p. 171.

5   Roger H. Davidson, 'Congress as a Representative Institution' in Uwe Thaysen, Roger H. Davidson, and Robert Gerald Livingston (eds), *The US Congress and the German Bundestag. Comparisons of Democratic Processes* (Boulder and Oxford: Westview Press, 1990), p. 49.

6   Ross K. Baker, *House, and Senate* (New York and London: W. W. Norton and Co., 1989), pp. 45–7

7   *Ibid.*, p. 57.

8   Barbara Sinclair, *The Transformation of the US Senate* (Baltimore and London: The Johns Hopkins Press, 1989), p. 213; John F. Bibby, *Congress Off the Record, The Candid Analyses of Seven Members* (Washington, D.C.: American Enterprise Institute, 1983), p. 51; and Burdett A. Loomis, *The New American Politician: Ambition, Entrepreneurship, and the Changing Face of Political Life* (New York: Basic Books, 1988), pp. 111–14.

9   Richard F. Fenno, *Congressmen in Committees* (Boston and Toronto: Little Brown, 1973), p. 1.

10 Glenn R. Parker, *Institutional Change, Discretion, and the Making of the Modern Congress* (Ann Arbor, MI: University of Michigan Press, 1992).

11 Samuel Kernell, *Going Public. New Strategies of Presidential Leadership* (Washington, D.C.: Congressional Quarterly Press, 1986), p. 25.

12 Robert H. Salisbury and Kenneth A. Shepsle, 'US Congressman as Enterprise', *Legislative Studies Quarterly*, 6 (1981), pp. 559–76; Burdett A. Loomis, 'The Congressional Office as a Small (?) Business: New Members Set Up Shop', *Publius*, 9 (1979), pp. 35–55.

13 The term was first used in David E. Price, 'Professionals and "Entrepreneurs": Staff Orientation and Policy Making on Three Senate Committees', *Journal of Politics*, 33 (1971), pp. 316–36; and David E. Price, *Who Makes the Laws? Creativity and Power in Senate Committees* (Cambridge, MA: Schenkman, 1972). See also Steven H. Schiff and Steven S. Smith, 'Generational Change and the Allocation of Staff in the US Congress', *Legislative Studies Quarterly*, 8 (1983), pp. 457–68 and David E. Price, *The Congressional Experience. A View From the Hill* (Boulder and Oxford: Westview Press, 1992), ch. 5.

14 Salisbury and Shepsle, 'US Congressman as Enterprise', p. 573.

15 Michael J. Malbin, 'Delegation, Deliberation, and the New Role of Congressional Staff' in Thomas E. Mann and Normal J. Ornstein (eds), *The New Congress* (Washington, D.C.: American Enterprise Institute, 1981), pp. 134–77.

16 Morris Fiorina, 'The Decline of Collective Responsibility', *Daedalus*, 109 (1980), p. 44.

17 US Congress. Joint Committee on the Organisation of Congress, Hearings. *Committee Structure*, 103rd Congress, First Session, April–May 1993.

18 Edward V. Schneier and Bertram Gross, *Legislative Strategy. Shaping Public Policy* (New York: St Martin's Press, 1993), p. 55.

19 Robert Bendiner, *Obstacle Course on Capitol Hill* (New York: McGraw-Hill, 1964), p. 16.

20 The relevant authorities named after House parliamentarians and updated every two years are Asher C. Hinds, *Precedents of the House of Representatives* (Washington, D.C.: USGPO, 1907); Clarence C. Cannon, *Procedure in the House of Representatives,* H. Doc. 86–122. (Washington, D.C.: USGPO, 1960), and Lewis M. Deschler, *Deschler's Precedents of the House of Representatives* (Washington, D.C.: USGPO, 1977). Senate precedents are found in Floyd Riddick, *Senate Procedure, Precedents and Practices* (Washington, D.C.: USGPO, updated periodically).

21 Richard F. Fenno, 'The Senate Through the Looking Glass: The Debate Over Television', *Legislative Studies Quarterly*, 14 (1989), p. 346 and Richard F. Fenno, *Learning to Legislate. The Senate Education of Arlen Specter* (Washington, D.C.: Congressional Quarterly Press, 1991), pp. xii-xiii.

22 Hugh Heclo, 'Issue Networks and the Executive Establishment' in Anthony King, ed., *The New American Political System* (Washington, D.C.: American Enterprise Institute, 1978), p. 99; and Robert H. Salisbury, John P. Heinz, Robert L. Nelson, and Edward O. Laumann, 'Triangles, Networks, and Hollow Cores: The Complex Geometry of Washington Interest Representation' in Mark P. Petracca (ed.), *The Politics of Interest: Interest Groups Transformed* (Boulder and Oxford: Westview Press, 1992), pp. 130–49.

23 Woodrow Wilson, *Congressional Government. A Study in American Politics* (Baltimore and London: The Johns Hopkins Press, 1981. Originally published 1885), p. 69.

24 US Congress. Joint Committee on the Organisation of Congress, Hearings. *Committee Structure*, 103rd Congress, First Session, April–May 1993, p. 776.

25 Kenneth Shepsle and Barry Weingast, 'The Institutional Foundations of Committee Power', *American Political Science Review*, 81 (1987), pp. 85–104; Keith Krehbiel, 'Why are Committees Powerful?' and a reply by Shepsle and Weingast in *American Political Science Review*, 81 (1987), pp. 929–45; and Keith Krehbiel and Douglas Rivers, 'The Analysis of Committee Power: An Application to Senate Voting on the Minimum Wage', *American Journal of Political Science*, 32 (1988), pp. 1151–74.

26 Steven S. Smith, *Call To Order. Floor Politics in the House and Senate* (Washington, D.C.: The Brookings Institution, 1989), ch. 6.

27 See, for example, Barry R. Weingast, 'Fighting Fire With Fire: Amending Activity and Institutional Change in the Postreform Congress', in Roger H. Davidson (ed.), *The Postreform Congress* (New York: St Martin's Press), pp. 142–68.

28 Smith, *Call To Order*, pp. 141–5 and ch. 6; Sinclair, *The Transformation of the US Senate*, pp. 111–25.

29 Fenno, *Congressmen in Committees*, p. 1.

30 Richard L. Hall, *Participation in Congress* (New Haven and London: Yale University Press, 1993) and Richard L. Hall, 'Participation, Abdication, and Representation', in Lawrence C. Dodd and Bruce I. Oppenheimer (eds), *Congress Reconsidered*, 5th edn (Washington, D.C.: Congressional Quarterly Press, 1993), p. 168–9; John E. Owens, 'Good Public Policy Voting in Congress: An Explanation of Financial Institutions Politics', *Political Studies*, 43 (1995), pp. 82–3; and Charles L. Clapp, *The Congressman. His Work As He Sees It* (Washington, D.C.: Anchor Books, 1963), pp. 264–8.

31 US. Congress. Joint Committee on the Organisation of Congress, *Organisation of the Congress*, Final Report, vol. ii, 103rd Congress, First Session, p. 231; and Center for Responsive Politics, *Congressional Operations: Congress Speaks – A Survey of the 100th Congress* (Washington, D.C.: Center for Responsive Politics, 1988), pp. 65–6.

32 Steven S. Smith and Christopher J. Deering, *Committees in Congress*, 2nd edn (Washington, D.C.: Congressional Quarterly Press, 1990), p. 140. See also Roger H. Davidson, 'Subcommittee Government: New Channels for Policy-making' in Mann and Ornstein, *The New Congress*, pp. 99–133.

33 Exclusive committees were Appropriations, Rules and Ways and Means; major committees are Agriculture, Armed Services, Banking, Education and Labor, Energy and Commerce, Foreign Affairs, Judiciary, and Public Works and Transportation; and non-major committees were Budget, District of Columbia, Government Operations, House Administration, Merchant, Marine and Fisheries, Natural Resources, Post Office and Civil Service, Science, Space and Technology, Small Business and Veterans' Affairs. Standards of Official Conduct was exempt.

34 Richard F. Fenno, 'If, As Ralph Nader Says, Congress is "The Broken Branch", How Come We Love Our Congressmen So Much?' in Norman J. Ornstein (ed.), *Congress in Change. Evolution and Reform* (New York: Praeger, 1975), p. 282, but cf. Steven S. Smith, 'Informal Leadership in the Senate: Opportunities, Resources, and Motivations', in John J. Kornacki (ed.), *Leading Congress. New Styles, New Strategies* (Washington, D.C.: Congressional Quarterly Press, 1990), p. 73.

35 Fenno, *Congressmen in Committees*, pp. 147, 190–1.

36 Lawrence C. Dodd and Bruce I. Oppenheimer, 'Maintaining Order in the House. The Struggle for Institutional Equilibrium', in Dodd and Oppenheimer, *Congress*

Reconsidered, 5th edn, pp. 51–3; and Janet Hook, 'The Influential Committees: Money and Issues', *Congressional Quarterly Weekly Report*, January 3 1987, pp. 22–3.

37 Gabriel Kahn, 'Hyde Battles Away On Judiciary Panel', *Roll Call*, February 20 1995, pp. 1 and 15.

38 Gary C. Cox and Matthew D. McCubbins, *Legislative Leviathan. Party Government in the House* (Berkeley, CA and Oxford: University of California Press, 1992), pp. 27–9.

39 See also Christopher J. Deering, 'Career Advancement and Subcommittee Chairs in the US House of Representatives: 89th to 99th Congress.' A paper presented to the Midwest Political Science Association, Chicago, Illinois, April 1986 and David Twenhafel, ed., *Setting Course. A Congressional Management Guide*, 4th edn (Washington, D.C.: Congressional Management Foundation, 1992), p. 73.

40 Andrew Taylor, 'Freshmen Shift the Balance on House Banking Panel', *Congressional Quarterly Weekly Report*, January 30 1993, p. 209.

41 The typology works better for House committees because senators are much less likely to cite the influence goal, and generally less sure of and less intense about their preferences. As a result, Senate committees often fall into the mixed constituency–policy category.

42 In 1965, the House Democratic Caucus stripped John Bell Williams (D.MS) and Albert Watson (D.SC) of their seniority because they had supported Barry Goldwater the Republican candidate for president in 1964. In Williams' case, the effect was to deny him the chair of the House Interstate and Commerce Committee. Two years later, Adam Clayton Powell (D.NY) was deprived of his chair of the Education and Labor Committee for misuse of House funds; and in 1969, John Rarick (D.LA) was deprived of his seniority because he supported George Wallace, the third party candidate in the 1968 presidential election. Most recently, in 1981, following his conviction in the 'Abscam' scandal, Raymond Lederer (D.PA) was refused any committee assignments even though he had been a member of the prestigious Ways and Means Committee in the previous two Congresses.

43 Smith and Deering, Committees in Congress, p. 212. See also David W. Rohde, *Parties and Leaders in the Post-Reform House* (Chicago: University of Chicago Press, 1991), pp. 77–8.

44 Jill Zuckman, 'Most House Chairs Hold On; Freshmen Win Choice Posts', *Congressional Quarterly Weekly Report*, December 12 1992, p. 3788; David S. Cloud, 'Rostenkowski's Challenge: Delivering For Clinton', *Congressional Quarterly Weekly Report*, February 6 1993, p. 257.

45 Smith and Deering, *Committees in Congress*, 2nd edn, ch. 3. Not listed here, being a woman was apparently an important requirement to becoming a member of the Senate Judiciary Committee in 1993, following the bungling of the interrogation of Anita Harris during the committee's hearings on the nomination of Judge Clarence Thomas to the Supreme Court in 1991. Ultimately, the committee's membership was increased to accommodate the two new women senators, Feinstein and Moseley-Braun (D.IL).

46 On the efforts of freshman Congresswoman Carrie Meek (D.FL) to win a seat on the House Appropriations Committee, see Jill Zuckman, 'All the Right Moves', *Congressional Quarterly Weekly Report*, December 12 1992, p. 3786. See generally, Irwin Gertzog, 'The Routinization of Committee Assignments in the US House of Representatives', *American Journal of Political Science*, 10 (1976), pp. 693–712;

Kenneth A. Shepsle, *The Giant Jigsaw Puzzle. Democratic Committee Assignments in the Modern House* (Chicago: University of Chicago Press, 1978).

47 Following the death of William Natcher (D.KY), chair of the House Appropriations Committee, in 1994 over twenty Democrats were reported to be seeking the assignment.

48 Until 1994, members of the House Budget Committee (except the Speaker's leadership appointee) served for six years in any ten (although this rule may be waived). House rules for the 104th Congress (1995–6) changed the term limits on Budget Committee members to four terms in any six Congresses The rationale for rotating membership in the case of the House Budget Committee is to allay fears that the committee might become too powerful; and in the case of the House and Senate Select Intelligence Committees, to encourage effective oversight.

49 Data calculated from Larry Makinson, *PACs in Profile. Spending Patterns in the 1992 Elections* (Washington, D.C.: Center for Responsive Politics, 1993); Larry Makinson, *The Price of Admission. Campaign Spending in the 1992 Elections* (Washington, D.C.: Center for Responsive Politics, 1993); and Larry Makinson and Joshua F. Goldstein, *Open Secrets: The Encyclopaedia of Congressional Money and Politics* (Washington, D.C.: Center for Responsive Politics, 1994).

50 The Center for Public Integrity, *Well-Healed. Inside Lobbying for Health Care Reform* (Washington, D.C.: The Center for Public Integrity, 1994), pp. A65–A75.

51 Davidson, 'Subcommittee Government: New Channels for Policy-making', p. 111.

52 Richard L. Hall and Frank W. Wayman, 'Buying Time: Money Interests and the Mobilisation of Bias in Congressional Committees', *American Political Science Review*, 84 (1990), pp. 797–820.

53 Fenno, *Congressmen in Committees*, chs. 2 and 3.

54 Smith and Deering, *Committees in Congress*, 2nd edn, pp. 139–48, 156–9; Randall Strahan, *New Ways and Means. Reform and Change in a Congressional Committee* (Chapel Hill, NC and London: University of North Carolina Press, 1990), p. 107.

55 John R. Hibbing, 'Contours of the Modern Congressional Career', *American Political Science Review*, 85 (1991), pp. 405–28; Richard L. Hall, 'Participation and Purpose in Committee Decision-making', *American Political Science Review*, 81 (1987), pp. 105–28; Strahan, *New Ways and Means*; John F. Manley, *The Politics of Finance. The House Committee on Ways and Means* (Boston: Little Brown, 1970); Fenno, *Congressmen in Committees*, ch. 4; C. Lawrence Evans, *Leadership in Committee. A Comparative Analysis of Leadership Behavior in the US Senate* (Ann Arbor, MI: University of Michigan Press, 1991), ch. 4; John E. Owens, 'Extreme Advocacy Leadership in the Pre-Reform House: Wright Patman and the House Banking and Currency Committee', *British Journal of Political Science*, 15 (1985), pp. 187–205; Owens, 'Good Public Policy Voting in the US Congress'.

56 Mary Jacoby, 'Obey, Smith Battle Today', *Roll Call*, March 21 1994, p. 30.

57 Kahn, 'Hyde Battles Away On Judiciary Panel', p. 15.

58 Beth M. Herschen and Edward I. Sidlow, 'The Recruitment and Career Patterns of Congressional Committee Staff: An Exploration', *Western Political Quarterly*, 39 (1986), pp. 701–8; Price, 'Professionals and "Entrepreneurs"', pp. 316–36; and Christine DeGregorio, 'Professionals in the US Congress: An Analysis of Working Styles', *Legislative Studies Quarterly*, 13 (1988), pp. 459–76.

59 Phil Duncan (ed.), *Politics in America 1994* (Washington, D.C.: Congressional Quarterly Press, 1993, pp. 1350–2.

60 See David Maraniss, 'Power Play: Chair's Gavel Crushes Gas Decontrol Vote', *Washington Post*, November 20 1983, p. A1; Richard E. Cohen, *Washington At Work: Back Rooms and Clean Air* (New York: Macmillan, 1992); and Richard E. Cohen, 'Domineering Dingell Doesn't Dominate', *National Journal*, June 6 1992, p. 1366.

61 On the importance of context and style in committee leadership, see Fenno, *Congressmen in Committees*, p. 133; Strahan, *New Ways and Means*, ch. 5; and Smith and Deering, *Committees in Congress*, p. 124; and Owens, 'Extreme Advocacy Leadership'.

62 Smith and Deering, *Committees in Congress*, p. 124.

63 Quoted in Strahan, *New Ways and Means*, p. 104; Rochelle L. Stanfield, 'Plotting Every Move', *National Journal*, March 26 1988, pp. 794–5.

64 Sara Brandes Crook and John R. Hibbing, 'Congressional Reform and Party Discipline: The Effect of Changes in the Seniority System on Party Loyalty in the US House of Representatives', *British Journal of Political Science*, 15 (1985), pp. 207–26.

CHAPTER 5

Congressional parties and legislative decision-making

Much debate has surrounded the impact of party leaderships and organisations – the third set of organisational structures we will examine. In a constitutional system characterised by power sharing, mixed representation and institutional competition it is unrealistic to expect central party organisations to provide what Charles O. Jones calls 'substance-oriented policy leadership' of the type found in British and other European party systems.[1] If such a leadership style was attempted in Congress or the country at large, it would be resented and fiercely opposed by most members and voters.

Party organisations

Despite the conventional wisdom that parties are rather unimportant in the life of Congress, the perception of members of Congress is rather different. 'Newly elected members of Congress,' Congressman David Price (D.NC) has noted, 'when they come to Washington . . . immediately confront the fact that the House is a party-led chamber.'[2] In fairly quick succession, newcomers attend orientation sessions organised by the majority and minority leaderships, vote for a leader and adopt caucus or conference rules, House members vote for their party's nominee for Speaker strictly along party lines, senators their president *pro tempore*, and then are assigned to various committees by their party colleagues. In the House and Senate chambers, Democrats and Republicans sit in different segments – the majority to the right of the presiding officer, the minority to the left. The parties have different conferences and cloakrooms in which to discuss tactics and strategy; and in floor debates are allotted equal time (assuming the minority on a particular bill is synonymous with the minority party). Committees and subcommittees are organised along party lines. All committee and subcommittee chairs are members of the majority party. If a party loses its majority in a chamber (as the Democrats did in both houses after the 1994 elections), it forfeits control of committee chairs; the referral and scheduling of legislation; the vast resources, staff and powers which accrue to committees; the possibility that it can enact its legislation; and, if it also controls the presidency, the political benefits of single-party government.

House caucuses and conferences

Each party in both houses organises a conference – or in the case of House Democrats, a caucus – for all party members. After the mid-1960s, these organisations became much more central to members' lives, especially in the House, than they had been previously. It was a reinvigorated House Democratic Caucus which moved in the 1970s to undermine the foundations of committee government by challenging the bastions of seniority and committee chairmanship power; and constructed in its place a new power structure based on decentralised sub-committees, strengthened central party leadership, and greater internal party democracy. Prompted by disenchantment with the passivity of their colleagues in the 1950s and 1960s, by the need to harness newer and younger members' talents and energies, and by newcomers insisting on greater participation in organisational and policy decisions, leaders of both parties in the 1970s embraced new strategies which sought to maximise colleagues' inclusion and participation in party affairs through the dissemination of information and broad consultation in the belief that such strategies would enhance partisan cooperation, enthuse members, and benefit their party.[3]

The House Democratic Caucus and the House Republican Conference each have a budget of about $1.5 million (1995), excluding funding for their leadership structures. They serve a number of functions for their respective members: (i) to provide a private forum in which party members may question committee and party leaders candidly on the tactics and substance of specific legislative proposals; (ii) to ratify committee assignments and chairmanships recommended by the steering committee; (iii) to approve rules changes; and (iv) to publicise the party's legislative efforts and the respective parties' 'spin' on the days events – particularly important for the majority party when the White House is controlled by the opposing party. Under Republican Conference chair Dick Armey (R.TX) in the 103rd Congress (1993–4), the Conference organised a 'rapid response truth squad' comprising the party's policy experts with special responsibility for producing and publicising the party's response to policy initiatives from the Clinton Administration and majority Democrats.[4] House Democrats followed the Republicans' example after they lost control of the House in 1994.

Democratic Caucus rules require monthly meetings (usually two are held) when Congress is in session; Republican Conference meetings are called by the Conference Chair after consultation with the Republican leader. Fifty members in both parties may petition extraordinary meetings. Both parties have mechanisms for expelling members (by a two-thirds) but only the Democrats stipulate conditions for expulsion and discipline: Rule I (103rd Congress) states that all Democrats are bound, if they wish to retain their membership, to support Caucus decisions in the House on important organisational matters: including the election of the Speaker, other House officers and committee chairs; the assignment of party members to committees; the adoption of House rules designating the agenda-setting powers of the Speaker; full and subcommittee chairs, and committee jurisdictions; Rules Committee recommendations on how floor bills may be amended; and appeals against the Speaker's ruling. Although there is no explicit binding requirement to vote for Caucus' proposals for House rules (taken immediately after the election of a Speaker and before committee assignments are allocated), voting is usually along party-lines. Caucus rules also prohibit members from campaigning for non-Democratic candidates in any partisan federal election. Congressmen John Bell Williams (D.MS) and Albert Watson (D.SC) were stripped of their seniority by the House Democratic Caucus in 1965 for supporting the Republican candidate for president Barry Goldwater in 1964; and in 1969, John Rarick (D.LA) was deprived of his seniority because he supported George Wallace, the third party candidate in the 1968 presidential elections.

The consequences of voting against Caucus policy and legislative recommendations are much less drastic; although the threat of widespread desertion from the party is certain to influence party and committee leaders. Not since the 1970s have Caucus rules bound or instructed Democratic members to vote for or against a specific legislative measure – and even then, some Democrats ignored Caucus instructions and no action was taken against them. Only very rarely has the Steering and Policy Committee (DSPC) and after 1994 the Policy Committee endorsed specific legislation as being important to the party. In May 1993, eleven Democratic subcommittee chairs voted against President Clinton's budget reconciliation package but over protests from colleagues the Caucus again took no disciplinary action. If, however, the Caucus does expel a member he/she automatically loses his/her committee assignments and all accrued committee seniority. Even then, the consequences may be less than onerous.[5]

Both House party organisations have committee structures designed to reflect the diversity and inclusiveness of each. Most important on the Republican side is the Steering Committee, modelled on the now-defunct Democratic Steering and Policy Committee. Created in December 1994 to replace the older Republican Committee on Committees, it is firmly under the control of the Republican leadership and is located in the Speaker's office. Composed of twenty-seven members (104th Congress), it includes all House Republican leaders, the chairs of the four most important committees, and is chaired by the Speaker when the party is the majority (see Table 5.1). The Steering Committee's responsibilities include nominating committee members and chairs, establishing legislative priorities, and scheduling items for House and Conference consideration.

The seemingly permanent minority status of the House Republicans before 1994 led the party to place great emphasis on policy development and publicity.[6] Before the Steering Committee was created, the Policy Committee was the most important committee, then chaired by the Republican leader but now led by a separately elected chair. In the 104th Congress (1995–6) the Policy Committee comprised forty-one members, including all the elected Republican leaders, the

Table 5.1. Composition, functions, and officers
of party organisations in the House and Senate

	HOUSE		
	DEMOCRATS		
Organisation	Membership	Function	Officers
Democratic Caucus	All House Democrats	Nominates candidate for the Speaker; elects the Democratic Leader, Majority Leader (if the majority), Majority/Minority Whip, Caucus chair, vice chair, DCCC chair; nominates committee members and chairs; disciplines members; considers rules changes and resolutions; considers policy issues and pending legislation; binds members to vote for Speaker, other House offices, committee chairs and committee members; and publicises party policies.	Chair and vice chair, elected for no more than two consecutive terms every 2 years.
Democratic Steering Committee	Speaker and Majority Leader or Minority Leader, co-chair, 2 vice chairs, Speaker and Majority Leader or Minority Leader, Majority or Minority Whip; Caucus chair; Caucus vice chair, chair of the DCCC; 4 deputy chief whips; 12 regional representatives elected by the Caucus; the chairs/ranking members of the Appropriations, Budget, Rules, and Ways and Means Committee, and 10 members appointed by the Democratic Leader.	Nominates Democratic committee members and chairs; schedules matters for House and Caucus consideration (in majority); recommends to the Caucus that a committee or subcommittee chair is vacant; recommends the removal of members' committee assignments.	Chair (who is the Democratic Leader); co-chair and 2 vice chairs appointed by the Democratic Leader.
Policy Committee	Speaker and Majority Leader or Minority Leader, Majority or Minority Whip, Caucus chair, Caucus vice chair, 4 chief deputy whips, and 6 vice chairs.	Analyses and develops party positions on important national issues; coordinates policy; establishes legislative priorities; drafts legislation and devises floor strategies; coordinates messages and speeches; makes recommendations to the Caucus; publicises and promotes party's principles in the press.	Chair, 6 vice chairs appointed by the Democratic Leader.
Democratic Congressional Campaign Committee	Speaker, one Democrat elected from each state or territory with party representation in the House; and 8 other members appointed by the Speaker.	Raises and distributes campaign money; provides electoral services and assistance to Democratic candidates for the House.	Chair, nominated by the Democratic Leader and elected by the Caucus every 2 years

HOUSE			
REPUBLICANS			
Organisation	Membership	Function	Officers
Republican Conference	All House Republicans	Nominates candidates for the Speaker; elects Republican Leader, Majority Leader (if the majority), Republican Whip, Conference chair, vice chair, secretary, NRCC chair; ratifies committee assignments and chairs (or ranking members); considers rules changes and resolutions; considers policy issues and pending legislation; considers recommendations from the Steering and Policy committees and publicises party policies.	Chair, vice chair, and secretary, elected by the Conference every 2 years
Steering Committee	Speaker and Majority Leader or Minority Leader; Majority or Minority Whip; Conference chair, Policy Committee chair, NRCC chair, 10 elected regional representatives (including 1 for small states); and the chairs/ranking members of the Appropriations, Budget, Rules, and Ways and Means Committees; 2 sophomore members; and 2 freshman members.	Nominates Republican committee members and chairmen; considers resolutions on party policy, legislative and scheduling priorities; schedules matters for Conference consideration; and appoints ad hoc committees to conduct special studies or investigations.	Chair, who is Speaker or Minority Leader.
Policy Committee	Policy Committee chair, Speaker, Majority Leader or Minority Leader, Majority or Minority Whip, Conference chair, Conference vice chair, Conference secretary, and NRCC chair; chairs of the Appropriations, Budget, Rules, and Ways and Means Committees; 10 elected regional representatives; 2 sophomore members; 2 freshman members; and 10 regional representatives appointed by the Speaker/Republican leader.	Analyses and develops party positions on important national issues and legislation; makes recommendations to the Conference; publicises and promotes party's principles.	Chair, elected by the Conference every 2 years
National Republican Congressional Committee	Chair, Speaker, Majority Leader or Minority Leader, Majority or Minority Whip, Conference chair, Conference vice chair, Conference secretary, Policy Committee chair, and 22 members of the Conference appointed by the NRCC chair.	Raises and distributes campaign money and provides electoral services and assistance to Republican candidates for the House.	Chair elected by the Conference every 2 years.

SENATE			
DEMOCRATS			
Organisation	Membership	Function	Officers
Democratic Conference	All Democratic senators	Nominates candidate for Majority Leader, elects the Democratic leader, Majority/Minority Whip, Conference secretary; nominates committee members and chairs; considers rules changes and resolutions; considers policy issues and pending legislation; binds members to vote for Majority Leader, other Senate offices, committee chairs and committee members; and publicises party policies.	Chair (who is the Majority/Minority Leader), and secretary all elected by the Conference every 2 years.
Democratic Policy Committee	Majority/Minority Leader, co-chair, 4 vice chairs, 13 Democratic senators appointed by the leader as vacancies occur. Majority/Minority Whip, Conference Secretary are ex offico.	Analyses and develops party positions on important national issues; drafts legislation and devises floor strategies; makes recommendations to the Conference; publicises and promotes party's principles.	Chair (who is the Majority/Minority Leader); co-chair and 4 vice chairs, all appointed by the leader.
Democratic Steering and Coordination Committee	Chair, Majority/Minority Leader, Majority/Minority Whip, Conference Secretary, Chief Deputy Whip, and 15 Democratic senators appointed by the leader as vacancies occur.	Nominates Democratic committee members and chairs; considers resolutions on party policy, legislative priorities; schedules matters for Senate and Conference consideration; communicates with the House and outside interest groups.	Chair and 6 vice chairs appointed by the leader.
Democratic Senatorial Campaign Committee	Chair.	Raises and distributes campaign money and provides electoral services and assistance to Democratic candidates for the Senate.	Chair appointed by the leader.

chairs of the Appropriations, Budget, Rules, and Ways and Means Committees, a large number of regional representatives, and two members each from the two most recent intakes of Republican members (Table 5.1). Over recent years, the Policy Committee has specialised in issuing fiery partisan statements on major legislative issues, such as the following on crime legislation in 1993:

> What the House Democrats did this week was a crime. They used every trick in their legislative book to prevent meaningful votes on tough measures to restore safety to our streets and security to our homes . . . So while the

SENATE			
REPUBLICANS			
Organisation	Membership	Function	Officers
Republican Conference	All Republican senators	Nominates candidate for Majority Leader, elected the Republican leader, Majority/Minority Whip, Conference chair and secretary, Policy Committee chair, RSCC chair; ratifies committee assignments and chairs; considers rules changes and resolutions; considers policy issues and pending legislation; binds members to vote for Majority Leader, other Senate offices, committee chairs and committee members; and publicises party policies.	Chair and secretary elected by the Conference every 2 years.
Republican Policy Committee	Chair, Majority/Minority Leader, Majority/Minority Whip, Conference chair, Conference Secretary, chairs/ranking members of all standing committees and Select Committee on Intelligence.	Analyses and develops party positions on important national issues; drafts legislation and devises floor strategies; makes recommendations to the Conference; publicises and promotes party's principles.	Chair elected by the Conference every 2 years.
Republican Committee on Committees	Chair and 5 other Republican senators.	Recommends Republican committee assignments to the Majority/Minority Leader.	Chair elected by the Conference every 2 years.
National Repulican Senatorial Committee	Chair and 15 other Republican senators.	Raises and distributes campaign money and provides electoral services and assistance to Democratic candidates for the Senate.	Chair elected by the Conference every 2 years.

country bleeds, the House is gagged. While the public lives in fear, House Democrats fear to vote in public.[7]

Besides its partisan publicity role, the Policy Committee provides a private forum for developing policy and issue positions, conducting research, publishing issue papers, and organising publicity events for Republican members.[8] Before it was abolished in December 1994, the committee shared this role with the Research Committee and a number of task forces. In the 101st Congress, for example, the Research Committee organised over forty task forces aimed at influencing debate in the media and in issue networks on issues ranging from acid rain to western lending to communist counties.[9] The third and final element in House Republican members' party structure is the National Republican Congressional Committee which provides financial and other assistance to Republican candidates for the House. Until very recently, its work was not well coordinated with Conference activities and it was heavily in debt. Under the current chair, Bill Paxon (R.NY), it has worked much more closely with the House Republican leadership.

Most important on the Democratic side is the Steering Committee (formerly the Democratic Steering and Policy Committee) which is effectively the executive committee of the Caucus. Composed of thirty-eight members (104th Congress), including all elected House Democratic leaders, it is co-chaired by the Democratic Leader and his appointee and has responsibility for nominating committee members and chairs, establishing legislative priorities, and scheduling items for House and Caucus consideration (see Table 5.1). Somewhat confusingly, Democrats also have a Leadership Advisory Group composed of thirteen Democrats to advise their leader. Until 1994, responsibility for developing party policy and assisting the leadership in defining and publicising the party's policy agenda was assigned to the Speaker's Working Group on Policy Development, consisting of thirty-one members (half from the DSPC). However, following the party's electoral defeat, Democrats adopted a version of the House Republican's model by creating a separate Policy Committee. This committee supposedly acts as a 'counsel of elders' for the party, has responsibility for establishing and implementing the party's policy agenda, and operates separate suborganisations for policy, communications, and research. The new Policy Committee is composed of fifteen members (104th Congress) and is chaired by the Democratic Leader. Responsibility for raising and allocating campaign money is assigned to the Democratic Congressional Campaign Committee (DCCC) whose chair is nominated by the Democratic Leader and elected by the Caucus.

Party organisations in the Senate

Although both parties in the Senate have a number of committees with almost identical functions to those in the House, party organisation in the Senate is not as elaborate – primarily because of the chamber's smaller size. Democratic and Republican Conferences meet weekly (usually Tuesday lunchtime) to consider current legislative strategies and policy issues informally and dispense with various organisational tasks; and at the beginning of each Congress, choose leaders and approve rules changes. To a great extent, the activism of these organisations depends very much on the dispositions of individual leaders; although over recent years senators have generally emulated their House colleagues by seeking to use party conferences and committees to demand better party services, and greater opportunities to influence party policy-making. Central party leaders have responded to these demands by gearing party structures to emphasise greater inclusiveness and maximum participation. Thus, after he was elected Majority Leader (and chair of the Policy Committee) in 1989, Senator George Mitchell (D.ME) rejuvenated the Democratic Policy Committee (DPC) – following a period of dormancy in the late 1970s and 1980s under the leadership of Senator Robert Byrd (D.WV) – and appointed Senator Tom Daschle (D.SD) as co-chair in 1989. Under Daschle's leadership, this committee rather than the Democratic Conference (which does not have separate staff or offices) assumed primary responsibility for developing yearly legislative agendas for the Conference; holding weekly meetings; sponsoring retreats and seminars on particular policy questions; and for providing Senate Democrats with timely and in-depth information on pending issues, schedules, and leaders' statements and views. In these ways, the DPC 'carved out an important niche for itself as a discussion forum and a service provider' in ways which, in many cases, mirrored practices initiated by the Senate Republican Policy Committee in the 1970s.[10] When Daschle became Democratic Leader in December 1994, he retained his chair of the Policy Committee and appointed an ally as its co-chair. Democratic committee assignments are the responsibility of the 25-member Democratic Steering and Coordinating Committee which until 1989 was also chaired by the Democratic Leader but is now chaired by one of his/her leading lieutenants. Democratic senators may not sit on both the Policy and Steering and Coordination Committees at the same time. Daschle also established a new Technology and Communication Committee with responsibilities for improving Democrat senators' communications with groups outside Washington, and appointed another ally as its chair.

Senate Republican party organisation follows a similar division of responsibilities but leadership positions of the Conference, the Policy Committee, the Committee on Committees (seven members), and the National Republican Senatorial Committee are all elected by the Conference, as in the House. Senate Republicans also combine their policy development and coordination roles within one powerful committee – the 22-member Policy Committee – the members of which (except the chair) are all committee chairs/ranking members or in leadership positions.

At the core of these elaborate party organisations in the House and Senate are, of course, the party leaderships who play much more significant roles in the day-to-day business of Congress than twenty or thirty years ago.

Majority party leadership

Majority party leadership in the house

Largely as a result of developments since the 1970s – a period dominated by the Democratic Party until 1994 – majority party leadership in the House has been strengthened significantly. Helped by the chamber's stronger party orientation, by better coordination of party organisation and policy-making through the more extensive network of party committees, by stronger accountability to ordinary majority members, by a huge expansion in resources (almost $6 million in 1995) and party staff far greater than the increase either in members' personal staff or committee staff, by split party control of Congress and the presidency, majority leaders have become much more prominent and more significant players both within their parties and the House.

Majority leadership is vested primarily in the increasingly potent office of the Speaker, who is leader of the majority party *and* the chamber's presiding and chief administrative officer. During the era of committee government in the 1940s, 1950s, and 1960s, the combination of a divided majority party and autonomous and unaccountable committee chairs confined even a skilful speaker like Sam Rayburn (D.TX, 1941–6; 1949–52; 1955–61) largely to brokering accommodations. Even as recently as the 1970s, Speaker Carl Albert (D.OK, 1972–7) observed that he would 'never do anything without the consent of my committee chairmen'.[11] With the reactivation of the Democratic Caucus, the curtailing of committee chairs' power in the 1970s, the declining ideological heterogeneity of majority Democrats, and the need felt by House Democrats for help in enacting legislation and countering Republican power in the White House, the Speaker's formal powers and political influence in the 1980s were strengthened to a magnitude not seen since the early twentieth century. As a result, at least since the 1970s, the Speaker has become unequivocally *the* pre-eminent political force in the House. Since 1994, the Republican Speaker Newt Gingrich (R.GA) has exploited the opportunity provided by the ending of Democratic control to expand even further the office's powers. Under his speakership, Republican party power has been consolidated much more around his office which functions as a sort of parliamentary leadership challenging and competing with Democratic presidential leadership and eclipsing leadership from the Senate.

The Speaker is, of course, only the most important member of an increasingly large majority leadership team. Table 5.2 shows the majority leaderships for the 103rd (1993–4) and 104th (1995–6) Congresses. Besides the Speaker, the majority leadership includes the Majority or Floor Leader, the Majority Whip, and the Caucus or Conference Chair and Vice Chair – all of whom are elected by the party caucus or conference, depending on whether Democrats or Republicans are the majority. (The Chair and Vice Chair of the Democratic Caucus are limited to two consecutive full terms; and the Chair and Vice Chair of the Republican Conference normally may not be a standing committee chair or ranking member.) Under Democratic majorities in recent years, a core group comprising the Speaker, the Majority Leader, the Majority Whip, the Chief Deputy Whips (all appointed by the Speaker), and the Chair and Vice-Chair of the Democratic Caucus coordinated majority leadership activities through frequent informal contacts with one another and Caucus members, and through regular meetings of the whips (every Thursday morning), the DSPC (about twice a month), with Senate leaders, and (when there was a Democrat in the White House) with the president. On the basis of the party's 1994 election victory, power in the Republican-controlled House became much more centralised in the office of the Speaker and, correspondingly, the power and influence of other Republicans leaders (although not their election) came to depend greatly on the Speaker's discretion. One early indication of this shift was Speaker Gingrich's refusal to grant the request of House Majority Whip Tom DeLay (R.TX) the same budget as the outgoing Democratic whip, and to confine the Majority Whip's office largely to vote-counting and shepherding legislation to passage. While DeLay's budget was cut, that of Majority Leader Dick Armey (R.TX) was increased by more than half. An internal leadership memorandum also indicated that coordination of the staff of leadership offices and the tasks of chief party spokesperson and strategist would rest with the Speaker.[12]

In the contemporary House, the Speaker has an impressive array of formal powers, and a sizeable budget ($2.1 million in 1995). As the chief presiding officer, he/she opens each daily session, rules on procedural issues, decides which members will be recognised to speak and offer amendments, judges the results of voice and standing or division votes, refers bills to committees, and appoints the chair of the Committee of the Whole (the parliamentary mechanism through which the House considers most legislation). As leader of the party, he/she also (i) influences and controls the House's schedule; (ii) influences committee and conference assignments; (iii) appoints and removes majority members of the Rules Committee (all of whom either serve in the majority's whip organisation or are party loyalists); (iv) appoints and removes majority members of the House Oversight Committee (introduced in 1995); (v) appoints *ad hoc* oversight committees, subject to House approval; and (vi) controls the party's public and media relations. As the House's chief administrative office, he/she also commands substantial administrative and public relations resources which since January 1995 have expanded significantly and become more centralised.[13]

Contemporary Speakers' capacity to shape the House's agenda is substantial – as long as they have the support of their party bases. Beginning with the House's internal reforms of the mid-1970s, and enhanced by the pro-active styles of Democratic speakers Tip O'Neill (D.MA, 1977–86) and Jim Wright (D.TX 1987–9) – against the background of deficit politics and split-party control – a steady increase in the Speaker's involvement in policy-making occurred. As many newly elected Republicans perceived Gingrich as the reason for their election in 1994, his power as Speaker was enhanced and authority within the House centralised much further – even though the new majority also limited his tenure of the office (with Gingrich's approval) to four consecutive terms.

A series of reforms introduced by the Democrats in the mid-1970s gave the Speaker powers (against which there was no appeal) to refer bills to more than

Table 5.2. House party leaderships, 103rd and 104th Congresses

103RD CONGRESS			
Democrats		Republicans	
Position	Holder	Position	Holder
Speaker	Thomas Foley (WA)	Minority Leader	Robert Michel (IL)
Majority Leader	Richard Gephardt (MO	Minority Whip	Newt Gingrich (GA)
Majority Whip	David Bonior (MI)	Conference Chair	Dick Armey (TX)
Caucus Chair	Steny Hoyer (MD)	Conference Vice Chair	Bill McCollum (FL)
Caucus Vice Chair	Vic Fazio (CA)	Conference Secretary	Tom Delay (TX)
Chief Deputy Whips	Butler Derrick (SC) Barbara Kennelly (CT) John Lewis (GA) Bill Richardson (NM)	Chief Deputy Whip	Robert Walker (PA)
Floor Whip	Martin Frost (TX)	Deputy Whips	Joe Barton (TX) Tom DeLay (TX) Dennis Hastert (IL) Nancy Johnson (CT) Jon Kyl (AZ) Gerald Solomon (NY)
Deputy Whips	Tom Bevill (AL) Bill Heffner (NC) Norman Mineta (CA) Charles Rangel (NY) Martin Sabo (MN) Patricia Schroeder (CO) Charles Stenholm (TX) Estaban Torres (CA) Jolene Unsoeld (WA) Alan Wheat (MO) Pat Williams	Assistant Deputy Whips	Thomas Bliley (VA) John Boehner (OH) Dan Burton (IN) Paul Henry (MI) Robert Livingstone (LA) Bill Paxon (NY) Pat Roberts (KS) Olympia Snowe (ME)
Whip Task Force Chairs	Bart Gordon (TN) David Obey (WI)	Regional Whips	4
At-Large Whips	56		
Assistant/Zone Whips	14		

one committee, to decide which parts of a bill would go to which committees and in which order, to impose time limits on the first committee in a sequential referral, and to re-refer a measure after it has been amended by one committee so as to fall within the jurisdiction of another committee.[14] As a result, by the early 1990s, most multiple referrals were routine. Even though multiple referrals did not involve the Speaker personally, the significance of this new strategic power *vis-à-vis* the standing committees was unmistakable. Effectively, the leader of the majority party had the capacity both to prevent a single committee or a group of committees from obstructing a bill and to impede a bill he/she or, more importantly, the majority party did not like by sending it to a number of committees

104TH CONGRESS			
Republicans		Democrats	
Position	Holder	Position	Holder
Speaker	Newt Gingrich (GA)	Minority Leader	Richard Gephardt (MO)
Majority Leader	Dick Armey (TX)	Minority Whip	David Bonior (MI)
Majority Whip	Tom DeLay (TX)	Caucus Chair	Vic Fazio (CA)
Conference Chair	John Boehner (OH)	Caucus Vice Chair	Barbara Kennelly (CT)
Conference Vice Chair	Susan Molinari (NY)	Chief Deputy Whips	Rosa DeLauro (CT)
			Chet Edwards (TX)
			John Lewis (GA)
			Bill Richardson (NM)
Conference Secretary	Barbara Vucanovich (NV)	Ex-Officio Whip	Joe Moakley (MA)
Chief Deputy Whip	Dennis Hastert (IL)	Parliamentarians	Barney Frank (MA)
			Bob Wise (WV)
Deputy Whips	Cass Ballinger (NC)	Deputy Whips	Tom Bevill (AL)
	Jim Bunning (KY)		Bill Heffner (NC)
	Mike Crapo (ID)		Eddie Bernice Johnson (TX)
	Barbara Cubin (WY)		Norman Mineta (CA)
	John Doolittle (CA)		Charles Rangel (NY)
	Tom Ewing (IL)		John Reed (RI)
	Tillie Fowler (FL)		Bobby Rush (IL)
	Porter Goss (FL)		Martin Sabo (MN)
	Tim Hutchinson (AR)		Patricia Schroeder (CO)
	Rick Lazio (NY)		Charles Stenholm (TX)
	Bob Ney (OH)		Estaban Torres (CA)
	Randy Tate (WA)		Pat William (MT)
	Bill Zeliff (NH)		
Assistant Deputy Whips	39	At-Large Whips	45
		Regional Whips	12

and/or by refusing to impose a time limit on committee deliberations. Thus, in the 99th Congress, for example, Speaker O'Neill referred a Republican-sponsored economic recovery bill jointly to four committees, but sent an almost identical Democratic-sponsored bill to a single committee which was expected to consider it sympathetically.[15] More than this, successive Democratic Speakers used the multiple referral device to influence the impact of particular committees. In 1993, for example, Speaker Tom Foley (D.WA) awarded jurisdiction over President Clinton's entire health care bill to the strongly led and centrist Energy and Commerce, and Ways and Means committees rather than to the highly fractious and liberal Education and Labor Committee. In January 1995, the new Republican majority instituted a major change enabling the Speaker to designate a committee 'of primary jurisdiction' – although he/she could still refer parts of bills to other committees, and whole bills sequentially to other committees.

The Speaker's influence over committees has also increased as a result of majority members' concerns over the budget deficit and the consequent introduction of a congressional budget timetable (Table 4.8) and a requirement that portions of the budget be coordinated and agreed as a unified whole. The effect of these changes was to centralise budget-making power and, with the support of the Democratic majority, to enhance the influence of the Speaker. The new House and Senate Budget Committees reported budget resolutions which more or less bound committees to authorise expenditures and programmes which complied with them. Against a background of growing demands for fiscal restraint (reflected in passage of the Gramm-Rudman-Hollings Deficit Reduction Act in 1985), split-party government, and deepening ideological divisions between the parties after 1980, O'Neill and Wright transformed the traditional role of the Speaker as 'nurturer and process manager' of the budget to dominant player in a policy area which has dominated Congress' agenda since the late 1970s. Under directions from the Speaker, the Rules Committee began to limit the number of floor amendments to the Budget Committee's first budget resolution; and for the first time since the coup against 'Uncle' Joe Cannon in 1910, the leader of the majority party in the House became involved in budget policy-making *within* committees, and in negotiating budget agreements with the president and Senate leaders.[16]

In other important policy areas – such as trade, crime, transportation, environmental protection, and health care – the Speaker, at the behest of the Democratic majority, became closely involved in packaging discrete bills into enormous omnibus legislation, reauthorisations and continuing resolutions, often running to hundreds or thousands of pages. Again, the general effect was to centralise authority and influence over content and scheduling in the hands of the Speaker (and the majority party) – because only he/she had the resources and prerogatives required to manage and coordinate such complex measures. In the 100th Congress (1987–8), for example, Speaker Wright used the multiple referral procedure to require six committees to report the omnibus trade bill within a short period of time and then personally brokered the subsequent inter-committee bargaining in order to move the legislation to the floor. The investment by the majority of so much authority and influence in one office, of course, carries risks for the holder. If a Speaker fails to use his influence aggressively or fails to meet the expectations of his party colleagues and defers to committee leaders – as Speaker Foley often had to – legislative stalemate and political damage to the majority party may result. For example, in 1991, Foley was sharply criticised by majority Democrats for deferring too much to the chairs of the Public Works and Ways and Means committees in a long-running dispute over the highway and mass transit funding bill. When a similar dispute developed in 1993 between the Public Works Committee and the Transportation Subcommittee of the Appropriations Committee, the leadership quickly moved in and effected a compromise.

The majority party has also been willing to allow their leadership to exercise greater influence over the flow of legislation to the floor – through expanded use of suspending the rules and by increasing the Speaker's influence over the Rules Committee. On the House floor, the Speaker exercises absolute discretion (subject to the will of the majority) over the recognition of members for the purpose of offering motions to suspend the rules. Historically, the rules were suspended for passing non-controversial bills, such as the naming of a post office or the minting of a new coin; in which case a two-thirds majority is required, debate is limited to forty minutes, and no amendments are permitted. Between 1973 and 1977, however, majority Democrats increased the number of days on which suspensions could be considered and made provision for clustering several votes on suspension motions into a specific time period. As a result, the leadership has made increasing use of suspensions – to the extent that by the early 1990s the number of bills brought to the floor under suspensions far exceeded those brought to the floor under all types of rules. In the 102nd Congress (1991–2), 52 per cent of all bills and joint resolutions were considered under suspension of the rules, compared with 27 per cent in the 94th Congress (1975–6).[17] The advantage of these 'fast track' procedures for gaining rapid approval of emergency legislation are obvious. However, much to the annoyance of the Republican minority, Democratic majority leaders used suspensions increasingly to seek approval of controversial legislation on which there was significant partisan disagreement, and to approve bills which forced the minority to cast difficult votes on popular programmes. Not surprisingly, the increasing use of suspensions to call up controversial bills led to an increasing number failing.

The Rules Committee – the House's legislative gatekeeper, and once the bastion of the conservative coalition (see Chapter 2) – is now very much an arm of the majority leadership. Since 1975, the Speaker has enjoyed the power to appoint all the committee's majority members (including the chair) subject to Caucus or Conference ratification. In consequence, the committee's role was transformed fairly swiftly from one of obstructing to expediting majority party legislation and generally serving as the 'eyes and ears' of the leadership.[18] The committee also offered the floor managers of bills the opportunity to preview their legislation before taking it to the floor. Under the chairmanship of Richard Bolling (D.MO, 1979–82), a leading lieutenant of Speaker O'Neill, the committee began granting a new category of 'special' or restrictive rules in addition to the simple 'open' (any germane amendments) and 'closed' (no amendments) rules. With the support of majority Democrats, these new types of rules limited to varying degrees the ability of members to offer floor amendments and allowed certain specific actions to be ruled in order. So, whereas 75 to 85 per cent of the rules reported from the Rules Committee were open in the middle and late 1970s, by the 103rd Congress (1993–4), 70 per cent were closed and 73 per cent were 'restrictive'.[19] A good example of how such rules affect House debate occurred in May 1993 when the House considered the Omnibus Budget Reconciliation bill. Floor debate on the bill was governed by H Res 186 – a restrictive rule which ruled out of order 19 Democratic and 32 Republican amendments, ruled in order 7 Democratic and 1 Republican substitute offered by the ranking minority member of the Budget Committee which could not then be amended, and waived all points of order. Undoubtedly, the adoption of this rule helped the Democratic majority and President Clinton win passage of the legislation, although not without costs. When the Republicans took over the House in 1995, they approved a House rule which required the Rules Committee to stipulate waivers of points of order in special rules as much as possible.

Somewhat ironically, after complaining that the Democrats used too many closed rules and promising that three-quarters of bills would be granted open rules, when they took control of the House in 1995, the new Republican majority imposed a closed rule on the very first motion of the new Congress – to adopt the rules of the House. Inevitably, the Republicans' commitment to open rules conflicted with the party's promise to legislate its Contract With America within 100 days, and with Democrats' wish to take advantage of open rules to offer numerous amendments. By February 1995, a preliminary analysis showed that about two-thirds of the majority Republicans' rules were closed.[20] Moreover, coupled with this development was a new rule affecting so-called 'limitation amendments' to appropriations bills. Under the new rule, committee chairs will no longer be able to block amendments to strike specific items affecting spending programmes within their committee jurisdictions from appropriations bills without the permission of the House majority leader. The likely effects of this will be a flood of limitations amendments offered by majority members seeking to dismantle federal programmes without hearings in authorising committees.

In the contexts of increased numbers of floor amendments, electronic voting (which makes members' floor voting records accessible to the public), multiple referral, the increasing power of subcommittees, and the reduced power of committee chairs, special rules provide the majority with huge advantages on the House floor. They help the leadership manage floor votes, reduce uncertainty, conserve precious floor time, protect committee compromises and bargains, provide political cover for majority members, and advance the agenda of the majority while allowing the minority to challenge selected but significant provisions of a bill. Nonetheless, their use serves to enhance partisanship, reduce opportunities for the minority, and increase the level of risk for the majority leadership. House majority Democrats lost six rules in the 103rd Congress (including one on a highly salient crime bill) – with consequent political embarrassment for the party.

House rules give the Speaker the power to select conferees. Although in practice these decisions are usually left to the committee(s) which report a measure, multiple referral and the relaxation of rigid adherence to committee seniority in the appointment of conferees does allow the Speaker discretion to choose conferees from a number of different committees, to select conferees in addition to those chosen by a committee chair (depending on his relationship with the chair and the nature of legislation under consideration), and to veto conferees he/she does not want. In July 1993, for example, Speaker Foley took the apparently unprecedented step of appointing four Democratic and six Republican freshmen to the 214-member conference on the 1993 budget reconciliation bill. He did this because many freshmen, who might be electorally vulnerable in 1994, felt the need to demonstrate to their electorates that they were taking action on the budget deficit. The Speaker also has discretion to specify which House conferees will handle particular parts of a conference bill; and is often closely involved in the conference itself, arbitrating among several committee delegations and seeking to protect the House's position *vis-à-vis* the Senate.

As a result of important institutional and contextual changes since the 1970s, the contemporary Speaker is then in a much better position that any of his predecessors since Cannon to try to ensure majority rule in the House. Even so, it is important to note that Speakers are only as powerful as their party bases will let them become.[21] If a Speaker becomes powerful, he runs the risk of losing his base of support and trust. If a Speaker decides to exert his/her authority and influence and is unsuccessful, he runs a similar risk. In early 1995, Speaker Gingrich appeared to be all-powerful because many new Republican members saw him as the reason they were elected. However, speakership power, like prime ministerial power, is basically elastic. As time passes, inevitably Gingrich will find greater difficulty in sustaining his party base and will have to relinquish some power.

Many of the day-to-day tasks of majority leadership are not undertaken by the Speaker in person. They are performed by the Majority Leader who works closely with the Speaker and other majority leaders, and is widely seen as his/her heir-apparent.[22] These tasks include: formulating the majority party's legislative programme; scheduling and guiding it through the House; keeping a watchful eye on committee chairs to ensure action is taken on legislation important to the party; and, when the party also controls the presidency, coordinating the schedule with the White House.

At the beginning of a Congress, the scheduling problem is that there is too little legislation; at the end, too much. Setting the House schedule is a thoroughly partisan exercise. Initially, it involves extensive consultation between rank and file majority members and other majority leaders. Majority leaders then determine the schedule according to two primary needs: bringing legislation to the floor which will benefit the party; and keeping off the floor certain legislation or issues which will not benefit the party, the leadership opposes, or it believes will not pass the Senate. Copies of the schedule for the forthcoming week are distributed at the weekly whip meeting and then announced by the Majority Leader on the floor on Thursday afternoon. Once a decision is made to bring legislation to the floor, the Majority Leader notifies the whips (named after the equivalent system in the British House of Commons) who then seek to galvanise rank and file support and gather information on levels of support and likely parliamentary and political problems during floor consideration.

In the 1940s and 1950s, Speaker Rayburn ran the Democratic majority in the House 'out his back pocket', relying heavily on an informed personal network of trusted colleagues for information, and bargaining with a few important committee chairs to build coalitions. Rayburn's last Whip, Carl Albert (D.OK) 'didn't have anything to do' (his chief staffer evidently asked to be reassigned to Albert's district office) while his deputy whip had 'double nothing to do'.[23] Although there was a formal whip system – consisting of a whip, a deputy whip, and about eighteen regionally-elected zone whips who were all appointed by the Speaker – it rarely operated as an efficient and reliable vehicle for gathering information on Democrats' voting intentions. A number of factors combined to bring about change in the 1970s: majority Democrats began insisting on more inclusive and participatory party organisation – many wanted to be whips – and after a Republican won the White House in 1968, the party was deprived of the services of Democratic presidents' congressional liaison staffs. The volume of legislation and floor amendments also increased and electronic voting was introduced making floor politics more unpredictable and in greater need of monitoring and involvement by leaders. As a result, the majority whip system was extended and strengthened so that by the 103rd Congress (1993–4), as many as 94 Democrats (36 per cent of the Democratic Caucus) were members, over half of whom appointed by the Speaker. As Table 5.2 shows, special efforts were made to include diverse elements of the party: Majority Whip David Bonior's chief deputy whips include two southerners, a woman, and a black (also a southerner). As the size of the majority whip organisation increased, Democratic leaders formalised a division of labour whereby the elected zone whips (who may not necessarily be party loyalists) were given primary responsibility for gathering information and counting votes, and the appointed officers were made responsible for maximising party support. Although Republican leaders created a significantly smaller whip organisation of 58 members in the 104th Congress (1995–6), it is substantially larger than their operation as the minority in the previous Congress, and significantly larger than the Democrats' organisation in the 1950s and 1960s. As in the British House of Commons, a large whip system is now an essential part of majority party management of the House.

Under Democratic control before 1995, majority whips convened weekly whip meetings which they used to obtain vital information about the wishes and moods of members, to explain their decisions to a wide cross-section of the party, and to negotiate concessions in order to maximise party support. Occasionally, they provided forums in which whips challenged leaders' decisions and ultimately influenced party strategies. As part of their effort to persuade majority Democrats not listed on the now-routine whip counts to support the party position, the Democratic leadership also created whip task forces to facilitate passage of major legislation, such as the 1993 budget reconciliation bill, four to five weeks before the leadership planned a vote. About seventy such whip task forces operated in each of the 100th, 101st and 102nd Congresses.[24] When legislation reached the floor, majority whips stationed themselves at strategic points round the floor to try to persuade wavering colleagues to support the party; with the most senior whips assigned to key positions by the entrances (see Figure 5.1). Majority members were warned that if they did not support the party, their vote would be 'remembered'. Separate lists were kept by the Majority Whip on procedural votes (considered important tests of party loyalty) and major legislation, indicating which Democrats had supported and opposed the party. These were consulted by party leaders when appointments to task forces, overseas visits, and desirable committee assignments were under consideration, and shared with the Clinton White House.

By the 1990s then it is clear that the majority leadership is now much more involved in 'working the House floor' to influence legislative outcomes than in previous decades. According to data compiled by Barbara Sinclair, whereas the majority leadership was involved in slightly less that half the items on the House's legislative agenda during the 91st Congress (1969–10), and in only 28 per cent of items was there 'major' leadership involvement, by the 101st Congress (1989–90), leadership involvement had jumped to 68 per cent of legislative items and major involvement to 54 per cent.[25]

Not only has the frequency of leadership involvement increased but also its nature. In the Congress of the 1940s, 1950s, and 1960s, involvement by House leaders consisted largely of responding to requests from committee chairs to help win floor approval for their committees' legislation. In the 1990s, majority leaders are far more involved at all stages of the legislative process. In the early stages, and following consultations with rank and file majority members, they make a determined attempt to set the House's agenda rather than leaving it to committee chairs. When a committee fails to write a bill which will satisfy most of the majority party or most of the House – and the legislation is important to the majority party – leaders intervene. Not only can majority party leaders invoke sanctions against committees – assuming they have the support of their party – even more importantly, they now have the resources and whipping organisation with which to become involved in gaining floor passage of preferred legislation. The *quid pro quo* for committees who wish to receive the leadership's assistance is that their legislation must reflect the majority party's policy agenda. Indeed, in today's party-oriented environment, committees are likely to act responsibly and positively to party pressures, not only because ordinary members and chairs fear

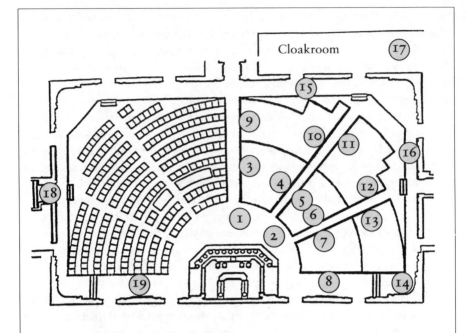

1. 1 Chief Deputy Whip;
   1 Whip Task Force Chair;
   2 At-Large Whips;
   1 Assistant Whip.

2. 1 Deputy Whip;
   3 At-Large Whips;
   1 Assistant Whip.

3. 3 At-Large Whips;
   2 Assistant Whips.

4. Floor Whip;
   3 At-Large Whips;
   1 Assistant Whip.

5. 1 Whip Task Force
   Chair; 3 At-Large Whips;
   1 Assistant Whip.

6. 2 Deputy Whips;
   3 At-Large Whips;
   2 Assistant Whips.

7. 2 Deputy Whips;
   2 At-Large Whips;
   1 Assistant Whip.

8. 3 At-Large Whips;
   2 Assistant Whips.

9. 1 Deputy Whip;
   3 At-Large Whips;
   1 Assistant Whip.

10. 1 Deputy Whip;
    3 Assistant Whips.

11. 1 Deputy Whip;
    2 At-Large Whips;
    1 Assistant Whip.

12. 1 Chief Deputy Whip;
    3 At-Large Whips;
    2 Assistant Whips.

13. 1 Deputy Whip;
    2 At-Large Whips;
    2 Assistant Whips

14. 4 At-Large Whips.

15. 1 Deputy Whip;
    3 At-Large Whips.

16. Entrance from Cannon
    and Longworth
    Buildings: Majority Whip;
    3 At-Large Whips
    (including the dean of
    the California delegation).

17. 1 Deputy Whip;
    4 At-Large Whips.

18. Entrance from Rayburn
    Building: 1 Chief Deputy
    Whip; 2 At-Large Whips;
    1 Assistant Whip.

19. 1 Chief Deputy Whip;
    2 At-Large Whips;
    2 Assistant Whips.

Figure 5.1. House Democrats' Whip plan, 1993. *Source*: Timothy J. Burger, 'Inside the Democrats' Whip Plan', *Roll Call*, September 20 1993, p. 20.

invoking the wrath of the Caucus or Conference who may remove them, but also because they recognise the legitimacy of their party's wishes. In the 1990s, there have been many examples of this type of close involvement in committees' work by majority leaders. In 1991, for example, Speaker Foley asked Majority Whip Bill Gray (D.PA) – who was also the most senior black member of the House – to work with the House Judiciary Committee and other Democrats to weaken a civil rights bill passed by the committee so that it might pass on the floor. Ultimately, Foley supported a substitute amendment on the floor which was based on a compromise bill negotiated by Gray.

Majority leaders now also monitor the flow of major legislation right from its inception to help ensure that majority members have important legislative accomplishments to report to their constituents. In the 103rd Congress (1993–4), for example, Speaker Foley and the Democratic majority leadership were heavily involved in moving forward legislation on major health care reform, crime, education, lobbying reform, clinic access, and environmental legislation – much of which was requested by the new Democratic administration. Once legislation was reported out of committee, majority leaders used the Rules Committee aggressively to structure members' choices, reduce legislative uncertainty; and once legislation reached the floor, sought to maximise party support. In the Republican-controlled 104th Congress, the majority leadership undoubtedly worked extremely closely with the committees to implement the party's Contract With America – helped substantially by a clear policy agenda, committee chairs' transparent dependence on the Speaker and the Conference, and the willingness of rank and file Republicans to follow the central leadership.

Finally, at the behest of rank and file majority members, House majority leaders have also adopted higher public and media profiles since the 1970s. Under conditions in the 1980s of Democratic control of Congress and a Republican president with formidable communication skills in the White House, Democratic leaders began to articulate alternative Democratic policy goals and deny Republican presidents a free hand in defining the political agenda. Speakers O'Neill, Wright, and Foley responded by hiring press officers and calling daily 15-minute press conferences. With a Democrat in the White House, Speaker Gingrich took this development several steps further in 1995 by insisting that his daily news conferences were televised nationwide on C-SPAN, while day-to-day responsibilities were delegated to other majority leaders. As a result of their frequent exposure on television, contemporary House speakers and majority leaders have become well-known national political figures – acting almost as leaders of the opposition, able to command air-time in the manner of the White House, and unmistakably in competition with the president. Richard Gephardt, Majority Leader between 1989 and 1994, made a point, for example, of providing the media with a Democratic message of the day relating to the party's major legislative goals. His Republican successor, Dick Armey (R.TX), adopted a similar role.

Majority leadership in the Senate

As we should expect, party organisation and leadership in the Senate is rather less formalised and weaker than in the House. There is no equivalent to the House Speaker. The Constitution made the vice president the president of the chamber but except for ceremonial occasions he/she rarely takes the presiding chair, is prohibited from speaking unless granted permission by the Senate, and cannot vote unless votes are tied.[26] In his absence, the Senate elects its own President Pro Tempore (a position which is usually awarded automatically to the most senior member of the majority party), although in practice many different senators take turns presiding over debates. Leadership of the majority party is exercised by the Majority Leader. Lacking the presiding officer's prerogatives and powers, however, he/she enjoys far less discretion over proceedings than does the House Speaker – with the result that Senate floor politics are much less predictable. Thus, in February 1993 Senate Democratic leaders and the Clinton White House were twice ambushed successfully by Republican senators. On the first occasion, they used the threat of a floor debate to force President Clinton to delay lifting the prohibition on homosexuals in the armed forces; and on the second occasion introduced and then won approval by a large majority for an amendment which restricted the admission to the US of aliens with AIDS. Had this threat been made in the House, the Speaker would likely have rescheduled the vote. Indeed, the only significant power the Senate's rules provide for the Majority Leader is the right to be recognised first when other senators are seeking recognition. Almost all other powers rest on the consent and cooperation of other senators. For example, the Majority Leader needs the consent of the Minority Leader before exercising various powers, such as referring a measure to more than one committee (multiple referral) or temporarily increasing the membership of a standing committee to ensure dominance for the majority party. When consent and cooperation are not forthcoming – as in the closing months of the 103rd Congress when Republicans saw the possibility of winning the Senate in the 1994 elections – there is little a majority leader can do except threaten to keep the Senate in session.

Like majority leaders in the House, the primary responsibility of the Senate Majority Leader is to manage the flow of legislation to and from the floor. In the absence of many procedural devices available to House majority leaders, this task in the Senate is even more difficult, more so in recent years. Proceedings are deliberately slow and unpredictable because Senate rules place so few constraints on senators' floor activities. 'The Senate', Senator J. Bennett Johnston (D.LA) once observed, 'is run for the convenience of one senator to the inconvenience of 99.'[27] Whereas the House operates according to majority rule; the Senate is run on minority rule. Getting senators to attend the floor – even to offer their own amendments, make speeches, consult on unanimous consent agreements – or to cast their vote are major problems, as any visitor to the Senate chamber can attest. As a result, roll call votes are frequently left open longer than the fifteen minutes required by Senate rules; quorum calls are frequently used to gain senators' attendance; and often votes are rerun or delayed to suit the convenience of particular senators. Since there is no general germaneness rule, individual senators may circumvent or ignore committee decisions by offering bills on the floor as amendments to almost any measure under consideration; or, they may introduce floor amendments unrelated to a bill currently under consideration. Formal rules are constantly adjusted – even ignored – so as to accommodate the wishes of individual senators. Since the 1970s, unpredictability on the Senate floor has been augmented further by a sharp increase in the number of floor amendments. In the 1950s, the Senate floor functioned primarily to ratify decisions made by the committees. After the 1970s, demands by individual senators that their bills be scheduled as well as those from committees increased; and floor amendments to committee bills became routine, with the result that committee legislation was rarely approved unamended.[28]

A variety of procedural devices are available to senators to obstruct the chamber's business. Debate on almost all legislative measures is governed by unanimous consent agreements which specify on an informal basis the length of debate, restrictions on non-germane amendments, and dates and times for final votes, and require the assent of every single senator. Requests for unanimous consent – notice of which must be given to senators in advance – inevitably leave leaders prey to the obstructionist tactics of individual senators who can simply put a 'hold' on to delay or prevent floor consideration of a bill or nomination, with the accompanying implied threat that he/she will conduct an extended debate on the measure if demands are not met. 'The rules around here are such', Senator Howard Metzenbaum (D.OH) once observed, 'that one determined member can wreak havoc with the schedules.'[29] Even if a bill or nomination is reported unanimously out of committee, there is nothing to stop an individual senator from putting a 'hold' on. Even worse, there is no public record of which senator has put on the hold or the conditions attached to it. Once a measure reaches the Senate floor, it may be subject to the well known filibuster (Rule II) whereby one or more senators may speak for an unlimited time on any bill, amendment, or motion to obstruct further business. Cloture – the process by which a filibuster may be ended other than by unanimous consent – requires an affirmative vote by at least sixty senators. The best-known filibuster occurred from February 29 to March 5 1960 when a group of southern senators debated civil rights for 125 hours and 16 minutes; the longest individual record is held by Senator Strom Thurmond (R.SC) who talked for 24 hours and 18 minutes against the 1957 Civil Rights bill. Since 1970, filibusters have been used much more frequently, often routinely, by senators of varying ideological persuasions. Including those held on civil rights measures, there were only 29 motions to invoke cloture between 1959 and 1970. After 1970, there were a mean 39 per Congress;[30] and in the 103rd Congress (1993–4), there were an unprecedented 55 filibusters. In April 1993, a solid bloc of 43 Republican senators denied Senate Majority Leader George Mitchell (D.ME) cloture on President Clinton's economic stimulus/supplemental appropriations package. In the same year, five other presidential measures were delayed or killed by Republican filibusters – the first time ever that a minority party in the Senate has used the filibuster in a partisan way to block important presidential initiatives.[31] In August 1994, Mitchell himself threatened a filibuster on health care reform unless Senate Republicans allowed votes on amendments. Subsequently, Republicans filibustered bills on campaign finance and the California desert.

Since 1970, successive majority leaders have resorted to a number of strategies to forestall obstructionism and delay in order to expedite the majority party's business. First, they have initiated changes to the Senate's rules which make it easier to cut off debate through cloture. In 1975, Majority Leader Mike Mansfield (D.MT, 1961–76) succeeded in persuading senators to reduce the two-thirds majority for cloture to three-fifths (60 votes); and in 1979, Mansfield's successor, Robert Byrd (D.WV) successfully moved to limit all floor debate after cloture to 100 hours (subsequently reduced in 1986 to 30 hours). Although the number of filibusters has not fallen, it is evident from the 101st and 102nd Congresses (1991–4) that cloture has been sought more readily – even routinely – by the Majority Leader on an increasing number of measures; and now seems to be accepted by senators as a legitimate device for managing business. Second, mirroring increasing use of restrictive rules in the House, Senate majority leaders have made increasing use of complex unanimous consent agreements – or time agreements – for tactical purposes. It is now usual for a time agreement to stipulate the subject of each floor amendment which will be permitted, the name of the senator sponsoring it (and controlling debate time in support of the amendment), the total time permitted for debate on such an amendment (including a specific time at which the amendment will be voted on),[32] and most recently prohibitions against non-germane amendments. Such time agreements are sought particularly when bills are complex and controversial, and require careful consultation with the Minority Leader. Third, during his tenure as Majority Leader between 1989 and 1994, Senator George Mitchell (D.ME) won the support of majority Democrats for reaffirming the traditional definition of holds as giving senators 24 hours' notice of a measure which concerned them or to which they objected being brought up. Finally, in a further attempt to expedite business senators agreed in 1988 to a change in their working week which provided for three five-day weeks on legislative business and every fourth week in their states.

As in the House, Majority Leaders have sought to use party organisation to encourage greater collegiality and inclusiveness within a chamber which is highly individualistic. At the prompting of rank and file senators, Senate majority leaders began in the 1980s and 1990s to use their party conferences more as collective instruments for managing rather exercising control over their parties.

Assisted by larger budgets for party and leadership activities ($5.2 million in 1994), as Minority and Majority Leader, Robert Byrd used the Democratic Conference between 1977 and 1989 to 'test the waters, figure where the significant majority is as a party and uses that to decide on the agenda, what to bring up on the floor and force to a vote.'[33] Mitchell took this process much further by consulting with and encouraging more participation by a broader range of Democratic senators. Besides appointing Daschle, a junior senator, as co-chair of a revitalised Democratic Policy Committee, Mitchell selected one of his defeated opponents in the contest for Majority Leader, Daniel Inouye (D.HI), as chair of the Democratic Steering Committee and conservative Democrat John Breaux (D.LA) first as chair of the Democratic Senatorial Campaign Committee and then as Chief Deputy Whip. Under Mitchell's leadership, various other services were made available through party channels: weekly 'whip notices' alerting party senators to forthcoming floor business; expert advice on legislation, policy problems, and political matters; electronic mail facilities; clearing houses for job applications; in-house cable television providing up-to-date information on floor developments; analyses of floor voting records; professional assistance with producing newsletters and graphics; and production assistance for broadcast messages and programmes. In contrast with Byrd's somewhat exclusive leadership style, Mitchell broadened the majority leadership structure by adding the new whip posts of Assistant Floor Leader and Chief Deputy Whip (see Table 5.3); sharing floor management duties with Majority Whip Wendell Ford (D.KY), Daschle (D.SD), and the new Assistant Floor Leader Barbara Mikulski (D.MD); and made extensive use of whip task forces to coordinate party strategy on important legislation, especially when more than one committee had jurisdiction over a bill. All these actions served to reinforce a more collegial approach to majority leadership, to solidify support for the party's position, and allow Mitchell to engage in other party activities inside and outside Congress – including the party's message in the mass media around the country.[34] So successful was Mitchell's leadership strategy that his effectiveness was compared favourably with Lyndon Johnson, the legendary cloakroom arm-twister of the 1950s. At the beginning of 1995, the newly elected Republican Majority Whip Trent Lott (R.MS) promised a more active larger whip organisation, including a Chief Deputy Whip, two deputy whips, and six regional whips (see Table 5.3).

Yet, despite the undoubted strengthening of Senate party organisation and leadership, it remains true nevertheless that the chamber's individualistic character precludes leaders from the demanding roles played by their colleagues in the House. The primary role of Senate whips is not to twist arms but to monitor floor developments and maintain communications with the party membership. As Senator Jay Rockefeller (D.WV) argued in the Senate debate on health care reform in 1994: 'The Majority Leader can only offer the rest of us the opportunity to act; he has no powers further than that. Then, it's up to us.' The task of counting votes on a floor bill – on the rare occasions they are required – falls to

Table 5.3. Senate party leaderships, 103rd and 104th Congresses

| 103RD CONGRESS | | | | 104TH CONGRESS | | | |
| Majority Democrats | | Minority Republicans | | Majority Republicans | | Minority Republicans | |
Position	Holder	Position	Holder	Position	Holder	Position	Holder
Majority Leader	George Mitchell (ME)	Minority Leader	Bob Dole (KS)	Majority Leader	Bob Dole (KS)	Minority Leader	Tom Daschle (ND)
Majority Whip	Wendell Ford (KY)	Assistant Minority Leader	Alan Simpson (WY)	Majority Whip	Trent Lott (MS)	Minority Whip	Wendell Ford (KY)
Conference Chair	George Mitchell (ME)	Conference Chair	Thad Cochran (MS)	Conference Chair	Thad Cochran (MS)	Conference Chair	Tom Daschle (ND)
Conference Secretary	David Pryor (AR)	Conference Secretary	Trent Lott (MS)	Conference Secretary	Connie Mack (FL)	Conference Secretary	Barbara Mikulski (MD)
Assistant Floor Leader	Barbara Mikulski (MD)	Deputy Whips (15)		Chief Deputy Whip	Judd Gregg (NH)	Chief Deputy Whip	John Breaux (LA)
Chief Deputy Whip	John Breaux (LA)			Deputy Whips (3)	Slade Gorton (WA) James Inhofe (OK) Rick Santorum (PA)	Deputy Whips (4)	Jeff Bingaman (NM) Joseph Lieberman (CT) Patty Murray (WA) Charles Robb (VA)
Deputy Whips (4)	Patrick Leahy (VT) Bob Graham (FL) Tom Harkin (IO) Barbara Boxer (CA)			Regional Whips (6)	Hank Brown (CO) Daniel Coats (IN) William Cohen (ME) Paul Coverdell (GA) Kay Bailey Hutchinson (TX)	Assitant Floor Leader	Byron Dorgan (ND)
Assistant Whips (4)	John Kerry (MA) Charles Robb (VA) Byron Dorgan (ND) Patty Murray (WA)						

the bill's managers, who are the relevant committee's leaders, with some assistance from the whips. The weakness of the Senate whipping system is well illustrated by Mitchell's predicament in 1991 when he requested Majority Whip Senator Wendell Ford (D.KY) to count votes on legislation to abolish the honoraria system (whereby members of Congress received fees for giving speeches at interest group functions) and award members a pay increase. Ford opposed the legislation and, not surprisingly, was not effective in rounding up votes.[35] Day-to-day chores of tracking down senators for important votes, requesting their attendance on the floor, and counting votes are left to majority and minority party staff and the conference secretaries.

Lacking the procedural prerogatives of the House Speaker and the House's elaborate whip network, Senate Majority Leaders have been confined traditionally to acting as managers, enablers, mediators, brokers, 'middlemen', even janitors,[36] of their more stately minoritarian chamber. Their attempts to lead their party in the Senate in particular directions or promote the president's agenda (if their party also controls the White House) have depended primarily on their ability to exploit the right to be recognised first; on the fairly minimal levels of deference accorded them on scheduling; and their management and bargaining skills. More recently, however, majority leaders have sought to enhance their influence by expanding their policy leadership role.

Urged on by their Senate party colleagues and benefiting from greater party cohesion and policy polarisation between the parties, they have chosen to become more assertive on policy matters. Senators Robert Byrd, Howard Baker (R.TN, 1981–4) and Mitchell, in particular, accepted responsibility for preparing fairly detailed legislative agendas for their parties. In 1987 and 1988, Byrd worked with House Speaker Jim Wright to develop a legislative agenda to counter President Reagan's, in time for the 1988 elections; and during his tenure as leader, the number of staff quadrupled and many policy specialists were added. Byrd's successor as Democratic leader George Mitchell pursued the role of policy leader particularly enthusiastically. Well before Bill Clinton proposed a health care reform bill, in 1991 Mitchell worked with Senators Kennedy (D.MA), Riegle (D.MI), and Rockefeller (D.WV) to produce a Democratic health care bill for the Senate. Between 1991 and 1994, Mitchell was intimately involved in deciding the content and political strategy to be adopted on almost all important legislation brought to the Senate floor: including the civil rights bill in 1991; the Brady (handgun control) bill and major energy and transportation legislation in 1992; budget reconciliation in 1993; and in 1994 legislation on family leave compensation, voter registration, abortion counselling, campaign finance, and many aspects of foreign policy. To facilitate stronger policy leadership, Mitchell expanded the leadership staff by over 50 per cent and revitalised the Democratic Policy Committee, appointing one of his loyal supporters as co-chair and providing for a budget of $1.2 million (1993). Given the institutional and political constraints precluding the type of substance-oriented policy leadership found in European parliaments, and the formidable power and influence exercised by individual senators, these policy-leading efforts were truly significant.

As the Senate Majority Leader's policy leadership role has become more important, so has his/her ability to speak for the party in public – particularly in front of the television cameras – become an important part of the job. In the 1950s, Majority Leader Lyndon Johnson (D.TX, 1955–61) was a very effective spokesperson for the Democratic majority; but at a time when television was not so important in politics, an ability to perform well as the party's spokesperson was not seen as important, and was not a major factor in choosing a majority leader. Johnson's successors, Mike Mansfield and Robert Byrd, were not very effective.[37] Since the 1980s, however, as the demands of the job changed, as Senate Democrats witnessed the greater involvement of O'Neill and Wright in the House, and as the national press concentrated their coverage of the Senate increasingly on senior members in leadership positions,[38] the leader's ability to perform well on television became crucial. Byrd's Republican successor after 1980 – Bob Dole (R.KS), a leader known for his partisan wit and perceptive comments – was particularly adept at ensuring his party gained maximum press exposure. George Mitchell was elected Majority Leader in 1989 at least partly because of his effectiveness on television during the House–Senate Iran-Contra hearings in 1986. As leader, Mitchell was particularly sensitive to the public relations demands of his post, particularly before 1993 when Republicans took full advantage of the media attention on a Republican president. Like Dole, Mitchell regularly appeared with committee chairs at press conferences on major legislative initiatives and held daily press briefings while the Senate was in session. He appeared twice as many times on television per year as his predecessor Byrd.[39] One of the first actions of Mitchell's successor as Democratic leader, Tom Daschle (D.SD), in the 104th Congress (1995–6) was to create a new Democratic Committee on Technology and Communications to improve the party's public relations and articulate better its policies.

The central role of parties in organising Congress, selecting leaders, structuring decision-making, facilitating agreement, and informing the public and the media of the work of government leads immediately to the important question: how much influence do parties have on congressional outcomes? To what extent does party *qua* party shape decision-making? Do congressional parties offer genuine policy alternatives? Are the voting responses of Democrats and Republicans different? And how much are party differences based on ideology and principle and how much on satisfying constituents and winning re-election?

Congressional decision-making

Considerable scholarly attention has been given to how and why members of Congress decide how they will vote on the hundreds of roll call – or yea and nay – votes held on the House and Senate floors in any one session. As a result, although important differences of interpretation remain over which factors are most important and when they are important, we now know a great deal about the various influences on roll call voting and the calculus of congressional decision-making.

Party influence

In most of the literature on congressional politics, the traditional measure of party voting in each chamber is fairly minimal: the percentage of recorded floor votes on which *a bare majority* of one party opposes a majority of the other party. Figure 5.2 shows that in only 15 of the 42 years since 1953 have a majority of House Democrats opposed a majority of Republicans on more than half the recorded votes; in the Senate, this occurred in only 7 years. In the late 1960s and 1970s, the percentage often dropped below 30 per cent in the House and below 40 per cent in the Senate. Even at the high levels achieved in both houses since 1985,[40] party voting is weak – especially when compared with the British House of Commons. If a party vote was defined as one in which 90 per cent of one party opposes 90 per cent of the other party very few votes in Congress would qualify.[41] In the 104th Congress, for example, Democrats voted unanimously on only 20 out of 1,094 House votes (less than 3 per cent) and on only 66 out of 724 Senate votes (9 per cent). These low levels of partisanship should not be surprising given the discussion in Chapter 3. As Melissa Collie has observed: 'When candidates tend to win on their own outside the legislature, they tend to act on their own inside the legislature.'[42]

Research by Patterson and Caldeira has shown that House party voting tended to increase sharply when party conflict among the electorate is high – notably during periods of polarisation on economic, labour-management, and social justice issues – and when the House and the president are controlled by the same party. In the less partisan Senate, the most important factor is presidential leadership, particularly when the president is of the same party as the Senate majority (as in 1993). As might be anticipated, newly elected members tend to be more partisan than their seniors. In 1993, for example, House Democratic freshmen were 6 per cent more partisan than all House Democrats; House Republicans, 5 per cent more partisan; Senate Democrats, 8 per cent more partisan; and Senate Republicans, 10 per cent more partisan. Other research by Rohde has concluded that four sets of factors are crucial. The most important are electoral: policy partisanship increases when members of one party are elected with constituency preferences similar to their party colleagues but different from those of the

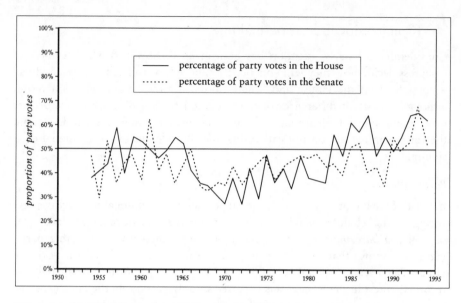

Figure 5.2. Number of times a majority of one party voted against a majority of the other party in the House and Senate, 1954–1994.

opposing party. So, the election of many liberal Democrats in the late 1950s and 1960s led directly to a strengthening of Democratic Party organisation in the House (the creation of the Democratic Study Group and the reinvigoration of the House Democratic Caucus) which in turn produced increased party voting. In a similar way, the enfranchisement and mobilisation of black voters in the south led directly to the election of less conservative southern Democrats which in turn led to greater Democratic party unity. The second set of factors are institutional differences between the House and the Senate. As we emphasised in the earlier discussion, House majority leaders have a stronger array of powers at their disposal than do Senate leaders who must contend with the prerogatives and privileges of individual senators. Third are personal factors – such as the personality, style, and ideology of leaders; for example, Jim Wright compared with Tom Foley; Bob Michel compared with Newt Gingrich. Finally, the nature of the legislative agenda must be taken into account; for example, votes on foreign policy are generally less partisan than those on domestic policy.[43]

Even though partisanship is weaker than in the British House of Commons and other legislatures, important policy issues do divide Democrats and Republicans. Major studies by Clausen and Sinclair found that the congressional parties were divided on agricultural assistance, social welfare, and economic management issues, and on legislation favouring labour unions and the poor, and regulating private businesses. Party was a less useful guide to voting on civil rights,

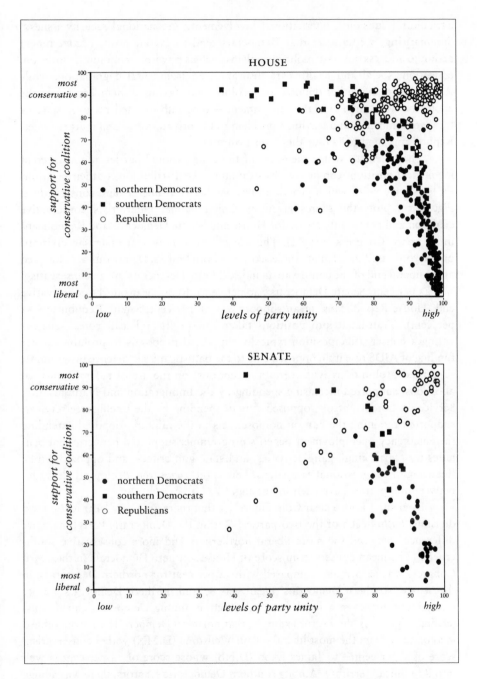

Figure 5.3. House and Senate conservatism and partisanship, 103rd Congress. *Source: Congressional Quarterly.*

agricultural subsidies, international involvement, and national security issues.[44] Summarising, we can say that Democrats tend to favour positive government action to address domestic policy problems such as poverty, economic dislocation, education, social and health care insurance, environmental degradation, while Republicans have either opposed such solutions or favoured them less. Given the choice between involving the government – especially the federal over state or local government – and leaving a problem to the private sector and market forces, Republicans tend to favour the latter positions.

The extent to which members of the congressional parties adopt different ideological positions can be seen by examining the distributions of their positions on legislative votes which generate divisions between liberals and conservatives. Figure 5.3 plots the scores given by Congressional Quarterly's conservative coalition and party unity scores for House and Senate Democrats and Republicans in the 103rd Congress (1993–4). The scattergrams show sharp partisan divisions on the votes used to calculate these scores: in both houses, Democrats are clustered at the liberal end of the conservatism index (House Democrats' mean conservatism was 44 per cent, Senate Democrats', 40 per cent), Republicans to the conservative end (House Republicans' mean support was 88 per cent, Senate Republicans 83 per cent). Translated into positions taken on specific roll call votes, senators voting a conservative position typically supported proposals to prohibit further funding of AIDS research; opposed cuts to the ballistic missile defence programme; supported prohibitions (with certain exceptions) on the use of federal funds for abortions; supported increasing spending by the Immigration and Naturalisation Service on border patrols; opposed cuts in spending by the intelligence services; supported retaining the ban on homosexuals in the military; opposed extending the emergency unemployment benefits programme; supported new criminal penalties for 'carjacking', gang activities, and state gun crimes; and opposed public financing of congressional campaigns.[45] Since the 1970s, the ideological cleavages between the parties have been increasing.[46]

Even so, it is also clear from Figure 5.3 that there are fairly clear ideological divisions *within* each of the two parties. Within the Democratic Party, there are differences between the more liberal northerners and more conservative southerners. (The mean conservatism score of House southern Democrats in the 103rd Congress was 62 per cent compared with 32 per cent for northern Democrats; in the Senate, southern Democrats' mean was 67 and northern Democrats' 30 per cent.) However, even a north–south distinction among Democrats can be misleading. Figure 5.3 shows, for example, that northern Democratic senators ranged ideologically from the most liberal – Paul Wellstone (D.MN) with a conservatism score of 5 per cent – to James Exon (D.NB) whose score of 74 per cent is well into Republican territory. Among southern Democratic senators, there was a huge disparity between Richard Shelby (D.AL, who switched to the Republicans in 1994) who had a conservatism score of 95 per cent – very similar to those of many Republicans – and Dale Bumpers (D.AR) with a score of 45 per cent, well into northern Democratic territory. Similar wide discrepancies exist among House Democrats. Narrower discrepancies also exist among Republicans, especially in the Senate as Figure 5.3 shows. For example, Senators James Jeffords (R.VT), Mark Hatfield (R.OR), and John Chafee (R.RI) are all positioned well within the Democrat's ideological territory, and a considerable distance from party colleagues such as Jesse Helms (R.NC) and Phil Gramm (R.TX). Of course, much depends on the sample of roll call votes and, therefore, the measure of ideology used. If a measure of support for labour unions was used – an index compiled by the American Federation of Labor-Congress of Industrial Organisations – the differences between northern and southern Democrats is much narrower: just 9 per cent difference (northern Democrats' mean score was 84 per cent; southern Democrats', 75 per cent.) Even so, the coalitional nature of congressional parties is one of their basic features and often results in cross-partisan or bipartisan voting patterns such as the coalition of conservative Democrats and Republicans.[47]

The inevitable corollary to such ideological diversity is that there are wide variances in the degrees to which House members and senators support their party colleagues. As Figure 5.3 shows, one House Democrat – Gene Taylor (D.MS) – supported his party on only 37 per cent of party unity votes, while in the Senate Jeffords supported his Republican colleagues on less than 4 in 10 votes. Even so, in the 103rd Congress, 82 per cent of House Democrats and 78 per cent of House Republicans, and 87 per cent of Senate Democrats and 79 per cent of Senate Republicans supported their party colleagues on at least 80 per cent of party unity votes in their respective chambers.

Having established that party, ideology, and region structure congressional voting, let us now consider the dynamics of legislative voting: how do members of Congress decide which way to cast their votes? What are the most important factors which influence their choices? Focusing on floor decision-making, we will begin by considering the question posed earlier, concerning the role and influence of central party leaders, then explain the importance of other influences, and finally report an explanation of how members decide.

Party leaders' influence

Although central party leaders have certainly become more involved and more decisive in organising their parties and chambers, as we showed earlier, their influence and authority remain far from overwhelming – and is certainly much weaker than that of their predecessors in the nineteenth century, and their con-temporaries in the British House of Commons. Contemporary party leaders in Congress lack what former House member and student of Congress Richard Bolling has called 'the institutional tools of leadership'.[48] In the contemporary electoral context, they also lack the clearly defined constituency bases of their nineteenth-century predecessors, which helped produce cohesive parties and far stronger party leadership. If contemporary leaders need the vote of a recalcitrant party colleague on the floor, they cannot threaten with any conviction to influence whether or not the colleague receives his/her party's nomination at the next election. They may be able to deny such a colleague a preferred committee assignment or even a committee chair. However, other constraints – such as the seniority norm or the need to represent different ideological sections of the party or the fear that a colleague may defect to the other party – may preclude such action. At the beginning of the 104th Congress (1995–6), even Speaker Gingrich felt compelled for the sake of party unity to nominate a number of senior moderates to committee chairs.

Central party leaders do not enjoy the powers of parliamentary leaders because their party colleagues have been unwilling to give them such powers. Their effectiveness depends much more on a combination of personal and contextual factors: their leadership styles (are they assertive, accommodating, and skilled in parliamentary strategy?); the institutional context (what is their power *vis-à-vis* committee chairs?), the partisan context (what is their party's majority? how cohesive is their party?); and the issue context (what type of issue is involved in a particular vote?). The interactions of central leaders with the president and the wider external environment – including constituents, interest groups, and the mass media – are also important.

In the contexts of split-party control, a cohesive Democratic majority in the House, and budget deficit policy constraints, Speaker Tip O'Neill (D.MA) pursued 'a participatory, middleman style' in the early 1980s which 'encouraged members to express their preferences, and for the leader to consider them before deciding how to act'. In contrast, O'Neill's successor, Jim Wright (D.TX), 'forged a leader-initiated relationship with House Democrats in the context of an economic recession, a Republican president weakened by the Iran-Contra scandal, and the Democrats regaining control of the Senate'.[49] The leadership style of Speaker Foley (D.WA) was different again. Finding he had to contend with powerful committee chairs, he pursued a leadership strategy which was much more conciliatory and respectful of the policy-making roles of committees and, according to critics, led to some embarrassing defeats.[50] In the more individualistic Senate, Majority Leaders Dole and Mitchell pursued selective approaches to bill management and policy leadership. Only on very important issues – such as budget reconciliation, foreign policy, health care, and environmental issues – did they maximise their efforts to influence their party colleagues.[51]

How significant are central party leaders' actions in encouraging party voting? How much attention do legislators – particularly those who are party colleagues – pay to their leaders when they make their yeas and nays on the chamber floors? The answer, not surprisingly, is very little. The positions and pleas of central party leaders evidently do not figure prominently in the decision-making calculus of members of Congress. In his study of House floor voting,

John Kingdon found that House members spontaneously mentioned their party leadership as an influence on their decisions only 10 per cent of the time. It was of major importance for only 5 per cent of Kingdon's sample of members, and of no importance at all on 63 per cent of votes. The influence exercised by committee chairs and ranking members was equally unimpressive.[52] Of six 'actors' considered as possible influences on House members' floor voting decisions – constituency, fellow members of Congress, party leadership, interest groups, the administration, and congressional staff – party leaders were the least important – although the leadership of the president's party was found to have more (but still minimal) influence on its members, particular juniors, than the leadership of the non-presidential party.

Research by Froman and Ripley identified certain conditions under which House Democratic leadership in the 1960s was effective. Their research showed that party colleagues are likely to be most responsive to the calls of their leaders when those leaders are committed, active, and in agreement with one another; when the issue is seen as procedural rather than substantive; when the visibility of an issue to the general public and/or the action to be taken is low; when the state delegation is not involved in bargaining for specific provisions; and, most importantly, when constituency opposition is slight.[53] These findings reinforce the point made earlier that, unlike in parliamentary systems where party is normally the overwhelming influence and leaders make policy decisions which receive almost automatic support from followers – almost in a top-down manner – party leadership in the Congress is much more conditional. Congressional parties act responsibly – in the sense that they devise policies which are offered to the electorate and implement them if elected as the majority – in extremely limited circumstances. Only when sufficient party legislators in Congress can agree important policy proposals can they behave as disciplined parties. Only in these circumstances will the use of the tools of leadership (the Rules Committee, scheduling powers, the whip system, etc.) be effective.[54]

Constituency influence

It is, of course, voters who elect and reelect members of Congress – not parties. What happens when the position of a member's party or party leadership conflicts with his/her perception of constituency opinion? Kingdon's study found that House party leaders' positions conflicted with party members' perceptions of constituency opinions on about half the votes in his sample – although often House members did not see a conflict between their party leadership's position and their constituents'.[55] To what extent then, and under what conditions does constituency influence floor decision-making? And what is the relationship between party and constituency?

It is not difficult to find examples of constituency opinions influencing a legislator's vote. After voting with 57 other Democrats against a rule providing for a ban on assault weapons, Congressman Charles Wilson (D.TX) explained that the alternative would be 'just like putting a gun in your mouth in rural Texas'. On the same vote, Congressman Christopher Shays (R.CT) also defied his party, disregarded threats that he would be denied his party's financial support in the 1994 elections, and explained the importance of the legislation for crime prevention programmes in his district.[56] That members of Congress frequently respond positively to perceived constituency opinion is supported by Kingdon's study which shows that legislators are likely to vote with their constituents on almost half the votes on which they recognise their constituency has taken a position. Members mentioned constituency factors as important on over one-third of votes (more than any other influence) and considered constituency to be of major or decisive importance on almost four out of ten votes.[57]

In one sense, finding that the roll call decisions of members of Congress accord regularly with the wishes of their constituents is not surprising. Presumably, voters elect representatives whose views reflect their own; those representatives *should* cast their votes in Congress to reflect the views of people they represent. Indeed, there is a very strong empirical relationship between the ideology of districts and the ideological positions of their representatives in Congress: liberals tend to represent liberal districts; conservatives, conservative districts. Figure 5.4 shows this relationship for the 103rd Congress using Bill Clinton's percentage of

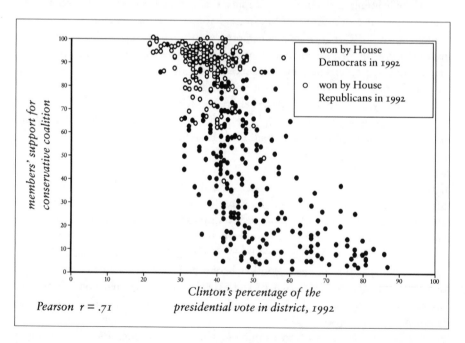

Figure 5.4. House members' conservatism and district conservatism.

the presidential vote in each House district as a surrogate for a district's conservatism (i.e. assuming that more liberal districts would have voted for Clinton; more conservative districts for George Bush).

The relationship between legislators and constituents is, however, more complex than this. Some constituents are (or are anticipated to be) more attentive than others. When these attentive constituents feel strongly about a particular issue – such as gun owners in a rural district on the issue of gun control laws or car makers in an urban district about air pollution legislation – the legislator is wise to respond by voting his constituency. Thus, in August 1994 when Congress was considering health care legislation – an issue which generated intense feelings among voters – Congressman Peter Hoagland (D.NB), for example, explained his opposition to a bill offered by his own party leaders in terms of his own policy preferences and those of his constituents:

> I have very serious problems with the Gephardt [health care] bill because it is really a Trojan Horse for a government-run single-payer system . . . In addition . . . [the bill] would also take customers away from the insurance industry. In Omaha [Hoagland's home district], we have nine insurance companies including Mutual of Omaha which employs 10,000 people, and Blue Cross/ Blue Shield of Nebraska, which employs many thousands of people. Now, if we move 75 million more Americans into Medicare, why then these people can't buy health insurance policies from the private sector, from Mutual of Omaha or Blue Cross/Blue Shield.[58]

Indeed, Kingdon found in his study that members and their constituents were in remarkable agreement on those issues most salient to the member's constituents and where constituency opinions were most intense.

Health care was obviously a major issue in 1994. In the 1990s, other issues – such as abortion, gun control, and welfare – also attract the intense attention of constituents and interest groups. Members of Congress do not need, however, to vote in agreement with their constituencies on every issue; only on those about which voters feel intensely. Many issues do not attract the intense attention of constituents. So, if a legislator feels strongly about an issue and perceives that his/her constituents are generally ambivalent or indifferent, the member may be able to vote his/her own policy preferences with impunity and ignore constituents' views. Even when constituent opinion is intense, so long as the member avoids a series of 'wrong' votes against various constituency groups (which may be as few as two or three in any session), the member can usually afford to vote his own policy preferences. For members in marginal seats, however – like Congressman Hoagland – there is an absolute need to avoid 'wrong' votes and to stick fairly closely to the views of 'the median voter' on most issues if they are to avoid defeat.[59] But, for all members there is always the risk that 'latent or unfocussed opinions can quickly be transformed into intense and very real opinions with enormous political repercussions'.[60] Legislative term limits, the savings and loan and House bank scandals are good examples of latent issues erupting in recent elections.

The influence of constituency on legislative voting also varies with the type of issue and according to how constituency is defined. Some issues more than others invite constituency influence. In an extensive study of patterns of House and Senate floor voting between the 1980s, Clausen found that constituency influence was particularly strong on civil rights legislation and proposals to limit farm subsidies; but was much weaker in voting on legislation concerned with social welfare, agricultural assistance, international involvement, and national security commitments.[61]

Constituency influence on legislative voting depends not only on the intensity of local opinions and on the type of issue under consideration but also on how a member's constituency is defined. In Chapter 3, we referred to Fenno's concepts of nested constituencies: members of Congress perceive a personal constituency, a primary constituency, a re-election constituency, and a geographic constituency. A member of Congress can depend on the first two almost willy nilly. It is the re-election constituency – the voters from whom he expects to receive support at the next election – that he/she needs to cultivate and, presumably, will be influenced by. How members of Congress cultivate different re-election constituencies can be seen from the relationships between senators from the same state who are members of different parties. Many same-state senators' ideological positions differ sharply. In the 103rd Congress (1993–4), for example, Washington state was represented by Republican Slade Gorton and Democrat Patty Murray (conservative coalition scores of 90 and 24). Other states' senators also show similar disparities: New York senators Moynihan (Democrat) and D'Amato (Republican) had scores of 16 and 82 respectively; and Iowa senators Harkin (Democrat) and Grassley (Republican) had scores of 13 and 75. These differences are explained by members of Congress having different re-election constituencies: in the cases of the Republican senators, conservative re-election constituencies; for Democrats, liberal ones.[62] The implication is that legislators' voting records are responses to discrete blocs of voters – their re-election constituencies – as well as reflections of their own policy preferences. We will return to this important point later. Before doing so, however, let us consider briefly another factor in congressional decision-making: the question of interest group influence.

Interest group influence

Interest group influence is a favourite topic of discussion in relation to congressional decision-making. For a variety of reasons, Congress is the natural focus of interest group activity: (i) one of the institution's most important functions is to represent different interests; (ii) its decentralised institutional structure and weak parties promote interest group activity; (iii) the system of constituency representation and the practice of contemporary electoral politics encourage members of Congress to become sensitive to the interests of powerful constituency groups; and (iv) the level of ideological conflict inside and outside Congress is not high. More recent developments further encourage the view that interest groups are influential: the proliferation of groups and their political action committees since the 1970s; an increased tendency to locate their headquarters in Washington, D.C.; their enhanced information processing capacities, enabling them to mobilise their members more efficiently; the development of single-issue lobbying (on issues such as abortion and gun control); the further erosion of party activities and capacities; the growing importance of public interest groups such as Common Cause and various consumer and environmental groups; and the intensification of lobbying activities by business corporations, state and local government, and foreign interests.[63]

Interest groups have much to offer in the legislative process and, thereby, influence policy outcomes. Interest group lobbyists have expert knowledge of Congress' internal operations and have access to influential committee and sub-committee members. They have access to vital policy information which members of Congress need. Many have access to enormous financial resources which can be directed in the form of campaign contributions and other electoral assistance to well-placed members on relevant committees. Last, but by no means least, they have the capacity to mobilise their membership in the districts and states of House members and senators – often through high volumes of 'inspired' constituency communications orchestrated by national officials in Washington – in support of or opposition to specific bills and amendments which affect their interests.

Whether and to what extent they exert influence on legislative voting is a matter of considerable scholarly and popular debate. Kingdon's study found that interest groups were neither the most nor the least important influences on how House members voted on the floor. Members spontaneously mentioned interest groups as being important influences in just under one-third of cases – less than the percentage of times constituency and fellow members were mentioned, but more frequently than party leaderships. As with constituency influence, the salience of the specific legislative issue is crucial – the higher the salience, the greater the importance of interest groups in members' calculations. When, however, the effects of other actors were controlled, interest group influence was almost nil. Kingdon found this to be true regardless of legislators' party, their seniority, or the nature of their district. The main explanation for this conclusion is that members of Congress do not consider interest group influence in their decision-making calculations *unless an interest group has some connection with their constituencies*. Indeed, many members dismiss the efforts of Washington-based lobbyists if they have no connection with their constituency because electoral sanctions cannot be used against them.[64] The importance of a constituency connection can be seen from the example of the National Rifleman's Association

(NRA) which orchestrated opposition to an omnibus crime bill in August 1984. The organisation's political strength lies not so much in its wealth or the skill of its lobbyists in Washington (although these are important) but in its membership of three million intensely loyal gun owners who are organised into potent well-organised grass-roots contact organisations. The same is true of other mass membership groups, like veterans' organisations who successfully opposed attempts to abolish the House and Senate Veterans' Affairs committees in 1994.

However, whether an interest group influences legislative voting on a specific bill depends on a number of other factors, including whether or not legislators feel they have no alternative but to support a group; whether or not powerful interest groups are on both sides of a legislative conflict; and whether or not interests are seeking to defend the policy status quo. These same factors also determine whether the giving of campaign contributions to well-placed committee members influences congressional outcomes. A study of House voting on the Firearms Owners Protection Act of 1986 concludes, for example, that contributions made by the NRA and Handgun Control did affect how members voted.[65] However, other studies have not found a positive relationship. A broad study of 120 PACs emphasised the diversity of their organisations, goals and strategies; and found that their 'return on investment' was limited to gaining access to legislators' time.[66] In many cases, interests on different sides of an issue contribute to many different legislators, thereby diffusing the political influence of any one set of interests.[67] Although systematic evidence that PACs buy or rent votes does not exist, a study of PACs' influence in committees found that the receipt of campaign contributions increased members' attendance and involvement in legislative negotiations in order to assist contributors.[68]

While it would be foolish to conclude that interest groups never influence members' voting decisions, there is no convincing evidence that the practice is widespread. Indeed, it is likely that interest group influence will be constrained by other actors and variables, including the legislator's re-election constituency, party, and his/her own policy values and ideological predispositions. However, separating these diverse influences is in practice an intractable problem which is almost impossible to answer: do House members and senators vote the same way as an interest group *because of* that interest group's activities? Or, would the legislator have voted the same way as the group in any case because he/she supports the values and interests the group espouses? A study of congressional voting on national defence issues found, for example, that defence contractors PACs gave more money to conservatives than to liberals 'not because conservatives need more financial support to influence their votes but because the PACs recognise the powerful effects of ideological predispositions on defense voting.'[69] We will investigate further the importance of legislators' personal policy preferences in the next section.

Legislators' policy preferences and the calculus of decision-making

Earlier in this chapter, we explained how the yeas and nays of House members and senators on floor votes may be arrayed along liberal–conservative continua, and how legislators' voting patterns vary according to the type of policy issue under consideration. Research on congressional committees has reached similar conclusions.[70] Legislators' policy preferences are reinforced by the views of their re-election constituencies back home, by their wish to vote consistently on the same or similar issues over time, and by their choice of congressional colleagues from whom they accept information and advice on how they should vote.[71] An important question raised by these findings is whether the general policy attitudes and dispositions of members of Congress (whether they are conservative or liberal) can readily be applied to specific bills and amendments which are often highly technical, whose ideological or policy content is not readily apparent, and on which members do not have well-informed or intense opinions.[72]

In his influential study, Kingdon provides what is undoubtedly the most convincing explanation of how members of Congress make their individual voting decisions, and how legislators' ideological predispositions and policy preferences interact with constituency, party, and interest group influences.

Following an examination of the roles and influence of various factors acting upon House members' voting decisions – the legislator's constituency, trusted congressional colleagues, party leaders, interest groups, the administration, and congressional staff – Kingdon concludes that no one actor is preeminently influential. He interprets the process by which individual legislators reach their voting decisions as a sequential search for consensus.[73] Within what he calls 'the consensus mode of decision' (see Figure 5.5), the legislator proceeds through a sequence of five steps. *First*, he/she decides (often subconsciously or implicitly) whether or not an impending vote is controversial. If the vote is not controversial, he/she votes with all other members; given the pressures of time on legislators, there is little point in studying an issue over which there is no controversy. If there is controversy, the legislator proceeds to the next decision-making step. At this *second* step, he/she determines whether or not there is a consensus among his/her immediate 'field of forces' – those people who are members of the legislator's re-election constituency, trusted congressional colleagues, party leaders, interest group allies, the administration (if of the same party), and staff with whom he/she normally agrees – *and* his/her own policy attitudes on the particular issue. If, at this stage, the members' personal field of forces (which will be configured differently for every single legislator) is free of conflict, he/she votes with the consensus. If, however, there is no consensus within the member's field of forces (for example, elements of his/her re-election constituency may oppose one another, or interest group allies may oppose the president of his/her party), the legislator proceeds to a *third* step. At this step, the legislation determines whether any of his/her personal goals are particularly important, considering first

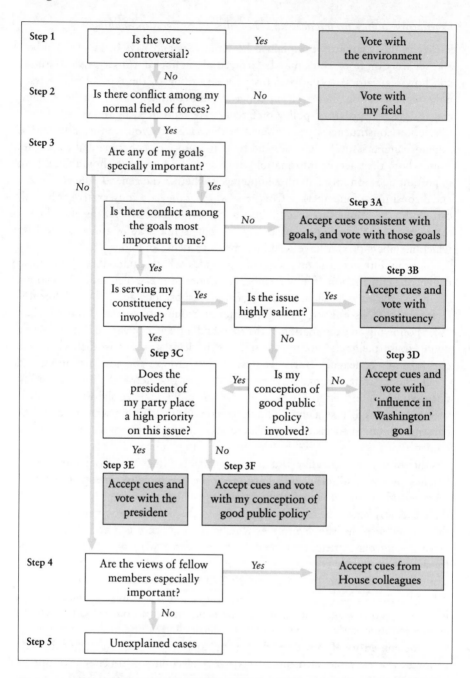

Figure 5.5. Kingdon's model of House floor decision-making. *Source*: John W. Kingdon, *Congressmen's Voting Decisions*, 3rd edn (Ann Arbor, MI: The University of Michigan Press, 1989), p. 244.

whether serving the constituency is most important (as Congressmen Wilson and Shays did on the 1994 crime bill), then whether the president of his/her party is placing a high priority on the issue, and then whether good public policy is the most important goal. If the legislator decides one of his/her goals is particularly important in making the particular voting decision, he/she votes with the goal. If none of these goals is important enough, he/she proceeds to the *fourth* step and votes in most cases with trusted congressional colleagues, sometimes quite blindly. A *fifth* step (unexplained cases) is provided for members whose decision-making process does not follow the consensus mode.

The plausibility of Kingdon's explanation is that members of Congress do not have to involve themselves in an extended search for information or to review systematically the opinions of *all* actors who may conceivably influence a voting decision. These few simple decision rules govern almost all voting decisions made on the House floor (and probably in committee too). A few points are worth emphasising. First, note that if there is no consensus among the legislator's field of forces, he/she considers first whether there is a constituency interest. Although he/she may not ultimately vote with his/her constituency, constituency is always the first consideration – hardly surprising since most members of Congress wish to be re-elected. Second, note that if the constituency is not involved, and there is a conflict between pursuing good public policy and building personal influence in Washington, the member votes with his policy goals, unless he/she is of the same party as the president and the president identifies the vote as a 'must pass' issue, in which case he/she supports the president. The implication in this sequence is that the legislator's strong personal policy dispositions are more important than considerations of personal prestige and influence, such as supporting the party leadership or trading favours. Third, note the importance once again of the salience of an issue. If the constituency goal is involved, the member weighs serving constituents against policy and/or prestige goals. If the issue has implications for the constituency *and* is highly salient (attentive constituents will notice and disapprove of a vote), constituency considerations determine the voting choice. If, on the other hand, the issue is not highly salient the member has greater latitude to allow his/her policy views and/or prestige considerations to determine the decision.

The key elements in these sequences then are the search for consensus, and the importance of members' own policy preferences in deviating from a consensus. As Kingdon explains, the legislator:

> prefers his own policy attitude, unless he is pulled away from it under specified circumstances. Thus, a high-priority request from a president of his own party or an intense constituency preference on a high-salience issue may overrule his own attitude. Short of those rather extraordinary circumstances, the legislator's goal of promoting his conception of good public policy carries the day. In the event that this policy goal is not relevant to

the decision, for example, when the member does not care much about the issue, then he prefers the constituency in the high-salience case and the intra-Washington influences in the rest.[74]

Despite the importance attached to legislators' own policy attitudes, Kingdon's is not an ideological explanation of decision-making. Instead, policy attitudes are general long-term factors which help determine whether or not a legislator will be susceptible to specific voting cues provided by short-term influences such as party leaders, interest groups, the president, congressional colleagues, and staff. The stronger a member's long-term predispositions, the less likely are short-term influences to influence his/her vote. Implicit in the sequence of decision rules is that members of Congress behave purposively. Legislators are not just swept along by constituents, interests groups, the president, party leaders, and other actors; they have discretion and autonomy in interpreting information and selecting cues.

Implicit in this view, furthermore, is that on some occasions a particular legislator may be persuaded to vote a particular way for purely idiosyncratic, personal reasons. No matter how complex legislative voting models are, they cannot explain why, for example, such a strong opponent of government regulation as Senator Strom Thurmond (R.SC) strongly supports legislation requiring warning labels in advertising for alcoholic drinks (his daughter was knocked down by a drunken driver); or why Senator Robert Dole (R.KS) has developed a special concern for Armenia (an Armenian doctor helped him recover from serious injuries in World War II).[75]

In Chapters 6–8, the focus shifts away from Congress to the presidency. We begin by examining the institutional development of the office, and then consider in successive chapters how the contemporary institution is organised, how the office interacts with the American electorate, and how presidents decide.

Notes

1   Charles O. Jones, 'Senate Party Leadership in Public Policy' in David C. Kozak and John D. Macartney (eds), *Congress and Public Policy. A Source Book of Documents and Readings* (Homewood, IL: Dorsey, 1982), p. 175.

2   David E. Price, *The Congressional Experience. A View from the Hill* (Boulder and Oxford: Westview Press, 1992), p. 82.

3   See Barbara Sinclair, 'Parties in Congress: New Roles and Leadership Trends', in L. Sandy Maisel (ed.), *The Parties Respond. Changes in American Parties and Campaigns* (Boulder, CO and Oxford: Westview Press, 1994).

4   William F. Connelly and John J. Pitney, *Congress' Permanent Minority? Republicans in the US House* (Latham, MD and London: Littlefield Adams, 1994), p. 43.

5   For example, in 1981, the Democratic Caucus removed Congressman Phil Gramm (D.TX) from the Budget Committee, following his support for the Reagan Administration's budgetary policies and betrayal of Democratic legislative strategies to House Republicans. Gramm immediately resigned from the Caucus and became a

Republican, sought and won re-election to the House in a special election, and was reassigned to the Budget Committee by his new party ahead of five other Republicans with greater seniority.

6   John B. Bader and Charles O. Jones, 'Republican Parties in Congress: Bicameral Differences', in Lawrence C. Dodd and Bruce I. Oppenheimer (eds), *Congress Reconsidered*, 5th edn (Washington, D.C.: Congressional Quarterly Press, 1993), p. 311.

7   Quoted in Connelly and Pitney, *Congress' Permanent Minority?*, p. 44.

8   William F. Connelly, 'The House Republican Policy Committee. Then and Now'. Paper presented to the Annual Meeting of the American Political Science Association, Washington, D.C., September 1989.

9   John J. Pitney, 'Republican Party Leadership in the US House'. Paper presented to the Annual Meeting of the American Political Science Association, San Francisco, August–September 1990.

10 Donald C. Baumer, 'Senate Democratic Leadership in the 101st Congress' in Allen D. Hertzke and Ronald M. Peters (eds), *The Atomistic Congress. An Interpretation of Congressional Change* (Armonk, NY and London: M. E. Sharpe, 1992), pp. 293–332, 305; and Steven S. Smith, 'Forces of Change in Senate Party Leadership and Organisation' in Dodd and Oppenheimer, *Congress Reconsidered*, 5th edn, p. 274. On the Republican Policy Committee in the 1970s, see John G. Stewart, 'Central Party Organs in Congress' in Harvey C. Mansfield (ed.), *Congress Against Itself* (New York: Praeger, 1975), pp. 20–33.

11 John J. Rhodes, *The Futile System* (Garden City, NY: EMP Publications, 1976), p. 30.

12 Timothy J. Burger, 'DeLay Won't Get Budget Bonior Had', *Roll Call*, December 19 1994, pp. 1 and 17.

13 Previously 'non-partisan' offices – such as the Clerk, the Chief Administrative Officer, the House Inspector-General, the Sergeant at Arms, the Parliamentarian, and even the Chaplain, responsible for running the House's day-to-day operations now fall directly under the Speaker's control.

14 On the growth of multiple referrals, see Roger H. Davidson, Walter J. Oleszek, and Thomas Kephart, 'One Bill, Many Committees: Multiple Referrals in the House of Representatives, *Legislative Studies Quarterly*, 13 (1988), pp. 3–28; and Garry Young and Joseph Cooper, 'Multiple Referral and the Transformation of House Decision Making', in Dodd and Oppenheimer, *Congress Reconsidered*, 5th edn, Table 9.1.

15 Roger H. Davidson and Walter J. Oleszek, 'From Monopoly to Interaction: Changing Patterns in Committee Management of Legislation in the House'. Paper presented to the Annual Meeting of the Midwest Political Science Association, Chicago, April 1987, p. 28.

16 Daniel J. Palazzolo, *The Speaker and the Budget. Leadership in the Post-Reform House of Representatives* (Pittsburgh and London: University of Pittsburgh Press, 1992).

17 US Congress. Joint Committee on the Organisation of Congress, *Organisation of the Congress*. Final Report. Volume II (Washington, D.C.: USGPO, December 1993), p. 40.

18 See Bruce I. Oppenheimer, 'The Rules Committee: New Arm of Leadership in a Decentralised House', in Dodd and Oppenheimer, *Congress Reconsidered* (New York: Praeger, 1977), pp. 96–116; David W. Rohde, *Parties and Leaders in the Post-Reform House* (Chicago: University of Chicago Press, 1991), p. 97.

19 'Open Versus Restrictive Rules', unpublished mimeo, Office of the Minority Staff, House Rules Committee, August 1994. See also Stanley Bach and Steven S. Smith, *Managing Uncertainty in the House of Representatives. Adaptation and Innovation in Special Rules* (Washington, D.C.: The Brookings Institution, 1988), pp. 12–33, 116–17.

20 Mary Jacoby, 'Six Weeks Into Majority, GOP Asks: How Open Should Open Rules Be?', *Roll Call*, February 13 1995, p. 20.

21 Joseph Cooper and David W. Brady, ' Institutional Context and Leadership Style: The House From Cannon to Rayburn', *American Political Science Review*, 75 (1981), pp. 411–25.

22 Although promotion is not automatic and requires an affirmative vote by the majority caucus or conference and the House, all recent Speakers have been succeeded by the next person down on the leadership ladder. Gingrich was Minority Whip before becoming Speaker in 1995; Foley was Majority Leader before 1989, as were his predecessors Wright, O'Neill, and Albert.

23 Barbara Sinclair, *Majority Leadership in the US House* (Baltimore and London: John Hopkins University Press), p. 55. See also D. B. Hardeman and Donald C. Bacon, *Rayburn. A Biography* (Austin, TX: Texas Monthly Press, 1987).

24 Barbara Sinclair, 'House Majority Leadership in the Era of Divided Control', in Dodd and Oppenheimer, *Congress Reconsidered*, 5th edn, p. 248.

25 *Ibid.*, p. 239.

26 In 1993 and 1994, vice president Al Gore used his casting vote from the chair to win Senate approval for a number of measures supported by President Clinton, most notably in June 1993 when he provided the deciding vote on the budget reconciliation bill budget. Vice President George Bush did the same to gain Senate approval for President Reagan's Strategic Defense Initiative in 1987 .

27 Steven V. Roberts, 'Life, or Lack Thereof, in the Senate', *New York Times*, November 22 1985, p. B8, quoted in Walter J. Oleszek, *Congressional Procedures and the Policy Process* (Washington, D.C.: Congressional Quarterly Press, 1989), p. 25.

28 Barbara Sinclair, *The Transformation of the US Senate* (Baltimore and London: John Hopkins University Press, 1989), pp. 111–25.

29 Quoted in Ross K. Baker, *House and Senate* (New York and London: W. W. Norton and Co., 1989), p. 74.

30 Joint Committee, *Organisation of the Congress*, Vol. II, pp. 54–7. See also Sinclair, *The Transformation of the US Senate*, p. 116; and Bruce I. Oppenheimer, 'Changing Time Constraints on Congress: Historical Perspectives on the Use of Cloture' in Dodd and Oppenheimer, *Congress Reconsidered*, 3rd edn, pp. 396–7.

31 John B. Gilmour, 'Senate Democrats Should Curb Use of the Filibuster', *Roll Call*, January 24 1994, p. 5.

32 See also Steven S. Smith and Marcus Flathman, 'Managing the Senate Floor: Complex Unanimous Consent Agreements Since the 1950s', *Legislative Studies Quarterly*, 14 (1989), pp. 349–74.

33 Fred R. Harris, *Deadlock or Decision. The US Senate and the Rise of National Politics* (New York and Oxford: Oxford University Press, 1993), p. 183.

34 Smith, 'Forces of Change in Senate Party Leadership and Organisation', p. 275; Richard E. Cohen, 'Making His Mark', *National Journal*, May 20 1989, p. 1232; and Baumer, 'Senate Democratic Leadership in the 101st Congress', p. 310–11.

35 Phil Duncan (ed.), *Politics In America 1994. The 103rd Congress* (Washington, D.C.: Congressional Quarterly Press, 1993), p. 608.

36 Roger H. Davidson, 'Senate Leaders: Janitors for an Untidy Chamber', in Dodd and Oppenheimer, *Congress Reconsidered*, 3rd edn, pp. 225–52.

37 Robert L. Peabody, *Leadership in Congress. Stability, Succession and Change* (Boston and Toronto: Little Brown, 1976) and Randall B. Ripley, *Power in the Senate* (New York: St Martin's Press, 1969).

38 Stephen Hess, *The Ultimate Insiders. US Senators in the National Media* (Washington, D.C.: Brookings Institution, 1986), p. 23.

39 Smith, 'Forces of Change', pp. 282, 284.

40 Partisanship also increased within committees in the 1980's. See Daniel S. Ward, 'The Continuing Search for Party Influence in Congress: A View from the Committees', *Legislative Studies Quarterly*, 18 (1993), pp. 211–30.

41 See A. Lawrence Lowell, 'The Influence of Party Upon Legislation in England and America', *Annual Report of the American Historical Association*, I (1901), pp. 321–543. Using Lowell's stricter criterion, only about 17 per cent of House votes recorded in various sessions between 1921 and 1948, and as few as between 2 and 8 per cent between 1950 and 1967, qualified as party votes. Julius Turner, *Party and Constituency. Pressure on Congress* (Baltimore and London: Johns Hopkins University Press, 1951), p. 23 and Julius Turner and Edward Schneier, *Party and Constituency. Pressure on Congress* (Baltimore and London: The Johns Hopkins University Press, 1970), p. 17.

42 Melissa P. Collie, 'Universalism and the Parties in the US House of Representatives, 1921–80,' *American Journal of Political Science*, 32 (1988), pp. 865–83.

43 Samuel C. Patterson and Gregory A. Caldeira, 'Party Voting in the United States Congress', *British Journal of Political Science*, 18 (1988), pp. 111–31; David W. Rohde, 'Electoral Forces, Political Agendas, and Partisanship in the House and Senate' in Davidson (ed.), *The Post-Reform Congress*, pp. 27–46.

44 Aage R. Clausen, *How Congressmen Decide* (New York: St Martin's Press, 1973); Aage R. Clausen and Carl E. Van Horn, 'The Congressional Response to a Decade of Change, 1963–1972', *Journal of Politics*, 39 (1977), pp. 624–66; Barbara Sinclair, *Congressional Realignment, 1925–1978* (Austin, TX: University of Texas Press, 1982); Barbara Sinclair, 'Agenda, Policy and Alignment Change from Coolidge to Reagan' in Dodd and Oppenheimer, *Congress Reconsidered*, 3rd edn, pp. 291–314.

45 Bob Benenson, 'Clinton Keeps Southern Wing on His Team in 1993', *Congressional Quarterly Weekly Report*, December 18 1993, p. 3435. On long-term trends, see Keith T. Poole and R. Steven Daniels, 'Ideology, Party and Voting in the US Congress, 1959–1980', *American Political Science Review*, 79 (1985), pp. 373–99 and William R. Shaffer, 'Party and Ideology in the US House of Representatives,' *Western Political Quarterly*, 25 (1982), pp. 92–106.

46 Jerome M. Chubb and Santa A. Traugott, 'Partisan Cleavage and Cohesion in the House of Representatives, 1861–1974', *Journal of Interdisciplinary History*, 7 (1977), p. 383 and Smith, 'Forces of Change', pp. 265 and 268.

47 Mack C. Shelley, *The Permanent Majority. The Conservative Coalition in the US Congress* (University, AL: University of Alabama Press, 1983).

48 Richard Bolling, 'Committees in the House', *The Annals of the American Academy of Political and Social Science*, 161 (1974), p. 4.

49 Palazzolo, *The Speaker and the Budget*, pp. 216–22.

50 Lawrence C. Dodd and Bruce I. Oppenheimer, 'Maintaining Order in the House: The Struggle for Institutional Equilibrium' in Dodd and Oppenheimer, *Congress Reconsidered*, 5th edn, pp. 56–7.

51 Smith, 'Forces of Change', p. 286.

52 John W. Kingdon, *Congressmen's Voting Decisions*, 3rd edn (Ann Arbor, MI: University of Michigan Press, 1989), p. 112.

53 Lewis A. Froman and Randall B. Ripley, 'Conditions for Party Leadership: The Case of the House Democrats', *American Political Science Review*, 59 (1965), pp. 52–63.

54 Rohde, *Parties and Leaders in the Post-Reform House*, p. 31; Peabody, *Leadership in Congress*, p. 9.

55 Kingdon, *Congressmen's Voting Decisions*, pp. 117–18.

56 Kenneth J. Cooper, 'Gun Control Opponents Prevail in Major Defeat for Clinton', *Washington Post*, August 12 1994, p. A1; Ann Devroy, 'Surprise Vote Blocks House Action on Crime Bill', *Washington Post*, August 12 1994, pp. A1 and A12.

57 Kingdon, *Congressmen's Voting Decisions*, pp. 30–1.

58 Interview with Hoagland on National Public Radio, *Morning Edition*, August 15 1994.

59 The median voter thesis has its origins in James H. Kuklinski, 'Representatives and Elections: A Policy Analysis', *American Political Science Review*, 72 (1978), pp. 165–77.

60 R. Douglas Arnold, *The Logic of Congressional Action* (New Haven, CT: Yale University Press, 1990), p. 68.

61 Clausen, *How Congressmen Decide*, pp. 73 and 77.

62 See Morris P. Fiorina, *Representatives, Roll Calls and Constituencies* (Lexington, MA: D. C. Heath, 1974); Charles S. Bullock and David W. Brady, 'Party, Constituency and Roll Call Voting in the US Senate', *Legislative Studies Quarterly*, 8 (1983), pp. 29–43; and Catherine R. Shapiro, David W. Brady, Richard A. Brody, and John A. Ferejohn, 'Linking Constituency Opinion and Senate Voting Scores: A Hybrid Explanation', *Legislative Studies Quarterly*, 15 (1990), pp. 599–621.

63 Burdett A. Loomis and Allan Cigler (eds), *Interest Group Politics*, 4th edn (Washington, D.C.: Congressional Quarterly Press, 1994); Kay Lehman Schlozman and John T. Tierney, *Organised Interests and American Democracy* (New York: Harper and Row, 1986); and Mark P. Petracca (ed.), *The Politics of Interest: Interest Groups Transformed* (Boulder and Oxford: Westview Press, 1992).

64 Kingdon, *Congressmen's Voting Decisions*, p. 147.

65 Laura I. Langbein and Mark A. Lotwis, 'The Political Efficacy of Lobbying and Money. Gun Control in the US House, 1986', *Legislative Studies Quarterly*, 15 (1990), pp. 413–40.

66 Janet M. Grenzke, 'Shopping in the Congressional Supermarket: The Currency Is Complex', *American Journal of Political Science*, 33 (1989), pp. 1 and 12; John R. Wright, 'PACs, Contributions, and Roll Calls: An Organizational Perspective', *American Political Science Review*, 79 (1985), p. 411.

67 John E. Owens, 'The Impact of Campaign Contributions on Legislative Outcomes in Congress: Evidence from a House Committee', *Political Studies*, 34 (1986), pp. 285–95.

68 Richard L. Hall and Frank W. Wayman, 'Buying Time: Money Interests and the Mobilisation of Bias in Congressional Committees', *American Political Science Review*, 84 (1990), pp. 797–820.

69 Richard Fleisher, 'PAC Contributions and Congressional Voting on National Defense', *Legislative Studies Quarterly*, 18 (1993), p. 406.

70 Glenn R. Parker and Suzanne L. Parker, *Factions in House Committees* (Knoxville, TN: University of Tennessee, Press, 1985); Joseph K. Unekis and Rieselbach, *Congressional Committee Politics. Continuity and Change* (New York: Praeger, 1984); and John E. Owens, 'Good Policy Voting in the US Congress: An Explanation of Financial Institutions Politics', *Political Studies*, 43 (1995), pp. 66–91.

71 See Richard F. Fenno, *Home Style: House Members in Their Districts* (Boston and Toronto: Little Brown, 1978); Herbert Asher and Herbert Weisberg, 'Voting Change in Congress: Some Dynamic Perspectives on an Evolutionary Process', *American Journal of Political Science*, 22 (1978), pp. 394–425; Kingdon, *Congressmen's Voting Decisions*, pp. 75–82.

72 Donald R. Matthews and James A. Stimson, 'Decision-making by US Representatives' in Sidney Ulmer (ed.), *Political Decision-making* (New York: Van Nostrand, 1970), pp. 20–1.

73 The following discussion is taken from Kingdon, *Congressmen's Voting Decisions*, pp. 242–50.

74 Kingdon, *Congressmen's Voting Decisions*, p. 249.

75 Martha Angle, 'The Human Truth About Politics', *Congressional Quarterly Weekly Report*, May 22 1993, p. 1326.

PART 2

The presidency

CHAPTER 6

The institutionalisation of the presidency

Constitutional and historical roots

The position of the president in the American political system has been controversial from its very beginning. As a self-conscious Republic, Congress was not only the evident first branch of government, but the primary locus of authority drawn from public consent. Congress was a legislative assembly, but more than that it embodied the assemblage of a sovereign people. The main powers of the new federal government were accordingly enumerated in the section of the United States Constitution devoted to the Congress (i.e. Article I). With such a post-revolutionary emphasis upon popular sovereignty and legislative centrality, there was little room in theory for a strong executive presence. And yet, despite the unfavourable circumstances and in the face of bitter criticism, the Founding Fathers devised a forceful executive and laid the foundation for its later development into an alternative source of popular expression.

Americans emerged from their revolutionary struggle against the British government with a highly developed animus against executive figures amd authority. Executive power was equated with the crown. As the empire in British law was conceived as the King's empire, the American colonies were administered in principle by the crown in the form of royal governors. In practice, governors, for much of the eighteenth century, ruled in conjunction with the indigenous assemblies which became increasingly sophisticated in their use of political and procedural manoeuvres designed to undermine the governor's position. When Britain sought to undo this evolutionary development by reintroducing a strict mercantilist economic order and an enhanced form of central control (1764), the colonists regarded it as an unwarranted invasion of their liberties as English men and women.[1] The unresolved problem of the British empire was clearly exposed – i.e. subjects in the colonies possessed fewer rights amd protections than subjects in Britain simply because of where they lived. As most Americans had been deeply immersed in the Whig culture of Britain, they interpreted the British efforts at colonial taxation and coercion as affirming not only that the colonies were governed according to the arbitrary use of royal prerogative, but that, as far as they were concerned, the Glorious Revolution of 1688 had yet to be extended to the colonies. For sound propaganda and political reasons, therefore, the colonists' Declaration of Independence was an indictment of a royal, rather than a British, abuse of power. The Declaration made explicit reference to George III and his 'history of repeated injury and usurpations, all having in direct object the estab-lishment of an absolute tyranny over these states.'[2] As a consequence, the document that marked the birth of American liberty, was an assault upon the corruptive force of monarchy. It was designed both to draw support for the American rebellion from Whigs in Britain, and to mobilise American opinion for the ensuing revolutionary struggle. In respect to the first aim, it was effective. As far as the second objective was concerned, it succeeded absolutely. The *raison d'être* of the War of Independence (1776–81) and the identity of the newly emancipated states were firmly based upon a reaction against monarchy, crown prerogative, executive force, and indeed any form of external restraint.

The suspicion of executive power was clearly evident in the structure of the new state constitutions. Even though the governor in the state would now be of indigenous origin the detestation of the old royal governors was such to ensure that the states went to great lengths to ensure that their powers remained limited.[3] In most states the governor had no veto or power of appointment. In New England and New York, governors were elected, but elsewhere they were appointed by the legislative assembly. In all states, the governor could be checked by a council and removed from office by impeachment. Although each governor was expected to act as the commander-in-chief of their state's militia, the legislature retained control of military appointments and promotions. In every state, the governor and the executive department was constituted a separate branch of government not to ensure independence, but primarily to keep the governors and the corruptive element of the executive force away from the legislative assembly.[4]

At the national level, the suspicion of executive power was commensurately greater. The danger of imperialism went hand in hand with the danger of royalism. After the common effort of the *American* War of Independence by the *Continental* Army, the newly emancipated states went their separate ways. Liberation was liberation for the states. The only national entity was a weak Congress with no independent authority. It had no taxing powers and no armed forces. In the states, there was at least a recognition that an executive function existed in government – i.e. a role that the assembly could not perform. But at the national level, such was the prejudice against an executive, that even the need for such an agency was denied. What govenment structures existed were regarded as appendages to the Congress. Departments were run by legislative committees. Secretaries of the departments not only had to report to such committees, but had to receive administrative directions from them. There was a 'president' under the Articles of Confederation, but he was merely the presiding officer of the Congress. The only other executive entity was a committee that came into existence when Congress was in recess. It had very few powers and could only act when nine out of the thirteen states consented to a course of action. In post-revolutionary America, a national executive was only necessary when Congress was not in session. It was not there to fulfil functions that Congress could not do; it was only there to perform tasks in Congress's absence.[5]

Between 1781 and 1787, America was set on a course of decentralisation and devolution from the original base point of centralism provided by the British empire and the crown in particular.

Figure 6.1 provides a schematic expression of America's departure from both geographical and political centralism under the Articles of Confederation. The two appeared interlinked in that movement towards political decentralisation brought with it movement towards legislative supremacy and *vice versa*. With decentralisation, however, came the risk of social disintegration. The fervour of autonomy led to states discharging all responsibility and obligations to their neighbours. Each state had its own tariffs, coinage, laws of contract and armed forces, and its own foreign policy. By 1787, enough disquiet had been generated over the capacity of the states to maintain internal order, to provide collective security against European imperial powers, and to maximise America's economic potential for 55 *prominenti* to meet in Philadelphia to revise the Articles of Confederation. Notwithstanding the various disputes concerning the extent to which America faced a crisis during these years, or the degree to which the Founding Fathers' intentions were coloured by their decision to extend their property rights,[6] the fact remains that the Founding Fathers believed it was vital to redesign American government by creating a potent federal level of authority

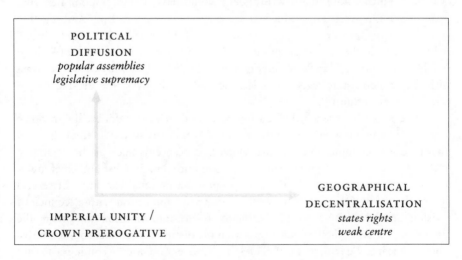

Figure 6.1. Post-revolutionary developments in political authority.

capable of defending the Republic, regulating its expansion and providing a settled legal and financial basis to the country's economic activity. Some of the Founding Fathers were nationalists who wanted a dominant federal government with a veto over state legislation. Others believed that such change was both unnecessary and unacceptable. They pressed for measures to restrain the new government and to ensure that the separate sovereignties of the states, and especially the small states, were preserved in the new arrangement.[7] Amidst the intense enthusiasm and suspicion that surrounded the Founding Fathers' secret deliberations, one feature was assured of attracting particular notoriety.

The shape, function, and power of the new executive would be the litmus test of just how radical a scheme of government the Founders were proposing to the American public. More than any other single component, the executive would reveal the Founding Fathers' motives and intentions, their level of political risk-taking and their willingness to repudiate conventional republican wisdom. Accordingly, when the Founding Fathers unveiled their new Constitution, the arrangements for the executive department were to say the least highly controversial. Bearing in mind the circumstances at the time, the precedents available in the states, and the traditional animosity surrounding such an office, it would not have been unreasonable for the Founders to have proposed a plural executive appointed by Congress and working alongside an advisory council. It might have been expected that each part of such a plural executive would have a tenure of two years or less, would be ineligible for re-election and would be devoid of any veto power. But such expectations were quite misplaced for the Founding Fathers proposed a single chief executive serving for four years and operating without a council, with no limits on re-election, and without any arrangements for a rotation of offices. Furthermore, the new president would have a veto, appointment and treaty-making powers, an established salary, and the power of pardon, together with the customary role of commander-in-chief of the armed services and a broad right of access to the generic properties of executive power.[8] In the view of Wilfred Binkley, 'the sorry spectacle of impotent state executives of 1787 . . . in contrast with the despotic state legislatures led the Fathers to invest the President with extraordinary authority'.[9]

The executive branch devised by the Founders was undoubtedly an office with considerable potential for power, but also for criticism. The final shape of the office was certainly not the one which had been envisaged at the beginning of the convention. Even James Madison, a committed nationalist and chief architect of the Constitution had originally proposed a national executive of several offices elected by Congress who would operate in conjunction with a 'council of revision' and who would not be eligible for re-election. Madison and others like him began to change their minds towards a more distinctive and vigorous executive when it became clear that the Philadelphia Convention was becoming a matter of state bargaining and negotiation rather than the rational consideration of abstract governmental theory. After the smaller states had insisted upon compromising the principles of representation by population and of unicameralism through the establishment of a Senate, the nationalists believed that the prospects for an effective central government were massively diminished. It was partly out of desperation, therefore, that those of nationalist disposition turned to the presidency to compensate for what they saw as the increasing parochialism of both the convention and the emergent character of the Constitution.[10]

In the final weeks of the Convention, the presidency was effectively redesigned and granted a dramatic increase in power and status. In order to enhance his independence, and to promote responsibility for the administration, the plural executive and council of revision were scrapped in favour of a single president acting clearly on his own. He would be elected neither by the Congress nor by the state legislatures but by a special electoral college, again to improve his chances for independence. And in addition to the president's specific powers, the office was afforded a general grant of executive authority: 'The Executive Power shall be vested in a President of the United States of America.'[11] In contrast to Congress, whose legislative powers were precisely stipulated, the presidency's executive authority was not reduced to a set of enumerated components. This may have been because the executive function is by its very nature resistant to exact definition. Nonetheless, the phrase bestowing executive power to the president was conspicuously vague and open-ended in nature. It was 'sufficiently ambiguous so that no one could say precisely what it meant . . . Indeed, the common rules of constitutional construction that then prevailed assumed that general terms might imply more than the enumerated powers that followed.'[12] All of these features reflected the hopes that the nationalists had in the capacity of the presidency to neutralise the localised and particularistic distractions of the Congress and to act, in Gouverneur Morris' phrase, as 'the general guardian of the national interests'.[13]

The anti-federalists, who opposed the states' adoption of the Constitution, immediately drew atention to the presidency which in their view was courting corruption. According to their classical republican outlook, the chief danger to any structure of government would always come from the executive. For the Founders wantonly to recreate a national executive figure within six years of America having rid itself of George III was tantamount to a counter-revolution. In the same way that decentralisation and legislative power coincided with one another after the acquisition of independence, so the Founders were accused of reversing the process by providing a return to central government with a corresponding revival of executive power. James Madison accepted the premise but not the conclusion. America's experience between 1781 and 1787 demonstrated that the primary source of danger in a republic was paradoxically the people itself acting in its assemblies. 'The legislative department is everywhere extending the sphere of its activity and drawing all its power into its impetuous vortex.'[14] It was the executive department that required protection from the legislature, not the other way around. The Constitution's apologists insisted that the presidency was utterly benign in nature, heavily constricted by checks and balances, disciplined by elections, and conditioned by the fact that '[i]n republican government, the legislative authority necessarily predominates'.[15]

The anti-federalists were not at all convinced. Federalists claimed that they had no intention of reinstating a monarchical estate in America and that the design of the presidency had been modelled on states like New York and Massachusetts whose governors had considerable authority.

> Indeed, by drawing selectively from the state constitutions it was possible to argue from precedent that sanction for every feature of a strong national executive could be found in one or another of these charters of Americanism.[16]

To the anti-federalists, this was not the point. There was a world of difference between a strong governor within the established confines of an integrated state, and a potent chief executive in a system that sought to join the states together in a sprawling national entity. The federal nature of the American republic was threatened not only with union but also with empire because the Founding Fathers had recklessly made available a potential monarch. Edmund Randolph called the presidency 'the foetus of monarchy'[17] and worked ceaselessly to have it aborted by opposing the Constitution's ratification.

Although the anti-federalists failed to prevent the states' acceptance of the federal Constitution, their arguments remained as a potent constraint upon the presidential office and its subsequent development. What power pertained to the president was more potential than actual, more inherent and problematic than explicit and clear-cut. The executive office represented the dark continent of the Constitution. It was capable of arousing powerful and emotive references to monarchy, to corruption and, thence, to an entire pathology of republican degeneration. The magisterial figure of George Washington serving as the first president disarmed the sceptics, but only temporarily.

The presidency remained, and still continues to be, a controversial office, the outer limits of which are always susceptible to extension and by the same token also open to dispute. Of all the Framers' creations, the presidency is the one structural feature of the Constitution that can only be comprehended and satisfactorily accounted for in terms of a process of development. Such development has often been episodic and reversible.[18] It is only with the benefit of 200 years of hindsight that it is possible to impose a sense of an ordered progression upon the office. In reality, the status and legitimacy of the presidency had depended upon individual presidents establishing different roles for the office, which over time have accumulated into the conglomeration of functions that today characterises the modern presidency.

Presidents, precedents, and institutionalisation

The individual incumbents who have contributed to the presidency in this way and who in the process have provided the landmarks in the evolution of the office are portrayed in Table 6.1.

Table 6.1. Key precedents in the development of the pre-modern presidency

President	Period in Office	Contribution
G. Washington	1789–1797	republican trustee
T. Jefferson	1801–1809	party leader
A. Jackson	1829–1837	democratic populist
A. Lincoln	1861–1865	national guardian
T. Roosevelt	1901–1909	international leader
W. Wilson	1913–1921	programmatic reformer

In the embryonic period of the new Republic, George Washington (1789–97) deployed his personal stature as the successful commander of America's forces in the war for independence to establish the first vital precedent for the office. It was his occupation of the position for eight years which allowed it to survive its controversial origins. Thomas Jefferson (1801–9) developed the office into that of party leader. As the victor in the first presidential election to feature two organised, competitive, and bitterly opposed parties (i.e. the Federalists and the Jeffersonian Republicans), Jefferson used his position to maximise other benefits of government for his party. According to Louis Koenig:

> Of all the presidents, Thomas Jefferson is unsurpassed in the authority he asserted as party leader and in the fealty he commanded for state and local party organisations. He held sway by means of a thoroughly formulated theory of party principles and functions and a sure grasp of the means of party action.[19]

In spite of Jefferson's radicalism he was nevertheless a patrician – part of that old colonial gentry which had dominated the politics of the new Republic for over forty years. It was not until the election of Andrew Jackson (1829–37) that the presidency became identified with populist representation and democratic leadership. In contrast to the sophisticated elitism of the east, Jackson was an uncultivated westerner who embodied the insurgency of the 'back country'. Jackson not only exploited the extension of the franchise that had occurred in the 1820s, but sought to further the democratisation of America by an extensive turnover in government personnel (e.g. spoils system) and a general assault upon privilege. These changes set against the popular election of members of the electoral college, the onset of party conventions, and the development of national campaign organisations, set American politics on a course of democratic progression.

Abraham Lincoln (1861–5) linked the presidency with the very survival of the federal union. The Civil War (1861–65) threatened to split the United States into two sections. Lincoln dramatised the role of president as guardian of the nation and guarantor of the Republic. His reliance upon executive orders and his initiative in unilaterally claiming prerogative rights as an executive in wartime set the standard for future presidents to defy constitutional procedure and the strict observance of the rule of law in the pursuit of the national interest in times of emergency.

The presidency of Theodore Roosevelt (1901–9) firmly associated the office with the United States as a global power along with the international responsibilities as well as the opportunities that such a position entailed. 'Despite his sincere loyalty to the democratic game, this herald of modern American militarism and imperialism displayed in his political character many qualities of recent authoritarianism.'[20] Roosevelt's personal identity with masculine assertion and overseas adventure was publicly merged with America's own adolescent emergence as a world force not just in the economic sphere but in the field of international relations (e.g. Russo-Japanese peace settlement 1905), force projection (e.g. the expansion of the United States Navy), foreign intervention (e.g. the construction of the Panama Canal), and even military engagement (e.g. the Spanish–American War of 1898). As a consequence, America's expansionism became closely associated with Roosevelt's own expansionist and thoroughly functional conception of the presidency's role. In his own words,

> I declined to adopt the view that what was imperatively necessary for the Nation could not be done by the President unless he could find some specific authorization to do it. . . Under this interpretation of executive power I did and caused to be done many things not previously done by the President and the heads of the departments. I did not usurp power but I did broaden the use of executive power.'[21]

The next president to make a distinctive contribution to the office was Woodrow Wilson (1913–21). He wanted to use the presidency to bring about a reformulation of American society through a programme entitled 'The New Freedom'. Wilson provided both the intellectual and political momentum to what he regarded as a necessary series of measures designed to restore social liberty through the use of the federal government. State intervention to regulate the banking system, to limit the power of the 'trusts' (i.e. monopolies), and to outlaw child labour in inter-state industries followed Wilson's election. His reforms associated the presidency with the welfare of society, with the responsibilities of a positive state, with an executive obligation to address injustice and with the need to offer a domestic programme for government policy as a qualification for the White House.

All these chief executives are universally recognised as 'great presidents'.

Greatness in this context relates to their mastery of events, their influence upon history, and the shaping of their country's destiny. In particular, it relates to 'their ability to magnify their own department and their own powers, at the expense of the other branches'.[22] Each of the presidents mentioned above established and refined a particular role for the presidency. They created a series of strands drawn from the raw materials of the Constitution and bequeathed by them to their successors. The effect was roughly cumulative in nature in that Lincoln, for example, was not only a war leader but a democratic leader (e.g. Jackson), and party leader (e.g. Jefferson) as well. Woodrow Wilson drew upon all five previous roles and extended the position further to a sixth. They were all landmark presidents, but they did not create an indelible change in the scenery. Such figures represented the peaks in a very uneven development in which a great president like Lincoln could be followed by a series of largely anonymous under-achievers.

It was not until Franklin D. Roosevelt and the twin crises of the Great Depression and World War II (1933–45) that all the precedents were fused together into an overwhelming political force which not only changed the face of politics in the United States but established the presidency in a position of permanent centrality in American government (see Figure 6.2).

After Franklin Roosevelt, all subsequent presidents *had* to fulfil, or try to fulfil, the full range of executive roles, in order to remain in office. A satisfactory response to a range of concurrent responsibilities was now seen as a minimal requirement. Franklin Roosevelt was the first modern president and, as a consequence, he set in motion the modern presidency in which the principle of an

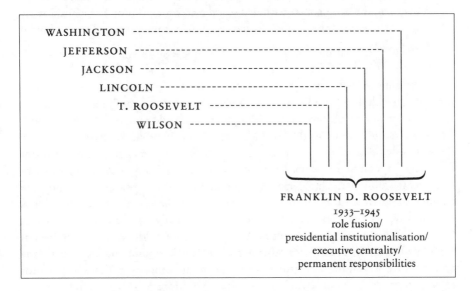

Figure 6.2. The accumulation of precedents in the modern presidency.

executive driven government was assimilated and the means to achieve it were granted institutionalised status.

It was during the Roosevelt period that the merits of, and the national need for, a strong presidency came to be acknowledged as a long-term basis. Franklin Roosevelt himself set the standards and provided the archetypal model of a strong modern presidency. In the words of William E. Leuchtenberg, Roosevelt

> took an office which had lost much of its prestige and power in the previous twelve years and gave it an importance which went well beyond what even Theodore Roosevelt and Woodrow Wilson had done . . . Under Roosevelt, the White House became the focus of all government – the fountainhead of ideas, the initiator of action, the representative of the national interest.[23]

Roosevelt 'introduced a positive conception of responsibility and emphasised as never before, the dynamic role of the federal government'[24] in fulfilling that responsibility. Under Roosevelt, the 'presidency began to undergo not a shift but rather a metamorphosis'.[25] By energising the presidency, he stimulated the government into an altogether more direct and imaginative agency of social action. One distinguished disciple of Roosevelt and the New Deal had no doubt that his appeal and lasting effect lay in the fact that:

> Franklin Roosevelt brought government to the people. He personalised the role of government and brought better understanding of that social contract so vital for a democracy – the direct relationships of the people to their government and the government to the people. This conception of government and the people has continued – and today people look to the presidency more than ever as the people's office and the central force in political affairs.[26]

When Roosevelt died in office, he left behind not only a vast infrastructure of government intervention, but an enhanced social expectation of state responsibility established by years of New Deal measures and extensive wartime management. As a result, it is commonly asserted that 'the successors of Franklin Roosevelt have all been in his shadow – as much in power and style as in issues and policy'.[27] There are qualifications to this view, but it is also true that following Roosevelt it was simply assumed that any president was necessarily an aggregate of functions that were imperative to modern government – namely head of state, chief executive, premier diplomat, chief legislator, commander-in-chief, party leader, popular tribune, national security overseer and manager of the American economy. It is only after Roosevelt that the federal government finally appears to have become fully established as the focal point of America's national life and as the indispensable pre-condition to America's further social and economic development. It is only after Roosevelt that the growth of presidential authority appears to conform to a pattern of inevitable and irreversible evolutionary progression. Rexford Tugwell may have been right in saying that 'the president was not a person he was an institution'.[28] What is certain is that he made the presidency into an institution and institutionalised its place in American government and society.

Executive government as a source of presidential power

Roosevelt did not just bequeath expectations and responsibilities to his successors. His bequest took a physical form in the shape of government buildings, budgets, and personnel. During Roosevelt's period of office, the federal government literally grew in size for as more areas of social provision and economic regulation were covered by the New Deal, Washington D.C. radically changed shape to accommodate the new bureaucracies. American central government had undergone dramatic expansions before, but these were only during periods of war. After the emergencies were over, governments contracted accordingly. The enlargement of the federal government during the New Deal was exceptional in three main respects. First, unprecedented growth took place during peacetime. Second, government was expanded even while the economy was contracting. And third, government expenditure and employment never returned to pre-New Deal levels, even after the twin crises of the Depression and World War II had been resolved. In the ten years before the New Deal (1922-32), the federal budget averaged $3.36 billion, while federal civilian employment stood at an average of 566,000. By 1936 when nearly all the New Deal reforms had been set in place, the federal budget had grown to $8.5 billion and civilian employment to 867,000. The federal budget as a proportion of the Gross National Product (GNP) had risen from 4.7 per cent in 1931 to 9.0 per cent in 1935. World War II, of course, massively increased these levels (from $9.06 billion in 1940 to $98.4 billion in 1945; from 1.04 million civilian employees in 1940 to 3.82 million in 1945). Even though the federal government contracted in size after the high water mark of the war, it has never returned to the low water mark of the 1920s. While civilian employment has remained steady at around 3 million, the federal budget has continued to grow throughout the post-war period (see Table 6.2).

Table 6.2. The growth of the federal budget – outlays in billions of dollars

Year	Dollars
1945	92.7bn
1950	42.6bn
1955	68.4bn
1960	92.2bn
1965	118.2bn
1970	195.7bn
1975	332.3bn
1980	590.9bn

Year	Dollars
1985	946.4bn
1986	990.3bn
1987	1,003.9bn
1988	1,064.1bn
1989	1,143.2bn
1990	1,252.7bn
1991	1,323.8bn
1992	1,381.8bn
1993	1,474.9bn

Source: Statistical Abstract of the United States: 1993, 113th edn (Austin: Reference Press, 1993), p. 328.

The expansion of the federal government is often seen as a monument to the sort of heroic and enlightened presidential activism in society which Roosevelt did so much to establish as a model of executive leadership and responsibility. Strongly associated with this perspective is the belief that since the federal government is to such a large extent personified by the president and legitimised by his constitutional position as chief executive, the entity of Washington government is given a form, an identity, and a direction drawn from the occupant of the White House – i.e. its chief agent and main benefactor. As a consequence, the federal government is often equated with 'presidential government' both from a factual point of view as an empirical condition and also from a normative perspective, whereby presidents are expected to maximise their control of government for the sake of social improvement, administrative efficiency, and democratic accountability.[29] But appearances can be deceptive. The real extent to which the federal government in Washington can be construed as an amalgam to a condition of presidential government remains a subject of intense dispute.

As chief executive, the president is nominally the head of the executive branch of the federal government. As such, he is the chairman of the largest single organisation in American society. It employs nearly 5 million civilian and military personnel and its budget accounts for 22 per cent of the GNP making it the biggest single consumer in the United States. There are, for example, 142,000 federal employees engaged in procuring goods and services for the government. Their work amounts to approximately 20 million contract actions per annum. Their responsibilities reach into every corner of American life – from building nuclear missiles to regulating the stock market, from constructing dams and highways to underwriting mortgages, from defining advertising standards to protecting bears in national parks. For example, the federal government in the form of such agencies as the Bureau of Land Management, the US Forest Service, the Bureau of Indian Affairs, and the Defense Department have jurisdiction over nearly half the land mass of eleven western states. The scale of the federal bureaucracy's presence in

American society together with its expenditure, specialisation, and continuity gives the presidency enormous opportunities to draw from its resources.

In Washington where information is always thought to be synonymous with power, the federal bureaucracy can provide any president with a wealth of economic, social, and even political intelligence. The president can use the bureaucracy as a clearing house for advanced information that will enhance the administration's decision-making powers by allowing executive choices to be made as the basis of a careful assessment of the feasibility, legality and political prudence of the various alternatives. The bureaucracy's necessary links with society make it a representative institution in its own right. Each part of the bureaucracy invariably develops linkages with that sector of society with which it is most closely associated. In the continuous battle for information, an astute president can plug into these networks and exploit the oppurtunities they offer for consultation, learning, and warning which will enable an administration to spot problems in advance and to respond sensitively towards grassroots objections to actual or projected government policy. For example, it is by no means uncommon for a president's legislative proposals to be devised and refined by executive agencies working in collaboration with their social and economic clients in the private sector.

Accurate information is particularly important in foreign affairs and national security for the executive branch's primary *raison d'être* lies in this field. In any examination of the federal bureaucracy, it is important not to overlook the obvious fact that it is the executive branch which possesses the federal government's means of physical coercion. The president not only has access to such forces, his executive role is based upon being central to all decisions involving any major deployment of such force. As a consequence, being chief executive means that it is possible to authorise the seizure of steel mills (e.g. President Truman), to send federal marshals into the south to enforce desegregation (e.g. President Kennedy), and to direct government agencies to subject political opponents to surveillance and harassment (e.g. President Nixon). Through his position at the apex of a hierarchial command structure a president can choose to invade a foreign country (e.g. President Bush in Panama (1990) and Iraq (1991), President Clinton in Haiti (1994)); to impose a naval blockade (President Kennedy and Cuba (1962)); to bomb overseas targets (e.g. President Reagan and Tripoli (1986), President Bush and Baghdad (1991)); to run a secret war (President Nixon and Cambodia (1969–73)); to conduct a rescue mission (e.g. President Carter in Iran (1980)); to engage in forceful intervention to relieve famine (e.g. Presidents Bush and Clinton in Somalia (1992–3)); and ultimately to place American forces on full alert in readiness for a possible global confrontation to threaten nuclear devastation (e.g. President Kennedy in 1962, President Nixon in 1973). In the same way that the president has access to this magnitude of force, so he can expect a commensurate degree of physical protection to preserve both the organisational and democratic integrity of decision-making in such a sensitive and potentially grave area of policy direction. Apart from 24-hour personal security by specialist units of the bureaucracy (e.g. secret service) which constitute a praetorian guard around the figure of the president, extraordinary measures exist to preserve the presidency in time of war. For example, one of the most closely guarded secrets of the Cold War was the 'Outpost Mission', which covered arrangements for evacuating the president from Washington after a nuclear attack. An elite helicopter force (2857th Test Squadron) with heavy protection against radiation would snatch the president from the remains of the White House and take him to one of the large underground sites reserved for government relocation outside Washington. If the president could not be rescued from the White House bunker, another force was permanently on stand-by with cutting equipment and cranes to ensure that the official with number one priority in a post-nuclear administration would survive to maintain the semblance of government.[30]

Presidential use of bureaucracy is not limited to simple force. The executive branch and its place in American society can provide the chief executive with opportunities for influence and persuasion. For example, given that the federal government spends over 20 cents of every dollar in the American economy, the bureaucracy constitutes in its own right a power in the marketplace. Presidents can use this presence as an instrument of economic management and by doing so, extend their leverage into areas where no formal authority exists.

In 1965, for example, President Johnson used the market power of the federal government to prevent a major corporation (i.e. Aluminium Corporation of America – ALCOA) from increasing its prices by an amount which the Johnson Administration regarded as unacceptably inflationary in effect. President Johnson had no authority to coerce a private company into revoking its pricing policy. Nevertheless, he made up for the deficiency by asking his Secretary of Commerce to warn ALCOA that the administration would take 200,000 tons of aluminium from the government's stockpile of strategic materials and dump them on the domestic market if ALCOA did not rescind its price increase. Bearing in mind the deflationary effect of such a course of action, ALCOA cancelled the price rise.

Presidents can also use the federal bureaucracy to educate and condition the private sector, and even the public at large, to improve standards of conduct. The federal bureaucracy has, for example, pioneered procedures against sexual and racial discrimination in employment. The most dramatic instance of a president seeking to use the executive branch as a model for social reform came in 1948. In the late 1940s, President Truman found it impossible even to contemplate the plausibility of an effective civil rights act. Congressional opinion and the structure of the Democratic Party precluded such a bold reform coming through changes in the law. Nevertheless Truman decided to press the issue by force of example. He appointed blacks to the federal courts and to high-level administrative institutions. But perhaps most significantly, he issued an executive order in 1948 which began the process of racial desegregation in the armed forces. In 1993, President Clinton sought to emulate Truman by using an executive order to end discrimination against gay men and women in the armed services.

Of course, presidents can avail themselves of the bureaucracy for less laudable and altogether more personal and partisan motives. Incumbent presidents are regularly accused of using their discretionary spending powers to stimulate the economy to coincide with re-election campaigns. President Nixon abused his position to achieve other objectives. He demanded that the Internal Revenue Service subject those on his political 'blacklist' to prolonged and intrusive financial scrutiny. Before his downfall, it is clear that he intended to intensify this use of bureaucratic counter-measures in his second term of office.

> I want the most comprehensive notes on all those who tried to do us in. They didn't have to do it. They are asking for it and they are going to get it. We have not used the power in this first four years as you know. We have never used it. We have not used the Bureau [Federal Bureau of Investigation] and we have not used the Justice Department but things are going to change now.[31]

More recently, during George Bush's re-election campaign in 1992, the president demonstrated the power of incumbency in distributing federal largess for electoral purposes. Bush was conscious of the need to hold states in the south and mid-west and, therefore, over a period of two days during early September 1992 he announced the following measures:

- The federal government's acceptance of all the costs of emergency disaster relief in Louisiana and Florida following the destruction caused by Hurricane Andrew.
- The rebuilding of the Homestead Air Force base (Florida) which had been destroyed by the hurricane but which had also been earmarked as a likely contender for closure following the end of the Cold War.
- The lifting of a ten year old ban on the sale of F16 advanced fighters to Taiwan, allowing General Dynamics (Texas) to secure a $4 billion contract.
- The upgrading of the M1 Tank built in Michigan, even though the administration had long blocked the measure.
- An increase in federal relief to cotton farmers in south Texas.
- A rise in subsidies for American wheat exports which would benefit the grain farmers of South Dakota.
- The administration's acceptance of the V–22 tilt rotar aircraft (with Bell Helicopter Textron of Texas as a prime contractor) despite the fact that 'every year since 1989, Secretary (of Defence) Cheney had attempted to eliminate the V–22's funding, arguing that a $33 billion program simply [could] not be afforded within the shrinking defense budget'.[32]

Bearing in mind President Bush's commmitment to reducing the federal deficit, his two-day spending spree on behalf of the federal bureaucracy was a remarkable display of executive action.

In the event, President Bush lost the election not least because he was seen as having failed to provide a substantive sense of domestic purpose for his administration. While presidents may try to use the government to appeal to specific constituencies through pork barrel politics they are also expected to give a clear direction to the positive state. Whether it is President Roosevelt's 'New Deal' or President Johnson's 'Great Society', President Nixon's 'New Federalism' or President Clinton's 'New Covenant', they have all helped to establish a prevailing assumption that presidents can and should be at the helm of federal bureaucracy, in order to fulfil electoral promises of social and economic improvement, to justify their position as chief executive, to satisfy the principle of democratic responsibility, and to invest the federal government with a renewed commitment to society's welfare and the nation's interest.

Executive government as a limitation of presidential power

At first sight the idea that the federal bureaucracy might constitute a constraint upon the presidency seems implausible and contrary to the Weberian rationale of such an organisation,[33] in which the power of functional specialisation is inversely proportional with the unified and generalised authority of its political leadership. As the only nationally elected official in the federal government, and the only elected component of the entire executive branch, the president would appear to be in a wholly predominant position in relation to Washington's bureaucracy. He faces a cabinet who have all been selected by him, who generally have no explicit political constituency or party power base, who are responsible solely to the president, and who are likely to remain in Washington for a considerably shorter period than the chief executive.[34] The dependency culture of the American cabinet together with the development of an increasingly professional civil service would seem to make the president into an unassailable *de facto* as well as a *de jure* chief executive. And yet, nothing could be further from the truth.

Presidential power *from* the bureaucracy cannot be equated with presidential power *over* the bureaucratic structure. Far from being a presupposition of the presidential condition, the federal bureaucracy is an organisation which is highly resistant to external control. It not only has a capacity to deflect, defer, and obstruct administrative direction from the White House, it possesses political resources in its own right which it can deploy to preserve its independence.[35] So prodigious is the bureaucracy's ability to frustrate external supervision that gaining even some measure of control over the executive branch is widely regarded as being one of the chief executive's most difficult tasks. Many would say that it ranks as *the* most arduous problem in any administration.[36]

Because presidents invariably fail in such a task, the customary conclusion is that instead of providing an instrument of presidential government, the federal bureaucracy actually offers only an illusion of it. Furthermore, it is 'an "illusion" in the fullest sense of the word for it is based on appearances that mislead and deceive'. So much so in fact, that 'far from being in charge or running government, the president must struggle even to comprehend what is going on'.[37]

The capacity of unelected and unaccountable civil servants to frustrate the high profile democratic and leadership credentials of a president, is attributed to three main factors: first, constitutional and legal constraints; second, structural and organisational dynamics; and third, political limitations.

The presidency's chances of controlling the executive were compromised at the onset by the Constitution. While executive power may be lodged with a president, Congress has always retained the power to organise the executive branch, to set its budget, and to supervise its conduct in implementing the body of statute law passed by the legislature. In addition, the president can only make senior appointments with the advice and consent of the Senate. Because of the adoption of a formal separation of powers scheme in the Constitution, the executive branch has traditionally been a servant with two masters. As a consequence, the president's position of chief executive means constitutionally that he possesses the chief power within the executive branch, not that he has any formal claims to a monopoly of power over it. A new president quickly finds that the federal bureaucracy is altogether less geared to policy than it is to law. Cabinet secretaries often have to remind a president who is enthusiastic for rapid change that it is they who are responsible for carrying out the statutory obligations of government. They are also bound to enforce legal and financial commitments through methods laid down by administrative law, in order to prevent both the unreasonable exercise of bureaucratic discretion and any unwarranted political intrusion by the White House.

Regulatory commissions and the legislative veto provide two archetypal illustrations of a president's legal capacity to act as a chief executive officer. Legislative vetoes will be examined in Chapter 11. Commissions are formally part of the executive branch yet because they are adjudged by Congress as fulfilling quasi-legislative and quasi-judicial roles, and because they are explicitly assigned to provide an independent regulatory function, these commissions are legally protected from presidential influence.

Presidents can appoint commission members but they cannot dismiss them and because their tenures are both fixed and staggered it prevents a president from making sudden and sweeping changes to a commission's membership. For example, each of the seven members of the Federal Reserve Board has a fourteen-year term of office. The appointments are made on a rolling basis which ensures that in a single four-year term, a president under normal circumstances would only be able to appoint or reappoint two members of the Board. Commissions, therefore, are often substantial organisations supervising major areas of social and economic activity (e.g. Federal Communications Commission, Federal Trade Commission, Securities and Exchange Commission, Equal Employment Opportunity Commission, Consumer Product Safety Commission, Occupational Safety and Health Review Commission). Although they are often located within executive departments, they are nevertheless legally protected structures whose legitimacy is based upon the independence of its decisions and the need for organisational autonomy to serve the public interest. For example, even though a modern president is ultimately responsible for the management of the national economy, he has no control over monetary policy because of the independence of the Federal Reserve Board which sets American interest rates. President Clinton found this to be one of the most painful of his initiation rites into Washington politics. Clinton came to realise that his administration's financial position and, by extension, his entire reform package would be conditional upon decisions taken by the Federal Reserve Board, and upon the reaction of the bond market in particular to the Federal Reserve's movement on interest rates. Bob Woodward captures the moment of understanding in his description of an early meeting of Clinton's economic advisers.

> It was possible that the Fed would lower rates, and it was possible that the credibility of a deficit reduction plan would cause inflation fears to recede and the bond traders to cut long term interest rates . . . 'But after ten years of fiscal shenanigans,' Blinder [Alan Blinder, professor of economics at Princeton and deputy to Laura Tyson, chairperson of the Council of Economic Advisors] quickly pointed out, referring to the unrealized promises of Reagan and Bush to cut the deficit, 'the bond market will not likely respond' . . . Clinton's face turned red with anger and disbelief. 'You mean to tell me that the success of the program and my reelection hinges on the Federal Reserve and a bunch of fucking bond traders?' he responded . . . Clinton, it seemed to Blinder, perceived at this moment how much of his fate was passing into the hands of the unelected Alan Greenspan and the bond market.[38]

The second main reason for the difficulties presidents face in exerting control over the bureaucracy lies in its composition and organisation. American bureaucracy was a late developer. It emerged long after the main framework of government had become established. In the words of Robert J. Williams, the federal bureaucracy has grown

> in a sporadic, *ad hoc* way and its structures and activities have never been consciously integrated or co-ordinated. . . The reality is that there is no such thing as the federal service because each part is the product of a unique institutional skirmish. Instead there is a collection of federal personnel

systems which may be formally joined together but which in practice enjoy a high degree of effective autonomy.[39]

The civil service lacks both an historical identity and an *esprit de corps*. As such, there is little in the American culture of government employment to counter the centrifugal tendencies of American policies. Left to themselves, agencies will tend to move progressively away from the orbit of the chief executive and towards the stronger gravitational field of the policy jurisdiction itself together with the social and economic interests incorporated within it.

American presidents are constantly confronted with a bureaucracy which is in Arthur Schlesinger's view, 'sprawling and undisciplined neither especially responsive to its political chiefs nor especially dependent on their protection'.[40] What was the product of incremental growth, in a system largely devoid of any conception of the state, has remained an incoherent and chronically accessible organisation in which structure is accepted as being interchangeable with process and policy.[41] One way in which this situation can be improved is by reorganising the executive branch to reduce the wastage and duplication that arise from such decentralisation; to improve the coordination of government services in the same areas which are often randomly distributed throughout several different agencies; and to allow an altogether more rational use of administrative reasons. Despite the logic behind the quest for government reorganisation, presidents are rarely permitted to carry out such structural alterations because it is Congress which has the final authority on such matters and Congress has generally been loath to disrupt the bilateral relationship that exists between executive agencies and congressional committees. Any rearrangement of the government would threaten Congress' system of committees that in the main replicates the current organisational pattern of the federal bureaucracy.

President Johnson, for example, failed in his effort to consolidate the Departments of Commerce and Labor into one organisation. President Nixon's grandiose plan to merge several departments into four large units also came to nothing. Some changes have been accomplished – four new departments have been created since 1977 (Table 6.3).

Table 6.3. The growth of cabinet level departments

Department	Year	President	Personnel (1991)
State	1789	Washington	25,699
War/Defense	1789	Washington	1,012,716 (civ.)
Treasury	1789	Washington	166,433
Interior	1849	Polk	81,683
Agriculture	1862	Lincoln	125,640
Justice	1870	Grant	90,821
Commerce (formerly part of Commerce and Labor, 1903)	1913	Wilson	38,087

Department	Year	President	Personnel (1991)
Labor (formerly part of Commerce and Labor, 1903)	1913	Wilson	17,938
Housing and Urban Development	1965	Johnson	14,998
Transportation	1966	Johnson	69,831
Energy	1977	Carter	19,539
Health and Human Services (formerly part of Health, Education and Welfare, 1953)	1980	Carter	129,483
Education (formerly part of HEW, 1953)	1980	Carter	5,081
Veterans Affairs	1988	Reagan	256,145

Source: J.P. Pfiffner, *The Modern Presidency* (New York: St Martin's Press, 1994); *Statistical Abstract of the United States: 1993*, 113th edn (Austin: Reference Press, 1993), p. 343.

Nevertheless, the structure of government remains 'organisationally incoherent' with programmes 'scattered throughout a crazy quilt of bureaus and divisions in the more than one hundred ·executive departments and agencies', where the placement of a government responsibility within the administrative structure has 'little to do with rational concepts of management'.[42]

Even when changes have been made, there is no assurance that the alterations have been appropriate to more effective management, or motivated by non-political considerations. The Department of Defense, for example, was formed in 1949 when all the service departments were placed under one integrated structure. But forty years later, inter-service rivalry and conflict were still rampant and ensuring a low level of coordination in military planning. In 1988, for example, the rapid expansion of military spending under President Reagan had led to nearly fifty different electronic combat systems and to over forty separate infra-red imaging projects designed to meet similar needs.

Of course, any chief executive will be frustrated by the organisation for which he or she is responsible. Large administrative structures possess their own inherent limitations. Those who work within them interpret such limits as the consequences of rational thoroughness, professional experience, and institutional continuity. In Washington, the sheer operational complexity of such a large organisation as the federal bureaucracy generates its own indigenous restrictions. Delays are seen as inevitable. It has been estimated that it takes from six to eight months for a presidential directive to be translated into agency action. In some cases the time between decision and implementation can be as great as three years. In the words of one observer:

> decision-making may be the President's prerogative if he claims it, but only the organizations under him can implement his decisions. And large organizations have characteristics that tend to blunt the sharpness of decisions . . . Policies are executed according to preconceived plans and standard operating procedures – the only possible method by which large organizations can act.[43]

The federal budget also fails to provide a president with an arena of open choice. Budgets have incidental properties of their own. Because they are invariably the product of stable decision processes, they are devised incrementally, in which the previous year's budget is both the norm and the projected basis for all subsequent allocations.[44] During recent years, the effects of 'incrementalism' have been compounded by the fact that a rising proportion of the federal budget is designated as 'uncontrollable expenditure' to the extent that it is composed of legal entitlements and prior contractual obligations. In 1970, the proportion of the budget containing uncontrollable spending was 61.5 per cent. In 1980, it stood at 70 per cent. By the 1990s, such 'uncontrollable' spending was accounting for over three-quarters of all federal expenditure.

All these legal and administrative constraints may be evident, but it does not prevent presidents – especially incoming presidents – from believing that such inherent limitations are more apparent than real and that they are condoned and perpetuated by politically motivated interests within the bureaucracy. This leads to the final factor in the president's problems in substantiating his position as chief executive. As politicians with a limited tenure of office, all presidents are disposed to the view that the scope for bureaucratic responsiveness to change is kept artificially small by a politicised bureaucracy intent upon protecting its entrenched policies, resources, and position.

It is customary for Republican presidents to suspect the federal bureaucracy of being a fifth column for the Democratic Party. This is because the rise of the bureaucratic state in America was largely instigated by liberal Democratic presidents intent upon a more activist and interventionist government. Civil servants were thought to be Democratic in conviction, Democratic in electoral choice, and Democratic in their defence of established programmes and their advocacy of further government expansion. Incoming Republican presidents have regularly condemned the federal bureaucray for acting as a trustee for Democratic programmes in which self-interest, employment protection, and simple inertia would ensure bureaucratic opposition to all presidential efforts at rationalisation and the diminishment of government. In a classic study of the problem, Joel Aberbach and Bert Rockman used survey evidence to corroborate the claim that a gap existed in the values and beliefs between those serving in the Nixon administration and members of the civil service. Aberbach and Rockman not only found 'a career civil service with very little Republican representation, but even more pointedly . . . a social service bureaucracy dominated by administrators ideologically hostile to many of the directions pursued possessed by the Nixon administration'.[45]

Presidential belief in the political bias of the civil service and in its capacity to frustrate White House policy, is not, however, confined to Republican incumbents. It is also endemic in Democratic administrations and it extends much further than the Pentagon which is regarded as having close ties with the Republicans because of their attachment to patriotic expression and national defence.

Notwithstanding the more or less explicit partisanship of some parts of the civil service it is evident that the bureaucracy is politicised in a much more subtle and persuasive sense than mere party affiliation. At one level, civil servants can be expected over time to acquire an affinity both with the agencies for whom they work and with the programmes for which they are responsible. From loyalty, experience, and specialised knowledge comes resistance to political change and the impulse to use their access to advance information to confront political superiors.

At another level is the permeation of social and economic interests into the bureaucracy. Either consciously or unconsciously the boundary between society and government, between private and public sectors, becomes progressively indistinct until civil servants not only adopt the perspectives of cognate groups lying outside government, but cooperate with them to protect their joint interests. This cross-penetration of perspectives and interests is what must alarm presidents about the executive branch. It is why so many chief executives believe that sooner or later cabinet members will 'go native' and succumb to the entrenched interests of their departments. It is also why many commentators have claimed that those who serve in the cabinet are a president's 'natural enemies'.[46]

Bureaucratic potential for political non-cooperation and even confrontation is further enhanced by the presence of the civil service's alternative master, i.e. the Congress. It is the Congress that provides the arena in which White House policy can be challenged by forces inside and outside the bureaucracy. It is the Congress which allows the bureaucracy's implicit political constituencies to be mobilised and fully expressed in an adversarial context. The fragmentation of Congress into specialist committees facilitates not only a parallel fragmentation of the bureaucracy, but also the development of political alliances between components of Congress and the bureaucracy together with their outside client-based interests. These communities of mutual political interest are often referred to as 'iron triangles'.[47] The term evokes the notion of a permanent sub-government, independent of presidential direction, resistant to unacceptable change and largely autonomous in nature.[48] 'Iron triangles' are consistent with the more conventional metaphor of executive agencies as 'a chain of traditional citadels defended like forts against presidential incursion'.[49] Both suggest that the growth of the executive branch has produced not so much an extension to it as a wholly different entity – i.e. a *de facto* fourth branch of government.

More recently, Hugh Heclo has claimed that 'iron triangles' are a misnomer because they suggest a permanence and solidity which no longer exists in many of the relationships between government and outside interests. They have been superseded by 'issue-networks'. Heclo prefers this term because it conveys the wider and more diffuse composition of policy alliances that have come to prevail in contemporary American government.

Iron triangles and subgovernments suggest a stable set of participants coalesced to control fairly narrow public programs which are in the direct economic interest of each party to the alliance. Issue networks are almost the reverse image in each respect. Participants move in and out of the networks constantly. Rather than groups united in dominance over a program, no one, as far as one can tell, is in control of the policies and issues. Any direct material interest is often secondary to intellectual or emotional commitment.[50]

These groupings of shared knowledge make the old consensus politics of the mutual adjustment of interests far more difficult because they promote not merely an intransigent morality, but a morality of intransigence. Constituents of 'iron triangles' could 'at least be bought off by giving them some of the material advantages that they crave[d]. But for issue activists it is likely to be a question of policy choices that are right or wrong'. The 'influence of the policy technicians and their networks permeates everything the White House may want to do'.[51] A president is, therefore, confronted with the difficulty of trying to exert political leadership in a situation in which the more closely political administrators become identified with the various specialised policy networks the further they became separated from the ordinary citizen[52] and, thereby, from a solid foundation of public support.

Benefits and problems of control devices

Whether presidents are frustrated by the material force of iron triangles or by the more transcendent properties of policy technocracy, their position in the executive branch is continuously compromised by legal structural and political forces beyond their control. The presidency's legitimacy within contemporary American politics is closely linked with the idea that as the federal government increases in scale it remains susceptible to the president's political supervision. To the extent that it is seen not to be reducible to the chief executive's authority or control, the president's own political position suffers accordingly – which in turn further undermines his position to exert discipline. A lack of effective presidential direction, therefore, is both an administrative and a political problem, not least to the political system as a whole. The response to this syndrome of an institutionalised control, has been a series of attempts to strengthen the presidency's structural position and improve its capacity to act as a chief executive.

By far the most significant of these efforts at augmentation is the Executive Office of the President (EXOP). It is essentially an aggregate organisation consisting of several specialised units geared to providing the president with the sort of administrative resources required to engage the executive branch. The Executive Office of the President is designed to compensate for the president's solitary status against the big battalions of the executive departments and to tilt the balance away from the forces of bureaucratic decentralisation and towards the extension of central presidential authority. The origins of the Executive Office lay in the rapid expansion of the federal government during the New Deal when even a highly resourceful president like Franklin Roosevelt risked being overwhelmed by the burgeoning executive branch. The Brownlow Committee of Administrative Management was set up to study the problem and in 1937 it reported that the President needed 'help'.[53] The help it had in mind were not the customary reform ideas of executive reorganisation or measures intended to increase efficiency and economy. The Committee laid unprecedented emphasis upon the need for the president to be reaffirmed as the centre of the executive branch and to be afforded the managerial instruments to translate his formal position into an actual condition.[54] A nervous Congress took two years to approve Brownlow's recommendations and in 1939 Roosevelt took ownership of an Executive Office that in subsequent years would rapidly grow into a major institution.

The main substance of the original bequest to the president, and the entity which continues to provide the bulk of the 'help', is the budgetary office. The Bureau of the Budget was moved from the Treasury Department to the Executive Office and reorganised into a much more active instrument of administrative management. The Bureau was already well versed in pooling, correlating and revising the financial estimates of the various departments of government. It now performed this function for the president rather than for the Treasury. Furthermore, it was given a new responsibility of 'legislative clearance' – i.e. monitoring and coordinating departmental requests on proposed legislation. Ostensibly the Bureau's interest lay in the financial implications of legislation for the federal budget. But it was not long before the Bureau spilled over into the substance of legislation. Accordingly, the Bureau became 'the president's sole agent for clearing departmental drafts for proposed legislation obtaining agency advice on enrolled bills, and advising the president on measures passed by Congress'.[55]

This elite corps of approximately 500 economists and accountants was a permanent invitation for presidents progressively to press their claims to supervise the executive branch. But to a president like Richard Nixon who was convinced that the civil service was infested by the opposite party and who was intent upon a holy war on Washington bureaucracy, even the Budget Bureau was found wanting. In President Nixon's view, it was not only insufficiently managerial in function but also professionally neutral to the point of suspicion in such a partisan contest. Instead of a Bureau that merely prevented clashes in policy, Nixon wanted an outfit that could actively piece together comprehensive omnibus programmes from different sources, that could evaluate executive programmes in relation to the administration's substantive goals and principles; and that could take the latter and translate them into coordinated and coherent programmes. In 1970, Nixon achieved his objectives when Congress approved the reorganisation of the Budget Bureau into the appropriately named Office of Management and Budget.

The Office of Management and Budget has since become the most powerful single administrative unit in Washington. It is now responsible for the overall management of the federal government in respect to personnel, resources and policies.[56] It also provides a permanent invitation to presidents to push its remit further and further in the drive to acquire greater central control over government – even if this is at the expense not just of the agency's reputation for professional 'neutral competence', but of the stability provided by its 'institutional memory'.[57] Since its formation, the Office of Management and Budget has assumed responsibility for examining the substance of executive programmes, for assessing the ways in which they are implemented, and even for engaging in the actual implementation of policy. Under President Reagan, the Office of Management and Budget (OMB) was given yet another central function. The Office of Management and Budget was pressed into service for Reagan's crusade to reduce the scale of federal regulation in American society. Under Executive Order 12291 (1981), Reagan greatly enlarged the OMB's authority to subject the regulations from independent agencies to stringent oversight and central clearance. In 1985, President Reagan went even further with Executive Order 12498 which required agencies to produce yearly estimates of *anticipated* policy agendas and decisions for OMB review.

The Office of Management and Budget has been instrumental in the institutionalisation of the presidency but it has by no means been the only active agent in the process. Its precedent has been copied – albeit on a smaller scale – on a variety of occasions for a variety of reasons. Two of the most significant additions to the Executive Office came after World War II when the responsibilities the president had acquired during the 1930s and 1940s for the state of the economy and for the nation's defence were formally recognised by Congress and translated into statutory obligations. In 1946, the Employment Act declared it is the policy of the federal government 'to promote maximum employment, production and purchasing power' in the national economy. To assist the president in his obligation to monitor the economy and to report on its performance, a Council of Economic Advisers (CEA) was created and placed in the Executive Office. A year later, the presidency was provided with a National Security Council (NSC) to advise him on all matters relating to defence. After an uncertain beginning when President Truman suspected that Congress had set up the agency to ensure that post-war presidents would not enjoy the same level of personal discretion in foreign policy-making that Roosevelt had acquired in World War II, the National Security Council was gradually transformed into the principal presidential instrument in the planning and coordination of American foreign policy. It became a highly influential body not just in the day-to-day conduct of American foreign policy, but in the handling of international crises, especially during the Cold War era. Its prominence has led to friction between the president's National Security Adviser and mainline agencies (especially the State Department) becoming a common condition of American government.

Other elements of the Executive Office have come and gone. Some of its original components (e.g. National Resources Planninng Board, Office of Government Reports) and units required by wartime conditions (e.g. Office of Emergency Management, Office of War Mobilisation) have been eliminated. Newer agencies have taken their places (e.g. Domestic Council, Special Action Office for Drug Abuse) only to be replaced by others (e.g. Office of Policy Development, Office of Drug Abuse Policy). No consistent pattern is discernible either in respect to the number of agencies within the Executive Office or to the substantive content of their jurisdictions.[58] The placement of different agencies within the Executive Office are prompted by different motivations – sometimes to protect an agency from mainline departments (e.g. Office of Economic Opportunity), sometimes to give visible expression to a president's concern for an issue (e.g. Energy Policy Office, Office of Consumer Affairs), and sometimes to generate specific administrative benefits (e.g. Domestic Council). President Clinton, for example, made a point of naming the agency designed to spearhead the drive towards American economic recovery, the National Economic Council (1993). It was a conscious effort to draw on the established authority of the National Security Council in an attempt to give emphasis to Clinton's electoral commitment to reorder American security priorities in the post-Cold War world. The Executive Office, therefore, will vary with each president in both the number and composition of its constituent units. While President Carter had 15 components to his Executive Office, President Reagan had between 10 and 11. In 1994, President Clinton's Executive Office had 11 elements (see Table 6.4).

Table 6.4. The component elements and staffing levels of the Executive Office of the President (EXOP) – 1994

Title	Number of principals and staff assistants
White House Office	220
Council of Economic Advisers	17
Council on Environmental Quality	4
National Security Council	55
Office of Management and Administration	46
Office of the National Aids Policy Coordinator	7
Office of National Drug Control Policy	16
Office of Policy Development	34
Office of Science and Technology Policy	43
Office of the United States Trade Representative	28
Office of Management and Budget	567

Source: (Washington: Carroll Publishing Co., 1994), pp. 133–42

The only parts of the Executive Office to have had a continuous existence from the Office's formative period in the late 1930s and 1940s are the White

House Staff, the OMB, the CEA, and the NSC. These still provide the backbone of the Executive Office with the OMB accounting for the lion's share of the personnel (i.e. approximately one third).

If it is the OMB which has the professional prestige, there can be little doubt that it is the White House staff which provides the EXOP with its most potent and politically controversial element. The White House staff permits the president to bring his most trusted personal advisers and associates into the highest reaches of government, where they are expected to act as a countervailing force on behalf of the president against the many interests in the executive branch competing for authority. The Brownlow Committee originally recommended six presidential assistants who 'should be possessed of high competence, great physical vigour, and a passion for anonymity'.[59] By 1941, the White House staff had grown to 53. In 1973, it had increased to 542. Because of the controversy generated by President Nixon's White House staff in the Watergate scandal (1973–4), subsequent presidents have regarded it as politically prudent to try and reduce the size of their staff. By 1977 the level of stood at 394. In 1982 the figure was 394 and by 1985 the staff was registered at 367. In 1991, the level stood at 347. Such statistics, however, have to be treated with caution as they can be kept artificially low through the practice of seconding staff from other agencies on a temporary basis. Much of the staff is engaged in housekeeping and secretarial activities. The actual number of presidential assistants is in the region of 25. Exact figures and assignments at this level are also imprecise not only because the organisation varies across different administrations, but because each president will redefine job descriptions and shift responsibilities amongst advisers within a single administration. Apart from a few exceptions (e.g. press relations/media communications, legislative liaison), the White House Office is not broken down into permanent and precise compartments. The emphasis is on adaptability and flexible response.

The growth in the scale and power of the White House staff is widely seen as epitomising the rise of the modern presidency. The staff provide the most graphic expression of the centrality of the presidency and its *raison d'être* in contemporary American government. In strictly formal terms, the staff is supposed to be merely the extension of the president with no separate identity of its own and with no right to perform any function that the president himself would not be able to fulfil by himself. The real position is that 'in three critical areas – control of the executive branch, political outreach and policy advice – the presidential staff have enabled the president to do things he would otherwise be unable to do on his own'.[60] Such has been the impact of the White House staff on the strength of the presidency that it amounts to 'the emergence of a presidential branch of government separate and apart from the executive branch'.[61]

With power, status, and position comes controversy and even notoriety. For example, two of the most serious political and constitutional scandals in recent American history have centred upon the White House staff (i.e. the Watergate scandal and the Iran–Contra affair of 1986–7). The criticisms most commonly lodged against the White House are as follows:

- Through their physical proximity and access to the president, a disproportionately small number of aides is given disproportionate influence at the highest level of government.

- They are often seen as unrepresentative of the country as a whole, with many coming from the president's home state (e.g. President Kennedy's 'Irish mafia', President Carter's 'Georgia mafia', President Clinton's 'Arkansas mafia'); and regarded as unqualified for the position they hold – many having served as campaign managers and organisers.

- Staff are appointed without congressional approval and are protected from congressional scrutiny by executive privilege. Because they are unelected, unaccountable, and irremovable, for many critics 'it [is] not the functions performed by the White House staff that [is] at issue, it [is] the fact that the White House staff perform[s] them'.[62]

- In the guise of administrative officers, the White House staffers are, or become, political activists and even hire executives.

- Staffers are the eyes and ears of the president but in performing this function they continually post the risk of appropriating not just his arms and legs, but also his mind (see Chapter 7).

- Staff assistants can both isolate presidents from other centres of power and sources of advice, and at the same time overwhelm presidents by drawing additional issues into the White House that could be more easily resolved outside it.

- The White House office further exacerabates the presidential–cabinet relations, substituting coercive direction for consensual coordination by undermining cabinet secretaries' authority and projecting them deeper into departmental 'nativism'.

- The inexperience and zeal of such staff can lead to the usurpation of presidential authority and even to actions that reach beyond the limits of legality.

- The political priorities of the staff can generate a lack of respect for the rights of other parts of the government, an unwillingness to acknowledge the validity of alternative viewpoints, and a desire to nullify the system's traditional checks and balances. Political aggression and limited horizons can lead the White House staff to conclude that 'the separation of powers is an anathema. They have wonderful ideas, apparently, only to see them sabotaged in the bureaucratic labyrinth. How dare those bureaucrats get in the way! . . . It is as if the Presidency were the government. The President's men tend to see themselves not as part of a larger system, but as the system itself.'[63]

- Given that the White House staff represents the president's closest aides and real choices for advice, the staff is seen as an extension of the president's person and as a characterisation of his administration. This being so, the staff attracts extensive scrutiny from the media and the president's opponents, leading on occasions to it becoming a lightning rod for political controversy, and thereby a device for challenging the president himself.

- In providing a president with his own mini-bureaucracy, White House staff merely replicates rather than resolves the problems of bureaucracy. As a consequence, the White House staff is not so much a method of effective executive control so much as a substitute for one.

Despite the profusion and gravity of these complaints and the acknowledgement that the White House office remains politically and constitutionally ambiguous, it is by convention left largely alone. There have been very few moves by Congress either to subject it to sustained oversight, or to confront its legal immunities or to challenge its present form and function. The dearth of moves against the White House staff as a governmental entity is symptomatic of a larger and more generalised deference towards the institutionalisation of the presidency. The White House staff, and the Executive Office of the President as a whole, is tolerated out of a sense of realism which recognises that while presidential institutions came as a belated response to the institutionalisation of the federal bureaucracy, they have nevertheless been assimilated as both a necessary and legitimate feature of American government.

Deinstitutionalisation?

It is that self same presidential institutionalisation which has been responsible for the new alternative strategy of controlling the federal bureaucracy. Instead of simple reform or reorganisation, recent presidents have used their public prestige and political position to popularise the issue of *reducing* the federal bureaucracy as an act of communal will against priviledge, wastage, and over-regulation. Presidential populism against the 'fourth branch of government' was especially prominent in the Reagan Administration. Instead of acting as a chief executive and defending the interests of his civil servants, Reagan used the role of chief executive to distance himself from government in general and from the civil service in particular. His public rhetoric dramatised the existence of a trial of strength between himself and the dark forces of bureaucratic incrementalism. Reagan extended control by a process of debilitation and demoralisation (e.g. salary reductions, diminished retirement benefits and the end of 'cost of living' adjustments). The heavy artillery was provided by the Grace Commission which in effect let loose thousands of industrialists and business executives into the federal bureaucracy, in order to demonstrate the inefficiency of government and the need for 'top-down' corporate management structures. The Commission depleted its authority by its exaggerated claims of possible savings, its heavy-handed ideological style, its underestimation of congressional opposition and its abrasive and over-blown report running to 38 volumes and 2,478 recommendations. Even though very few of its recommendations were ever implemented, the Grace Commission set the combative tone of the Reagan presidency in relation to its own administrative machinery.[64] But in spite of severe budget cuts in 1982, across the board reductions in staff, blanket targets for privatisation levels in agencies, and a flamboyant war against bureaucracy, President Reagan failed to prevent the restoration of expenditure growth and the consequent increase in the federal deficit.

As another professional outsider who had successfully run for the presidency by campaigning against the citadel of Washington government, Bill Clinton instituted a different kind of panacea. Instead of mere reduction, the emphasis was now on 'reinvention' – a contemporary buzz word popularised by David Osborne and Ted Gaebler's book *Reinventing Government*[65] which advocated the need for an altogether more fluid and entrepreneurial approach in the public sector. The term reinvention of government was prompted by the belief that modern conditions were making traditional 'industrial era' bureaucracy redundant. The old ideal of programmes delivered to passive recipients and implemented by a detached professional and hierarchically organised elite directed by executives according to strict operational rules, was claimed to be inefficient, wasteful, and unworkable. With such a chronic and systematic deficit problem, more could be and had to be, elicited from existing resource levels. Osborne and Gaebler demonstrated how this could be achieved. It involved a radical change not merely in government organisation but in public service philosophy (e.g. competition in service delivery, contracting out, treating recipients as customer consumers, output oriented management, decentralised budgetary incentive schemes, performance review).

Osborne and Gaebler identified ten guiding principles of governmental reinvention:

1. *Catalytic government:* steering rather than rowing.

2. *Community-owned government:* empowering rather than serving.

3. *Competitive government:* injecting competition into service delivery.

4. *Mission-driven government:* transforming rule-driven organisations.

5. *Results-oriented government:* funding outcomes, not inputs.

6. *Customer-driven government:* meeting the needs of the customer, not the bureaucracy.

7. *Enterprising government:* earning rather than spending.

8. *Anticipatory government:* prevention rather than cure.

9. *Decentralised government:* from hierarchy to participation and teamwork.

10. *Market-oriented government:* leveraging change through the market.

Clearly inspired by Osborne and Gaebler's evangelism, President Clinton instituted the National Performance Review (NPR) – an extensive study of the federal bureaucracy conducted by 250 government employees headed by Vice-President Al Gore. The staff was divided into twenty-two 'Agency Reinvention Teams' with a brief to examine organisational structures, financial management, budgeting, personnel, procurement, regulatory systems and programme design. In the spirit of reinvention, the NPR report published in September 1993 was only a fraction of the size of the Grace Commission's findings. It advocated the rationalisation of agency jurisdictions; the decentralisation of budget formulation; greater consultation between the OMB and other agencies; the streamlining of government procurement procedures; greater discretion for managers to contract out; the devolution of decision-making; increased local flexibility in hiring, firing, and incentive schemes; the reduction of government monopolies; a greater usage of performance targets; and a movement towards a general deregulation within governmental agencies. According to the Clinton Administration, the NPR promised to save $108 billion and to reduce federal employment by 252,000 over five years. The administration claimed that its programme was different from that of the Reagan presidency in that it had been largely produced by federal employees and envisaged a pragmatic partnership between workers and management. Nevertheless, it can be claimed that the motivation behind NPR was very similar to that of the Grace Commission. According to Charles Goodsell, for example:

> The reinvention movement has turned the Washington establishment and much of the public management fraternity back in the direction of the mind-set of the Reagan era. Once again we are assuming that public servants do not serve and that bureaucracy does not work ... [T]he overall emphasis of the administration has been to revert to the posture of correcting problems, not building on strengths. The vice-president's claim on the day before his report was presented that American government is 'failing the American people' captures this sentiment succinctly.[66]

The populist scepticism attached to the current administration culture is quite clear from the NPR's preamble which states that government workers 'fill out forms that should never have been written, follow rules that should never have been imposed and prepare reports that serve no purpose and are often never even read. In the name of controlling waste, we have created paralysing inefficiency.'[67]

Even though the success of the NPR will in the end depend on Congress, the Review itself shows that the presidency's drive to control the bureaucracy remains a central feature both of Washington politics and of the presidency's political role. The presidency's own institutionalisation remains in fact largely dependent upon the need to supervise the bureaucracy. Given the nature of administrative and management principles drawn from the models of reinvention or re-engineering,[68] such control will increasingly take the form of bureaucratic *de*institutionalisation, with the presidency providing the central direction to the release of market dynamics within the executive branch. The contemporary institutionalisation of the presidency, therefore, promises to become not an extension to bureaucratic institutionalisation so much as a point of disjunction from which the bureaucracy's institutional nature is progressively diminished.

Notes

1 See C. Bonwick, *The American Revolution* (Basingstoke, Macmillan, 1991); E. S. Morgan, *The Stamp Act Crisis: Prologue to Revolution* (Chicago: University of Chicago Press, 1953); E. S. Morgan, *The Birth of the Republic* (Chicago: University of Chicago Press, 1956).

2 'Declaration of Independence, 1776' in R. D. Heffner (ed.), *A Documentary History of the United States*, rev. edn (New York: Mentor, 1976), p. 16.

3 G. S. Wood, *The Creation of the American Republic, 1776–1787* (Chapel Hill: University of North Carolina Press, 1969), ch. 4.

4 M. Cunliffe, *American Presidents and the Presidency* (London: Fontana, 1972), ch. 1.

5 J. B. Saunders, *The Presidency of the Continental Congress, 1774–1789* (Chicago: University of Chicago Press, 1930); M. Jensen, *The New Nation: A History of the United States During the Confederation, 1781–1789* (New York: A. A. Knopf, 1950).

6 C. A. Beard, *An Economic Interpretation of the Constitution of the United States* (New York: Macmillan, 1913).

7 J. N. Rakove, 'The Great Compromise: Ideas, Interests and the Politics of Constitution Making', *William and Mary Quarterly*, 64, 3 (July 1987), pp. 424–57.

8 T. E. Cronin (ed.), *Inventing the Presidency* (Lawrence: University of Kansas Press, 1989); E. S. Corwin, *The President: Office and Powers, 1789–1984* (New York: New York University Press, 1984), ch. 1; A. S. Diamond, 'The Zenith of the Separation of Powers Theory: The Federal Convention of 1787', *Publius: The Journal of Federalism* (Summer 1978), pp. 45–70; R. F. Jones, 'The Founding Fathers and the Creation of the Executive Branch' in P. C. Dolce and G. H. Skau (eds), *Power and the Presidency* (New York: Scribner, 1976); C. C. Thach, *The Creation of the Presidency* (Baltimore: Johns Hopkins University Press, 1969).

9 W. E. Binkley, *President and Congress*, 3rd rev. edn (New York: Vintage, 1962), p. 29.

10 J. N. Rakove, "The Great Compromise': Drafting the American Constitution, 1787', *History Today*, 37 (September 1987), pp. 19–25.

11 Article III, Section 1.

12 R. M. Pious, *The American Presidency* (New York: Basic Books, 1979), pp. 29, 30.

13 Gouverneur Morris quoted in Rakove, '"The Great Compromise": Drafting the American Constitution', p. 24

14 James Madison, 'Federalist Paper No 48' in J. Madison, A. Hamilton, and J. Jay, *The Federalist Papers* (New York: Mentor 1961), p. 309.

15 James Madison, 'Federalist Paper No 51' in Madison *et al.*, *The Federalist Papers*, p. 322.

16 Cunliffe, *American Presidents and the Presidency*, p. 32.

17 Quoted in R. M. Pious, *The American Presidency*, p. 27.

18 F. McDonald, *The American Presidency: An Intellectual History* (Lawrence: University Press of Kansas, 1994).

19 L. Koenig, *The Chief Executive*, 3rd edn (New York: Harcourt Brace Jovanovich, 1975), p. 127.

20 R. Hofstadter, *The American Political Tradition and the Men Who Made It* (London: Jonathan Cape, 1967), p. 206.

21 Quoted in Binkley, *President and Congress*, p. 235.

22 J. M. Burns, *Presidential Government: The Crucible of Leadership* (Boston: Houghton Mifflin, 1973), p. 81.

23 W. E. Leuchtenberg, *Franklin Roosevelt and the New Deal, 1932–1940* (New York: Harper and Row, 1963), p. 327. See also W. E. Leuchtenberg, 'Franklin D. Roosevelt: The First Modern President', in F. E. Greenstein (ed.), *Leadership in the Modern Presidency* (Cambridge: Harvard University Press, 1988), pp. 7–40.

24 D. Perkins, *The New Age of Franklin Roosevelt, 1932–45* (Chicago: University of Chicago Press 1957), p. 2.

25 F. E. Greenstein, 'Change and Continuity in the Modern Presidency', in A. King (ed.), *The New American Political System* (Washington, D.C.: American Enterprise Institute, 1978), p. 445.

26 H. H. Humphrey, *The Political Philosophy of the New Deal* (Baton Rouge: Louisiana State University Press, 1970), p. x.

27 G. McConnell, *The Modern Presidency* (New York: St Martin's Press, 1967), p. 13.

28 Quoted in A. M. Schlesinger, Jr., *The Imperial Presidency* (London: Andre Deutsch, 1974), p. 522.

29 Burns, *Presidential Government*; T. E. Cronin, *The State of the Presidency*, 2nd edn (Boston: Little, Brown, 1980), ch. 3; F. E. Greenstein, 'Change and Continuity in the Modern Presidency' in King (ed.), *The New American Political System*, pp. 47–52.

30 *Time*, 10 August 1992.

31 *The White House Transcripts: The Full Text of the Submission of Recorded Presidential Conversations to the Committee on the Judiciary of the House of Representatives by President Richard Nixon*, intro. R. W. Apple, Jr. (New York: Bantam, 1974), p. 63.

32 J. J. Tritten and P. N. Stockton, *Reconstituting America's Defense – The New United States National Security Strategy* (New York: Praeger, 1992), p. 78.

33 See R. Bendix, *Max Weber: An Intellectual Portrait* (London: Methuen, 1966), pp. 423–30.

34 H. Heclo, *A Government of Strangers* (Washington, D.C.: Brookings Institution, 1977).

35 R. E. Neustadt, *Presidential Power and the Modern Presidents: The Politics of Leadership from Roosevelt to Reagan* (New York: Free Press, 1990), ch. 4. See also R. Rose, *The Postmodern President: The White House Meets the World* (Chatham: Chatham House, 1988), ch. 9; F. E. Rourke, 'Grappling with the Bureaucracy', in A. J. Meltsner (ed.), *Politics and the Oval Office* (San Francisco: Institute for Contemporary Studies, 1981), pp. 123–40; P. Woll and R. Jones, 'Bureaucratic Defense in Depth', in R. E. Pynn (ed.), *Watergate and the American Political Process* (New York: Praeger, 1975), pp. 215–24.

36 T. E. Cronin, 'Presidents as Chief Executives' in R. G. Tugwell and T. E. Cronin (eds),

The Presidency Reappraised (New York: Praeger, 1974), pp. 234–65; R. Maranto, 'The Administrative Strategies of Republican Presidents From Eisenhower to Reagan', *Presidential Studies Quarterly*, 23, 4 (Fall 1993), pp. 683–97; E. Sanders, 'The Presidency and the Bureaucratic State' in M. Nelson (ed.), *The Presidency and the Political System*, 2nd edn (Washington, D.C.: Congressional Quarterly Press, 1988), pp. 379–409; H. Seidman and R. Gilmour, Politics, *Position and Power: From the Positive to the Regulatory State*, 4th edn (New York: Oxford University Press, 1986).

37 H. Heclo, 'Introduction: The Presidential Illusion' in H. Heclo and L. M. Salaman (eds), *The Illusion of Presidential Government* (Boulder: Westview, 1981), p. 1.

38 B. Woodward, *The Agenda: Inside the Clinton White House* (New York: Simon and Schuster, 1994), p. 84.

39 R. Williams, 'Policy, Process and Power: Understanding American Bureaucracy', in R. Williams (ed.), *Explaining American Politics: Issues and Interpretations* (London: Rouledge, 1990), pp. 99, 101.

40 Schlesinger, *The Imperial Presidency*, p. 249.

41 T. M. Moe, 'The Politics of Bureaucratic Structure', in J. E. Chubb and P. E. Peterson (eds), *Can the Government Govern?* (Washington, D.C.: Brookings Institution, 1989), pp. 267–329; S. S. Skowrenock, *Building a New American State* (New York: Cambridge University Press, 1982).

42 J. A. Califano, *A Presidential Nation* (New York: Norton, 1975), p. 21.

43 D. A. Peppers, '"The Two Presidencies": Eight Years Later', in A. Wildavsky (ed.), *Perspectives on the Presidency* (Boston: Little, Brown, 1975), p. 464.

44 A. Wildavsky, *The Politics of the Budgetary Process*, 4th edn (Boston: Little, Brown, 1984).

45 J. D. Aberbach and B. A. Rockman, 'Clashing Beliefs within the Executive Branch: The Nixon Administration Bureaucracy', *American Political Science Review*, 70, 2 (June 1976), p. 467; see also R. Nixon, *The Memoirs of Richard Nixon* (London: Sidgwick and Jackson, 1978), pp. 768–9.

46 The phrase is generally attributed to President Eisenhower's Budget Director, Charles Dawes. The full quotation is: 'Cabinet members are vice presidents in charge of spending, as such they are the natural enemies of the President', quoted in H. Seidman, *Politics, Position and Power: The Dynamics of Federal Organization* (New York: Oxford University Press, 1970), p. 72.

47 T. Lowi, 'How the Farmers Get What They want', in T. Lowi and R. Ripley (eds), *Legislative Politics, USA,* 3rd edn (Boston: Little, Brown, 1973), pp. 184–91.

48 D. Cater, *Power in Washington* (New York: Random House, 1964); T. Lowi, 'American Business, Public Policy, Case Studies and Political Theory', *World Politics*, 16 (July 1964), pp. 677–715; R. Ripley and G. A. Franklin *Bureaucracy and Policy Implementation* (Homewood: Dorsey, 1982); R. Ripley and G. A. Franklin, *Congress, the Bureaucracy and Public Policy*, 4th edn (Homewood: Dorsey, 1987).

49 E. J. Hughes, *The Living Presidency: The Resources and Dilemmas of the American Presidential Office* (Baltimore: Penguin, 1974), p. 48.

50 H. Heclo, 'Issue Networks and the Executive Establishment', in King, *The New American Political System*, p. 102.

51 *Ibid.*, p. 121.

52 *Ibid.*, p. 118.

53 See F. Mosher (ed.), *'The President Needs Help'* (Lanham: University Press of America, 1988).

54 J. Hart, *The Presidential Branch* (New York: Pergamon, 1987), pp. 24–36.

55 L. Fisher, *President and Congress: Power and Policy* (New York: Free Press, 1972), pp. 53–4.

56 L. Berman, *The Office of Management and Budget and the Presidency, 1921–1979* (Princeton: Princeton University Press, 1979).

57 H. Heclo, 'OMB and the Presidency: The Problem of "Neutral Competence"', *Public Interest*, 38 (1975); T. M. Moe, 'The Politicised Presidency', in J. E. Chubb and P. E. Peterson (eds), *The New Direction in American Politics* (Washington, D.C.: Brookings Institution, 1989), pp. 235–71.

58 J. P. Burke, *The Institutional Presidency* (Baltimore: Johns Hopkins University Press, 1992), chs 3–7.

59 Quoted in Burke, *The Institutional Presidency*, p. 1.

60 J. Hart 'The President and his Staff' in M. Shaw (ed.), *From Roosevelt to Reagan: The Development of the Modern Presidency* (London: C. Hurst, 1987), p. 203.

61 N. W. Polsby, 'Some Landmarks in Modern Presidential-Congressional Relations', in A. King (ed.), *Both Ends of the Avenue* (Washington, D.C.: American Enterprise Institute, 1983), p. 20. See also P. Arnold, *Making the Managerial Presidency: Comprehensive Reorganization Planning, 1905–1980* (Princeton: Princeton University Press, 1986); T. E. Cronin, 'The Swelling of the Presidency', in Pynn, *Watergate and the American Political Process*, pp. 204–15; Hart, *The Presidential Branch*, chs 4, 6, 7; S. Hess, *Organizing the Presidency*, 2nd edn (Washington, D.C.: Brookings Institution, 1988); G. King and L. Ragsdale, *The Elusive Executive Executive* (Washington, D.C.: Congressional Quarterly, 1988).

62 Hart, *The Presidential Branch*, p. 120.

63 A. Wildavsky quoted in G. Hodgson, *All Things To All Men: The False Promise of the Modern American Presidency* (Harmondsworth: Penguin, 1984), p. 98.

64 C. T. Goodsell, 'The Grace Commission: Seeking Efficiency for the Whole People', *Public Administration Review*, 44, 3 (May/June 1984), pp. 196–204.

65 D. Osborne and T. Gaebler, *Reinventing Government: How the Entrepreneurial Spirit is Transforming the Public Sector* (Reading: Addison-Wesley, 1992).

66 C. T. Goodsell, *The Case for Bureaucracy: A Public Administration Polemic*, 3rd rev. edn (Chatham: Chatham House, 1994).

67 Quoted in M. Walker, 'Onward Clinton Soldiers in Faith', *Guardian Weekly*, 12 September 1993.

68 M. Hammer and J. Chompey, *Reengineeering the Corporation* (London: Allen and Unwin, 1993).

CHAPTER 7

The public presidency

Presidents are party leaders. At no point is the significance of the party connection more pronounced than when a candidate is selected as president. At that climactic point in an electoral campaign, a party leader lays claim to national leadership on the grounds of a successful party-based campaign to utilise electorates across the United States in favour of the candidacy. A successful presidential election campaign is generally characterised by, and attributed to, a display of party unity. Candidates claim to qualify for high office through the acquisition of their party nominations. Furthermore, they rely on party supporters, workers, and voters throughout the country to provide the inertial force for overall victory. A successful presidential campaign, therefore, appears to fuse party and nation together in an integrated exercise of popular sovereignity, organised through a stable two-party system covering the country. As such, a presidential victory is seen to coincide with the majority preferences of a national voting constituency lodged in their millions for either the Democratic or Republican Party leader. To complete the apparent correlation between national party politics and presidential electioneering, it has been customary in American history for newly elected presidents to be accompanied by party majorities in Congress.

Federal conditions and party divisions

Appearances, however, can be deceptive. What may seem to be a large integrated exercise in mass voting is in reality a highly fragmented and often incoherent form of popular consent. Apart from the fact that a large portion of the electorate does not turn out to vote in presidential elections[1] (i.e. an average of 47 per cent) each election is in effect an assemblage of fifty discrete state elections for seats in the Electoral College which is the body that officially selects the president. While the basis of the Electoral College has been considerably democratised since its inception in 1787, it remains a distinctively federal institution. It not only gives disproportionate weight to the smaller states over the larger states, it also acts as a device for aggregating separate state elections together on a 'winner-takes-all' bloc basis. Instead of acting as a device for integrating votes into a global popular vote, the Electoral College remains a collective body providing a federal framework for national leadership selection. Acknowledging the indivisibility and legitimacy of state sovereignty, the Electoral College ensures that individual votes are accumulated together but only as far as the sub-unit level of the state within the federation. The arrangement carries the risk of the popular vote winner ending up the loser in the Electoral College because of the distribution of votes around the country (see Table 7.1). Nevertheless, the risk of the Electoral College's capricious mechanics denying the presidency to the winner of the popular vote is considered less significant than the need to sustain the federal nature of the electoral system.[2]

Table 7.1. Distortions of the popular vote in the Electoral College – presidential elections 1876, 1888

(I) PRESIDENTIAL ELECTION: 1876		
Candidate	Popular Vote	Electoral College Votes
S. J. Tilden (Democrat)	50.94%	184
R. B. Hayes (Republican)	47.95%	185
P. Cooper (Greenback)	0.97%	0
Others	0.14%	0
(II) PRESIDENTIAL ELECTION: 1888		
Candidate	Popular Vote	College Votes
G. Cleveland (Democrat)	48.66%	168
B. Harrison (Republican)	47.82%	233
C. B. Fisk (Prohibition)	2.20%	0
A. J. Streeter (Union Labor)	1.29%	0
Others	0.03%	0

The federal influence is not just limited to the Electoral College; it extends to the structure and operating ethics of the parties themselves. For the most part, national parties are national in name only. Each party reflects the federal origins and organisations of the political system. While it is true that the characteristics of the federal government have evolved into a more centralised arrangement, the national parties have not developed with the same speed. They remain closely aligned to the formalities of America's more traditional federal balance between nation and state. Since parties are essentially in business to win offices and acquire power, it is wholly consistent in a federal system characterised by state and local sovereignty that parties should concentrate on competing for the one million elective posts available in the 83,000 units of American government. This represents power in its most immediate localised sense. Parties were formed to compete at this level – conditioned by each state's political system, rules and regulations, traditions and interests. In essence, the development of national parties was a bottom-up process in which local parties and party systems came to identify with a national dimension of conflict and attachment at the federal level.[3] Identification, however, is not the same as equivalence. While state parties are part of a system of nationally organised parties, the former retain a substantial sphere of local autonomy as befits a federal union. In fact, national and state party organisations retain a high degree of independence from one another and consequently find it difficult to develop a common approach to policy and strategy. They are, to use the customary description, a 'loose federation' of localised groupings: 'groups in such confusing array of relationships with one another that no chart or diagram could ever generalize their contacts accurately'.[4]

The lack of any clear political and structural hierarchy in the American federation remains a powerful constraint in the development of national parties. 'Within the American structure, there are limits beyond which centralization and coherence in the parties may not go'.[5] In such a system, 'decentralization and lack of cohesion in the party system are based on the structural fact of federalism'.[6] The nationalisation of the Democratic and Republican parties, therefore, has remained an intermittent and highly provisional process in which state and local parties constantly calculate the balance of advantage to be gained by investing in collaborative efforts for a common cause. A presidential election has customarily been the only period when the national party organisations have come fully into existence. This reflects not only the scale of coordination required to win in such an election but also the central fact that the presidency is the only nationally elected office in the American system. Given the huge significance of the federal government in contemporary American society, state and local parties readily coalesce every four years to form alliances to fight the presidential election. To a very great extent, a presidential election is the *raison d'être* of the national party system. It is the one central occasion that mobilises Democrats and Republicans across the fifty states to vote *as if* they belonged to national parties and behaved like national party supporters. The chimera is short lived. Just as an election marks the high water mark of the parties' collective enterprise on a national level, so the period after the election throws into high relief the customary centrifugal forces of American politics. The national organisation of a party normally deteriorates in the face of the urgent preoccupations of state issues and local contests. Accordingly, the vast bulk of party activity reverts to the norm of decentralised electoral campaigning – a disaggregated condition which to Bert Rockman represents its defining characteristic

> [O]ur parties rarely have progressed much past local and personal factions
> . . . What the Constitution fragmented and what the culture reinforced, the
> party system for the most part has been unable to counter. Anemic as they
> typically have been at the national level, the American parties have tended
> to adapt and to reflect their environment rather than overcome and redirect
> it. In so doing, they have reflected a politics that failed to join purpose with
> organization.[7]

Even though elected fellow Democrats and Republicans are present in the Congress, they cannot be relied upon to act as cohesive entities either in supporting or opposing the figure in the White House. Although they are members of the federal government and are assembled in the nation's capital, the structural constraints and electoral conditions of the separation of powers system precludes any sustained institutional partnership between members of the same party in the legislative and executive branches. The differences in tenures, constituents, and mandates not only within Congress but between members of Congress and the presidency deter the formation of collective security arrangements across institutional boundaries. Far from encouraging collaboration, the traditions and incentives of a system of separated powers inhibit the sense of common identity required to make any social bridgeheads across the divide between the legislative and executive branches. Members of Congress and presidents are not sufficiently dependent upon one another for the maintenence of their tenure in Washington, or for the development of their political careers, to recognise party unity as an overriding principle of government. In essence, they lack mutual need – i.e. the root compulsion to cooperate together for political survival and advancement. They do not require each other to remain in office. Therefore, they do not have the incentives to transform parties into devices for collective government and political responsibility. The benefits of partnership and party obligation are invariably outweighed by the need for individual licence to attend to local anxieties, to preserve idiosyncratic majorities, and to minimise electoral vulnerability by the individual cultivation of constituencies.[8]

Even individual members of the same party in the same institution cannot be relied upon to show solidarity. As we observed in Chapter 3, congressional policy is individualistic and entrepreneurial in nature. Fellow party members compete with one another to campaign against the collective entity of Congress as a national institution. The separation of powers structure, therefore, may be characterised as a horizontal division of powers in contrast to the vertical division of federalism, but in essence the localism of federal arrangements provides the fuel for the legislature and executive remaining institutionally separate from one another. In this respect, the division between the Congress and the presidency is an expression of the same federal disaggregation that weakens party structures and inhibits the full development of a two-party system. In place of responsible parties with the cohesion and discipline to reorganise government in line with voter preferences and to deliver policy programmes, American parties are habitually dismissed as merely agents of – instead of antidotes to – decentralisation. They are condemned for failing to provide a national dimension to political activity which would counteract the prevailing culture of candidate-centred campaigns, customised coalition-building and exaggerated constituency service. In such a context, presidents are commonly seen as party leaders without parties to lead.

The presidency and the promise of national leadership

The indictment of American parties can be overdrawn. It must be borne in mind that the two main parties do span the United States and provide the basis of organised political debate and activity across what is a sub-continent. The Democratic and Republican parties dominate electoral competition in a variety of time-zones and climates. It is also important to acknowledge not only that the United States has had a recognisable party system since 1800, but that it has played a central role in the political development of the country. Parties were particularly significant during the formative stages of the Republic. In the view of William Chambers, political parties made five major contributions to the establishment of America's political system. First, they helped to define and maintain a national arena of political authority by directing debate and resources to what was an initially fragile central government. Second, parties helped to reduce factional divisions within the country by offering large inclusive frameworks for accommodation. Third, with the rise of mass politics, parties were able to respond to the demands of participation by providing an apparatus of widespread involvement in decision-making. Fourth, parties helped to translate what was an abstract Constitution into a viable and responsive form of government. The capacity of parties to channel America's major economic, social, and regional forces into a national arena of engagement legitimised both the government and the parties themselves. Finally, as the chief mediating structures between people and government, American parties have been agents of socialisation. They have encouraged the establishment of a core of shared attitudes and loyalties amongst Americans and have assisted in the creation of a common identity which has accordingly reduced the potential for alienation and polarisation in the federal union.[9] The influence of these contributions is still evident in the party system today. For example, more Americans identify with one or other of the two parties than those who do not have such an allegiance.[10] Candidates for elective office find it very difficult to compete effectively without the designation of a major party label. The occasions when politicians have switched parties have been conspicuously few in number; and the opportunities to establish successful third parties have been very limited and usually confined to short-lived surges of non-conformism. Parties organise the distribution of power inside Congress; they devise national rules covering the procedures of local parties; they run national committees and conventions; recruit leaders for office; and provide national support services for their candidates. To James Macgregor Burns, all this is enough to call the party system a 'second constitution because it does much of what a constitution does. Parties allot power, reserve power, distribute power, organise power, make government possible in many cases and, hence, in their own way, they act like constitutions'.[11]

Evidence of an underlying stratum of party organisation and attachment is particularly noticeable at the presidential level. Without the nomination of one of the main parties, a presidential aspirant effectively has no chance of becoming the nation's chief executive. Every president has been a member of a mainline political party and every president relies on his own party for the basis of congressional support and for the means of his own re-election.[12] By the same token, 'party success depends in large measure on a capacity to recruit presidential candidates who can win the presidency, as presidential elections have become a central test of party strength'.[13] Given the sectional nature of America's political development and traditions, and the absence of deep polarising divisions over the socio-economic order, it might be concluded that the American party system maximises the potential for political organisation. In the view of one senior American politician, 'in any other country, the Democrats would be four or five parties and the Republicans two or three'.[14] As a consequence, while the presidency and party system provide a rudimentary form of national policy-making and accountability, they should perhaps not be expected to exceed their very limited capacity in this field and, thereby, risk what little organisational integrity exists at such a level.

While the presidency may be said to be chiefly responsible for the high expectations of party government and, therefore, indirectly culpable for the successive bouts of disillusionment that came in their wake, the office's sheer capacity for embodying national objective and common identity continue to evoke optimism over the system's potential for party cohesion. Presidential election campaigns are longer than they used to be; they involve more contenders and resources; and attract a greater volume of voters than they did in the past.[15] As a consequence, they lead to a climactic sense of national choice and popular mandate. This encourages a disposition towards politics of national revival and a cultural preoccupation with the ensuing course of the presidency. Given the level of public attention directed to the presidency and the democratic reforms of the selective processes surrounding the office, it might be thought that the modern presidency had either satisfied the needs of party leadership, or else supplanted the party dimension with a functional equivalent based upon executive authority. Neither conclusion would be correct. The presidency still raises hopes for the system and these hopes are still expressed in terms of unfulfilled party government. The presidency's position as a party leader continues to suggest the need for party integration as a remedy for the systematic disarray of American government. The disjunction between the singularity of the chief executive and the multiplicity of the rest of the federal government transforms the presidency into a critical frame of reference for what is required to fulfil the system's potential. The relationship between the responsibilities of the presidential office and the organisation of national parties continues to be regarded as both a central fault in the political system and, likewise, a source of final redemption. Just as the problems of the presidency are often reducible to party, so the problems of the American party system are most evident at the presidential level.

Forty years ago, parties were criticised for their organisational incoherence and indiscipline; their lack of resistance to pressure from large and well organised interest groups; their ineffectual techniques of policy formulation; their inability to integrate sufficiently to translate electoral promises into law; and their overall failure to provide for popular choice, responsible government, and democratic accountability. One celebrated report on America's two-party system observed 'that the national and state party organisations are largely independent of one another, each operating within its own sphere, without appreciable common approach to problems of party policy and strategy'.[16] It concluded that 'organizational forms have not been overhauled for nearly a century. The result is that the parties are now probably the most archaic institutions in the United States.'[17] Today the criticisms are virtually identical in substance and purpose. If anything, they are more severe in their indictment of decay[18] and more pressing in the urgency for reform.[19]

The implications of such criticisms are profound for the presidency and for its ascribed role in integrating government in the cause of responsive decision-making, purposive national policy, programmatic action, and accountable administration. The irony of such contemporary complaints is that they come at the end of a reform process that has wrought immense changes in the relationship between presidency and party – changes which were prompted by presidential politics and which were designed to increase the integrity of the president as party leader. The important question raised by such developments is whether the presidency has been weakened, not in spite of them, but because of them.

Primary elections as solutions and problems

By far the most significant change in the party system to affect the contemporary presidency has been the increased usage of primary elections to select delegates to each party's national convention. As the main purpose of any convention is to select the party leader for the forthcoming presidential election, the device of primary elections opened up the nomination process to wider participation amongst party supporters. Before primary elections took a grip on the process, state delegations to a party convention tended to be organised hierarchially with control resting primarily with state party *apparatchiks* whose function was to maximise personal and local benefits from the process of insider-dealing and bargaining that characterised the party conventions during the first half of the century. It was customary for delegations to be chosen by local party caucuses and conventions where pressure from local party machines could be brought to bear. In spite of the undemocratic overtones to the selection of such state delegations their leaders did at least provide the national party with both a network of political communication and exchange, and a form of collective consciousness and historic memory that lent continuity to the quadrennial conventions.

Moreover, these party careerists actually chose their leader within a party arena and they did so to serve their view of the party's interests. It is true that to many the interests of their party were coloured by considerations of federal patronage, subsidies, and contracts. But it is equally the case that self-interest drove the delegates towards the selection of the candidate that could win national office and, by doing so, optimise the chances of party gains in the thousands of state and local elections that always coincide with a presidential election (i.e. the alleged 'coat-tails effect'). Party regulars in such old style conventions proceeded on the overriding principle that a national election could only be won by mobilising party organisations around the country with the selection of a leader who could minimise the divisions within a party and, thereupon, appeal to the general public from a unified party base.

Primary elections have now become the most conspicuous feature of the presidential selection process.[20] Given their contemporary prominence in presidential elections, it is often thought that they are an essentially modern device. But this is not strictly the case A dozen states had presidential primary elections as early as 1912, but the momentum was not maintained. Some primaries were abandoned in the 1920s and 1930s. For the next fifty years, primaries were regarded as a minority or supplemental alternative. Of the delegates that were elected, many were not bound to support particular candidates in the convention. Unknown or unfavoured candidates might participate in primary elections to show their strength and to impress the party professionals but such victories were far from decisive. In 1960, John Kennedy successfully defused doubts over both his Catholicism and his capacity to appeal to regions outside New England by entering and winning a number of primary elections.[21] The success of the Kennedy campaign is widely regarded as a watershed leading, thereafter, to primary based campaigns. It was a crucial precedent in campaigning but it did not in itself lead to any increase in the emphasis given to primary elections within the party system.

The decisive break with the past came after the 1968 Democratic Party convention when an insurgency movement against the Johnson administration was seen to be precluded from the national convention by what appeared to be a moribund oligarchy of white middle-class and middle-aged party placemen. In conditions of civil strife, the party managers nominated Vice- President Hubert Humphrey as party leader, but in doing so conceded the need for an inquiry into party structure and delegate selection. The McGovern-Fraser Commission recommended the elimination of the unit rule; an end to *executive officio* delegates; a limitation on the number of delegates chosen by state committees to 10 per cent; a ban on delegate selection concluded before the election year; and a requirement that women, youth, and minority groups be represented in 'reasonable relationship' to each state's population. These new rules were included in a range of reforms undertaken by the Democratic Party between 1968 and 1972.[22]

Although presidential primaries were not specifically recommended in the

Commission's report, a net effect of the reforms was a dramatic rise in their adoption by states either seeking to replace prohibited methods of delegate selection, or trying to avoid altogether the new stringent regulations imposed upon party caucuses. Between 1968 and 1972, the number of presidential primaries rose from 17 to 23 and the proportion of delegates selected by primaries increased from 41 per cent to 66 per cent. In 1968, the proportions of women, youth, and black delegates were 13 per cent, 2. 6 per cent and 5. 5 per cent respectively. By 1972, the commensurate figures were 40 per cent, 21 per cent and 15 per cent.[23] The convention's composition was different in another respect. Many of the delegates were amateurs – new not only to conventions but also to Democratic Party politics. They were issue and candidate enthusiasts, whose zeal had displaced established cadres of party professionals and managers.[24]

The new rules favoured the grassroots insurgency of George McGovern's own campaign for the presidency in 1972. McGovern won enough primaries to secure the nomination before the convention even assembled. Although Vice-President Hubert Humphrey entertained the prospect of winning the nomination, he entered the race too late to amass enough delegates from the primaries to deadlock the convention. 'While most of us paid him [McGovern] little mind, he had put together a phenomenally successful coalition of people, many of whom had never before tasted political power . . . Party regulars and labor felt excluded'.[25] Old style party leadership, home grown from within the party structure, was at an end. George McGovern may have lost the ensuing presidential election, but he

Table 7.2. The expansion of presidential primaries

	Democratic Party			Republican Party		
Year	Number of primaries	Votes cast	Percentage of delegates from primary 'states'*	Number of primaries	Votes cast	Percentage of delegates from primary 'states'*
1960	16	5,686,664	38.4	15	5,537,967	38.6
1964	16	6,247,435	41.4	17	5,935,339	45.6
1968	17	7,535,069	48.7	17	4,473,551	47.0
1972	23	15,993,965	66.5	22	5,188,281	58.2
1976	30	16,052,652	76.1	29	10,374,125	70.4
1980	35	18,747,825	81.1	36	12,690,451	78.0
1984	30	18,009,217	67.1	29	6,575,651	66.6
1988	37	23,230,525	81.4	38	12,169,003	80.7
1992	40	20,179,973	88.0	30	13,025,824	85.4

Note: Primaries include binding and nonbinding presidential preference primaries as well as primaries selecting national convention delegates only without indication of presidential preference. Prior to 1980, votes cast in the delegate-only primaries are not included in the total votes cast.

* 'States' include all jurisdictions having delegates.

Source: H. W. Stanley and R. G. Niemi, *Vital Statistics on American Politics*, 4th edn (Washington, D.C.: Congressional Quarterly Press, 1994), p. 148.

had demonstrated how a political figure could gather by a personal coalition and effectively take over the party at the national level. The pattern was set and the number of primaries rose sharply in the ensuing years. Through a mixture of state law and sustained pressure at the national party level, the Republican Party followed the Democratic Party's lead until it too reached a point where over 80 per cent of its delegates were chosen through primary elections (see Table 7.2).

Within four years Jimmy Carter, a largely unknown ex-governor of Georgia, mastered the strategy of presidential primaries and won the Democratic nomination over the objections of the party. At the same time, Ronald Reagan launched a major challenge to President Ford by competing successfully in the Republican presidential primaries. Ford won 13 primaries (affording 889 delegates) and eventually secured the nomination, but in winning 10 primaries (affording 839 delegates), Ronald Reagan demonstrated that an incumbent president could no longer be assured of his party's renomination. As it was, Ford only prevailed over Reagan by 1,180 to 1,069 votes in the Republican Convention. Any president looking for re-election now had to enter the primaries, in order to re-establish his leadership. Presidential primary elections had become not merely a necessary, but a sufficient, condition to securing leadership nominations. Waiting for a party's national convention to stake a claim to the leadership was no longer a viable strategy. Anyone adopting such a tactic would find that he or she was six months too late (see Table 7.3).

Table 7.3. The accumulation of delegates prior to a party convention – e.g. Democratic Party 1992

Date	State	New delegates		Cumulative delegates*		Clinton % of delegates
		Clinton	Other	Clinton	Tsongas/Brown	
18 Feb.	New Hampshire	9	9	9	9	.2%
25 Feb.	South Dakota	3	12	12	21	.3
3 Mar.	Colorado	14	32			
	Georgia	54	22			
	Maryland	29	38	148	25	6.7
	Idaho	0	18			
	Utah	5	18	198	145	4.6
7 Mar.	South Carolina	36	7	184	25	8.3
	Arizona	15	26			
	Wyoming	4	9			
	Democrats abroad	0	7			
8 Mar.	Nevada	5	12			
10 Mar.	Florida	87	61			
	Louisiana	59	1			
	Massachusetts	0	94			
	Mississippi	39	0			

Date	State	New delegates		Cumulative delegates*		Clinton % of delegates
		Clinton	Other	Clinton	Tsongas/Brown	
	Oklahoma	38	7			
	Rhode Island	6	16			
	Tennessee	56	12			
	Texas	94	33			
	Delaware	3	11			
	Hawaii	16	4			
	Missouri	34	43			
	Texas	0	69	707	428	16.5
17 Mar.	Illinois	107	57			
	Michigan	74	57	947	559	22.1
24 Mar.	Connecticut	21	32	991	589	23.1
5 Apr.	Puerto Rico	51	0			
7 Apr.	Kansas	27	9			
	Wisconsin	35	47			
	New York	101	143	1265	803	29.5
28 Apr.	Pennsylvania	112	57	1586	857	37.0
5 May	Indiana	55	22			
	North Carolina	72	12			
	District of Columbia	17	0	1735	880	40.5
12 May	Nebraska	13	12			
	West Virginia	31	0	1784	888	41.6
19 May	Oregon	29	18	1860	945	43.4
26 May	Arkansas	30	6			
	Kentucky	34	18	1877	944	46.1
2 June	California	191	157			
	Alabama	43	12			
	Montana	8	8			
	New Jersey	80	25			
	New Mexico	17	8			
	Ohio	113	38	2511	1159	58.6

* Cumulative totals include delegates chosen in second-level caucuses and superdelegates.

Source: R. K. Baker, 'Sorting Out and Suiting Up: The Presidential Nominations', in G. M. Pomper *et al.*, *The Election of 1992: Reports and Interpretations* (Chatham: Chatham House, 1993), p. 53.

The rise of presidential primary elections has been a highly significant development in American politics. 'The selection of Presidential nominees is a crucial point – some would contend the *most* critical point – in the democratic governance of the United States today'.[26] As such, primary elections attract fierce controversy not just over the effects attributed to them but over the relative merits and demerits of such effects upon the selection process and, ultimately, upon the presidency itself. The arguments can be broken down into four main categories – i.e. considerations of (i) time, (ii) cost, (iii) representativeness and (iv) party.

Arguments against primaries: time

The growth in primary elections has increased the election campaign to at least ten months and because of the need for pre-primary organisation, the elongation can be said to extend to two years. The length of the process is alleged to lead to political over-exposure, public weariness and candidate exhaustion. Successive primary elections are accused of being a 'tortuous, fatiguing and cruel'[27] process that succeeds only in killing off promising candidates and damaging the survivors. Walter Mondale recounts that one former candidate had told him 'three years after the campaign had ended that he still hadn't recovered emotionally or physically from the ordeal'.[28] The commitment required even to enter the primaries is so great that candidates who enter either need to have no other political obligations, or else be prepared to neglect their political offices for the sake of presidential ambition. Even when the primary season is apparently shortened by timetabling the larger states early in the process, the net effect is to lengthen the pre-primary scramble for candidate resources and exposure.

Arguments against primaries: cost

Because of the financial costs involved in competing in primary elections, the advantage lies with those candidates who are either well financed to begin with or who are capable of raising funds and servicing debts as they go along. This provokes anxieties that resourcing takes precedence over campaigning and successful candidates are those who are adept at acquiring financial backing rather than providing leadership and policy direction. The massive expenditure incurred by primaries is directed to the mutual destruction of runners within their own parties – the alleged effect of which is to deny the party organisations of much needed funds that would otherwise have been donated to them. For example, in the early manouevrings for the 1996 Republican nomination, promising candidates (e.g. Jack Kemp, Dick Cheney) had been forced to stand down as early as February 1995 because of lack of funds. The most notable departure from the field was Dan Quayle who, despite formidable name recognition as a former vice-president, also felt compelled to withdraw on grounds of cost. The task of raising an estimated $500,000 a week to reach the $20 million threshold for an effective primary campaign was not only thought to be beyond his reach but would have constituted a permanent distraction to the actual task of running a campaign (e.g. decisions on policy and electoral strategy).

Arguments against primaries: representativeness

Primary elections are associated with low turnouts, multiple choice and plurality victories. As a consequence, they are reputed to be unrepresentative in nature and capricious in effect. The sequence of primaries (e.g. the disproportionate weight given to the first bout in the small unrepresentative state of New Hampshire) is held to be unfair to those candidates whose regional strengths or other support bases are not tested in the early primaries. The fact that minority victories can be secured from minority turnouts and that results are given meaning by variable and media selected criteria, results in primary elections being seen as arbitrary and volatile in nature rather than a rational selection process.

Arguments against primaries: party

By their very nature, primaries induce and maximise party divisions by transforming the leadership into a publicly competitive process. The need of each aspirant to differentiate himself or herself from each other in a forum of public appraisal places a low premium upon party unity. As aspirants compete for different constituencies on individual candidate-centred grounds, they publicise personal and policy distinctiveness and, in doing so, delay and even jeopardise party integration just prior to the critical period of a presidential election. Since a multiplicity of candidates and, therefore, of splits is far more likely to occur in the 'out party' than in the party occupying the White House, primary elections can be said to compound the organisational disadvantages of challenging an incumbent president.

Primary elections transfer leadership recruitment from the party organisations to an open process of public preference by transitory participants without a permanent stake, or even interest, in either national party.

> The crucial qualifications of a presidential candidate now are his ability to raise money and to appeal to the public at large through television. Whether the candidate is acceptable to, and capable of working effectively with, the members of his party in the Congress and the other party leaders on whom he will depend for his support has not been a criterion that the voters deemed important – or would have the information to apply if they did.[29]

As a consequence, 'the party elite that includes the party's senators and representatives has lost the means to defend itself against the election of an outsider to the White House'.[30] With peer review in decline, it is now a positive advantage for a candidate to run as an 'outsider' not just against Washington government but against his or her own party establishment. To cut parties off from the process of nomination is 'to deprive them of incentives to organise, and to set them prematurely at the mercy of the masses of people whose information at the primary stage is especially poor'.[31] As a consequence, parties are undermined to the extent of having to accept leaders chosen for them.

Although presidential primaries remain one of the most controversial elements of the political process, they are not without their apologists. For any criticism, there is a more than adequate response.

Arguments for primaries: time

The length of the primary season provides a thorough testing of both the candidates and their organisations. It provides time for policies to be discussed, issues to be explained and candidates to be appraised. The primary election process allows the contenders to prove not only their personal endurance and capacity to withstand stress but also their political and management skills. While aspirants seek to inform the public, it is widely accepted that contenders are themselves educated by the experience of having to campaign in all areas of the country. In highly publicised and pressurised conditions, time can reveal character and with it a contender's ability to fulfil the different roles of a highly individualised office.

Arguments for primaries: cost

While it is true that primary elections are expensive there is little evidence that financial contributions to candidates would be given to party organisations in the absence of such elections. It can also be claimed that funds are a reflection, rather than the cause of, public support. Moreover, because of the emphasis given to small states in the nomination process (e.g. Iowa, New Hampshire), it is possible for poorly financed candidates to engage in effective low cost 'meet the people' campaigns. In 1984, for example, Senator Gary Hart began his campaign with a 2 per cent level of support amongst Democrats in New Hampshire but within two weeks he had arrested the momentum of the front-runner (Walter Mondale) by winning the primary in that state. While the costs of presidential elections continue to rise, mostly because of the expense of television, the issue of costs has at least been partially resolved by the provision of public matching funds made available through the campaign finance reforms of the 1970s (see pp. 240–4).

Arguments for primaries: representativeness

Notwithstanding the problematic nature of what is and what is not representative, it is possible to claim that primary elections are not as inherently unrepresentative as they are reputed to be.[32] Because it is necessary to form alliances and build coalitions in public, candidates have to accumulate as wide a range of groups and interests as possible – including minority interests that contenders would not have otherwise tried to incorporate in their campaigns. It is claimed that the net effect has been to produce party leaders that represent the greatest volume and broadest range of voters. It can also be asserted that primary elections provide a more representative process than the preceding arrangements because the primary system now 'provides for a much larger number of party members participating in the presidential nomination process by means of voting for their preferred candidates'.[33] Apart from the evident representation of minority groups in the reformed nomination structures, the selection process itself can be painfully representative of party factions and divisions. For example, in 1976 Democratic supporters had a choice between Edward Kennedy (liberal Democrat), Jimmy Carter (centre Democrat), and George Wallace (southern conservative Democrat). In 1984, Walter Mondale (traditional New Deal Democrat), Gary Hart ('new Democrat') and Jesse Jackson (black Democratic activist) battled it out for the Democratic Party nomination. In 1988, the Republican nomination was bitterly contested between George Bush (Ivy League – Wall Street moderate Republican), Bob Dole (mid west – Main Street conservative Republican), and Pat Robertson (religous right), while in 1992 Pat Buchanan (libertarian and religious right) publicly opposed the renomination of President Bush

Arguments for primaries: party

It is because different shades of opinion within parties are openly expressed through primary elections that the eventual winners can claim to have secured their nominations fairly. When factions have been electorally defeated, deep splits are arguably less likely to occur. For example, there used to be a profusion of disputes at the conventions over the selection, distribution, and accreditation of delegates. But with the onset of increased primary elections there has been a marked reduction in these damaging diversions. Conventions may not actually choose the party leaders anymore, but the affirmation given to the nominees by the assembled delegates still evokes the importance of popular leaders and potential winners for party morale and unity. Primaries not only give parties extensive publicity (especially the 'out' party) but also the appearance at least of being an intermediary between government and people. Primaries can help to unify a party and to maximise a party's electoral advantage. Martin Wattenberg demonstrates that the 'greater the margin a nominee accumulates over his closest rival in the primaries, the better he does in the general election'.[34]

While it is true that primary elections do make parties more susceptible to incursions by ideological wings and unrepresentative issue activists, for the most part primaries lead to the nomination of those contenders who led the poll ratings at the beginning of the process. Susceptibility to unelectable lurches to either left or right, however, should not be exaggerated. 'Because they want to win, party activists are unlikely to go on an ideological binge'.[35] Primaries produce winners of proven popularity and the capacity to win a presidential election still remains the best agent for organisational cohesion.

These arguments for and against primaries are ongoing and problematic. Because of the positive and negative values attached to them, there is little chance that the differences can ever be resolved. The situation is further compounded by the fact that any single feature of primary elections could be interpreted as a plus or a minus depending upon circumstances and the effect upon favoured candidacies. Perhaps the only contribution that political science can make to the debate is to inform by empirical research. One notable example of such enlightenment in recent years has been provided by Larry Bartels.[36] In spite of the wealth of *prima facie* evidence suggesting that primary elections are arbitrary in nature and capricious in effect, Bartels assembles an impressive array of statistical evidence in support of the proposition that primary elections are far less erratic than they appear to be. By carefully tracking the changing state of public information about candidates throughout the primary election season – together with measurements of broad public ideology (i.e. liberalism–conservatism); emotional affect towards the contenders; the geographical distribution of underlying support; and the public perception of each candidate's chances of ultimate victory – it is possible to view the outcomes in terms of an explicable process of informed public opinion.

Notwithstanding the contributions of such research, primary elections continue to generate sweeping criticism of the system and a profusion of rhetoric on the need for change. According to James Ceaser, for example, the nominating process has become the 'least stable of all the major national institutions. It has also been the most deficient. Flawed in concept it has been harmful in operation and, if continued in the form of the past decade . . . it could threaten the well-being of the entire political system'.[37] Reformers press for the primary election campaign period to be shortened and for more delegates to be not only chosen by the party but to be independent of pre-convention pledges to candidates. Some reforms have occurred. The Democrats pioneered measures to reinstate party experience in the national convention by reserving delegate places for party officials and public office-holders. While the proportion of 'super-delegates' have increased from 14 per cent of the convention in 1984 to 19 per cent in 1992, there is little evidence that their presence leavened the impact of the primary elections in the selection process.

A device to shorten the length of the primary election process has been 'Super Tuesday' – a date in early March when a whole series of states have their primaries on the same day (see Figure 7.1). It was originally conceived to maximise the south's influence upon the selection process and to produce an early and decisive front-runner that would burn off lesser candidates, save costs, and facilitate party unification. The results of the three Super Tuesdays in 1984, 1988, and 1992, however, have been less than decisive in foreclosing divisions by producing

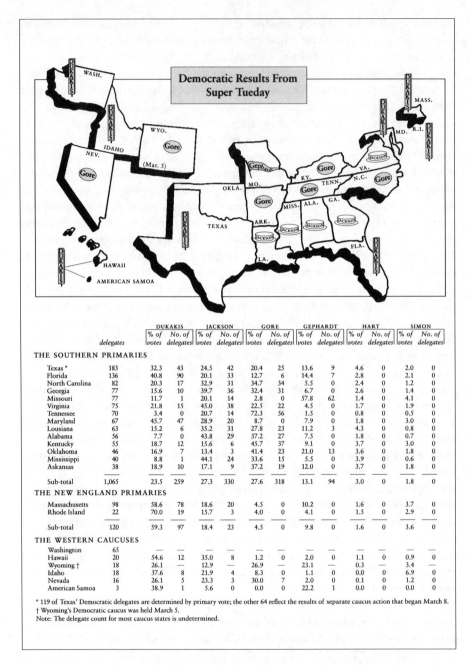

	delegates	DUKAKIS % of votes	No. of delegates	JACKSON % of votes	No. of delegates	GORE % of votes	No. of delegates	GEPHARDT % of votes	No. of delegates	HART % of votes	No. of delegates	SIMON % of votes	No. of delegates
THE SOUTHERN PRIMARIES													
Texas *	183	32.3	43	24.5	42	20.4	25	13.6	9	4.6	0	2.0	0
Florida	136	40.8	90	20.1	33	12.7	6	14.4	7	2.8	0	2.1	0
North Carolina	82	20.3	17	32.9	31	34.7	34	5.5	0	2.4	0	1.2	0
Georgia	77	15.6	10	39.7	36	32.4	31	6.7	0	2.6	0	1.4	0
Missouri	77	11.7	1	20.1	14	2.8	0	57.8	62	1.4	0	4.1	0
Virginia	75	21.8	15	45.0	38	22.5	22	4.5	0	1.7	0	1.9	0
Tennessee	70	3.4	0	20.7	14	72.3	56	1.5	0	0.8	0	0.5	0
Maryland	67	45.7	47	28.9	20	8.7	0	7.9	0	1.8	0	3.0	0
Lousiana	63	15.2	6	35.2	31	27.8	23	11.2	3	4.3	0	0.8	0
Alabama	56	7.7	0	43.8	29	37.2	27	7.5	0	1.8	0	0.7	0
Kentucky	55	18.7	12	15.6	6	45.7	37	9.1	0	3.7	0	3.0	0
Oklahoma	46	16.9	7	13.4	3	41.4	23	21.0	13	3.6	0	1.8	0
Mississippi	40	8.8	1	44.1	24	33.6	15	5.5	0	3.9	0	0.6	0
Askansas	38	18.9	10	17.1	9	37.2	19	12.0	0	3.7	0	1.8	0
Sub-total	1,065	23.5	259	27.3	330	27.6	318	13.1	94	3.0	0	1.8	0
THE NEW ENGLAND PRIMARIES													
Massachusetts	98	58.6	78	18.6	20	4.5	0	10.2	0	1.6	0	3.7	0
Rhode Island	22	70.0	19	15.7	3	4.0	0	4.1	0	1.5	0	2.9	0
Sub-total	120	59.3	97	18.4	23	4.5	0	9.8	0	1.6	0	3.6	0
THE WESTERN CAUCUSES													
Washington	65	—	—	—	—	—	—	—	—	—	—	—	—
Hawaii	20	54.6	12	35.0	8	1.2	0	2.0	0	1.1	0	0.9	0
Wyoming †	18	26.1	—	12.9	—	26.9	—	23.1	—	0.3	—	3.4	—
Idaho	18	37.6	8	21.9	4	8.3	0	1.1	0	0.0	0	6.9	0
Nevada	16	26.1	5	23.3	3	30.0	7	2.0	0	0.1	0	1.2	0
American Samoa	3	38.9	1	5.6	0	0.0	0	22.2	1	0.0	0	0.0	0

* 119 of Texas' Democratic delegates are determined by primary vote; the other 64 reflect the results of separate caucus action that began March 8.
† Wyoming's Democratic caucus was held March 5.
Note: The delegate count for most caucus states is undetermined.

Figure 7.1. Indecisive outcome from a 'Super Tuesday'. Results from Democratic primaries and caucuses, 1988. *Source*: *Congressional Quarterly Weekly Report*, March 12 1988, p. 638.

outright winners. The proposal by California in 1994 to shift the primary elections for its huge Democratic and Republican delegations from June to March may in the future tilt the balance in favour of an early resolution of the leadership competition in each party.

Despite the criticisms surrounding the primary election process, it appears unlikely that the emphasis upon it will be diminished in the near future. Local and national dynamics sustain a momentum in favour of primary elections. The Democratic Party, for example, attempted to arrest the trend towards primaries in the 1980s by shortening the selection process, limiting proportional representation (i.e. denying delegates to those candidates who failed to acquire a 20 per cent level of votes) and encouraging the reintroduction of state caucuses for delegate selection. The number of primaries did fall (see Table 7.2), but by 1992 the level of primaries had recovered and accounted for more delegates than ever before (i.e. 90 per cent). Moreover, caucuses had become so open and binding upon delegates that they were no longer the vehicles of old style party politics. Some simply graduated into primary elections, while others had become so democratised in procedure and substance that they had become the equivalent of primary elections in the emphasis given to mass participation and loss of party autonomy. The resumption of the drive towards high public participation in delegate selection and, therefore, leadership recruitment has left reformers with a limited agenda of integrating primaries into a single simultaneous national primary.[38]

Dollar democracy

The effect of primaries upon the national parties and leadership selection and presidential politics in particular has been further compounded by the reforms to campaign financing. During the 1970s, a series of federal election finance laws were passed, in order to regulate an area of political activity that had become the subject of widespread public anxiety. The misuse and abuse of campaign funds, together with the inferred conjunction of money and political influence led to a series of measures designed to register and regulate the financial contributions, receipts and expenditures related to federal elections. The Federal Elections Campaign Act (FECA) of 1971 together with the amendments added in 1974, 1976, and 1979 were designed to identify the sources and limits of campaign contributions to candidates, and thereupon to monitor campaign spending to ensure that it squares with its demarcated origins. The base point of the reforms was that candidates could only receive donations from three main sources (i.e. individuals, parties, and political action committees or PACs). By bringing the flow of money to the surface, it also became possible to cap the size of donations with a set of maximum limits – $1,000 per election from an individual; $5,000 per election from a PAC; and a variable sum based on each state's voting age population from a national party organisation.[39]

The reforms reflected and, thereby, endorsed the centrality of the candidate in contemporary elections. The emphasis of financial regulation was placed upon a set of bilateral relationships between donations and the candidate as the end-user. Each candidate was now fully responsible for his or her campaign. Apart from having to organise a team of accountants to maintain a tightly integrated record of every campaign transaction, the reforms distanced candidates even further from their parties. Candidates came to rely increasingly upon individuals and PACs for what were becoming ever more expensive campaigns.[40] In the past, candidates could rely on sizeable bloc donations by national and state party organisations. They could also hope to attract the generous support of 'fat cat' millionaire contributions. But under the new regime, party contributions have shrunk to less than 1 per cent of the contributions made to candidates running for Congress. About a third of such contributions now come from PACs. But over half come from individual contributions. Because the fat cats have been killed off – in so far as single contributions are concerned – successful candidates are those who are adept at appealing to a profusion of kittens whose small contributions characterise contemporary electoral fundraising. Given that the average cost of running a campaign for a Senate seat now stands at $2.5 million, contenders need to engage in the highly expensive but politically lucrative process of propagating large numbers of small donations – independent of party organisation and obligation.

Presidential candidates operate under the same basic rules, but because the costs of running for the presidency are so much greater and the opportunities for the abuse of campaigning advantages are commensurately more extensive, the financial rules for candidate selection and the presidential election itself depart from the congressional norm in a number of important respects. During the pre-nomination stage, the national parties have to remain officially neutral towards the contenders in the primaries and caucuses. This places such an enormous financial burden upon those challenging for the party nominations that it can jeopardise the democratic process. To alleviate the candidate's burden of generating national organisations to engage effectively in the nomination process, the FECA includes a provision for a system of publicy funded matching grants. Once a candidate proves the seriousness of his campaign by raising at least $5,000 in individual contributions of $250 or less in at least 20 states – thereby triggering the eligibility target of $100,000 – then he or she qualifies for federal funds that match every *individual* contribution[41] dollar for dollar for all donations up to $250. If candidates decide to opt into the scheme then they have to comply with a number of contractual stipulations – the chief of which is the acceptance of state spending limits and an aggregate maximum expenditure of private and public funds during the pre-nomination stage (i.e. $20.2 million in 1984; $23.1 million in 1988; $27.6 million in 1992).[42] In 1988, the federal government subsidised this stage by $67.5 million. These public funds, which amounted to nearly a third of all expenditures made by the contenders, were channelled directly to the candidate organisations to be deployed at their discretion.

'Dollar democracy' was extended even further with the FECA's arrangements for the period of the presidential election. Once the party nominees have been chosen, then they are given the further option of having their election expenses covered in full by public funding. Following the Watergate scandal with its revelations of 'slush funds' and 'money laundering', and the alleged scandal of the 1972 presidential election when President Nixon outspent his Democratic challenger George McGovern by $60 million to $20 million, Congress attempted to restore some integrity and equity to the democratic process. It did so first by allowing the presidential campaign of both the main parties to be financed from the public purse, and second by limiting both campaigns to the same expenditure ceiling.[43] In 1976 that ceiling stood at $21.8 million. With adjustments for inflation, the ceiling has risen from $29.4 million in 1980 to $40.4 million in 1984. In 1988, it stood at $46.1 million and by 1992 it had reached $55.5 million.[44]

The principle behind the reform is that the main party candidates are performing a competitive and beneficial function and, as such, should be supported by the equal provision of public resources. Even though many in the Republican Party have objected to the principle of public funding (especially Ronald Reagan), all Republican presidential candidates since the inception of the reform have joined their Democratic counterparts in opting for Treasury money along with its spending ceilings. In 1992, each party was given only $5.5 million of public assistance and was held to a formal expenditure limit of $10.3 million. Given that a presidential election is traditionally the *raison d'être* of a national party, the FECA conspicuously underwrites the marginal significance of parties in contemporary presidential elections. It does so not just by the disparity of funds reserved to the parties relative to the candidate, but by the way the limits serve to relegate national party organisations to a general service function separate from the main competitive interplay at the leadership level.

At first sight, it might be thought that such public provision had largely excluded the role of parties supporting their own candidates. After the excesses of the Nixon Administration when government position was exploited to fill Republican Party coffers, the intention of campaign finance reform was to minimise the role of party in presidential elections. Nevertheless, loopholes or expansion joints were not only left in but were progressively developed during succeeding years to give the parties a much greater influence than is normally acknowledged. Because the main emphasis of the FECA and the accompanying Federal Election Commission lies with the flow of money into and out of candidate accounts, it necessarily has less authority over, and therefore less concern with, the movement of money elsewhere in the electoral system. A distinction grew between, on the one hand, 'hard money' within the purview of the FECA and subject to stringent reporting and accounting arrangements, and on the other hand 'soft money' which falls outside the FECA channels but which nevertheless can have a material effect on candidates and campaigning.[45]

One of the chief sources of 'soft money' was the Supreme Court decision of *Buckley* v. *Valeo* (1976).[46] In this case, the Court reviewed the FECA and found the principle of limiting campaign expenditure to be constitutionally invalid. To the Court, such constraints represented an inherent violation of the Constitution's First Amendment guarantee of free expression. Candidates could now spend as much of their own money on their election campaigns as they wished. Candidate organisations could also make unlimited expenditures if they chose to reject public funding and its contractual obligations.[47] Following *Buckley* v. *Valeo*, the:

> availability of public funds became . . . [the] incentive, the big carrot for controlling the costs of campaigning . . . There was now a link between public funding and limits on spending; for the first time one now had to have acceptance of the former to impose the latter. Public funding increasingly became not an end in itself but a means to the goal of limiting campaign spending.[48]

In 1985, the Court also ruled out limits on organisations which committed resources to campaigns on an independent basis. For example, although a PAC is limited to a direct $5,000 contribution to a candidate, it can spend an unlimited volume of money on behalf of, or in the interests of, a candidate – provided that such 'independent expenditure' is not made with the cooperation, or prior consent, of the candidate.[49] As long as the records of such contributions are lodged with the FEC then no rules are broken. By 1984, for example, PACs were spending $15.3 million in support of President Reagan's re-election campaign.[50]

Independent expenditures like this have an intermediate status between 'hard' and 'soft' money. Even though the monies may be spent outside the candidate organisations, they not only originate in hard money contributions but their usage is recorded and accounted for. Something akin to this device is employed by parties. In addition to the contributions made direct to the candidates, national and state party organisations can make 'coordinated expenditures' on behalf of, and often in conjunction with, candidates. Even though such semi-direct expenditures are categorised as party rather than candidate funds, they are limited by the FECA on a state by state basis. But other party expenditures for the benefit of presidential candidates are not capped by the FECA. Since the 1979 amendments to the FECA, state and local parties have been permitted to spend unlimited amounts on 'grassroots' functions for presidential candidates. Such notionally independent expenditures can be directed to voter registration drives and electoral mobilisation campaigns. These can be of material benefit to contenders in a presidential election – especially when the timing of such activities is coordinated to achieve the optimum advantage for a party leader.[51] Neither contributions to state parties nor expenditures made by them are covered by the FECA. Many states still allow corporations and unions to make direct contributions to party committees. And fat cats at the state level are still running wild, making over $100,000 donations to state and local parties on the understanding that they will serve the interests of one or other presidential candidate.

By seeking to preserve the structure and voluntarism of local parties, Congress's 1979 amendments to the FECA formally excluded contribution and spending limits from 'party building' activities. As a result, the parties have become the command and control centres of 'soft money' which is defined as money raised and spent 'outside of the restrictions of federal law (and often to circumvent those restrictions) with the intention, nonetheless, of influencing the outcome of a federal election, directly or indirectly',[52] i.e. an election otherwise governed by the FECA. Soft money represents the conjunction of mutual interest with a plausible denial of complicity. In 1988, for example, presidential candidates Michael Dukakis and George Bush accepted public funding for their presidential election campaigns and were, therefore, prohibited from accepting private funds. Nevertheless, they both engaged in generating private unregulated contributions ($23 million by the Democrats and $22 million by the Republicans) that were channelled into state and local party accounts where they could be strategically coordinated within each party to maximum national effect. When soft funds and local activities are taken into account together with the scale of the support services provided by the Democratic and Republican National Committees, it is evident that the party organisations are not exactly the impoverished and declining accomplices to presidential candidates that they are often reputed to be.[53]

But even though parties still make a substantial contribution to presidential election campaigns, they cannot change the nature and dynamics of modern campaigning. Resources are still centred on candidates. Parties do not dominate, let alone monopolise election funds. Party resources are just one component in a range of funding sources, the chief of which are direct individual donations in the pre-nomination stage. Instead of parties fielding candidates for office, it is candidates who appropriate party resources for their own use. The drive remains one of entrepreneurial competition between candidate organisations each seeking to customise an electoral coalition into a self-financing aggregate capable of prevailing over opposition. At the pre-nomination stage, the successful contenders are necessarily those that are effective in soliciting a high volume of small con-tributions, often through the use of direct-mailing techniques. The objective is to use resources to acquire public visibility and to develop electoral momentum. Accumulated funds are also a measure of popular appeal. 'The ability of one candidate to raise more money than another is, like having more volunteers, a legitimate demonstration of public support'.[54]

Fund-raising success is further enhanced with the addition of federal match-ing grants, which in turn generates more intense competition amongst contenders both to claim available public funds and to reduce their opponents' access to such funds. Matching grants are criticised for aiding and abetting fratricide. They are also criticised for prolonging the pre-nomination competition by helping to extend the life of failing candidacies and by forcing contenders to begin their campaigns increasingly early, in order to qualify for public funds and, thereupon, to use them as advance collateral for private campaign loans. Moreover, because the eligibility formula has not been adjusted for inflation since the FECA amendments in 1974, it means that candidates now find it approximately four times easier to qualify for federal funds than was the case in the mid-1970s. This of course means that the $250 maximum federal matching grant has also decreased in value but such a devaluation must be balanced by the advances in computer-generated devices for soliciting donations on a mass scale. But perhaps the most significant consequence of such federal support is the way it lends legitimacy to the electoral function of candidate organisations and, in doing so, further encourages the detachment of presidential candidates from party obligation and solidarity. This dynamic is extended in the general election where parties are not only narrowly limited in the contributions they can make to candidates, but are formally required to make independent expenditures in order to give assistance over and above such limits. In the global expenditure of funds spent in presidential elections, it is evident that candidates rely on the parties and their soft money for the donkey work of party building, voter registration, and electoral administration – thus freeing the candidates to channel the lion's share of their public funding directly into personal promotion and direct candidate-centred campaigns to mass rather than party audiences. Just as the pre-nomination stage, and especially the primaries, serve to place the emphasis upon the contenders to construct their own electoral organisations and their own leadership constituencies, so the dynamics of campaign financing also help to ensure that the cultivation of bilateral relationships between leaders and public is extended to the general election.

Political television and media politics

Television provides another key element to the linkage between primary elections and campaign finance. So central has television become to the strategy and conduct of presidential elections that it provides a third component to a process that integrates candidate-centred campaigns with independent fund-raising and expenditure and self-generated public communications. The net effect is a deepening interrelationship between politics and presentation in which the former is increasingly personalised and the latter is progressively publicised. It is a relationship that has had profound implications both for the presidential election process and for the presidency itself. In 1952, only 46. 7 per cent of American households possessed a television. By 1960, the figure had grown to 89. 4 per cent.[55] During the 1960s, the potential for a national television audience was largely fulfilled not simply through the increasing volume of television ownership but by the development of the three national networks (i.e. NBC, ABC, CBS). By 1990, the percentage of television households had risen to 98.2 per cent. Half of households now had access to cable television and the average number of television sets per household had reached two for the first time since records began.[56]

Table 7.4. Number and circulation of daily newspapers (1958–1990)

Year	Number	Circulation (in millions	Circulation as a percentage of population
1958	1778	58.7	33.6%
1965	1751	60.4	31.1%
1975	1756	60.7	28.1%
1985	1676	62.8	26.3%
1990	1611	62.3	24.9%

Source: H. W. Stanley and R. G. Niemi, *Vital Statistics on American Politics* (Washington, D.C.: Congressional Quarterly Press, 1994), p. 148.

While the number of newspapers during this period showed a slight decline, the number of television stations mushroomed from 862 in 1970 to 1,442 in 1990.[57] And although daily newspaper circulation remained level, it declined in relation to the growth in population (see Table 7.4). Television's evening news audience by contrast increased dramatically. In the period from 1965 to 1984, for example, the audience figures more than doubled from 18.4 million to 45.6 million.[58] Television is now not only the main source of news and political information for the American public, but the source with the most credibility and authority.[59] It is also the primary means by which political leaders seek to present themselves and their policies and records to a mass audience. The same is true for aspiring leaders who wish to displace those established in positions of leadership. While the press is still important as an interpretive intermediary in leader–public relations (e.g. the press is still credited with setting the campaign agenda for the electronic media), there is no doubt that it is television which provides the key instrument of political communications and which allows presidential aspirants to acquire public attention by gaining direct access to the voters' living rooms.[60] It is this capacity that has transformed television's political status over the last 25 years from significant to pre-eminent. Albert Hunt believes that the change was complete by 1984:

> Although television started in the 1940s, by 1960 it had only begun to approach maturity. By 1984 it was abundantly clear that American political elections were driven by television. Any modern presidential campaign is dominated by the awesome importance of television coverage.[61]

To Robert Donovan and Ray Scherer, the watershed came a little later:

The waves of changes that began with the televising of the national conventions in 1948 had, by 1988, transformed the mode, mechanics, and theater of elective politics . . . While not the only determinant of a candidate's popularity, television has become an unavoidable threshold to political power.[62]

But to Tom Wicker, the celebrated print journalist, television had become predominant as early as 1980. In that year, he observed that:

Presidential politics, today, it is reasonably fair to say, *is* television. Party politics has given way to media politics, and the full consequences of that momentous shift probably are yet to be seen: among them, surely, is the loss of function of the traditional parties and the widening gap between the media arts of running for president and the grinding politics of governing the country.[63]

Table 7.5. Responses by political professionals to the question 'what has been the single greatest change in electioneering in the past decade?'

Single greatest change	%
Importance/impact/use of television	43
Federal election laws	14
Money in politics	11
Use/integration of modern technology and consultants	9
Role of the computer	6
Reduced role of the parties	3
Negative campaigning	3
Other responses	11

Source: F. I. Luntz, *Candidates, Consultants and Campaigns: The Style and Substance of American Electioneering* (Oxford: Basil Blackwell, 1988), p. 16.

The altered reputation of political television is well captured by an opinion poll (Table 7.5) which questioned leading political professionals on what in their view constituted the single greatest change in electioneering over the decade from 1978 to 1988. To Frank Luntz, who produced the poll, the 'impact of television in recent years cannot be overstated'.[64] And nowhere has this fusion of television and political salesmanship been more evident than in presidential primary elections.

To succeed in a primary election campaign, a candidate needs to be able to make an appeal to as wide a constituency as possible. During the pre-nomination stage, a party is not available to help a candidate. Even if it could provide direct assistance, this would not necessarily amount to an advantage. With the decline of party attachment and the corresponding increase in independent voting behaviour, a party could not be assured of allegiance to a favoured candidate should it decide to make a public endorsement of a particular contender. If party loyalty can no longer be relied upon in a general election when the party leadership has been resolved, then the influence of any party recommendation would be negligible – and even possibly counterproductive – in the multiple candidacy conditions of primary elections. Candidates, therefore, have to build a relationship with the public, in order to establish a relationship with the party as a national organisation. For any particular candidate, this means acquiring personal visibility and public recognition. It is essential for a contender to differentiate himself or herself from the pack of other contenders. This can be done most effectively through television.

Television in this sense fulfils a basic electoral need of conveying candidates to the voting public which will select the party leaders for the parties. A leadership aspirant will seek to cultivate the media in two main ways. First, by using campaign strategies (e.g. scheduling statements and speeches to gain maximum coverage; creating attractive photo-opportunities; ensuring appearances possess a visual quality for television; providing 'sound-bites' for newscasts; addressing groups that will evoke a positive response from a television audience) to attract as much television news coverage as possible. On a broader scale, campaign management will attempt to influence how an election is defined – i.e. the identification of key issues, the criteria of leadership and the proportion of the vote needed to rank as a 'success'. It is essential for a candidate to recognise and cultivate what is widely regarded to be the power elite of presidential politics.[65] Broadcast journalists and editors are the key intermediaries between aspiring presidents and access to the news together with its propagated judgements and interpretations. To James Barber, the foremost task of a presidential candidate today

> is not building a coalition of organized interests, or developing allegiances with other candidates or politicians in his party, or even winning over the voters whose hands he shakes. If he has his priorities straight, he is first and foremost a seeker after favourable notice from the journalists who can make or break his progress . . . Smart candidates recognize that power and hurry to adapt their strategies to it. They learn to use journalism, as journalism uses them. If the journalists are the new kingmakers, the candidates are the new storytellers, active plotters of drama they hope will win [elections] for them.[66]

Contemporary candidates seek not merely to be included in news reports, but to influence the content of the news itself. As such, it is equally the case that campaigns are now directed more to achieve media coverage than to make direct contact with the voters.

This leads to the second way in which candidates attempt to use the media for their own advantage. In order either to challenge or to reinforce the effect of the media's campaign coverage, candidate organisations will make their own efforts to reach the audience by market research, private polling, and especially television advertising. Even though privately purchased television time can be wasteful because of the mismatch between political constituencies and media outlets, television advertising can be a very effective way for a candidate to generate a niche market in public sensibilities.[67] It can create the maximum impact in the minimum time. Television advertising provides a candidate with some measure of independence from the established priorities of the media outlets. It also permits a campaign to increase the level of candidate awareness across several states at the same time – a capacity which is becoming increasingly important with the drive to compress the length of the primary election season (e.g. Super Tuesday). As a consequence, television advertising has now become an established part of the competition for leadership nominations; a competition made all the keener with the absence of any equal air time provision for candidates.

Public expenditures are such that a campaign which takes its case directly to the public is no longer regarded as an exceptional and audacious attempt to circumvent the process of leadership selection, so much as a minimal requirement in a contemporary process that relies upon such candidate-generated self-promotion. Not to participate would be different but it would be a largely invisible and irrelevant distinction to a public now thoroughly accustomed to the competitive drive towards candidate outreach. It is rather more the fact that exposure denotes a personal ability or effort to acquire it. While exposure in itself will not assure a candidate of public attachment, non-exposure almost invariably leads to public indifference because it suggests a deliberate opting out of the process of public presentation. This joint cultivation of television communications amounts to a massive outlay of resources. To be successful, candidates need to hire media consultants, marketing specialists, polling experts, 'spin doctors', and experienced campaign managers.[68] Many professionals will not join a campaign unless they are satisfied it is adequately resourced. It often becomes necessary, therefore, for a candidate to give priority to fund-raising, in order to give the campaign sufficient credibility to attract top quality personnel. Money in itself is not a sufficient condition[69] for success, but it is a necessary requirement, especially for the huge expense of television. Whether it is for audience research, or for media market-testing, or for the technical weaponry needed for video warfare, the costs are immense. Some aspirants can be deterred from even entering the race either because of their own financial limitations or because of the daunting size of other candidates' campaign funds. Other contenders drop out because they cannot afford to stay in. Others hope that with an optimal deployment of initial funding the momentum will be created for a surge in public support and with it further resources for more television. All candidates, however, are aware that television is the prime medium of electioneering and that, compared with the labour-intensive but limited dimensions of traditional party communications, it is a highly sophisticated and rapidly adaptable conduit to the public. Candidates are also painfully aware of the expense and pitfalls of television as well as the controversies that surround it.

The role of the mass media in politics and especially elections has provoked a number of deep and long-standing debates. Highly contentious speculations surround the relationships between modern electioneering and the personalised 'horse-race' style of campaign reporting; between passive election coverage and active candidate selection; between political bias and structural bias in the media; and between the level of public information and the commercial constraints and priorities of television companies.[70] Other problematic areas include the extent to which the media's pre-selection of favourites and 'also rans' become self-fulfilling projections; whether the candidates' manipulation of the media is greater than the exploitation of the candidates by the media; whether images and issues are mutually exclusive; the rate at which the media influences, or is influenced by, public opinion; and 'whether television emphasizes those attributes of style and personality that contribute to effective leadership'.[71] These issues are not susceptible to any precise resolution. What is evident as far as primary elections are concerned, however, is the existence of an underlying dynamic in primary elections which, while being conspicuously affected by such disputes, nevertheless possesses an integrity of its own. The dynamic in question is the close interplay between individual campaigning, fund-raising and media exposure.

Just as the public provision of the FECA helps to foster multiple candidacies for leadership positions, so it also increases the demand for television exposure. Each candidate seeks to maximise his media coverage, in order to break away from the pack. The FECA's limits on campaign spending has supported the trend by 'concentrating official campaign spending into television, as it offers a cost-effective way of promoting a candidate in the market'.[72] While contenders compete for television outlets and for the resources to pay for them, money is dependent upon a candidate's telegenic appeal and an ability to handle the media to achieve the maximum effect. Money is required not just to buy air time, but to establish a campaign, in a state like New Hampshire, long enough to generate the level of local news coverage needed to gain public recognition and popular interest before election day.

The crowded schedule of primary elections has the effect not only of intensifying the need for money and television, but of doing so when candidates are most dependent upon assistance. The drive for resources and exposure places such an enormous strain upon a candidate's organisation both to acquire funds and to optimise their use, that the handling of electioneering, fund-raising and media marketing becomes a measure of candidate competence. Just as the ability to win primary elections is closely connected to a capacity to acquire donations and manage the media, so money and television maintain the momentum towards primary elections. Those successful politicians who are most adept at generating financial resources and public exposure are the least likely to press for any diminution of primary elections. On the contrary, it is precisely because of their competitive edge in maximising financial backing and public attention that they will be instrumental in maintaining the spiral towards candidate autonomy, self-finance, and television populism. The net effect, as Doris Graber makes clear, is that votes are no longer mobilised through party solidarity or group identity but through largely unmediated appeals to consumer choice, or individual intuition, or even personal prejudice:

> During the 1940s, when social scientists first investigated the impact of the mass media on the outcome of presidential elections, party allegiance was the most important determinant of the vote. It was followed by voters' feelings of allegiance to a social group, assessment of the candidate's personality, and consideration of issues, in that order. Since the full flowering of the electronic age more than two decades later, the order has been reversed. The candidate as a personality has become the prime consideration at the presidential level. Second are issues associated with the candidate, followed by party affiliation and group membership. When voters base their decisions on a candidate's personality or stand on issues, the media become more important because they are the chief sources of information about these matters. Correspondingly, political parties take on less importance.[73]

The independence of a candidate from his or her party, which is first set in motion during the selection process is sustained in the general election. Despite the appearance of a party embodied in its national convention and purposefully engaged in leadership selection, a modern American party in essence only ratifies the pre-selection of its leaders. Leadership choice may be a point of culmination for the leader and his or her entourage, but it in no way marks a metamorphosis of the party. There is no climactic fusion of party elements into an electoral solidarity. Notwithstanding the basic organisational characteristics of a two-party system (e.g. head-to-head presidential debates, dual party tickets, and electoral strategies and voting behaviour that are largely zero-sum in character), modern presidential elections no longer consist of *party* campaigns exclusively deployed against one another. It is no longer a contest of party elites appealing to party solidarity in support of programmes of party policy. It is now more a choice of candidates made on the basis of personalised appeals and candidate-related issues.

Party dealignment and candidate-based electioneering

The emphasis upon candidates is partly residual in that the party structure is no longer as stable as it used to be in the 1930s, 1940s, and 1950s. Since the dissipation of Roosevelt's New Deal coalition (i.e. the south, eastern blue collar workers, industrial unions, Catholic immigrants, western farmers, middle-class progressives, opinion-forming intelligentsia) an alternative governing coalition has failed to materialise.[74] Instead of *re*alignment, there has been *de*alignment in which an increasingly fluid electorate has demonstrated variable and even volatile attachments to different parties.[75] In addition to the rising incidence of ticket-splitting and the well-documented decline in party identification, the proportion of voters who have a neutral view towards both parties has increased from 13 per cent in 1952 to 36 per cent in 1984[76] – i.e. a very large pool of floating voters who can be, and very often are, pivotal in determining election outcomes. With the diminishment of reliable party support 'the belief that one should vote the man rather than the party has now become part of the American consensus' and as such 'most voters now view parties as a convenience rather than a necessity'.[77] The personalisation of presidential elections, however, has also been a direct result of the campaigns run by presidential candidates themselves. Their own electoral strategies have contributed to the view that the party organisations are mainly 'shells within which the real contest is played'.[78] Candidates have increasingly used the party as a platform not just to make direct appeals over the party's head to the public but to demonstrate their distance from the party's traditional and organisational moorings. It is now common for newly selected presidential candidates to make no mention of their own parties and to refuse to campaign actively for their parties' congressional and local tickets. Theirs is a national media campaign that requires total concentration upon maximising the individual political benefits to be accrued from the necessarily personalised format of mass media coverage. The presidential campaign is judged explicitly on personal appeal and competence irrespective of the important, if implicit, role played by party attachment and organisation. This can lead to campaigns where cultivated symbolism can threaten to displace the consideration of issues and policies.

President Ronald Reagan's 1984 re-election campaign, for example, had as its central theme the celebration of the president's first term as a cultural affirmation of America itself. The centrepiece was the party's convention in Dallas where Reagan introduced himself by way of a video presentation of Reagan's America followed by an acceptance speech in which the torch of the Los Angeles Olympics was linked to the torch of the Statue of Liberty, and to the mission and promise of the new world which it evoked.

To Jane Mayer and Doyle McManus, the performance typified the essential style of the candidate-centred appeal:

> His speech made no reference to any plans to cut government spending further – Social Security or otherwise. It made no explicit promise to continue the defense buildup. It never mentioned either Nicaragua or Lebanon. Instead, Reagan delivered a moving soliloquy on the Olympic games taking place that summer, likening the runners' torch to 'another torch, the one that greeted so many of our parents and grandparents . . . Miss Liberty's torch'. The speech wove together many strands of the nation's

lore, entwining his presidency with hope, excellence, athleticism, and patriotism, and finally placing his reelection bid on a symbolic plane completely above partisan politics. It was everything the strategists . . . could have hoped for.[79]

The Reagan campaign continued to emphasise cultural verities at the expense of any new political agenda. Despite the weakness of his administration's record and the dearth of policy ideas, Reagan successfully fused together a disarming political optimism with a 'feel good' nostalgia for the simplicities and certainties of the 1950s. Reagan's motif that 'it was morning again in America' combined a 'regressiveness of story with the utmost sophistication of special effects'.[80] With his use of political symbolism 'Reagan not only represent[ed] the past, but resurrect[ed] it as a promise of the future'.[81] Reagan's packaging of a past made accessible through presidential symbolism was not only central to his re-election campaign, it was strongly implicated in the emphatic nature of his victory when high public reputation appeared to transcend low policy approval.[82]

The apparent displacement of policy substance was arguably even greater in 1988 when George Bush cancelled out Michael Dukakis' 16 point opinion poll lead (i.e. 58–42 per cent in August 1988) by a deliberate strategy of negative television campaigning. Bush's campaign team exploited the suggestive nature of television imaging to damage Dukakis' personal standing by portraying him as hypocritical, unpatriotic, incompetent, and soft on crime. Television advertisements distorted Dukakis' record when he was Governor of Massachusetts. The most notorious featured the case of Willie Horton, a black and convicted murderer who committed rape and murder while on a weekend pass from a Massachusetts prison. Even though most states had a prisoner-furlough programme and even though it was a wholly exceptional case, Dukakis was accused of having operated a 'revolving door prison policy' in which murderers and rapists were set loose in the community.[83] While television 'technology brought the menacing image of Willie Horton into millions of American homes',[84] the same technique was used to build on the suburban fear of crime and to convey the message that George Bush, in contrast to Michael Dukakis, supported the death penalty. Similar techniques were used to discredit Dukakis on such issues as pollution control and national pride. Bush's campaign manager, Lee Atwater, was reported to have said 'that the sky was the limit on Dukakis' negatives'.[85] Although Bush overhauled Dukakis in the polls and then prevailed in the election, it led to widespread unease that the presidency had been decided by television and in particular the exploitation of television stage-craft to undermine the political reputation of one of the candidates. Criticism was levelled at the Bush campaign not just for its distasteful strategy but for the way it appeared to achieve success by deliberately furthering the process in which visual suggestion and association are given greater weight than policy statements, and the fair consideration and analysis of substantive proposals.[86]

Of course style and image are not the same as material conditions and political choices. It is possible to exaggerate the significance of presentation in electoral outcomes. Causal factors in voter behaviour are multiple and complex in nature. They range from party attachments, individual decisions and group solidarity to past government performance, prospective policy evaluation, and the state of the economy. In the leading predictive models of presidential elections, for example, the level of economic growth is generally the major variable.[87] But economic indicators are not the whole story. Presidential approval is also highly significant. 'While presidential approval and economic conditions are themselves positively correlated, each exerts an independent influence on the vote, with presidential approval appearing to be more important'.[88] Presidential approval is not only a far more diffuse category, it is one which is susceptible to leadership skills in evoking a sense of past achievement and future confidence. But the real significance of the modern presidency's preoccupation with image communications lies less with actual elections and more with the permanent political landscape that conditions presidential conduct and strategy throughout the four-year term of office. The emphasis upon the continuous public projection of the presidency is not wholly reducible to electoral considerations. The intensification of the presidency's engagement with the public during electoral periods serves merely to underline the extent to which a president is today always expected to be in public contact. For a president, the difference between elections and normal periods is one only of degree – not of kind. The cultivation of public links and the maintenence of conspicuous pre-eminence to national audiences have become necessary features of presidential life. So much so in fact that it is said to have led to a qualitatively different kind of presidency – i.e. a 'public presidency' with a distinctive set of demands, resources, and implications.

The public presidency and the 'permanent election'

In the United States, commentators have repeatedly drawn attention to the way that presidents have sought to compensate for their weaknesses in Washington by appealing directly to the public for support. Presidents have exploited the individuality of the office to project themselves as the focal embodiments of popular concern and the public interest. In 'going public',[89] it is claimed that presidents generate a personal following in the country which displaces the traditional need for political negotiation and accommodation within Washington.

> A White House faced with the prospect of fishing for the votes of hundreds of congressional minnows can turn to the publicity resources of the Oval Office to create public support for a proposal before it is discussed with Congress. If successful in this, a President need not bargain for votes; instead, members of Congress are forced to support a White House proposal by the tide of public opinion that the President has created.[90]

The increased incidence of public appearances, televised addresses, and political trips have massively enhanced the presidency's centrality in American politics. It has reached the point where presidents are able not just to 'speak directly to voters over the heads of Congress and organised interests' but to 'overrule the influence of these traditional adversaries'.[91] This in turn has projected presidents into 'the limelight of American politics, and citizens come naturally to organize their political thinking and focus their hopes for the future around the White House'.[92]

According to Samuel Kernell, who has done most to popularise the term 'going public', the change in the presidency's relationship with the public is the product of a systematic change in American politics from 'institutionalised pluralism' to 'individualised pluralism'.[93] Instead of a pattern of stable power blocs (e.g. 'conservative coalition', sectional/regional groupings, party leaders, congressional committee 'barons', a manageable media and a limited number of 'big interests') in which presidents could negotiate alliances and build coalitions, the position is now far more unstable, fluid, and multilateral. With the penetration of the federal government into so many spheres of society and the rise of issues that cross-cut traditional political allegiances – together with the decentralisation of Congress and the erosion of parties – presidents have had to forgo private accommodation for public salesmanship. They have done so both as a means to counter the smaller but less disciplined and more intransigent power centres that arise in Washington and as a way of assembling temporary coalitions from splintered interests and groupings on an issue by issue basis. As a consequence, presidents are now more actively involved in using their positions and lending their public status to acquiring support for policies by direct and more undifferentiated appeals to the public. The scale and depth of this trend towards a 'public presidency' has been so dramatic that it is widely regarded as being one of the most important and revealing developments in American politics over the last generation. In the words of James Pfiffner, 'contemporary presidents have the capacity to reach the public in ways that could not have been imagined by earlier presidents, and they have consciously formed their strategies of governing to exploit that capacity'.[94]

The need to respond to such a changing environment has led to a number of tangible organisational changes in the White House. The Office of Political Affairs ensures that presidents now have substantial influence over their parties and in particular over their operations in mobilising partisan political support. Another function now institutionalised in the White House is the administration's relationships with interest groups. The Office of Public Liaison is assigned the task of coordinating the presidency's contacts and negotiations with the ever increasing profusion and fragmentation of represented interests. A function once performed by national parties, the management of administration-interest group relations and the organisation of interest group support for presidential politics is now conspicuously lodged in the White House.

But most significant of all is the White House Office of Communications whose status and power in the modern presidency bears testament to the central importance of media outreach to the nation beyond Washington. As all power centres in Washington have become more susceptible to public pressure, it has become doubly necessary for the presidency both to compete and actively to cultivate closer and more immediate linkages between the White House and its national constituency. The Office of Communications evolved out of the Press Office and came to provide a very different set of services to that experienced at a time when the presidency worked closely with a small White House press corps (1930s-1960s). While the Press Office used to manage media relations by furnishing the press corps with White House information on a reactive day-to-day basis, the Office of Communications was formed not only to coordinate information across the entire executive branch but also to produce a more proactive and strategic use of information that would be confined neither to the national press corps, nor to improvised daily releases.[95]

Today the Office organises the dissemination of information to optimum effect; it mobilises cabinet offices and senior administration figures around single daily themes; it provides a news service and information source to media channels outside Washington; and it is actively involved in generating public support for the administration's policy agenda. With the rapid growth in White House re-porters, in television news channels and in the importance of the media, and especially television, in interpreting the administration's actions and shaping its reputation for competence, the Office of Communications is the keeper of the presidential image in an environment where public appearance carries all manner of political implications. While the style and organisation of the Office of Communications can change,[96] the needs it responds to do not. The presidential imperative to reach the public makes it essential that the president should exploit the media's resources to gain the maximum effect. Such is the importance of 'going public' and 'spin control' that the Office can provide the means of bypassing the national media and communicating directly with local media outlets through satellite and cable link-ups. In his study of the Office of Communications, John Maltese concludes that both the cultivation and abandonment of the Washington media are important elements in a modern president's armoury.

> Although an important part of spin control is maintaining a good working relationship with media representatives – especially the elite media who cover the White House on a regular basis – it is equally important to know when to circumvent them. The office often attempts to avoid the filter of intermediary reporters by taking messages directly to the people . . . Those in the public relations call it 'disintermediation'. Whatever the process is called, the Office of Communications represents an institutionalized mecha-nism for getting around the media. However, the office must use such 'end-runs' sparingly or risk alienating the influential opinion-makers who cover the white House.[97]

As modern communications develop, presidential opportunities to extend the techniques of going public expand commensurately. President Clinton, for example, not only exploited the 'narrow-casting'[98] channels of local media outlets during the 1992 presidential election, he continued to use them while in office. Clinton's clear preference for direct contact with his audiences through shows such as CNN's *Larry King Live* have often taken precedence over set piece press conferences. Clinton's political compulsion for immediacy with the public, in order to exert control over the policy agenda, has been further extended to include 'electronic town hall meetings' covered by local television stations but linked by satellite to numerous other television stations and to multiple television audiences who would be able to put questions to the president. Such meetings were employed both to cut out media middlemen in an effort to revive the partnership between 'the rulers and ruled' which Clinton avowed in the election campaign, and to generate public pressure upon members of Congress and other centres of resistance in Washington. In a town hall meeting in Detroit in February 1993, for example, the president used the occasion to arouse support for his economic programme. His intention was made quite clear. 'Listen to what I say. Decide whether you think it's fair and tell me and your senators and congressmen whether you think I'm right or wrong'.[99]

President Clinton has not limited his experiments in media populism to such meetings. Guided by his media technology consultant, Jeff Weller, the president has made a concerted attempt to exploit interactive techniques in the drive to circumvent the media establishment of national anchormen and pundits. He has engaged in live television 'talk-ins' with audiences in the White House Rose Garden and he has pioneered the use of on-line computer access to White House statements, briefings and speeches. The Clinton Administration has also championed the use of e-mail communications direct to the White House and set up the White House 'computer forum' which provides a data base of e-mail messages to 'Clinton Pz' (i.e. the president's computer identity) and with it an in-house barometer of public opinion. President Clinton in general has made a conscious effort to be seen to be accessible and responsive to ordinary Americans. Just as the public appears to be more willing to contact such a president,[100] so Bill Clinton himself is not above making an in-flight call to a local radio programme from Air Force One in order to participitate in a live talk-show,[101] or permitting an album of his impromptu saxaphone solos to be released under the title 'The President Blows'.

The public presidency is not simply an instrumental device to achieve a set of policy objectives. Neither is it a matter of choice, or timing, or experimentation. It represents a driving need to be permanently engaged in the public arena and to be lodged persistently in media schedules. Not being in the public eye is no longer regarded as presidential. It is now a defining condition of the presidency to be not merely represented in the media, but to be an integral part of what has become a media community of pollsters, reporters, columnists, commentators, media consultants, advertising producers, campaign strategists, political scientists, and information spokespersons who are all bound togther by an ascribed public interest in presidential scrutiny and speculation. To Michael Kelly, it is a community that has its own rules, beliefs, language and culture. Its central object and justification is the president – 'the architect and ultimately the victim of the world's most elaborate personality cult'.[102]

Just as '[p]ersonal popularity is now a necessary, and perhaps sufficient condition for running for the presidency',[103] so public exposure between elections has become an integral feature of presidential politics. It can even be claimed that going public has become 'a political objective in itself' in which policies are 'judged, not so much in terms of their intrinsic character, as in terms of their suitability for political marketing'.[104]

It is precisely this emphasis upon presentation and personalisation that creates concern over the extent to which government and campaigning – political leadership and public exposure – have become indistinguishable from one another. Seen in this context, the public presidency is less a departure from the norms of governing and more an extension to the imperatives of campaigning. The public presidency, therefore, is an integral feature of what Sidney Blumenthal calls 'the permanent campaign'[105] in American politics, in which parties have been all but superseded as organising agents of political participation by mass media communication, personalised appeals, and image cultivation. The breakdown of parties and party-based candidate selection has led in one sense to more entrepreneurial and independent presidents. But in another way, it has produced presidents without governing coalitions, without stable levels of support, and without conclusive mandates for any policy agenda. This leads to presidents having to generate support 'on the hoof' – accumulating fragments of consent, temporarily disarming opponents and retailing images and proposals, whilst continuously working to maintain a basis of prospective electoral strength. The public presidency is an exterior reaction to interior weaknesses and one that subjects presidents to an array of cross-pressures as professional governance becomes compounded with public communication. 'I haven't been out there as much as I should have been', an exasperated President Clinton told his audience in a Cleveland shopping mall 17 months into his presidency. 'I have been doing huge heavy lifting, and long meetings on health care and the economy. And I've been forced to deal with a lot of other issues. You can't carry on a totally continuous campaign. It's simply not possible'.[106]

Notes

1   See W. D. Burnham, 'The Turnout Problem' in A. J. Reichley (ed.), *Elections American Style* (Washington, D.C.: Brookings Institution, 1987), pp. 97–133; R. A. Teixeira, *Why Americans Don't Vote: Turnout Decline in the United States, 1960–*

1984 (New York: Greenwood, 1987); F. F. Piven and R. A. Cloward, *Why Americans Don't Vote* (New York: Pantheon, 1989).

2 For more on the issues raised by the Electoral College, see N. R. Peirce and L. D. Longley, *The People's President* (New Haven: Yale University Press, 1981); W. Berns, *After the People Vote* (Washington, D.C.: American Enterprise Institute, 1992); M. J. Glennon, *When No Majority Rules: The Electoral College and Presidential Succession* (Washington, D.C.: Congressional Quarterly Press, 1992); D. W. Abbott and J. P. Levine, *Wrong Winner, The Coming Debacle in the Electoral College* (New York: Praeger, 1991).

3 See W. N. Chambers and W. D. Burnham (eds), *The American Party Systems: Stages of Development* (New York: Oxford University Press, 1967); R. Hofstadter, *The Idea of a Party System* (Berkeley: University of California Press, 1970).

4 W. H. Riker, *Democracy in the United States*, 2nd edn (New York: Macmillan, 1965), p. 278.

5 D. B. Truman, 'Federalism and the Party System' in A. Wildavsky (ed.), *American Federalism in Perspective* (Boston: Little, Brown, 1967), p. 107.

6 *Ibid.*, p. 107.

7 B. A. Rockman, *The Leadership Question: The Presidency and the American System* (New York: Praeger, 1984), p. 64.

8 D. Mayhew, *Congress: The Electoral Connection* (New Haven: Yale University Press, 1974); T. E. Mann, *Unsafe At Any Margin: Interpreting Congressional Elections* (Washington, D.C.: American Enterprise Institute, 1978).

9 W. N. Chambers, 'Party Development and the American Mainstream', in Chambers and Burnham, *The American Party Systems*, pp. 3–32.

10 Despite the rise in independent voting, two-thirds of Americans still identify themselves as Democrats and Republicans. See W. E. Miller, 'Party Identification and the Electorate of the 1990s', in L. S. Maisel (ed.), *The Parties Respond: Changes in American Parties and Campaigns*, 2nd edn (Boulder: Westview, 1994), pp. 103–22.

11 J. M. Burns, 'The Presidency and the Party System' in F. Kinsky (ed.), *Crisis and Innovation: Constitutional Democracy in America* (New York: Basil Blackwell, 1988), p. 65. See also A. Ranney and W. Kendall, *Democracy and the American Party System* (New York: Harcourt, Brace and Co., 1956); A. Ranney, *The Doctrine of Responsible Party Government* (Urbana: University of Illinois Press, 1954).

12 A. M. Schlesinger, Jr., *History of Presidential Elections, 1789–1968* (New York: Chelsea House, 1971).

13 J. D. Lees, 'The President and his Party', in M. Shaw (ed.), *From Roosevelt to Reagan: The Development of the Modern Presidency* (London: C. Hurst, 1987), p. 46.

14 Tip O'Neill quoted in Burnham, 'The Turnout Problem', Reichley (ed.), *Elections American Style*, p. 106.

15 S. J. Wayne, *The Road to the White House* (New York: St Martin's, 1992); J. W. Ceaser, *Presidential Selection* (Princeton: Princeton University Press, 1979); H. Asher, *Presidential Elections and American Politics*, 4th edn (Homewood: Dorsey, 1988); J. Kessel, *Presidential Campaign Politics: Coalition Strategies and Citzen Response*, 3rd edn (Homewood: Dorsey, 1988); E. H. Buell and L. Sigelman, *Nominating the President* (Knoxville: University of Tennessee Press, 1991).

16 *Toward a More Responsible Two Party System: A Report of the Committee on Political Parties* (New York: American Political Science Association, 1950), p. 26.

17   *Ibid.*, p. 27.

18   E. C. Ladd, *Where Have All the Voters Gone: The Fracturing of America's Political Parties*, 2nd edn (New York: Norton, 1982); W. J. Crotty, *American Parties in Decline*, 2nd edn (Boston: Little, Brown, 1984).

19   D. S. Broder, *The Party's Over: The Failure of Politics in America* (New York: Harper and Row, 1972); W. E. Hudson, *American Democracy in Peril: Seven Challenges to America's Future* (Chatham: Chatham House, 1995), chs 2, 5. J. L. Sundquist, 'Strengthening the National Parties', in Reichley (ed.), *Elections American Style*, pp. 195–221; J. M. Burns, *Cobblestone Leadership: Majority Rule, Minority Power* (Norman: University of Oklahoma Press, 1990); G. S. and B. D. Black, *The Politics of American Discontent: How a New Party Can Make Democracy Work Again* (New York: Wiley, 1994).

20   W. J. Crotty and J. Jackson III, *Presidential Primaries and Nominations* (Washington, D.C.: Congressional Quarterly Press, 1985).

21   T. H. White, *The Making of the President, 1960* (London: Jonathan Cape, 1964).

22   A. Ranney, 'Political Parties: Reform and Decline' in Anthony King (ed.), *The New American Political System* (Washington, D.C.: American Enterprise Institute, 1978), pp. 213–47.

23   Figures from B. I. Page and M. P. Petracca, *The American Presidency* (New York: McGraw-Hill, 1983), p. 98. For information on the further development of minority representation in succeeding national conventions, see F. J. Sorauf and P. A. Beck, *Party Politics in America*, 6th edn (Glenview: Scott, Foresman, 1988), pp. 335–7.

24   J. J. Kirkpatrick, *Dismantling the Parties: Reflections on Party Reform and Party Decomposition* (Washington, D.C.: American Enterprise Institute, 1978); N. W. Polsby, *Consequences of Party Reform* (New York: Oxford University Press, 1983); B. E. Shafer, *Quiet Revolution: The Struggle for the Democratic Party and the Shaping of Post-Reform Politics* (New York: Sage, 1983); M. Plissner and W. J. Mitofsky, 'The Making of the Delegates 1968–1988', in S. J. Wayne and C. Wilcox (eds), *The Quest for National Office* (New York: St Martin's, 1992), pp. 154–60; E. C. Kamark and K. M. Goldstein, 'The Rules Do Matter: Post-Reform Presidential Nominating Politics', in Maisel (ed.), *The Parties Respond*, pp. 169–98.

25   H. H. Humphrey, *The Education of a Public Man: My Life and Politics* (London: Weidenfeld and Nicolson, 1976), p. 436.

26   Crotty and Jackson, *Presidential Primaries and Nominations*, p. 3.

27   S. Hess, *The Presidential Campaign: An Essay*, rev. edn (Washington, D.C.: Brookings Institution, 1978).

28   W. F. Mondale, *The Accountability of Power: Toward a Responsible Presidency* (New York: McKay, 1975).

29   J. L. Sundquist, *Constitutitonal Reform and Effective Government* (Washington: Brookings Institution, 1986), p. 185. See also T. Sandford, *A Danger of Democracy: The Presidential Nominating Process* (Boulder: Westview, 1981); S. Keeler and C. Zukin, *Uninformed Choice: The Failure of the New Presidential Nominating System* (New York: Praeger, 1983).

30   Sundquist, *Constitutional Reform and Effective Government*, p. 185.

31   N. W. Polsby and A. Wildavsky, *Presidential Elections: Strategy of American Presidential Elections* (New York: Charles Scribners, 1964), p. 156.

32   For more on this debate, see P. M. Miller, M. E. Jewell and L. Sigelman, 'Divisive Primaries and Party Activists: Kentucky, 1979 and 1983', *Journal of Politics*, 50 (2)

(May 1988), pp. 459–70; A. Ranney, 'The Representativeness of Primary Electorates', *Midwest Journal of Political Science*, 12 (2) (May 1968), pp. 224–38.

33   W. J. Crotty, 'Two Cheers for the Presidential Primaries', in T. E. Cronin (ed.), *Rethinking the Presidency* (Boston: Little, Brown, 1982), p. 65.

34   M. P. Wattenberg, 'From a Partisan to a Candidate-Centered Electorate', in King (ed.), *The New American Political System, Second Version* (Washington, D.C.: American Enterprise Institute, 1990), p. 153. See also P. R. Abramson, 'Generational Change and the Decline of Party Identification in America: 1952–1974', *American Political Science Review*, 70 (2) (June 1976), pp. 769–78; L. D. Epstein, *Political Parties in the American Mold* (Madison: University of Wisconsin Press, 1986), pp. 256–63.

35   A. I. Abramowitz and W. J. Stone, *Nomination Politics: Party Activists and Presidential Choice* (New York: Praeger, 1984), p. 135. Nonetheless, evidence exists that suggests that party organisation does suffer from primary elections by creating divisions at the grassroots level – leading to diminished participation and electoral assistance in the subsequent presidential election by supporters of beaten candidates in closely fought primary election encounters. See W. J. Stone, 'Prenomination Candidate Choice and General Election Behavior: Iowa Presidential Activists in 1980', *American Journal of Political Science*, 28 (2) (May 1984), pp. 361–78.

36   L. Bartels, *Presidential Primaries and the Dynamics of Public Choice* (Princeton: Princeton University Press, 1988).

37   J. W. Ceaser, 'Improving the Nomination Process' in Reichley (ed.), *Elections American Style*, p. 29.

38   For a criticial examination of the problems posed by a national primary, see A. Wildavsky, *The Beleaguered Presidency* (New Brunswick: Transaction Books, 1991), ch. 15.

39   H. E. Alexander, *Financing Politics*, 3rd edn (Washington, D.C.: Congressional Quarterly Press 1984); H. E. Alexander and M. Bauer, *Financing the 1988 Election* (Boulder: Westview, 1991); M. Malbin, *Money and Politics in the United States: The View from the Inside* (Washington, D.C.: Center for Responsive Politics, 1988); F. J. Sorauf, *Money in American Elections* (Glenview: Scott, Foresman, 1988); L. J. Sabato, *Paying for Elections: The Campaign Finance Thicket* (New York: Priority, 1989).

40   L. J. Sabato, *PAC Power* (New York: Norton, 1985); F. I. Luntz, *Candidates, Consultants and Campaigns: The Style and Substance of American Electioneering* (Oxford: Basil Blackwell, 1988); Citizen Action, *Hidden Power: Campaign Contributions by Large Individual Donors, 1989–90* (Washington, D.C.: Citizen Action, 1991); D. Clawson, *Corporate PACs and Political Influence* (New York: Basic Books, 1992).

41   Because PAC contributions are ineligible for matching grants, they are relatively less attractive to presidential campaign organisations and, as such, there is a relative disincentive on the part of PACs to make contributions to presidential contenders.

42   Candidates are permitted to spend an extra 20 per cent of such totals to cover fundraising costs.

43   Third parties can also acquire public funds for competing in a presidential election, but they have to surpass a threshold of 5 per cent of the popular vote. The resources received are calculated on a sliding scale that rises along with the share of the popular vote gained. The disadvanatge for the minor parties is that they can only receive the funding after the election. The only real benefit from such a system is that the

amount in question can effectively be claimed twice over – once after the initial qualifying election and again four years later when the same sum can be procured prior to the next presidential election.

44 Candidates are permitted to draw on a limited allocation of party funds over and above their ceiling of public funds. In 1992, for example, both George Bush and Bill Clinton were each allowed to spend an additional $10 million from party sources on top of thier allocation of $55 million of public funds.

45 E. Drew, *Politics and Money: The New Road to Corruption* (New York: Macmillan, 1983).

46 *Buckley* v. *Valeo* 424 US (1976).

47 The most notable example of a candidate waiving the opportunity of acquiring public matching funds remains John Connally in 1980. Because he wished to concentrate his resources in certain key states, he declined public funding and, thereupon, retained discretion over the state by state distribution of his campaign resources.

48 F. J. Sorauf, *Inside Campaign Finance: Myths and Realities* (New Haven: Yale University Press, 1992), p. 152.

49 *Federal Election Commission* v. *National Conservative Political Action Committee*, 466 US 935 (1985).

50 Members of Congress and other prominent politicians can set up their own individual PACs to promote favoured policies and to provide donations to favoured candidates. Such PACs can also form the financial and organisational basis to a 'pre-pre-nomination' campaign for the presidency. In fact, the foundation of a PAC is often seen as a sign of a politician's presidential ambitions. Such PACs allow an aspirant to test public opinion and to amass funds prior to any formal declaration of a candidacy. On a more practical level, the PAC device also allows candidates to circumvent the normal limits on the raising of funds for individual campaigns. See R. K. Baker, *The New Fat Cats: Members of Congress as Political Beneficiaries* (New York: Priority, 1989).

51 See P. S. Herrnson, *Party Campaigning in the 1980s* (Cambridge: Harvard University Press, 1988); F. J. Sorauf and S. A. Wilson, 'Political Parties and Campaign Finance: Adaptation and Accommodation Toward a Changing Role', in Maisel (ed.), *The Parties Respond*, pp. 235–54.

52 Sorauf, *Inside Campaign Finance*, p. 147.

53 See A. J. Reichley, 'The Rise of National Parties' in J. E. Chubb and P. E. Peterson (eds), *The New Direction in American Politics* (Washington, D.C.: Brookings Institution, 1989), pp. 191–5; J. A. Schlesinger, 'The New American Party System', *American Political Science Review*, 79 (4) (December 1985), pp. 1152–69; C. P. Cotter and J. F. Bibby, 'Institutionalization of Parties and the Thesis of Party Decline', *Political Science Quarterly*, 95 (1) (Spring 1980), pp. 1–27; P. S. Herrnson, 'The Revitalization of National Party Organizations', in Maisel (ed.), *The Parties Respond*, pp. 45–68.

54 Luntz, *Candidates, Consultants and Campaigns*, p. 225.

55 *The American Almanac: The Statistical Abstract of the US 1974*, intro. B. J. Wattenberg (New York: Grosset and Dunlap, 1973), p. 693.

56 *Statistical Abstract of the United States, 1991* (Washington, D.C.: US Government Printing Office, 1991), p. 556.

57 *Ibid.*, p. 556.

58   Figures drawn from R. K. Baker, G. M. Pomper, and W. C. McWilliams, *American Government*, 2nd edn (New York: Macmillan, 1987), p. 141.

59   D. A. Graber, *Mass Media and American Politics* (Washington, D.C.: Congressional Quarterly Press, 1989), ch. 5. See also L. Erbing, E. Goldenberg and A. Miller, 'Front Page News and Real World Cues: A New Look at Agenda-Setting by the Media', *American Journal of Political Science*, 24 (1) (February 1980), pp. 16–49; S. Iyengar, M. Peters and D. R. Kinder, 'Experimental Demonstrations of the "Not So Minimal" Consequences of Television News Programs', *American Political Science Review*, 16 (4) (December 1982), pp. 848–57; S. Iyengar and D. R. Kinder, *News That Matters: Television and Public Opinion* (Chicago: University of Chicago Press, 1987).

60   Graber, *Mass Media and American Politics*, ch. 6; M. Linsky (ed.), *Television and Presidential Elections* (Lexington: Lexington Books, 1983); A. Ranney, *Channels of Power: The Impact of Television on American Politics* (New York: Basic Books, 1983); C. McDowell, 'Television Politics: The Medium in the Revolution', in P. Duke (ed.), *The Politics of Upheaval* (New York: Warner, 1986), pp. 217–39; S. Mickelson, *From Whistle Stop to Sound Bite: Four Decades of Politics and Television* (New York: Praeger, 1989); M. Schram, *The Great American Video Game: Presidential Politics in the TV Age* (New York: William Morrow, 1987); R. P. Hart, *Presidential Communication in the Modern Age* (Chicago: University of Chicago Press, 1987); D. Owen, *Media Messages in Presidential Elections* (Westport: Greenwood, 1991); C. Allen, *Eisenhower and the Mass Media: Peace, Prosperity and Prime Time Television* (Chapel Hill: University of North Carolina Press, 1993); M. A. Watson, *Expanding Vision: American Television in the Kennedy Years* (New York: Oxford University Press, 1990); R. J. Donovan and R. Scherer, *Unsilent Revolution: Television News and American Public Life, 1948–1991* (Cambridge: Cambridge University Press, 1992).

61   A. R. Hunt, 'The Media and Presidential Campaigns', in Reichley (ed.), *Elections American Style*, p. 57.

62   Donovan and Scherer, *Unsilent Revolution*, p. 239.

63   T. Wicker, 'The Elections: Why the System Has Failed', *New York Review of Books*, 14 August 1980.

64   Luntz, *Candidates, Consultants and Campaigns*, p. 16.

65   M. J. Robinson, 'Where's the Beef?: Media and Media Elites in 1984', in A. Ranney (ed.), *The American Elections of 1984* (Washington, D.C.: American Enterprise Institute, 1985). The changing nature of the 'media elite' is examined in E. O'Shaughnessy, N. Leman, and D. Halberstam, 'The New Establishment', *Vanity Fair*, 57 (10) (October 1994), pp. 109–59.

66   Quoted in A. Bakshian, *Winning the White House: An Insider's Guide to American Presidential Elections* (Bolton: Ross Anderson, 1984), pp. 94–5.

67   R. K. Goodwin, *One Billion Dollars of Influence: The Direct Marketing of Politics* (Chatham: Chatham House, 1988); F. C. Arterton, *Media Politics: The News Strategies of Presidential Campaigns* (Lexington: Lexington Books, 1984); E. Diamond and S. Bates, *The Spot: The Rise of Political Advertising on Television*, rev. edn (Cambridge: MIT Press, 1988). N. J. O'Shaughnessy, *The Phenomenon of Political Marketing* (Basingstoke: Macmillan, 1990), chs 5, 8, 9; M. D. McCubbins with J. H. Aldrich, F. C. Arterton, S. L. Popkin, and L. J. Sabato, *Under the Watchful Eye: Managing Presidential Campaigns in the Television Era* (Washington, D.C.: Congressional Quarterly Press, 1992)

68 L. J. Sabato, *The Rise of Political Consultants: New Ways of Winning Elections* (New York: Basic Books, 1981); Luntz, *Candidates, Consultants and Campaigns, passim*; D. Chagal, *The New Kingmakers* (New York: Harcourt Brace Jovanovich, 1981); R. E. Denton and G. C. Woodward, *Political Communication in America* (New York: Praeger, 1985); O'Shaughnessy, *The Phenomenon of Political Marketing*, ch. 7; B. Schieffer and G. P. Gates, *The Acting President: Ronald Reagan and the Men Who Hepled Create the Illusion That Held America Spellbound* (New York: Dutton, 1989).

69 Note the conspicuous failures of super-wealthy individuals like John Connolly and Pete DuPont to acquire their party's nomination in 1980 and 1988 respectively.

70 For example, see M. J. Robinson, and M. A. Sheehan, *Over the Wire and on TV: CBS and UPI in Campaign '80* (New York: Sage, 1983); H. E. Bardy and R. Johnson, 'What's The Primary Message: Horse Race or Issue Journalism?' in G. R. Orren and N. W. Polsby (eds), *Media and Momentum: The New Hampshire Primary and Nomination Politics* (Chatham: Chatham House, 1987), pp. 127–86.

71 P. Woll and R. H. Winstock, *America's Political System: A Test With Cases*, 5th edn (New York: McGraw-Hill, 1991), p. 477.

72 P. J. Davies, *Elections USA* (Manchester: Manchester University Press, 1992), pp. 43–4.

73 Graber, *Mass Media and American Politics*, p. 197.

74 K. A Anderson, *The Creation of a Democratic Majority, 1928–1936* (Chicago: University of Chicago Press, 1979); J. M. Allswang, *The New Deal and American Politics* (New York: Wiley, 1978); W. D. Burnham, *Critical Elections and the Mainsprings of American Politics* (New York: Norton, 1970).

75 See H. Norputh and J. Rusk, 'Partisan Dealignment in the American Electorate: Itemising the Deductions since 1964', *American Political Science Review*, 76 (3) (September 1982), pp. 522–37; N. H. Nie, S. Verba, and J. R. Petrocik, *The Changing American Voter* (Cambridge: Harvard University Press, 1976); M. P. Wattenberg, 'The Hollow Realignment: Partisan Change in a Candidate-Centered Era', *Public Opinion Quarterly*, 51 (Spring 1987); M. P. Wattenberg, *The Rise of Candidate Centered Politics* (Cambridge: Harvard University Press, 1991).

76 Martin P. Wattenberg, *The Decline of American Political Parties, 1952–1988* (Cambridge, MA: Harvard University Press, 1986).

77 Wattenberg, 'From a Partisan to a Candidate-Centered Electorate', in King (ed.), *The New American Political System*, Second Version, p. 149.

78 Quoted in Bakshian, *Winning the White House*, p. 78.

79 J. Mayer and D. McManus, *Landslide: The Unmaking of the President, 1984–1988* (London: Fontana, 1989), p. 33

80 G. Wills, *Reagan's America: Innocents At Home* (London: Heinemann, 1988), p. 377.

81 *Ibid.*, p. 377.

82 S. M. Lipset, 'Beyond 1984: The Anomalies of American Politics', *PS: Political Science and Politics*, Spring 1986.

83 See J. E. White, 'Bush's Most Valuable Player', *Time*, 14 November 1988. See also K. H. Jamieson, *Dirty Politics: Deception, Distraction and Democracy* (New York: Oxford University Press, 1992).

84 Donovan and Scherer, *Unsilent Revolution*, p. 248.

85 *Ibid.*, p. 246.

86   See M. R. Hershey, 'The Campaign and the Meida' in G. M. Pomper *et al.*, *The Election of 1988: Reports and Interpretations* (Chatham: Chatham House, 1989); D. Kellner, *Television and the Crisis of Democracy* (Boulder: Westview, 1990).

87   M. S. Lewis-Beck and T. Rice, 'Forecasting Presidential Elections: A Comparison of Naive Models, *Political Behavior* (1984) pp. 39–51; D. A. Hibbs, Jr., 'President Reagan's Mandate from the 1980 Elections: A Shift to the Right?, *American Politics Quarterly*, 10 (1982), pp. 387–420; R. C. Fair, 'The Effect of Economic Events Votes for President: 1984 Update', *Political Behavior* (1988); A. I. Abramowitz, 'An Improved Model for Predicting Presidential Election Outcomes', *PS: Political Science and Politics* (Fall 1988), pp. 843–7.

88   J. E. Campbell and T. E. Mann, 'Forecasting the 1992 Presidential Election: A User's Guide to the Models', *The Brookings Review*, Fall 1992, p. 23.

89   S. Kernell, *Going Public: New Strategies of Presidential Leadership* (Washington, D.C.: Congressional Quarterly Press, 1986).

90   R. Rose, *The Postmodern President: The White House Meets the World* (Chatham: Chatham House, 1988), p. 35.

91   R. J. Barrilleaux, *The Post-Modern Presidency: The Office after Reagan* (New York: Praeger, 1988), p. 134.

92   G. C. Edwards III, *The Public Presidency: The Pursuit of Popular Support* (New York: St Martin's, 1983), p. 5.

93   Kernell, *Going Public*, p. 25.

94   J. Pfiffner, *The Modern Presidency* (New York: St Martin's, 1993), p. 36. See also B. Miroff, 'The Presidency and the Public: Leadership as Spectacle', in M. Nelson (ed.), *The Presidency and the Political System*, 2nd edn (Washington, D.C.: Congressional Quarterly Press, 1988), pp. 271–91; M. Edelman, *Constructing the Political Spectacle* (Chicago: University of Chicago Press, 1988); J. Tulis, *The Rhetorical Presidency* (Princeton: Princeton University Press, 1987); K. K. Campbell and K. H. Jamieson, *Deeds Done in Words: Presidential Rhetoric and the Genres of Governance* (Chicago: University of Chicago Press, 1990); T. J. Lowi, *The Personal President: Power Invested, Promise Unfulfilled* (Ithaca: Cornell University Press, 1985). For an extension of Lowi's thesis into the 1980s, see C. A. Rimmerman, *Presidency by Plebiscite: The Reagan-Bush Era in Institutional Perspective* (Boulder: Westview, 1993).

95   D. S. Broder, *Behind the Front Page: A Candid Look at How the News is Made* (New York: Simon and Schuster, 1987); F. Cormier, J. Deakin, and H. Thomas, *The White House Press on the Presidency: News Management and Co-Option* (Lanham: University Press of America, 1983); R. E. Denton, Jr. and D. F. Hahn, *Presidential Communication* (New York: Praeger, 1986); J. Kumar and M. B. Grossman, *Portraying the President: The White House and the News Media* (Baltimore: Johns Hopkins University Press, 1981); M. J. Rozell, 'President Carter and the Press: Perspectives from White House Communications Advisers', *Political Science Quarterly*, 105 (3) (Fall 1990), pp. 419–34; Graber, *Mass Media and American Politics*, pp. 235–54; H. Schmertz, 'The Media and the Presidency', *Presidential Studies Quarterly*, 16 (1) (Winter 1986), pp. 11–21.

96   J. A. Maltese, *Spin Control: The White House Office of Communications and the Management of Presidential News*, 2nd edn (Chapel Hill: University of North Carolina Press, 1994).

97   *Ibid.*, p. 216.

98 A. Ranney, 'Broadcasting, Narrowcasting, and Politics' in King (ed.), *The New American Political System*, Second Version, pp. 175–201; L. King with M. Sencel, *On The Line: The New Road to the White House* (New York: Harcourt, Brace, 1993); T. Rosentiel, *Strange Bedfellows: How Television and the Presidential Candidate Changed American Politics, 1992* (New York: Hyperion, 1993).

99 Quoted in M. Fletcher, 'Clinton preparing bitter medicine to turn round the economy', *The Times*, 15 February 1993.

100 President Clinton received more letters during his first five months in office than President Bush received in the whole of 1991 or 1992. The White House was forced to take on an extra 200 volunteers to open and process the 22,000 letters that poured in every day.

101 The phone call was made at a height of 30,000 feet to radio station KMOX in St Louis on 24 June 1994.

102 M. Kelley, 'David Gergen, Master of the Game', *New York Times Magazine*, 31 October 1993. See also F. Smoller, *The Six O'Clock Presidency: A Theory of Presidential Press Relations in the Age of Television* (New York: Praeger, 1990); M. Foley, *The Rise of the British Presidency* (Manchester: Manchester University Press, 1993), pp. 91–103.

103 Rose, *The Postmodern President*, p. 97.

104 *Ibid.*, p. 36.

105 S. Blumenthal, *The Permanent Campaign*, rev. edn (New York: Simon and Schuster, 1982).

106 Quoted in M. Walker, 'Clinton sets out to sell his presidency', *The Guardian*, 11 May 1993.

CHAPTER 8

Decision-making in the White House

To make decisions, it is necessary to acquire information, to determine options to identify issues, to choose a course of action, and ensure its implementation. At first sight, the president would appear to be provided with an effective decision-making structure in the form of a cabinet.[1] Through this forum, departmental secretaries can pool their specialist information and draw together the results of their consultations with client groups, to give the president a wide range of policy advice and a sound basis for making informal choices and feasible commitments. By the same token, the cabinet also has the potential to coordinate policies within the government machine and to ensure that presidential purposes are clearly reflected in the implementation of policy on the ground.

The collective deficiencies of the president's cabinet

The formal means exist by which the cabinet can translate such potential into actuality. The Cabinet Room, for example, is located next door to the Oval Office and is officially reserved only for cabinet meetings. In addition to its prestigious location, the cabinet possesses its own secretariat, responsible for preparing and circulating the agendas and for following through cabinet decisions. The cabinet secretary was introduced by President Eisenhower who was intent upon maximising his use of the cabinet both as a decision-making body and as a device for delegating responsibility from the White House to the executive departments. With this in mind, Eisenhower convened an average of thirty-four cabinet meetings a year during his presidency.[2] But although the cabinet secretary's office remains in existence, no president since Eisenhower has ever used the cabinet to the same extent. On the contrary, it has been customary for modern presidents to look elsewhere for their administration's source of central decision-making and collective identity; President Eisenhower's attachment to the cabinet, therefore, was wholly exceptional. It remains significant less as a precedent and more for throwing into relief the normal pattern of presidential–cabinet relations, in which the potential for cabinet decision-making is denied rather than affirmed.

It is true that incoming presidents almost invariably claim that it is their intention to reinstate cabinet government and, as such, they set themselves the task of working closely with their cabinets. It is equally conventional for presidents to overlook these commitments and progressively diminish the role of the cabinet during their tenure in the office. In one sense, it is quite logical for presidents to begin their period in office with an affinity to the cabinet. Faced with the immensity of the federal bureaucracy, it is only to be expected that a president would wish to rely upon his cabinet team of chosen lieutenants – all of them freshly appointed, many of them new to Washington, and each of them swearing allegiance to their benefactor.

But the honeymoon never lasts for long. Just as it is rational for a president to want to use the cabinet for his chosen purposes, so in another sense it is just as understandable for him increasingly to discard the decision-making capabilities of the cabinet. Harold Seidman explains,

> Presidents operate under very rigid time restraints. What they want, they want now. They are impatient with solutions that go beyond the next congressional election, and their maximum time span is four years. They say they welcome disagreement and dissent, but cannot understand why Cabinet members do not share a presidential perspective. The fiefdoms are fractious, and the machinery of Government moves too slowly to suit their purposes. Their experience . . . has given them neither the knowledge nor the aptitude to energize the executive establishment, so far as possible they attempt to by-pass and neutralize it.[3]

Such was President Kennedy's urgency for reform that it was not long before he concluded that 'cabinet meetings are simply useless. Why should the Postmaster General sit there and listen to a discussion of the problem of Laos? . . . I don't know how presidents functioned with them or relied on them in the past'.[4] In contrast to Eisenhower who convened ten cabinet meetings in the first eighty days of his presidency, Kennedy 'held only three meetings in his first eighty days in office and less thereafter'.[5] Kennedy was so disenchanted with the cabinet as an instrument of government that he even abolished the cabinet secretary's office.

Kennedy's frustrations typified those of every modern president except Eisenhower. As a consequence, the cabinet is widely regarded as an inappropriate body for the role assigned to it and for the decisions expected of it. The successive disappointments of the American cabinet have led many observers to conclude that cabinet decision-making is inherently incompatible with the political system. 'Although presidents, usually while introducing their newly appointed cabinet members to the press, like to talk about cabinet government as their goal, cabinet government is an impossibility in the American system'.[6] Again, 'if cabinet government is defined in the strong sense – as the president governing only indirectly through the way his department and agency heads decide to act as a group – then the proposition is dangerously unrealistic. It is significant that no president has ever left office extolling the virtues of cabinet government.'[7]

Several reasons exist that explain the retarded development of the American cabinet as a decision-making body. First, it is assembled *after* the president has entered ofice. Its members have not fought the election together as an aspiring government team and have no political *esprit de corps* from years of purposeful collaboration. Second, because the president is the only elected office-holder in the executive branch, cabinet members have no political base, or claim to authority, comparable to the chief executive. Third, a president does not have a free choice in the selection of the cabinet. By convention, he is expected to have a geographically and politically balanced cabinet. It is also prudent to include representatives of minorities, figures who can command respect in Congress and even, on occasion, a political opponent. Fourth, a president must proceed on the basis that a cabinet member should be acceptable to his or her allocated department. Apart from the problems of acquiring Senate confirmation of an unacceptable secretary-designate, it is not in the president's own interests to have a secretary that incurs bureaucratic hostility and, therefore, even greater opposition from a department than would otherwise be the case.

Fifth, a large proportion of the cabinet are necesssarily strangers to the president – i.e. specialist managers in their own discrete fields, brought to Washington to fulfil specific administrative functions.[8] Cabinet recruitment on these lines leads not so much to a mature political hierarchy, but to an uneasy disjunction between the president, with explicit political responsibilities for the national interest, and 'the government' and cabinet with its implicit attachments to the sphere of structural bureaucratic and interest group policies. Sixth, the belief that much of his cabinet is operating in a different political dimension, and that it is incapable of objective and collective decision-making, can lead to a disdainful presidential posture towards the cabinet. President Truman's view of the cabinet is especially significant as he addressed his comments directly to the members of his cabinet at their first meeting. The entry in his personal diary records the occasion:

> [Cabinet] Held Cabinet Meeting – explained to Cabinet members that in my opinion the Cabinet were simply a Board of Directors appointed by the President, to help him carry out policies of the Government; in many instances the Cabinet could be of tremendous help to the President by offering advice whether he liked it or not but when the President [gave] an order they should carry it out. I told them I expected to have a Cabinet I could depend on and take in my confidence and if this confidence was not well placed I would get a Cabinet in which I could place confidence . . . [T]hat is the way I intend to run this.[9]

The absence of collective responsiblity, together with the lack of dependence of cabinet members upon government success and re-election for their career development, can provoke presidents into attempts to stamp their singular authority upon the cabinet. President Clinton, for example, has been known to subject his cabinet to outbursts of sarcasm and wrath prompted by his infuriation over Washington politics and his own programme's lack of progress.[10] Presidents Nixon (1973) and Carter (1979) went so far as to sack their entire cabinets as a demonstration of their presidential authority. More commonly, the conditions under which presidents coexist with their cabinets lead to the latter being progressively ignored by the chief executive. In the view of many who occupy the White House, the indifference is mutual. As John Ehrlichmman once caustically observed: 'We only meet them [i.e. cabinet members] at the White House Christmas Party; they go off and marry the natives [i.e. civil servants and bureaucratic interests]'.[11]

There are qualifications to this pathology of cabinet government. It can be pointed out that cabinet secretaries are not necessarily a president's 'natural enemies',[12] but can be a 'president's natural allies' motivated by party loyalty and ideological solidarity. Instead of being cowed by clientelism, they can be 'more loyal to party principles than even their presidents'.[13] It can also be argued that the strength of organised interests even in the traditionally client-based departments have been weakened (i) by changes in the presidential nomination process which have diminished the influence of traditional group attachments in the selection of nominees; (ii) by the trend away from appointing prestigious figures to the cabinet towards selecting experts or managers with proclaimed loyalty to the president;[14] (iii) by the enhanced significance of central budgetary control; and (iv) by the profileration and fragmentation of interests in an increasingly heterogeneous group culture. Even though the cabinet can be regarded as a body less susceptible to entrenched interests than it used to be and as an entity able to provide an important outlet for actual and symbolic political representation, it nevertheless remains an undeveloped centre of decision-making. From the perspective of the theory of institutionalisation, the American cabinet lacks autonomy, corporate identity, and organisational coherence and integrity − 'the cabinet has little sense of self − rather it has many selves'.[15]

The politics of cabinet selection

Because one of Bill Clinton's key campaign promises had been to appoint a government that would 'look like America' and 'reflect the diversity of America', he devoted more time to the selection of his cabinet than any president before him. Cabinet selection was part of a much larger process to ensure greater minority represenation in the senior levels of the bureaucracy. According to Thomas Edsall, 'no previous president ha[d] been as explicit about diversity as a criterion for cabinet and government appointments'. Although the president denied that he was 'bean counting' it became clear that something akin to a quota system was being applied to the process of selection. Clinton's personnel office broke each state down into its component minorities of blacks, women, Hispanics, and Asians for the purposes of allocating appointments. Applicants were subjected to the 'egg test', in order to determine the extent to which they could contribute towards achieving balances of ethnicity, gender, and geography in the profile of federal employment.

The prolonged process of acquiring proportional representation in the federal bureaucracy bore fruit. By the end of 1993, 14 per cent of federal appointments were black (a figure slightly higher than that warranted by the 12 per cent of Americans who are black); 9.5 per cent were Hispanic and 3 per cent were Asian (both figures corresponding to the minorities' level in the population as a whole). The male/female split was not far from being equal (i.e. 54 per cent/46 per cent respectively).

The quota system was not applied with the same rigour to the level of cabinet posts. Nevertheless, Clinton's cabinet included five women (Janet Reno, Donna Shalala, Hazel O'Leary, Carol Browner, Madeleine Albright); three blacks (Mike Espy, Ron Brown, Jesse Brown); and two Hispanics (Federico Pena, Henry Cisneros). Other balances were implicit in his selection. Experienced Washingtonians like Warren Christopher and no fewer than three ex-members of Congress (e.g. Lloyd Bentsen, Les Aspin, Leon Panetta) were mixed with notable 'outsiders' (e.g. Espy, Pena, O'Leary). 'New Democrats' (e.g. Richard Riley, Robert Reich) were offset by liberals (e.g. Shalala). Free traders (e.g. Reich) were combined with protectionists (e.g. Bentsen); intellectuals (e.g. Reich, Shalala) with political fixers (e.g. Ron Brown, Mickey Kantor); 'greens' (e.g. Bruce Babbitt, Al Gore) with business sympathisers (e.g. Bentsen, Ron Brown); and financial conservatives (e.g. Bentsen) with deficit cutters (e.g. Panetta).

Such diversity may have had enormous symbolic value, but it was also prompted by Clinton's need to appease major factions in the Democratic Party. By not giving any particular grouping a clear ideological supremacy, the president sought to ensure that he would remain the central arbitrator and that most of the major decisions would, therefore, be reserved for him. Although the cabinet was carefully chosen by Clinton, this was not the same as saying that it was *his* cabinet. Decisions were designed to be his through the diversity and disjunctions of the cabinet's membership.

Contraction as a response to the problem of decision-making

In recognising the weakness of the cabinet, presidents have helped to undermine it further. As a decision-making body, it has continually disappointed presidents because it has failed to match its institutionalisation as a coordinative force in government with the institutionalisation of departmental interests. Indeed, it is precisely because the cabinet is normally so effective in giving multiple expression to the entrenched interests of the bureaucracy that presidents increasingly turn to the executive office, and to the White House staff in particular, as a forum of executive decision-making. As presidents turn progressively inward to compensate for their perceived lack of outreach in the executive branch, they not only serve to verify this self-assessment, but strengthen their resolve to split policy-making from policy implementation and wherever possible to leave the executive with the residual role of carrying out decisions to the exclusion of helping to shape them.

The compulsive drive by presidents to wrest discretionary decision-making for the bureaucracy has taken many forms. In the early days of the modern presidency, for example, President Roosevelt employed a competitive approach to administration in which overlapping jurisdictions and even duplicate responsibilities 'reserved the big decisions for the president'.[17] Roosevelt's deliberate cultivation of insecurity and anxiety in the government machine 'brought him an effective flow of information . . . kept the reins of decision in his own hands, made for administrative flexibility and stimulated subordination to effective performance'.[18] The legendary disorder of the Roosevelt administration, however, was not a model that could be repeated by his successors. More conventional means were created through the development of the EXOP (see pp. 209–15).

Another arrangement to assist decision-making has come into existence by convention and evolution, rather than by conscious creation. This is the informal demarcation by presidents of an inner and outer cabinet. According to Thomas Cronin, the former is distinguished from the latter by its physical, political, and personal proximity to the president and by its high priority for national responsibilities.[19] By the same token, the outer departments are distinguished by their close relationships with client groups and by the inevitable advocacy of client and bureaucratic-based interests on the part of the departmental secretaries. Although presidents will often begin their period of office by treating all cabinet members on an equal footing, it is generally accepted that with time the inherent cross-pressures have their effect. They lead to the emergence of a progressively isolated outer cabinet with restricted access to the president in contrast to the inversely proportional reliance by the president upon a conspicuous inner cabinet. To Cronin, the inner and outer cabinets are distinguished by departments, by the type of people asked to serve in them, and by the type of responsibilities, interests, and likely conduct associated with them.

Jeffrey Cohen has advanced a more sophisticated ranking that allows for three rather than two sub-cabinets.[20]

(i) Inner Cabinet
Defense
Justice
State
Treasury

(ii)   Old Outer Cabinet
Agriculture
Commerce
Interior
Labor Veterans' Affairs

(iii)   New Outer Cabinet
Education
Energy
Health & Human Services
Housing & Urban Development
Transportation

Even though the Veterans' Affairs Department was only created in 1988, it is ranked as an old outer cabinet department because of its extensive history as an independent agency prior to its change of status.

Cohen posits the existence of both older and newer outer cabinets. While the former consists of established departments working within 'environments that are dominated by one strong interest', the latter is composed of the more recently established departments with 'more complex environments . . . [accommodating] many, often conflicting, interests'.[21] In the cabinet pecking order, the older outer cabinet retains special status because of the focused nature of their interests. The newer outer departments often serve multiple and competing interests within issue areas that are redistributive in nature and, therefore, more controversial and likely to generate conflict within and between departments. As a consequence, the newer outer cabinets are more unmanageable and resistant to their marginal isolation by the White House.

For an innovative president like Richard Nixon, even the extensive apparatus of the EXOP and the availibility of an ultra-zealous inner cabinet was not enough to satisfy his requirements. President Nixon wanted to arrest the inertial properties of the positive state and rearrange its priorities. As the federal government was the chief political issue to Nixon, it followed that government organisation could be equated with policy. As such, President Nixon embarked on a strategy to acheive a *de facto* government reorganisation by the White House taking over the hierarchy of the executive branch. The president sought to capture the initiative in decision-making by colonising the senior political and civil service positions of the administration with Nixon loyalists and by thrusting White House bureaucratic intervention to the point where presidential aides became line executives. Ironically, his crusade of 'counter-bureaucracy' in many instances had the reverse effect with the White House staff bogged down in implementation, while departments and agencies moved in to fill the policy vacuum.[22] President Nixon's other approach to the problem was to designate four 'super-secretaries' to be in charge of four functional areas of policy (i.e. human resources, community development, economic affairs, and natural resources). The four offices would not only be Nixon loyalists with closer access to the president than other secretaries but would merge the role of presidential adviser with that of departmental secretary. This provocative attempt to politicise the bureaucracy further by explicitly diminishing the role of the cabinet in favour of four presidential councillors of state (i.e. an inner inner cabinet) foundered because of the Watergate scandal.[23]

Another strategy to keep those in cabinet and sub-cabinet positions away from the 'permanent government' and closer to the White House was devised by the Reagan Administration. In addition to the most stringent control over appointments to ensure loyalty to the 'Reagan revolution', the administration attempted to reconstruct the governmental structure itself in an attempt to facilitate the Reagan agenda.[24] The main element in this 'administrative presidency' strategy was that of 'cabinet councils'. These were specialist bodies of selected cabinet secretaries and representatives of the Executive Office of the President who met on a regular basis as a set of policy teams. The seven councils were designed not merely to achieve government coordination in a range of policy areas (e.g. economic affairs, human resources, food and agriculture, legal policy)[25] but, just as significantly, to keep the cabinet secretaries in close contact with the White House.

It is accepted that some of the councils (e.g. the Cabinet Committee on Economic Affairs) achieved a measure of success. Nevertheless, the experiment foundered on a number of rocks.[26] First, they only covered a handful of issue areas and even within these areas they were used to address only second level problems. 'The linkage here was mostly between the White House and sub-cabinet officials, and this not only tended to push secretaries out of the picture but also *increased* tensions between the White House and the secretaries, and among the secretaries of the participating departments as well'.[27]

Second, their status was further affected by the way they drew cabinet secretaries to the White House only to block their access to the president himself. Issues were expected to be dealt with by discussion within the councils.[28] Efforts to short-circuit such collective review, by taking problems directly to the president, were strongly discouraged. 'Of course, an individual cabinet secretary might still try to end-run the councils and lobby the President on his or her own, but White House staffers were continually on guard against this possibility, and Reagan himself appears to have been generally unreceptive to special appeals of this kind'.[29] To a senior cabinet officer, like Treasury Secretary Don Regan, cabinet councils were 'cumbersome and redundant'.[30]

> I began to suggest that a more orderly process was needed for discussing economic policy directly with the President. The practice of operating through lieutenants . . . created an irksome atmosphere. It was difficult, not to say impossible, to convince White House aides that any matter was important enough to be brought directly to the President for a decision. 'Bring that up in the Cabinet Council on Economic Affairs (CCEA)', the

Presidential aides would say in a kindly way. 'See if they understand what you're trying to do and see if they agree'. I would do so, but this was not usually a method that was capable of producing decision and action. As chairman of the CCEA, I was usually able to bring the members to an eventual consensus on a given question. In the absence of a consensus or choice of options, the President could not be petitioned for a decision.[31]

Finally, the councils began to be seen by executive branch components less as a means for consultation and joint policy-making and more as a device for ensuring that the departments' own policy development activities coincided with the central strategic positions of the White House. In President Reagan's second term, Don Regan became White House chief of staff and was instrumental in the elimination of the cabinet councils system (April 1985) in favour of an altogether more centralised policy apparatus centred upon his own office (i.e. the functions performed by the councils were absorbed into the National Security Council, the Domestic Council, and the Economic Council).

All these instances of presidents seeking both to draw decisional choices into the orbit of the White House and by the same token to ensure that policy selections are fully implemented by the federal bureaucracy, follow a very similar pattern of successive contraction in the circle of decision-makers. From initial intentions to use the full cabinet, the president invariably lapses into an inner cabinet and, thereupon, with remarkable consistency the centre for primary decision implodes further into the White House staff. In this way, numerical contraction comes to coincide with geographical contraction within the intimacy of the West Wing (see Figure 8.1).

Presidents even find that their own staff – ostensibly the most deinstitutionalised element in the government – possesses institutional properties that give it a continuity in organisation and performance independent of individual presidents. In John Burke's view, the 'staff is a large-scale organisation with many bureaucratic characteristics: complexity, fragmentation, competition, and self-serving advocacy. One such characteristic is the emergence of complex work routines, which often stifle originality, generate intrastaff controversy, and reduce differences on policy to their lowest common denominator'.[32]

The difficulties posed by the White House staff itself can lead, very often directly against a president's stated intentions, to the elevation of, and subsequent reliance upon, a White House chief of staff. Presidents Ford, Carter, and Reagan vouched that they would not repeat President Nixon's mistake of vesting excessive power in the White House, and with that in mind refused to acknowledge any need for a White House chief of staff. Nevertheless, all three found that a collegiate staff in which every senior aide had comparable access to the president, was in practice wholly unworkable. The 'spokes of the wheel' format, as this type of organisation is called, led to fragmentation and delay. For the president at the hub of such an arrangement, it led to political and decisional overload. Presidents

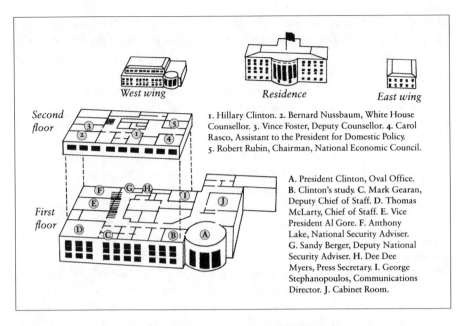

West wing

Residence

East wing

Second floor

1. Hillary Clinton. 2. Bernard Nussbaum, White House Counsellor. 3. Vince Foster, Deputy Counsellor. 4. Carol Rasco, Assistant to the President for Domestic Policy. 5. Robert Rubin, Chairman, National Economic Council.

First floor

A. President Clinton, Oval Office. B. Clinton's study. C. Mark Gearan, Deputy Chief of Staff. D. Thomas McLarty, Chief of Staff. E. Vice President Al Gore. F. Anthony Lake, National Security Adviser. G. Sandy Berger, Deputy National Security Adviser. H. Dee Dee Myers, Press Secretary. I. George Stephanopoulos, Communications Director. J. Cabinet Room.

Figure 8.1. Location of senior White House personnel at the beginning of the Clinton Administration. *Source*: *Time*, February 8 1993.

Ford, Carter, and Reagan were all prompted 'by the difficulty of controlling [such] a large staff organisation'[33] into revising their earlier opposition to hierarchy and opting for a White House chief of staff (e.g. Donald Rumsfeld, Hamilton Jordan, and Don Regan respectively).[34]

In the case of Presidents Bush and Clinton, they deferred at the beginning of their administrations to the need for a chief of staff, albeit with limited powers (i.e. John Sununu and Thomas 'Mack' McLarty respectively). Sununu went on to concentrate his influence in an aggressive and overweening way. Ultimately, he became an embarrassment to President Bush and had to be replaced in 1991. While John Sununu had attracted such epithets as 'Big Bad John', The Abominable No-Man', 'The Saddam Hussein of Bureaucrats', and 'The Fat Little Pirate', Thomas McLarty was quickly considered to be too accommodating and ineffectual for a White House chief of staff. 'Mack the Nice' or 'Mack the Knifeless',[35] as he was called, allowed a *de facto* 'spokes of the wheel' arrangement to develop under the cover of an ostensibly centralised system. As a consequence, the Clinton presidency was seen to lose focus, direction, and even competence in the first eighteen months of office. McLarty's inability either to impress upon Clinton the need for delegation, or to restrict the number of people having direct access to the president, led in June 1994 to McLarty being replaced by Leon 'the Leg Breaker' Panetta, whose brief it was to produce order from chaos and to separate

Clinton from his numerous friends. Such is the pressure on a president to reduce his contacts in the face of growing public criticism that it is likely President Clinton will come, like Presidents Carter and Reagan before him, to rely increasingly upon the personal support and political guidance of the First Lady.

In one sense, the retreat into progressively smaller concentric circles of advisers can be interpreted as part of a president's life cycle, in which grand gestures towards national consensus and collaborative action become increasingly displaced by multiple opposition, gridlock, and accusations of failed leadership. Anxiety and suspicion lead to withdrawal, defensiveness, and even isolation, exacerbated by the prospect of electoral defeat, or by the onset of a lame duck status. In another, and much deeper, sense it can be claimed that the reduction of a president's governing circle is not a function of time so much as an illustration of the real essence of the presidency itself. Arguably, it is only when the presidency is subjected to extended duress that the inherent singularity of the office is fully revealed. According to this perspective, no matter how extensive and institutional-ised the apparatus surrounding the president may be, the interior core that gives meaning to the office remains the individual. Ultimately, it is through the indi-vidual incumbent and his political purposes and skills that an administration's policies, organisation, decisions, and achievements can be comprehended and appraised. In Fred Greenstein's words, 'if the potentialities and limitations of the presidency are a function of its incumbent's performance, it follows that [an] understanding of the presidency as an institution of government must be rooted in an understanding of how individual presidents have carried out their respon-sibilities'.[36]

The individual as the normative and empirical foundation of presidential decision-making

The emphasis upon the individual within the presidency and the importance attached to the relationship between *how* a president comes to a decision and *what* is decided upon have given rise to a whole genre in the study of the office. By far the most prominent contribution to this analytical perspective has been Richard Neustadt's *Presidential Power*.[37] In this ground-breaking study, Neustadt laid emphasis on the operational realities of being president. In the process, he sought to distance the presidency from the more traditional forms of scholarly examination that stressed the office's constitutional position, its legal powers and its formal claims to hierarchical command. Instead of conceiving the presidency as a list of discrete functions, Neustadt located the office within a highly political and bureaucratic environment, from which presidents could not escape, and through which they had to realise their objectives by harnessing scarce resources and engaging in protracted negotiation. Because those around him possessed their own access to political and organisational power, a president could not depend on the power to command, but had to rely instead upon his own skills in motivating others to cooperate with him. He had in effect 'to induce them to believe that what he want[ed] of them [was] what their own appraisal of their own responsibilities requir[ed] them to do in their own interest, not his'.[38]

If a president were to rely upon constitutional declarations of position, or on a formal hierarchy of executive decision-making, he would quickly find himself in an isolated and impotent position. Successful presidents are those who understand the provisional nature and marginal qualities of power. They sense the sources of power and the opportunities for acquiring it within a complex organisation. They grasp the central reality that power is reciprocal in nature, drawn as it is from an enclosed environment, in which every constituent element is interconnected to, and interdependent upon, every other element. To Neustadt, power is always a two-way street. A source of power for a president (e.g. party, executive branch, Congress), therefore, is also by its very nature a potential limitation of power.[39]

Neustadt's pioneering and highly influential book sought to extricate the presidency from the conventional understanding that likened the office to a set of clothes bequeathed to the incumbent. To Neustadt, this notion was a fallacy. There were no clothes. Any president who proceeded on this assumption would remain naked. All that a president is given is an opportunity to make his own clothes – i.e. his own presidency. Since power is always provisional and precarious, a president must not only constantly protect his sources of influence, but continually seek to maximise his power by bargaining and mutual accommodation. For example, more significant than any formal allocations of 'power' is the state of a president's public prestige and professional reputation. A chief executive whose political skills are highly regarded in Washington helps to produce a favourable impression amongst the general population, which in turn further enhances his leverage in Congress and the bureaucracy. By the same token, a president who loses authority either in the country or in Washington will find the spiral works in reverse, in which case his professional reputation and public prestige will drag one another down to produce a presidency with rapidly declining influence.

To Neustadt, the presidency is a place for professional politicians who have a sixth sense for the mercurial nature of power and for its ever present limitations. Presidents need the will to acquire power. Because the presidency is an idiosyncratic office, it requires individuals with an exceptional capacity for improvising and cultivating influence, and for shrewdness and judgement in working with the other participants in the political system. Just as there is a need for forceful presidential leadership, in order to redeem the chronically fragmented structure of American government into a semblance of order and coordination, so Neustadt believes that such a need can only be met by 'experienced politicians of extraordinary temperament'.[40] To Neustadt, the presidency is a position of unique significance and as such it 'is not a place for amateurs'[41] but for professionals who know how to help themselves to power. 'The more determinedly a president seeks power, the more he will be likely to bring vigor to his clerkship. As he does so he contributes to the energy of government'.[42]

Neustadt's conception of the presidency has attracted a considerable variety of criticism. For example:

- Neustadt stands accused of unnecessarily confining presidential power to persuasion, therefore overlooking alternative sources of influence. Presidents may not always have to resort to persuasion especially when they are able to appeal to shared values and ideological commitments. Compliance can occur through extended personal loyalty to the president, through the dynamics of a group identity, or through a coincidence of principles amongst dispersed participants.[43]

- Although a president cannot rely on the power of command that does not mean it is totally redundant as a leadership device. It can be effective in a direct sense especially during crisis situations, and it is usable in an indirect sense as a basis for authority upon which additional techniques of influence can be built.[44]

- His notion of an optimum fit between the presidency and its modern role on the one hand, and a presidential type correlated with such a role on the other hand, is criticised as a normative judgement disguised as an empirical revelation. Neustadt is often suspected of partisan bias in that his prescribed role of government is interventionist, his prescribed role of presidential leadership is activist, and his model fit between man and office is provided by the presidency of Roosevelt.

- Neustadt is also regarded as America's Machiavelli[45] because of the emphasis he places on calculation and manipulation in the pursuit of power and because he implies that power carries its own morality separate from any normative purposes that may be served by such power.

- The appropriation and misuse of executive power by such compulsive power-seekers as Lyndon Johnson and Richard Nixon is said to highlight the failure of Neustadt's methodology 'to distinguish between the use and abuse of presidential power'.[46] As a result, Neustadt's thesis can be interpreted as not only legitimising and encouraging the drive for power, but also overlooking the possibility of power being accumulated to the point of excess, which over the late 1960s and 1970s became the 'central issue in almost all writing about the presidency'.[47]

Neustadt has responded to these criticisms by making a number of adjustments to his perspective of the presidency. He concedes, for example, maximising power cannot be a president's sole criterion for making decisions and that candidates for the office should have 'drive' as opposed to being 'driven men'.[48] But such modifications represent only minor shifts of emphasis in what remains a basically unchanged conception of presidential power. According to the latest edition of *Presidential Power* (1990),[49] recent presidencies have served only to vindicate Neustadt's original conclusions. The thrust and authority of Neustadt's vision, therefore, continues undiminished. An effective presidency is still seen to be dependent upon a president's experience, temperament, and judgement for the position. Presidents not only make decisions in the immediate sense of choosing options, they have to condition such decisions in accordance with their own personal dimension of influence cultivation. In effect, a president continually needs to 'buttress prospects for his future influence while making present choices'.[50] With Neustadt, there is never any doubt that it is the president who must make the key decisions, if for no other reason than it is only he who can judge what is right for his unique position and, therefore, what is right for the presidency.

The mainstream genre of presidential analysis, that Neustadt helped to establish and which stresses the centrality of the president in decision-making, has been strengthened even further by the work of James Barber. His key text, *The Presidential Character: Predicting Presidential Performance in the White House*[51] proceeds on the premise that if the nature of the presidency is one of personal power, then the office can best be explained by studying not merely the individual president but what lies beneath the person and determines his character, his behaviour, and ultimately, his decisions. This form of study attempts to go one step further than conventional biography by seeking to explain the developmental process in character formation and then to examine the ways in which character or personality determine a president's actions in office. According to Barber, who must be regarded as representing the vanguard of this form of study, a president's character is crucial to the understanding of the office – 'the connection between his character and his Presidential actions emerges as paramount'.[52] The basic objective of this type of analysis is to trace influences from childhood to adulthood, from personality to action, and from the subconscious to political decision. It has been claimed that such analysis can even provide a predictive capacity and that this could be, and moreover should be, used to assess the suitability of prospective presidential candidates.

Barber's scheme of anaysis is based upon a general theory of political personality which is itself derived from the relationship between an individual's psychological composition and the environment to which that person reacts and within which he will arrive at decisions. Barber refers to three elements in an individual's personal development. First is character, determined largely in childhood, which provides a basic outlook upon life, experience, and oneself. Second is a person's 'world view' which embraces wider ideas of cause and effect in society and conceptions of human nature and moral conflict. This outlook on the world is normally formed by the end of adolescence. The third constituent, 'style', is connected to early adulthood and relates a person's habitual way of performing the roles that he or she has adopted or has been allocated to – i.e. how a person actively translate himself or herself into positions dealing with other people and their expectations and judgements. Although all three elements 'fit together in a dynamic package',[53] Barber gives primary significance to character. 'It is what life has marked into a man's being . . . character is a person's stance as he confronts experience'.[54]

When these three cumulative developmental stages, and their dynamic inter-relationships, are applied to presidents and their position in an ever changing political environment (i.e. the 'power situation' and the 'climate of expectations'), it is possible to make generalisations and even predictions, concerning how a given president will react to a given situation. Barber claims not merely that '[p]residential character – the basic stance a man takes toward his [p]residential experience – comes in four varieties' but that 'the most important thing to know about a [p]resident or candidate is where he fits among these types'.[55] The typology is derived from the interplay of two criteria – namely, the amount of energy a president invests in the office (active or negative), and the degree of emotional satisfaction derived from his political activity (positive or negative). The two criteria produce a four-fold table to which any president can be assigned on the basis of a biographical investigation into the formation of his character. As character is a fixed property, a president cannot help but betray his inner strengths and weaknesses in the decisions he makes under stressful conditions in such an exposed position (see Table 8.1).

Table 8.1. Barber's typology of presidential characters

	Affect toward the Presidency	
	Positive	Negative
Active	Thomas Jefferson Franklin Roosevelt Harry Truman Gerald Ford Jimmy Carter George Bush Bill Clinton	John Adams Woodrow Wilson Herbert Hoover Lyndon Johnson Richard Nixon
Energy Directed toward the Presidency	'consistency between much activity and the enjoyment of it, indicating relatively high self-esteem and relative success in relating to the environment . . . shows an orientation to productiveness as a value and an ability to use his styles flexibly, adaptively.'	'activity has a compulsive quality, as if the man were trying to make up for something or escape from anxiety into hard work . . . seems ambitious, striving upward, power-seeking . . . stance toward the environment is aggressive and has a problem in managing his aggressive feelings.'
	James Madison William Taft Warren Harding Ronald Reagan	George Washington Calvin Coolidge Dwight Eisenhower
Positive	'receptive, compliant, other-directed character whose life is a search for affection as a reward for being agreeable and co-operative . . . low self-esteem (on grounds of being unlovable).'	'low self-esteem based on a sense of uselessness . . . in politics because they think they ought to be . . . tendency is to withdraw, to escape from the conflict and uncertainty of politics by emphasizing vague principles (especially prohibitions) and procedural arrangements.'

Source: J. D. Barber, *The Presidential Character: Predicting Performance in the White House*, 4th edn (Englewood Cliffs: Prentice Hall, 1992); M. Nelson, 'The Psychological Presidency', in M. Nelson (ed.), *The Presidency and the Political System* (Washington, D.C.: Congressional Quarterly Press, 1988), p. 164.

Of the four types, active-positives are the most beneficial to the presidency. They have successfully overcome the crises of psychological development and are able to bring their confidence and self-esteem to bear in conditions requiring personal drive, but also flexibility and an ability to use criticism constructively. The type most ill-suited to the presidency are the active-negatives. As they lack security and self-esteem, their ambition for political office is fuelled by a compulsion for domination and control. Politics is a means of compensation for personal inadequacy and while this can produce extraordinary leadership, it can also lead to destructive behaviour. An active-negative personality is brittle and, therefore, unable to adapt to disappointments or unexpected developments. As a consequence, he/she is likely to engage in rigid defensiveness, in aggression towards opponents, and in the translation of leadership into a fixed position of intransigence. To Barber, active-negatives are a danger both to themselves and to the government as a whole for they will not only pursue failed policies but also undermine the system's democratic norms in an attempt to retain their authority. Active-negative characters, therefore, need to be identified and avoided in any presidential election.

Barber's work proceeds on Neustadt's premise that the modern presidency requires active and purposeful personalities. While Neustadt stresses the importance of the right presidential techniques, Barber gives emphasis to the needs for presidents to possess the right temperament for the job. Passive characters are deemed to be implausible in, and inappropriate to, a position of political leadership. But as Barber makes clear, active presidents can be differentiated into two types – positive and negative. Drawing on the turbulent experience of the presidencies of Johnson and Nixon, he develops Neustadt's conception of the presidency in three highly significant ways. First, he roots presidential performance not merely in political experience but in personal developmental experiences and psychological composition. Second, he differentiates active presidents into two types – active-positive being the optimum fit for the presidency and active-negative being unfit and dangerous for the office. And third, Barber claims that his theory is predictive. Once a personality has been assigned to the four-fold typology, then that person's behaviour, performance, and record in the presidency could be anticipated from psychological indicators. Like Neustadt, Barber has encountered a profusion of criticism. The most significant indictments are given below.

The typology is condemned as inadequate and inaccurate. Barber's two criteria for the formation of the types are criticised as being neither properly explained nor fully comprehensive. They are further criticised for being neither purely political nor purely psychological categories, but an indeterminate mixture of properties. Instead of four types, a more sensitive measure of personality could produce a greater number of more accurate types.[56] The four-fold classification also fails to recognise that an individual president may move from one behavioural category to another, that some may be true hybrids, and that there is a 'strong possibility that the very talented political leaders are likely to be a combination of active-positve and active-negative characteristics'.[57]

Another point of criticism is the complaint that psychological analysis of this type is too deterministic in the way it assigns present and future decisions to past experience and subconscious motives. Barber claims that he does not reduce political behaviour directly and exclusively to pre-existent psychology conditions formed in childhood. It is true that he does not explicitly allude to a causal chain from early family experiences to adult political decisions as some studies have done.[58] But despite his references to 'world view' and 'style' he does give primary weight to 'character' which, by his own specifications, is rooted in childhood.

Another point at issue is the belief that Barber's typology is the product of circular reasoning. By making inferences about the inner character of a president's exterior behaviour, Barber is accused of then confining and structuring his observations of such a president to coincide with and reaffirm his initial allocation of a personality type. Presidents 'are so presented in terms of the models active and passive (positive and negative) . . . that one begins to wonder if Barber has not selected illustrations to fit the categories'.[59] The same criticism is extended to the typology itself. Once the four-fold classification has been established, then all succeeding presidents must be pressed deductively into one of the four categories, irrespective of whether they warrant the addition of other dimensions of character.

Like Neustadt, Barber is accused of introducing value judgements into an empirical anaysis by emphasising the need to fill the presidency with the right characteristics (i.e. active-positives). The latter not only fit the functional demands of the presidency, they fit the contemporary requirements of an active and positive government in American society. As a consequence, the models of active-positives well adjusted to the personal demands of the White House have tended to be from the liberal wing of the Democratic Party (e.g. Roosevelt, Truman, Kennedy) – thereby raising the suspicion that the evaluation of presidents is determined more by the substance of their policies than by their personal performances as chief executive.

In Fred Greenstein's *The Hidden Hand Presidency*,[60] Barber's categories are thrown into disarray by the revelation that while President Eisenhower appeared and acted as a passive-negative president, his motivations, behaviour, and achievements were wholly out of line with the premises of such a character type. 'A covert preoccupation with getting political results while appearing nonpolitical was central to Eisenhower's leadership style'. It was also 'in many ways the obverse of such classic depictions of forceful presidential leadership as Richard Neustadt's *Presidential Power*'.[61]

In public, Eisenhower seemed to be idle, aimiable, ineffectual, and politically naive. But to Greenstein, he was not out of his depth at all but a workaholic with highly developed political skills and instincts. Contrary to his reputation, Eisenhower did not rely upon formal organisational structures producing consensual recommendations, but took measures to receive a variety of advice and to experience a projection of debate. As for his geniality, that was reserved for public consumption. Behind the scenes, he was irascible, scheming, devious, and even duplicitous. He self-consciously divided his public self from his private self and in the process largely subjected his personality to the overriding priority of his political objectives – i.e. to sustain the post New Deal status quo and to cultivate national unity and tranquillity during the Cold War. Style and purpose were, therefore, congruent with one another. Instead of aggressive leadership by self-assertive active-positives, Eisenhower showed that discretion and subtle leadership could be very effective in achieving the aims set by the president. In Greenstein's view,

> The argument of *The Hidden Hand Presidency* is that being in effect a public head of state and a private prime minister, Eisenhower succeeded in resolving the contradictions inherent in the presidential role. In so doing he was able to enjoy exceptional public support. In taking Eisenhower to be a political innocent, his contemporaries failed to recognize that a president who distanced himself from his administration's politics thereby protected himself from blame for those of his administration's policies that were controversial. The very practices that led political observers to underestimate Eisenhower were central to his leadership, including that of working through intermediaries on his administration's more contentious policies and actions.[62]

While Greenstein does not claim that Eisenhower's methods and objectives can or should be adopted by different presidents at other times, he does challenge Barber's necessary conjunction between an active-positive personality, effective political leadership, and the fulfilment of the executive role in government. Such a challenge must be implicit in Greenstein's revision of Eisenhower, otherwise it is tantamount to claiming that an active-positive figure could effectively disguise himself as a passive-negative personality over two terms of office. Similar problems are raised by the attributed success of Ronald Reagan's presidency. Both Eisenhower's and Reagan's periods in office prompt the question of whether different models of presidential leadership are merely different means to the same end, or different means to different ends.

In general, critics point to the difficulty of relating psychology to politics especially in light of the fact that there is no uniformly accepted theory of personality. Just as 'more than one model of personality may explain a given action . . . so motivation for specific actions usually draws upon more than one level of personality'.[63] Given that each individual is a complex set of variables operating at different levels of personality, the relationship between character and political style and leadership decisions will be problematic to say the least. The complexity can be gauged by Figure 8.2 which provides a rudimentary guide to the profusion of possible interactions.

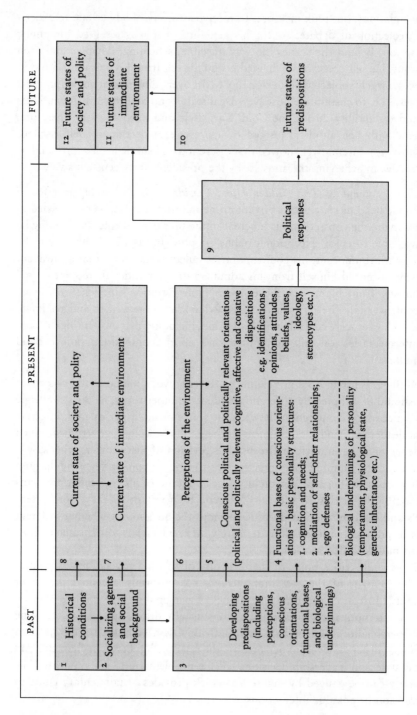

Figure 8.2. Greenstein's comprehensive map for the analysis of personality and politics. *Source:* F. I. Greenstein, 'Can Personality and Politics be Studied Systematically?', *Political Psychology*, 13 (1) (1992), p. 115.

Apart from the technical difficulties of ascertaining character and the practical problems of applying it to political analysis, there is the additional question of whether character in the deep sense of a core psychology does explain political action.[64] The products of other levels of personality (e.g. ideological belief, personal values, leadership style, political skill) allegedly not so dependent upon character development may be equally, or more, responsible for a presidential decision or policy.

Notwithstanding these many complaints and objections, James Barber has succeeded in highlighting the significance of the presidency as a highly individualised office. In the view of Michael Nelson, the critiques are a reflection of his contribution – i.e. 'a concentration (albeit an overconcentration) on the importance of presidential personality in explaining presidential behaviour, a sensitivity to its nature as a variable (power does not always corrupt; nor does the office always make the man), and a boldness in approaching the problems voters face in predicting what candidates will be like if elected'.[65] The widespread currency of Barber's assumptions and categories have not only helped to shape the public's discussion of the office but have provided a powerful affirmation of the presidency's cultural characterisation as an individual writ large – thereby equating presidential explanation with psychological analysis.

Although there is a social predisposition to view the presidency as the embodiment of the incumbent's individuality and to regard decision-making in the White House as a derivate of the president's thought processes, the president and his personality nevertheless provide only a partial explanation of how decisions are made at this level of government. Even if personality theorists could resolve all the problems concerning the reliability of their methods and the validity of the conclusions, it is very far from certain that they would be in a position to explain the collective behaviour of politicians, or even the relationship between a single politician and others. Quite the contrary in fact. Character may explain the president but it will not account for the presidency. While Neustadt and Barber acknowledge the significance of the environment that surrounds the president and conditions what is possible for him to achieve in office, their emphasis upon the conscious design of individual leaders is such that the environment tends to be overlooked. And yet, the position and effectiveness of a leader is ultimately dependent upon his or her interaction with a political environment which is for the most part beyond control, and which provides a powerful limitation upon any leader's autonomy and freedom of action. A presidential decision, therefore, has to be seen less as a product of personal will and more as a form of negotiation between the president and the political environment. While a decision is an attempt to make an active impression upon the environment, the decision itself will have been a response to environmental pressures and a product of the conditioning constraints of a president's political position.

The corrective dimension of the political environment

The president's most immediate environment is the executive branch. As has already been described, presidents go to great lengths to reduce the environmental constraints of bureaucracy. Whether it is executive reorganisation, cabinet councils, legislative clearance or central budgeting, they are all designed to inhibit the restrictions of the executive branch upon the chief executive. All modern presidents now attempt to reshape the flow of communications and decisions at the highest executive levels by laying their own template of organisation upon the White House Office and its connections to the outside world. One of the most important things to know about a new president, therefore, is his White House organisation chart because that will show how he intends to structure his immediate environment.

Having established such a chart, one of the most difficult things for a president will be to keep to it in practice. This is because an organisational plan is an attempt to create order in an inherently disordered and unpredictable situation where disruptive external forces will always compromise the integrity of any interior flow of information, advice, and influence.

Another, and arguably more significant, way that a president structures his immediate environment is through his political style. The way a president defines his needs and aims to his staff will inevitably influence how it will operate. In other words, the organisation and conduct of the staff will intuitively reflect the president's personal orientation to information, conflict, decision-making, and overall management.[66] Despite being within the White House and working in close proximity to the president, therefore, the staff can – albeit inadvertently – project and amplify a president's weaknesses even to the point of undermining his authority both inside and outside the White House. In this way, the staff can become part of the environmental problem for a president. President Carter, for example, believed he could micro-manage the government. His demand for information and his unwillingness to delegate decisions led to him working for eighteen hours a day and being thoroughly submerged in detail. His efforts to control even his immediate environment were self-nullifying because the staff had intuitively assisted him into a position of overload from the wider environment.

President Reagan, on the other hand, wanted to reserve only the major strategic decisions for himself and was content to delegate the rest to the point of negligence. According to one of his aides, it was difficult 'to get Reagan to concentrate on the specifics of the problem' because on most subjects he was 'not really looking to make a decision'.[67] His chief of staff, Don Regan, described the president's decision-making style as a:

> baffling system, in which the President seldom spoke, while his advisers proposed measures that contradicted his ideas and promises, created uncertainty in a situation that cried out for action. I thought that I understood

the President's philosophy. But how did he want it carried out, if at all? Casual exchanges in Cabinet meetings and other large gatherings were enough to give the necessary guidance . . . The President himself sent out no strong signals. He listened, encouraged, deferred. But it was a rare meeting in which he made a decision or issued orders.[68]

After the revelation of the Iran-Contra scandal (1986–87), for example, President Reagan's numerable and variable defences included that he had not been properly informed of developments by his staff; that his staff had misled him and usurped his policy-making authority; that he had not even made a decision to sell arms for hostages; that if he had come to such a decision, he had not realised it at the time, or could not recall whether he had done so. Both his Secretary of State, George Schultz, and his Secretary of Defense, Casper Weinberger, repeatedly warned the president in 1985 that even if the plan was not conceived as an exchange of weapons for hostages, it would be made to look as if it were just such a deal.

In his televised address to the American nation in March 1987, Reagan accepted responsibility for the policy but still expressed bafflement. 'A few months ago, I told the American people I did not trade arms for hostages. My heart and my best intentions still tell me that is true, but the facts and the evidence tell me it is not'.[69] In his memoirs, it is clear that Reagan had not changed his mind: 'Whatever the truth of the matter, the Iranian initiative was made to look like an arms-for-hostage deal . . . To this day I still believe that the Iranian initiative was not an effort to swap arms for hostages'.[70] If anything, Reagan saw himself as a victim of his own staff which 'had done things they hadn't advised me of'.[71] But it was Reagan, and his attitudes to decision-making, that had created such a staff system in the first place.[72]

On occasions, a president's immediate environment can become so structured that it creates a barrier to open decision-making. The barrier can be material in nature when White House aides reduce and even eliminate outside access to the president (e.g. Reagan's White House). More insidious still is the restriction of fresh ideas and information by a White House staff that becomes so insular that it develops a form of frozen thinking. Although it may arise unintentionally and unconsciously, once the syndrome of positions and perspectives becomes established it forms an enclosure around the decision-makers who assimilate only the information that is consistent with the increasingly orthodox outlook of the group. Irving Janis describes this effect as 'groupthink'.[73] Shared commitments and experiences in a situation of stress produces a group loyalty which culminates in a resistance to re-examine positions in the light of new facts. Additional information is intuitively screened by the group. If it is compatible with 'groupthink', it is instinctively ignored. Critical warnings are, therefore, misread or discarded. The main symptoms of 'groupthink' Janis identified are outlined below.

1. An illusion of invulnerability, shared by most or all the members, which creates excessive optimism and encourages taking extreme risks.

2. Collective efforts to rationalise in order to discount warnings which might lead the members to reconsider their assumptions before they recommit themselves to their past policy decisions.

3. An unquestioned belief in the group's inherent morality, inclining the members to ignore the ethical or moral consequences of their decisions.

4. Stereotyped views of enemy leaders as too evil to warrant genuine attempts to negotiate, or as too weak and stupid to counter whatever risky attempts are made to defeat their purposes.

5. Direct pressure on any member who expresses strong arguments against any of the group's stereotypes, illusions, or commitments, making clear that this type of dissent is contrary to what is expected of all loyal members.

6. Self-censorship of deviations from the apparent group consensus, reflecting each member's inclination to minimise to himself the importance of his doubts and counterarguments.

7. A shared illusion of unanimity concerning judgements conforming to the majority view (partly resulting from self-censorship of deviations, augmented by the false assumption that silence means consent).

8. The emergence of self-appointed mindguards – members who protect the group from adverse information that might shatter their shared complacency about the effectiveness and morality of their decisions.

The main outcome is that the more a group becomes subjected to groupthink, the poorer and more non-rational its decisions will be. In fact, it can be claimed that under these conditions no decisions will be made at all because all decisions will essentially be the same.

The combination of a small number of individuals selected for their loyalty, working in close proximity to the president, and being directly responsible for the management of policies made by the group, makes the White House into a potential hot-house for 'groupthink'. Although the paranoiac defensiveness of the Nixon White House provides the archetypal example of 'groupthink',[74] all presidents are vulnerable to its distortions of political reality. Incoming presidents may insist that their White House will be permanently enlightened by a plurality of viewpoints, but after a year or so a beleaguered president and his staff can easily become a victim of 'groupthink'. The phenonemon demonstrates that the utility of psychological analysis of the presidency is not limited to the individual but can embrace the dynamics between the president and his advisers. It also shows that attempts by the president to control his environment can backfire and turn into a self-imposed constraint. While presidents may use the White House staff in an attempt to impose order and direction upon the immediate political environment, the social psychology of groupthink can invest that environment with a mind of its own. Instead of autonomy, there is merely conformity, delusion, and even escapism.

For the most part, presidents find it difficult, either consciously or unconsciously, to structure much of the environment that confronts them. More often than not, they simply have to deal with what is given – executive agencies, regulatory commissions, Congress, parties, courts, state governments, interest groups, the media etc. This is not to say that the presidency is locked in a static set of conditions. Diagrams of decision-making used to feature a series of concentric circles with the president always occupying the central area. The objective was to illustrate gradations of influence upon policy, culminating in the chief executive where the buck was always assumed to stop.

One of the problems with such diagrams is that they often succeed in conveying the reverse impression from that which was intended. They can be interpreted as presenting the president under siege – surrounded by circular barriers that not only prevent decisions from reaching the White House, but represent the progressive outer diminishment of presidential influence rather than the progressive concentration of decision-making capacity. But the main problem with such diagrams is that they are inherently two-dimensional and static in nature. They fail to illustrate the constant flux in the political environment. They do not acknowledge the dynamics of interaction that exist between the presidency and the political environment. And they fail to recognise the different layers of environmental conditions that a president must take into account in reaching decisions. The presidency is lodged in a crowded and confined political environment but it is also an environment which is changeable and multi-dimensional in nature and open to constant interpretation by decision-makers who wish to maximise what it will assimilate.

In reaching decisions, presidents have to take account of a profusion of environmental variables that will structure the conditions in which decisions are made, shape the available choices, and determine the extent to which decisions will be followed by effective action. These variables are not confined to the material specifics of a president's political position – e.g. his margin of victory in the election; his party's majority, or lack of one in Congress; his opinion poll ratings; the time remaining in his period of office etc. Other structural, if less evident, variables are just as significant. For example, presidents are constrained by the availability and accuracy of information; by the level of analysis given to such information, especially in respect to likely outcomes; by the timescale in which a decision needs to be made; by the technical feasibility of a course of action; by the resources required to translate a decision into effective action; by the weight of previous commitments either from a president's predecessors and earlier policies; and by the authority of the decision-makers and the legitimacy of their options.[75]

The problem of the current federal deficit provides an example of virtually all these constraints. The immense burden of $3,000 billion of accummulated public debt was bequeathed to the presidents of the 1990s by their predecessors, and by Ronald Reagan in particular. The level of interest repayment alone on a deficit of this order accounts for approximately 15 per cent of the federal government's yearly budget. When other long-term contractual obligations are taken into account (e.g. social security, government procurement), it is clear that the spending options of any contemporary president will be heavily circumscribed. The difficulty of predicting the performance of the national economy, moreover, constrains the level of reliable information and analysis upon which decisions can be made. Drastic action to cut the deficit might not only backfire on the economy and worsen the situation, but might be untenable on grounds of legal obligation (e.g. breach of contract), constitutional authority (e.g. alleged usurpation of power), political prudence (e.g. electoral damage/defeat), and public philosophy (e.g. charges of contempt for the cultural norms of equity, security, and social provision).

The political environment can impress itself upon a president in other ways. Environmental circumstances can change. The political environment in crisis conditions will be different from the environment in normal conditions. Decisions on big issues will be differently structured to decisions on small issues – which is not the same as saying that decisions on the latter are any easier to make or to impose than the former. A liberal president will confront an environment which will be dissimilar to the environment of a conservative president. A president intent upon change – be it liberal reform or new right radicalism – will operate under different conditions to a president content with consensus and consolidation. The type of issue will also have an important bearing on the president's position. 'Redistributive policy', for example, which involves the reallocation of social goods and values, tends to give emphasis to the centralised position of the presidency. 'Distributive policy' on the other hand, which involves the allocation of particularised benefits to specific group interests, tends to give emphasis to the decentralised elements of government and stable coalitions of interests associated with them.[76]

The most distinctive classification of issue types is the putative division between foreign policy and domestic policy. They used to be considered as two separate environments in which the presidency was necessarily predominant in the former on grounds of functional capacity and Cold War imperatives. The distinction is less clear today because of the increasing interdependency of national economies and the reduction of superpower tensions. Nevertheless, the area of foreign policy is still more likely to yield instances of presidential prerogative than domestic policy. President Reagan, for example, invaded Grenada, intervened in the Lebanon, bombed Libya and supported a guerrilla war in Nicaragua. There is still a greater probability that foreign policy will provide an 'ambiguous environment [in which] new situations and political roles that are only sketchily defined by formal rules provide great latitude for actors' personalities to shape their behaviour. Structural environments', on the other hand, such as 'bureaucratised settings and contexts in which there are well-developed and widely known and accepted norms',[77] are more common in domestic policy and tend to constrain the behaviour of an individual decision-maker like the president. The irony of foreign policy-making is that by liberating the president from the customary restrictions of the domestic environment, it only projects the president out into the altogether more complex and volatile environment of international relations and its multiple constraints, intractable conflicts, and concealed traps. President Bush, for example, decided to send troops to Somalia in 1992 to facilitate the provision of humanitarian assistance for a limited period of time. Once there, both he and his successor found it very difficult to reverse the process and to disengage American forces from the country. Throughout 1993, therefore, Somalia became part of the environmental parameters within which President Bill Clinton had to operate.

As we can see a president's freedom of action is conditioned by a rich variety of factors.[78] No one factor exactly matches the influence of another. Nonetheless, there is one institution which does typify many of the problems confronting a president in making decisions and in trying to convert such decisions into policies. The relationship between the president and Congress is not only central to the actual process of policy formulation in the United States, it is critical to any understanding of the relationship between the presidency and its political environment. No entity other than Congress better illustrates the variable nature of presidential influence and the need for negotiation that comes from possessing an incomplete authority to fulfil the presidential role. For most presidents, Congress does not merely exemplify the environmental limits to decision-making discretion, it embodies them. Accordingly, the study will now proceed to examine the relationship between the presidency and Congress.

Notes

1   G. R. Hoxie, 'The Cabinet and the American Presidency, 1789–1984', *Presidential Studies Quarterly*, 14 (2) (Spring 1984), pp. 209–30.

2   R. F. Fenno, *The President's Cabinet* (Cambridge: Harvard University Press, 1959).

3   H. Seidman, *Politics, Position and Power: The Dynamics of the Federal Organization* (New York: Oxford University Press, 1970), p. 75.

4   A. M. Schlesinger, Jr., *A Thousand Days: John F. Kennedy in the White House* (London: Mayflower Dell, 1967), p. 541.

5   J. P. Burke, *The Institutional Presidency* (Baltimore: Johns Hopkins University Press, 1992), p. 93.

6   B. Rockman, 'The Style and Organization of the Reagan Presidency', in C. O. Jones (ed.), *The Reagan Legacy: Promise and Performance* (Chatham: Chatham House, 1988), p. 13

7   H. Heclo, 'One Executive Branch or Many?', in A. King (ed.), *Both Ends of the Avenue: The Presidency, the Executive Branch and Congress in the 1990s* (Washington, D.C.: American Enterprise Institute, 1983), p. 26.

8   H. Heclo, *Government of Strangers: Executive Politics in Washington* (Washington, D.C.: Brookings Institution, 1977).

9   Quoted in R. H. Ferrell, *Off the Record: The Private Papers of Harry S. Truman* (New York: Harper and Row, 1980), p. 29.

10 B. Woodward, *The Agenda: Inside the Clinton White House* (New York: Simon and Schuster, 1994), pp. 164–6.

11 Quoted in R. P. Nathan, *The Plot That Failed: Nixon and the Administrative Presidency* (New York: Wiley, 1975), pp. 39–42.

12 Seidman, *Politics, Position and Power*, p. 72.

13 G. K. Wilson, 'Are Department Secretaries Really a President's Natural Enemy?', *British Journal of Political Science*, 7 (3) (July 1977), p. 297.

14 N. W. Polsby, 'Presidential Cabinet Making', *Political Science Quarterly*, 43 (1) (March 1978), pp. 15–26.

15 J. E. Cohen, *The Politics of the US Cabinet, Representation in the Executive Branch, 1789–1984* (Pittsburgh: University of Pittsburgh Press, 1988), p. 15.

16 T. B. Edsall, 'Clinton, So Far', *New York Review of Books*, October 7 1993.

17 A. M. Schlesinger, Jr., *The Coming of the New Deal* (London: Heinemann, 1960), p. 518.

18 *Ibid.*, p. 520.

19 T. E. Cronin, *The State of the Presidency*, 2nd edn (Boston: Little, Brown, 1980), pp. 247–86.

20 Cohen, *The Politics of the US Cabinet*, pp. 122–45.

21 *Ibid.*, p. 125.

22 Nathan, *The Plot That Failed: Nixon and the Administrative Presidency*.

23 R. P. Nathan, *The Administrative Presidency* (New York: Wiley, 1983).

24 P. M. Benda and C. H. Levine, 'Reagan and the Bureaucracy: The Bequest, The Promise and The Legacy', in Jones (ed.), *The Reagan Legacy*, pp. 102–42.

25 The five original cabinet councils established in 1981 were: (i) the Cabinet Council on Economic Affairs, (ii) the Cabinet Council on Commerce and Trade, (iii) the Cabinet Council on Human Resources, (iv) the Cabinet Council on Natural Resources and Energy, and (v) the Cabinet Council on Food and Agriculture. Two additionaal councils were added in 1982. They were (i) the Cabinet Council on Legal Policy and (ii) the Cabinet Council on Management and Administration.

26 C. Campbell, *Managing the Presidency: Carter, Reagan, and the Search for Executive Harmony* (Pittsburgh: University of Pittsburgh Press, 1986).

27 Cohen, *The Politics of the US Cabinet*, p. 30.

28 J. Pfiffner, *The Strategic Presidency: Hitting the Ground Running* (Chicago: Dorsey, 1988), pp. 62–4.

29 Benda and Levine, 'Reagan and the Bureaucracy', in Jones (ed.), *The Reagan Legacy*, p. 111.

30 D. T. Regan, *For the Record: From Wall Street to Washington* (London: Heinemann, 1988), p. 235.

31 *Ibid.*, pp. 187–8.

32 Burke, *The Institutional Presidency*, p. 43.

33 *Ibid.*, p. 107.

34   S. Kernell and S. Popkin (eds), *Chief of Staff* (Berkeley: University of California Press, 1986).

35   Nicknames drawn from J. Cassidy 'Washington celebrates as Sununu faces the axe', *Sunday Times*, 30 June 1991; 'White House fears Leon the Leg Breaker', *Sunday Times*, 3 July 1994.

36   F. I. Greenstein, 'Introduction: Toward a Modern Presidency', in F. I. Greenstein (ed.), *Leadership in the Modern Presidency* (Cambridge: Harvard University Press, 1988), pp. 1–2.

37   R. E. Neustadt, *Presidential Power: The Politics of Leadership* (New York: Wiley, 1960).

38   *Ibid.*, p. 46.

39   *Ibid.*, ch. 3.

40   *Ibid.*, p. 195.

41   *Ibid.*, p. 181.

42   *Ibid.*, p. 185.

43   P. W. Sperlich, 'Bargaining and Overload: An Essay on Presidential Power', in A. Wildavsky (ed.), *Perspectives on the Presidency* (Boston: Little, Brown, 1975), pp. 406–30.

44   J. Hart, 'Presidential Power Revisited', *Political Studies*, 25 (1) (March 1977), pp. 48–61.

45   See W. T. Bluhm, *Theories of the Political System* (Englewood Cliffs: Prentice-Hall, 1965).

46   Hart, 'Presidential Power Revisited', p. 56.

47   *Ibid.*, p. 56.

48   R. E. Neustadt, *Presidential Power: Leadership with Reflections on Johnson and Nixon* (New York: Wiley, 1976), p. 27.

49   R. E. Neustadt, *Presidential Power and the Modern Presidents. The Politics of Leadership From Roosevelt to Reagan* (New York: Free Press, 1990).

50   *Ibid.*, p. 317.

51   J. D. Barber, *The Presidential Character: Predicting Performance in the White House* (Englewood Cliffs: Prenctice-Hall, 1972).

52   *Ibid.*, p. 445.

53   *Ibid.*, p. 6.

54   *Ibid.*, p. 8.

55   *Ibid.*, p. 6.

56   A. L. George, 'Assessing Presidential Character', in Wildavsky (ed.), *Perpsectives on the Presidency*, pp. 91–134; See also E. C. Hargrove, 'Presidential Personality and Revisionist Views of the Presidency', *American Journal of Political Science*, 17 (4) (November 1973), pp. 819–35; J. H. Qualls, 'Barber's Typological Analysis of Political Leaders', *American Political Science Review*, 71 (1) (March 1977), pp. 182–211; L. P. Stark, 'Predicting Presidential Performance from Campaign Conduct: A Character Analysis of the 1988 Election', *Presidential Studies Quarterly*, 22 (2) (Spring), pp. 295–309.

57   E. C. Hargrove, *The Power of the Modern Presidency* (New York: A. A. Knopf, 1974), p. 77.

58   For example see the work of Bruce Mazlish: *In Search of Nixon: A Psychohistorical Inquiry* (New York: Basic Books, 1972); *Kissinger: The European Mind in American Policy* (New York: Basic Books, 1976).

59   E. C. Hargrove, 'Presidential Personality and Leadership Style', in G. C. Edwards
     III, J. H. Kessel, and B. A. Rockman (eds), *Researching the Presidency: Vital Ques-
     tions, New Approaches* (Pittsburgh: University of Pittsburgh Press, 1993), p. 96.

60   F. I. Greenstein, *The Hidden Hand Presidency: Eisenhower as Leader* (New York:
     Basic Books, 1982).

61   F. I. Greenstein, 'Leadership Theorist in the White House', in Greenstein (ed.),
     Leadership in the Modern Presidency, p. 78.

62   F. I. Greenstein, 'The Hidden Hand Presidency: Eisenhower as Leader, a 1994
     Perspective', *Presidential Studies Quarterly*, 24 (2) (Spring 1994), p. 235.

63   Hargrove, *The Power of the Modern Presidency*, pp. 69, 73.

64   F. I. Greenstein, 'Can Personality and Politics Be Studied Systematically?', *Political
     Psychology*, 13 (1) (March 1992), pp. 105–28.

65   M. Nelson, 'The Psychological Presidency', in M. Nelson (ed.), *The Presidency and
     the Political System* (Washington, D.C.: Congressional Quarterly Press, 1988), p. 197.

66   A. George, *Presidential Decision-Making in Foreign Policy: The Effective Use of
     Information and Advice* (Boulder: Westview, 1980).

67   Quoted in G. T. Church, 'How Reagan Decides', *Time*, 13 December 1982.

68   Regan, *For The Record*, p. 189.

69   Quoted from 'Reagan's Televised Address on the Tower Board Investigation, March
     4 1987', *Congressional Quarterly Alamanac, 1987, 100th Congress, 1st Session, 1987*,
     Volume XLIII (Washington, D.C.: Congressional Quarterly Press, 1988), p. 121.

70   R. Reagan, *An American Life* (London: Arrow, 1991), pp. 528, 540.

71   *Ibid.*, p. 541.

72   For an extended examination of the linkage between on the one hand the organisation
     and operation of presidential advisory systems and on the other presidential person-
     ality and management, see Colin Campbell's typology of (i) 'priorities-and-planning';
     (ii) 'broker-politics'; (iii) 'administration-politics'; and (iv) 'survival-politics' cate-
     gories in C. Campbell, *Political Executives and Key Bureaucrats in Washington,
     London and Ottawa* (Toronto: University of Toronto Press, 1983), and Campbell,
     Managing the Presidency.

73   I. Janis, *Victims of Groupthink: A Psychological Study of Foreign Policy Decisions
     and Fiascos*, 2nd edn (Boston: Little, Brown, 1982), pp. 197–8.

74   J. Dean, *Blind Ambition: The White House Years* (London: Star/W. H. Allen, 1977).

75   T. C. Sorensen, *Decision-Making in the White House: The Olive Branch and The
     Arrows* (New York: Columbia University Press, 1963).

76   T. Lowi, 'American Business, Public Policy, Case Studies, and Political Theory',
     World Politics, 16 (4) (July 1964), pp. 677–715.

77   Greenstein, 'Can Personality and Politics Be Studies Systematically?', p. 110.

78   For an approach that combines the wider political environment with the inner context
     of the president's immediate advisers as well as presidential character, see J. P. Burke
     and F. I. Greenstein, 'Presidential Personality and National Security Leadership: A
     Comparative Analysis of Vietnam Decision-Making', *International Political Science
     Review*, 10 (1) (January 1989), pp. 73–92.

Congress and the presidency

CHAPTER 9

Legislating together

The framers of the Constitution invested all legislative power in a Congress consisting of two chambers (Article 1, Section 1). The president's role within the separated system would be limited and secondary. Alexander Hamilton insisted in Federalist Number 75:

> The essence of the legislative authority is to enact laws, or, in other words, to prescribe rules for the regulation of the society; while the execution of the laws and the employment of the common strength, either for this purpose or for the common defense, seem to comprise all the functions of the executive magistrate.[1]

Nevertheless, the framers did not give the Congress complete legislative power. In Article 1, Section 7, they stipulated that for legislation to become law it must be signed by the president, thereby opening the possibility of a presidential veto which could only be overridden by a two-thirds majority in both houses. In Article 2, Section 3, they imposed on the president several responsibilities with respect to legislation: to provide Congress 'with information of the state of the Union, and recommend to their consideration such measures as he shall judge necessary and expedient'; to call 'on extraordinary occasions' one or both houses of Congress into session;[2] to adjourn them if they could not reach agreement; and to 'take care that the laws be faithfully executed'.

The Constitution and the growth of the presidency-centred tradition

The framers of the Constitution wanted a separated system in which the legislature and the executive would be both independent of, and dependent on, one another. Eschewing a parliamentary system along British lines, the power to make laws would be shared between the two institutions, and each would be elected or appointed by different political constituencies at different times. With the industrialisation and democratisation of the United States in the late nineteenth and early twentieth centuries, together with the national government's progressive involvement in economic regulation, social provision, and international affairs, the presidency acquired an increasingly prominent role in the political system. In the process, the traditional pre-modern presidency was transformed – contrary to the framers' expectations – into the modern presidency.

We explained in Chapter 6 that what Americans now understand about, and perhaps more importantly what they expect of their presidents, is coloured greatly by the modern presidency which crystallised during the tenure of Franklin D. Roosevelt. Roosevelt's presidency also reinforced a presidency-centred perspective in the literature on American government and law-making which still continues today. According to this perspective, the president was the 'single institutional repository of coherent political leadership',[3] central to the policy-making process, and essential for providing the country with political change. The key aspects of this approach were as follows: first, the framers of the Constitution constructed a governmental system with a built-in proclivity to inertia and institutionalised conflicts – an 'invitation to struggle' in Edward Corwin's famous phrase[4] – in which Congress is evaluated according to the extent to which it cooperates with or disagrees with the president.[5] Second, congressional–presidential relations are portrayed as a zero-sum game in which the ascendancy of the presidency occurs at the expense of Congress' power and *vice versa*.[6] Third, despite the increased assertiveness of Congress since the 1970s (which is sometimes seen as detrimental),[7] the presidency is seen as permanently and necessarily ascendant in the modern era. Fourth, presidential pre-eminence is accepted as not only a descriptive fact but also a prescriptive norm of contemporary American government. According to this perspective, it is only through a pro-active president elected with a national mandate that the separated system can function and respond to the major social and economic problems of American society.[8] This leads to the fifth and final element which is the attributed need to engage in institutional reform in order to enhance the president's role as leader and manager of national government – thereby affording coherence to the national policy-making process.[9]

The legislative presidency

With the emergence of the modern Rooseveltian presidency, presidents assumed the role of legislative leader and began to invest heavily in ways of improving their ability to win congressional approval for legislation they wanted. What Stephen Wayne calls 'the legislative presidency' was born.[10] Pre-modern or traditional presidents took an interest in Congress' actions – as the Constitution and political realities required – but they were not expected to initiate policy proposals or act as legislative leaders of Congress; and Congress felt no obligation to act on their recommendations. A presidential message to Congress was, in James Bryce's magnificent simile, 'like a shot in the air without practical result'.[11] Beginning in 1921, when Congress gave the president broad initiating powers to submit an annual budget, presidential efforts increased to win congressional approval for major legislative proposals formulated by the president. After 1932, legislative leadership by the president became a serious business.

Personally inclined to using his personal influence to win congressional approval for his proposals, confronted by massive social, economic, and political upheaval, and blessed with huge Democratic majorities in Congress (313–117 in the House and 60–35 in the Senate), Roosevelt became engrossed in the legislative process – often delivering messages to Congress in person. He sent draft bills and made arrangements for them to be introduced by sympathetic legislators. (President Lincoln had tried this 70 years earlier and had been rebuffed. Taft had done the same in 1910, with the same result. Three years later Wilson succeeded in having his bills introduced, but his action was seen as illegitimate, even unconstitutional.)[12]

During this period, it became accepted that the president *would* lead Congress; and Congress came to accept that the president *should* provide a lead. The sea change in congressional–presidential relations ushered in in the 1930s is well captured by Schlesinger's splendid description of the first 100 days of the Roosevelt Administration:

> On Thursday, March 9, at noon, a breathless five days after the inauguration, Congress convened. Almost at once it received a message from the President: 'I cannot too strongly urge upon the Congress the clear necessity for immediate action [on the banking crisis].' Chairman Henry B. Steagall of the Banking and Currency Committee read aloud the only available copy of the proposed banking legislation. Debate was limited to forty minutes, and even before this time expired members began calling 'Vote! Vote!' Shortly after four o' clock, the House passed unanimously and without a roll call the bill few of its members had even seen. In the meantime, the Senate, which had been awaiting printed copies, decided to substitute the House version and open its own debate . . . Just before seven-thirty, the Senate passed the bill 73 to 7. An hour later, it was at the White House. The whole affair, from the first introduction to the final signature, had taken less than eight hours.'[13]

In a special session of Congress which met for just over three months in 1933, Roosevelt sent 15 messages and guided 15 major laws to enactment. Congress did not so much consider Roosevelt's legislation as salute it as it passed by.

The expectation in Congress that the president should and would become heavily involved in initiating, advocating, and supporting his administration's legislation was sustained after Roosevelt's death. Immediately, on assuming office in 1945, President Truman followed Roosevelt's practice and sent a lengthy message to Congress outlining his legislative proposals. Two years later when he refused to send Congress a draft price control bill, the president was roundly criticised by Republican leaders. Eisenhower received a similar rebuke from congressional leaders in 1953 when he refused to submit an annual legislative programme.[14] Since then, all presidents have submitted annual legislative programmes to Congress, as well as annual budgets and various reports. President-elect Kennedy even agreed his legislative priorities with Democratic leaders in Congress before he was inaugurated. Indeed, Kennedy and Johnson were so vigorous in proposing new social and economic legislation and so involved in setting Congress' legislative agenda, monitoring congressional deliberations, and influencing members' judgements that by the end of the 1960s 'it seemed that the legislative power of the presidency had extended beyond the mere suggestion of policy to the declaration of it.'[15] Presidents Nixon, Ford, Carter, Reagan, and Bush all initiated detailed legislative proposals, and were active in winning support for them in Congress. Indeed, Congress expects the White House to provide Congress with the central elements of its legislative agenda and often refuses to move in a policy area before receiving a specific proposal from the president. House Ways and Means chairman Dan Rostenkowski (D.IL) declared a few weeks after the 1992 presidential election, 'we owe it to . . . Bill Clinton *to let him set the agenda*'. Like Kennedy, Clinton also agreed his legislative agenda with Democratic congressional leaders before he was inaugurated.

Regardless of their personal styles, legislative strategies, policy objectives, White House organisation, and levels of enthusiasm for close personal involvement, all presidents since Franklin Roosevelt have sought to exercise legislative leadership in Congress, provide Congress with a primary agenda, and establish its legislative priorities. All congresses since the 1930s have expected presidents to exercise legislative leadership and have subjected the vast majority of presidential legislation to serious attention.

The changed expectations of the president's role in the legislative arena led in the 1950s to the creation of formal institutions within the White House. Even after the creation of the Executive Office of the President in 1939, Roosevelt had no formal congressional liaison office to lobby Congress. But the importance he attached to congressional relations was evident in a number of aspects of White House organisation: in the president's assignment of specific White House staff to liaise with congressional leaders; in the development of the Bureau of the Budget into a central clearance mechanism within the executive branch for advising and coordinating legislative proposals on behalf of the president; in the use of various Washington lawyers to help draft legislation and lobby Congress; in the distribution of executive patronage and other assistance to persuade opponents and waverers to support the president's legislation; in the frequent use of the presidential veto; and in the attention Roosevelt gave to the marshalling of public opinion in support of his legislative efforts[16] – all key aspects of the contemporary legislative presidency. During Truman's presidency (1945–53), the president's special counsel was given specific responsibility for directing the formulation and presentation of the president's annual legislative programme, which was outlined in the annual State of the Union message to Congress. Thereby, an embryonic congressional liason staff was formed, the most important members of which were located in the Bureau of the Budget. Despite his personal misgivings about leading Congress, President Eisenhower furthered the institutionalisation of the legislative presidency. He instituted regular meetings at the White House with congressional leaders, became intimately involved in the details of congressional bargaining on important legislation, and created the first official legislative liaison office in the White House under the direction of Major General Jerry Persons. The office had separate sections for House and Senate liaison, and employed experienced lobbyists, including a former member of Congress and staff borrowed from the Department of Defense.[17]

Presidents Kennedy and Johnson attached even greater importance to congressional liaison and integrated liaison staff into policy development networks within the White House. Kennedy appointed Larry O'Brien as his most highly paid adviser, with the title Special Assistant to the President for Congressional Relations and Personnel, and gave him complete authority to speak on behalf of the president. Under O'Brien's direction, politically experienced congressional liaison staff with valuable regional knowledge and connections in Congress were appointed to the Office of Congressional Relations (OCR). During the Kennedy and Johnson administrations, O'Brien and his staff maintained meticulous records of legislators' support for the president and feted members of Congress with patronage and favours. Johnson himself was personally involved in the OCR's work even to the extent of making detailed judgements about legislative strategy. In the early part of his presidency, liaison staff were allowed direct access to the president.[18] In the Nixon and Ford administrations, legislative liaison was given a high priority, although congressional relations and policy development were less pro-active.[19] As Congress remained under Democratic control, OCR staff in these Republican administrations 'worked the Hill' even more closely than their Democratic predecessors – usually from the Republican Whip's office in the House and the vice president's non-ceremonial office in the Senate. In the 1970s, then, under conditions of split-party or divided government the now-familiar features of contemporary congressional liaison became an accepted part of the legislative process. Since the beginning of Reagan's presidency, staff of what is now called the Office of Legislative Liaison have been located within the White Office itself, rather than in the old Executive Office building next door where they languished under President Carter. Presidents Reagan, Bush, and Clinton all appointed people with considerable experience of working in or with Congress to their OLA operations.[20]

Undoubtedly, the growth of the modern presidency and the development of the legislative presidency changed the relationship between the president and Congress and helped focus attention to a much greater extent than previously on presidential leadership. Once it became expected that presidents would lead Congress, not surprisingly their leadership styles, ideologies, temperaments, and skills became relevant variables in congressional–presidential relations. Indeed, the wide acceptance of the presidency-centred approach led after 1952 to the misguided practice of rating presidents yearly according to how much support 'their' legislative proposals received from Congress. Presidents who received the strongest support, according to Congressional Quarterly, were Johnson in 1965 (93 per cent), Eisenhower in 1953 (89 per cent), Kennedy in 1963 (87 per cent), and Clinton in 1993 and 1994 (86 per cent). Those who received the lowest levels of congressional support were Bush in 1992 (43 per cent), Reagan in 1987 (44 per cent), Reagan in 1988 (47 per cent), Nixon in 1973 (51 per cent), and Eisenhower in 1959 (52 per cent). While these scores have the virtue of showing that some presidents are more successful than others, and that presidential success rates vary from year to year, their presidency-centred premise is misleading and they are methodologically flawed.[21] Other aspects of the presidency-centred approach have also had resonance in accounts of contemporary congressional–presidential relations. Most notable is the belief that intense institutional conflict between the president and Congress is an unavoidable consequence of constitutional design and that Congress' organisation, together with the individualism and parochialism of its members, preclude coherent law-making. Despite the widespread currency of this presidency-centred perspective and the depth of the analytical tradition that accompanies it, this approach is nevertheless distorted and misleading. In short, it grossly understates the extent to which Congress and the president interact and work together to create laws.

Institutional competition within a separated system

Our approach to congressional–presidential relations starts from the premise that the Constitution deliberately engendered institutional competition between Congress and the president. The United States does not have a parliamentary or presidential system. It has, in Charles O. Jones' phrase, a separated system.[22] The president is not the legislature nor is he part of it. If he wants legislation, he must seek the approval of Congress and, most importantly, win sufficient votes from legislators to secure passage of his legislation. If the Congress wants legislation, it can approve it without the president's consent, so long as they can override the president's veto should it be exercised. Anthony King put this crucial point in stark relief, first from the perspective of the White House and then from Congress:

> [U]nder the American system, you [the president] need votes all the time and all kinds of votes: votes for and against bills, votes for and against amendments, votes to appropriate funds, votes not to appropriate funds, votes to increase the budget, votes to cut the budget, votes to enable you to organise the executive branch, votes to strengthen you (or not to weaken

you) in your dealings with administrative agencies, votes to sustain your own vetoes, votes to override legislative vetoes, votes in the Senate to ratify the treaties you have negotiated and to confirm the nominations you have made, votes (every century or so) in opposition to efforts to impeach you. You need votes to enable you to build up a record, to win re-election, to win – who knows? a place in history. Indeed, come to think of it, you need votes in Congress to enable the government to function at all . . . The only kind of votes that you as president do not need, impeachment apart, are votes to sustain you in office . . . In short, you are heavily dependent on Congress.

And what is the perspective of legislators from Capitol Hill?

Suppose you are a congressman or senator, sitting in your office at the other end of the avenue on Capitol Hill . . . As you sit there in your office reading your mail or talking to somebody on the telephone, what are your aims in life? Much, of course, depends on how old you are and whether you hope someday to run for a higher office (possibly the Senate if you are in the House, perhaps the presidency itself). But in the normal course of events, you probably have three goals . . . to be reelected . . . to be a big noise in the House or the Senate . . . [and] to play your part in seeing to it that the United States of America is well governed, according to your lights or maybe according to the lights of your constituents.[23]

In order to win votes in Congress, a president must inform legislators of the specific details of his proposals, make clear what the likely effects of legislation are, relate them to existing policies, provide House members and senators with good reasons why they should support him, and participate actively in negotiations with Congress to build winning coalitions. However, a president cannot escape the basic differences of the two institutions to policy-making. As the only official elected by a country-wide constituency, as the federal official held most responsible for American well-being and prosperity, as the occupant of an office with unique responsibilities in foreign policy, the president is likely to bring a national perspective to the business of legislating. Members of Congress, in contrast, are likely to regard legislation from a regional or local perspective. The frequency of elections to Congress, the marginal role played by political parties in congressional elections, and members' attentiveness to their constituencies – all mean that it is likely that they will consider first and often last the effects of legislative proposals on their states and districts, rather than their consequences for the whole country. They will protect their constituency interests – if necessary directly – by demanding special provisions or opposing the measure outright, or indirectly by guarding the jurisdictional claims of congressional committees of which they are members. They will likely insist that their policy and constituency expertise is injected into legislative proposals. Often, they will develop their own policy alternatives completely separate from the president's efforts.

How then might the president and Congress temper the inevitable conflict between them? What factors in their relations might encourage cooperation and enable the two institutions to work together?

Presidential leadership skills

One of the most familiar themes of the presidency-centred approach to congressional–presidential relations is the importance of presidential leadership skills. In his classic book, *Presidential Power*, Richard Neustadt argued that the power of the president is 'the power to persuade'. Presidents acquire personal reputations as either skilled or unskilled in the arts of persuasion. 'The men he would persuade', argues Neustadt, 'must be convinced in their own minds that he has skill and will enough to use his advantages.' And personal reputation is something over which a president can exercise greatest influence.[24]

In order to establish a reputation and maximise his power over Congress, a president needs to be personally skilful, shrewd, and manipulative. It is necessary for a president to know and understand the needs of members of Congress, consult with them, especially leaders, and give them advance notice before initiating major policy proposals. These actions then need to be followed up using all available resources to persuade members either to support the president's policy or not oppose it. Favours may need to be exchanged with members; political and personal assistance provided; personal appeals made; and Cabinet members, congressional leaders, and influential people in members' constituencies utilised to help. If these methods of persuasion are not successful, a president may need to twist arms and make threats. And a president must be able to compromise, and know when to compromise. If compromises are offered too early he will be deemed weak; too late and accusations of stalemating the legislative process will be made.[25]

Neustadt's recommendations for maximising presidential power over Congress seemed to be borne out by President Johnson's experiences with Congress, who observed after he left the White House:

> There is but one way for a president to deal with Congress, and that is continuously, incessantly, and without interruption. If it's really going to work, the relationship between the president and Congress has got to be almost incestuous. He's got to know them better than they know themselves. And, then, on the basis of this knowledge, he's got to build a system that stretches from the cradle to the grave, from the moment a bill is introduced to the moment it is officially enrolled as the law of the land.[26]

Johnson, of course, was a former Majority Leader of the Senate. As president, he was intimately involved in the legislative process. Apparently his favourite reading was the *Congressional Record*. He required staff to provide him on a daily basis with detailed memoranda on their legislative contacts, special problems, noteworthy conversations, all of which he digested rapidly and thoroughly.[27]

Not all presidents have these skills, however. Of recent presidents, Ronald Reagan certainly did. Although not a former member of Congress, he showed respect for congressional prerogatives and reached out to members for support, courting key members including Democratic House Speaker 'Tip' O'Neill, and seeking the advice of congressional Republicans for important Cabinet positions.[28] In his first two years, President Clinton also received high marks for the skill with which he courted Congress. He demonstrated awareness of the need to involve himself deeply in the business of finding votes and the caring and feeding of the needs, interests, and egos of members of Congress. Following Reagan's example, he toured House and Senate office buildings to pay courtesy visits to congressional leaders. According to his director of legislative liaison, Clinton made fifteen personal visits to Capitol Hill in his first eleven months in office.[29] Legislators were also invited regularly to the White House. Working with an experienced legislative liaison staff and Cabinet colleagues, he was intimately involved in cajoling the House and Senate to support his 1993 budget package. Clinton personally telephoned many Democratic opponents of the plan on the day of the House vote to try to persuade them to support him. After the vote, the *Washington Post* reported

> Rep. Sam Coppersmith (D.AZ), a freshman . . . was whipped to death. Two calls from Clinton on the day of the vote; multiple contacts from the [House] whips. Bleary-eyed and obviously troubled, Coppersmith seemed to be in a daze late Thursday night after the vote. 'By God, it's hard to say "No" to the President', said Coppersmith. 'I think I said, "Mr. President. I can't say Yes."' According to Coppersmith, Clinton had told him that a defeat would make financial markets go haywire, that there would be adjustments to the budget package in the Senate, that he would get another crack at the plan.[30]

In order to win votes in the House and Senate, the president made last-minute concessions on energy taxes, cuts in social entitlements, agricultural subsidies, and import restrictions on peanuts and tobacco. One House member who voted with the president learned that a military installation projected to move from his district 'may stay put'; another won a personal visit to his district by the Treasury Secretary; and so on.[31] Clinton and his staff mounted a similarly intensive effort in November 1993 on the vote to approve the North American Free Trade Agreement (NAFTA). Working closely this time with the House Republican leadership, he defined the issue, took the propaganda initiative, demonstrated considerable legislative finesse and made the necessary compromises and bargains to overcome opposition within his own party to win the vote. In the immediate aftermath, he was dubbed 'Lyndon Baines Clinton'.

While Reagan and Clinton are seen as skilful negotiators with Congress, President Carter adopted a 'holier than thou' attitude to Congress and showed incredible naivety in his legislative dealings. As president-elect, he insisted that congressional leaders go to Georgia to meet him. In office, members of Congress felt slighted. Carter did not consult with relevant committee chairs before introducing major legislation and failed to inform members of patronage appointments and projects affecting their districts and states. In a now-famous episode, Carter began his presidency by proposing to eliminate nineteen water projects near and dear to members in seventeen states. Even after four years of dealings with Congress, '[he] remained a stranger in a strange land'.[32] Similarly, Kennedy did not win congressional support for federal aid to education because 'he did not understand the need to wheel and deal with passion for what he believed to be right . . . and he did not seem to know . . . that politics cannot be played from a distance'. And President Nixon 'lacked the skill and, to some extent, the will to press' for his welfare reform plan, supposedly his highest domestic priority.[33]

Besides possessing useful personal skills, a president must be good at manipulating the legislative context and exploiting leadership opportunities when they arise. Most importantly, a president should select carefully a limited number of priority issues with which he/she wishes to be identified. He needs to direct Congress' attention to those issues, frame them as the president sees them so as to channel Congress' decision-making choices, and provide legislators with a clear lead on those priorities. 'Nothing an individual president can do breeds success like clear priorities.'[34] If we examine some recent examples, again we find contrasting experiences.

In his first year, Reagan concentrated on spending and taxation – issues on which Republicans and conservative Democrats in Congress could agree. He then proceeded to take advantage of Congress' budget reconciliation process, which provided for a few up-and-down votes early in the session, to manoeuvre the Democrat-controlled House into supporting his budget package. Once a president is able to score victories in Congress like this – and the more important and resounding those victories are – the greater legislative momentum, prestige, and influence he acquires. In contrast, President Carter wasted his agenda-setting advantages in his early years by sending to Congress large numbers of complex proposals which were often contentious and divided his own party. President Clinton also made the mistake of failing to control the agenda when in early 1993 his legislative presidency became embroiled by a decision to lift the ban on homosexuals in the military. As a consequence, he was required to expend valuable political resources at an initial stage of his presidency on this issue rather than on other issues more important to Congress and the voters, such as the budget, health care, and welfare on which he had focused in his election campaign. Only after this *débâcle* and a reorganisation of White House staff did Clinton concentrate his legislative efforts on a narrower range of priority issues, including deficit reduction, health care (subsequently abandoned in late 1994), and NAFTA.

In order to influence Congress' legislative priorities, a president must also be skilful in determining what the legislative process in Congress can deliver at any given time. When we examined in Chapter 4 what members of Congress did in one particular week in 1993, we made the point that Congress has its own agenda and pace which may not be the president's. We also showed that the legislative process in Congress is sequential, iterative, and serial. It is possible, therefore, that a president's legislative proposals may fail not because of congressional opposition (although this is bound to exist on many issues) but because of Congress' own crowded agenda, because members' priorities conflict, or because House and Senate rules inhibit consideration. As a former congressional leader Lyndon Johnson, for example, was well aware of these potential pitfalls and was careful not to overload Congress' agenda. He sent bills 'one by one rather than in a clump' and 'when the agendas of the receiving committees were clear so that they could be considered right away'.[35] Jimmy Carter was oblivious to these considerations – at least in his early years. Some of Bill Clinton's early legislative efforts also fell foul of these problems. Clinton's health care legislation, for example, was sent to Congress nine months after the announcement of his intention to do so leaving insufficient time for the 103rd Congress to consider such a highly complex bill extending to 1,700 pages. Congressional committees did not begin working on the legislation until well into 1994, and by the time the legislation reached the floors, legislators were thinking about the year-end adjournment and the 1994 mid-term elections.

Finally, if the president is going to exert influence on Congress, it is important that he/she demonstrate a good sense of timing, that Congress' mood should be read accurately, and that adjustments be made accordingly. 'I have watched the Congress from either the inside or the outside, man and boy, for more than forty years,' former President Johnson observed, 'and I've never seen a Congress that didn't eventually take the measure of the President it was dealing with.'[36] Typically, this period is only a year, often less. During this honeymoon, Congress tends to be impressed by the previous November's results which gave the president an electoral victory and, as a result, is usually more cooperative in this period. It is sensible for presidents – as Johnson, Reagan and, eventually, Clinton did – to act quickly. Events such as Kennedy's assassination may unexpectedly provide presidents with windows of opportunity, but these cannot be anticipated.

Although considerable emphasis is placed on presidents' legislative skills in interpretations of presidential-congressional relations, it seems nevertheless unwise to overestimate what Burns calls the 'skills mystique'.[37] Various empirical studies conclude that although presidential leadership skills should not be ignored, presidents' success rates with Congress show little variance between presidents reputed to be highly skilled (like Johnson) and others thought to be less skilled or unskilled (such as Carter). Edwards, for example, concludes that 'presidential legislative skills are not closely related to presidential support in Congress . . . In most instances presidents exercise them at the margins of coalition building, not at the core.'[38] This is not to say, however, that anecdotes and case studies which point to the importance of presidential skills[39] are necessarily inaccurate.

Presidential popularity

A second factor which is widely regarded as influencing presidential-congressional relations is the president's popularity. Once elected, presidents are watched carefully. Their performance in office is assessed frequently by opinion pollsters who regularly ask voters whether or not they approve or disapprove of the president's handling of his job. As Figure 9.1 shows, presidents' approval and disapproval ratings have fluctuated considerably from president to president and from month to month within the term of office of any one president. President Reagan's quarterly average approval ratings, for example, ranged from 63 per cent down to 38 per cent; President Bush's from 78 per cent to 37 per cent; and President Clinton's from 55 per cent to 42 per cent. If a president's approval ratings are high, it is assumed that he is powerful and as a consequence members of Congress will support the president's proposals; if they are low, it is assumed he is politically weak and members of Congress will not be concerned about opposing his proposals. This popularity-compliance connection rests on two principles: first, most members of Congress want to be reelected next time and look for cues which will tell them what they need to do and say to win re-election from their constituents; and second, most members believe that they should represent their constituents' opinions. Legislators have few means of measuring and evaluating current opinions on issues and politics among folks back home. If they consider their re-election constituencies to coincide with or be a part of the president's constituency, they may use public evaluations of the president as surrogate measures of public opinion in their constituencies. If the president is popular with the public, so the theory goes,[40] members of Congress (who often feel electorally vulnerable) will reason that their prospects for re-election will be enhanced if they support a popular president. Alternatively, if the president's popularity is low – as Bill Clinton's was in 1994 – legislators may choose to distance themselves from him in order to protect themselves. When, for example, the crime bill supported by the president was refused a rule in the House in August 1994, one administration official offered the president's low popularity as an explanation:

> Who would have thought that so many of these guys would think it was safe to vote against a crime bill? Republicans and Democrats must be pretty damn sure the president will be incapable of using the vote against them in

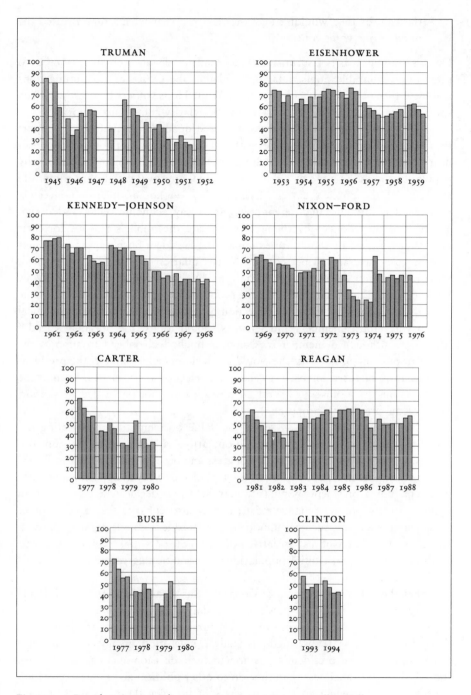

Figure 9.1. Presidents' approval ratings, 1945–1994. *Source*: Gallup Poll.

the Fall, or they wouldn't take the risk in a year when crime is rated the number one voter concern.[41.]

On this reading, it is not surprising that presidents devote so many resources to projecting favourable public images;[42] and that the Office of Communications and the Office of the Press Secretary in the White House offices have grown. Even so, there are good reasons to question the popularity-compliance theory.

Although a number of studies have used quantitative analysis to support the theory that presidential popularity affects congressional support for the president's legislative proposals,[43] there are good theoretical reasons to question why popularity should be a major factor. Presidential approval ratings are composite measures of the public's current feelings: they do not distinguish between a president's performance in different policy areas (say, economic policy and foreign affairs) and they do not by themselves indicate the public's reasons for their evaluations. Figure 9.1 shows, for example, that President Bush's approval ratings shot up to an average 78 per cent in the last quarter of 1990. As it happened, these ratings were based almost entirely on his performance in the Gulf War. Bush's approval ratings for handling the economy were far lower during the same period. Since approval ratings are reflections of general feelings, there is no logical reason why House members and senators should follow the president's lead.[44] Moreover, although a member of Congress might feel obliged to support the president on a major issue he/she would not feel obliged to support the president on legislation opposed intensely by his/her re-election constituency. Even at the height of Bush's popularity, liberal Democrats were not persuaded to support many of the president's proposals.

Like presidential skills, it seems the value of a high approval rating lies essentially at the margins. Presidential popularity, as measured by the approval ratings, serve to remind members of Congress and other political actors in Washington of the potential political costs they might have to pay in opposing a popular president. For a president, popularity may help him decide whether or not an opportunity for political change exists; it may also enhance the value of other presidential resources, such as support for the president among his own party in Congress, the efficacy of his legislative skills, and the potential for public support. In these respects, presidential popularity is a conditioning rather than a determining factor.

For the individual member of Congress, this means that he/she will decide whether or not to support the president's legislative proposals on the basis of that individual's strategic calculations of the electoral and other costs and benefits of doing so. In fact, as John Kingdon's study shows, most members do not give much weight to the president's position in their decision-making calculations. Indeed, they give much less than they do to other political actors. Based on data collected in 1969 (when government was split between the parties), Kingdon's study showed that in fully 61 per cent of House floor voting decisions, the administration was regarded by legislators as of no importance whatsoever, of minor importance in 21 per cent, and of major importance in 14 per cent. As a predictor of legislators' voting decisions, the administration's position fared even worse; although not surprisingly legislators of the president's party pay greater attention to the administration than do the opposition party, and junior members of both parties pay more attention than do seniors.[45] Far more important to legislators, as we explained in Chapter 5, are constituency factors and members' own policy preferences. Members of Congress know, moreover, that incumbents seldom lose their re-election bids because they have supported or opposed a president – even a popular one – on a specific set of roll call votes. Much more important is whether or not members are ideologically in tune with the district or state; and, as we showed in Chapter 5, most are.

Having reintroduced into the discussion the importance of what happens in Congress, let us now examine the extent to which congressional conditions make it easier or more difficult for a president to be influential and for the two institutions to work together.

The president and congressional partisanship

It is simply to state an obvious but essential truth that a president's influence with Congress depends on party arithmetic as well as on the strength of congressional party loyalties. As we showed in Chapter 5, party is an important source of influence in Congress; presidents are *de facto* party leaders. Table 9.1 shows that since 1932 the differences between congressional party contingents vary from enormous to minuscule: in the House, between 244 in the 75th Congress to just 8 in 1953; and in the Senate, from 58 in 1937 to 1 in 1953 and 1955. Some presidents (almost all Democrats) have enjoyed huge arithmetic majorities for their parties – as Roosevelt did in the 74th and 75th Congresses (1933–8), Johnson in the 89th Congress (1965–6), and Carter in the 95th Congress (1977–8) – while others have not. President Eisenhower, a Republican, had a party majority of only 8 in the House and 1 in the Senate when he became president in 1953. Some presidents, however, find that one or both houses of Congress are controlled by the opposing party – for example, Truman in the 80th Congress (1947–8), Eisenhower in the 84th, 85th, and 86th Congresses (1955–60), Nixon, Ford, Reagan, and Bush throughout their presidencies, and Clinton in the 104th Congress (1995–6). Indeed, the period from 1946 to 1996 has seen split-party government most of the time. Obviously, when presidents' parties have arithmetic majorities in Congress, they have substantial political advantages, as President Johnson found in the 89th Congress and President Reagan to a lesser extent in the 97th Congress (1981–2). However, a president with a super-majority of seats is not necessarily more advantaged. We will come back to the impact of partisan majorities on the president's strategic position a little later.

Table 9.1. Party control of Congress and the presidency, 1931–1995

	PRESIDENCY			HOUSE					SENATE				
				Membership			Gains/Losses		Membership			Gains/Losses	
Election Year	President	Popular Vote Majority	Congress	Democrats	Republicans	Others	Democrat	Republican	Democrats	Republicans	Others	Democrat	Republican
1930	Hoover (R)		72nd	220	214	1	+53	-53	47	48	0	+8	-8
1932	Roosevelt (D)	7,050,000	73rd	313	117	5	+113	-113	60	35	1	+13	-13
1934	Roosevelt (D)		74th	322	103	10	+9	-14	69	25	2	+9	-10
1936	Roosevelt (D)	11,073,102	75th	333	89	13	+11	-14	75	17	4	+6	-6
1938	Roosevelt (D)		76th	262	169	4	-71	+80	69	23	4	-8	+8
1940	Roosevelt (D)	4,964,561	77th	268	162	5	+7	-8	66	28	2	-3	+4
1942	Roosevelt (D)		78th	222	209	4	-45	+46	57	38	1	-8	+9
1944	Truman (D)	3,594,993	79th	242	191	2	+21	-19	57	38	1	-1	+1
1946	Truman (D)		80th	188	246	1	-53	+55	45	51		-11	+11
1948	Truman (D)	2,188,054	81st	263	171	1	+76	-76	54	42		+9	-9
1950	Truman (D)		82nd	235	199	1	-27	+27	49	47		-5	+5
1952	Eisenhower (R)	6,621,242	83rd	213	221	1	-24	+24	47	48	1	-2	+2
1954	Eisenhower (R)		84th	232	203		+19	-18	48	47	1	+2	-2
1956	Eisenhower (R)	9,567,720	85th	234	201		+2	-2	49	47		0	0
1958	Eisenhower (R)		86th	283	153		+49	-48	64	34		+15	-13
1960	Kennedy (D)	118,574	87th	263	174		-20	+21	64	36		-2	+2
1962	Kennedy (D)		88th	258	176		-4	0	68	32		+4	-4

Election Year	President	Popular Vote Majority	Congress	HOUSE Membership Democrats	Republicans	Others	HOUSE Gains/Losses Democrat	Republican	SENATE Membership Democrats	Republicans	Others	SENATE Gains/Losses Democrat	Republican
1964	Johnson (D)	15,951,378	89th	295	140		+38	-37	68	32		+2	-2
1966	Johnson (D)		90th	248	187		-48	+48	64	36		-3	+3
1968	Nixon (R)	510,314	91st	243	192		-7	+7	58	42		-5	+5
1970	Nixon (R)		92nd	255	180		+12	-12	55	45		-2	+2
1972	Nixon (R)	17,999,528	93rd	244	191		-13	+13	57	43		+2	-2
1974	Ford (R)		94th	291	144		+48	-48	61	38		+3	-4
1976	Carter (D)	1,682,970	95th	292	143		+2	-2	62	38		0	0
1978	Carter (D)		96th	277	158		-12	+12	59	41		-3	+3
1980	Reagan (R)	8,420,270	97th	243	192		-33	+33	47	53		-12	+12
1982	Reagan (R)		98th	269	166		+26	-26	46	54		0	0
1984	Reagan (R)	16,877,890	99th	253	182		-15	+15	47	53		+2	-2
1986	Reagan (R)		100th	258	177		+5	-5	55	45		+8	-8
1988	Bush (R)	7,077,023	101st	260	175		+3	-3	55	45		+1	-1
1990	Bush (R)		102nd	267	167	1	+8	-8	56	44		+1	-1
1992	Clinton (D)	5,805,344	103rd	256	178	1	-11	+11	55	45		-1	+1
1994	Clinton (D)		104th	203	231	1	-53	+53	47	53		-8	+8

Source: Congressional Quarterly.

Note: Democratic control is indicated by shaded areas.

313

The extent to which a president is able to take advantage of his party's control of Congress depends also on the extent to which he can gain their support. Although such support is by no means automatic in a separated system, presidents receive considerably more support from their own party in Congress than they do from the opposition party. Levels of support among the president's party also varies from administration to administration, between the House and Senate, and between the two parties. The strongest support was that given by House Democrats for Democratic presidents (especially Kennedy and Johnson) and by House Republicans for Republican presidents (especially Ford and Reagan). House Democrats were much more generous in their support for Republican presidents than were Republicans in their support for Democratic presidents. In the Senate, as we have suggested in earlier chapters, partisanship was more muted.[46] Table 9.2 shows that these patterns were also evident in the 102nd (1991–2) and 103rd (1993–4) Congresses:

Table 9.2. Party support in Congress for Presidents Bush and Clinton, 103rd and 104th Congresses

		HOUSE			SENATE		
Congress	President	Democrats	Republicans	Difference	Democrats	Republicans	Difference
102nd (1991–92)	Bush	32%	74%	42%	38%	78%	40%
103rd (1993–94)	Clinton	79%	44%	35%	89%	37%	51%

Cells are the mean levels of support for the president in each party

Source: Congressional Quarterly

These patterns of congressional party support for presidents are not surprising. Members of the president's party in Congress are likely to share the same political goals and policy preferences. They derive electoral support from similar coalitions and can anticipate being judged at the next election at least partly on the president's record. They share similar emotional attachments to their party and the president, and may actively distrust the opposition party. Members of the president's party in Congress are also more likely to be recipients of presidential patronage and favours. For these reasons, it was not surprising to see and hear expressions of support for President Clinton from his party in the House and the Senate in 1993. 'I'm going to do my best to be supportive', declared Senator Herb Kohl (D.WI) in the early months of Clinton's presidency. 'We need to remember that his success is ours and to the extent that he fails, we fail.' 'We have to demonstrate to the American people that we can govern', insisted House Chief Deputy Whip John Lewis (D.GA) in similar vein.[47]

Even so, congressional parties are not conspicuous for their institutional discipline or for their resources of coercive force. As we showed in Chapter 5, each congressional party includes members with widely divergent views and central party leaders' disciplinary powers are limited. The capacity of parties and presidents to structure voting is much weaker than in strong party systems such as Britain's; and since the 1950s, electoral ties between presidents and their party colleagues in Congress have weakened considerably as the advantages of incumbency have reduced the effects of winning presidential candidates' coat tails. In the 1932 and 1936 elections, Roosevelt's popularity in the presidential elections produced long coat tails in the congressional elections helping elect large numbers of Democrats to the House and Senate. By the 1984 elections, 45 per cent of House districts were yielding different results in presidential and House elections – usually a Democrat winning the House seat and the Republican candidate winning the presidential vote in the district.[48] Although the percentages of seats with discrepant outcomes fell in 1988 and again in 1992 (to only 24 per cent), the numbers of House seats affected continued to remain high with large numbers of members winning their seats by larger percentages than the president. In the 1992 elections, Clinton won a higher percent of the vote than did the winning Democratic congressional candidate in only 12 House seats, although his showing in certain states, such as California, was credited with saving some Democratic seats; in no state did Clinton win a higher percentage of the vote than the winning Democratic candidate for the Senate.[49] On the basis of these results, it would not have been surprising if many congressional Democrats had concluded that they were more representative of their districts and states than the president and, in many cases as Table 9. 3 shows, failed to support proposals supported by President Clinton.

Table 9.3. House Democratic support for President Clinton on selected votes, 104th Congress

Date	Issue	Vote	Percentage Voting with Clinton
February 1993	Family and medical leave – pass	265–163	89%
March 1993	1994 budget resolution – approve	243–183	96%
March 1993	Economic stimulus bill – vote on rule	240–185	95%
June 1993	Aid to Russia – amendment to amount	140–289	82%
June 1993	Restrict use of federal money for abortion	255–178	62%
August 1993	1994 budget resolution – approve conference report	218–216	84%
September 1993	Give president discretion on homosexuals in military	169–264	61%
November 1993	Extend deadline for troops leaving Somalia	226–201	88%
November 1993	Brady handgun control bill – passage	238–189	73%
November 1993	North American Free Trade Agreement – approve	234–200	40%
November 1993	Across-the-board spending cut (Penny-Kasich)	213–219	78%
February 1994	Create Department of Environmental Protection – rule	191–227	76%
March 1994	Balanced budget constitutional amendment – approve	271–153	61%
March 1994	1995 budget resolution – approve further cuts	202–216	83%
May 1994	Ban manufacture and possession of assault weapons – pass	216–214	70%

Date	Issue	Vote	Percentage Voting with Clinton
May 1994	Abortion clinic assess – approve	214–174	82%
June 1994	End unilaterally UN arms embargo on arms to Bosnia – pass	244–178	53%
August 1994	Crime bill – rule	210–225	77%
August 1994	MFN status for China – renew	280–152	59%
October 1994	Lobbying disclosure – adopt conference report	306–112	92%
October 1994	Withdraw US troops from Haiti immediately	205–225	86%
November 1994	Implement GATT – pass	288–146	65%

Source: Various Congressional Quarterly Weekly Reports.

The appropriate conclusion to draw is Neustadt's: 'What the Constitution separates, our parties do not combine.'[50] Compared with the position of a British prime minister that of an American president in respect of his legislative party is weak. He cannot withdraw the party whip or discipline party members because he has no control whatsoever over a legislator's membership of a congressional party caucus or conference. Neither can he have congressional dissidents 'deselected' as party candidates because he has no influence over congressional nominations. Indeed, far from using coercion, a president must tread carefully even when dealing with members of his own party. 'Party loyalty or responsibility means damn little', complained President Kennedy in 1962. 'They've got to take care of themselves first. [House members] all have to run this year – I don't and I couldn't hurt most of them if I wanted.'[51] Nor should he try to hurt them. It would be far worse for a member of his party in Congress to lose office than for a president not to receive the member's support on a single vote.

The president and legislators' ideologies

If party is a weak link between presidents and Congress, is ideology a basis of agreement? We noted in Chapter 5 how important legislators' ideological predispositions and policy attitudes are as influences on decision-making in Congress. Although ideology is closely correlated with party, many members of Congress hold ideological preferences outside their party's mainstream: conservatives in the Democratic Party; liberals and moderates in the GOP.

Legislators' ideologies and policy preferences are likely to provide bases of support for a president for several reasons which have been discussed in previous chapters. First, as we showed in Chapter Three, most individuals want to become members of Congress because they are interested in politics and have fairly well developed and often intensely held attitudes towards aspects of public policy. Various studies have shown also that once elected, the policy attitudes of members of Congress remain fairly stable over time, and especially one or two presidential terms.[52] Second, as we showed in Chapter 5, most legislators' ideological and

316

policy dispositions tend to be in tune with their re-election constituencies, thereby reducing the risk of conflict between their own views and those held intensely by constituents. Third, members of Congress tend to seek and receive political and policy information and voting cues from congressional colleagues and others with whom they usually agree,[53] which has the effect of reinforcing patterns of decision-making along ideological and partisan lines.

Presidents also vary according to their ideological predispositions. Assigning presidents an ideological score according to the percentages of times they supported the positions of Americans for Democratic Action (a liberal organisation) and Americans for Constitutional Action (a conservative group) on congressional votes, Jon Bond and Richard Fleisher scored Kennedy and Johnson as liberals, Ford and Reagan as conservatives, and Eisenhower a moderate (but conservative on domestic policy).[54]

It is not surprising to find, then, that policy positions adopted by presidents tend to generate a congressional support pattern along ideological and attitudinal lines. Presidents Kennedy and Johnson relied for most of their legislative successes on the support of a '*de facto* liberal coalition',[55] but a number of their proposals also received the support of a number of moderate Republicans. Presidents Nixon and Reagan relied on the support of many conservative southern Democrats, as well as Republicans. President Carter worked frequently with Republicans, often because his centrist proposals ran counter to the Democratic Party's traditional liberal base in Congress. Figure 9.2 shows that President Clinton's strongest

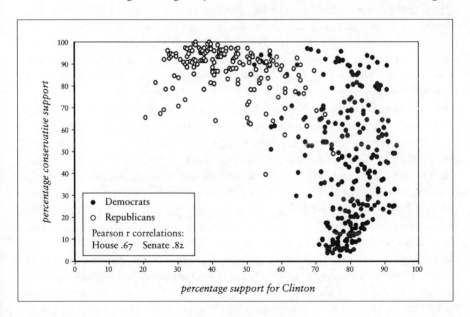

Figure 9.2. House members' support for President Clinton, 103rd Congress.

congressional supporters in the 103rd Congress (1993–4) were liberals and moderates; his strongest opponents were conservatives. In consequence, as President Clinton found when he sought congressional support for NAFTA in 1993, presidents must often rely on the support of bipartisan congressional coalitions for their proposals. Generally, as Bond and Fleisher found from their studies of congressional–presidential relations from Eisenhower to Reagan, the greater the ideological differences between a president and Congress, the less congressional support the president will receive from both parties and especially from the party which is not the president's.[56] Ideology, therefore, is often an important factor in congressional–presidential relations.

Even so, as we found with party, there are limits to the extent to which ideology can link legislators to the president. One reason is that most members of Congress do not wish to appear in the eyes of voters as ideologues at the extremes of the liberal–conservative spectrum, mainly because most voters' attitudes and preferences are not located there. As Kingdon has noted, ideology is much less useful as a decision-making guide for legislators positioned in the middle of the ideological spectrum.[57] A second reason is that many votes in Congress which are important to the president – particularly those on distributive issues like farm subsidies, trade, public works, and military contracts – involve members' constituency interests. Congressional votes on NAFTA, GATT (the General Agreement on Tariffs and Trade), cuts to the superconducting super collider project, and higher grazing fees on public lands are examples of Democrats opposing President Clinton in response to constituency pressures (see Table 9.4). A third reason is that ideological coalitions in Congress – such as the conservative coalition – are unlike the congressional parties in that they do not have formal organisational structures which might be utilised in support of presidential efforts to win votes. One of President Clinton's problems in the 1990s was that as a centrist 'new Democrat' he depended for support on centrist members of Congress who by definition were a minority and did not enjoy the benefit from a formal organisational structure cutting across extant party lines (see Figure 9.2).

In their innovative study which sought to assess the extent to which undisciplined and ideologically diverse congressional parties link the policy preferences of presidents and Congress, Bond and Fleisher identified four conceptually distinct party factions with which every president must deal. First is the president's political base which includes those legislators most predisposed to support the president's preferences, because they share both a party affiliation and an ideological perspective (i.e. liberal Democrats for Democratic presidents and conservative Republicans for Republican presidents). Second are the cross-pressured members of the president's party. Third are cross-pressured members of the non-presidential party. Cross-pressured legislators are those with ideological outlooks outside their party's mainstream (i.e. conservative Democrats and liberal Republicans) who often find their partisan and ideological allegiances at odds.

Fourth are members of the opposition political base, i.e. legislators who are the direct opposite of those who are members of the president's political base. From their analysis of these congressional party factions between 1953 and 1993, Bond and Fleisher found that the political bases of presidents in the House varied from between 223 (51 per cent of the membership) in 1977–8 (Carter and the 95th Congress) to as few as 120 (28 per cent of the House) in 1975–6 (Ford and the 94th Congress). In the Senate, the president's base varied between 51 (Johnson and the 89th Congress) and 23 (Ford and the 94th Congress). In almost all cases then the votes of a president's party base were insufficient to determine the outcome (see Table 9.4).[58] In consequence, all presidents need to reach out far beyond their party bases to cross-pressured party colleagues as well as to cross-pressured members of the opposition party.

In practice, however, presidents' difficulties in winning votes in Congress do not end here. Bond and Fleisher found that at least since the 1950s the president's party base in Congress frequently failed to unify behind him. Most recent presidents received the support of at least three-quarters of their party on only 60 per cent of roll call votes where there was conflict (columns 4 and 6 in Table 9.4). In the extreme case, President Ford's base in the House in the 93rd Congress united with him on only 18 per cent of votes. In successive Congresses, Presidents Eisenhower, Nixon, Ford, and Reagan regularly received 75 per cent support from their party bases on less than 50 per cent of House votes, slightly higher in the Senate. Only in the exceptional circumstances of the 87th through 90th Congresses did Presidents Kennedy and Johnson consistently enjoy the support of at least 75 per cent of their party bases on about 90 per cent of roll call votes. In 1993, Bill Clinton won the support of at least 75 per cent of his party base on 74 per cent of House votes and 79 per cent of Senate votes.[59]

When the president seeks the support of Congress, central and committee party leaders play a crucial role in helping unite the president's party base behind his legislative positions. In the House, every president from Eisenhower to Reagan received the support of his party's floor leader on at least 80 per cent of important votes; in the Senate, levels of central leader support ranged from 100 per cent (for Kennedy) to just 70 per cent (for Ford). Importantly, when the floor leader of the president's party supported the president, support from members of his party's congressional base increased significantly regardless of whether or not the president had a party majority. The supportive roles played by Speaker Foley, House Majority Leader Gephardt, and Senate Majority Leader Mitchell in successfully mustering votes for President Clinton's budget reconciliation bill in 1993 supports this conclusion; as does the negative effect of Senate Majority Leader Byrd's less supportive stances on President Carter's legislative efforts. Bond and Fleisher also found, however, that if the president's party was the minority in Congress, positions adopted by central and committee leaders had little effect on improving the president's prospects of success.[60]

This analysis demonstrates very clearly then how the partisan and ideological composition of Congress places real limits on a president's ability to win congressional approval of legislation. In a multivariate analysis which sought to measure the effects of presidential skills and popularity, Congress' partisan and ideological composition, and various other factors on presidential success in

Table 9.4. Percentages of votes on which presidents' party bases in Congress unified for the president, 1953–1993

Congress	President	HOUSE		SENATE	
		Number of legislators in president's party base	Percentage of votes on which base unified in favour of president	Number of legislators in president's party base	Percentage of votes on which base unified in favour of president
83rd	Eisenhower	201	62%	36	70%
84th	Eisenhower	129	32%	44	53%
85th	Eisenhower	178	29%	34	55%
86th	Eisenhower	141	53%	23	58%
mean	*Eisenhower*		43%		59%
87th	Kennedy	188	88%	42	78%
88th	Kennedy	166	95%	45	64%
mean	*Kennedy*		90%		74%
88th	Johnson	166	92%	45	80%
89th	Johnson	203	93%	51	63%
90th	Johnson	180	80%	44	44%
mean	*Johnson*		87%		61%
91st	Nixon	160	30%	31	56%
92nd	Nixon	156	64%	32	73%
93rd	Nixon	157	52%	28	56%
mean	*Nixon*		49%		60%
93rd	Ford	157	18%	28	42%
94th	Ford	120	53%	25	69%
mean	*Ford*		45%		60%
95th	Carter	223	57%	44	65%
96th	Carter	230	58%	51	50%
mean	*Carter*		57%		57%
97th	Reagan	168	41%	43	72%
98th	Reagan	150	49%	43	61%
mean	*Reagan*		46%		68%
103rd*	Clinton	222	74%	50	79%

Source: Bond and Fleisher, *The President in the Legislative Arena*, Tables 4.1 and 4.6; and Bond and Fleisher, 'Clinton and Congress: A First-Year Assessment', *American Politics Quarterly*, 23 (1995), p. 366–7.

* First session only.

Congress, Bond and Fleisher found only congressional variables to have strong and significant effects. Not surprisingly, the greatest change in the probability of president's being successful was associated with changing the president's party base from a majority to minority; and the effects of high presidential skills and presidential popularity were extremely weak and inconsistent. Echoing Edwards' verdict, presidential influence in Congress is 'at the margins'.[61]

Like Mark Twain's cat who avoided cold as well as hot stoves, it is important that we draw the right conclusions here. The importance of Congress' partisan and ideological composition and the marginal significance of presidential skills and popularity do not mean that who is elected president does not matter. Clearly, it does matter. Presidents make important autonomous decisions about which bills they will send to Congress, about which bills they will give a high priority, about their responses to congressional initiatives, about appointments, about how they organise their presidencies, and about how they will respond to the changing political and policy environment. All these decisions involve personal choices by the president. All these decisions interact with the strategic environment in which Congress and the president relate to one another, which cannot be controlled by the president alone, the Congress alone, or even by both together.

The strategic environment for legislating

'Presidents are not created equal, politically or otherwise', Jones has argued.[62] Recent presidents may be placed into five categories according to the strategic circumstances in which they entered the White House and, in particular, how they achieved their party's nomination and what were the results of the election. Six presidents were initially nominated by their parties and subsequently elected, three were renominated and re-elected, three were non-elected presidents, two were elected vice-presidents, and one was an elected heir-apparent.[63] Of the elected presidents, Eisenhower in 1952 and Reagan in 1980 were elected by substantial margins but Kennedy in 1960, Nixon in 1968, Carter in 1976, and Clinton in 1992 only won by narrow margins. All three re-elected presidents (in the second category) – Eisenhower in 1956, Nixon in 1972, and Reagan in 1984 – won by landslides. Presidents in the last three categories were all 'takeover' presidents. In the third category, Truman, Johnson, and Ford all entered the White House as a result of the death or resignation of their predecessor; and took over their predecessor's organisation and priorities. The first two of these, constituting the fourth category, subsequently won their party's nomination and were elected themselves on their own efforts. And finally, uniquely, Bush was an heir-apparent president who was nominated and elected after serving with his predecessor.

From this classification, it is evident that six of the most recent presidents, falling into the last three categories, entered the White House as beneficiaries of circumstances. They were not elected initially in their own right; and probably would not have been had they sought the presidency. Only three out of the ten presidents since World War II – Eisenhower (1952), Johnson (1964), and Reagan (1980) – entered the White House under optimal conditions: in that they successfully contested their party's nomination and won the presidential election by a landslide; and their party made substantial gains in Congress that were associated with their campaigns. Most post-war presidents, however – Truman (1948), Kennedy (1960), Nixon (1968), Carter (1976), Bush (1988), and Clinton (1992) – had to make do with less than optimal conditions. Eisenhower (1956), Nixon (1972), and Reagan (1984) won re-election by huge margins but found that Congress remained under the control of the opposite party. Furthermore, as Table 9.5 shows, even those presidents whose tenures began in optimal conditions found subsequently that their strategic circumstances deteriorated as their party's base in Congress was reduced after the next mid-term elections: Truman faced a Congress controlled by the opposition party after less than two years, Eisenhower found the same after 1954, as did Clinton after 1994; and Reagan faced both houses under the control of the opposition party after 1986. Indeed, in the period 1946 to 1996 there has been split-party government a majority of the time; and since 1968, this pattern has occurred on 83 per cent of occasions.

Depending on how they become president and the varying strategic circumstances in relation to Congress which they face, it is logical that different presidents should pursue different governing strategies with Congress which reflect what they can reasonably be expected to accomplish.[64] What is an appropriate policy strategy for one president may not be appropriate for another, and what is appropriate for a president in any two-year period may be inappropriate for the same president in another period, if strategic circumstances change. If the party of a newly elected president also does well in the congressional elections, it is likely that a president will be able to pursue an 'assertive' policy strategy, at least until the next election – as Johnson did after Kennedy's death and again after the 1964 elections, and Reagan did after the 1980 elections. However, when a president wins office by a narrow margin and the congressional results are not clear – as Truman found after 1948, Kennedy after 1960, Nixon after 1968, Carter after 1976, and Clinton after 1992 – the strategic circumstances are not so advantageous. Logically, in such circumstances, a president should pursue a 'compensatory' strategy wherein he seeks to augment claims for congressional support by finding supplementary ways of authenticating his leadership – for example, by pursuing the sort of 'going public' strategy outlined in Chapter 7. Re-elected presidents who return to the White House with strong personal support but face a Congress elected on different messages may be best advised to pursue a 'guardian' strategy which protects their earlier achievements – as Eisenhower did after 1956, Nixon after 1972, Reagan after 1984, and Bush after 1988. Finally, the optimal policy strategy for takeover non-elected presidents is to depend on the legacy of their predecessor and adopt either a 'custodial' strategy – as Truman and Johnson did

Table 9.5. Patterns of party control of Congress and the presidency, 1945–1996

			Congress		
Congress	President	President's Party	House	Senate	Party Control
79th	Truman	Democrat	Democrat	Democrat	Single
80th	Truman	Democrat	Republican	Republican	Split
81st	Truman	Democrat	Democrat	Democrat	Single
82nd	Truman	Democrat	Democrat	Democrat	Single
83rd	Eisenhower	Republican	Republican	Republican	Single
84th	Eisenhower	Republican	Democrat	Democrat	Split
85th	Eisenhower	Republican	Democrat	Democrat	Split
86th	Eisenhower	Republican	Democrat	Democrat	Split
87th	Kennedy	Democrat	Democrat	Democrat	Single
88th	Kennedy/Johnson	Democrat	Democrat	Democrat	Single
89th	Johnson	Democrat	Democrat	Democrat	Single
90th	Johnson	Democrat	Democrat	Democrat	Single
91st	Nixon	Republican	Democrat	Democrat	Split
92nd	Nixon	Republican	Democrat	Democrat	Split
93rd	Nixon/Ford	Republican	Democrat	Democrat	Split
94th	Ford	Republican	Democrat	Democrat	Split
95th	Carter	Democrat	Democrat	Democrat	Single
96th	Carter	Democrat	Democrat	Democrat	Single
97th	Reagan	Republican	Democrat	Republican	Split
98th	Reagan	Republican	Democrat	Republican	Split
99th	Reagan	Republican	Democrat	Republican	Split
100th	Reagan	Republican	Democrat	Democrat	Split
101st	Bush	Republican	Democrat	Democrat	Split
102nd	Bush	Republican	Democrat	Democrat	Split
103rd	Clinton	Democrat	Democrat	Democrat	Single
104th	Clinton	Democrat	Republican	Republican	Split

in 1945 and 1963 – or a 'restorative' strategy as Ford did in 1974. Most recent presidents have recognised the strategic limitations placed on their presidencies and pursued optimal strategies with Congress. For different reasons, four did not: Truman (1948), Nixon (1972), Carter (1976), and Clinton (1992), all of whom pursued assertive strategies when strategic conditions warranted compensatory strategies – in each case not without success.

Another important element of the strategic context in which the president and Congress legislate is the more permanent policy environment which is centred primarily on Congress. As we showed in an earlier chapter, Congress' legislative agenda is far larger than the president's; and most of the policy issues which face a president exist already before an incumbent enters the White House. Indeed, it is likely that these issues were the focus of much of the rhetoric and debate in the presidential election campaign. The president then enters a policy debate which has usually ensued for some time. James Sundquist makes this point well in his study of policy-making in the 1950s and 1960s when he writes that:

> The ultimate results were, in a sense, *compelled by the circumstances of the problems themselves* [our emphasis]. Though the imagination and skill and doggedness of the political actors were indeed remarkable, these men [Eisenhower, Kennedy and Johnson] nevertheless seem as actors, following a script that was written by events.[65]

Following a review of the nature and ambitiousness of the policy agenda of each post-war presidential administration, of the major events which influenced that agenda, and of the president's impact on subsequent agendas, Jones' study concludes that very few presidents have the resources to change the policy agenda significantly. Congressional approval of President Johnson's expansion of social welfare programmes in 1964 and 1965, and of President Reagan's new revenue and spending priorities in 1981 are exceptions. The best that most can hope to achieve is to become 'part of a continuous though changing government'[66] wherein policy choices are constrained.

Legislating together

Given then the limitations imposed on congressional–presidential relations by strategic conditions – as well as the constitutional and institutional limitations – it is clear that an interpretation of the legislative process which rests primarily on presidential efforts and presidential success is mistaken and leads typically to unrealistic expectations of what a separated system can deliver. It is not surprising, therefore, to find that a number of studies of congressional–presidential relations emphasise the role of both Congress and the president *legislating together*, as 'tandem institutions' within a separated system of checks and balances.[67] In a study completed many decades ago, Chamberlain found after examining the legislative histories of various proposals between 1873 and 1940 that congressional influence was preponderant in twice as many cases as presidential influence – although the number of cases of presidential preponderance increased dramatically after 1933. Twelve of the ninety pieces of legislation (13 per cent) were approved, moreover under conditions of split-party government. Chamberlain concluded that 'the president is [not] less important than generally supposed but that Congress is more important', because the length of time in which issues and legislation remained under legislators' consideration ensured that most important statutes had deep legislative roots. The effect of presidential attention, Chamberlain argued, was to elevate a bill 'from the obscurity of just another bill to the prominence of an administration measure. Administration experts had participated by drafting a new bill but there was not very much in the new bill that had not been present in one or more earlier drafts.'[68] A total of 79 out of 90 acts reviewed in the study were found to have their origins in previous congressional bills.

A follow-up study of legislation considered between 1940 and 1967 also gave Congress a major role in initiating new policies.[69] Steven Shull's analysis of legislating between 1953 and 1975 found that Congress was dominant in more policy areas than was the president, including farm policy, public works, and crime. Most significantly, the typical pattern was a mixture of executive and legislative leadership.[70] Jones' analysis of the legislative histories of twenty-eight important enactments over the post-war period also found many different patterns of institutional interaction but, as in Shull's study, the most common pattern of law-making was balanced participation by both institutions. Balanced participation, with the president assigning a high priority to the proposal, occurred in five cases (18 per cent); and genuinely balanced participation – the most frequent pattern of institutional interaction – occurred in ten cases (36 per cent). Major bills enacted through truly balanced participation included the National Housing Act of 1949, the Atomic Energy Act of 1952, the Civil Rights Act of 1957, the Clean Air Act of 1963, the Occupational Safety and Health Act of 1970, Social Security Reform of 1983, and the 1990 budget. Like the previous studies, Jones' analysis found that presidential preponderance was atypical. Presidents were preponderant in six cases (21 per cent) and Congress in seven cases (25 per cent). A brief review of enactments in 1993 and 1994 show a similar pattern. Measures such as the Family and Medical Leave Act, the Motor Voter bill, the Interstate Banking Act, and the crime bill had long gestation periods in Congress before they were promoted by President Clinton.

Focusing on particular Congresses, rather than enactments, Jones also found that balanced participation occurred just as frequently under single as split-party government.[71] In cases of single party government, balanced participation usually resulted from a Democratic president operating from a weak electoral base while his party maintained substantial majorities in the House and Senate – as in the cases of Truman in the 79th Congress, Kennedy in the 87th Congress, Carter in the 95th, and Clinton in the 103rd Congress. Here, presidents enjoyed advantages arising either from their surprising victories or the freshness of their messages but members of Congress reasoned that they could nevertheless act independently from the president because they did not owe their election to his coat tails. In cases of split-party or divided government, balanced interaction between Congress and the president was related to congressional Democrats retaining their majorities at the same time that voters elected a Republican president – for example, Eisenhower in 1956, Nixon in 1968 and 1972, and Reagan in 1984 – sometimes by landslides.

Table 9.6. Party control of Congress and the presidency and patterns of
institutional interaction, 1945–1994

President and Congress	Institutional Interaction	Party Control
Truman		
79th	Balanced	Single
80th	Congressional	Split
81st	Balanced	Single
82nd	Balanced/Congressional	Single
Eisenhower		
83rd	Balanced	Single
84th	Balanced	Split
85th	Balanced	Split
86th	Congressional	Split
Kennedy/Johnson		
87th	Balanced	Single
88th	Balanced/Presidential	Single
89th	Presidential	Single
90th	Balanced	Single
Nixon/Ford		
91st	Balanced	Split
92nd	Balanced	Split
93rd	Balanced/Congressional	Split
94th	Congressional (stalemate)	Split
Carter		
95th	Balanced	Single
96th	Balanced/Congressional	Single
Reagan		
97th	Presidential	Split
98th	Balanced	Split
99th	Balanced	Split
100th	Congressional	Split
Bush		
101st	Congressional	Split
102nd	Congressional (stalemate)	Split
Clinton		
103rd	Balanced	Single

Source: Charles O. Jones, *The Presidency In A Separated System* (Washington, D.C.: Brookings Institution, 1994)
p. 291.

Importantly, in the context of contemporary debate in the United States about government stalemate and 'gridlock', Jones' analysis makes clear that over the post-war period, split-party government was associated with a number of different patterns of interaction between Congress and the president, not just stalemate. As Table 9.6 shows, when control of government was split between the parties in the 80th, 86th, 100th, and 101st Congresses, Congress was preponderant. When government was divided in the 84th, 85th, 91st, 92nd, 93rd, 98th, and 99th Congress, there was balanced interaction. Only in the 94th and 102nd Congresses was there stalemate. Just as single party control does not guarantee institutional cooperation, so split-party government does not lead necessarily to stalemate. Under conditions of split-party government, the separated system continued to produce laws. Mayhew's detailed analysis of important laws enacted between 1946 and 1990 showed that 152 out of a sample of 267 (57 per cent) became law. A study by Jones of a smaller sample of the legislation selected by Mayhew also found that production of major legislation was not interrupted by split-party government: 16 of the 28 selected laws, including the Taft-Hartley Labor-Management Relations Act of 1947, the 1949 European Recovery Act, the Federal Aid Highway Act of 1956, the 1974 Budget and Impoundment Control Act of 1974, the Economic Recovery Act of 1981, the Omnibus Trade Act of 1988, and the Deficit Reduction Act of 1990 were all enacted by when Congress and the presidency were controlled by different parties.[72] Mayhew explained the continuation in legislative production as a function of congressional norms, electoral incentives, presidential leadership skills, events and public mood, all of which provided 'anchors of constancy'. The key for Jones is a set of party-based negotiating activities which leads to the creation of winning coalitions. Sometimes these activities are bipartisan (when Congress and the president agree on the need for policy action); sometimes co-partisan (where party control of Congress and the president is split and where legislative proposals are developed in parallel either by each institution or by the two parties in the House and Senate); and sometimes cross-partisan (where an important segment of one party works with and supports the other party – often the president's party – which initiates policy). Jones found few examples of bipartisanship in his sample of enactments but many examples of cross-partisanship – notably when southern conservative Democrats joined with Republicans to form a conservative coalition in support of a Republican president.[73]

The message which comes out loud and clear from this empirical research is that the business of legislating in the American separated system is a shared process. It is about Congress and the president legislating together. It is not about the extent to which Congress approves or fails to approve a set of proposals worked out exclusively within the executive branch. 'When it comes to making laws in Washington,' Jones observes, 'it is never done solely in the White House, it is sometimes done largely on Capitol Hill, and it is normally done with a substantial amount of cross-institutional and cross-partisan interaction through elaborate sequences featuring varying degrees of iteration.'[74] Contrary to presidency-centred interpretations which suggest that America's national government can only function properly when the president is dominant and/or Congress and the presidency are controlled by the same party, presidents find that when they enter the legislative arena they must accommodate themselves to a continuing process of law-making, which is based on Congress. On occasion, they may be crucial players in this process, particularly in designating legislative priorities, but often they are not – and Congress continues to produce legislation without them or parallel to their own efforts.

Having explained in this chapter how the separated system introduces considerable fluidity and imprecision into the relationship between Congress and the president in the legislative arena, in the next chapter we examine in detail the different components of the separation of powers and how and to what extent the Supreme Court has resolved the inevitable jurisdictional disputes between the legislature and the executive arising from it.

Notes

1 James Madison, Alexander Hamilton, and John Jay, *The Federalist Papers* (New York and Toronto: New English Library, 1961), p. 450.

2 This idea was floated in late 1994 as President Clinton tried to persuade Congress to approve health care legislation. The last president to invoke this power was Truman who in 1948 called Congress back into session to consider important price control, housing and other legislation. No president has used the power to adjourn Congress.

3 Mark A. Peterson, *Legislating Together. The White House and Capitol Hill From Eisenhower to Reagan* (Cambridge, MA and London: Harvard University Press, 1990), p. 3.

4 Edward S. Corwin, *The President: Office and Powers* (New York: New York University Press, 1940), p. 200. James L. Sundquist refers to 'the constitutional dilemma', see his *Constitutional Reform and Effective Government*, rev. edn (Washington, D.C.: The Brookings Institution, 1992), ch. 1.

5 The most egregious formulation of this view is Huntington's: 'Congress can defend its autonomy only by refusing to legislate, and it can legislate only by surrendering its autonomy . . . If Congress legislates, it subordinates itself to the President; if it refuses to legislate, it alienates itself from public opinion. Congress can assert its power or it can pass laws; but it cannot do both.' Samuel P. Huntington, 'Congressional Responses to the Twentieth Century', in David B. Truman (ed.), *The Congress and America's Future* (Englewood Cliffs, NJ: Prentice Hall, 1965), p. 6.

6 Thomas E. Cronin, *The State of the Presidency*, 2nd edn (Boston: Little, Brown, 1980), pp. 138–40.

7 See, for example, Lloyd Cutler, 'To Form a Government', *Foreign Affairs*, 59 (1980), pp. 127–39; Charles M. Hardin, *Presidential Power and Accountability* (Chicago: University of Chicago Press, 1974); Huntington, 'Congressional Responses to the

Twentieth Century'; and Barry M. Blechman, *The Politics of National Security. Congress and US Defense Policy* (New York and Oxford: Oxford University Press, 1990).

8   Woodrow Wilson, *Constitutional Government in the United States* (New York: Columbia University Press, 1908), p. 49; Richard E. Neustadt, *Presidential Power* (New York: John Wiley, 1960), p. 185; Robert A. Dahl, *The New American Political (Dis)Order* (Berkeley, CA: Institute of Governmental Studies Press, 1994), p. 18.

9   James L. Sundquist, 'Needed: A Political Theory for the New Era of Coalition Government in the United States', *Political Science Quarterly*, 103 (1988–9), pp. 613–35; Cutler, 'To Form a Government'; Nelson W. Polsby, *Consequences of Party Reform* (New York: Oxford University Press, 1983), pp. 105–14; and Dahl, *The New American Political (Dis)Order*, pp. 19–23.

10   Stephen Wayne, *The Legislative Presidency* (New York: Harper and Row, 1978).

11   James Bryce, *The American Commonwealth* (New York: Macmillan, 1889), vol. 1, p. 58.

12   Wilfred Binkley, *President and Congress* (New York: Random House, 1947), p. 298; Wilfred E. Binkley, 'The President as Chief Legislator', *Annals of the American Academy of Political and Social Science*, 307 (1956), p. 95.

13   Arthur S. Schlesinger, *The Age of Roosevelt. The Coming of the New Deal* (Boston: Houghton Mifflin, 1958), pp. 7–8.

14   Susan M. Hartman, *Truman and the 80th Congress* (Columbia, MO: University of Missouri Press, 1971), p. 122; Richard E. Neustadt, 'Presidency and Legislation: Planning the President's Programme', *American Political Science Review*, 49 (1955), p. 1015.

15   Wayne, *The Legislative Presidency*, p. 20.

16   Between 1933 and 1945, Roosevelt vetoed 138 public bills, 60 of which were of national significance. Richard A. Watson, *Presidential Vetoes and Public Policy* (Lawrence, KS: University Press of Kansas, 1993), pp. 32–6; Wayne, *The Legislative Presidency*, pp. 85–91; Fred I. Greenstein, 'Change and Continuity in the Modern Presidency', in Anthony King (ed.), *The New American Political System* (Washington, D.C.: American Enterprise Institute, 1978), pp. 47–53.

17   Greenstein, 'Change and Continuity', p. 59; Wayne, *The Legislative Presidency*, p. 39; Nigel Bowles, *The White House and Capitol Hill: The Politics of Prseidential Persuasion* (Oxford: Oxford University Press, 1987), p. 17.

18   Theodore C. Sorensen, *Kennedy* (London: Pan Books, 1965), pp. 394–5; Bowles, *The White House and Capitol Hill*, esp. ch. 2; and John Hart, *The Presidential Branch. From Washington to Clinton* (Chatham, NJ: Chatham House, 1994), pp. 190–3.

19   Wayne, *The Legislative Presidency*, pp. 22, 158–61; Bowles, *The White House and Capitol Hill*, p. 186.

20   John E. Owens, 'Clinton and Congress: An Early Assessment', *Politics Review*, 3 (1993), p. 7.

21   Norman J. Ornstein, Thomas E. Mann, and Michael J. Malbin (eds), *Vital Statistics on Congress, 1993–1994* (Washington, D.C.: Congressional Quarterly Press, 1994), pp. 195–6; and Steve Langdon, 'Clinton's High Victory Rate Conceals Disappointments', *Congressional Quarterly Weekly Report*, 31 December 1994, pp. 3619–23 and 3654. The scores' limitations are discussed in George C. Edwards, *At the Margins. Presidential Leadership of Congress* (New Haven, CT and London: Yale

University Press, 1989), ch. 2; Peterson, *Legislating Together*, Appendix B; Jon Bond and Richard Fleisher, *The President in the Legislative Arena* (Chicago and London: University of Chicago Press, 1990), pp. 60–6; and Charles O. Jones, *The Presidency in a Separated System* (Washington, D.C.: The Brookings Institution, 1994), p. 193.

22 Jones, *The Presidency in a Separated System*, pp. 1–2.

23 Anthony King, 'A Mile and a Half Is a Long Way', in King (ed.), *Both Ends of The Avenue* (Washington, D.C.: American Enterprise Institute, 1983), pp. 247–8.

24 Richard E. Neustadt, *Presidential Power and the Modern Presidents. The Politics of Leadership From Roosevelt to Reagan* (New York: Free Press, 1990), pp. 29, 50, 54, and 68.

25 George C. Edwards, *Presidential Influence in Congress* (San Francisco: W. H. Freeman, 1980), chs 5–7; and Reo Christenson, 'Presidential Leadership of Congress', in Thomas E. Cronin (ed.), *Rethinking the Presidency* (Boston: Little, Brown, 1982), pp. 255–70.

26 Doris Kearns, *Lyndon Johnson and the American Dream* (New York: Harper and Row, 1976), p. 226; Bowles, *The White House and Capitol Hill*, pp. 54–6, 102–4, 126–7.

27 Kearns, *Lyndon Johnson and the American Dream*, p. 233; Wayne, *The Legislative Presidency*, p. 151; Bowles, *The White House and Capitol Hill*, pp. 47–8.

28 James P. Pfiffner, *The Strategic Presidency. Hitting the Ground Running* (Chicago: Dorsey Press, 1988), p. 144; Thomas P. O'Neill, *Man of the House. The Life and Political Memoirs of Speaker Tip O'Neill* (New York: Random House, 1987), p. 344; Charles O. Jones, 'Ronald Reagan and the US Congress: Visible-Hand Politics', in Charles O. Jones, *The Reagan Legacy. Promise and Performance* (Chatham, NJ: Chatham House, 1988), pp. 34–7.

29 Howard Paster quoted in the *Washington Post*, November 23 1993, p. A19.

30 Kevin Merida, 'On Key Votes, House Whips Start Cracking',*Washington Post,* May 31 1993, p. A6.

31 George Hager and David S. Cloud, 'Democrats Pull Off Squeaker in Approving Clinton Plan', *Congressional Quarterly Weekly Report*, May 29 1993, p. 1340; 'The Grease Factor: Bargains With Congress', *Newsweek*, June 7 1993, p. 18; and David Von Drehle, 'The Royal Treatment. Clinton Woos Backbencher Like a Peer', *Washington Post*, May 28 1993, p. A1.

32 Irwin B. Arieff, 'Carter and Congress: Strangers to the End', in Congressional Quarterly, *Almanac 1980* (Washington, D.C.: Congressional Quarterly Press, 1980), p. 5 quoted in Charles O. Jones, *The Trusteeship Presidency. Jimmy Carter and the United States Congress* (Baton Rouge, LA and London: Louisiana State University Press, 1988), p. 200; Charles O. Jones, 'Presidential Negotiation With Congress', in King (ed.), *Both Ends of the Avenue*, pp. 118–23.

33 Barbara Kellerman, *The Political Presidency. Practice of Leadership From Kennedy Through Reagan* (New York: Oxford University Press, 1984), pp. 88 and 155.

34 Peterson, *Legislating Together*, p. 267. In his study of legislating between 1953 and 1984, Peterson shows that presidents' least consequential initiatives were more than twice as likely to be denied active consideration by Congress than were those of the greatest consequence. Almost 40 per cent were ignored (p. 183).

35 Edwards, *Presidential Influence in Congress*, p. 119.

36 Rowland Evans and Robert Novak, *Lyndon B. Johnson: The Exercise of Power* (New York: Signet, 1968), pp. 514–15; Lyndon B. Johnson, *The Vantage Point.*

Perspectives of the Presidency 1963–1969 (New York: Popular Library, 1971), pp. 441 and 443.

37 James MacGregor Burns, *The Power To Lead. The Crisis of the American Presidency* (New York: Simon and Schuster, 1984), p. 38.

38 Edwards, *At the Margins*, p. 211; Bert A. Rockman, *The Leadership Question: The Presidency and the American System* (New York: Praeger, 1984).

39 For example, Terry Sullivan, 'Headcounts, Expectations, and Presidential Coalitions in Congress', *American Journal of Political Science*, 32 (1988), pp. 567–88; and Brad Lockerbie and Stephen A. Borelli, 'Getting Inside the Beltway: Perceptions of Presidential Skill and Success in Congress', *British Journal of Political Science*, 19 (1989), pp. 97–106.

40 See for example Neustadt, *Presidential Power*, pp. 40 and 71; Edwards, *At the Margins*, pp. 102–7; Samuel Kernell, *Going Public: New Strategies of Presidential Leadership* (Washington, D.C.: Congressional Quarterly Press, 1986).

41 Ann Devroy, 'Surprise Vote Blocks House Action of the Crime Bill', *Washington Post*, August 12 1994, p. A14.

42 Barbara Hinckley, *The Symbolic Presidency: How Presidents Portray Themselves* (New York: Routledge, 1990), ch. 1; Lyn Ragsdale, 'The Politics of Presidential Speechmaking, 1949–1980', *American Political Science Review*, 78 (1984), pp. 971–84; cf. George C. Edwards, *The Public Presidency. The Pursuit of Popular Support* (New York: St Martin's Press, 1983), ch. 2.

43 Charles W. Ostrom and Dennis M. Simon, 'Promise and Performance: A Dynamic Model of Presidential Popularity', *American Political Science Review*, 79 (1985), pp. 334–58; Edwards, *Presidential Influence in Congress*, pp. 108–10; and Douglas Rivers and Nancy Rose, 'Passing the President's Program: Public Opinion and Presidential Influence in Congress', *American Journal of Political Science*, 29 (1985), pp. 183–96.

44 Jones, *The Presidency in a Separated System*, p. 118; Edwards, *At the Margins*, ch. 6; Paul C. Light, *The President's Agenda. Domestic Policy Choice From Kennedy to Carter* (Baltimore and London: Johns Hopkins University Press, 1983), pp. 73 and 82; and Jon R. Bond and Richard Fleisher, 'The Limits of Presidential Popularity as a Source of Influence in the US House', *Legislative Studies Quarterly*, 5 (1980), pp. 69–78.

45 John W. Kingdon, *Congressmen's Voting Decisions*, 3rd edn (Ann Arbor, MI: The University of Michigan Press, 1989), ch. 6.

46 Edwards, *At the Margins*, pp. 40–4.

47 David S. Broder, 'Democrats Worrying. Clinton's Problems Raise Fears for 1994', *Washington Post*, June 9 1993, p. A16; Kitty Cunningham, 'With Democrat in White House, Partisanship Hits New High', *Congressional Quarterly Weekly Report*, December 18 1993, pp. 3432–33.

48 Gary C. Jacobson, *The Politics of Congressional Elections*, 3rd edn (New York: Harper Collins, 1992), pp. 158 and 162).

49 Owens, 'Clinton and Congress', p. 7.

50 Neustadt, *Presidential Power*, p. 29.

51 Sorensen, *Kennedy*, p. 383.

52 John R. Hibbing, *Congressional Careers. Contours of Life in the US House of Representatives* (Chapel Hill, NC: University of North Carolina Press, 1991), ch. 5; Kingdon, *Congressmen's Voting Decisions*, pp. 274–8; Aage R. Clausen, *How Congressmen Decide. A Policy Focus* (New York: St Martin's Press, 1973).

53 Kingdon, *Congressmen's Voting Decisions*, ch. 3.
54 Bond and Fleisher, *The President in the Legislative Arena*, p. 164.
55 Louis Koenig, *The Chief Executive*, 4th edn (New York: Harcourt Brace Jovanovich), 1981, p. 167.
56 Bond and Fleisher, 'The Limits of Presidential Popularity', p. 75; and Richard Fleisher and Jon R. Bond, 'Assessing Presidential Support in the House: Lessons From Reagan and Carter', *Journal of Politics*, 45 (1983), pp. 748–53.
57 Kingdon, *Congressmen's Voting Decisions*, p. 268.
58 Bond and Fleisher, *The President in the Legislative Arena*, ch. 4; and Jon R. Bond and Richard Fleisher, 'Clinton and Congress: A First Year Assessment', *American Politics Quarterly*, 23 (1995). This approach is a variation on a theme pursued in James MacGregor Burns, *The Deadlock of Democracy: Four Party Politics in America* (Englewood Cliffs, NJ: Prentice Hall, 1963).
59 Bond and Fleisher, *The President in the Legislative Arena*, pp. 94–9; and Bond and Fleisher, 'Clinton and Congress', table 4.
60 Bond and Fleisher, *The President in the Legislative Arena*, pp. 134–49.
61 *Ibid.*, pp. 224–9.
62 Jones, *The Presidency in a Separated System*, p. 27.
63 *Ibid.*, pp. 28–41.
64 *Ibid.*, pp. 48–51; and Charles O. Jones, *Separate But Equal Branches. Congress and the Presidency* (Chatham, NJU: Chatham House, 1995), p. 251.
65 James L. Sundquist, *Politics and Policy. The Eisenhower, Kennedy, and Johnson Years* (Washington, D.C.: The Brookings Institution, 1968), p. 507.
66 Jones, *The Presidency in a Separated System*, p. 181.
67 Peterson, *Legislating Together*.
68 Lawrence H. Chamberlain, *The President, Congress and Legislation* (New York: Columbia University Press, 1946), p. 454.
69 Ronald C. Moe and Steven C. Teel, 'Congress As Policymaker: A Necessary Reappraisal', *Political Science Quarterly*, 85 (1970), pp. 443–70.
70 Steven A. Shull, *Domestic Policy Formation. Presidential–Congressional Partnership?* (Westport, CT.: Greenwood Press, 1983), p. 166. Even at the height of presidential ascendancy, a few studies pointed to Congress' independent policy-making role. See John S. Saloma, *Congress and the New Politics* (Boston: Little, Brown, 1969); Sundquist, *Politics and Policy;* and Gary Orfield, *Congressional Power: Congress and Social Change* (New York: Harcourt Brace Jovanovich, 1975).
71 Jones, *Separate But Equal Branches*, pp. 10–13. A valuable study of banking laws enacted between 1823 and 1986 shows that 92 per cent were passed without presidential involvement. See Jean Reith Schroedel, *Congress, the President, and Policy-making. A Historical Analysis* (Armonk, NY and London: M. E. Sharp, 1994).
72 David R. Mayhew, *Divided We Govern. Party Control, Law-making, and Investigations, 1946–1990* (New Haven, CT: Yale University Press, 1991); Jones, The Presidency in a Separated System, ch. 8; and Schroedel, *Congress, the President, and Policy-making*, p. 185
73 Jones, *The Presidency in a Separated System*, pp. 19–23, 270–3.
74 *Ibid.*, p. 273.

CHAPTER 10

Interpreting the separation of powers

If there is a single theme that characterises the relationship between the presidency and Congress, and which conditions both their political behaviour and their relative contribution to policy, then there is little doubt that it is the separation of powers which provides such a defining property. The separation of powers not only provides the central organising principle of the federal government but typifies the Constitution's underlying purpose of rendering government power safe by demarcation and division. By explicitly allocating power to functionally discrete entities of government, the Constitution's designers are regarded as having set in motion a mechanism of competitive interplay between institutions that has ensured a self-perpetuating dispersal of power and, with it, the preservation of individual liberties. The separation of powers format establishes the institutional structures and operational rules of the political game in Washington, while at the same time generating a dynamic imprecision within government that ensures jurisdictional tensions and demarcation disputes at the highest levels of government. It is through the separation of power and its associated checks and balances, therefore, that the presidency and Congress confront one another and also learn to coexist together. The distinctive features of Washington politics – the language of institutional differentiation, the strategies of contested authority, and the appeals for constitutional legitimacy – are derived from, and expressed through, the principles and technicalities of the separation of powers. It is the latter that provides an underlying framework of constitutional reference which does not merely inform debate. It motivates and energises political engagement and penetrates the political calculations of every office-holder in Washington.

The conceptual, structural and cultural components of separated powers

At its most basic level, the separation of powers refers firstly to the acceptance that government can be reduced conceptually to three main functions; secondly to the conscious belief that government can be structurally designed to reflect these functions; thirdly to the belief that in the American system just such a framework has been achieved; and lastly to the political value attached to its existence and influence at the centre of government. The three functions in question are the legislative functions (i.e. law-making), the executive function (i.e. law implementation), and the judicial function (i.e. law interpretation and judgement). These differentiated functions possess a conceptual and chronological order in that a law must first be enacted before it can be carried out and then subsequently adjudicated and refined in contested cases. Conceptual priority and chronology are also significant in the specific circumstances of America's adoption of a system of separated powers. As a highly self-conscious Republic, the republican assembly possessed pride of place in the states and in the original Articles of Confederation. In constructing a federal government, the Founding Fathers' point of departure was that the legislature would be the first branch of government. To many of their contemporaries, an executive was an optional extra and at the very least a dangerous luxury. Nevertheless, to many of the Fathers, it was the assembly which had become a source of instability and which required a separate and forceful executive to redress the balance. A powerful executive department was established in response to the pre-existing norm of a sovereign assembly. The third element – that of federal judiciary – was certainly established by the founders but the exact scope of its power was not given close consideration. The Supreme Court's claims to judicial review were developed incrementally through precedent and case law until, at a much later point in the Republic's history, it became evident that the three separate institutions were comparable in constitutional weight and political standing.

The fundamental rationale of the separation of powers is that by identifying the three constituent elements of government and, thereupon, creating and sustaining a division between them, the ever present possibility of government lapsing into arbitrary rule would be averted. Montesquieu's book *The Spirit of the Laws* (1748)[1] had done much to popularise the idea of the separation of powers amongst the elites of the American colonies in the pre-revolutionary period. To Montesquieu, the success and stability of the British Constitution was attributable to the way it had evolved into a structure in which the three functions of government were performed by three more or less separate institutions of government (i.e. legislature – Parliament; executive – government/monarchy; judiciary – courts). It is immaterial whether Montesquieu was correct or not in his estimation of the separation achieved in the British system. What is clear is that his theorem on separated powers as the keystone of a stable and benign structure of government was assimilated in America as a form of received wisdom. It quickly acquired the status of republican authority. As a consequence, it was never a matter of *whether* the new states and the new federal government would adopt the separation of powers system. It was only ever a question of *how* it would be achieved. But even this more limited question posed a number of very demanding problems especially to the Founding Fathers.

The most difficult was squaring a separation of powers with a fully developed system of checks and balances. Although these two devices are now uniformly seen as being integral to one another, there is in fact no necessary connection between them. A separation of powers is based upon qualitative differentiation and even an implicit hierarchy of functions. Checks and balances on the other hand, proceed on the assumption of an interaction between necessarily homogeneous and coequal entities. The former envisages isolation, specialisation, and independence while the latter is synonymous with connections, friction, and interdependence. The former was a contemporary doctrine derived from the increased functional segmentation of the state following the Glorious Revolution and the emergence of a constitutional monarchy with an increasingly assertive Parliament. Checks and balances, on the other hand, were drawn from the ancient doctrine of mixed government, in which the best and most sustainable form of governance was considered to be one which incorporated an aggregate of class interests.[2] Montesquieu's conception of separated powers in the British Constitution strongly implied a parallel system of checks and balances drawn from the elements of mixed government which were still so evident in the British context (i.e. monarchy – crown, aristocracy – House of Lords, and democracy – House of Commons). The anomaly of the two principles fused together was a product of Britain's long constitutional history.

Montesquieu's model, therefore, was only of limited value to the Founding Fathers who were not merely engaged in reinventing government from first principles, but were doing so from an intellectual and cultural attachment to classlessness. The American Revolution had formally banished monarchy and aristocracy. Only the people and republicanism remained. It was difficult to claim that checks and balances were the national accoutrements of separated powers without compromising the principles of republicanism. What could possibly check and balance the people represented in the legislation if it were not something other than the people? It was surely a matter of logic that 'contrary to republican tradition, separation of powers compel[led] Americans to abandon the supremacy of the legislature'.[3] This was precisely the argument put forward against the Constitution by the Anti-Federalists, who were wary of the 'danger of insidious usurpation by the few, the inevitable and persistent pressure of the "artful and ever active aristocracy"'.[4] They criticised the Founders not only for recklessly seeking to contrive an indigenous aristocracy (i.e. Senate) and even a monarchy (i.e. presidency), but also for blending them into a mixed government capable of removing majoritarian threats to privilege.

The Founding Fathers certainly wished to devise a central government robust enough to withstand the divisions and volatility of American society and 'to secure the public good . . . against the danger of . . . a [majority] faction'.[5] Nevertheless, they were also well aware that they could not afford to antagonise a public uncertain and even fearful of central authority. James Madison, the chief architect of the Constitution, defended the creation by firmly attaching himself to Montesquieu's first principle. To Madison, '[t]he accumulation of all powers, legislative, executive and judiciary in the same hands, whether of one, a few, or many, and whether hereditary, self-appointed, or elective, may justly be pronounced the very definition of tyranny'.[6] The objective was to keep the different elements of government as separate as possible, in order to recreate the *effect* of the old and much valued British Constitution, prior to its Hanoverian corruption. The checks and balances of the British model had been drawn from its mixed government traditions subsequently projected on to an emergent framework of richly differentiated institutions. The Founding Fathers were seeking to reverse the process by starting with a full separation of powers and moving on to the virtues of checks facilitated by functional and institutional divisions. The chief problem with this inversion of British constitutional development was that it begged the central question of whether the three powers could – or even should – be checking one another, given that they were supposed to be intrinsically separate.

Madison's response was two-fold. First, he pointed out that the three powers were not totally self-contained entities.

> Experience has instructed us that no skill in the science of government has yet been able to discriminate and define, with sufficient certainty, its three great provinces – the legislative, executive, and judiciary . . . Questions daily occur in the course of practice which prove the obscurity which reigns in these subjects, and which puzzle the greatest adepts in political science.[7]

In a private letter to Thomas Jefferson, Madison conceded the impossibility of rigorously differentiating the three branches from each other. The branches between the legislative, executive and judiciary 'consist in many instances of mere shades of difference'.[8] Montesquieu himself had implied as much. In Madison's view, Montesquieu's 'own words impart . . . that where the *whole* power of one department is exercised by the same hands which possess the *whole* power of another department, the fundamental principles of a free constitution are subverted'.[9] Some overlap and imprecision was, therefore, acceptable within the meaning of separation. According to Madison, Montesquieu 'did not mean that these departments ought to have no *partial agency* in, or no *control* over, the acts of the other'.[10]

Madison's equation of functional mixture with mutual restraint leads to his second response. The complete separation of powers was not only conceptually and institutionally implausible, it was also unnecessary to satisfy the objectives of separation – i.e. governmental control. On the contrary, some sharing of functions ensured competition, friction and, therefore, restraint. Imprecision and mixture provided the points of contact for institutions to interact with one another and to limit each others' sphere of influence. Muddle was rationalised as creative tension and as the necessary means to interior equilibruim. To Madison, 'a dependence on the people is, no doubt, the primary control on the government; but experience has taught mankind the necessity of auxiliary precautions'.[11] The inexactitude of separated powers, and the competitive and adversarial behaviour induced by such a lack of delineation, provided the motive force behind these 'auxiliary precautions', which would enable government to control itself. To the founders, checks and balances served the republican cause. The subdivision of government into distinct departments would prevent the usurpation and abuse of power by factions – even a majoritarian faction. Individual liberties, minority rights, and the public interest would accordingly be served not only – or even primarily – through representative government, but by the autonomous control of government through its own internal structure of division and debilitation. To the objection that no alternative social order or authority could legitimately defy the popular assembly in a republic, the defenders of the Constitution justified their scheme of checks and balances by reference to the overarching objective of republican government. In a framework heavily dependent upon functional analysis (i.e. legislature-executive-judiciary), the Founding Fathers relied upon their notion of republicanism's function (security against arbitrary government) to validate the existence of checks and balances and the mutual frustration that they would generate within the political system.

The clarity of the ulterior motive has never managed to diminish the muddle surrounding the separation of powers and its problematic relationship with the ancient mixed government doctrine of checks and balances. Enormous confusion still exists over whether one is the precondition, or the agency, or conclusion of the other. The separation of powers can be seen as the rationale for checks and balances. By the same token, the scheme of checks and balances can be taken as the rationale for separated powers. Logically the qualitative differentiation of the separate branches still does not really square with the idea of checks which depends upon the homogeneity of material units and the interchangeability of power between different branches. Nevertheless, if the muddle generated by the Founding Fathers has not been resolved, the legitimacy of the muddle itself has been resolved in favour of the utility of disaggregated and countervailing powers. The problem of the undemocratic nature of checks and balances was quickly defused by a blanket of democratic terminology. Fearful though they were of the mass, the Founding Fathers had no alternative other than to work with both the Revolution's populist and democratic impulses and its intellectual abandonment of alternative social authority. The Founding Fathers' solution to the problem of democracy was couched in democratic terms. Under the cover of a generalised attribution of government to representative democracy, '[t]he ideas and vocabulary that had formerly been applied to monarchy, aristocracy and democracy were firmly transferred to the legislative, executive and judicial branches of government'.[12] Separated powers, and checks and balances, were defined not as an attempt to frustrate the popular assembly, so much as a way of translating different expressions of the populace into government. To Gordon Wood, the House of Representatives 'lost its exclusive connection with the people'.[13] Democracy had spread by force of association.

Representation was now identified simply with election; thus, all elected officials, and even those not elected such as judges, were considered somehow 'representative' of the people. Consequently, the older classical ideas of democracy and mixed government that went back to Aristotle became irrelevant in describing the new American political system. Democracy rapidly became a generic label for all American government.[14]

This being so, democracy would be served not only directly through elections and the communication of popular will, but equally through the interplay of representative institutions which would ensure that 'if any one of them sought to get out of line . . . [it] would bump up against another element of public authority'.[15]

The imagery of comparable parts of government set against themselves has given the political system a mechanistic property that strongly suggests a form of calculable and predictable self-regulation. Functions and powers instrumental to produce a highly complex system of institutional dynamics provides an inherent restraint upon government. It can even be said to rank as an alternative form of constitution, in which power is limited not so much by legal barriers but by the blind and spontaneous processes of conflicting governmental units. To Charles McIlwain, this does not represent an adaption of constitution, so much as a mutation of it. In McIlwain's view, the constitutional objective of limiting government is not the same as, nor is it served by, the weakening of government.

Among all the modern fallacies that have obscured the true teachings of constitutional history, few are worse than the extreme doctrine of the separation of powers and the indiscriminate use of the phrase 'checks and balances'. The true safeguards of liberty against arbitrary government are the ancient legal limitation and the modern political responsibility. But this responsibility is, I think, utterly incompatible with any extended system of checks and balances.[16]

Be this as it may, what is clear is that the separation remains a defining characteristic of national government and one that relies for its authority upon its easy accessibility as a concept and upon its simple symmetry as a timeless exchange of institutional forces.

The contemporary significance of the separation of powers

The reason for devoting so much space to the origins of the separation of powers structure is because its background has a direct bearing on the shape and conduct of modern American politics at the national level. Whether it is the existence of institutional competition, the framework of the electoral and party systems, the strategies of political calculation and negotiation, the vocabulary and criteria of political argument, or the nature of policy-making, they have all in one way or another been thoroughly conditioned by America's fusion of separated powers and reciprocal checks. As such the principle and practice of separated powers have been at the root of practically every feature described and issue raised in this book. Washington policy is both permeated by references to the simplistic categories and formalities of the separation of powers scheme, and characterised by the compulsive reduction of complex conditions and positions to the simplicities of the scheme's principles of differentiation and interaction.[17]

In some respects of course the US separation of powers *is* a simple doctrine affording clear and direct consequences. Three functions are roughly translated into three institutions. The division is maintained by the basic injunction preventing any individual from serving in more than one institution at any one time. This starkly unequivocal requirement effectively removed at one stroke any possibility that the federal government might evolve into a parliamentary system with a strong cabinet to link the legislature and executive together. Attempts to make a permanent bridge across the gap between the presidency and Congress have always foundered on the rocks of institutional rivalry and the mutually exclusive ranks of its personnel. Even as early as the first Congress (1789–91), members of the House of Representatives refused to allow Secretary of Trade, Alexander Hamilton, to make his financial report in person to the House. Hamilton wished to follow the precedents from the old Confederation Congress and initiate British ministerial practices by establishing a presence in the legislature. It was widely suspected at the time that Hamilton saw himself not merely as the equivalent of a crown minister, but as a prospective prime minister. His charismatic leadership and his close relationship with President Washington, made such a position a realistic possibility, especially in a Congress as yet unstructured by party lines. Nevertheless, Hamilton's request to report to the House of Representatives in person was rejected. To Wilfred Binkley, the proposal 'so lightly disposed of by Congress was unquestionably of momentous consequence in our constitutional development'.[18] The separation of powers held and a vital precedent against external control and leadership was established. By the end of the second Congress, the hostile reaction of the House against Hamilton's ministerial pretensions was such that it made his 'position as secretary scarcely tenable'.[19]

Even with the asset of a developed two-party system, the separation of powers principle still acted as a gulf between the two elected bodies of the presidency and Congress. It has been on only very rare occasions that the gap has sufficiently diminished to allow for a congenial and productive partnership between the two branches (i.e. 1933–5, 1964–5, 1981). President Lyndon Johnson, for example, enjoyed such spectacular success in Congress during the mid-1960s that it seemed as if the separation of powers had been neutralised.

> He blended and obscured the usual relationship between the President and the Congress, mingling previously distinct functions together until he involved each branch in both proposing and disposing of legislation. He was

seeking to fashion an American version of the British parliamentary system, arrogating to himself the role of the British Cabinet . . . 'The trick was,' Johnson later mused, 'to crack the wall of separation'.[20]

But it was only ever a crack, and a very limited and temporary one at that. The wall was swiftly re-erected once President Lyndon Johnson faltered in his mastery of Congress. Even though Johnson continued to enjoy large Democratic majorities in Congress, the two institutions grew apart during the final three years of Johnson's presidency (1966–8). The period bore testimony to Richard Neustadt's observation that 'what the Constitution separates our political parties do not combine. The parties are themselves composed of separated organisations sharing public authority'.[21] In other words, while parties might normally be expected to provide a conjunction between the two branches of elective branches of government, the separation of powers in the US has prevailed over attempts to reorganise the constitutional structure along the lines of party government. In Johnson's case, his spectacular fusion of legislative and executive forces was conspicuously shortlived. Nothing structural remained of his previous influence and, therefore, nothing could prevent the relapse of Johnson's linkage back to the customary norm of separated and adversial powers. Indeed the relationship between the presidency and Congress deteriorated so dramatically after 1966, that the enmity and acrimony between the institutions was far greater in the late 1960s that it had been prior to President Johnson's accession to the presidency.

The elegance and simplicity of the separation of powers is also strongly evoked by the intervention of the Supreme Court as a referee in the jurisdictional disputes between the presidency and Congress. Just as the separation of powers fuels conflict over institutional borders and generates charges and counter-charges of usurpation, so the principle also implies that such differences can be resolved by constitutional reference. The intervention of the Supreme Court in such disputes gives dramatic expression not only to the concept of three separate, co-equal and interactive powers, but also to the underlying supposition of a discernible delineation of constitutional functions and powers. Such cases have produced decisions uncovering boundary lines and clarifying claims to rightful possession. Furthermore, because these decisions feature judges arbitrating between national political institutions, they rank as some of the most significant cases in American constitutional history.

The Supreme Court and presidential restraint

In *Ex parte Milligan* (1866),[22] for example, the Supreme Court found that President Lincoln had acted unconstitutionally in establishing military commissions in areas where the civil courts were operating normally. Military courts in conditions of civil insurrection were only legitimate in those areas directly affected by armed conflict. When such courts were established outside a theatre of war, they infringed 'one of the plainest of constitutional provisions'[23] – i.e. that courts must be ordained and established by Congress. They could not be 'justif[ied] on the mandate of the president, because he is controlled by law, and has his appropriate sphere of duty, which is to execute, not make, the law'.[24] Even though Lincoln was the commander-in-chief at a time of civil war, the Supreme Court was nevertheless attentive to the implications of martial law to civil liberties, and was prepared to reprimand the president on grounds of acting beyond his powers as chief executive. The Court also found against Lincoln in *Ex parte Merryman* (1861).[25] In this case, the president was censured for giving his military officers the power to suspend the writ of *habeas corpus* wherever armed insurrection warranted such an action. Apart from the fact that only Congress could legitimately suspend such a fundamental civil right, the Supreme Court pointed out that the civil courts were still operational in the area where Merryman was arrested. No satisfactory reason, therefore, existed for the military to deny a civilian trial. If the president could suspend *habeas corpus* in such circumstances, then the Court concluded that the Constitution had conferred upon him 'more regal and absolute power over the liberty of the citizen than the people of England have thought it safe to entrust to the crown'.[26]

Another president in the full flight of his emergency powers as commander-in-chief was brought to ground by the Supreme Court in 1952. During the Korean War, President Truman ordered the seizure of American steel mills in order to avert a strike and, therefore, to prevent any disruption to the supply of military equipment. In *Youngstown and Tube Co. v. Sawyer* (1952),[27] the Supreme Court declared such an action to be an unconstitutional extension to his executive obligations to enforce federal law. The Court pointed out that Congress had previously considered, and rejected, just such a power for the president in the field of labour relations. If a prerogative of this sort was not derived from an act of Congress, then it could only be attributed to the president's inherent powers under Article II of the Constitution. The Court could find no such implied authority. On the contrary, it was clear that the president had usurped his position. The nation may have been at war, but the separation of powers remained intact.

> In the framework of our Constitution, the President's power to see that the laws are faithfully executed refutes the idea that he is to be a lawmaker. The Constitution limits his functions in the law-making process to the recommending of laws he thinks wise and the vetoing of laws he thinks bad.[28]

Despite the burgeoning size and responsibilities of modern executive government and the discretionary powers that flow to the chief executive as a consequence, the Supreme Court has nevertheless acted in several landmark cases to remind presidents that they continue to operate within a system of separated powers. In *Humphrey's Executor v. United States* (1935),[29] the Supreme Court restricted the president's power to remove officers of the federal government. Franklin Roosevelt had dismissed Humphrey from the Federal Trade Commission because of a difference of political outlook. The Roosevelt administration cited the case of *Myers* v. *United States* (1926)[30] in which the Supreme Court decided that where executive officers were concerned a president had an unrestricted power of removal – even in circumstances where Congress had provided a statutory limitation upon dismissals. But the Federal Trade Commission neither occupied a place in the executive branch, nor exercised any executive powers. Even though it was an administrative body designed to implement legislative policies, it was intended to do so 'without executive leave'.[31] It was meant to be 'entirely free from the control or coercive influence, direct or indirect'.[32] As a consequence, a president could not remove any member of such a commission. His removal power was limited to 'purely executive officers'.[33] Commissioners could only be removed on grounds of personal misbehaviour (e.g. negligence, malfeasance), and not on the basis of political allegiance or the substance of decisions. Because the function of a commission was not exclusively executive in character, the Court concluded that the commissioners were not exclusively subject to presidential control.

The Supreme Court's usage of the separation of powers and of functional analysis to protect commissions from executive intrusion was again in evidence in *Wiener* v. *United States* (1958).[34] In this case, President Eisenhower had removed three members of the War Claims Commission. Unlike the legislation setting up the Federal Trade Commission, the War Claims Commission contained no statutory provision for granting, limiting, or denying the president's removal power. But the Court did not equate silence with licence. The fact it was a commission meant that, on functional grounds, it was not exclusively executive in nature and therefore should not continually be dependent upon the chief executive for its decisions and personnel. Although Congress had not set any statutory limits on the president's power of executive removal, the Court judged that, on the basis of its creation, it must have meant the commissioners to be independent of the president. Bearing in mind the function of a commission, the clear inference was:

> that Congress did not wish to have hang[ing] over the Commission the Damocles' sword of removal by the President for no reason other than that he preferred to have on that Commission men of his own choosing.[35]

The Court further restricted the power of the chief executive within the executive branch in *Morrison* v. *Olson* (1988).[36] This case involved the status of independent counsels who, under the authority of the Ethics in Government Act (1978), are appointed to investigate, and where necessary, prosecute high ranking executive officials. An independent counsel is appointed by a federal court on the advice of the Attorney General. Such a counsel can only be removed by the Attorney General on grounds of 'good cause' (i.e. personal misbehaviour). The president complained that these 'special prosecutors' were not performing quasi-judicial or quasi-legislative functions. They were engaged in executive law enforcement activities and, as such, should be removable by the chief executive. On this occasion, the Court agreed that according to the letter of the separation of powers, an independent counsel was executive in character. Nevertheless, the spirit of the separation of powers, and especially its associated system of checks and balances, determined that the arrangement of independent counsels should remain unchanged. In the Court's view, the 'good cause' rubric did not unnecessarily restrict the executive's powers of discretion in the area of removal. It was acknowledged that the Ethics in Government Act involved some curtailment of presidential authority.

> It is undeniable that the Act reduces the amount of control or supervision that the Attorney General and, through him, the President exercises over the investigation and prosecution of a certain class of alleged criminal activity. The Attorney General is not allowed to appoint the individual of his choice; he does not determine the counsel's jurisdiction; and his power to remove a counsel is limited.[37]

But despite these restrictions upon the chief executive and senior executive figure of the Attorney General, the Court believed that the key factor was one of need. What was at issue was whether a president needed to have a stronger removal of power over independent counsels in order 'to perform his constitutional duty'. The Court thought not: 'we simply do not see how the President's need to control the exercise of that discretion is so central to the functioning of the Executive Branch as to require as a matter of constitutional law that the counsel be terminated at will by the President'.[38] It was not a question of always trying to maximise the separation of the three branches wherever possible. It was more a matter of tolerating inter-branch and inter-functional ambiguity up until the point when such imprecision compromises the effective functioning of a department of government.[39]

Presidential powers have been curtailed by the Supreme Court's interpretation of the separation of powers in other ways. In *Train* v. *New York City* (1975),[40] the Supreme Court rejected the Nixon Administration's claim of executive discretion in federal government expenditure. President Nixon had withheld funds provided by Congress for the control and alleviation of water pollution. The Clean Water Act had authorised the construction of a series of waste treatment plants. The president's refusal to spend the amount reserved for these installations was based both upon precedents of budgetary discretion by chief executives in the pursuit of responsible financial management and upon ambiguities in the legislation itself. The Court was not impressed and declared that the president had no authority to countermand the expenditure of such substantial sums explicitly reserved by Congress for a set purpose. To Louis Fisher, the decision was significant for the way that 'important constitutional principles were underscored: the authority of the Congress to mandate spending; the President's obligation to carry out the laws; and the legitimacy of court order to compel presidential action'.[41]

The question of presidential privacy and executive priviledge was raised in *Nixon* v. *Administrator of General Services* (1977).[42] A congressional statute had authorised the General Services Administration to sift through President Nixon's papers, in order to determine which were of a private nature and which should be open to public disclosure. President Nixon complained that this amounted to a denial of presidential privilege and an infringement of the separation of powers. But the Supreme Court was more sanguine. By 7 to 2, the Court held the test of whether the separation of powers had been breached was the extent 'to which it prevents the Executive Branch from accomplishing its constitutionally assigned functions'.[43] The Supreme Court alluded to the 'contemporary realities of our political system'[44] and to the 'pragmatic flexible approach of Madison'[45] in its dismissal of President Nixon's fundamentalist approach of a complete separation of independent powers. In the Court's view, nothing in the arrangement for monitoring President Nixon's papers 'render[ed] it unduly disruptive of the Executive Branch'.[46]

Without doubt, the most dramatic example of the Supreme Court defying a president came in *United States* v. *Nixon* (1974)[47] when the Court ordered the president to relinquish tape recordings of private White House conversations that would establish the truth or otherwise of presidential statements on the Watergate scandal. The president had successfully defied a succession of government agencies in gaining access to what he regarded as necessarily secret executive discussions. Frustration led to the Supreme Court for redress. The president's position was that the tapes of private White House conversations were in their own right private and protected by the convention of executive privilege. Furthermore, the dispute was in Nixon's view an internal executive matter. As the executive had exclusive authority over the prosecution of cases, it was the chief executive who had the final say over what evidence should be used in any given case. According to the president's counsel, any attempt by the Court to adjudicate in an intra-branch dispute would be an intrusion into the jurisdiction of another branch of government.

The Court did not regard the president's position as an adequate defence. The special prosecutor had not only been given full independence by the president, he had been granted 'explicit power to contest the invocation of executive privilege'.[48] The Court declared that the case was justiciable and proceeded to hear the case. In answer to Nixon's claim that the separation of powers precluded a judicial review of executive privilege, the Court pointed out that it was the 'ultimate interpreter of the constitution'.[49] Its judicial power could not be shared. 'Any other conclusion would be contrary to the basic concept of the separation of powers and the checks and balances that flow from the scheme'.[50] In response to President Nixon's position that executive privilege was absolute because of the separation of powers, the Court stated that: 'neither the doctrine nor the need for confidentiality of high level communications . . . can sustain an absolute unqualified presidential privilege of immunity from judicial process under all circumstances'.[51] To do so would be to 'upset the constitutional balance'.[52] Nixon's third line of defence was that executive privilege would always outweigh a subpoena in such circumstances. Here the Court concluded that because the case involved criminal proceedings and the need for specific materials as evidence, a 'generalised interest in confidentiality . . . [could] not prevail over the fundamental demands of due process of law'.[53] As a consequence, the Court ordered the release of the tape recordings. Because the evidence derived from them proved President Nixon's complicity in the Watergate 'cover-up', his resignation followed soon after.

The Supreme Court and congressional constraint

Supreme Court censure has not been confined to the executive branch. The US Congress has also been subjected to critical judicial review in relation to the separation of powers. In the New Deal period, for example, the Supreme Court invalidated several government programmes because Congress was deemed to have compromised its own legislative function. In successfully passing reform legislation, Congress was censured for failing in its legislative duties by delegating law-making responsibilities away to the administrative apparatus set up to implement such programmes. Congress accepted that the attempt by government to regulate areas of the national economy necessarily involved the need for discretion in administrative rule-making, in order to accommodate the scale and complexity of the undertaking. As long as it issued authoritative guidelines, then Congress assumed administrative officers could subsequently issue regulations within the parameters laid down in the enabling legislation. The Supreme Court disagreed. In *Schecter Corporation v. US* (1935),[54] for example, the centrepiece of Roosevelt's New Deal programme, the National Recovery Agency, was struck down by the Supreme Court on grounds that its arrangements amounted to an unconstitutional delegation of legislative authority by Congress. 'Instead of prescribing rules of conduct, it authorises the making of codes to prescribe them'.[55] The delegation was not confined to a single act or group of acts described by reference to a standard. It was in effect a 'roving commission to inquire into evils and upon discovery to correct them'.[56] The remit included whatever was necessary for the interests of the industry concerned: 'This is delegation running riot'.[57]

The conservatism of the Supreme Court at the time made such a free-wheeling agency as the NRA difficult to accommodate within the separation of powers doctrine. By 1941, the Supreme Court had changed both in personnel and outlook. It recognised the need for, and requirements of, the regulatory state. In the *Opp Cotton Mills* v. *Administrator* (1941),[58] the Court rationalised the change to agency rule-making. Because the standards and procedure had been set by Congress then there was 'no failure in the performance of the legislative function'.[59] The Constitution was 'not to be interpreted as demanding the impossible or the impractical'.[60] As such, Congress could not be expected to prescribe administrative decisions 'in advance for all cases'.[61] Accordingly, 'the exercise of [administrative] judgement within prescribed limits' was acceptable because 'the essentials of the legislative policy and its formulation as a rule of conduct'[62] had been satisfied. Just as the appraisal of facts in relation to a prescribed policy 'involve[d] the exercise of judgement',[63] so the Supreme Court's own assessment of standards and procedures defined by Congress was also inevitably subjective. With the exponential development of federal regulation, the Supreme Court progressively abandoned the task of appraising standards and requirements. Even delegated legislation devoid of defined statutory standards has become accepted by the Supreme Court on utilitarian grounds – i.e. that such standards may exist by other means (e.g. self-imposed administrative standards, budgetary sanctions, guidance from the legislative history of enacted laws, the force of accumulated precedent), and that regulation might sometimes be more effective without the sort of detailed statutory provision that would allow litigants to avoid regulation by way of highly technical disputes. If the Court has sometimes relaxed its stance against delegated legislation by adopting a more pragmatic approach to the separation of powers, other cases show that it is not averse to sudden lapses into a more fundamentalist approach to institutional relationships.

In *Bowsher* v. *Synar* (1986),[64] the Court invalidated a key point of the Gramm-Rudman Deficit Reduction Act (1985) on the grounds that it breached the separation of powers between the presidency and Congress. Although the Act itself had been woven together by both branches, the Court found that the central device of automatic spending cuts to control the budget deficit was unconstitutional. In the Court's view, the Comptroller General, who had been given the task of calculating and mandating the expenditure cuts, was an officer of the Congress. As such, he was performing an executive role while being theoretically removable by the legislature. According to the Court, this anomaly could only be resolved by formally recognising the Comptroller General as part of the legislature, thereby precluding him from executive duties. As the Deficit Reduction Act depended upon the officer to make the cuts, that part of the legislation was declared unconstitutional. Even though the independence of the Comptroller General from Congress had always been taken as read, the Court adopted a conspicuously 'mechanical notion of executive–legislative relations'.[65] The Court ignored both the fact of Congress' development of legislative oversight and the legitimacy of such a legislative role. As far as it was concerned the Constitution did 'not contemplate an active role for Congress in the supervision of officers charged with the execution of the laws it enacts'.[66]

A much more characteristic and far-reaching reversion to basics occurred with the Supreme Court's sudden attack on legislative vetoes in 1983. Over a period of fifty years, Congress had employed the device of the legislative veto as a way of allowing the executive to attend to its vast regulatory obligations whilst at the same time accommodating the discretionary powers, that those responsibilities entailed, within a structure of congressional control. Executive discretion was made conditional upon active congressional intervention in administration *after* the passage of legislation. Regulatory licence would be given by Congress on the understanding that any subsequent decision made within the remit of such a licence would be liable to a selective veto by the legislature.

From 1932 onwards a rich variety of vetoes evolved within the apparatus of a rapidly developing regulatory state. Some legislative vetoes could only be enforced by both houses of Congress through a concurrent resolution. Others could be applied by one chamber or even by one committee within the House or Senate. But even though legislative vetoes had become an integral instrument of government management and had acquired legitimacy as a convention through fifty years of usage, the Supreme Court challenged them in 1983. In *Immigration and Naturalization Service* v. *Chadha* (1983)[67] and other related cases, the Court declared that legislative vetoes by concurrent resolution, or by one house or one committee, were unconstitutional on grounds that they infringed the separation of powers. Congress could not second-guess laws it had passed into executive hands. Chief Justice Burger argued that action taken by Congress through legislative vetoes was 'essentially legislative'[68] in character and as such needed to conform to the regular legislative process in which decisions were made by both houses of Congress and presented to the president for approval. Once Congress has passed a law, it cannot retain discretionary powers over its implementation except by returning to the established legislative process (i.e. by formally revising the law). To do otherwise would be to allow Congress to engage in activities that are the preserve of the executive branch. In strong contrast to the accommodating outlook that the Court showed towards the separation of powers in *Nixon* v. *Administrator of General Services* (1977), the judgement was doctrinaire and unyielding in the face of custom and practicality. The fact that the device is 'efficient, convenient and useful in facilitating functions of government . . . will not save it if it is contrary to the Constitution. Convenience and efficiency are not the primary objectives – or the hallmarks – of democratic government'.[69] The Constitution divided government into three categories and it was the Court's obligation to preserve them.

> The hydraulic pressure inherent within each of the separate Branches to exceed the outer limits of its power, even to accomplish desirable objectives, must be resisted.[70]

The position of those who were mystified by the iconoclasm of a judgement which affected over 200 veto provisions in 126 laws was perhaps best conveyed by Justice Byron White's dissenting opinion. The Court had not only removed a key device through which executive and independent agencies were made accountable to Congress,[71] it had struck down 'in one fell swoop provisions in more laws enacted by Congress than the court has cumulatively invalidated in its history'.[72] What had been a 'necessary check on the unavoidably expanding power of the agencies'[73] and an 'important . . . political invention that allow[ed] the President and Congress to resolve major constitutional and policy differences'[74] had been declared void in unnecessarily sweeping terms by the Court.

The Supreme Court and executive licence

Landmark cases in the area of the separation of powers are not confined to prohibitory judgements. The Supreme Court does not simply curtail; it can condone, guide, and even encourage. This has particularly been the case with the executive branch. The legislature is more straightforward in that the collective powers of the federal government are formally allocated to Congress in its legislative capacity as an originator of statute law. For the most part, to test the constitutionality of Congress is to examine whether its laws supersede the powers stipulated in the Constitution's allotment of federal powers. The executive branch, on the other hand, is a more reactive institution officially geared to implementing law. If a federal law is unconstitutional, therefore, it is primarily the fault of Congress, as it is the source of the offending law – not the executive whose task it is merely to carry out the law. Nonetheless, the executive is not always so passive in nature. It is reactive in another and more contentious sense. As the agency with the government's means of physical coercion at its disposal, it is thought to possess an inherent responsibility to respond to changing events and to threats to both the social order and the nation's security. Such a discretionary prerogative is assumed to be in the public interest. It is accepted as the *raison d'être* of an executive force. In this context, actions undertaken by an executive cannot always be expected to be derived from specific laws, or even be reducible to any legal sanction. They may even be contrary to statute law.[75] It is the Supreme Court which in many respects has taken on the responsibility for allowing the American chief executive to develop in this direction. The relationships between statute law and administrative discretion, between executive prerogative and a constitutional order, and between the presidency and the nebulous language of Article II have often been left to the Court to resolve by constitutional construction. In fact, the rise and legitimation of the modern presidency can be said to be largely attributable to the Court's creative role in enlarging the scope of executive licence from within the formal constraints of a constitutional system.

In the *Prize Cases* (1863),[76] the Supreme Court recognised that the chief executive had an interior property which was not reducible to constitutional prescription but which was contingent upon the force of circumstances facing government. The case considered the legality of President Lincoln's blockade of southern ports and the seizure of ships and cargoes from those seeking to break the blockade. The plaintiffs claimed that in the absence of a state of war, a blockade was illegal in international law. As no war had been declared by Congress, then Lincoln's act of war was an unconstitutional usurpation of congressional powers. The Supreme Court disagreed. The decision over whether hostilities warranted a blockade was a question to be decided by the president who was duty bound to meet the situation of war 'in the shape it prescribed itself without waiting for Congress to baptise it with a name'.[77] A president is 'bound to resist by force . . . without waiting for any special legislative authority'.[78]

The case of *In re Neagle* (1890)[79] provided further elucidation of the fact that the presidency possessed not only powers implied in the Constitution, but also powers inherent in the nature of the executive function. The Supreme Court found that in some circumstances an executive order could rank as a legitimate substitute for an act of Congress. This was because a president's executive function was not limited to statutes enacted by Congress but extended to 'any obligation fairly and properly inferable from [the Constitution], or any duty . . . derived from the general scope of . . . duties under the laws of the United States'.[80] The Court reiterated the point. The president's duty of executing the laws was not 'limited to the enforcement of acts of Congress . . . according to their *express terms*', but included also 'the rights, duties and obligations growing out of the Constitution itself, our international relations, and all the protection implied by the nature of the government under the Constitution'.[81]

Perhaps the most expansive construction of Article II by the Supreme Court came in the 1930s when the modern foundations of the presidency's pre-eminence in American foreign policy-making were laid down. The emphasis lay upon the needs of foreign policy and the functional capacity of the chief executive to satisfy those needs were firmly established in US v. *Curtiss Wright Export Corporation* (1936)[82] (see Chapter 11). They were further developed in US v. *Belmont* (1937)[83] when the Court upheld President Roosevelt's decision to establish diplomatic relationships with the Soviet Union in 1933. This was not a treaty but an 'executive agreement' made on the basis of the president's authority in foreign affairs and national security. The plaintiffs complained that an executive agreement could not supplant the property rights they held under New York law. The state had refused to recognise the forcible confiscation of American assets by the Soviet Union. The Court, however, recognised the executive agreement as a valid international compact concluded by the president with the authority involving the 'external powers of the United States [which were] to be exercised without regard to state laws or policies'.[84] The national government had clear priority in such an area and the president had 'authority to speak as the sole organ of that government . . . That the negotiations, acceptance of the assignment and agreements and understandings in respect thereof were within the competence of the president may not be doubted'.[85]

The freedom of manoeuvre granted to the chief executive by the Supreme Court can reach alarming proportions. The most notorious example concerned the occasion in February 1942 when President Roosevelt issued an executive order enpowering the Secretary of War to designate military areas from which persons could be excluded to prevent espionage and sabotage. The Secretary of War duly created a military area covering California, Oregon, Washington, and parts of Arizona. From that zone, 112,000 Japanese-Americans were forcibly removed and taken away to 'relocation centres'. Despite the fact that a large majority of the detainees were natural-born American citizens and that no evidence was produced to justify such a blanket invasion of civil liberties, the Supreme Court found the action taken by the civil and military authorities to be constitutional. Even though the key judgement (*United States* v. *Korematsu* (1945)[86] came two years after the evacuation when it was clear that the policy had been an over-reaction to the widespread panic over a possible Japanese invasion, the Court was not prepared to challenge either the executive's use of prerogative in the field of national security, or the rights of military judgement during wartime. As it was impossible to 'bring about an immediate segregation of the disloyal from the loyal',[87] a mass expulsion was a 'military imperative. The need for action was great, and the time was short'.[88]

On occasions like these, the Court sees its role as one of squaring the meaning of executive power in a constitutional structure with the social need for executive power, in a rapidly changing international context. During the global tensions of the Cold War when the United States believed itself to be in a position of sustained nuclear peril, the Court was only too well aware that any attempt to confine the executive within narrow constitutional boundaries risked being not only conceptually implausible but also politically dangerous. The Court's endorsement of executive authority in foreign affairs was tantamount to investing the office with an extra-constitutional status. The Court could be accused of deploying 'constitutional philosophy to shore up presidential actions that were otherwise legally suspect'.[89] Others claimed that it was simply a matter of democratic survival that 'in a time of crisis, a democratic constitutional government must be temporarily altered to whatever degree is necessary to overcome the peril'.[90] Another view was that the strain of the Cold War had simply reaffirmed an integral, but often concealed, dimension of executive power in the American Republic. This was that the executive possesses 'extra constitutional power, and its existence as an essential part of the office must be acknowledged if we are to understand the presidency of our time'.[91]

The limits of judicial management

Although landmark decisions by the Supreme Court have been very significant in the development of the political system in general, and of the separation of powers in particular, they can be misleading. They give the impression that all constitutional disputes arising between the presidency and the Congress either have been, or can be settled by such high profile forms of adjudication. They suggest that the imprecision arising from the operational practicalities of separated institutions can always be resolved by reference to a constitutional precision made available by the Court. Such inferences are misguided for three main reasons.

First, when the Supreme Court decides to move into a field, it cannot help but get its boots muddy. In seeking to clarify an issue, it almost invariably finds that in the process it has created fresh confusion. In reaching its decision, it inadvertently disturbs precedents, understandings, conventions, and traditions. Muddy footprints can smudge not only the final decision but many of the contributory components of the Court's argument. The Supreme Court's tradition of allowing concurring opinions to be presented by justices who have reached the same conclusion through different routes clearly poses a challenge to judicial coherence at the best of times. But even when the Court is united in a decision, it finds it very difficult to avoid giving multiple answers to constitutional questions. In deciding against an individual action of an individual president, for example, the Court can in the process affirm, by implication, the constitutionality of broad swathes of discretionary power accumulated in the presidential office.

In the case of *United States* v. *Nixon* (1974),[92] the Court refuted the president's claim to executive privilege over tape recordings requested for a criminal prosecution. Yet in reaching its decision, it could not avoid touching upon the subject and, therefore, the validity of executive privilege in general. Far from challenging it, the Court recognised a 'presumptive privilege for presidential communications'.[93] Moreover the 'privilege is fundamental to the operation of government and inextricably rooted in the separation of powers under the Constitution'.[94] The need for candour and objectivity amongst presidential advisers requires a secrecy which in turn 'calls for great deference from the courts'.[95] To the Court, it was in fact 'necessary, in the public interest, to afford presidential confidentiality the greatest protection'.[96] President Nixon may have lost the battle, therefore, but the presidency won the war over the legitimacy of executive privilege.

The *second* factor behind the Supreme Court's maintenance of constitutional inexactitude lies in its avoidance of deciding certain categories of cases. In order to regulate the flow of cases into its dockets, the Supreme Court has developed a series of conventions that guides the selection of cases and massively reduces the number accepted for judgement. In effect, they are devices by which the Court has 'avoided passing upon a large part of all the constitutional questions pressed upon it for decision'.[97] For example, the Court maintains a very restrictive policy towards the question of litigants' legal standing, towards the extent to which disputes are authentic 'cases and controversies', and towards whether constitutional questions requiring resolutions are raised by the cases presented. Probably the most notable convention is the Court's practice of defining judgement on what it construes to be 'political questions'. The designation of a question as 'political' is of course a political judgement by the judiciary in its own right. In returning such questions to the more explicitly political branches of government, the Court in effect refuses to hear them on grounds that they fall outside the criteria for judicial decision. In the Court's view they are better resolved by means that do not involve formal constitutional pronouncements. Implicit in such declarations is the assertion that some cases simply do not lend themselves to adjudication – i.e. that there are some controversies which raise matters *beyond* the reach of the Constitution as a body of fundamental and determinate law. Such a position flies in the face of '*Madison* v. *Marbury*'s basic assumption that the Constitution is judicially declarable law'.[98] Nevertheless, the Court has often found it prudent to assimilate such a proposition rather than to confront it by challenging the political branches in cases where the Supreme Court considers the final authority to be either in another branch of government, or in the interplay between the branches of government.

The Supreme Court has traditionally been predisposed to regard disputes over the separation of powers as political questions. This inclination comes from (i) a basic unwillingness to assume an explicitly judgemental role over two branches that are ostensibly equal in status to the judiciary; (ii) a recognition that political choice is not only accommodated but actively encouraged within the Constitution; (iii) a belief that some events, reactions, and judgements are not readily reducible to judicial assessment or to judicially enforceable remedies; and (iv) an understanding that political contestants will attempt to use the courts to translate political differences into demarcation disputes over the separation of powers and to substitute judicial rulings for political decisions or non-decisions. As a consequence, the Supreme Court has been very wary over the separation of powers. In the words of Justice Frankfurter,

> Clashes between different branches of the government should be avoided if a legal ground of less explosive potentialities is properly available. Constitutional adjudications are apt by exposing differences to exacerbate them.[99]

The most notable area in which the Supreme Court has conspiciously sought to diminish the 'explosive potentialities' of constitutional definition has been that of foreign policy and national security. Against an initial background of joint participation and responsibility for foreign affairs, the Court has generally resolved the question of the overall control of foreign policy in favour of the executive because of its responsive and discretionary capabilities:

[T]he very nature of executive decisions as to foreign policy is political, not judicial. Such decisions . . . are delicate, complex and involve large elements of prophecy . . . They are decisions of a kind for which the Judiciary has neither aptitude, facilities nor responsibility.'[100]

The Court has been loath to intervene in disputes over foreign policy between the president and Congress. It is customary for such disputes to be categorised as 'political questions' and, therefore, non-justiciable in character. To the Court, each branch has its own 'resources available to protect and assert its interests'.[101] Moreover, any attempt by the courts to resolve such differences would be misplaced. Questions 'relating to foreign affairs is an area into which we should not and do not prematurely intrude. History shows us that there are too many variables to lay down any hard and fast constitutional rules'.[102] For the most part, Congress has deferred to the *force majeure* of executive policy-making, especially during a period of sustained tension like that of the Cold War. Opposition to a chosen course in foreign policy, therefore, has normally been construed as a matter of political dispute irrespective of the constitutional implications for the separation of powers.

In 1973, political accommodation gave way to intransigence in the form of a sustained attempt by Congress to revise the constitutional balance in foreign affairs. Congress sought to restore some of its constitutional stock in the field of national security by passing the War Powers Resolution, which threatened to limit the presidency in the deployment of military forces – that most sensitive of executive prerogatives. President Nixon vetoed the legislation stating that it was unconstitutional as it took away 'authorities which the president had properly exercised under the Constitution for almost 200 years'.[103] Moreover, it would 'lead to extreme confusion and dangerous disagreements concerning the prerogatives of the two branches'.[104] But the veto was overridden and the resolution became law. This controversial measure intended to calibrate any future American troop deployments by the president with a measure of congressional participation both in the initial deployment, and in the continued presence of US armed forces, in areas of hostilities. The objective of the legislation was to revive Congress' powers in the declaration of war and by the same token to enhance its position in terminating undeclared wars. Even though the War Powers Resolution was reputed to be a major constitutional innovation, it has never in twenty years been tested constitutionally by the Supreme Court. As it stands, the legislation is not unconstitutional, but then again it has not received any verification by the Supreme Court. To the Court, the origins and operation of the War Powers Resolution are political questions which need to be resolved by exchanges between the presidency and Congress. Disputes over the constitutionality of wars in Vietnam and Cambodia prior to the War Powers Resolution had been classified as political questions and, therefore, were not justiciable. Despite the passage of the War Powers Resolution, disputes over the constitutionality of more recent wars in

El Salvador, Nicaragua, Grenada, the Middle East, and the Persian Gulf have likewise been dismissed by the courts as political in nature. Even cases brought by members of Congress claiming that the Reagan Administration had breached the War Powers Resolution were dismissed by lower federal courts as political questions. To the courts, members of Congress had legislative remedies at hand. If they chose not to exercise them and to defend their prerogatives, it was not up to the judiciary to compensate for their lack of collective will.[105] The Supreme Court saw no reason to dispute such judgements and, therefore, never accepted any of the cases on appeal. The fact that cases were often argued out between different sets of congressmen and senators in court only reaffirmed that these were political questions to be left to politicians.[106]

Landmark judgements by the Supreme Court in 'great cases' fail to characterise the working properties of the separation of powers for a *third* reason. This factor is the simple, but far-reaching, practice of political participants working cooperatively to neutralise the potential and actual divisions generated by a separation of powers framework. Such a framework is replete with opportunities to engage in constitutional claims and counter-claims over the jurisdictional distribution of power. Political differences can quickly ramify into conflicting constitutional constructions of rightful legislative, executive, or judicial authority. Political disputes can degenerate into debilitating constitutional or institutional intransigence with branches accusing other branches of jurisdictional intrusion, institutional usurpation, and constitutional subversion. Such is the expense in time, resources, and political energy in arousing the force of constitutional fundamentalism that participants often find that they have more to gain by cooperating with one another in ways that blur the distinctions of separated powers, but which make government governable on a day to day basis. Proceeding on the assumption that the 'great ordinances of the Constitution do not establish or divide fields of black and white',[107] they cultivate a world of grey half-tones through which the separation of powers is made operational. Both the spirit and the utility of what in Washington is termed 'comity' is evident in numerous conventions that acknowledge the separation of powers but which seek to diffuse its effects. For example, even though presidents have never formally recognised the constitutionality of the War Powers Resolution, they have not openly defied its provisions. On the contrary, they have both acknowledged its existence and claimed to have acted in accordance with its stipulated procedures. Admittedly, such compliance has followed the letter rather than the spirit of the law. For example, President Carter consulted with, and notified, a very limited number of senior members of Congress just prior to the Iran hostage rescue mission in 1980. President Reagan also insisted that his notification of, and consultation with, Congress over the invasion of Grenada was consistent with the War Powers Resolution. But like Carter, Reagan's contact with Congress amounted to a *fait accompli* as armed forces were already deployed, or being deployed, when such 'discussions' took place.[108]

In August 1983, President Reagan saw the value of congressional support for his risky and possibly open-ended deployment of a US Marine force in Lebanon. He agreed to conform to the procedure of the War Powers Resolution by issuing a formal hostilities report which would trigger the clock envisaged in the Resolution and, thereby, provide a set period during which Congress could review, and possibly veto, the president's deployment of forces. But as part of the deal, Congress agreed that the clock should run for eighteen months instead of the stipulated sixty days. By not resorting to intransigent positions on either side of an irreconcilable divide over the separation of powers, both parties gained. Instead of a debilitating stalemate, an accommodation was reached which acknowledged each other's claims within a separation of powers framework but which did not pursue any sort of final settlement. It was an interim but workable solution. Congress was able to reiterate its prerogative powers in an actual war setting where the lives of American service personnel were at risk. It also secured an undertaking that both the number and the role of the Marine force would remain limited. The president, on the other hand, had tied Congress to his policy in Lebanon and as a consequence made it difficult for Congress to generate public opposition to him should the policy fail. While the president agreed to the principle of a running clock, he was careful to distance himself from giving recognition to the War Powers Resolution itself. After signing the agreement, he issued the following statement:

> I do not and cannot cede any of the authority vested in me under the Constitution as President and as Commander in Chief of the United States Armed Forces. Nor should my signing be viewed as any acknowledgement that the President's constitutional authority can be impermissibly infringed by statute.[109]

Congress waived its objectives in the interests of an agreement. Like President Reagan, members of Congress suspended their full claims under the separation of powers for the sake of a productive engagement, instead of a principled standoff.

A similarly cooperative response was evoked by the Supreme Court's decision to invalidate legislative vetoes.[110] At first sight, this was a victory for the executive branch until, that is, Congress began to consider the alternatives available to it. Instead of increasing the discretion available to the executive, Congress threatened a regime of legislation that would be limited in time and scope. The president and executive agencies would be forced to return to Congress repeatedly for formal extensions to temporary authority. If Congress could only intervene in administration by changing the law, then it would not only give less away in any future legislation, but would constrain executive discretion by the time-consuming and wholly uncertain process of statute amendment. As an executive victory threatened to turn to ashes in the obduracy of a separation of powers standoff, executive officials and members of Congress quickly joined forces to maximise their positions by using alternative means to retain as much of the legislative veto structure as possible. Administrators cooperated with Congress to reinstate the effect of legislative vetoes by taking their previous arrangements out of public law and relying instead on private and informal means. Many agencies are required to 'notify' congressional committees about the implementation of programmes. Notification before *Chadha* was the preliminary condition of a legislative veto. After *Chadha*, it became the private equivalent of a veto provision. It was politically prudent for an agency to withdraw an action once an oversight agency had responded negatively to a notification. The retaliatory action available to Congress, should such an agreement break down, secured the adherence of executive officials to what was an informal pact. There have been many examples of such veto replacements since *Chadha* (e.g. opting for a joint resolution of approval or disapproval; limiting appropriations; and shortening periods of authorisation).

In the words of Louis Fisher, 'forms . . . change but not power relationships and the need for a *quid pro quo*'.[111] To Fisher, it should not have been surprising that following the Court decision 'a number of windows [were] raised and new doors constructed, making the executive structure as accommodating as before for shared power'.[112]

The politics of separated powers

After 200 years, the separation of powers remains the matrix within which the chief institutions of national government interact with one another. Just as the separation of powers shapes and energises national policies so political forces and issues are expressed through the system of separated powers. The US's experience of the separation of powers continues to condition not only the strategies of policy engagement, but also the terms of political argument and the criteria of political success. The framework of separated powers is not confined to an interrelationship of institutions. The structure is ingrained with its own language, political conventions, and social temperament. It evokes a profusion of legal and constitutional ramifications, while at the same time fostering an extravagant political rhetoric. For example, voluminous legal argument is expended upon the nature and extent of the three different powers. Courts proceed to hear cases on the understanding that they can distinguish institutions by reference to functions and *vice versa*. Complex interpretations revolve around conundrums such as whether the outward reach of an evolving executive branch implies a limit set by another institution or function, or whether a developing executive has any necessary connection with the diminution of another element of the tripartite system.

By the same token, the separation of powers can encourage the most unrestrained and flamboyant hyperbole. In the late 1960s and early 1970s, the common complaint was that the US possessed an 'imperial presidency'. It was accused of

usurping power from Congress by undermining the Republic's checks and balances. For much of the 1970s and 1980s, it was the courts which were accused
of destabilising the constitutional balance. 'The shift from judicial supervision of
procedure *in the courts* to control of *legislative* policy making'[113] was described
as 'a truly extraordinary transformation'.[114] The 'imperial judiciary' was alleged
to regard the Constitution less as a set of fundamental principles and more as an
invitation 'to make constitutional law and, where necessary, to remake it'.[115] By
the late 1980s, it was Congress that was being increasingly criticised for exceeding
its powers. Congress was alleged to have engaged in micromanaging the executive
branch; to have delegated 'more and more of the traditional law-making responsibilities to the federal courts and to "independent agencies"';[116] and to have used
investigations by independent counsels to present 'interbranch disputes over policy
as executive branch violations of the criminal law'.[117] Critics claimed that the
'imperial Congress' posed 'a threat to the separation of powers'[118] and that it was
time to 'defeat congressional imperialism against the executive'.[119]

Charges of imperialism are part of the protocol of arguments spawned by
the separation of powers. Just as the imperialism of the British crown was the
scandal which provoked the American Revolution and which the US Constitution
was designed to prevent in the future through the establishment of divided powers,
so charges of contemporary imperialism are designed to imply the corruption of
the system through an imbalance in its components. Liberty may be threatened
but a ready solution is always at hand in the form of action to reinstate the old
equilibrium. Usurpation is always seen as reversible. The problems of the Republic
are thereby reduced to power relationships between the institutional units that
collectively constitute the balance of powers. Almost any issue can have separation
of powers implications, or can be invested with such implications for political
reasons.

Because of this and the fact that balance and harmony are indeterminate,
and even aesthetic, concepts in the realm of political institutions, the capacity for
separation of powers disputes is matched only by the impermanence of contemporary solutions and the unavailability of final answers. While equilibrium
continues to be the central objective, it nevertheless remains a contested and highly
relative condition.

The potential for disaggregation and incoherence is of course reduced by
long-standing conventions. These extend beyond the areas mentioned above to
embrace practices pursued by both the presidency and Congress to protect the
Supreme Court from political pressures, in order to limit the scope for inter-branch
dispute. For example, the executive may be reluctant to give a Supreme Court
decision its full support. It may be slow to respond and engage in dilatory action,
but it will proceed on the premise of giving full legitimacy to court decisions and
to its own responsibility to implement them. For its part, Congress refuses to
challenge the Supreme Court's scope of appellate jurisdiction. Apart from one

wholly exceptional case following the Civil War when Congress prevented the Court from reviewing a piece of Reconstruction legislation, Congress has not changed the Court's jurisdiction. Congress has left it untouched even though the jurisdiction is conditioned by 'such exceptions, and under such regulations as the Congress shall make'.[120] It is generally agreed that the issue is not 'whether Congress possesses the basic power to make exceptions to the Appellate jurisdiction of the Supreme Court, but whether there are any limits on that power, and if so, what they are'.[121] Doubts exist over whether Congress can discriminate against particular types of cases. Legislative discrimination like this was attempted on numerous occasions in the 1980s when Republican dissidents in Congress sought to restrict the Supreme Court's authority to hear appeals in cases involving abortion, school prayer, and bussing. Significantly, they all failed to secure passage. Where the independence of the judiciary is concerned, Congress has invariably erred on the side of caution.

A similar convention prevails in the selection of Supreme Court justices which involves both the president and the Senate. In giving consideration to a Supreme Court appointment, the Senate traditionally assesses a nominee's judicial competence rather than his or her political allegiances or constitutional convictions. Furthermore, it is customary for the Senate to defuse the potential for political division by deferring to the president's choice. The force of this tradition is reflected in the success rate of 92.6 per cent that twentieth-century presidents have achieved with their Supreme Court nominations. It is only on rare occasions, therefore, that a controversial appointment strains these conventions to the limit. The veil of assessing only a nominee's judicial status can then be torn away to reveal an underlying struggle in which discussions over legal competence are clearly expressions of political division.[122]

A case in question occurred in 1987 when President Reagan selected Judge Robert Bork for the Supreme Court. Because Bork was perceived in liberal circles as a radical conservative who would not only challenge the Supreme Court's precedents but give the Court a decisive conservative majority, his appointment was widely regarded as a blatant attempt to politicise the Court. His nomination was considered in the light of the Court's past record and of its likely future performance with Bork on the bench. As different coalitions of interest groups amassed in support of and in opposition to the nomination, Bork was subjected to a prolonged and critical examination by the Senate's Judiciary Committee.[123] It sought to elicit his opinions on certain litmus test questions (e.g. abortion), in order to predict his likely judgements as a Supreme Court justice. Even though Reagan attached his declining political prestige to Bork's case, the corrosive atmosphere generated by the nomination ensured its defeat.

After the factionalism that surrounded the nomination of Judge Robert Bork to the Court in 1987, there was widespread concern that the controversy had brought the law into disrepute.

Several public figures . . . resented the public aspect of the debate, fearing that the integrity of the law would be compromised by rubbing shoulders with the vulgarity of politics itself.[124]

Those responsible must also have been mindful of a possible public backlash against any explicit politicisation of the Supreme Court. If it was good politics for a majority of the Senate to defeat Bork's nomination, it was equally good politics for both President Reagan and the Senate to return the nomination process to its customary opaqueness and equanimity.

From the public contentiousness generated by the Bork nomination, the Reagan and Bush administrations resorted to a policy of nominating non-controversial and even anonymous judges to the Court. Anthony Kennedy's anodyne performance in the Senate Judiciary Committee's hearings won him the Supreme Court seat previously earmarked for Bork. After the rancour generated by the Bork nomination, the Senate rushed to approve him by 97 votes to 0. In 1990, President Bush followed the precedent and nominated David Souter to replace Justice William Brennan. Souter, who was virtually unknown outside his home state of New Hampshire, was similarly neutral and uninformative in the public hearings conducted by the Judiciary Committee. Bush sought to defuse the problem of Supreme Court nominations by publicly disavowing the use of ideological litmus tests in his choices for the Court.

> He insisted that potential nominees would not even be asked their views on abortion. In return, he expected the Senate, including the Judiciary Committee, to show the same reticence. In this way, the President invoked the tradition that nominees should not be asked specific questions on issues likely to come before them in constitutional cases. This tradition, however, had clearly been infringed during the Bork nomination. The Bush strategy was by no means guaranteed success: it demanded that the one question to which everyone wanted an answer was the one question which should never be asked.[125]

The Senate responded in kind. Even though the balance of the Court's philosophy was supposedly at stake again, the Senate approved Souter's nomination by 90 votes to 9. The Senate's approval of David Souter reaffirmed Michael Comiskey's assertions about the general process of Supreme Court nominations: (i) that 'nominees do not want to reveal how they will vote on controversial issues or even to outline their approach to such issues in a way that might signal their future votes'; (ii) that nominees are usually able to 'hide their beliefs on vital constitutional issues'; and (iii) that 'senators of both parties share a powerful incentive not to insist on full disclosure of a nominee's views' because by not uncovering such views senators are able to 'avoid a politically risky vote on a nominee of known, controversial beliefs'.[126]

The low profile policy was less easy to maintain in 1991 when President

Bush had to replace the highly distinguished Justice Thurgood Marshall. Because Marshall had been the first black member of the Court and the only black Justice since his appointment in 1967, President Bush had very little choice other than to replace Marshall with another black judge. His subsequent nomination of Clarence Thomas was controversial, therefore, not because of his race but because of his deeply conservative views on affirmative action for racial minorities. The appointment looked contrived. Thomas had only been a judge for one year. It was widely believed that Bush had appointed him to the Court of Appeals for the District of Columbia in 1990 in preparation for the Supreme Court nomination to replace Marshall. It was also evident that if Thomas had been white, he would never have been nominated. It was not simply that doubts were expressed over his professional competence.[127] It was that there were better black candidates available for selection.

Thomas' nomination was clearly designed to outflank liberal critics opposed to yet another conservative being placed on the Court. Once again, the Republican administration guided and coached its nominee through the Judiciary Committee hearings. As Bush assured the Senate that no ideological vetting on policy positions had taken place, Thomas sought to avoid all controversy by refusing to volunteer his views on contested cases. The opaqueness of his answers prompted an exasperated Michael Kramer to conclude that:

> [H]e was an empty vessel. For all that he revealed about his legal philosophy, he may as well have been wearing a bag over his head. When pressed on matters of moment in the US, he backed away from almost every opinion he had ever expressed. Incredibly, he told Senators that he had 'no opinion' on *Roe* v. *Wade*, thus marking himself as probably the only person in the US without a view on the Supreme Court's landmark decision.[128]

The Judiciary Committee itself had to be careful in these circumstances. According to convention, it is only supposed to assess a nominee's legal proficiency, not to evaluate ideological leanings and policy positions. To do so would compromise the Supreme Court's formal apolitical and non-partisan status, visibly undermine the Court's reputation for impartiality, and in the process bring the Court itself into disrepute. Because of these traditional inhibitions, there was very little doubt that Clarence Thomas' nomination would be confirmed by the Senate. To the administration, everything was going to plan until the hearings were suddenly and dramatically derailed into open controversy, not on the basis of policy but on grounds of the judge's personal conduct. The forensic examination of legal philosophy fell into disarray as Judge Thomas was confronted by allegations of past sexual harassment made by his former colleague Anita Hill, a law professor from the University of Oklahoma.

The Thomas issue turned into a moral question of which side was telling the truth. In the process, the Judiciary Committee compromised itself by attempting to perform the function of a court of law in seeking to assess evidence and arrive at a judgement in a contested case. The divisiveness of the original nomination was compounded by the divisiveness of both the charges and the Senate's reaction to them, which were variously described as partisan, prejudiced, and sexist. Although Clarence Thomas' nomination was approved by a vote which reflected the polarisation his selection had caused (i.e. 52 in favour to 48 votes against the nomination), the reputation of the Bush Administration and the Senate was harmed. However unintentionally, they were both seen as being responsible for gratuitously bringing the Supreme Court into direct contact with partisan politics and Washington struggles.[129]

Normality was resumed when President Clinton nominated Judge Ruth Bader Ginsburg to the Court in July 1993. Her professional reputation as a careful and disciplined judge and her personal standing as a 'non-political'[130] figure with a 'non-ideological approach'[131] gave her nomination an immediate appeal. She drew support from liberals for her work in the law of sexual discrimination, while the backing she received from Justice Antonin Scalia and Robert Bork ensured that there would not be a conservative campaign against the nomination. The Senate approved the choice by 96 to 3.

Conventions that reduce the centrifugal forces of separated powers are deep set and integral both to the relationship between the presidency and Congress, and to the day to day functioning of government. They help to ensure that 'while the Constitution diffuses the power the better to secure liberty, it also contemplates that practice will integrate the dispersed powers into a workable government'.[132]

But conventions spawned within the separation of powers do not in themselves resolve the problems of fragmentation and incoherence that always remain central to a framework of separated powers. Cooperative practices and traditions may moderate the effect of division, but they do not provide the unity that so many American reformers have advocated in the past and continue to champion in the present. Critics complain that the separation of powers and effective government are mutually exclusive conditions. They point to the way that separated powers generate interminable disputes over precedents, jurisdictions, and authority. They condemn the separation of powers for the American system's innumerable opportunities for minority obstruction and for the evasion of political accountability that ensues from such a structure. They point to the occasions of extensive delay in policy-making and to periods when government inaction is so protracted that it amounts to paralysing immobilism or 'gridlock'.[133]

The diagnoses and prognoses are very familiar. The remedial solutions are equally well worn (see Chapter 12), but they remain unused and untried. This is partly because of the difficulty of achieving reform in such a complex and disaggregated system. But it is mostly because of a traditional impulse in American political culture that equates disjointed and disabled government with safety and liberty. The separation of powers is not merely a structural concomitant of

American democracy. Neither is it simply an integral component of such a system of democracy. Rather, it is its defining characteristic. It is central to the operational nature of the system, but also to the substance and meaning of its democratic credentials. The separation of powers does not compromise or break down a political unity that would otherwise come into existence. It is instead symptomatic of America's acceptance of different dimensions of democracy, whose interrelationships may be problematic but which nevertheless coexist with one another in an unresolved condition of imprecision and tension. It is this attachment to a plurality of institutions and expressions of democracy that resists serious criticism of the system and retards the reformers' drive for change. The next chapter will explore the problematic implications of these divergent structures and protocols of democracy for the policy-making process.

Notes

1 C. L. de S. Montesquieu, *The Spirit of the Laws*, trans. T. Nugent, intro. F. Neumann (New York: Hafner, 1949).

2 See M. J. C. Vile, *Constitutionalism and the Separation of Powers* (London: Oxford University Press, 1967); W. B. Gwyn, *The Meaning of the Separation of Powers: An Analysis of the Doctrine from its Origin to the Adoption of the United States Constitution* (New Orleans: Tulane University Press, 1965); C. M. Walsh, *The Political Science of John Adams: A Study in the Theory of Mixed Government and the Bicameral System* (New York: Knickerbocker, 1915).

3 H. C. Mansfield, Jr., *Constitutional Soul* (Baltimore: Johns Hopkins University Press, 1991), p. 148.

4 H. Storing, *What the Anti-Federalists Were For* (Chicago: University of Chicago Press, 1981), p. 52.

5 J. Madison, 'Federalist Paper No. 10', in J. Madison, A. Hamilton and J. Jay (eds), *The Federalist Papers*, intro. C. Rossiter (New York and Toronto: New American Library, 1961), p. 80.

6 J. Madison, 'Federalist Paper No. 47', in Madison *et al.*, *The Federalist Papers*, p. 301.

7 J. Madison, 'Federalist Paper No. 37', in Madison *et al.*, *The Federalist Papers*, p. 228.

8 Thomas Jefferson quoted in L. Fisher, 'A Political Context for Legislative Vetoes', *Political Science Quarterly*, 93 (2) (Summer 1978), p. 228.

9 J. Madison, 'Federalist Paper No. 47', in Madsion *et al.*, *The Federalist Papers*, pp. 302–3.

10 *Ibid.*, p. 302.

11 J. Madison, 'Federalist Paper No. 51', in Madison *et al.*, *The Federalist Papers*, p. 322.

12 Vile, *Constitutionalism and the Separation of Powers*, p. 151.

13 G. S. Wood, 'Democracy and the Constitution', in R. S. Goldwin and W. A. Schambra (eds), *How Democratic is the Constitution?* (Washington, D.C.: American Enterprise Institutute, 1980), p. 16.

14 *Ibid.*, pp. 15–16.

15 M. S. Evans, *Clear and Present Dangers: A Conservative View of America's Government* (New York: Harcourt Brace Jovanovich, 1975), p. 23.

16 C. H. McIlwain, *Constitutionalism: Ancient and Modern*, rev. edn (Ithaca: Cornell University Press, 1947), pp. 141–2.

17 M. Foley, *Laws, Men and Machines: Modern American Government and the Appeal of Newtonian Mechanics* (London: Routledge, 1990).

18 W. E. Binkley, *President and Congress*, 3rd rev. edn (New York: Vintage, 1962), p. 44

19 *Ibid.*, p. 48.

20 D. B. Kearns, *Lyndon Johnson and the American Dream* (New York: Harper and Row, 1976), pp. 221–2.

21 R. E. Neustadt, *Presidential Power: The Politics of Leadership* (New York: J. Wiley, 1960), p. 33.

22 *Ex parte Milligan* (1866), 4 Wall 2.

23 *Ibid.*, 4 Wall 122.

24 *Ibid.*, 4 Wall 121.

25 *Ex parte Merryman* (1861), 17 Fed. Cas. 144, No. 9, 487.

26 *Ex parte Merryman* (1861).

27 *Youngstown Sheet and Tube Co. v. Sawyer* (1952), 343 US 579.

28 *Ibid.*, 343 US 587.

29 *Humphrey's Executor v. United States* (1935), 295 US 602.

30 *Myers v. United States* (1926), 272 US 52.

31 *Ibid.*, 295 US 628.

32 *Ibid.*, 295 US 629.

33 *Ibid.*, 295 US 628.

34 *Wiener v. United States* (1958), 357 US 349.

35 *Ibid.*, 357 US 356.

36 *Morrison v. Olson* (1988), 487 US

37 *Ibid.*, 487 US 695–6.

38 *Ibid.*, 487 US 691.

39 *Ibid.*, 487 US 691. For more on the nature of the separation of powers controversy generated by the issue of indepedent counsels, see M. R. Levin, 'Prosecuting Tyranny', *National Review*, 46 (7) (April 18 1994); K. J. Harriger, 'Separation of Powers and the Politics of Independent Counsels', *Political Science Quarterly*, 109 (2) (Summer 1994), pp. 261–86.

40 *Train v. New York* (1975), 420 US 35.

41 L. Fisher, *Constitutional Conflicts Between Congress and the President*, 3rd rev. edn (Lawrence: University Press of Kansas, 1991), p. 197.

42 *Nixon v. Administrator of General Services* (1977), 433 US 425.

43 *Ibid.*, 433 US 443.

44 *Ibid.*, 433 US 441.

45 *Ibid.*, 433 US 442.

46 *Ibid.*, 433 US 445.

47 *United States v. Nixon* (1974), 418 US 683.

48 *Ibid.*, 418 US 695.

49 *Ibid.*, 418 US 704.

50 J. Madsion quoted in *ibid.*, 418 US 704.

51 *Ibid.*, 418 US 706.

52   *Ibid.*, 418 US 707.
53   *Ibid.*, 418 US 713.
54   *Schecter Corp.* v. *United States* (1935), 295 US 495.
55   *Ibid.*, 295 US 541.
56   *Ibid.*, 295 US 551.
57   *Ibid.*, 295 US 553.
58   *Opp Cotton Mills* v. *Administrator* (1941), 312 US 126.
59   *Ibid.*, 312 US 144.
60   *Ibid.*, 312 US 145.
61   *Ibid.*, 312 US 146.
62   *Ibid.*, 312 US 145.
63   *Ibid.*, 312 US 144.
64   *Bowsher* v. *Synar* (1986), 106 US 3181.
65   L. Fisher, 'The Administrative World of *Chadha* and *Bowsher*', *Public Administration Review*, 47 (3) (May/June 1987), p. 213.
66   *Bowsher* v. *Synar* (1986), 106 US 3187.
67   *Immigration and Naturalization Service* v. *Chadha* (1983), 462 US 919. The related cases were: *Process Gas Consumers Group, et al., Appellants* v. *Consumer Energy Council of America, et al.* 463 US 1216; *Interstate Natural Gas Association of America, et al., Appellants* v. *Consumer Energy Council of America, et al.*, 463 US 1216; *Petrochemical Energy Group, Appellant* v. *Consumer Energy Council of America, et al.*, 463 US 1216; *American Gas Association* v. *Consumer Energy Council of America, et al.*, 463 US 1216; *United States Senate, Appellant* v. *Federal Trade Commission, et al.*, 463 US 1216; *United House of Representatives, Appellants* v. *Federal Trade Commission, et al.*, 463 US 1216.
68   *Immigration and Naturalization Service* v. *Chadha*, 462 US.
69   *Ibid.*, 462 US 944.
70   *Ibid.*, 462 US 951.
71   *Ibid.*, 462 US 967.
72   *Ibid.*, 462 US 1002.
73   *Ibid.*, 462 US 1002.
74   *Ibid.*, 462 US 972.
75   H. C. Mansfield, Jr., *Taming the Prince: The Ambivalence of Modern Executive Power* (New York: Free Press, 1989).
76   *Prize Cases* (1863), 67 US 635.
77   *Ibid.*, 67 US 669.
78   *Ibid.*, 67 US 668.
79   *In re Neagle* (1890), 135 US 1.
80   *Ibid.*, 135 US 59.
81   *Ibid.*, 135 US 63.
82   *United States* v. *Curtiss Wright Export Corp.* (1936), 299 US 304.
83   *United States* v. *Belmont* (1937), 301 US 324.
84   *Ibid.*, 301 US 331.
85   *Ibid.*, 301 US 330.
86   *United States* v. *Korematsu* (1945), 323 US 214.
87   *Ibid.*, 323 US 219.
88   *Ibid.*, 323 US 223-4.

89   R. Y. Funston, *A Vital National Seminar: The Supreme Court in American Political Life* (Palo Alto: Mayfield, 1977), p. 46.

90   C. Rossiter, *Constitutional Dictatorship: Crisis Government in Modern Democracies* (New York: Harcourt Brace, 1948), p. 5.

91   R. S. Hirschfield, 'The Power of the Contemporary President', in A. Wildavsky and N. W. Polsby (eds), *American Governmental Institutions: A Reader in the Policy Process* (Chicago: Rand McNally, 1968), p. 137.

92   *United States* v. *Nixon* (1974), 418 US 683.

93   *Ibid.*, 418 US 708.

94   *Ibid.*, 418 US 708.

95   *Ibid.*, 418 US 706.

96   *Ibid.*, 418 US 715.

97   *Ashwander* v. *Tennessee Valley Authority* (1936), 297 US 288.

98   L. H. Tribe, *The Constitutional Structure of American Government: The Separation and Division of Powers* (Mineola: Foundation, 1978), p. 72.

99   *Youngstown Sheet and Tube Co.* v. *Sawyer* (1952), 343 US 579, 595.

100 *Chicago & S. Air Lines* v. *Waterman S. S. Corp.* (1948), 333 US 103.

101 *Goldwater* v. *Carter*, 444 US 996.

102 *Ibid.*, 617 F. 2d 697.

103 R. Nixon, 'Veto of the War Powers Resolution, October 24 1973', *Public Papers of the Presidents of the United States: Richard Nixon, Containing the Public Messages, Speeches, and Statements of the President, 1973* (Washington, D.C.: United States Government Printing Office, 1975), p. 893.

104 *Ibid.*, p. 894.

105 For an examination of how this outlook dissuaded the Supreme Court from taking up the federal district court cases of (i) *Lowry* v. *Reagan* (1987) in which 110 members of Congress challenged America's reflagging of Kuwaiti oil tankers in the Persian Gulf; and (ii) *Dellums* v. *Bush* (1990) in which 56 members of Congress sought to restrain the president from engaging in the Gulf War (1990–1) without prior congressional consent, see M. J. Glennon, 'The Gulf War and the Constitution', *Foreign Affairs*, 70 (2) (Spring 1991), pp. 84–107.

106 For example, see *Crockett* v. *Reagan*, 558 F. Supp 893 (D. D. C. 1982); *Crockett* v. *Reagan*, 720 F. 2d. 1355 (D. C. Cir. 1983). Even when the Supreme Court accepts that a foreign policy case is not a sufficiently political question to exclude it from judgement, the Court has taken congressional inaction as a form of implicit approval of executive action. In *Dames and Moore* v. *Regan* (1981), for example, the Court regarded the absence of congressional objections to comparable presidential actions in the past as a positive source of executive authority. 'We are thus clearly not confronted with a situation in which Congress has in some way resisted the exercise of Presidential authority' (453 US 688). Because Congress had not engaged in resistance, the Supreme Court saw no reason to compensate for its inaction.

107 *Springer* v. *Philippine Islands*, 277 US 189, 202.

108 M. Rubner, 'The Reagan Administration, the 1973 War Powers Resolution, and the Invasion of Grenada', *Political Science Quarterly*, 100 (4) (Winter 1985–6), pp. 627–47.

109 Quoted in C. W. Kegley Jr. and E. R. Wittkopf, *American Foreign Policy: Pattern and Process*, 3rd edn (Basingstoke: Macmillan, 1987), p. 447.

110 *Immigration and Naturalization Service* v. *Chadha* (1983), 462 US 919.

111   Fisher, *Constitutional Conflicts Between Congress and the President*, p. 149.

112   *Ibid.*, p. 152.

113   R. Berger, *Government By Judiciary* (Cambridge: Harvard University Press, 1977), p. 241.

114   For example, see M. Walles, 'Imperial Government or Imperial Judiciary', *Political Quarterly*, 62 (2) (April–June 1991), pp. 273–84.

115   W. Berns, 'Government by Lawyers and Judges', *Commentary* (June 1987), p. 19.

116   G. S. Jones and J. A. Marini (eds), *The Imperial Congress: Crisis in the Separation of Powers* (New York: Pharos, 1988), p. 1.

117   *Ibid.*, p. 320.

118   *Ibid.*, p. 1.

119   *Ibid.*, p. 320.

120   Article III, Section 2.

121   D. G. Barnum, *The Supreme Court and American Democracy* (New York: St Martin's Press, 1993), p. 211.

122   See J. A. Segal, 'Senate Confirmation of Supreme Court Justices: Partisan and Institutional Politics', *Journal of Politics*, 49 (4) (November 1987), pp. 998–1015.

123   See R. Hodder-Williams, 'The Strange Story of Judge Robert Bork and a Vacancy on the United States Supreme Court', *Political Studies*, 36 (4) (December 1988), pp. 613–37; R. H. Bork, *The Tempting of America: The Political Seduction of the Law* (London: Sinclair-Stevenson, 1990), pp. 267–349.

124   Hodder-Williams, 'The Strange Story of Judge Robert Bork', p. 636.

125   R. McKeever, 'Courting the Congress: President Bush and the Appointment of David Souter', *Politics*, 11 (1991), p. 29.

126   M. Comiskey, 'Can the Senate Examine the Constitutional Philosophies of Supreme Court Nominees?', *PS* (September 1993), p. 495.

127   The American Bar Association's Standing Committee on the Federal Judiciary rated Thomas as only 'qualified' for the Supreme Court. This was in marked contrast to 'well qualified' which had been the customary ranking accredited to nominees over the previous twenty years.

128   M. Kramer, 'Shame on them all', *Time*, October 21 1991.

129   See T. M. Phelps and H. Winternitz, *Capitol Games: Clarence Thomas, Anita Hill and the Story of a Supreme Court Nomination* (New York: Harper Collins, 1992).

130   'No wows necessary', *The Economist*, June 19 1993.

131   J. Biscupic, 'With Ginsburg, Clinton Court would radiate to the center', *International Herald Tribune*, June 16 1993. See also 'Clinton's Choice of Ginsburg signals moderation', *Congressional Quarterly Guide to Current American Government*, Fall 1993 (Washington, D.C.: Congressional Quarterly Press, 1993), pp. 80–5.

132   *Youngstown Sheet and Tube Co.* v. *Sawyer* (1952), 343 US 579, 635.

133   For example, see D. Robinson (ed.), *Reforming American Government: The Bi-centennial Papers of the Committee on the Constitutional System* (Boulder: Westview, 1985); J. L. Sundquist, *Constitutional Reform and Effective Government* (Washington, D.C.: Brookings Institution, 1986).

CHAPTER 11

Policy-making controversies

The relationship between the presidency and Congress in a system of separated institutions has a profound influence upon the policy-making capacity of government. It does so not just in the general sense of policy outcomes, but in the operational presuppositions that are cultivated in a framework designed around functional and jurisdictional demaraction. These working assumptions condition public attitudes, structure political debate, and shape the means and ends of policy. By the same token, they also evoke intense dispute both on analytical and normative grounds. What separate institutions can do and should do, how they fulfil their roles and what they actually achieve, either singly or together, become political issues in their own right. Such institutional controversies, woven as they are into the instruments and objects of political dispute, have immense consequences for policy-making. Likewise, it is in the policy-making process that these controversies become most evident. It is for this reason, that the present chapter is dedicated to examining the character and implications of two controversies which are arguably the most significant, and very often the least well understood, points of friction within the governing process.

Controversy I: That foreign-policy making is executive in nature and as such necessarily supersedes the normal dynamics of the separation of powers.

Even though the distribution of powers in the Constitution can be construed as providing the presidency and Congress with 'an invitation to struggle for the control of foreign policy',[1] it often appears that the facts of international life have occasioned an inherent and irrevocable presidential supremacy in the field of foreign and defence policy. The pre-eminence of the modern presidency in what is still seen in America as a distinctively modern sphere of government can be ascribed to two main influences.

Foreign policy as an executive prerogative

The *first* influence is the nature of the executive office itself, which carries with it an obligation to respond to any explicit dangers to the security of the state with the forces of physical coercion at the office's disposal. Only the executive has the runctional capacity of initiative and decision, and of secrecy and despatch, to react with the speed and singleness of purpose required to take action in the national interest.[2] An executive's immediate access to the sources of force brought with it a social trust not to abuse such a privilege but, at the same time, a *de facto* authority to deploy force when circumstances required it.

As the United States became increasingly involved in the outside world, the implicit nature of the executive's wider functions became more apparent and unavoidable. The rise of the modern presidency therefore was a correlate of the rise of the United States to a world power. America's successful development as a world power, in the dangerous and even anarchic conditions of international relations, was seen as going hand in hand with a comparable progression of its political system towards expanded executive power in the defence of American democracy. The transformation amounted to 'a centrifugal-centripetal effect: as American military and economic power moved outward, political power consolidated a home'.[3]

The *second* major influence behind the enhancement of presidential power in foreign affairs was the massive economic and social mobilisation undertaken by the United States first to engage in the total warfare of World War II and, thereafter, to sustain a comparable level of social preparedness during the Cold War. The Soviet threat in particular was instrumental in shifting attitudes away from a reversion to old patterns of decision-making. It led instead to a permanent military and national security establishment in 'peacetime', devoted to maintaining the social disciplines required for global ideological confrontation and to providing the appropriate level of threat to deter Soviet aggression and contain international communism.

The presidency's central position in this apparatus was widely accepted as amounting to a qualitative change in the political relationships between the presidency and Congress. Prior to World War II, Congress had been a functioning partner in foreign policy-making and had successfully frustrated President Roosevelt's objective of implicating the United States in the war at an earlier stage. Congress' isolationist attempts to keep America out of the war through the neutrality legislation of the 1930s was seen in the 1940s, and thereafter, to have been misguided, myopic, and dangerous. Congress' efforts at appeasement were so thoroughly discredited in favour of presidential expertise and foresight that the legislature largely abandoned the field of foreign policy-making. Because of the intensity of the Cold War and its potential for producing sudden crises, the emphasis was placed upon emergency executive powers. Congressional acquiescence reflected the social consensus on the irrefutable necessity to confront communism – even by means that compromised constitutional arrangements.[4]

The governing ethos of the Cold War posture was not one of a temporary dispensation from normal constitutional and political processes but of a permanent and open ended condition of preparedness, in which institutions like Congress conspired in their own marginalisation. The prospect of total war required a totality of discretion in areas touched by national security. The level of executive licence was such that a separate constitution was said to have come into existence in the field of foreign policy. The Supreme Court endorsed such a dichotomy by allowing the traditional arrangements of balanced institutional participation in foreign affairs to be superseded by executive dominance. The Court had laid the foundations of the president's transformation in the landmark case of *US v. Curtiss-Wright Export Corporation* (1936)[5]. Pressed by the growth of international instability that accompanied the rise of European totalitarianism and dictatorship in the 1930s, the Court responded with an exposition which all but excused the presidency from constitutional constraint in the area of international relations.

The Court recognised that the presidency possessed not only powers implied in the Constitution, but also powers inherent in the nature of the executive function. The president's position was not limited to constitutional provisions and acts of Congress, but was drawn from historical precedent, forces of circumstance, and the 'nature of foreign negotiations'. As a consequence, the president was afforded 'a degree of discretion and freedom from statutory restriction which would not be admissible were domestic affairs alone involved'. The Court concluded that the president possessed a 'very delicate plenary and exclusive power . . . as the sole organ of the federal government in the field of international relations'.[5] Ever since 1936, presidents have referred to the *Curtiss-Wright* decision as the basis of their independent authority in foreign affairs. In the Cold War, it formed the backbone of presidential claims to a unified political command structure commensurate with the extremity of the threat posed by communist forces. Judicial silences, evasions and deferments in the area of the presidency's foreign policy powers preserved the thrust of *Curtiss-Wright* and with it the legitimacy of the president's claim to act on behalf the American nation.

The transition to presidential pre-eminence was exemplified by the position of Congress in the post-war system. The dominant foreign policy posture in Congress became one of 'self-restraint on the part of the leadership' based on the principle 'that the President knew better than they and that the nation must speak with only one voice'.[6] Senator Arthur Vandenberg, chairman of the illustrious Senate Foreign Relations Committee, set the tone in 1947 when he conceded that the Congress did not enjoy original jurisdiction in foreign relations' because that was 'the prerogative of the Chief Executive'.[7]

Compared to the self-conscious modernity and efficiency of the presidency, Congress was widely perceived to be an insular and negative institution suffused with constituency pressures and pork barrel politics, and irredeemably wedded to vote trading, log-rolling, and electoral gratification. Analysts and even distinguished senators continued to warn against leaving 'vast and vital decision-making powers in the hands of a decentralised, independent minded, and largely parochial minded body of legislators'.[8]

Such anxieties were misplaced. American foreign policy-making was characterised by a bipartisan consensus expressed through Congress' legitimation of an executive-directed posture. In the defence budget, for example, Samuel Huntington concluded that 'throughout the dozen years after Word War II . . . Congress never vetoed directly a major strategic programme, a force level recommendation, or a major strategic weapon system proposed by the administration in power'.[9]

Legislative oversight of defence expenditures was minimal. Apart from being largely distracted by the 'real estate' elements in the military budget, the Armed Services Committees were bastions of Congress' 'conservative coalition'. As such, they had a hawkish concern with approving and even increasing Pentagon costs, rather than with challenging and decreasing them. As Rep. Otis Pike (D.NY) remarked: 'The House Armed Services Committee doesn't control the Pentagon: the Pentagon controls the House Armed Services Committee'.[10] Congressional co-operation was evident in other areas. During the 1930s, the United States entered into 142 formal treaties. During the same period President Roosevelt concluded 144 executive agreements, which were international arrangements made at presidential level without congressional approval and often without its knowledge. During the 1950s, the number of treaties entered into stood at 138, compared to 2,229 executive agreements (i.e. a ratio of 1:16.2). The trend towards this foreign policy tool that deliberately excluded the Congress continued apace during the 1960s with 114 treaties and 2,324 executive agreements (i.e. a ratio of 1:20.4).

Congress was also prepared to waive its constitutional rights in the area of war powers. It accommodated President Truman's failure either to consult Congress over the Korean crisis, or to ask for its approval in deploying American forces into what was a theatre of war. Congressional cooperation on such a scale was not out of character for the time. According to Arthur Schlesinger Jr. : 'In the decade after Korea. Congress receded not alone from the effort to control the war-making power but almost from the effort to participate in it, except on occasions when national security zealots on the Hill condemned the executive branch for inadequate bellicosity.'[11] The same conditioned compliance was still evident in 1964 when Congress fell over itself to pass the Gulf of Tonkin Resolution in response to President Johnson's call for political support after North Vietnam had launched an allegedly unprovoked attack on two US destroyers. The expansive terms of the resolution were used by President Johnson as the equivalent of a declaration of war. Over the next four years while US force levels in Vietnam were climbing to over half a million personnel, President Johnson always carried the Tonkin Resolution in his pocket to remind his opponents of the instructions that had been vested in him by Congress – i.e. 'to take all necessary measures to repel any armed attack against the forces of the US and to prevent further aggression'.[12]

The pattern of congressional derogation seemed self-evident and firmly set as an immutable condition of *Pax Americana*. Commentators could assert in conclusive terms that in foreign affairs 'committees demur, parties are muted;

Congress looks to the President for leadership and accepts a very limited policy-making role'.[13] It was felt that Congress simply could not match the executive's sources of information, its techniques of appraisal, and its prodigious ability to 'set the framework in which policies were discussed'.[14] Even to question an executive action in such an international context of sustained crisis might jeopardise the political solidarity – or the outside perception of American resolution – that may have been central to the effectiveness of any tactical or strategic manoeuvre. As very few members of Congress would wish to be held publicly responsible for undermining the president's authority, and with it the integrity of American foreign policy, Congress was usually more than content to acquiesce in the face of the commander-in-chief's expressions of national unity.

The challenge

Just when this condition of executive pre-eminence seemed most secure and immune to change, it was suddenly challenged by Congress' encroachment into the previously sacrosanct areas of presidential prerogative. From its 'passive role of ratifying decisions made in the executive branch',[15] Congress began to reassert its constitutional rights and responsibilities in the determination of foreign policy. Legislative pretensions to power graduated from the early guerrilla warfare against President Nixon's management of the Vietnam war (e.g. 'end the war' amendments, fund cut-offs); on to generalized investigations and critical appraisals of America's foreign policy and national security arrangements (e.g. the composition of the defence budget; the costings, performance and strategic needs of individual weapon systems; the conduct of the CIA); and through to the establishment of long-term statutory procedures enabling Congress to acquire information and to sustain its rights of consultation and participation in the formulation of foreign policy (e.g. military deployments, arms sales, executive agreements). This was no longer the subservient Congress of 'low policy and real estate' pre-occupations, but an apparently transformed institution moving into the development of high strategic policy and into the very implementation of policy itself.[16]

Renewed legislative interests were translated into a prodigious array of statutory procedures to secure congressional access to information and to establish the legislature's claims to consultation, and even to participation in the foreign policy process. Congress could no longer be written off as a sleeping partner in the creation of foreign policy. It was 'through the use of its inherent but often dormant powers'[17] that Congress was striving towards active and sustained involvement. It dug into economic policy issues (international trade, foreign aid), roamed into high strategic and diplomatic fields (arms control, human rights, nuclear non-proliferation), and penetrated sensitive areas of intelligence acquisition and covert operations. As it did so, it laid down a profusion of ground rules, statutory conditions, and reporting requirements. 'Clearly the presidents of the

1970s were confronted with a Congress different from those [Congresses] that had willingly, at times enthusiastically, deferred to presidential leadership in the 1950s and 1960s.'[18]

Congress demonstrated that it was prepared to challenge the presidency's prerogatives in very sensitive areas. For example, Congress passed the War Powers Resolution over President Nixon's veto (1973). It suspended military assistance to a fellow NATO ally. Even though it was against the express wishes of the administration, Congress cut off the aid to Turkey following its invasion of Cyprus (1974). Congress effectively wrecked the 1974 trade agreement with the Soviet Union by inserting a human rights amendment that made the agreement conditional upon the liberalisation of Jewish emigration. Congress was also prepared to redefine American interests in Angola by terminating American support to the anti-communist forces engaged in that country's civil war. By 1975, Congress was even prepared to launch an investigative exposure of the CIA and National Security Agency's most secret domestic and foreign operations, ranging from the illegal surveillance of political opponents to the destabilisation of third world economies and the existence of assassination plots against foreign leaders. Even Henry Kissinger, the champion of private diplomacy and American *realpolitik*, had to come to terms with the changed status of Congress and the associated transformation of American foreign policy-making: 'The decade-long struggle in this country over executive dominance in foreign affairs is over. The recognition that the Congress is a co-equal branch of government is the dominant fact of national politics today.'[19]

The forcible intrusion of members of Congress and senators into international affairs appeared to defy both the accumulated precedents of the previous thirty years and the compulsive logic which had previously translated the rise of executive hegemony into an inevitable and simple imperative. It appeared that during the 1970s, 'an increasingly embittered Congress [had] set out to reverse the flow of power to the presidency under the guise of putting controls on the president at a time when the American people were hostile to him. Congress in truth was set on its own power grab'.[20] To many observers, that assault had been so successful that the 'trend toward presidential power had been significantly reversed'.[21] Although Congress was more structurally fragmented and atomised in outlook than ever, its behaviour was abrasive enough to create the widespread impression that foreign policy was now as amenable to legislative politics as it had been to bureaucratic politics. So extraordinary was the rise of Congress in this field that it was portrayed as nothing less than a revolution:

> Since the ending of the Vietnam War an entire system of power has been overturned . . . Chief among the power gainers was the congressional rank and file. Among the booty redistributed by the revolution was control over United States foreign policy, long a presidential prerequisite.[22]

Moreover, there was evidence to suggest that the renewed 'congressional ascendance was not just a swing of the pendulum' but a 'revolution that would not be unmade'.[23]

The effect of these structural and attitudinal changes have been to make foreign policy-making into a highly variable and sometimes quite random process in which old patterns coexist with new arrangements. In the 1980s, both the presidency and Congress worked to come to terms with the traumatic aftermath of the Vietnam War, the Watergate scandal, and the energy crisis. It was a highly ambiguous legacy. In one sense, Congress continued to make spectacular inroads into foreign policy-making. In the field of weapons procurement and arms control, for example, the Congress responded to the public's dismay over the perceived hawkishness of the Republican administration by 'shouldering its way into the process'[24] with a series of dramatic inroads into many of the country's most advanced strategic projects. In the 1986–9 period, the House of Representatives led the way with a series of measures that (i) banned the testing of nuclear weapons in excess of one kiloton; (ii) prohibited the production of new binary chemical weapons; (iii) banned the testing of anti-satellite weapons (ASAT) (iv) cut funding for the Strategic Defense Initiative (SDI) by nearly a half; (v) reduced the production and deployment of the MX missile; and (vi) made deep cuts in the funding of the B2 Stealth bomber.[25]

In 1972, Les Aspin (D.WI), a junior member of the House Armed Services Committee had cited several reasons for the committee's timidity in the face of Pentagon demands:

> The weapon systems are complicated, people don't like to vote against defense measures, and there's always that lurking fear that there's some secret classified document which shows that a thing is really necessary and not just the pet project of some general.[26]

By 1985, Les Aspin had become chairman of the committee. In contrast to earlier times he was pressed, not only by the committee but by the Democratic Caucus as a whole, to challenge the Pentagon's budgetary requirements and even its strategic thinking. Congress sought to compensate for the Republican defence build-up by forcing arms control and superpower negotiation on to the political agenda. Accordingly, it pressed the administration to maintain compliance with SALT 2; it forced President Reagan to incorporate Congress' own 'build down' proposal in the Strategic Arms Reduction Talks (START) process; it insisted that Reagan's START negotiating team included someone who would ensure that the negotiating position adopted by Congress would be put forward and actively pursued; and it pressured the administration into maintaining the established interpretation of the 1972 Anti Ballistic Missile (ABM) treaty which had the effect of first curtailing the testing and development of the SDI project and secondly delaying the deployment of laser-based and kinetic energy weapons into space –

thus allowing time for negotiation and possibly cancellation. The significance of these types of congressional intervention prompted Barry Blechman into the following conclusion:

> The congressional role has grown from that of a relatively minor actor, frequently outspoken but only sporadically consulted, rarely involved in actual decision-making and never in policy execution, to that of a player with star billing in the making of US national security policy and sometimes the lead role in US government decisions.[27]

It was clearly possible to locate instances like this of audacious congressional action taken in direct opposition to many of the administration's high priority policies. For example, through a succession of amendments named after their chief sponsor, Edward Boland (D.MA), the Congress progressively confined the Reagan Administration's freedom of action in supporting the Contra guerilla forces in Nicaragua. At first, the legislation restricted American aid to the inter-diction of military supplies from El Salvador to Nicaragua's Sandinista government and, in doing so, established that US assistance was not designed to overthrow the revolutionary Sandinista regime. Later, the legislation was tightened to impose a cap on funding with subsequent supplementary funds made conditional upon the submission of progress reports by the administration accounting for and defending its policy. In October 1984, the third Boland amendment finally cut off the flow of funds altogether.[30] Even though President Reagan had attached his personal prestige to the Contras in the Nicaraguan civil war, Congress was prepared to frustrate him to the point where he and his staff began to look for private, and ultimately illegal, methods of continuing the support for the guerilla forces.

In the case of South Africa the Reagan Administration's policy of 'construc-tive engagement' began to encounter serious congressional criticism in 1984. Reagan opposed economic sanctions because he believed they would undermine the reformist experiments of the Botha government in Pretoria. But by 1985, when the South African government declared a state of emergency, the anti-apartheid movement in the United States had become a serious centre of influence, calling on the American administration to invoke economic sanctions upon the South African regime as a way of bringing pressure to bear for change. In the absence of any administration support for such measures, 'it was for Congress to take the action itself, to use its institutional share of the shared powers to set the basic terms of US policy'.[28] The ensuing Anti-Apartheid Act (1985) prompted Reagan to issue an executive order imposing limited economic sanctions on South Africa. In 1986, Congress turned the screw by passing a far more comprehensive package of sanctions. Although this was vetoed by the president, Congress prevailed on the issue with the first veto override on a foreign policy issue since the War Powers Resolution in 1973.

By the same token, it was equally possible to discern instances of old institutional infirmities. It was still evident that Congress experienced severe problems in applying war power legislation to presidents who possessed the capacity to take the initiative in both military deployment and public opinion management (e.g. Grenada 1983, Libya 1986, Panama 1989). Congress was clearly discomforted over being seen to compromise America's intelligence agencies – especially following the intelligence fiasco surrounding the unforeseen Soviet invasion of Afghanistan in 1979. The zeal of the 1970s was accordingly relaxed through the reduction of committees monitoring intelligence activities from eight to two and by the abandonment of the project to produce an all-encompassing charter for the CIA.

Congressional reticence was equally apparent in the way that it failed to follow through on the new procedures that it had stipulated to keep itself informed. Executive agencies were statutorily required to produce regular reports to Congress on such subjects as arms control and human rights. But after setting up the infrastructure of control, Congress had become negligent in using the information to condition policy in any consistent or coherent manner. Finally the Iran–Contra scandal gave graphic illustration of the way that a determined section of the White House could not only circumvent the administration's own bureaucracy and foreign policy, but also defy the spirit and thrust of Congress' legal sanctions against supplying military aid to the Contra forces in Nicaragua. Traditional attitudes to presidential prerogative and foreign policy-making clearly remained in existence. The Iran–Contra affair in particular revived interest in the proposition that no matter how much Congress can attempt to engage in a full partnership with the presidency and irrespective of any avowed 'revolution' in legislative–executive relations, the legislature continues to have chronic problems in competing on equal terms with the presidency in foreign policy-making. To Harold Koh, the 1980s showed that very little had changed, i.e. that as a general rule 'the president almost always wins in foreign affairs' for three main and readily familiar reasons that become quite evident when the recent past is analytically reviewed:

> First, and most obviously, the president has won because the executive branch has taken the initiative in foreign affairs and has often done so by construing laws designed to constrain his actions as authorizations. Second, the president has won because, for all of its institutional activity, Congress has usually complied with or acquiesced in what the president has done, through legislative myopia, inadequate drafting, inadequate legislature tools, or sheer lack of political will. Third, the president has won because the federal courts have usually tolerated his acts, either by refusing to hear challenges to those acts or by hearing the challenges and then affirming presidential authority on the merits.[29]

The same indeterminate mix of congressional assertion and revelation coexisting with executive discretion and initiative has also characterised the 1990s. Congress continued to restrict both the research funding and equipment testing of SDI until in May 1993 Les Aspin, by then the Secretary of Defense, announced an end to the project. Congress also continued to press its case on the diplomatic front with moves in 1991 to link a renewal of China's 'Most Favoured Nation' trading status to improvements in human rights and democracy, and pressure in 1994 to encourage President Clinton to remove the economic embargo against Vietnam through a Senate resolution urging the abandonment of the policy. Seen in this light, 'certainly Congress [has] show[n] no sign of retreating from its assertive foreign and defense policy role'.[30]

At the same time signs of the older paradigm continued to make themselves felt. In August 1994, for example, it was disclosed that the CIA had managed to conceal from Congress the construction of an entire $350 million office complex in Washington. Disguised as a corporate centre for Rockwell International, the 'Stealth Building' had been designed to house the National Reconnaisance Office which operates US spy satellites. The Intelligence committees had not been informed of the costs, location, or even of the existence of the NRO's new headquarters. The building had been effectively concealed in the intelligence agencies $6 billion 'black budget' until senators discovered the project during a routine congressional audit of facilities.[31] In the same vein, a month later, Greenpeace issued a report revealing that the United States government had deceived Congress for seven years by illegally supplying Japan with secret and highly advanced nuclear technology to help in the construction of a reprocessing plant capable of extracting weapons grade plutonium. Greenpeace alleged that the transfer of such Sensitive Nuclear Technology (SNT) was contrary not only to US law but also to international non-proliferation agreements. 'Far from denying the charge, Energy Department officials acknowledged that Greenpeace had raised a "valid" question – which in public relations terms meant that the charge was more or less correct'.[32]

But perhaps the incident which best encapsulates the continuing problematic nature of Congress' position in foreign policy came in the build-up to the Gulf War during 1990–1. Initially each house had given its support through resolutions to President Bush's deployment of 200,000 troops to defend Saudi Arabia following Iraq's incursion into Kuwait. But when the president changed the policy objective from defence to one of offence against the Iraqi army, Congress was once again placed in the classic cleft stick. It could give the president a form of open-ended support, required both to maintain operational flexibility and a united front against aggression. Alternatively, it could oppose the commander-in-chief at a time of crisis and, thereby, undermine presidential and American leadership in the eyes of international opinion, and in the process risk American lives by giving encouragement, or at least dangerously mixed signals, to the other parties in such a critical dispute. In this case, Congress was basically unwilling to give advance authority for war, and yet was loath to disrupt President Bush's elaborate assemblage of an international military coalition geared to the meaningful threat of war. Many members of Congress

> felt that they were being manipulated, forced to go along when they had serious and essentially non-partisan reasons for not doing so yet. To have withheld approval would certainly have produced a constitutional crisis on who controls going to war, the last thing needed at the point where diplomacy had produced an international consensus.[33]

The situation was aggravated by President Bush's tendency to overlook Congress and the need to consult it in the development of his war strategy. 'Again and again Bush practically ignored Capitol Hill as he made his decisions. While the administration spoke positively of consultation with Congress, it engaged only in notification – and usually after the fact'.[34] For example, when President Bush decided to double the deployment of US troops on October 30 1990, he announced it as a *fait accompli*. The chairman of the Senate Armed Services Committee, Sam Nunn 'erupted, as he was first informed of the decision only an hour before its announcement and, because he was called on a public telephone at a restaurant, was not even afforded the courtesy of a confidential conversation with Defense Secretary Dick Cheney'.[35]

On January 8 1991, President Bush stated that while he did not need congressional approval for his policy, having such support would strengthen his position on the diplomatic front. Accordingly he asked for the passage of a resolution authorising the use of 'all necessary means' to implement the United Nations resolution calling for the exclusion of Iraqi forces from Kuwait. Bush's risky request paid off and a constitutional crisis was averted, but only just. The Senate narrowly approved the resolution by 52 to 47. While the Senate (and House) votes satisfied Congress' constitutional claims over war powers, it failed to resolve the central problem of what would have happened if Congress had refused to grant such authority. It is clear that irrespective of the congressional vote, Bush was irrevocably committed to launching the attack on the basis of his inherent powers as chief executive. To James Pfiffner, this represented

> an extraordinary claim on the part of President Bush to presidential war power to the exclusion of Congress. Over the history of the United States, most presidential military actions taken without congressional approval were either minor or taken [as a] needed quick military response . . . But President Bush's decision to take the offensive against Saddam Hussein was prepared over a number of months. It was quite obvious to all that the US was preparing for a major military offensive. If the president would not admit that such a situation fell under the war declaration clause of Article I of the Constitution, it is hard to see what the independent role of Congress would be in committing the nation to war.[36]

Members of Congress, therefore, may have felt vindicated by their participation but in the president's view congressional support was a useful adjunct to, rather than an indispensable component of, his policy.

New environments and disrupted orthodoxies

It is true that to a certain extent, the variable nature of the relationship between the presidency and Congress in such an area of policy-making reflects the ancient imprecision in the demarcation of jurisdictions and powers. However, it would be inaccurate to conclude that the 1990s have produced simply more of the same i.e. nothing more than an extension of old adversarial practices reduced for the purposes of simplification to allusions to recurrent cycles and alternating balances of pre-eminence.[37] The context of foreign policy-making in the 1990s has experienced such dramatic changes that the tension between the presidency and Congress is as much derived from these altered conditions as from the continuities of constitutional checks and balances.

1. The *distinction between foreign policy and domestic policy is increasingly breaking down* in the face of a 'globalisation' not only of economic organisations and markets but of social and political issues. It is not simply that more areas of domestic activity now have international implications – or a greater perception of such a wider dimension. It is not even the recognition that foreign and domestic issues can be conjoined into 'intermestic' hybrids. Globalisation refers to the progressive integration of economies and problems that results in an unbroken continuum between national and international policy-making. Domestic politics no longer stops at the water's edge because there is no longer such a discernible edge. Just as American interests became more tightly tied to an international context, so world problems impose themselves more forcibly upon the United States.

The internationalisation of American politics is most evident in explicitly economic areas like trade, tariffs, new materials, energy and the global integration of capital and currency markets.[38] In the mid-1970s, for example, 13 per cent of American production was tied to exports but by 1994 that figure had risen to over a quarter. Just as noteworthy has been the progressive globalisation of the industrial base of American defence. 'The Department of Defense has reported that the lead in developing one-quarter of the technologies most essential to American industry is held by non-US firms, and a growing proportion of the products and components needed for defense come from abroad.'[39]

But globalisation also extends to the growing international nature of other systemic problems and responses (e.g. pollution, global warming, nuclear proliferation, population growth, food and water supplies, terrorism, drug trafficking etc) These issues inject an international dimension into domestic politics. By the same token, they foster the projection of domestic contention into multilateral arenas. The interrelatedness of national economies and social conditions together with the collective action required to manage them result in a crowded and highly complex sphere of foreign policy-making in which the increasing interdependence of the participants is matched by the increasing interdependence of the issues.

2. The *end of the Cold War and the elimination of any 'clear and present danger'* to the United States has further complicated the context of foreign policy-making. The Cold War had generated a coherent international posture, a social consensus geared to anti-communism, and a military conception of national security. The collapse of the Soviet Union turned the US into the only remaining superpower and with it the prospect of an American hegemony over the post-Cold War world. It was thought that the United States would have granted freedom of choice in how and where it would use its influence. In reality, the US found the post-Cold War world to be highly unstable and dangerous. In losing a clearly defined framework for policy, the US has had to resort to a reactive form of leadership and to improvised policy-making in coming to terms with the profusion of problems unleashed by the Soviet Union's demise. The revival of nationalism, the onset of increased fragmentation, the threat of regional conflicts, and the demands for humanitarian intervention in the third world have all coincided with a greater realisation of America's relative economic decline, the growth of isolationist impulses towards giving priority to the national economy over international outreach, and an American public averse to protracted military engagements. The post-Cold War world, therefore, has led to severe anxieties over whether there exists any organising principles for policy in such a plural and volatile world; whether a president can summon up the public support required to sustain a military action or threat of action; whether previous arrangements with allies can survive the post-Cold War changes to the international system and especially the new priority of economic over security concerns; whether the national security apparatus designed with the ultimate military threat of the Cold War in mind is now an anachronism; and finally whether the United States any longer possesses a defined and consistent international role that can inform its foreign policy.[40]

3. The *sweep of globalisation and the uncertainty of the post-Cold War world* have helped to foster a profusion of active interests in the foreign policy field. While international affairs used to attract the intermittent interest of corporations, unions, trade associations, and ethnic groups on a specific and individualised basis, foreign policy is now the regular habitat of a greatly increased volume and range of interest groups. Given the evident salience of world conditions and international decisions upon most ostensibly 'domestic' activities and given the post-Cold War relaxation of the constraints and secrecy surrounding foreign-policy decisions, more interest groups have been more prepared to assert themselves more forcibly in foreign policy issues. Ethnic groups, citizen action and 'cause' organisations, foreign government embassies and not least mainline American economic and social interest groups have responded to the growing

interdependence of the world economy and to the new fluidity in the international system by participating laterally and longitudinally in the area of foreign policy.

4. During the Cold War when the emphasis was on survival and the interconnectedness of dangers, *a mystique surrounded both foreign policy and those who made it.* It was not merely that non-specialists had no access to classified information, or to alternative ideas or appraisals, it was the belief that they would not be able to comprehend them or use them properly even if they were given such access. Foreign policy was necessarily reserved for 'experts' in the shape of a 'foreign policy elite'. This was no ordinary American elite but the archetypal American elite drawn from the eastern WASP establishment.[41] The *débâcle* surrounding Vietnam, the rise of public cynicism, and the decline in presidential authority, the movement towards more open government, the growth of 'think tanks'[42] and the onset of satellite and cable television have utterly undermined the old restrictions on the sources of, and attitudes towards, information on international affairs. Instead of a near monopoly of foreign policy information and reflexive Cold War deference to presidential judgement, presidents are now besieged by a multiplicity of groups and organisations not only with information sources and evaluation techniques of their own but with the means and willingness to challenge a president's foreign policy decisions on tactical, strategic, and ethical grounds.[43] As the ambiguity and discretion of the old foreign policy elite has crumbled in the face of professional foreign policy publicists and activists dealing openly in a deregulated market place of ideas, a new media elite has ensured that the public's access to information is now equal to that provided by the president's own bureaucratic channels.[44] In fact, in many cases the information provided by news organisations like C-SPAN and CNN is superior to that available in the White House. As Micheal Deaver recalls, the Reagan White House would often adjourn to watch CNN:

> Any time there was a world crisis, where would we be? The president and all of us – we'd be back there in his little alcove with the television on. The National Security Council and the Situation Room would bring us bulletins, but we knew things from watching television ten minutes before the NSC and the Situation Room.[45]

5. The turmoil of the late 1960s and 1970s subverted the public's 'followership' of a unilinear foreign policy and of an integrated decision-making system. As the attentive and active sector of the public became more ideologically polarised, the mass public which had been traditionally inert 'became less passive and more distrustful, prone to swing left or right unpredictably in response to current fears and concerns'.[46] That legacy is still evident today. Presidents continually have to condition their foreign policy positions, statements and actions to the state, or likely state, of public opinion. While the connection between public opinion and foreign policy-making used to be seen as minimal in any direct sense,

it is now regarded as far more immediate and extensive than the old 'top-down model' of foreign policy leadership. 'Increasingly . . . despite its low level of interest in foreign affairs, the public insists upon being in the loop, especially when sacrifice and hard choices are involved. The public has come to feel that foreign policy competes with domestic problems for attention and resources'.[47]

The American public remains profoundly sceptical not only of overseas involvement but of foreign policy professionals associated with and often apparently preoccupied with the views and interests of allies and competitors. 'Presidents have a difficult time building and maintaining public support for their foreign policies because the public hears dissenting voices and is inclined to listen to them'.[48]

Furthermore, because the public now has access to sources of immediate information (CNN), presidents have to respond as much to the highly changeable foreign policy agenda set by television news pictures (Somalia, Bosnia) as to the more stable but less visible agenda of arms control, foreign aid, and trade. In the words of one of President Clinton's senior White House advisors:

> CNN has become a universal intervener. We are often forced to respond to them as much as to actual activity. Every meeting has to be a decision meeting. If there is no decision, the president is seen as indecisive. It practically defines our existence here.[49]

The public reputation of presidential authority and competence is now increasingly bound up with the management of foreign policy episodes and domestic opinion on camera. Because American public attitudes to foreign policy tend to be contradictory (e.g. the desire for peace and military might; the demand that the US 'do' something about famine and atrocities but that American forces should not get 'involved'; the need to focus on the domestic economy and limit overseas commitment while simultaneously retaining America's exceptional leadership role in the world) and because the Cold War conditions of leadership have declined so markedly, presidents are increasingly left to improvise and negotiate policies on site. These in turn generate criticisms that the White House has no coherent foreign policy and that the occupant is being led by opinion polls rather than leading the American public.

Congress' increasing assertiveness in the field of foreign policy is a reflection of this new political environment. The erosion of the Cold War consensus, the diminishment of the nuclear threat, and the proliferation of foreign policy options have interacted with normal congressional impulses towards public representation, political self-promotion, policy entrepreneurship, structural decentralisation, and multiple access points, to produce a far more open-ended policy framework than the old enclosed and presidentially centred model. Moreover, Congress has not confined itself to being merely an outlet for public scepticism and dissent. Because of electoral changes (especially in the south) which have undermined the sectional character of the 'conservative coalition' and made foreign policy conflict increasingly partisan in character, and because of internal reforms that have strengthened the Democratic party leadership (especially in the House of Representatives), Congress has developed the organisational integrity to present policy alternatives on an institutional basis.[50]

On those occasions when there is a measure of sustained agreement (especially within the majority party), the Congress has demonstrated that it is able to provide a collective approach to foreign policy through the use of party structures, floor procedures, and leadership powers. At the same time, individual members or groups of members have the political licence to 'go public' and exploit the networks that exist between Congress, interest groups, think tanks, and the mass media in an effort to influence the foreign policy agenda. The Congressional Black Caucus, for example, was instrumental in (i) publicising the atrocities of the military regime in Haiti; (ii) highlighting the injustice and alleged racism of the forced repatriation of Haitian refugees undertaken by the US Coast Guard; and (iii) pressuring the Clinton Administration to take action against the Haitian regime in 1994.

Congressional assertion in foreign policy has in effect become regular and unremarkable. 'Congressional activism on foreign policy is a fact of life in the 1990s.'[51] It is not a simple derivative of 'split-party control' in which Republican presidents are pitted against Democratic agendas on Capitol Hill; neither is it the product of an autonomous institutional cycle in which dominance alternates over time between Congress and the White House. Congress' emplacement in foreign policy-making has arisen from deep-set changes in the social, international, and attitudinal context. The prominence of Congress in such a sphere of policy-making is both a product and agent of the new permability between what were once issue boundaries. Even sub-fields of foreign policy (e.g. trade, foreign aid, equipment, intelligence, strategy, ethnic conflict, military deployment) that could be used to produce a typology of different legislative–executive weightings, are no longer as useful as they once were because of the growing penetration of interdependence.

The porous nature of foreign policy-making and the corresponding erosion of legislative–executive distinctions, however, is not the same as saying that the Congress has reached a position of equivalence with the presidency.[52] Congressional intervention is not congressional occupation. Congress remains a legislative assembly and as such possesses a number of congenital defects that retard, and will always retard, its functional capacity to assume joint command of foreign policy. Congress depends upon the executive for the day to day responsibility for foreign policy. Apart from anything else, 'a relatively centralized, coordinated foreign policy making system' is claimed to be a pre-requisite of the wider international system and '[because] of this international reality, presidents remain the most potent political force in the making of foreign policy'.[53] As such, Congress relies upon the president to be 'to a greater or lesser degree, a constant and insistent force in all foreign policy areas'.[54]

What Congress is intent upon is preserving its licence to intervene in the role of a loyal opposition. Its preference lies in addressing itself to the nation's mistakes and offering attractive solutions, but never to the extent of assuming responsibility for the delicate network of interdependent diplomatic under-standings and military arrangements which characterize the nature of foreign policy. This form of self-denial is, of course, synonymous with the prudential self-defence of blame avoidance and responsibility offloading. Just as Congress claims the right to intervene, it likewise assumes the equal right to withdraw at a moment's notice leaving the presidency to resume control. Notwithstanding such political constants, Congress constitutes a powerful conditioning factor in foreign policy and one that can often frustrate, embarrass, and inhibit presidential decision-making. The recent record of Congress reveals that it can and does intervene in foreign policy-making on the basis of providing legitimate alternatives and responsible choices; that it can generate a deterrent effect on policy-makers through the threat of open criticism and crippling publicity; that its members are not bound by narrow constituency interests but are informed more by personal ideology and 'conceptions of good public policy'[55]; and that in the absence of a foreign policy consensus, Congress can offer a valuable arena of debate and oversight, in which the government is placed in direct contact with the wider public allowing policy to be shaped and legitimised through channels of consent. Presidents may remain pre-eminent in the field but it is a primacy heavily circum-scribed and conditioned by an adversarial culture of scepticism and complaint that is often expressed most forcibly through Congress.

Presidents were always constrained even in the Cold War. But now while still publicly accepting an unrealistically full measure of responsibility for national security and foreign policy, presidents are not only more limited than they were before, but more visibly constrained, by the plurality of forces within the United States and by the instability of the post-Cold War world. Presidents continue to be judged by Cold War standards of policy coherence and social consensus – aided and abetted by the rhetoric of grand design and available solution on the part of presidents and presidential candidates. An explicitly domestic policy president like Bill Clinton, for example, was ultimately compelled to turn his attention to foreign policy and to have his political authority and credibility at home subverted by a foreign policy widely characterised as a set of floundering 'flip-flops'. In essence the foreign policy incoherence of the first post-Cold War president has not simply been a product of personal incompetence or inexperience. It is a derivative of what is now a highly ambiguous world matched commen-surately by the highly nebulous position of the contemporary presidency whose individual pre-eminence in foreign policy is as problematic as the US's own position as the lone superpower in the 'new world disorder'.

Controversy II: That Congress' role in the execution and administration of policy is not and should not be confined to monitoring and supervising the executive after the fact.

The controversy about congressional involvement in foreign policy-making is, of course, part of a wider controversy about the operation of the separation of powers in respect of policy execution and administration. The second controversy focuses on this wider controversy in the light of a range of policy areas where the changing international environment is not a major, direct constraint.

With the rise of the American administrative state in the late nineteenth century, it became an accepted precept of good public administration that the separation of powers should be interpreted to mean that the executive alone should execute, manage, and administer policy, while Congress' role should be confined to monitoring and supervising executive action after the fact. At least since the 1930s and the huge expansion of the administrative state in the New Deal, this passive model of congressional oversight has become hopelessly outdated. Much later, as policy entrepreneurialism became rife on Capitol Hill after the mid-1960s, Congress became involved in all areas and stages of policy-making, including policy execution and evaluation, often offering alternatives to, as well as monitoring and supervising, executive policies.[56] Notwithstanding charges of congressional 'micromanagement', Congress' involvement in policy execution and administration is an inevitable consequence of the separated system established by the Constitution, the continued growth of an extremely large and complex administrative state, and an assertive Congress.

Administration as an executive function

The framers of the Constitution gave little thought to Congress' power to oversee, review, and investigate executive activities – for the simple reason that they did not anticipate a complex bureaucratic state. Congressional involvement in the administration of policy only became controversial when the federal government grew rapidly in the late nineteenth century.

With the huge growth of the federal administrative state, public administrators as well as legislators and outside commentators articulated what was at the time the predominant perspective on public policy-making: that a distinction should be drawn between politics and administration. According to this neat, if dubious, formulation, politics involved making value judgements, accommodating diverse views and interests, responding to popular wishes, and was Congress' province; the administration and implementation of policy was a technical process requiring expertise, objectivity and the strict application of tried and tested bureaucratic principles, and was the executive's responsibility. Precepts of good public administration were married then with formal interpretations of the separation of powers to legitimate strict functional roles for the president and Congress: the president would execute and administer policy; Congress would formulate policies through legislation and confine its role in policy implementation to monitoring and supervising the administrative process after the fact in order to ensure that the laws were being faithfully executed and to secure information for use in the preparation of new legislation.

Support for this politics–administration distinction persisted from the late nineteenth century until well into the twentieth century. Writing in 1885, for example, Woodrow Wilson complained that Congress 'has entered more and more into the details of administration until it has virtually taken into its hands all the substantial powers of government. It does not domineer over the President himself, but it makes the Secretaries [who are 'the executive in fact'] its humble servants.'[57] Fifty years later, even in the midst of the New Deal, the Brownlow Report insisted that Congress' concern was policy formulation through law-making while administration was a presidential and executive responsibility. The report advocated giving the president greater influence over the policy-making functions of what it called 'the headless "fourth branch" of the government'.[58] Even as recently as the early 1960s, the strict politics–administration distinction found strong academic support. Joseph Harris, for example, argued that

> Legislative controls which are unduly detailed stifle initiative, make for inflexibility and inefficiency in the conduct of governmental programs; sometimes result in imposing the will of individual legislators, or small groups, in matters in which they do not speak for the entire legislature and which are best left to executive officials; and end in frustrating the basic will of the legislative body.[59]

Yet, under threat of being overwhelmed by the accelerating expansion of the federal bureaucracy, Congress retreated in the early twentieth century from detailed involvement in policy administration, decided to delegate more and more power to the executive and to limit it less.[60] In the Budget and Accounting Act of 1921, Congress effectively began the process of ceding control over the budget to the president. By the 1940s, as a result of President Roosevelt's 1939 re-organisation plan, the Bureau of the Budget was firmly within the ambit of the president allocating appropriations among competing executive agencies, as well as undertaking legislative clearance of every agency's policy proposals.[61]

With the wholesale expansion of the executive establishment during and after the New Deal, the emergence of the United States as a world power, American involvement in World War II and the onset of the Cold War, Congress delegated enormous policy-making discretion to executive agencies and the president – ordering the Interstate Commerce Commission to protect the 'public interest'; directing the Federal Trade Commission to police 'unfair methods of competition'; insisting that the Federal Communications Commission apply the standard of 'public convenience, interest or necessity'; requiring the Securities and Exchange Commission to ensure that firms do not 'unduly or unnecessarily complicate the structure' or 'unfairly or inequitably distribute voting power among security holders', and so on.[62] These and other delegations of authority were defended and promoted on a number of grounds. First, that Congress (or any other representative assembly) was incapable of devising detailed rules and regulations that addressed the full complexity of contemporary problems. Second, only professional administrators (within the executive) could provide the expertise, experience, initiative, and flexibility necessary for the efficient management of complex policies; and, following Brownlow's recommendations, the president was better placed than Congress to oversee the executive's work: the president could become 'chief executive in his own right, not merely as the agent of Congress'.[63] The legitimacy of the politics–administration distinction was upheld and the functional division of labour between Congress and the executive was reinforced.

Administration as a congressional interest

The growth of the administrative state in the twentieth century served, however, to undermine as well as reinforce the politics–administration distinction, and to make congressional involvement in the administration of policy much more likely.

In delegating policy-making authority, Congress was under no illusion that the executive agencies and the president would perform mere administrative functions, or that legislators would abdicate their policy-making responsibilities completely. Although the executive would henceforth exercise enormous policy-making discretion, legislators reserved the right to insist that administrative and presidential policy choices served congressional interests. Delegation would serve legislators' interests by shifting responsibility (and blame) for detailed policy decisions to others within the executive, thereby creating sufficient distance between elected representatives and policy recipients (their constituents). 'Why [should legislators] take political chances', Morris Fiorina has reasoned, 'by setting detailed regulations sure to antagonise some political actor or another? Why not require an agency to do the dirty work and then step in to redress the grievances that result from its activities?'[64] However, legislators also ensured that agencies and departments remained permeable to congressional intervention. So, when Congress legislated entitlements and regulations – the stuff of New Deal politics – members could be certain of influencing executive decisions in favour of their constituents.

In the immediate post-World War II period, however, Congress was unwilling to return to the intrusive involvement in policy administration so characteristic of the late nineteenth century. This was the heyday of committee government when congressional committees, their client groups, and executive agencies worked closely together in subgovernments. Formal oversight was confined to ensuring that agencies had faithfully executed the laws, and that regulations were based on sound, logical, and empirical premises. Although the 1946 Legislative Reorganisation Act directed newly strengthened House and Senate committees to 'exercise continuous watchfulness of the execution [of laws] by the administrative agencies', neither the level of oversight activity nor its character changed significantly.[65] The 'witch hunts' against alleged subversives by Senator Joseph McCarthy (R.WI) and others also reinforced the view – prevalent in the public administration school – that congressional interventions in policy administration would be irresponsible, unfair, and personally or ideologically motivated.

For several reasons, Congress' willingness to undertake oversight and its capacity to do so increased significantly from the 1960s onwards. *First*, the changing directions of public policy stimulated legislators to extend oversight beyond monitoring and supervision into more direct controls over the executive. The creation of a plethora of new social welfare and social regulatory agencies, such as the Civil Rights Commission, the Area Redevelopment Administration, the Office of Equal Opportunity, the Environmental Protection Agency, the Consumer Product Safety Commission, the Youth Conservation Corps, and the Occupational Safety and Health Administration during the Johnson and Nixon presidencies involved further massive delegations of policy-making discretion to the executive. Under conditions of single-party control, minority Republicans demanded 'comprehensive, continuing and systematic' oversight of executive activities.[66] After 1968, under conditions of split-party control, congressional Democrats increased their oversight activities as part of their efforts to resist the efforts of Republican administrations to undermine programmes they supported – and, in Nixon's case, to oppose the increasingly unpopular war in south-east Asia. Subsequently, in the 1980s and 1990s, legislators were encouraged to adopt more active, direct, and pre-emptive approaches to oversight as the electorate became more and more disenchanted with government in Washington, and as the fiscal climate tightened to prevent the enactment of new programmes or the expansion of old ones.[67]

Second, the new ways in which delegated authority was exercised by executive departments and agencies from the 1960s onwards encouraged greater congressional involvement in administration. Traditionally, the predominant means by which agencies fulfilled their congressional mandates was through case-by-case adjudication, where factual evidence and legal deductions were the sole bases for decisions and in consequence the impact on decision-making was typically small and incremental. From the late 1960s onwards, under pressure from the newly empowered public interest group movement, executive administrators resorted increasingly to issuing quasi-legislative rules which affected entire classes of individuals and types of actions instead of specific named parties. As a result, the rule-making process was effectively transformed into a 'surrogate political process' which frequently attracted powerful political interests on opposing sides,[68] and drew in legislators.

Third, the efforts of Presidents Nixon, Carter, and Reagan to utilise the mechanisms of the administrative presidency to ignore or bypass Congress; to impound congressionally appropriated funds; to badger executive officials in congressionally supported programmes; to oversee and control executive departments and agencies through increased use of their powers of budgeting, spending, reorganisation, and legislative clearance; and, in Reagan's case, to use the OMB to review agency regulations on a systematic basis[69] and to vet executive personnel for ideological correctness all generated congressional reaction.[70]

Indeed, the realities of enhanced presidential control over executive agencies and departments and an increasingly tenuous distinction between politics and administration led to the development of a new theory of executive hegemony over policy execution and administration.[71] Whereas the old public administration model argued for executive hegemony on the bases of efficiency, objectivity, expertise, and flexibility, the new formulation emphasised the executive's greater political accountability, responsiveness, and institutional capacity. Echoing prescriptions for the modern presidency, the new model insisted that the president should be allowed to manage and control policy administration and execution, and Congress should continue only to monitor executive policy-making after the fact, because the president is the only person within the political system who is accountable and responsible to the country as a whole, because only the president has the institutional capacity to oversee a huge, activist, pluralistic administrative state, and because Congress' highly fragmented authority structure and permeability preclude comprehensive oversight.[72] Newly embellished with democratic legitimacy, the new presidency-centred model – like its public administration predecessor – placed responsibility for policy administration squarely within the executive and marginalised congressional involvement. Not surprisingly, Congress reacted and reasserted its role in policy administration and execution.[73] Congress' response to the administrative presidency, Vietnam, then Watergate and the continued growth of 'big government' was to enhance its oversight capacity and strengthen members' incentives to look into executive activities. The Legislative Reorganisation Act of 1970 increased the staffs of congressional committees, required most committees to issue biannual oversight reports, and allowed each to determine whether programmes within their jurisdictions should be appropriated on an annual basis. As a result, more and increasingly expert committee staff were able to act as the eyes and ears of committee leaders, to maintain extensive contact networks with relevant officials in executive departments and agencies, and to develop information systems to enable them to keep track of developments in programmes under their committee jurisdictions. The capabilities and responsibilities of the Congressional Research Service were strengthened and the General

Accounting Office (an agency of Congress) was empowered to undertake pro-gramme evaluations. In the Congressional Budget and Impoundment Control Act of 1974, committees were authorised to undertake programme evaluations them-selves or by contract and to report to Congress; the GAO was further strengthened; a new Congressional Budget Office was established to provide Congress with independent budget data and analyses; and new House and Senate budget com-mittees were created. House and Senate rules were also changed to encourage members to undertake oversight, and specific committees were given special or shared oversight authority to conduct comprehensive reviews of specific subject areas within their jurisdictions.[74]

Fourth, then, driving Congress' determination to enhance its oversight ca-pacity was the influx of younger, more active members in the 1970s who were much more sceptical of the positive role of government. These newly elected policy entrepreneurs were willing to undertake highly public oversight activities on an individual basis to help ensure that executive behaviour better reflected their preferences. They appreciated the likely electoral and political benefits – through mass media attention and publicity back home and in Washington – of becoming more involved in policy administration and execution. As the centralised budgetary process deprived committees of opportunities to authorise new spending pro-grammes, they and their more senior colleagues also understood that such activities helped maintain their committees' power and budget positions. As a result, al-though oversight retained its essentially *ad hoc* and uncoordinated character, as previously, it became more extensive, much more visible, and more effective.[75]

Congressional controls over the administrative process

Viewed in constitutional and political terms, Congress' increased involvement in the execution and administration of policy was inevitable. Given that the Con-stitution gives Congress the supreme authority to determine national policy, it is logical that the legislature must be in a position to define policy in as much detail as it thinks fit.[76] Given that Congress would deny itself vital opportunities to determine policy content and outcomes if it did not intervene during policy administration and execution, legislators have strong incentives to become in-volved. When members of Congress discover – as a consequence of formal oversight activities or as a result of constituency casework – that an executive agency or department has departed from the meaning and spirit of a law or they become aware of how an abstract law they passed actually affects citizens and organisations at the grassroots, they are entitled, if not obliged, to make their views known and to call the agency to account.

The argument that Congress is closely involved in the administrative process can be taken further. As Louis Fisher has observed, 'The legislative function does not cease with a bill that creates an agency. Only by monitoring the operation of a law can members uncover statutory defects and correct agency misinterpretations.'[77] Only through regular oversight can legislators pass and revise laws intelligently and effectively. For legislators to be confined solely to obtaining information on the performance of programmes after the fact, and for them to be denied opportunities and the means to use the information to create remedial legislation is inconceivable and impractical in a separated system.

Beyond this functional rationale, it is important to understand that congressional policy-making – even though it is bound to be uncoordinated and unsystematic – is an integral 'total' process which defies a strict separation between legislating and oversight.[78] 'What we conventionally tend to think of as postenactment oversight', Christopher Foreman insists, 'is in many respects simply a continuation of preenactment politics.'[79] In reality, the congressional policy process is continuous, cumulative, involves considerable backing and filling, and occurs in many different arenas. Given that members of Congress will perceive so much at stake in the administration and execution of policy, oversight by the legislature cannot be regarded as separate from the legislative authorisation and appropriation processes; responsibility for conducting oversight cannot be assigned to specific legislators or legislative subunits; and administration and execution of policy cannot be recognised as the exclusive preserve of the executive. Within a separated system, administering and executing policy necessarily involves both Congress and the executive, as does legislating.

Under the Senate's advice and consent procedures, senators may explore the expertise, suitability, and policy preferences of the president's nominees for executive positions when they appear before the relevant committees at confirmation hearings. Although very few nominations are rejected, senators are provided with important opportunities to influence the president, his nominees, and subsequent policy. Often they extract commitments on the future direction of policy or promises that the committee be kept informed of proposed actions or that nominees will seek prior approval from relevant committees before taking action. Occasionally, they withhold final action on confirmation until a nominee or the administration agrees to make certain policy promises.

> *Example*: Following criticism that former Secretary of Defense Les Aspin had failed to provide combat commanders in Somalia with sufficient support, in February 1994, Senate Armed Services Committee members won a promise from William J. Perry, President Clinton's nominee to replace Aspin, that he would provide field combat commanders with the necessary support in any future engagements, and that he would reorganise the 'ineffective network of assistant secretaries' that had been established in the Pentagon under Aspin. Perry also pledged that the Administration would comply with senators' requests for increased funding for military operations and maintenance.[80]

Investigations tend to be the most spectacular form of congressional over-sight because they produce large volumes of written evidence and attract public attention through television. They are often an effective means by which Congress ensures executive accountability and have been recognised as such by the courts.[81] Even the threat of hearings may ensure executive compliance. However, whether congressional investigations result in changes in executive policies depends on a number of factors, including the capacity of the investigating committee, the prevailing relations between committees and executive agencies, and the willing-ness and ability of executive officials to cooperate with investigating committees. Undoubtedly, as the examples in Table 11.1 show, a number of important con-gressional investigations have led to changes in public policy, albeit not all positive. The notorious hearings held by the House UnAmerican Activities Committee and by McCarthy, for example, led to new internal security measures but they also prompted Congress to write new rules protecting witnesses appearing before congressional committees.

Much less clear is the impact of numerous periodic reports Congress requires from executive agencies, inspectors general (appointed to agencies to investigate fraud, inefficiency, and abuse of authority), the president, and from Congress' own support agencies – including the GAO (which conducts policy analysis, programme evaluation and management accounting), the CRS, the CBO, and the OTA – which comment on the performance of specific programmes.[82] Undoubt-edly, some of these reports do influence legislation.

Example: Reports by the GAO and the Energy Department's Office of Inspector General were used by the Oversight and Investigations Sub-committee of the House Energy and Commerce Committee as the basis for hearings on the funding of the superconducting super collider in June 1993. At a time when pressures to cut the budget deficit where intense, the reports highlighted examples of frivolous spending, cost overruns, and delays in building. In October 1993, the House voted to kill $11 billion in appropria-tions for the project and required the Energy Secretary to submit detailed plans to shut it down.[83]

However, whether or not executive or congressional reports have a systematic effect on policy is uncertain.[84] Some reports – like those on the emerging savings and loan crisis in the 1980s from the Federal Home Loan Bank Board, the GAO, and various congressional committees; and those by the Inspector General of the Department of Housing and Urban Development on the Moderate Rehabilitation Programme (MOD REHAB) – were ignored. Others have had more diffuse effects. While their specific recommendations may not be translated into legislation they have generated valuable information, helped Congress focus on broad rather than narrow policy concerns, kept alive certain issues, and legitimised particular policy ideas – what Johannes calls 'issue incubation' – which have

Table 11.1. The policy impact of major congressional investigations

	Investigation	Policy Impact
1950s	House UnAmerican Affairs Committee, Disloyalty and espionage in or near government ranks; Senate Foreign Relations Committee, Disloyalty in the State Department; Investigative Subcommittee of the Senate Government Operations Committee, Subversion in the State Department and the Army.	Passage of the McCarran Internal Security Act of 1950; and new safeguards for witnesses appearing before congressional committees to assure fairness, pertinency of questions, and witnesses' civil liberties.
1965–70	Senate Foreign Relations Committee, Misguided IndoChina Policy; Disastrous and deceptive IndoChina policy; Continued US overinvolvement in IndoChina.	Reduction and eventual end to congressional funding of the war effort in south east Asia; and passage of the War Powers Resolution of 1973.
1973–74	Senate Select Committee on Presidential Campaign Activities and House Judiciary Committee, Watergate break-in and cover-up.	Resignation of President Nixon; criminal indictment of top administration officials; passage of the Ethics in Government Act and the Federal Election Campaign Act of 1974.
1975–76	Senate Select Committee to Study Government Operations With Respect to Intelligence Activites and House Select Committee on Intelligence, Dubious covert operations by US intelligence agencies.	New statutory and executive orders to control intelligence agencies; passage of the Hughes-Ryan Act of 1974; passage of the Intelligence Accountability Act of 1980; and the creation of permanent House and Senate select committees on intelligence.
1977–78	House Government Operations Committee; Senate Governmental Affairs Committee; Senate Environment and Public Works Committee, Financial scandal in the General Services Administration.	New statutory controls over GSA contracting procedures; passage of the Inspector General Act of 1978.
1983–84	House Energy and Commerce Committee, Political favouritism, conflict of interest, and general laxness in toxic-waste cleanup by the Environmental Protection Agency.	Resignation of the EPA director; dismissal of other top EPA officials by President Reagan; Superfund budget increased; more vigorous enforcement of environmental laws.
1987–88	Senate Select Committee on Secret Military Assistance to Iran and the Nicaraguan Opposition and House Select Committee to Investigate Covert Arms Transations with Iran. Ill-advised arms-for-hostages deal with Iran.	National Security Decision Directive on Special Activities amending executive procedures for covert action; amendment of statutory reporting requirements; creation of a statutory Office of Inspector General in the Central Intelligence Agency; criminal indictment and imprisonment of executive officials.
1989–90	House Government Operations Committee; Corruption in Reagan's Department of Housing and Urban Development; Senate Committee on Banking, Housing and Urban Affairs.	Improvements in reporting to Congress by the Department of Housing and Urban Development; administrative reforms within the department; passage of the Department of the Housing and Urban Development Reform Act of 1989.

Sources: David R. Mayhew, *Divided We Govern, Party Control, Lawmaking, and Investigations, 1946–1990* (New Haven and London: Yale University Press), pp. 13–25 and US Congress, Joint Committee on the Organisation of Congress, House Report 103–413/Senate Report 103–215, *Organisation of the Congress*, Vol. 2 103rd Congress, First Session, pp. 154–5.

helped shape a policy environment conducive to change.[85] For example, the discovery in 1994 of a spy in the CIA and of the agency's secret satellite complex being built outside Washington led congressional intelligence committees to demand more effective counter-intelligence and less secrecy, and to some members calling for the agency's abolition.

Some of the most direct policy results of oversight are felt through Congress' appropriations, reauthorisation, and budgetary processes. Using Congress' power of the purse, the House and Senate Appropriations committees review the existing operations and activities of executive agencies and departments on an annual basis as a matter of course before deciding the level and conditions under which new appropriations will be granted. Appropriators exercise almost complete discretion in deciding whether or not a programme will be funded, stipulating in detail how appropriations are to be spent, earmarking funds for specific projects in members' districts and states, and attaching 'riders' (often after little public debate) which explicitly prohibit the use of funds for specified purposes. This is congressional involvement in administrative policy-making at its most direct.

> *Example*: In 1984, the Labor-Health and Human Services-Education Subcommittee of the House Appropriations Committee learnt that the Occupational Safety and Health Administration had given a compliance waiver to a Virginia company while it studied the effects of cotton dust standard on the company's workers. Congressman David Obey (D.WI), a leading member of the subcommittee, persuaded his colleagues to include language in the fiscal 1985 appropriations bill which forbade this 'inappropriate human experimentation'.[86]

As a result of annual appropriations reviews and decisions, major changes of policy in areas as diverse as public works, abortion, and foreign aid have resulted. In January 1995, the new Republican leaders of Congress made it clear that they would use the appropriations process to review and, if necessary, eliminate a number of programmes and agencies.

Besides the annual appropriations process, since the late 1950s Congress has exercised control over the executive by authorising federal programmes for specified periods of time. Temporary authorisations enhance the influence of authorising committees over the subsequent appropriations process because the annual authorisation normally is approved first and the amount set by authorisers directly influences the amount subsequently appropriated. However, temporary authorisations also allow Congress frequent opportunities to review an executive agency's activities, which often result in legislators redirecting them, redefining the agency's purposes, making changes in law, or if it lacks confidence in an agency imposing stronger controls or even reorganising it out of existence.

> *Example*: In 1993, hearings conducted by the House Education and Labor and Senate Labor and Human Resources committees to reauthorise Project

Head Start until 1993 revealed that despite increases in resources and improvements in management and oversight, the performance and quality of the programme had not fulfilled expectations. Sensing that questions about the programme's quality might threaten bipartisan support for reauthorisation, Health and Human Services Secretary Donna Shalala announced in March 1993 that the programme's coverage would be cut back and a bipartisan advisory committee would be appointed to deal with problems of quality. Ultimately, legislation to reauthorise the programmes was approved which followed closely the recommendations of the advisory panel, required the Secretary to improve the standards for Head Start centres, and stipulated that 25 per cent of new appropriations should be set aside for quality improvements.[87]

Since deficit politics has come to occupy such a central place in Washington's policy agenda, Congress' all-persuave budgetary procedures established by the Congressional Impoundment and Budget Control Act of 1974, the Gramm-Rudman-Hollings Balanced Budget and Emergency Deficit Control Act of 1985 (as amended), and the 1990 Budget Enforcement Act inevitably draw the House and Senate budget committees, the CBO, and the party leaderships into evaluating and reviewing existing authorisations and appropriations which then influence the content of subsequent budget resolutions.

Example: In its first fiscal 1994 budget resolution, Congress instructed authorisation committees to reduce the total for military pay by $2 billion; extend examination fees charged by the Federal Deposit Insurance Corporation to state chartered banks; require employees to report private health coverage in order to help avoid the cost of Medicare and Medicaid coverage; make savings from foreign service retirement; increase patent, trademark, recreation and mining fees; eliminate the option for federal employees to take lump-sum retirement benefits; and reduce federal pay.[88]

Critics of oversight through the budget process have argued that discretionary spending caps invoked by the 1990 Budget Enforcement Act tend to thwart new programme initiatives and favour older (usually entitlement) programmes which have established political constituencies.[89] 'Once a programme has been created', Senator William Cohen (R.ME) has argued, 'it is virtually impossible to cut it back. Indeed the pressure is on to expand it to satisfy a particular group.'[90] Although the termination of the superconducting super collider in 1993 is a good counter-example, Congress sometimes ignores the results of its own evaluations.

Example: In August 1994, the House and Senate approved $2.1 billion in continuing appropriations for the space station Alpha, a joint venture with Russia, despite a critical evaluation report from the GAO which concluded that Russian involvement would actually add $2 billion to NASA's estimated costs of a further $30 billion to assemble, launch and operate the station over 18 years, and that the venture was of dubious scientific value.[91]

A final powerful means by which Congress influences the execution and administration of policy is through several forms of veto. Supreme Court Justice Byron White observed in 1983 that 'the prominence of the legislative veto mechanism in our contemporary political system and its importance to Congress can hardly be overstated. It has become a central means by which Congress secures the accountability of executive and executive agencies.'[92] Legislative vetoes make power and discretion delegated to the executive directly contingent upon further congressional review and control by establishing mandatory waiting periods (usually 60 to 90 days) within a statutory delegation of authority during which Congress (or one of its committees) may disapprove action taken by an executive department or agency, or the president.[93] They are used most frequently where Congress wishes to control executive discretion but finds it difficult to define guidelines for an agency in the authorising statute and appropriations procedures are likely to be ineffective because money is not significant. Since 1932, well over 500 veto provisions have been enacted into law. By 1983, well over half of statutes containing congressional vetoes and over two-thirds of individual veto provisions had been enacted since 1969.

> *Example*: In March 1977, the US Food and Drug Administration proposed a ban on saccharin following tests in Canada suggesting its carcinogenic potential. In response to public outrage that no approved sugar substitute would be available (cyclamate, the only other substitute having been banned already), members of the House Interstate and Foreign Commerce Committee questioned the ban 'based on the results of a study in which rats were fed the equivalent of 800 bottles of diet soda a day, an amount hundreds of times higher than the average Americans could be expected to consume.' Months later, Congress approved the Saccharin Study and Labelling Act, the provisions of which included an 18-month moratorium on any possible FDA ban on the use of saccharin; a requirement that the FDA undertake further study and report the results to Congress; and a mandate that a two-sentence warning be placed on all food products containing saccharin.[94]

Congress often used vetoes to retain control over the shifting of funds by executive agencies across budgets after monies have been appropriated and to prevent 'reprogramming' (moving funds from one discrete activity to another) without congressional consent. These vetoes require agencies to report reprogrammings to the relevant appropriations subcommittees or full committees or to other relevant committees thereby affording these units or their chairs opportunities to disapprove them during pre-set waiting periods or allowing them to come into effect following congressional notification.

Example: In 1994, the Senate Appropriations Committee included provisions in the Department of Veterans Affairs and House and Urban Development, and Independent Agencies bill directing the funded departments and agencies 'to notify the chairman of the committee prior to each reprogramming of funds in excess of $250,000', and to notify the committee of reprogrammings of lesser amounts if they involved changes in agencies' future funding requirements. The committee also required departments and agencies to submit operating plans for its approval within 30 days of the bill's enactment.[95]

The upward trend in the use of all types of congressional vetoes might have been halted by a landmark US Supreme Court decision in 1983. In *Immigration and Naturalisation Service* v. *Chadha*, 462 US 919, the Court declared 'congressional' forms of the veto unconstitutional because they failed to provide for the president's signature and for the approval of both houses in Congress.[96] In response to the Court's decision, Congress withdrew most of the president's powers granted in the 1974 Budget Act to defer spending. However, Congress continued with impunity to enact congressional and other forms of veto. In the 16 months between the *Chadha* decision and October 1984, for example, Congress approved an additional 53 legislative vetoes (including some which involved the most controversial issues of the day). Between 1984 and 1994 probably more than 300 vetoes have been added, mostly of the committee type and all with the president's signature.[97]

While the size and scope of the federal government remains large and complex, while executive officials continue to demand wide discretion in administering delegated authority, and while members of Congress wish to exercise control without having to pass new legislation, the legislative veto will continue to be used by Congress as an important mechanism for influencing and controlling administrative policy-making and congressional–executive relations. Indeed, it is these forces of everyday Washington politics which explain why the legislative accommodations which were reached before *Chadha* persist, and why new accommodations between the two branches have been forged after the Court's ruling, sometimes in forms strikingly similar to the legislative veto ruled unconstitutional by the Court.[98]

In a wider sense, however, the dispute surrounding the veto goes to the heart of our second controversy. Leaving aside the legal controversies involved in the *Chadha* decision,[99] the arguments of opponents of the veto voice similar concerns to those used by the older public administration tradition against congressional intervention in administrative policy-making: that Congress use of veto mechanisms promotes *ad hoc*, arbitrary, and irrational policy outcomes; introduces 'unnecessary' political considerations into administrative policy-making; and increases the excessive influence of client groups operating within policy subsystems swirling around the relevant congressional committees and executive departments and agencies.[100] Congressional intervention in the administrative process is perceived as undesirable and detrimental to good public policy. 'Expert', 'objective', and 'judicious' administrators are seen as wiser than legislators.[101] The inevitable conclusion reached by the veto's critics is that only the executive should be involved in administrative decisions and that Congress should be confined to a supervisory role in which it may only seek to modify agencies' policies by passing remedial legislation *after the fact*. Implicitly or explicitly, theirs is a model of administrative policy-making which is fundamentally anti-political, barely conceals a basic lack of faith in politics and the processes of political negotiation and compromise which are such an important element in congressional–executive relations within a separated system.

Congress as co-manager of the executive

Regardless of their individual features, prescriptions which equate good public policy with executive predominance violate Madisonian principles. The constitutional doctrine of the separation of powers on which they are supposed to be based assumes no neat division of power between the legislature and the executive nor any sequential distinction between legislative and administrative processes. The Constitution implied a separated system in which Congress, the president, and courts share in the business of governing. There can be no constitutional basis, therefore, for assuming that policy discretion once delegated by Congress automatically becomes the exclusive preserve of the executive. Nor, as a practical matter, can there be. Given that administrative agencies now make very significant and highly discretionary policy decisions – which affect the balance of power among various social and political interest in the ways that legislative decisions do – it is inconceivable and undesirable that the currently assertive Congress, equipped with substantial staff capacity, invigorated by policy entrepreneurialism, and operating within the contemporary context of widespread public ambivalance towards the bureaucratic state and split-party government, would be debarred from exercising influence over administrative decisions.[102] And, on democratic grounds, there seems much to be said for political representatives in Congress exercising control and influence over appointed officials, who are likely to be constrained by professional perspectives and values at the expense of broader policy and political considerations; and much to be said for a second round of politics at the execution and administrative stages of policy-making.[103]

In some areas, Congress probably has been guilty of micromanaging executive agencies and departments,[104] but in other areas (such as oversight of the savings and loan industry and mismanagement at HUD) it has been remiss. Most important, however, is that just as Congress and the president share responsibility for creating legislation, these tandem or partner institutions share responsibility for co-managing administration policy-making. As the examples from environmental protection policy, Head Start, OSHA, military spending, clean water, the superconducting super collider, foreign policy and other areas demonstrate, congressional involvement in administrative policy-making is commonplace and intrinsic to the congressional policy-making process. Although those individuals and units of Congress who become involved in administrative policy-making – especially committees and their chairmen – may not be perfectly representative of the entire Congress;[105] although congressional involvement often may be motivated by partisan, ideological, and constituency considerations;[106] although subsystem loyalties often may prevail; although Congress may become caught up in the minutiae of detail at the expense of the wider picture;[107] and although oversight of the executive is not and probably cannot be truly comprehensive and continuous,[108] Congress' increased role in administrative policy-making seems to be a sensible adaptation to the conditions of the modern administrative state.[109] Even more important, Congress' right to intervene in administration fulfils an important requirement of republican government in America that policy decisions are based on accommodations among different majorities represented in separate institutions, elected at different times and by different means. An active role for Congress in the administration of policy seems a vital means by which the institutional balance of power may be sustained.

Notes

1   Edward S. Corwin, *The President: Office and Powers* (New York: New York University Press, 1940), p. 200.

2   See John Locke, *Two Treatises of Government*, intro. Peter Laslett (Cambridge: Cambridge University Press, 1960), p. 384.

3   Walter LaFeber, 'The Constitution and United States Foreign Policy: An Interpretation', *Journal of American History*, 74 (1987), p. 706.

4   James L. Sundquist, *The Decline and Resurgence of Congress* (Washington, D.C.: Brookings Institute, 1981), ch. 5.

5   *United States* v. *Curtiss-Wright Export Corporation*, 299 US 304.

6   Erwin C. Hargrove, *The Power of the Modern Presidency* (New York: Alfred Knopf, 1974), p. 164.

7   Michael Leigh, *Mobilising Consent: Public Opinion and American Foreign Policy 1937–1947* (Westport: Greenwood, 1976), p. 168

8   J. William Fulbright, 'American Foreign Policy in the Twentieth Century', *Cornell Law Quarterly*, 47 (1961), p. 7.

9   Samuel P. Huntington, *The Common Defense* (New York: Columbia University Press, 1961), p. 124.

10 Quoted in 'Armed Services: Advocates or Overseers?', *Congressional Quarterly Weekly Report*, March 25 1972, p. 673.

11 Arthur M. Schlesinger, Jr., *The Imperial Presidency* (London: Andre Deutsch, 1974), p. 169.

12 *Congressional Record*, 88th Congress, Second Session, August 7 1964, p. 18471.

13   Barbara Hinckley, *Stability and Change in Congress*, 2nd edn (New York: Harper and Row, 1978), p. 167.

14   Roger Hilsman, *To Move a Nation: The Politics of Foreign Policy in the Administration of John F. Kennedy* (New York: Doubleday, 1967), p. 557.

15   David J. Vogler, *The Politics of Congress*, 2nd edn (Boston: Allyn and Bacon, 1974), p. 239.

16   See Thomas M. Franck and Edward Weisband, *Foreign Policy by Congress* (New York: Oxford University Press, 1979); Hoyt Purvis and Steven J. Baker (eds), *Legislating Foreign Policy* (Boulder: Westview, 1984).

17   R. Haas, 'Congressional Power: Implications for American Security Policy', *Adelphi Papers*, No. 153 (London: IISS, 1979), p. 10.

18   James A. Nathan and James K. Oliver, *Foreign Policy Making and the American Political System*, 2nd edn (Baltimore and London: Johns Hopkins University Press, 1994), p. 118.

19   Quoted in LaFeber, 'The Constitution and United States Foreign Policy', p. 715.

20   Rowland Evans and Robert Novak, *The Reagan Revolution* (New York: Dutton, 1981), p. 18.

21   Joseph L. Nogee, 'Congress and the Presidency: The Dilemma of Policy-Making in a Democracy', in John Spanier and Joseph L. Nogee (eds), *Congress, the Presidency and American Foreign Policy* (New York: Pergamon, 1981), p. 189.

22   Franck and Weisband, *Foreign Policy by Congress*, p. 3.

23   *Ibid.*, p. 6.

24   Barry M. Bletchman, 'The New Congressional Role in Arms Control', in Thomas E. Mann (ed.), *A Question of Balance: The President, the Congress and Foreign Policy* (Washington, D.C.: Brookings Institution, 1990), p. 113.

25   James M. Lindsay, *Congress and Nuclear Weapons* (Baltimore and London: Johns Hopkins University Press, 1991).

26   Quoted in 'Armed Services Committees: Advocates or Overseers?', p. 675.

27   Blechman, 'The New Congresional Role in Arms Control', p. 109. See also Barry M. Blechman, *The Politics of National Security: Congress and US Defense Policy* (New York: Oxford University Press, 1990); Barry M. Blechman, 'The Congressional Role in Congressional Military Policy', *Political Science Quarterly*, 106 (1991), pp. 17–32.

28   Bruce W. Jentleson, 'American Diplomacy: Around the World and Along Pennsylvania Avenue', in Mann (ed.), *A Question of Balance*, p. 159.

29   Harold H. Koh, *The National Security Constitution: Sharing Power After the Iran-Contra Affair* (New Haven: Yale University Press, 1990), p. 117.

30   Barbara Hinckley, 'Governing Unheroically (and Sometimes Unappetizingly): Bush and the 101st Congress', in Colin Campbell and Bert A. Rockman (eds), *The Bush Presidency: First Appraisals* (Chatham, NJ: Chatham House, 1991), p. 173.

31   J. Kahn, 'Senators Detect CIA's Concealed Spy Centre', *Financial Times*, August 10 1994.

32   Quoted in Peter Pringle, 'Nuclear Pledge Goes to Waste', *The Independent*, September 12 1994.

33   W. C. Olson, 'The US Congress: An Independent Force in World Politics', *International Affairs*, 67 (1991), p. 559.

34   David Gergen, 'America's Missed Opportunity', *Foreign Affairs*, 71 (1992) p. 7.

35   *Ibid.*, p. 8.

36   James P. Pfiffner, *The Modern Presidency* (New York: St Martin's Press, 1994), pp. 183–4. See also James A. Nathan, 'Salvaging the War Powers Resolution', *Presidential Studies Quarterly*, 23 (1993), pp. 235–68. Michael J. Glennon, 'The Gulf War and the Constitution', *Foreign Affairs*, 70 (1991), pp. 84–101; Louis Fisher, 'Congressional Checks on Military Initiatives', *Political Science Quarterly*, 109 (1994–5), pp. 739–62.

37   See Michael Foley, *Laws, Men and Machines: Modern American Government and the Appeal of Newtonian Mechanics* (London: Routledge, 1990), ch. 4.

38   Stephen Burman, *America in the Modern World: The Transcendence of United States Hegemony* (Hemel Hempstead: Harvester Wheatsheaf, 1991), chs 4 and 9.

39   Theodore H. Moran, 'International Economics and National Security', *Foreign Affairs*, 69 (1990/91), p. 80.

40   See Michael J. Hogan (ed.), *The End of the Cold War: Its Meaning and Implications* (Cambridge: Cambridge University Press, 1992); Graham Allison and Gregory F. Treverton (eds), *Rethinking America's Security* (New York: Norton, 1992).

41   Charles W. Kegley, Jr. and Eugene R. Wittkopf, *American Foreign Policy: Pattern and Process*, 3rd edn (Basingstoke: Macmillan, 1987), pp. 261–8. For an examination of the decline of the old foreign policy elite, see James B. Judis, 'Twilight of the Gods', *Washington Quarterly*, 14 (1991), p. 55.

42   David M. Ricci, *The Transformation of American Politics: The New Washington and the Rise of Think Tanks* (New Haven: Yale University Press, 1993).

43   John T. Tierney, 'Interest Group Involvement in Congressional Foreign and Defense Policy', in Randall B. Ripley and James M. Lindsay (eds), *Congress Resurgent: Foreign and Defense Policy on Capitol Hill* (Ann Arbor: University of Michigan Press, 1993), pp. 89–111.

44   L. King with M. Sencel, *On The Line: The New Road to the White House* (New York: Harcourt, Brace, 1993); E. O'Shaughnessy, N. Leman and David Halberstam, 'The New Establishment', *Vanity Fair*, 57 (1994), pp. 109–59.

45   Quoted in Robert J. Donovan and Robert Scherer, *Unsilent Revolution: Television News and American Public Life, 1948–1991* (Cambridge: Cambridge University Press, 1992), p. 316.

46   Thomas E. Mann, 'Making Foreign Policy: President and Congress', in Mann (ed.), *A Question of Balance*, p. 12.

47   Daniel Yankelovich and J. Immerwahr, 'The Rules of Public Engagement', in Daniel Yankelovich and I. M. Destler (eds), *Beyond the Beltway: Engaging the Public in US Foreign Policy* (New York: Norton, 1994), pp. 43–4, 45.

48   Mann, 'Making Foreign Policy', p. 13.

49   Quoted in BBC Radio 4, *Analysis*, 'Paved With Good Intentions', November 25, 1993.

50   See David W. Rohde, 'Partisan Leadership and Congressional Assertiveness in Foreign and Defense Policy', in Deese (ed.), *The New Politics of American Foreign Policy* (New York: St Martin's Press), pp. 76–101.

51   James M. Lindsay, 'Congress and Diplomacy', in Ripley and Lindsay (eds), *Congress Resurgent*, p. 280.

52   Barbara Hinckley, *Less Than Meets the Eye: Foreign Policy Making and the Myth of an Assertive Congress* (Chicago: University of Chicago Press, 1994).

53   Paul E. Peterson, 'The President's Dominance in Foreign Policy Making', *Political Science Quarterly*, 109 (1994), p. 217.

54   Peter Woll, *Congress* (Boston: Little, Brown, 1985), p. 436.

55 James M. Lindsay, 'Testing the Parochial Hypothesis: Congress and the Strategic Defense Initiative', *Journal of Politics*, 53 (1991), p. 872.

56 We follow Ogul's more expansive definition of oversight meaning 'behaviour by legislators or their staffs, individually or collectively, which results in an impact, intended or not, on bureaucratic behaviour'. Morris S. Ogul, *Congress Oversees the Bureaucracy. Studies in Legislative Supervision* (Pittsburgh, PA: University of Pittsburgh Press, 1976). Cf. Joel D. Aberbach, *Keeping a Watchful Eye. The Politics of Congressional Oversight* (Washington, D.C.: Brookings Institution, 1990); and Allen Schick, 'Politics Through Law: Congressional Limitations on Executive Discretion', in Anthony King (ed.), *Both Ends of the Avenue. The Presidency, the Executive Branch, and Congress* (Washington, D.C.: American Enterprise Institute, 1983).

57 Woodrow Wilson, *Congressional Government. A Study in American Politics* (Baltimore and London: Johns Hopkins University Press, 1981), p. 49.

58 The Brownlow Report is President's Committee on Administrative Management, *Administrative Management in the Government of the United States* (Washington, D.C.: USGPO, 1937), pp. 3 and 40.

59 Joseph P Harris, *Congressional Control of Administration* (Washington, D.C.: Brookings Institution, 1964), p. 2.

60 The Supreme Court sanctioned congressional delegation of power to executive agencies in *Hampton* v. *US*, 276 US 394 (1928) so long as delegations are accompanied by 'intelligible standards or principles or guidelines'. Since 1935, the Court has not declared a delegation of power to be unconstitutional despite the broad and sweeping nature of many.

61 Sundquist, *The Decline and Resurgence of Congress*, p. 21.

62 Louis Fisher, *American Constitutional Law* (New York: McGraw-Hill, 1990), p. 226; and Schick, 'Politics Through Law', p. 163.

63 Schick, 'Politics Through Law', p. 160.

64 Morris P. Fiorina, 'Congressional Control of the Bureaucracy: A Mismatch of Incentives and Capabilities', in Lawrence C. Dodd and Bruce I. Oppenheimer (eds), *Congress Reconsidered*, 2nd edn (Washington, D.C.: Congressional Quarterly Press, 1981) pp. 342–3; see also Peter Woll, *American Bureaucracy*, 2nd edn (New York: W. W. Norton and Co., 1977), p. 173.

65 Ogul, *Congress Oversees the Bureaucracy*; Seymour Scher, 'Conditions for Legislative Control', *Journal of Politics*, 28 (1963); John F. Bibby, 'Congress' Neglected Function', in Melvin R. Laird (ed.), *The Republican Papers* (New York: Anchor, 1968), pp. 477–88; and Lawrence C. Dodd and Richard L. Schott, *Congress and the Administrative State* (New York and Chichester: Wiley, 1979, pp. 168–70.

66 Bibby, 'Congress' Neglected Function', pp. 477–88.

67 Aberbach, *Keeping a Watchful Eye*, pp. 98–101.

68 See Gary C. Bryner, *Bureaucratic Discretion. Law and Policy in Federal Regulatory Agencies* (New York and Oxford: Pergamon Press, 1987), pp. 24–30; Christopher H. Foreman, *Signals from the Hill. Congressional Oversight and the Challenge of Social Regulation* (New Haven, CT. and London: Yale University Press, 1988), pp. 28–9.

69 Notably, President Reagan's Executive Order 12291 issued in February 1981 which required all executive branch agencies to submit all proposed and final rules to the Office of Management and Budget (OMB), and to justify their regulations through cost-benefit analyses; and Executive Order 12498 which further required agencies

to submit yearly agendas of 'calendars' of all current and anticipated policy actions to OMB for review.

70 See Richard P. Nathan, *The Administrative Presidency* (New York: John Wiley, 1983); Sundquist, *The Decline and Resurgence of Congress*; especially chs 3 and 11; Harold Seidman, *Politics, Position, and Power. The Dynamics of Federal Organisation*, 2nd edn (New York: Oxford University Press, 1975), ch. 4; Terry Moe, 'The Politicised Presidency', in John E. Chubb and Paul E. Peterson (eds), *The New Direction of American Politics* (Washington, D.C.: Brookings Institution, 1981), pp. 235–72.

71 William F. West and Joseph Cooper, 'Legislative Influence v. Presidential Dominance: Competing Models of Bureaucratic Control', *Political Science Quarterly*, 104 (1990), pp. 585–9.

72 For these various arguments, see for example, David R. Mayhew, *Congress: The Electoral Connection* (New Haven, CT and London: Yale University Press, 1974); Morris P. Fiorina, *Congress: Keystone of the Washington Establishment* (New Haven, CT and London: Yale University Press, 1977); Sundquist, *The Decline and Resurgence of Congress*, p. 451.

73 In *Dole v. United Steelworkers of America*, 494 US 26 (1990), the Supreme Court restricted the president's use of the OMB to control agency rule-making. In September 1993, President Clinton issued an executive order restoring discretion to executive agencies to write rules and regulations reducing the role of the OMB in the administrative process.

74 For a summary of the changes, see US Congress, Joint Committee on the Organisation of Congress, House Report 103–413/Senate Report 103–215, *Organisation of the Congress*, Vol. 2 103rd Congress, First Session, pp. 155–6.

75 Matthew D. McCubbins and Thomas Schwartz, 'Congressional Oversight Overlooked: Police Patrols Versus Fire Alarms', *American Journal of Political Science*, 28 (1984), pp. 165–6; and Fiorina, 'Congressional Control of the Bureaucracy', p. 334.

76 See, for example, Charles S. Hyneman, *Bureaucracy in a Democracy* (New York: Harper and Row, 1950), p. 81.

77 Louis Fisher, *The Politics of Shared Power. Congress and the Executive*, 3rd edn (Washington, D.C.: Congressional Quarterly Press, 1993), p. 55.

78 Charles O. Jones, *The United States Congress. People, Place, and Policy* (Homewood, IL: The Dorsey Press, 1982), pp. 404–6. Cf. Schick, 'Politics Through Law', p. 165.

79 Foreman, *Signals From The Hill*, p. 12.

80 Pat Towell, 'Senate Swiftly Confirms Perry As Defense Secretary', *Congressional Quarterly Weekly Report*, February 5 1994, pp. 254–5.

81 Relevant cases include *McGrain v. Daugherty*, 273 US 177 (1927), *Eastland v. United States Servicemen's Fund*, 421 US 491 509 (1975), *Gulf Oil Corporation v. Federal Power Commission* (1977), and *US ex rel. Parco v. Morris* (1977).

82 By 1992, Congress required some 3,627 annual reports from executive departments and agencies. Joint Committee on the Organisation of Congress, *Organisation of Congress*, p. 152. On inspectors general, see Paul Light, *Monitoring Government: Inspectors General and the Search For Accountability* (Washington, D.C.: Brookings Institution, 1993).

83 Mike Mills, 'Oversight Questions Nag Effort to Save Super Collider Again', *Congressional Quarterly Weekly Report*, July 31 1994, pp. 2031–4.

84 John R. Johannes, 'Study and Recommend; Statutory Reporting Requirements as a

Technique of Legislative Initiative in Congress – A Research Note', *Western Political Quarterly*, 29 (1976), pp. 589–96. Cf. Ogul, *Congress Oversees the Bureaucracy*, p. 177; US Congress, Joint Committee on the Organisation of Congress, Committee Print S. Prt. 103–19, *Congressional Reorganisation: Options For Change*, 103rd Congress, First Session, p. 136; and Frederick C. Mosher, *The GAO: The Quest For Accountability in American Government* (Boulder, CO: Westview, 1979), p. 281.

85 Johannes, 'Study and Recommend'.

86 Foreman, *Signals From The Hill*, p. 113.

87 Jeffrey L. Katz, 'Head Start Funding Nears Legislative Crossroad', *Congressional Quarterly Weekly Report*, March 5 1994, pp. 541–6.

88 George Hager, 'Democrats Hail Quick Passage of Clinton's Budget Plan', *Congressional Quarterly Weekly Report*, April 3 1993, pp. 822–3.

89 See, for example, the comments of Senator Nancy Landon Kassebaum (R.KS) in US Congress, Joint Committee on the Organisation of Congress, Hearings. *Budget Process*, 103rd Congress, First Session, March 16 1993, p. 3.

90 US Congress, Joint Committee on the Organisation of Congress, Hearings. *Interbranch Relations*, 103rd Congress, First Session, June 24 1993, p. 67. See also Philip G. Joyce and Robert D. Reischauer, 'Deficit Budgeting: The Federal Budget Process and Budget Reform', *Harvard Journal of Legislation*, 29 (1992), p. 442 and Herbert Kaufman, *Are Government Organisations Immortal?* (Washington, D.C.: Brookings Institution, 1976), p. 64.

91 Jeanne Ponessa, 'Space Station's Fate Hangs On NASA Budget Debate', *Congressional Quarterly Weekly Report*, May 7 1994, pp. 1113–14.

92 Dissenting views in *Immigration and Naturalisation Service* v. *Chadha* (462 US 919).

93 Vetoes may be of several types: a one-house veto (by simple resolution of either house), a two-house veto (by concurrent resolution), a committee veto, and a committee chair's veto. See Joseph Cooper and Patricia A. Hurley, 'The Legislative Veto: A Policy Analysis', *Congress and the Presidency*, 10 (1983), pp. 3–5.

94 Foreman, *Signals From The Hill*, pp. 137–41. For further examples, see Table 16-2 in Joseph Cooper, 'The Legislative Veto in the 1980s' in Lawrence C. Dodd and Bruce I. Oppenheimer (eds), *Congress Reconsidered*, 3rd edn (Washington, D.C.: Congressional Quarterly Press, 1985), p. 369.

95 Allen Schick, *The Federal Budget. Politics, Policy, Process* (Washington, D.C.: Brookings Institution, 1995), pp. 170–1; and Fisher, *The Politics of Shared Power*, pp. 68–71.

96 In *Chadha*, the Court did not rule against 'law' forms of the veto, where veto action by Congress follows normal legislative procedures and involves agreement by both chambers and submission to the president for approval.

97 Louis Fisher, personal correspondence with the authors, February 1995; Fisher, *The Politics of Shared Power*, p. 81 and Cooper, 'The Legislative Veto', p. 385.

98 Fisher, *The Politcs of Shared Power*, pp. 80–4; Fisher, *American Constitutional Law*, p. 231; and Louis Fisher, 'The Legislative Veto: Invalidated, It Survives', *Law and Contemporary Problems*, 56 (1993), pp. 273–92. For specific examples, see Martha Liebler Gibson, 'Managing Conflict: The Role of the Legislative Veto in American Foreign Policy', *Polity*, 26 (1994), pp. 441–72; and Jessica Korn, 'Improving the Policymaking Process by Protecting the Separation of Powers: Chadha and the Legislative Vetoes in Education Statutes', *Polity*, 26 (1994), pp. 677–98.

99 See, for example, Fisher, *American Consitutional Law*, p. 231.

100 Antonin Scalia, 'The Legislative Veto: A False Remedy for System Overload', *Regulation*, 3 (1979), pp. 19–26 and Robert Gilmour, 'The Congressional Veto: Shifting the Balance of Administrative Control', *Journal of Policy Analysis and Management*, 2 (1982), pp. 13–25; and Barbara Hinkson Craig, *The Legislative Veto: Congressional Control of Regulation* (Boulder, CO: Westview Press, 1983), pp. 123–38.

101 See, for example, William T. Gormley, *Taming the Bureaucracy. Muscles, Prayers, and Other Strategies* (Princeton, NJ: Princeton University Press, 1989), p. 212.

102 Cf. Theodore, J. Lowi, 'Presidential Democracy in America: Towards the Homogenised Regime', *Political Science Quarterly*, 109 (1994), pp. 401–15 and the critique offered by former Congressman Bill Green at pp. 417–21. For a refutation of this abdication thesis, see D. Roderick Kiewiet and Matthew D. McCubbins, *The Logic of Delegation. Congressional Parties and the Appropriations Process* (Chicago and London: University of Chicago Press, 1991).

103 On the positive responses of bureaucrats to congressional intervention, see John R. Johannes, *To Serve The People: Congress and Constituency Service* (Lincoln, NE: University of Nebraska Press, 1984); and Ogul, *Congress Oversees the Executive*, pp. 162–75.

104 See, for example, James Q. Wilson, *Bureaucracy: What Government Agencies Do and Why They Do It* (Washington, D.C.: Brookings Institution, 1990), pp. 241–4; Gordon S. Jones and John A. Marini (eds), *The Imperial Congress. Crisis in the Separation of Powers* (New York: Pharos Books, 1988); Jeremy Rabkin, 'Micromanaging the Administrative Agencies', *The Public Interest*, 100 (1990), pp. 116–30.

105 Aberbach, *Keeping a Watchful Eye*, pp. 84–6, 123, 169; Morris P. Fiorina, *Congress. Keystone of the Washington Establishment* (New Haven, CT and London: Yale University Press, 1988), pp. 28–9; R. Douglas Arnold, *Congress and the Bureaucracy. A Theory of Influence* (New Haven, CT and London: Yale University Press, 1979).

106 See, for example, Foreman, *Signals From The Hill*, pp. 42, 103, 108, 115; and Aberbach, *Keeping a Watchful Eye*, p. 118.

107 James Q. Wilson, *The Investigators: Managing FBI and Narcotics Agents* (New York: Basic Books, 1978), p. 46; Paul Quirk, *Industry Influence in Federal Regulatory Agencies* (Princeton, NJ: Princeton University Press), p. 125; Aberbach, *Keeping a Watchful Eye*, p. 197.

108 McCubbins and Schwartz argue that Congress limits the time and effort devoted to the most controversial and politically salient elements of executive activities largely by responding primarily to 'fire alarms' set off by interest groups, the press, staff, and others – rather than by conducting 'police patrol' oversight involving active, direct, systematic, frequent, and planned examinations of executive activities. McCubbins and Schwartz, 'Congressional Oversight Overlooked'; cf. Aberbach, *Keeping a Watchful Eye*, pp. 97–104.

109 Samuel P. Huntington, 'Congressional Responses to the Twentieth Century', in David B. Truman (ed.), *The Congress and America's Future* (Englewood Cliffs, NJ: Prentice Hall, 1965), pp. 31–8.

CHAPTER 12

The Congress, the presidency and the democratic system

The Congress and the presidency are America's two foremost political institutions. Their pre-eminence is drawn both from their electoral connections in what is a self-consciously democratic system of government and from their national status located as they are at the centre of the federal government in Washington. Their significance to the American political system and to the operational characteristics of American democracy is also derived from the dynamics not only between the two institutions themselves, but between the different governing properties, cultural traditions, and social conceptions that are closely associated with them. An institutional duality at such a high level can provide a ready expression of political differences even to the extent of defining the nature of issues and structuring the organisation of political dispute in terms of legislative–executive contrasts. The representative properties of the Congress and the presidency are in fact as dependent upon the evident coexistence of these two institutions, together with their unresolved tensions and dilemmas, as they are upon the more direct linkages between electoral choice and government. Just as the Congress and the presidency can be claimed to be the most characteristic features of American government, so by the same token the interplay between them can be said to characterise American politics.

The peculiarity of the relationship between the Congress and the presidency can be summed up by the phrase that the Supreme Court used to legitimise segregation during the first half of this century – i.e. 'separate but equal'.[1] The Congress and the presidency are separate institutions with different electoral arrangements, constituencies, and political functions. And yet notwithstanding their clear differentiation in a separation of powers scheme, they are also commonly regarded as equal. The Congress and the presidency not only share a formal equity in status as constitutionally coequal bodies, they are assumed to be sufficiently comparable to one another to generate a continuous system of checks and balances. Given that the two institutions are structured into close proximity to one another in a separated system that presupposes a set of interactive dynamics between components, the Congress and the presidency are habitually viewed as two almost mutually inclusive bodies. In American political culture, they are instinctively referred to together as a composite entity – almost a binary unit in which one would be incomplete and incomprehensible without recourse to its partner.

Institutional proximity within a context of separated powers, however, cuts both ways. It gives the impression of comparability and with it the potential for institutional checks, but the capacity for such an exchange of forces also rests upon the existence and maintenance of distinct institutional entities. In the American system, it is this very element of differentiation that is underlined and given such resonance by the structural requirement of interaction. By pulling the two institutions physically together for the purposes of mutual checks, the system simultaneously dramatises their qualitative differences and throws their respective natures into high relief. Far from being coequal and comparable, the Congress and the presidency can be interpreted as being so fundamentally different from one another that their relationship remains highly ambiguous in character and deeply problematic to the system as a whole.

While the modern Rooseveltian presidency has generally been characterised as a purposive, positive, and progressive institution, the Congress has by contrast been portrayed as an ingrown, negative, and regressive body. During the 1933–63 period in particular Congress acquired what became a lasting reputation for sloth, obstructionism, myopia, fragmentation, and parochialism. Congress for the most part was identified with those forces of reaction and dissolution that a modern president was expected to nullify in the cause of programmatic government. Just as Congress was seen as denying the emergence of a parliamentary model of government, so the presidency was regarded as a functional substitute for party government. Congress' decentralised and disjointed organisation was thought to match the pluralistic nature of its multiple constituencies and the politics of particularised benefits that went hand in hand with subnational representation and local electoral strategies. In the development of the modern presidency, Congress was almost invariably seen as the deadweight of immobilism and insularity that the presidency was responsible for shifting in order to secure unity and movement within an otherwise chronically divided system.

In many ways, the presidency in this period was dependent upon this negative conception of Congress for its own identity and *raison d'être*. The president, as the most responsive and adaptive element within government, provided the system as a whole with the capacity for overcoming its devices of self-restraint in the service of the public and national interest in the shape of the positive state and the defence establishment. While Congress was regarded as a fixed quantity of given characteristics, the president was entitled 'both in law and conscience to be as big a man as he [could be]',[2] in order to provide the energy and vision to release the nation from its own constraints. The individuality of the office lent itself to the notion that there was a definable general interest and that this could only be expressed by the president acting in his capacity as the sole representation of the American people. Congress exemplified the more traditional American democracy of local communities (i.e. the Jeffersonian ethos) and groups (i.e. the Madisonian ethos) maintaining an immediate and tangible connection with representatives who were closely dependent upon their constituencies. Modern presidents by contrast asserted the existence of a national democracy centred upon their office. This not only provided a link between the broad mass of the citizenry and the federal government, but amounted to a *de facto* reconstitution of the American people into an organic community embodied and served by the centre and, in particular, by the centre-point in the form of the presidency. In Theodore Lowi's view 'presidential government was a genuine regime change – the Second Republic of the United States'.[3] As a consequence, presidential power was 'great precisely because it [was] truly the people's power'.[4]

The idea that a national community existed, that government gave expression to such a community, and that government could genuinely act in the interests of the community, all tended to converge upon the office of the presidency. This was no mere extension of congressional democracy but a wholly different conception of democracy which was animated by the idea that popular authority was vested in an explicitly executive power both through political sanction and through the more abstract proposition that the presidency represented the collective interest of the Republic both symbolically and substantively. Presidential power, therefore, was closely related to the concept of the public welfare. As such, presidents were able to assume, or to have ceded to them, vast tracts of functional discretion and prerogative power. Because the modernisation of government coincided with the modernisation of the presidency, the latter became analogous to the positive values of the bureaucratic state (e.g. efficiency, decisiveness, initiative, coherence, intelligence, accountability, and a commitment to ideals) while the Congress was increasingly assigned to a set of negative connotations (e.g. indiscipline, inaction, irresponsibility, unaccountability, prejudice, and an attachment to interests). The net effect was a polarity of institutions that, at the height of the modern presidency, was seen as accommodating two parallel organisations with distinct traditions, outlooks, and timescales; with separate constituencies, agendas, and roles; with distinct principles, methods and objectives; with different conceptions of representative government, political development, and democracy; and arguably with two separate constructions of America.[5]

This polarity was always something of a caricature. It was a duality overdrawn in the main by presidents and their supporters, who sought to explain the slow progress of liberal reforms in the 1950s and early 1960s by reference to the structural constraints at the disposal of conservative elements in Congress. Devices like the filibuster, the committee system, and the seniority rule in the hands of the southern Democratic bloc were thought to have given disproportionate power to Congress' conservative leaders who were able to frustrate allegedly popular majorities by ensuring that the net effect of congressional activity produced conservative results irrespective of input. As part of a modern president's role was to renew and articulate a defining public philosophy,[6] the conception of an arcane and regressive Congress became part of America's political discourse. Just as executive leadership was built up as a beacon of rationality, efficiency, and progress (see Chapter 11), so Congress was cast down into the darkness as a syndrome of recidivism – i.e. 'aged and rural-oriented committee chairpersons, malapportionment of Congressional districts . . . Congressional susceptibility to interest group pressure . . . Congresspersons as a bunch of stick-in-the-muds whose function has been to overrepresent the worst tendencies of their constituents and to prevent dynamic presidents from getting anything accomplished'.[7]

Today, it is evident that the hold which the 'conservative establishment' had over Congress in the late 1950s and early 1960s was less than invincible. Changes in public attitudes, the large influx of northern Democrats in the 1958 mid-term elections, the 1964 landslide election for Lyndon Johnson, together with the Great Society reforms demonstrated Congress' capacity for major change. The old congressional–presidential duality has also been subjected to a number of other correctives. For example, it has become increasingly clear that institutions are not material solids with sharply differentiated boundaries. Richard Neustadt's dictum that it is 'a government of separated institutions *sharing* powers'[8] has been thoroughly vindicated by numerous studies into the bilateral connections between the executive and legislative branches (e.g. subgovernments, issue networks) and into the different ways they can be coordinated to provide opportunities for 'legislating together' (e.g. presidential influence, the force of ideas, and the 'collusion of elites') (see Chapter 9).[9] It is now recognised that the presidency is as much the victim of bureaucratic government in the executive branch as it is of any conservative lock within Congress. By the same token, it is generally conceded that Congress can be as innovative in policy formulation, and as responsive and responsible in its decision-making, as the presidency – arguably even more so.

Congress' sheer responsiveness to social movements has led Bert Rockman to conclude that Congress has grown into 'an institution of munificent pluralism – one that mirrors extraordinarily well (more so than a mere 20 years ago) the remarkable diversity of the activist elements in the society it is elected to represent . . . By its unyielding diversity, and by virtue of the transition from an atmosphere of clubbiness to one of entrepreneurial aggressiveness, Congress has become more a conductor of political electricity than an insulator'.[10] The old polarity has also suffered from the 'imperial presidency' episode when the trend towards modernising government through presidential licence was suddenly shown to be flawed by the abuse of power and contempt for the rule of law. The related collapse of President Nixon's aggressive attempts to increase the responsiveness of the federal bureaucracy, by colonising government with White House zealots dedicated to the personal interests of the president (i.e. the 'administrative presidency'), was also prompted by a concern that internal checks and balances were being subverted. In both cases, the dangers of allowing stated necessity, efficiency, and convenience to determine the shape of government over and against democratic or constitutional principle were exposed and acted upon. If 'presidential government' had previously been rationalised as the chief means of redeeming an otherwise unsustainable political system, Congress, during this period, was seen as being instrumental in the revival of the system's governing principles. At the very least, it demonstrated that the political development of the presidency and the progressive power transference to the executive were not irreversible processes.

Despite the fact that the conditions, conceptions, and traditions supporting the idea of an institutional duality of presidential stimulus and congressional response have diminished – not least by the preponderance of conservative presidents facing relatively liberal Congresses since the late 1960s – the belief in its existence and in its utility as a political issue continues to be felt. The parameters of argument and analysis have remained in place. Presidents are still disposed to see Congress as the central condition of their predicament in Washington. Presidential strategies are informed by the underlying premise of an unbridgeable organisational and political disjunction in government that supports a set of autonomous dynamics immune to change and producing only inertial policy. As one of their number recently put it:

> Unlike members of Congress, the president is elected by all the people. He is the chief executive, and his principal responsibility is the security of the nation and its people . . . Too often, in my experience, Congress reminds us that it is a political organism. The central preoccupation of too many of its members is getting re-elected; too often, instead of legislative statesmanship, this produces cynical posturing and pandering to the campaign contributors that have the fattest wallets.'[11]

Presidents by the same token are criticised for disengaging from the politics of negotiation and coalition-building in favour of fostering a public presidency geared to generalised appeal and popular approval.[12] Presidents for their part have felt driven to such strategies because of the mismatch between high expectations and responsibilities on the one hand and poor political resources, weakened parties, and dissipated authority on the other – a mismatch widely perceived to lead to a process of built-in presidential failure and, with it, a decline in governmental competence.

For much of the time this congressional–presidential duality is a normal part of the politics of jurisdictional dispute and blame assignment associated with the separation of powers framework. Such a system facilitates the reduction of political issues into an expression of bifurcated institutional interests and activities. On occasion, the normal interplay and mutual frustration, of legislative–executive relations can be superseded by a sense that there exists a chronic systemic dysfunction which jeopardises not merely policy-making but the integrity of government itself. The relationship between the Congress and the presidency became an issue in its own right in the late 1950s and early 1960s. It surfaced again in the late 1970s when President Carter experienced severe problems with his reform legislation and in particular his energy programme. The disquiet over the disintegration of the Carter presidency, along with the economic ravages of stagflation, spawned a new diagnostic and liberal reform-minded literature on the problems of American government.[13]

Critics alluded to the deep structural and self-perpetuating constraints within the American system that were so all-pervasive they effectively denied the possibility of government and with it the opportunity for social programme and economic development. And when constraints were cited, there was no doubt which particular area of countermanding machinery lay at the root of the problem – the separation of powers and most notably the disjunction between the Congress and the presidency. Lloyd Cutler pointed to the

> structural inability of our government to propose, legislate and administer a balanced program for governing. In parliamentary terms, one might say that under the US Constitution it is not now feasible to 'form a government'. The separation of powers between the legislative and executive branches, whatever its merits in 1793, has become a structure that almost guarantees stalemate today . . . In each administration, it becomes progressively more difficult to make the present system work effectively on the range of issues, both domestic and foreign, that the United States must now manage.[14]

Alvin Toffler despaired at the 'almost total paralysis of political decision-making in connection with the life-and-death questions facing society' and concluded that the 'decision-making system itself [had] become a menace'.[15]

Critical appraisal brought in its wake a raft of reform proposals aimed at reducing the separation between the executive and legislative branches and, thereby, increasing the probability of a more unified system and, with it, the provision of popular choice and accountable government. Many of the proposals were in the form of constitutional re-engineering (e.g. a single six-year term for presidents, coordinated terms of office for presidents and members of Congress, cabinet seats for members of Congress). Others were geared to changing the party system in an attempt to structure a closer interdependence between the branches (e.g. linking the nomination procedures to produce a greater convergence among party candidates for presidential and congressional offices, providing for 'team tickets' of party candidates that deny voters the opportunity of ticket-splitting).

Interest in such schemes faded when President Reagan's entry into the White House appeared to herald a sharp change of direction for American government. Reagan's programme of free market conservatism, together with the organised pressure that was exerted to secure its passage, vindicated those traditionalists who always claimed that there was nothing wrong with the American system that fresh elections and new leadership could correct. But after the first year of the Reagan presidency, the glow of the conservative revolution quickly dimmed and the old syndrome of presidential–congressional competition reappeared. The system was once again characterised as being deadlocked to the detriment of America's social and economic welfare. Political gamesmanship and public posturing by Presidents Reagan and Bush, along with the Democratic majority leaders in Congress, lent weight to the alleged sterility of American government. The sense of drift and disarray was deepened by the apparent incapacity of government to address a series of profound problems, by the incidence of political scandals, and by the rising level of public cynicism over politics and the institutions of government. Against this background, Bill Clinton effectively made the gridlock of divided government into a full scale issue in the 1992 presidential election. He pressed his candidacy not just on policy grounds but as a way of uniting the presidency and Congress and, thereby, providing the grand remedy of 'good government'. It proved to be a chimera. The much vaunted unity of government evaporated within only two years when the Republicans won control of both the House and Senate in the 1994 mid-term elections. Such was the scale of the victory that at the very least it raised serious doubts over the idea of unified government being a political and structural solution in its own right.

From the various swings in the debate over the actual and rightful condition of legislative–executive relations, it is clear that the politics associated with the separation of powers foster two main conceptions of American government. These two constructs coexist with one another but they also remain in a position of constant tension that fluctuates according to political conditions. The two features that condition American perspectives on the operation and appraisal of government in Washington, and which are exemplified in the interactions between Congress and the presidency, are drawn from the separate components of the term 'democratic system'. Each element can be given a different emphasis in the equation. On the one hand is the term '*democratic* system' where the latter is informed and even determined by the weight given to the former. The reverse (i.e. 'democratic *system*') is a less obvious, but no less significant, characteristic of American politics. Both these features are particularly relevant to the way that the interrelationship between the presidency and Congress is conceived and deployed in the wider context of government. The democratic theme is most evident on those occasions when the presidency and Congress are alluded to as 'divided government'. The accent upon system by contrast becomes more prominent when the institutional relationship is seen as one of 'gridlock'.

The *democratic* system

Divided government refers to a condition when the presidency is controlled by one party, and one or both elements of Congress are controlled by the other party. The potential for internal tension is, thereby, maximised at precisely the time when the possibility for party linkages across the branches are minimised. Such an enhancement of the separation of powers has become a regular feature of American government over the past thirty years and has often been cited as evidence of a breakdown in government. It is true that references to divided government are often accompanied by critical acknowledgements of the deleterious effects that such an arrangement may have on the responsiveness and accountability of the system.[16] Nevertheless, these reservations do not amount to an indictment of the system. Divided government may be inconvenient but it is not a pathological condition revealing government to be inherently unmanageable. Far from being abnormal or atypical, divided government has been shown to be a relatively common condition in American history.[17] Moreover, it is alleged to be not merely consistent with the principles underpinning the separation of powers but the fullest expression of those principles.

Even though 'general accounts of the operation of American national government presuppose unified party control',[18] there is nothing implicit within the separation of powers that requires such party unity. According to David Mayhew, divided government has not made any material difference to the rate at which important legislation has been enacted. In a survey covering the period from 1946 to 1990, Mayhew demonstrates that the availability of presidential skills in political persuasion, the existence of external factors facilitating change, and the presence of public opinion in favour of presidential activism were not exclusive to periods of unified government. They were also present during periods of divided government and were instrumental in generating legislative success in spite of the institutional disjunction. Charles Jones is another who gives emphasis to the underlying 'creativity and flexibility' of what he sees as a subtle matrix of separate institutions that is always changing and has 'a seemingly infinite number of mutations'.[19]

Research has cast doubt on other negative features associated with divided government. For example, David Rohde has demonstrated that divided government is actually related to a strengthening rather than a weakening of parties within Congress. Although divided government is a result of weak party ties among voters, the division between institutions can stimulate organisational integration and ideological coherence by parties within competing institutions.[20] Morris Fiorina seeks to show that divided government is not the capricious outcome of arbitrary and disorganised choices. As the parties have polarised and have, thereby, come to offer different sets of policy benefits, voters balance their choices and arrive at an intermediate position between unified government controlled by the Democrats and unified government controlled by the Republicans.[21] Divided government, therefore, provides an approximation to the aggregate of preferences. Gary Jacobson also sees the electorate as making a purposeful decision in favour of divided government but he attempts to show that the choice is more deliberately two-dimensional – i.e. opting for the attractive elements of the Republican Party to offset the less appealing components of the Democratic Party and *vice versa*.[22] The net effect is claimed to be a premeditated conjunction of Republican presidents and Democratic Congresses. Although such studies can only infer the existence of sophisticated and purposeful ticket-splitting from survey evidence, they do serve as a reminder that divided government need not be an aberrational form of self-contradiction, but can represent a graduated choice affording democratic legitimacy to a condition of split control. It can even be claimed that divided government is the result of voters making ideologically consistent choices across different parties.[23]

It must also be borne in mind that when the direct question of the preferability of divided or unified government is asked in opinion polls, the response has often been in favour of the former. In 1989, for example, the public had a preference for divided government over unified government by 45 per cent to 35 per cent – a preponderance significantly higher than the 25 per cent of the electorate who actually engage in ticket-splitting.[24] This point was not lost upon the incoming Clinton Administration in 1993. Clinton's consultants Stanley Greenberg and James Carville saw Congress as the domestic equivalent of the old Soviet Union that would threaten the president's ability to manage the country. Private polling disclosed that while 23 per cent of respondents chose the capacity to handle foreign relations and protect national security as the most important presidential strength, 63 per cent opted for the ability to handle Congress and address domestic problems. When asked about the style a president should adopt for such a role, 53 per cent favoured cooperation with congressional leaders compared to only 35 per cent who wanted the president to challenge Congress head on and criticise it for its failings.[25]

> The conclusion was very clear to the two consultants: the public wanted a president to master but not overwhelm Congress. To extend the analogy with the Soviet Union, they wanted containment and peaceful coexistence, not conventional war, and certainly not thermonuclear war. They wanted an end to gridlock.[26]

According to this more positive perspective of the separation of powers, when the system produces divided government it can be made to work by achieving sufficient common purpose to reduce institutional differences and acquire provisional and intermittent forms of cooperation. Arguably, divided government can be said to be a purer expression of the underlying dynamics of American politics in that it makes explicit the profusion of interests and cross-pressures that characterise the system – even when the governing institutions are notionally joined together in unified government. The driving force in this perspective is society itself and in particular the democratic forces that translate social divisions into varied political propositions requiring high levels of consultation and negotiation before a movement-inducing consensus is achieved. To the extent that the system does not appear to produce socially and economically beneficial policies, the fault is seen to be that of American society – not the the political system which is simply responding to incoherent and contradictory pressures. If the political system in Washington seems to be in damaging disarray from divided government, this is in itself only a symptom of a deeper malaise within society itself. As such, there is no necessary connection between unified institutions and more effective government. In fact, as one study concluded '[d]ivided government is not inherently ineffective, nor does the restoration of unified government offer any guarantee of effective government.'[27] It can even be argued that divided government may be as proficient or even better than unified government in generating the breadth of collaboration required for innovative policy-making.

In the light of this pluralistic perspective, attempts to contrive party or institutional strategies to produce a unified government are unsound, unnecessary, and even undemocratic. They are unsound because such schemes will always fail. The parties reflect society's own diversities and cleavages. Efforts to impose integration upon them, or to place them into positions of integrated institutional power would exert further enormous strains upon the fabric of the parties leading in turn to deep splits and the possibility of a multi-party system. Schemes to contrive unified government are seen as unnecessary because as the elections of 1992 demonstrated, unified government was achieved quite spontaneously through conventional electoral means. By the same token, the Republican Party in the 1994 mid-term elections demonstrated that the supposed Democratic 'lock' on the House of Representatives could be picked after forty years by turning a solid Democratic majority of 78 into a Republican majority of 26 in one election. The Republicans showed how it was possible for a party to organise an electoral campaign based upon a common programme (i.e. 'Contract With America') and to win a victory sufficient to organise Congress to address itself fully to the programme.

Lastly, devices to unify government are dismissed on grounds that they are contrary to the principles of the separation of powers. Apart from the possible dangers arising from the unintended and unwanted consequences that can always arise from reforms, such schemes are condemned because they are seen as a frontal assault upon the central conception of equilibrium derived from separated, competing, and countervailing powers. Since the separation of powers is the most characteristic feature of America's governmental organisation, and since it evokes balance as the central motivating ideal of American democracy, attempts to tamper with it arouse severe anxiety and strong opposition from those socialised into its consensus-building virtues. The cultural disquiet generated by proposals for major reform is captured by Morris Fiorina's alarmism over the potential repercussions of unified government: '[T]here is always the theoretical possibility that an aggressive unified government could follow a policy path that would kill many of its constituents before it was held to account at the next election'.[28]

In sum, the Congress and the presidency are dual representative and governing entities that can and do converge when the conditions for political compromise and institutional accommodation are present. When such conditions are absent, it is considered pointless and even dangerous to try to stimulate its presence through organisational engineering.

The democratic *system*

The second construct of American government which is pertinent to the politics surrounding the Congress and the presidency is drawn from the idea that America's arrangements for representative government constitute an organisational system in their own right. Problems in such a system are systemic problems by definition and it is this connection between input, process, and output that leads periodically to concern that the system has an exceptional influence on the operation of government. Most recently, that concern has turned to anxiety with the growing belief that the structure of government is not only an independent frame of reference but one that persistently operates in accordance with the status quo. This condition is not simply a curable case of divided government, so much as a congenital deformity known as gridlock.

In the 1990s, the term gridlock has become part of the currency of political exchange as the system is seen to multiply and exacerbate the divisions arising from separated powers into a matrix of inaction, stagnation, and frustration. Gridlock has become the watchword for that perspective which sees government in a constant state of sub-optimisation, in which the high expectations of electoral promises always slump into troughs of disaffection, and where 'big government' paradoxically coexists with an ascribed state of ungovernability – even within government itself. In such a context, only the systemic autonomy suggested by a state of gridlock can explain how democratic pressures can be continuously frustrated, how the anomalies and perversities of the system can remain in existence, and how the entrenched interests and elites within government continue to prosper. William Hudson's indictment typifies the sense of impotence:

> For most of our history, we managed to overcome the antimajoritarian bias of the Constitution through a combination of presidential leadership and political party organisation. This system offered temporary and partial solution to governmental gridlock, but in the past few decades even this partial system no longer worked . . . [leaving] government inefficient, unresponsive and unaccountable.[29]

A good deal of circumstantial evidence is available to support the existence of gridlock. It includes the differential between the generally recognised public need for reform (e.g. welfare, education, medical provision, campaign contribution and government spending and taxation) and the system's evident lack of response to such problems; the profusion of PACs and the multiple articulation of special interests in search of particularised benefits combined with the rise of candidate-based electoral strategies; the existence of polls showing very low levels of approval for Congress as an institution coinciding with the apparently paradoxical continuation of high incumbency and re-election rates; the close links between PACs and incumbent members of Congress and, in particular, between PAC campaign contributions and the strong financial position of incumbents in relation to their challengers; the prevailing culture of immunity within Washington that has led in Congress' case to a refusal to apply its social legislation to its own activities and working conditions; the steep rise in the public's distrust of, alienation from, and non-participation in, government; and the general erosion of party composition, party competition, and electoral choice in a system where dealigned votes offer very little prospect of a regime renewal in the form of a party realignment.

Such *prima facie* evidence infers the presence of a closed system of governance with a built-in resistance to any substantive changes in policy or process. It is a system which is characterised by the absence of any comprehensible relationship between assessments of popular opinion or conceptions of the public interest and the performance of government. As such, 'much of our public policy falls into two unpleasant categories: policies that lead to excessive spending, far beyond what the public would accept if it had a direct choice, and policies of governmental inaction on issues where the public wants substantial change'.[30]

It is wholly unclear whether a disjunction between public preference and government activity actually exists, and whether whatever resistance that is present is motivated by any conscious intent. The old accounts of the 'deadlock of democracy'[31] were couched as a confrontation between two recognisable and purposive elements, each with its own set of ideas and plan of action. Liberals had an affinity with the presidency, while the conservatives' power base lay in Congress. Gridlock today has a far more amorphous character derived, as it is, from a more fragmented system in which the interrelationship of multiple agents can easily be interpreted as producing a spontaneous and unintended condition of self-nullification. While liberal presidents and the old 'conservative coalition' used to battle it out for control, the impression associated with gridlock is that of no one being in charge. To Bert Rockman, 'Brownian movement, the random movement of particles seems a more apt descript[ion] of the policy process in America than does deadlock'.[32] Whatever name it is given, those who object to it are seen as complaining over the consequences of their own volatility.

Whether or not gridlock is consciously or unconsciously created, the debate engendered by it has contributed towards a general disquiet over the functional integrity of government. It has coincided with an intensified awareness within political science of (i) the links between costs and incentives on an individual basis and the formation and operation of institutional structures at a more general level;[33] and (ii) the relationship between different processes and policy outcomes.[34] Gridlock has also provided a supportive context to those recent analyses of American government that have given emphasis first to the increasing role of bureaucracies and courts in the process of government, second to the declining importance of elections and voting choices, and third to the rising incidence of mutually subversive activities by both the presidency and the Congress.[35]

But gridlock has probably been most influential in the way it has provided a focus to the recent populist complaints against government. Sensing the existence of a deep dysfunction in society, recent populist insurgency has been swift to identify the cause as a dysfunction in government, in which the public interest has been routinely sacrificed by the deliberate manipulativeness of 'special interests'. The perceived immobilism of government is taken as being directly related to its unresponsiveness to basic needs and desires. Popular frustration with the state of the economy, with deep-set social problems, and with the apparent failure of both traditional liberal and conservative solutions finds collective expression in a reaction against government *per se* and in a revival of schemes to promote direct democracy and popular sovereignty. The revivalist sentiments of such 'anti-politics' is captured in the 'Contract With America' with its promise to secure legislation with such titles as The Taking Back Our Streets Act, The Citizen Legislature Act, and the Restoration of the American Dream Act.

Gridlock has fuelled traditional suspicions that government is always self-serving and inclined to privilege, waste, and inequity. Such suspicions have been fuelled by a profusion of polemical books and articles. Kevin Phillips, for example, refers in *Arrogant Capital* to the cynical parochialism of the American governing class located inside the 'Washinton beltway'. Its immunity to change comes not just from its concentration of special interest lobbyists but from the fact that it has become a vested interest in its own right.[36] Given that change is widely cited as a basic requirement and that it is seen to be a very remote prospect even with unified government (see Table 12.1), gridlock provides the *raison d'être* to calls for reform, for the creation of a third national party, and for the provision of non-partisan leadership by super-outsiders like Ross Perot.

On an analytical level, gridlock has a close correspondence to the term balance which is usually invoked in connection with separated powers and institutional checks. Both are subjective terms disguised as objective conditions. Gridlock infers immobilism and with it the notion that changelessness is to be deplored as a feature of government. It also implies both a need for change and the existence of an available programme of corrective policy solutions. But the need is denied by a process locked into itself. Gridlock is thus seen as either

Table 12.1. The perceived impossibility of substantial change
within the political system, 1993–1994

Question: Do you agree/disagree with the following statement?	Percent Who Agree			
	May 1992	Aug. 1992	Feb. 1993	May 1993
Current incumbents will *never* reform the political system	69	62	52	67
Special-interest groups have more influence than voters.	83	79	79	84
Congress is largely owned by special-interest groups	74	71	68	74
If Democrats and Republicans continue to run things, we will never get real reform	46	38	36	45

Adapted from data collected by a Gordon Black Poll.

Source: G. S. Black and B. D. Black, *The Politics of American Discontent: How a New Party Can Make Democracy Work Again* (New York: John Wiley, 1994), p. 179.

preventing the formation of majorities for government, or frustrating the expression of majority preferences. Such attributed 'irrationality' is rationally explained in terms of the system's own blind mechanical autonomy.

This conceptualisation of government is not immune to criticism. For example, allegations of gridlock coincide with the evident presence of 'big government' producing high volumes of legislation and regulation. The extent to which this condition is evaluated either positively or negatively will depend upon political argument over who or what gains most from the current arrangements. Liberals used to complain about the conservative consequences of government momentum. Now the situation is reversed. One person's gridlock, therefore, can be another's stability. Likewise, gridlock can be just as much a consequence of an excess of responsiveness and movement, as it can be of chronic unresponsiveness and lack of direction. It should also be acknowledged that successful institutions are, by their very nature, necessarily resistant to externally imposed change.[37] Gridlock, like imbalance or disequilibrium, is an attempt to characterise government in terms which appear to describe a physical condition but one which carries with it a host of unfavourable connotations on intuitive, aesthetic, and moral grounds. As gridlock is not a condition that ordinarily commands assent, its description is simultaneously a critique and a call for change – i.e. it is value-loaded and politically charged.

Notwithstanding the analytical limitations of the term, gridlock remains a potent weapon of dissent within a political culture that has always placed a premium upon government arrangements constituting a 'system'. At the most fundamental level, the American Constitution suggests the creation at a single point in time of a finished organisation of government. Institutions are enumerated, powers are delineated, and interrelationships are set in motion in what appears to be a unified and coherent government structure. Federal elections are predetermined to run according to a precise and wholly predictable two-year cycle. The sheer continuity of the arrangements has been so formidable that 'only a half dozen of the twenty-six amendments adopted since the Constitution was ratified have affected the governmental structure at all, and none has altered its essential architecture'.[38] The difficulty of the amendment procedures and the strong impression of an integrated system in operation has encouraged the perception of government as a 'machine that would go of itself'.[39] It is representative and even democratic in one respect but in another respect mechanistic in that it is perceived to possess its own timeless and autonomous dynamics.

The American system attracts criticism because it is seen by its detractors to have successfully defied evolutionary change. It is condemned for being premodern in organisation, structurally impervious to fundamental change, and self-disabling in its attachment to reciprocal checks and balances. The common indictment concerning the way an 'eighteenth-century constitution has become the major obstacle to achieving democratic government'[40] is no mere rhetoric. It springs from a belief in the historic continuity of American government as a system. By the same token, it is precisely because that idea of a government system is so closely bound up with American history and America's own national identity that such indictments and calls for change almost invariably fail to evoke premeditated and systemic change. Apart from the constitutional problems inherent in any large-scale reform, a strong cultural antipathy exists against constitutional revision because it would threaten to undermine the interdependency between the political community expressed in the formation and maintenance of the Constitution, and the constitutional system itself which continues to define the essence of America's political settlement and social consensus.

The ongoing tension between the joint components of democracy and system within America's democratic system is epitomised by the relationship between the Congress and the presidency. On the one hand, the two institutions provide extensive evidence of the translation of democratic pressures into responsive and representative government. On the other hand, the two institutions also show how the separate forms of democracy associated with their organisational and electoral characteristics are not reducible to a single expression of popular sovereignty, and how the anomalies between these two democracies are rationalised as the necessary supports to a dynamic and generally effective system of interactive exchange.

Within such a context, failures in the institutional system are often diagnosed as democratic problems. Likewise democratic faults can be given mechanistic solutions. The systemic failure evoked by the term gridlock is very much a system-minded response to governmental problems. It is also one that can legitimise systemic correctives designed to produce action without apparent risk to the larger constitutional structure. The Gramm-Rudman-Hollings Act (1985), for example, included the provision of successive yearly cuts in federal expenditures to achieve the objective of a balanced budget. The legislation was in effect a piece of machinery that enforced universal reductions on a Congress that approved of balanced budgets in principle but which, without some form of systematic coercion, was incapable of pursuing a course of financial self-control.

The same principle has been evident in the Republicans' Contract With America with its provisions for a balanced budget amendment to the Constitution and automatic term limits, not merely for the Speaker and committee chairs, but for all members of Congress outside in their constituencies. Term limits is an integral part of the Republican strategy to subject Congress to the same processes of deinstitutionalisation that the executive has experienced with Vice-President Gore's National Performance Review. In the same vein, it is a wholesale response to a mass of discrete problems – i.e. individual local incumbents who keep winning re-election in the face of intense public criticism of Congress as a whole. Notwithstanding the constitutional objections raised by the measure, it is clear that its popular appeal comes from the acceptability of substituting a mechanical device for conventional democratic politics, in order to produce what is considered to be a democratic outcome – i.e. to enforce electorates after a fixed period (e.g. 12 years) to relinquish their incumbent representatives in favour of new choices for the collective benefit of the institution. In short, where unattended democracy produces consequences that are considered to be neither right nor logical, then a more mechanical approach to redirect the system is condoned.

In the final analysis, complaints over the lack of cooperation between the Congress and the presidency overlook the consensus required to make a separation of powers system workable at all. This entails a social tolerance of two democratic institutions coexisting within a single hybrid system. While this sense of government as a system encourages speculation over institutional 'fixes' to problems, that same conception of systemic complexity deters any fundamental revision of powers and relationships because of the risk of unravelling the entire system of government. The Congress and the presidency, therefore, are representative institutions in two respects. They represent different dimensions of electoral choice and consent within a government ostensibly related to the singular entity of the American people. They also embody the problematic disjunctions between democracy and system that condition the operation of America's democratic system at the highest level of government.

Notes

1   The exact phrase is 'equal but separate' but it later became known as 'separate but equal'. See *Plessy v. Ferguson*, 163 US 537 (1896).

2   W. Wilson, *Constitutional Government in the United States* (New York: Columbia University Press, 1911), p. 70.

3   T. J. Lowi, 'Presidential Democracy in America: Toward the Homogenized Regime', *Political Science Quarterly*, 109 (3) (1994), p. 403.

4   T. J. Lowi, 'Presidential Power: Restoring the Balance', *Political Science Quarterly*, 100 (2) (Summer 1985), p. 185.

5   For example, see W. Kendall, 'The Two Majorities', *Midwest Journal of Political Science*, 4 (4) (November 1960), pp. 317–45.

6   K. W. Thompson, *The President and the Public Philosophy* (Baton Rouge: Louisiana University Press, 1981).

7   P. Strum, *Presidential Power and American Democracy* (Santa Monica: Goodyear, 1979), p. 30.

8   R. E. Neustadt, *Presidential Power: The Politics of Leadership* (New York: John Wiley, 1960), p. 33.

9   For example, see J. R. Bond and R. Fleisher, *The President in the Legislative Arena* (Chicago: University of Chicago Press, 1990); M. Derthick and P. J. Quirk, *The Politics of Deregulation* (Washington, D.C.: Brookings Institution, 1985); A. King and G. Alston, 'Good Government and the Politics of High Exposure', in C. Campbell and B. A. Rockman (eds), *The Bush Presidency: First Appraisals* (Chatham: Chatham House, 1991), pp. 249–86.

10 B. A. Rockman, *The Leadership Question: The Presidency and the American System* (New York: Praeger, 1984), pp. 25–6.

11 R. Reagan, *An American Life* (London: Arrow, 1991), pp. 483–4.

12 T. J. Lowi, *The Personal Presidency: Power Invested, Promise Unfulfilled* (Ithaca: Cornell University Press, 1985).

13 For example, see D. L. Robinson (ed.), *Reforming American Government: The Bicentennial Papers of the Committee on the Constitutional System* (Boulder: Westview, 1985).

14 L. N. Cutler, 'To Form A Government', in Robinson (ed.), *Reforming American Government*, pp. 12, 23.

15 A. Tofler, *The Third Wave* (London: Pan, 1981), pp. 402, 424.

16 J. L. Sundquist, *Constitutional Reform and Effective Government* (Washington, D.C.: Brookings Institution, 1986). See also J. L. Sundquist (ed.), *Beyond Gridlock: Prospects for Governance in the Clinton Years – and After* (Washington, D.C.: Brookings Institution, 1993).

17 D. Mayhew, *Divided We Govern: Party Control, Lawmaking, and Investigations, 1946–1990* (New Haven: Yale University Press, 1991). See also C. O. Jones, *The Presidency in a Separated System* (Washington, D.C.: Brookings Institution, 1994), pp. 12–14.

18 M. P. Fiorina, 'An Era of Divided Government', in G. Peele, C. J. Bailey, and B. Cain (eds), *Developments in American Politics* (Basingstoke: Macmillan, 1992), p. 351.

19 Jones, *The Presidency in a Separated System*, p. 285. See also D. K. Price, *The Unwritten Constitution: Science, Religion and Political Responsibility* (Baton Rouge: Lousiana University Press, 1983).

20 D. W. Rohde, *Parties and Leaders in the Postreform House* (Chicago: University of Chicago Press, 1991).

21 M. P. Fiorina, 'An Era of Divided Government', *Political Science Quarterly*, 107 (3) (Fall 1992), pp. 387–410. See also *Divided Government* (New York: Macmillan, 1992).

22 G. Jacobson, *The Electoral Origins of Divided Government: Competition in the US House Elections, 1946–1990* (Boulder: Westview, 1990). See also E. C. Ladd, 'Public Opinion and the "Congress Problem"', *Public Interest*, 100 (1990), pp. 62–7; B. E.

Shafer, 'The Notion of an Electoral Order: The Structure of Electoral Politics at the Accession of George Bush', in B. E. Shafer (ed.), *The End of Realignment: Interpreting American Electoral Eras* (Madison: University of Wisconisn Press, 1991), pp. 37–84.

23 P. Frymer, 'Ideological Consensus within Divided Party Government', *Political Science Quarterly*, 109 (2) (Summer 1994), pp. 287–311.

24 Quoted in R. M. Vallely, 'Divided They Govern', in W. D. Burnham (ed.), *The American Prospect: Reader in American Politics* (Chatham: Chatham House, 1995), p. 280.

25 Quoted in B. Woodward, *The Agenda: Inside the Clinton White House* (New York: Simon and Schuster, 1994), pp. 268–9. The same public sentiment was evident after the Republicans' victory in the 1994 mid-term elections. When asked how the Republican majority in Congress should conduct itself, 78 per cent said it should work *with* President Clinton, while only 14 per cent preferred the option of working *against* the president (*Time*, November 21 1994).

26 Woodward, *The Agenda*, p. 269.

27 R. K. Weaver and B. A. Rockman, 'Institutional Reform and Constitutional Design', in R. W. Weaver and B. A. Rockman (eds), *Do Institutions Matter?: Government Capabilities in the United States and Abroad* (Washington, D.C.: Brookings Institution, 1993), p. 472.

28 M. P. Fiorina, 'An Era of Divided Government', in Peele, Bailey, and Cain (eds), *Developments in American Politics*, p. 350.

29 W. E. Hudson, *American Democracy in Peril: Seven Challenges to America's Future* (Chatham: Chatham House, 1995), p. 34.

30 G. S. Black and B. D. Black, *The Politics of American Discontent: How A New Party Can Make Democracy Work Again* (New York: John Wiley, 1994), p. 10.

31 J. M. Burns, *The Deadlock of Democracy: Four Party Politics in America* (London: John Calder, 1963).

32 Rockman, *The Leadership Question*, p. 29.

33 For example, see M. D. McCubbins and T. Sullivan, *Congress: Structure and Policy* (New York: Cambridge University Press, 1987).

34 For example, see Weaver and Rockman (eds), *Do Institutions Matter?*

35 B. Ginsberg and M. Shefter, *Politics By Other Means: The Declining Importance of Elections in America* (New York: Basic Books, 1990).

36 K. Phillips, *Arrogant Capital: Washington, Wall Street and the Frustration of American Politics* (Boston: Little, Brown, 1994).

37 See N. W. Polsby, 'The Institutionalization of the US House of Representatives', *American Political Science Review*, 62 (1) (March 1968), pp. 144–67.

38 Sundquist, *Constitutional Reform and Effective Government*, p. 40.

39 M. Kammen, *A Machine That Would Go Of Itself* (New York: A. Knopf, 1986).

40 Hudson, *American Democracy in Peril*, p. 34.

Index